Fodor's 2013

NORTHERN
CALIFORNIA

Fodor's Travel Publications, New York,
www.fodors.com

Portions of this book appear in Fodor's

FODOR'S NORTHERN CALIFORNIA 2013
Writers: Cheryl Crabtree, Denise M. Leto, Reed Parsell, Christine Vovakes, Bobbi Zane

Editors: Daniel Mangin, Michael Nalepa, Maria Teresa Hart, Jess Moss

Production Editor: Carolyn Roth
Maps & Illustrations: David Lindroth and Mark Stroud, *cartographers;* Rebecca Baer, *map editor;* William Wu, *information graphics*
Design: Fabrizio La Rocca, *creative director;* Tina Malaney, Chie Ushio, Jessica Ramirez, *designers;* Melanie Marin, *associate director of photography;* Jennifer Romains, *photo research*
Cover Photo: (Mountain Vineyard, Napa Valley) Martin Sundberg/Uppercut/Getty Images
Production Manager: Angela L. McLean

ISBN 978-0-87637-129-9

ISSN 1543–1045

SPECIAL SALES
This book is available at special discounts for bulk purchases for sales promotions or premiums. Special editions, including personalized covers, excerpts of existing books, and corporate imprints, can be created in large quantities for special needs. For more information, write to Special Markets/Premium Sales, 1745 Broadway, MD 3-1, New York, NY 10019, or e-mail specialmarkets@randomhouse.com.

AN IMPORTANT TIP & AN INVITATION
Although all prices, opening times, and other details in this book are based on information supplied to us at press time, changes occur all the time in the travel world, and Fodor's cannot accept responsibility for facts that become outdated or for inadvertent errors or omissions. So **always confirm information when it matters,** especially if you're making a detour to visit a specific place. Your experiences—positive and negative— matter to us. If we have missed or misstated something, **please write to us.** Share your opinion instantly through our online feedback center at fodors.com/contact-us.

PRINTED IN SINGAPORE

10 9 8 7 6 5 4 3 2 1

CONTENTS

MAPS

ABOUT THIS GUIDE

Fodor's Ratings

Everything in this guide is worth doing—we don't cover what isn't—but exceptional sights, hotels, and restaurants are recognized with additional accolades. **Fodor's Choice**★ indicates our top recommendations; ★ highlights places we deem highly recommended; and **Best Bets** call attention to notable hotels and restaurants in various categories. Care to nominate a new place? Visit Fodors.com/contact-us.

Trip Costs

We list prices wherever possible to help you budget well. Hotel and restaurant price categories from **$** to **$$$$** are noted alongside each recommendation. For hotels, we include the lowest cost of a standard double room in high season. For restaurants, we cite the average price of a main course at dinner or, if dinner isn't served, at lunch. For attractions, we always list adult admission fees; discounts are usually available for children, students, and senior citizens.

Hotels

Our local writers vet every hotel to recommend the best overnights in each price category, from budget to expensive. Unless otherwise specified, you can expect private bath, phone, and TV in your room. For expanded hotel reviews, facilities, and deals visit Fodors.com.

TripAdvisor ⊙⊙

Our expert hotel picks are reinforced by high ratings on TripAdvisor. Look for representative quotes in this guide, and the latest TripAdvisor ratings and feedback at Fodors.com.

Restaurants

Unless we state otherwise, restaurants are open for lunch and dinner daily. We mention dress code only when there's a specific

requirement and reservations only when they're essential or not accepted. To make restaurant reservations, visit Fodors.com.

Credit Cards

The hotels and restaurants in this guide typically accept credit cards. If not, we'll say so.

Ratings		Hotels & Restaurants	
★	Fodor's Choice		
★	Highly recommended	🏨	Hotel
⟲	Family-friendly	🛏	Number of rooms
		⫶⦿⫶	Meal plans
Listings		✕	Restaurant
✉	Address	☖	Reservations
✉	Branch address	🏛	Dress code
☎	Telephone	⊟	No credit cards
🖷	Fax	⑤	Price
⊕	Website		
✎	E-mail	**Other**	
✉	Admission fee	⇨	See also
⊙	Open/closed times	☞	Take note
Ⓜ	Subway	🏌	Golf facilities
⊕	Directions or Map coordinates		

Experience
Northern California

WHAT'S NEW IN NORTHERN CALIFORNIA

Foodie's Paradise

Great dining is a staple of the California lifestyle, and a new young generation of chefs is challenging old ideas about preparing and presenting great food. Food-truck frenzy has created a movable feast up and down the state. Esteemed chefs and urban foodies follow the trucks on Twitter as they move around cities 24/7 purveying delicious, cheap, fresh meals. The Spencer on the Go truck hangs out in SoMa in San Francisco, dishing such delicacies as escargot puff lollipops.

Grape Expectations

California wine culture is alive and well and continue to grow beyond the traditional wine country of Napa and Sonoma. In the Central Valley and Shasta Cascade areas, winemaking is also expanding. The Turkovich Family Winery opened in the Central Valley town of Winters just west of Sacramento. The Truckee River Winery, near Lake Tahoe, claims to be the highest and coldest winery in the nation.

Suite Dreams

Hotels are coming back to life in a big way. Visitors to Yountville in the Napa Valley have another new lodging choice, the Bardessono, a LEED-certified hotel that sports an eco spa and an underground geothermal system. And Park Hyatt Aviara has taken over and renovated the former Four Seasons in Carlsbad.

All Aboard

Riding the rails can be a satisfying experience, particularly in California where the distances between destinations sometimes run into the hundreds of miles. You can save money on gas and parking, avoid freeway traffic, and see some of the best the state has to offer.

The best trip is on the luxuriously appointed Coast Starlight, a long-distance train with sleeping cars that runs between Seattle and Los Angeles, passing some of California's most beautiful coastline as it hugs the beach. For the best surfside viewing, get a seat or a room on the left side of the train and ride south to north from San Diego to Oakland.

Head for the Hills

Things are looking up for visitors to California's alpine recreation areas, thanks to a host of enhancements. Yosemite National Park observed its 120th birthday in 2011 with some new ways to see the park. Yosemite Guide Service offers guided day hikes, customized driving tours, and backpacking trips. You can also take Yosemite Audio Adventures CD tours with you as you explore the park.

Homegrown Hospitality

Agritourism in California isn't new, but it is on the rise, with farm tours and agricultural festivals sprouting up everywhere.

Wine country is a particularly fertile area—spurred by the success of vineyards, the area's lavender growers and olive-oil producers have started welcoming visitors. Sonoma Farm Trail Tours include walking the land and a farm-driven dinner with paired wines.

In the Central Valley, America's number-one producer of stone fruit, you can travel themed tourist routes (like Fresno County's Blossom Trail) and tour herb gardens, fruit orchards, organic dairies, and pumpkin patches.

WHEN TO GO

Because it offers activities indoors and out, San Francisco rates as all-season destinations. Early spring—when the gray whale migration overlaps with the end of the elephant seal breeding season and the start of the bird migration—is the optimal time to visit Point Reyes National Seashore. Yosemite is ideal in the late spring because roads closed in winter are reopened, and the park's waterfalls—swollen with melting snow—run fast. Autumn is "crush time" in all the wine destinations, from Napa/Sonoma in the north and the central coast. Snowfall makes winter peak season for skiers in Mammoth Mountain and Lake Tahoe, where runs typically open around Thanksgiving. (They sometimes remain in operation into June.)

Climate
It's difficult to generalize much about the state's weather beyond saying that precipitation comes in winter and summer is dry in most places. As a rule, inland regions are hotter in summer and colder in winter, compared with coastal areas, which are relatively cool year-round. Fog is a potential hazard any day of the year in coastal regions. As you climb into the mountains, seasonal variations are more apparent: winter brings snow (at elevations above 3,000 feet), autumn is crisp, spring can go either way, and summer is sunny and warm, with only an occasional thundershower in the southern part of the state.

Microclimates
Mountains separate the California coastline from the state's interior, and the weather can sometimes vary dramatically within a 15-minute drive. On a foggy summer day in San Francisco, you'll be grateful for a sweater—but head 50 miles north inland to Napa Valley, and you'll

likely be content in short sleeves. Day and nighttime temperatures can also vary greatly. Temperature swings elsewhere can be even more extreme. Take Sacramento: On August afternoons the mercury hits the 90s and occasionally exceeds 100°F. Yet as darkness falls, it sometimes plummets to 40°F.

Forecasts
National Weather Service
🌐 *www.wrh.noaa.gov.*

WHAT'S WHERE

The following numbers refer to chapters.

2 The Central Coast. Three of the state's top stops—swanky Santa Barbara, Hearst Castle, and Big Sur—sit along the scenic 200-mile route.

3 Monterey Bay Area. Postcard-perfect Monterey, Victorian-flavored Pacific Grove, and exclusive Carmel all share this stretch of California coast. To the north, Santa Cruz boasts a boardwalk, a UC campus, ethnic clothing shops, and plenty of surfers.

4 San Francisco. To see why so many have left their hearts here, you need to the city's iconic neighborhoods—posh Pacific Heights, the Hispanic Mission, and gay-friendly Castro.

5 The Bay Area. The area that rings San Francisco is nothing like the city—but it is home to some of the nation's great universities, fabulous bay views, and Alice Waters's Chez Panisse.

6 The Wine Country. Napa and Sonoma counties retain their title as *the* California wine country, by virtue of award-winning vintages, luxe lodgings, and epicurean eats.

7 The North Coast. The star attractions here are the natural ones, from the secluded beaches and wave-battered bluffs of Point Reyes National Seashore to the towering redwood forests.

8 Redwood National Park. More than 200 miles of trails, ranging from easy to strenuous, allow visitors to see these spectacular trees in their primitive environments.

9 The Southern Sierra. In the Mammoth Lakes region, sawtooth mountains and deep powdery snowdrifts combine to create the state's premier conditions for skiing and snowboarding.

10 Yosemite National Park. The views immortalized by photographer Ansel Adams—of towering granite monoliths, verdant glacial valleys, and lofty waterfalls—are still camera-ready.

11 Sequoia and Kings Canyon National Parks. The sight of ancient redwoods towering above jagged mountains will take your breath away.

12 Sacramento and the Gold Country. The 1849 gold rush that built San Francisco and Sacramento began here, and the former mining camps strung along 185 miles of Highway 49 replay their past to the hilt.

13 Lake Tahoe. With miles of crystalline water reflecting the peaks of the High Sierra, Lake Tahoe is the perfect setting for activities like hiking and golfing in summer and skiing and snowmobiling in winter.

14 The Far North. California's far northeast corner is home to snowcapped Mount Shasta, the pristine Trinity Wilderness, and abundant backwoods character that appeals to outdoorsy types.

0   75 mi

0   75 km

Crescent City
Klamath
Yreka
Goose Lake
Redwood National Park
8
Arcata
Eureka
Ferndale
Weaverville
Mt. Shasta
Burney
Shasta Lake
CASCADE RANGE
Alturas
Redding
14
Lassen Volcanic National Park
Susanville
Red Bluff
Garberville
Leggett
Eel R.
Chico
Paradise
Willows
Oroville
Grass Valley
Truckee
Reno
Pyramid Lake
NEVADA
Fort Bragg
Willits
Sacramento Valley
Mendocino
Ukiah
Yuba City
Boonville
Clear Lake
49
Auburn
Lake Tahoe
CARSON CITY
Point Arena
Gualala
7
Healdsburg
6
Woodland
Placerville
South Lake Tahoe
Jenner
Santa Rosa
Napa
Fairfield
SACRAMENTO
Elk Grove
12
Yosemite National Park
Bridgeport
Novato
Sonoma
Lodi
Jackson
Point Reyes National Seashore
4
Berkeley
Stockton
Sonora
10
Mono Lake
9
SAN FRANCISCO
Oakland
Modesto
SIERRA NEVADA
Mammoth Lakes
5
Fremont
Turlock
Yosemite Village
Bishop
Palo Alto
San Jose
Merced
Santa Cruz
Gilroy
Chowchilla
Big Pine
Castroville
San Luis Res.
Los Banos
Madera
Kings Canyon National Park
PACIFIC OCEAN
Monterey
Salinas
Fresno
Pacific Grove
3
Soledad
Visalia
11
Carmel
5
Tulare Lake Bed
Porterville
Sequoia National Park
Big Sur
Coalinga
Kernville
China Lake
San Simeon
Paso Robles
Bakersfield
Ridgecrest
San Luis Obispo
McKittrick
Santa Maria
Tejon Pass
TEHACHAPI MTS.
Lancaster
Lompoc
2
Santa Barbara
Ojai
Santa Barbara Channel
Ventura
Oxnard
Pasadena
San Joaquin Valley

NORTHERN CALIFORNIA PLANNER

Driving Around

Driving may be a way of life in California, but it isn't cheap (gas prices here are usually among the highest in the nation). It's also not for the fainthearted; you've surely heard horror stories about California's freeways, but even the state's scenic highways and byways have their own hassles. For instance, on the dramatic coastal road between San Simeon and Carmel, twists, turns, and divinely distracting vistas frequently slow traffic; in rainy season, mud slides can close the road altogether. ⚠ Never cross the double line when driving these roads. If you see that cars are backing up behind you on a two-lane, no-passing stretch, do everyone (and yourself) a favor and use the first available pullout.

On California's notorious freeways, other rules apply. Nervous Nellies must resist the urge to stay in the two slow-moving ones on the far right, used primarily by trucks. To drive at least the speed limit, get yourself in a middle lane. If you're ready to bend the rules a bit, the second (lanes are numbered from 1 starting at the center) lane moves about 5 mph faster. But avoid the far-left lane (the one next to the carpool lane), where speeds range from 75 mph to 90 mph.

Flying In

Air travelers beginning or ending their vacation in San Francisco have two main airports to choose from: San Francisco International (SFO) or Oakland International (OAK) across the Bay. The former lands you closer to the city core (ground transportation will take about 20 minutes versus 35), but the latter is less heavily trafficked and less prone to pesky fog delays. BART, the Bay Area's affordable rapid-transit system, serves both airports. So your decision will probably rest on which one has the best fares and connections for your particular route.

If your final destination is Monterey or Carmel, San Jose International Airport (SJC), about 40 miles south of San Francisco, is another alternative.

FAQ

I'm not particularly active. Will I still enjoy visiting a national park? Absolutely, the most popular parks have something for everyone. In Yosemite the ultrafit embark on 12-hour trail treks and mere mortals can hike Cook's Meadow—an easy 1-mile loop that's also wheelchair accessible. Or just hop on a free shuttle or drive yourself to sites.

What's the single best place to take the kids? For its sheer smorgasbord of activities, San Francisco is hard to beat. A cable-car ride is a no-brainer—but be sure to also take a spin on the historic F-line trolleys. Other classic kid-friendly SF sights include the Exploratorium, the San Francisco Zoo, Alcatraz, the Ferry Building, and the California Academy of Sciences. Or head to Musée Mécanique to see what kids played way before Nintendo's Wii came out.

California sounds expensive. How can I save on sightseeing? CityPass (☎ 888/330–5008 ⊕ www.citypass.com) includes admission and some upgrades for main attractions in San Francisco. Also, many museums set aside free-admission days. Prefer the great outdoors? An America the Beautiful annual pass (☎ 888/275–8747 ⊕ www.nps.gov) admits you to every site under the National Park Service umbrella. Better yet, depending on the property, passengers in your vehicle get in free, too.

NORTHERN CALIFORNIA'S TOP EXPERIENCES

Hit the Road

Kings Canyon Highway, Redwood Highway, Tioga Pass, 17-Mile Drive, the Lake Tahoe loop: California has some splendid and challenging roads. You'll drive through a tunnel formed by towering redwood trees on the Redwood Highway. If you venture over the Sierras by way of Tioga Pass (through Yosemite in summer only), you'll see emerald green meadows, gray granite monoliths, and pristine blue lakes—and very few people.

Go for the Gold

Though California's gold rush ended more than a hundred years ago, you can still feel the

'49er fever on the western face of the Sierra Nevada in Columbia, a well-preserved town populated by costumed interpreters, where you can pan for gold or tour a mine. Or visit Bodie, an eerie ghost town in the eastern Sierra that remains in a state of "arrested decay."

Think Globally, Eat Locally

Over the years California cuisine has evolved from a mere trend into a respected gastronomic tradition: one that pairs local, often organic or sustainable, ingredients with techniques inspired by European, Asian, and, increasingly, Indian and Middle Eastern cookery.

Embrace Your Inner Eccentric

California has always drawn creative and, well, eccentric people. And all that quirkiness has left its mark in the form of oddball architecture that makes for some fun sightseeing. Begin by touring Hearst Castle—the beautifully bizarre estate William Randolph Hearst built above San Simeon. And Lake Tahoe's Vikingsholm (a re-created Viking castle) is equally odd.

Be Transported

San Franciscans take cable cars seriously—and riding on one is a must-do. You may even want to visit the (free!) Cable Car Museum to get a handle on the inner workings or just ring a gripman's bell. *(See the Cable Car feature in the San Francisco chapter.)* But the city's options for vintage public transport doesn't end there: the lesser known F line streetcars are every bit as photogenic, and they have shorter lines.

Go Wild

California communities host hundreds of annual events, but some of the best are organized by Mother Nature. The most famous is the "miracle migration" that sees swallows flock back to Mission San Juan Capistrano each March. In Pacific Grove masses of monarch butterflies reliably arrive for their winter vacation every year in October. If you can't make it there, visit the butterfly sanctuary in the California Academy of Sciences in San Francisco.

People-Watch

Opportunities for world-class people-watching abound in California. Just saunter the rainbow-flagged streets of San Francisco's Castro neighborhood or the century-old boardwalk in time-warped, resiliently boho Santa Cruz.

NORTHERN CALIFORNIA TODAY

The People

California is as much a state of mind as a state in the union—a kind of perpetual Promised Land that has represented many things to many people. In the 18th century, Spanish missionaries came seeking converts. In the 19th, miners rushed here to search for gold. And, in the years since, a long line of Dust Bowl farmers, land speculators, Haight-Ashbury hippies, migrant workers, dot-commers, real estate speculators, and would-be actors has come chasing their own dreams.

The result is a population that leans toward idealism—without necessarily being as liberal as you might think. (Remember, this is Ronald Reagan's old stomping ground.) And despite the stereotype of the blue-eyed, blond surfer, California's population is not homogeneous either. Ten million people who live here (more than 28% of Californians) are foreign born—including former Governor Schwarzenegger. Almost half hail from neighboring Mexico; another third emigrated from Asia, following the waves of Chinese workers who arrived in the 1860s to build the railroads and subsequent waves of Indochinese refugees from the Vietnam War.

The Politics

What's blue and red and green all over? California: a predominantly Democratic state with an aggressive "go green" agenda. Democratic Governor Jerry Brown, who was elected to the office for the second time in 30 years on a promise to clean up the financial mess created under his predecessor Arnold Schwarzenegger, is moving the progressive agenda ahead with policies that make California the greenest state in the nation

supporting more green construction, wind farms, and solar panels.

The Economy

Leading all other states in terms of the income generated by agriculture, tourism, and industrial activity, California has the country's most diverse state economy. Moreover, with a gross state product of more than $2 trillion, California would be one of the top 10 economies *in the world* if it were an independent nation. But due to its wealth ($61,000 median household income) and productivity, California took a large hit in the recession that began in 2007. This affected all levels of government from local to statewide and resulted in reduction of services that Californians have long taken for granted.

But the Golden State's economic history is filled with boom and bust cycles—beginning with the mid-19th-century gold rush that started it all. Optimists already have their eyes on the next potential boom: high-tech and bio research, "green companies" focused on alternative energy, renewables, electric cars, and the like.

The Culture

Cultural organizations thrive in California. San Francisco—a city with only about 775,000 residents—has well-regarded ballet, opera, and theater companies, and is home to one of the continent's most noteworthy orchestras. Museums like San Francisco Museum of Modern Art (SFMOMA) and the de Young also represent the city's ongoing commitment to the arts. Art and culture thrive farther south in San Diego as well. Balboa Park alone holds 15 museums, opulent gardens, and three performance venues, in addition to the San Diego Zoo. And L.A. and its environs are the chief arbiters of movies, TV, and video production. Capitol Records

set up shop in L.A. in the 1940s, and this area has been instrumental in the music industry ever since. And now websites are coming to thrive in that creative landscape—Facebook, YouTube, and Google are California creatures.

The Parks and Preserves

Cloud-spearing redwood groves, snow-tipped mountains, canyon-slashed deserts, primordial lava beds, and a seemingly endless coast: California's natural diversity is staggering—and efforts to protect it started early. The first national park here was established in 1890, and the National Park Service now oversees 30 sites in California (more than in any other state). When you factor in 278 state parks—which encompass underwater preserves, historic sites, wildlife reserves, dune systems, and other sensitive habitats—the number of acres involved is almost as impressive as the topography itself.

Due to encroaching development and pollution, keeping these natural treasures in pristine condition is an ongoing challenge. For instance, Sequoia and Kings Canyon (which is plagued by pesticides and other agricultural pollutants blown in from the San Joaquin Valley) has been named America's "smoggiest park" by the National Parks Conservation Association, and the Environmental Protection Agency has designated it as an "ozone non-attainment area with levels of ozone pollution that threaten human health."

There is no question that Californians love their 278 state parks, 70 of which were scheduled to close in July 2012 due to budget cuts. Nearly every park has its grass-roots supporters, who volunteer to raise money, volunteer as rangers, and work other jobs to keep the parks open.

The Cuisine

California gave us McDonald's, Denny's, Carl's Jr., Taco Bell, and, of course, In-N-Out Burger. Fortunately for those of us with fast-clogging arteries, the state also kick-started the organic food movement. Back in the 1970s, California-based chefs put American cuisine on the culinary map by focusing on freshly prepared seasonal ingredients.

Today, this focus has spawned the "locavore" or sustainable food movement—followers try to only consume food produced within a 100-mile radius of where they live, since processing and refining food and transporting goods over long distances is bad for both the body and the environment. This isn't much of a restriction in California, where a huge variety of crops grow year-round. Some 350 cities and towns have certified farmers' markets—and their stalls are bursting with a variety of goods. California has been America's top agricultural producer for the last 50 years, growing more fruits and vegetables than any other state. Dairies and ranches also thrive here, and fishing fleets harvest fish and shellfish from the rich waters offshore.

NORTHERN CALIFORNIA TOP ATTRACTIONS

Yosemite National Park
(A) Nature looms large here, both literally and figuratively. In addition to hulking Half Dome, the park is home to El Capitan (the world's largest exposed granite monolith, rising 3,593 feet above the glacier-carved valley floor) and Yosemite Falls (North America's tallest cascade). In Yosemite's signature stand of giant sequoias—the Mariposa Grove—even the trees are Bunyanesque. Needless to say, crowds can be super-size.

San Francisco
(B) Population-wise, San Francisco is smaller than Indianapolis. But when it comes to sites (and soul), this city is a giant. Start working through the standard travelers' "to do" list by strolling across the Golden Gate Bridge, taking a ferry to Alcatraz, and hopping on the Powell–Hyde cable car. Just leave enough time to explore the diverse neighborhoods where San Francisco's distinctive personality—an amalgam of gold-rush history, immigrant traditions, counterculture proclivities, and millennial materialism—is on display.

Wine Country
(C) Although the vineyard-blanketed hills of California's original Wine Country are undeniably scenic, the wine itself (preferably accompanied by the area's famed cuisine) remains the big draw here. Budding oenophiles can educate their palettes on scores of tours and tasting sessions—provided they can elbow their way through the high-season hordes.

Point Reyes National Seashore

(D) Aside from the namesake seashore, this Marin County preserve encompasses ecosystems that range from woodlands and marshlands to heathlike grasslands. The range of wildlife here is equally diverse—depending on when you visit, expect to see gray whales, rare Tule elk, and almost 500 species of birds. December through March you can also see male elephant seals compete for mates.

Lake Tahoe

(E) Deep, clear, and intensely blue, this forest-rimmed body of water straddling the California–Nevada border is one of the continent's prettiest alpine lakes. That environmental controls can keep it that way is something of a miracle, given Tahoe's popularity. Throngs of outdoor adventurers flock to the California side to ski, hike, bike, and boat. On the Nevada side, where casinos are king, gambling often wins out over fresh-air activities—but natural wonders are never far away.

Gold Country

(F) California's gold rush was one of the most significant events in U.S. history. It saved the Union and helped open the western frontier, when Argonauts flooded a 300-mi-long stretch of the Sierra foothills. Remnants of the gold rush remain to this day in the towns, diggings, trains, museums, and culture that you'll encounter along historic Highway 49; it runs north to south from Loyalton near the Nevada border to Oakhurst, just south of Yosemite. Towns along the way, mostly updated and renovated, allow you to dig into the past and discover what the excitement was all about.

QUINTESSENTIAL NORTHERN CALIFORNIA

The Wine

If California were a country, it would rank as the world's fourth-largest wine producer, after Italy, France, and Spain. In those countries, where vino is barely considered an alcoholic beverage, wine drinking has evolved into a relaxing ritual best shared with friends and family. A modern, Americanized version of that mentality integrates wine into daily life in California, and there are many places to sample it. The Napa and Sonoma valleys come to mind first. However, there are other destinations for oenophiles who want a vintage vacation. You can find great wineries around Monterey Bay and Gold Country's Shenandoah Valley, too. All are respected appellations, and their winery tours and tastings will show you what all the buzz is about.

The Beach

California's beach culture is, in a word, legendary. Of course, it only makes sense that folks living in a state with a 1,264-mile coastline (a hefty portion of which sees the sun upward of 300 days a year) would perfect the art of beach-going. True aficionados begin with a reasonably fit physique, plus a stylish wardrobe consisting of flip-flops, bikinis, wet suits, and such. Mastery of at least one beach skill—surfing, boogie boarding, kayaking, Frisbee tossing, or looking fab while catching rays—is also essential. As a visitor, though, you need only a swimsuit and some rented equipment for most sports. You can then hit the beach almost anywhere, thanks to the California belief in coastal access as a birthright. The farther south you go, the wider, sandier, and sunnier the beaches become; moving north they are rockier and foggier, with colder and rougher surf.

Californians live in such a large and splashy state that they sometimes seem to forget about the rest of the country. They've developed a distinctive culture all their own, which you can delve into by doing as the locals do.

The Outdoors

One of California's greatest assets—the mild year-round weather enjoyed by most of the state—inspires residents to spend as much time outside as they possibly can. They have a tremendous enthusiasm for every imaginable outdoor sport, and, up north especially, fresh-air adventures are extremely popular (which may explain why everyone there seems to own at least one pair of hiking boots). But the California-alfresco creed is more broadly interpreted, and the general rule when planning any activity is "if it can happen outside, it will!" *Plein air* vacation opportunities include dining on patios, decks, and wharves; shopping in street markets or elaborate open-air malls; hearing almost any kind of music at moonlight concerts; touring the sculpture gardens that grace major art museums; and celebrating everything from gay pride to garlic at outdoor fairs.

The Automobile

Americans may have a love affair with the automobile, but Californians have an out-and-out obsession. Even when gas prices rev up and freeway traffic slows down, their passion burns as hot as ever. You can witness this ardor any summer weekend at huge classic- and custom-car shows held statewide. Even better, you can feel it yourself by taking the wheel. Trace an old stagecoach route through the mountains above Santa Barbara on Highway 154; track migrating whales up the coast to Big Sur; or take 17-Mile Drive along the precipitous edge of the Monterey Peninsula. Glorious for the most part, but authentically congested in some areas in the south, Highway 1 runs almost the entire length of the state, hugging the coast most of the way.

GREAT ITINERARIES

Day 1: Arrival/San Francisco

Straight from the airport, drop your bags at the lighthearted Hotel Monaco near Union Square and request a goldfish for your room. Chinatown, chock-full of dim sum shops, storefront temples, and open-air markets, promises unfamiliar tastes for lunch. Catch a Powell Street cable car to the end of the line and get off to see the bay views and the antique arcade games at Musée Mécanique, the hidden gem of otherwise mindless Fisherman's Wharf. No need to go any farther than cosmopolitan North Beach for cocktail hour, dinner, and live music.

Day 2: San Francisco

A Union Square stroll packs a wallop of people-watching, window-shopping, and architecture-viewing. In Golden Gate Park, linger amid the flora of the conservatory and the arboretum, soak up some art at the de Young Museum, and find serene refreshment at the Japanese Tea Garden. The Pacific surf pounds the cliffs below the Legion of Honor art museum, which has an exquisite view of the Golden Gate Bridge—when the fog stays away. Sunset cocktails at the circa-1909 Cliff House include a prospect over Seal Rock (actually occupied by sea lions). Eat dinner elsewhere: Pacific Heights, the Mission, and SoMa teem with excellent restaurants.

Day 3: Into the High Sierra

Pick up your rental car and head for the hills. A five-hour drive due east brings you to Yosemite National Park, where Bridalveil Fall and El Capitan, the 350-story granite monolith, greet you on your way to Yosemite Village. Grab information and refreshment before hopping on the year-round shuttle to explore. Justly famous sights cram Yosemite Valley:

massive Half Dome and Sentinel Dome, thundering Yosemite Falls, and wispy Ribbon Fall and Nevada Fall. Invigorating short hikes off the shuttle route lead to numerous vantage points. Celebrate your arrival in one of the world's most sublime spots with dinner in the dramatic Ahwahnee Hotel Dining Room.

Day 4: Yosemite National Park

Ardent hikers consider John Muir Trail a must-do, tackling the rigorous 12-hour round-trip to the top of Half Dome in search of life-changing vistas. The merely mortal hike downhill from Glacier Point on Four-Mile Trail or Panorama Trail, the latter an all-day trek past waterfalls. Less demanding still is a drive to Wawona for a stroll in the Mariposa Grove of Big Trees and lunch at the 19th-century Wawona Hotel. In bad weather, take shelter in the Ansel Adams Gallery. At sunset, drive up to Glacier Point for a breathtaking view.

Day 5: Gold Country South

Step into a living gold-rush town at Columbia State Historic Park, where you can ride a stagecoach and pan for riches. Sutter Creek's well-preserved downtown bursts with shopping opportunities, but the vintage goods displayed at J. Monteverde General Store are not for sale. A different sort of vintage powers the present-day bonanza of Shenandoah Valley, heart of the Sierra Foothills wine country. Taste your way through Zinfandels and Syrahs at boutique wineries. Amador City's 1879 Imperial Hotel places you firmly in the past for the night.

Day 6: Gold Country North

In Placerville, a mineshaft invites investigation at Hangtown's Gold Bug Mine, while Marshall Gold Discovery State Historic Park encompasses most of Coloma and preserves the spot where James Marshall's

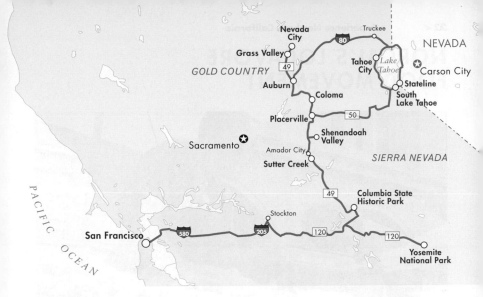

1849 find set off the California gold rush. Old Town Auburn makes a good lunch stop, but if you hold out until you reach Grass Valley you can try authentic miners' pasties. A tour of Empire Mine State Historic Park takes you into a mine, and a few miles away horse-drawn carriages ply the narrow, shop-lined streets of downtown Nevada City. Backtrack to Auburn or Placerville to overnight in historic or modern lodgings.

Day 7: To the Lake

Jewel-like Lake Tahoe is a straight shot east of Placerville on Highway 50; stop for picnic provisions in commercial South Lake Tahoe. A stroll past the three magnificent estates in Pope-Baldwin Recreation area hints at the sumptuous lakefront summers once enjoyed by the elite. High above a glittering cove, Emerald Bay State Park offers one of the best lake views as well as a steep hike down to (and back up from) Vikingsholm, a replica 9th-century Scandinavian castle. Another fine, old mansion—plus a nature preserve and many hiking trails—lies in Sugar Pine Point State Park.

Day 8: Lake Tahoe

With advance reservations, you can tour the ultraluxe 1936 Thunderbird Lodge and its grounds. The picture-perfect beaches and bays of Lake Tahoe–Nevada State Park line the Nevada shoreline, a great place to bask in the sun or go mountain biking. For a different perspective of the lake, get out on the azure water aboard the stern-wheeler MS *Dixie II* from Zephyr Cove. In South Lake Tahoe, another view unfurls as the Heavenly Gondola travels 2½ miles up a mountain. Keep your adrenaline pumping into the evening with some action at the massive casinos clustered in Stateline, Nevada.

Day 9: Back to the City/Departure

After a morning of driving, return your rental car in San Francisco and head to lunch at the Ferry Building, followed by a visit to the San Francisco Museum of Modern Art. Say good-bye to Northern California at one of the trendy bars in the downtown hotels.

NORCAL'S LOCAVORE FOOD MOVEMENT

Organic, local, and *sustainable* are buzzwords in Northern California, home to hundreds of small family farmers, sustainable ranchers, and artisan producers are leading the country's back-to-the-earth food movement.

When Alice Waters opened Chez Panisse in Berkeley in 1971, she sparked a culinary revolution that continues today. Initially called California cuisine, the cooking style showcased local, seasonal ingredients in fresh preparations. It also marked a new willingness by American chefs to experiment with international influences. As the movement spread, it became known as New American cooking. This "eat local, think global" ethos has lead to a resurgence of artisanal producers across the country.

The *locavore* (focused on sustainable, local foods) movement's epicenter is still Northern California. At the Ferry Plaza Farmers Market in San Francisco alone, farmers bring over 1,200 varieties of fruits and vegetables to market every year. Chefs proudly call out their purveyors on menus and Web sites, elevating humble vegetable growers to starring culinary roles.

FARMERS MARKETS

One of the best ways to taste Northern California's bounty is by stopping by the Ferry Plaza Farmers Market, held outside of the Ferry Building on the Embarcadero, at Market Street. Held on Tuesday and Saturday mornings, the market offers produce, meats, fish, and flowers from small regional farmers and ranchers, many of whom are certified organic.

It is also a great place to pick up items for a picnic. Prepared foods like tamales and pasta are available, as are specialties like jams, breads, and cheeses from local artisan producers.

Check ⊕ *www.cuesa.org* for hours.

FRUIT

Northern California's diverse climate makes it an ideal place to grow all types of fruit, from berries to stone fruit. Farmers' markets and restaurants abound with a staggering selection of produce: Blossom Bluff Orchards, south of San Francisco, offers more than 150 varieties of stone fruits, like apricots, nectarines, and peaches. North of the city, The Apple Farm grows 80 varieties of apples, pears, persimmons, quince, and French plums. The Bay Area is also one of the best places in the country to find rare fruit varieties like aprium, cherimoya, cactus pear, jujube, and loquat; California's famous Meyer lemons—sweeter and less acidic than common lemons—are celebrated in restaurant desserts.

VEGETABLES

Some chefs give top billing to their produce purveyors, like a recently observed menu touting a salad of Star Route Farm field greens with Picholine olives, sweet herbs, and goat cheese. Along with these tantalizing items, be on the lookout for locally grown artichokes, Asian vegetables, multihued beets and carrots, and heirloom varieties of tomatoes, squash, and beans.

MEAT

Family-owned ranches and farms are prominent in the region, with many raising organic or "humane certified"

beef, pork, lamb, and poultry. Upscale Bay Area restaurants are fervent about recognizing their high-quality protein producers. From recent menus at two well-known San Francisco restaurants: Wolfe Ranch quail and foie gras crostini with Murcott mandarins, smoked bacon and bok choy, and vanilla gastrique; and Prather Ranch lamb with fava greens, cranberry beans, crispy artichokes, and salsa verde.

FISH

Diners and shoppers will find myriad seafood from local waters, from farm-raised scallops to line-caught California salmon. On menus, look for Hog Island Oysters, a local producer that raises more than three million oysters a year in Tomales Bay. Sardines netted in Monterey Bay are popular in preparations like mesquite-grilled sardines with fava beans, French radish and fennel salad, and preserved Meyer lemon.

CHEESE

Restaurant cheese plates, often served before—or in lieu of—dessert, are a great way to experience the region's excellent local cheeses. Look for selections from Cypress Grove Chevre, popular for its artisan goat cheeses, and Cowgirl Creamery, a renowned local producer of fresh and aged cow's milk cheeses. Additionally, some shops and bakeries offer fresh local butter and cheeses.

THE ULTIMATE ROAD TRIP

CALIFORNIA'S LEGENDARY HIGHWAY 1

by Cheryl Crabtree

One of the world's most scenic drives, California's State Route 1 (also known as Highway 1, the Pacific Coast Highway, the PCH) stretches along the edge of the state for nearly 660 miles, from Southern California's Dana Point to its northern terminus near Leggett, about 40 miles north of Fort Bragg. As you travel south to north, the water's edge transitions from long, sandy beaches and low-lying bluffs to towering dunes, craggy cliffs, and ancient redwood groves. The ocean changes as well; the relatively tame and surfable swells lapping the Southern California shore give way to the frigid, powerful waves crashing against weatherbeaten rocks in the north.

Map labels:
- Ft. Bragg
- Mendocino
- SONOMA COUNTY
- Point Reyes National Seashore
- MARIN COUNTY
- Marin Headlands
- Sacramento
- San Francisco
- Santa Cruz
- 17-Mile Drive
- Monterey
- Carmel
- Big Sur
- Fresno
- Hearst San Simeon State Historical Monument
- San Luis Obispo
- Santa Barbara
- Santa Monica
- Los Angeles
- Long Beach

HIGHWAY 1 TOP 10

- Santa Monica
- Santa Barbara
- Hearst San Simeon State Historical Monument
- Big Sur
- Carmel
- 17–Mile Drive
- Monterey
- San Francisco
- Marin Headlands
- Point Reyes National Seashore

Give yourself lots of extra time to pull off the road and enjoy the scenery

STARTING YOUR JOURNEY

You may decide to drive the road's entire 660-mile route, or bite off a smaller piece. In either case, a Highway 1 road trip allows you to experience California at your own pace, stopping when and where you wish. Hike a beachside trail, dig your toes in the sand, and search for creatures in the tidepools. Buy some artichokes and strawberries from a roadside farmstand. Talk to people along the way (you'll run into everyone from soul-searching meditators, farmers, and beatniks to city-slackers and working-class folks), and take lots of pictures. Don't rush—you could easily spend a lifetime discovering secret spots along this route.

To help you plan your trip, we've broken the road into three regions (Santa Monica to Carmel, Carmel to San Francisco, and San Francisco to Fort Bragg); each region is then broken up into smaller segments—many of which are suitable for a day's drive. If you're pressed for time, you can always tackle a section of Highway 1, and then head inland to U.S. 101 or I-5 to reach your next destination more quickly.

WHAT'S IN A NAME?

Though it's often referred to as the Pacific Coast Highway (or PCH), sections of Highway 1 actually have different names. The southernmost section (Dana Point to Oxnard) is the Pacific Coast Highway. After that, the road becomes the Cabrillo Highway (Las Cruces to Lompoc), the Big Sur Coast Highway (San Luis Obispo County line to Monterey), the North Coast Scenic Byway (San Luis Obispo city limit to the Monterey County line), the Cabrillo Highway again (Santa Cruz County line to Half Moon Bay), and finally the Shoreline Highway (Marin City to Leggett). To make matters more confusing, smaller chunks of the road have additional honorary monikers. Just follow the green triangular signs that say "California 1."

HIGHWAY 1 DRIVING

- Rent a convertible. (You will not regret it.)
- Begin the drive north from Santa Monica, where congestion and traffic delays pose less of a problem.
- Take advantage of turnouts. Let cars pass you as you take in the ocean view and snap a picture.
- Mind your manners: Don't tailgate or glare at other drivers.
- If you're prone to motion sickness, take the wheel yourself. Focusing on the landscape outside should help you feel less queasy.
- If you're afraid of heights, drive from south to north so you'll be on the mountain rather than the cliff side of the road.
- Driving PCH is glorious during winter, but check weather conditions before you go as landslides are frequent after storms.

HIGHWAY 1: SANTA MONICA TO BIG SUR

Hearst Castle

THE PLAN

Distance: approx. 335 mi

Time: 3-5 days

Good Overnight Options: Malibu, Santa Barbara, Pismo Beach, San Luis Obispo, Cambria, Carmel

For more information on the sights and attractions along this portion of Highway 1, please see Los Angeles and Central Coast chapters

SANTA MONICA TO MALIBU (approx. 26 mi)

Highway 1 begins in Dana point, but it seems more appropriate to begin a PCH adventure in **Santa Monica.** Be sure to experience the beach culture, then balance the tacky pleasures of Santa Monica's amusement pier with a stylish dinner in a neighborhood restaurant.

MALIBU TO SANTA BARBARA (approx. 70 mi)

The PCH follows the curve of Santa Monica Bay all the way to **Malibu** and **Point Mugu,**

near **Oxnard.** Chances are you'll experience *déjà vu* driving this 27-mile stretch: mountains on one side, ocean on the other, opulent homes perched on hillsides; you've seen this piece of coast countless times on TV and film. Be sure to walk out on the **Malibu Pier** for a great photo opp, then check out **Surfrider Beach,** with three famous points where perfect waves ignited a worldwide surfing rage in the 1960s.

After Malibu you'll drive through miles of protected, largely unpopulated coastline. Ride a wave at **Zuma Beach,** scout for offshore whales at **Point Dume State Preserve,** or hike the trails at **Point Mugu State Park.** After skirting Point Mugu, Highway 1 merges with U.S. 101 for about 70 mi before reaching **Santa Barbara.** A mini-tour of the city includes a real Mexican lunch at **La Super-Rica,** a visit to the magnificent Spanish **Mission Santa Barbara,** and a walk down hopping **State Street to Stearns Wharf.**

SANTA BARBARA TO SAN SIMEON (approx. 147 mi)

North of Santa Barbara, Highway 1 morphs into the Cabrillo Highway, separating

Santa Barbara

from and then rejoining U.S. 101. The route winds through rolling vineyards and rangeland to **San Luis Obispo,** where any legit road trip includes a photo stop at the quirky **Madonna Inn.** Be sure to also climb the humungous dunes at **Guadalupe-Nipomo Dunes Preserve.**

In downtown San Luis Obispo, the **Mission San Luis Obispo de Tolosa** stands by a tree-shaded creek edged with shops and cafés. Highway 1 continues to **Morro Bay** and up the coast. About 4 mi north of Morro Bay, you'll reach **Cayucos,** a classic old California beach town with an 1875 pier, restaurants, taverns, and shops in historic buildings. The road continues through **Cambria** to solitary **Hearst San Simeon State Historical Monument**—the art-filled pleasure palace at **San Simeon.** Just four miles north of the castle, elephant seals grunt and cavort at the

Santa Monica

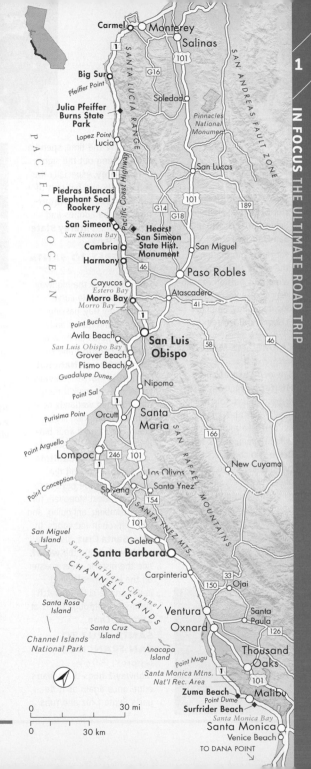

Big Sur

TOP 5 PLACES TO LINGER

- Point Dume State Preserve
- Santa Barbara
- Hearst San Simeon State Historical Monument
- Big Sur/Julia Pfeiffer Burns State Park
- Carmel

Piedras Blancas Elephant Seal Rookery, just off the side of the road.

SAN SIMEON TO CARMEL (approx. 92 mi) Heading north, you'll drive through **Big Sur,** a place of ancient forests and rugged shoreline stretching 90 mi from San Simeon to **Carmel.** Much of Big Sur lies within several state parks and the 165,000-acre **Ventana Wilderness,** itself part of the **Los Padres National Forest.** This famously scenic stretch of the coastal drive, which twists up and down bluffs above the ocean, can last hours. Take your time.

At **Julia Pfeiffer Burns State Park** one easy but rewarding hike leads to an iconic waterfall off a beach-front cliff. When you reach lovely **Carmel,** stroll around the picture-perfect town's mission, galleries, and shops.

HIGHWAY 1: CARMEL TO SAN FRANCISCO

San Francisco

THE PLAN

Distance: approx. 123 mi

Time: 2-4 days

Good Overnight Options: Carmel, Monterey, Santa Cruz, Half Moon Bay, San Francisco

For more information on the sights and attractions along this portion of Highway 1, please see chapters Monterey Bay, San Francisco, and Bay Area.

CARMEL TO MONTEREY

(approx. 4 mi)
Between **Carmel** and **Monterey,** Highway 1 cuts across the base of the Monterey Peninsula. Pony up the toll and take a brief detour to follow famous **17-Mile Drive,** which traverses a surf-pounded landscape of cypress trees, sea lions, gargantuan estates, and the world famous **Pebble Beach Golf Links.** Take your time here as well, and be sure to allow lots of time for pulling off to enjoy the gorgeous views.

Monterey

If you have the time, spend a day checking out the sights in **Monterey,** especially the kelp forests and bat rays of the **Monterey Bay Aquarium** and the adobes and artifacts of **Monterey State Historic Park.**

MONTEREY TO SANTA CRUZ (approx. 42 mi)

From Monterey the highway rounds the gentle curve of Monterey Bay, passing through sand dunes and artichoke fields on its way to **Moss Landing** and the **Elkhorn Slough National Estuarine Marine Preserve.** Kayak near or walk through the protected wetlands here, or board a pontoon safari boat—don't forget your binoculars. The historic seaside villages of **Aptos, Capitola,** and **Soquel,** just off the highway near the bay's midpoint, are ideal stopovers for beachcombing, antiquing, and hiking through redwoods. In boho **Santa Cruz,** just 7 mi north, walk along the **wharf,** ride the historic roller coaster on the **boardwalk,** and perch on the cliffs to watch surfers peel through tubes at **Steamer Lane.**

SANTA CRUZ TO SAN FRANCISCO (approx. 77 mi)

Highway 1 hugs the ocean's edge once again as it departs Santa Cruz and runs

Davenport cliffs, Devenport

northward past a string of secluded beaches and small towns. Stop and stretch your legs in the tiny, artsy town of **Davenport,** where you can wander through several galleries and enjoy sumptuous views from the bluffs. At **Año Nuevo State Reserve,** walk down to the dunes to view gargantuan elephant

FRIGID WATERS

If you're planning to jump in the ocean in Northern California, wear a wetsuit or prepare to shiver. Even in summer, the water temperatures warm up to just barely tolerable. The fog tends to burn off earlier in the day at relatively sheltered beaches near Monterey Bay's midpoint, near Aptos, Capitola and Santa Cruz. These beaches also tend to attract softer waves than those on the bay's outer edges.

Half Moon Bay

TOP 5 PLACES TO LINGER

- 17-Mile Drive
- Monterey
- Santa Cruz
- Año Nuevo State Reserve
- Half Moon Bay

seals lounging on shore, then break for a meal or snack in **Pescadero** or **Half Moon Bay.**

From Half Moon Bay to **Daly City,** the road includes a number of shoulderless twists and turns that demand slower speeds and nerves of steel. Signs of urban development soon appear: mansions holding fast to Pacific cliffs and then, as the road veers slightly inland to merge with Skyline Boulevard, boxlike houses sprawling across **Daly City** and **South San Francisco.**

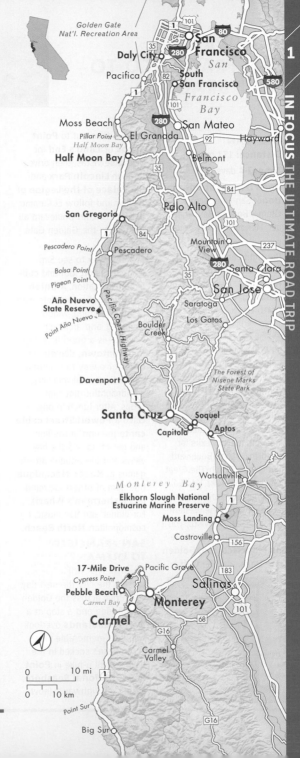

Golden Gate Nat'l. Recreation Area

San Francisco
Daly City
Pacifica
South San Francisco
San Francisco Bay
Moss Beach
Pillar Point
Half Moon Bay
Half Moon Bay
El Granada
San Mateo
Hayward
Belmont
Palo Alto
San Gregorio
Mountain View
Santa Clara
Pescadero Point
Pescadero
Bolsa Point
Pigeon Point
Año Nuevo State Reserve
San Jose
Saratoga
Los Gatos
Point Año Nuevo
Pacific Coast Highway
Boulder Creek
The Forest of Nisene Marks State Park
Davenport
Santa Cruz
Soquel
Capitola
Aptos
Watsonville
Monterey Bay
Elkhorn Slough National Estuarine Marine Preserve
Moss Landing
Castroville
17-Mile Drive
Cypress Point
Pacific Grove
Pebble Beach
Carmel Bay
Salinas
Monterey
Carmel
Carmel Valley
0   10 mi
0   10 km
Point Sur
Big Sur

HIGHWAY 1: SAN FRANCISCO TO FORT BRAGG

Mendocino Coast Botanical Garden

THE PLAN

Distance: 177 mi

Time: 2-4 days

Good Overnight Options: San Francisco, Olema, Bodega Bay, Gualala, Mendocino, Fort Bragg

For more information on the sights and attractions along this portion of Highway 1, please see San Francisco, Bay Area, and North Coast chapters

SAN FRANCISCO

The official Highway 1 heads straight through **San Francisco** along 19th Avenue through **Golden Gate Park** and the **Presidio** toward the **Golden Gate Bridge.** For a more scenic tour, watch for signs announcing exits for 35 North/Skyline Boulevard, then Ocean Beach/The Great Highway (past Lake Merced). The Great Highway follows the coast along the western border of San Francisco; you'll cruise past entrances to the **San Francisco Zoo, Golden Gate Park,** and the **Cliff**

Golden Gate Bridge

House. Hike out to **Point Lobos** or **Land's End** for awesome vistas, then drive through **Lincoln Park** and the **Palace of the Legion of Honor** and follow El Camino del Mar/Lincoln Boulevard all the way to the Golden Gate Bridge.

The best way to see San Francisco is on foot and public transportation. A **Union Square** stroll—complete with people-watching, window-shopping, and architecture-viewing—is a good first stop. In **Chinatown,** department stores give way to storefront temples, open-air markets, and delightful dim-sum shops. After lunch in one, catch a **Powell Street cable car** to the end of the line and get off to see the bay views and the antique arcade games at **Musée Mécanique** (the gem of otherwise mindless **Fisherman's Wharf**). For dinner and live music, try cosmopolitan **North Beach.**

SAN FRANCISCO TO OLEMA

(approx. 37 mi)

Leaving the city the next day, your drive across the Golden Gate Bridge and a stop at a **Marin Headlands** overlook will yield memorable views (if fog hasn't socked in the bay). So will a hike in **Point Reyes National Seashore,** farther up Highway 1 (now

Point Reyes National Seashore

called Shoreline Highway). On this wild swath of coast you'll likely be able to claim an unspoiled beach for yourself. You should expect company, however, around the lighthouse at the tip of Point Reyes because year-round views—and seasonal elephant seal– and whale-watching—draw crowds. If you have time, poke around tiny **Olema,** which has some excellent restaurants, and is home to the historic Olema Inn & Restaurant.

OLEMA TO MENDOCINO

(approx. 131 mi)

Passing only a few minuscule towns, this next stretch of Highway 1 showcases the northern coast in all its rugged glory. The reconstructed compound of eerily foreign buildings at **Fort Ross State Historic Park** recalls the era of Russian fur trading in California. Pull into **Gualala** for an espresso, a sandwich, and a little human contact

Point Reyes National Seashore

TOP 5 PLACES TO LINGER

- San Francisco
- Marin Headlands
- Point Reyes National Seashore
- Fort Ross State Historic Park
- Mendocino

before rolling onward. After another 50 mi of tranquil state beaches and parks you'll return to civilization in **Mendocino.**

MENDOCINO TO FORT BRAGG

(approx. 9 mi)

Exploring Mendocino you may feel like you've fallen through a rabbit hole: the weather screams Northern California, but the 19th-century buildings—erected by homesick Yankee loggers—definitely say New England. Once you've browsed around the artsy shops, continue on to the **Mendocino Coast Botanical Gardens;** then travel back in time on the **Skunk Train,** which follows an old logging route from **Fort Bragg** deep into the redwood forest.

The Central Coast

FROM VENTURA TO BIG SUR

WORD OF MOUTH

"I was blown away by the immense outdoor pool at the Hearst Castle. It is huge, and yet incredibly serene in its surroundings. The Castle is situated on top of the hills in the San Simeon area and allows for massive views of nearly 360 degrees around."

—photo by L Vantreight, Fodors.com member

WELCOME TO
THE CENTRAL COAST

TOP REASONS TO GO

★ **Incredible nature:** Much of the Central Coast looks as wild and wonderful as it did centuries ago. The area is home to Channel Islands National Park, two national marine sanctuaries, state parks and beaches, and the vast and rugged Los Padres National Forest.

★ **Edible bounty:** Land and sea provide enough fresh regional foods to satisfy even the savviest of foodies—grapes, strawberries, seafood, olive oil . . . the list goes on and on. Get your fill at countless farmers' markets, wineries, and restaurants.

★ **Outdoor activities:** Kick back and revel in the casual California lifestyle. Surf, golf, kayak, hike, play tennis—or just hang out and enjoy the gorgeous scenery.

★ **Small-town charm, big-city culture:** Small, friendly, uncrowded towns offer an amazing array of cultural amenities. With all the art and history museums, theater, music, and festivals, you might start thinking you're in L.A. or San Francisco.

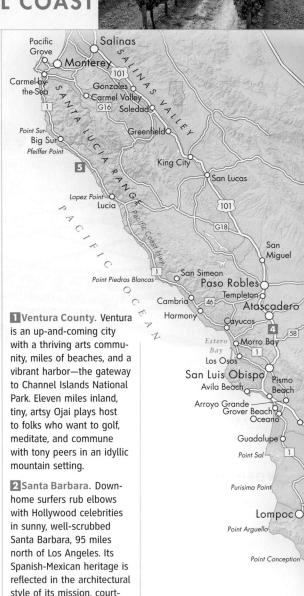

1 Ventura County. Ventura is an up-and-coming city with a thriving arts community, miles of beaches, and a vibrant harbor—the gateway to Channel Islands National Park. Eleven miles inland, tiny, artsy Ojai plays host to folks who want to golf, meditate, and commune with tony peers in an idyllic mountain setting.

2 Santa Barbara. Down-home surfers rub elbows with Hollywood celebrities in sunny, well-scrubbed Santa Barbara, 95 miles north of Los Angeles. Its Spanish-Mexican heritage is reflected in the architectural style of its mission, courthouse, and many homes and public buildings.

3 **Santa Barbara County.** Wineries, ranches, and small villages dominate the quintessentially Californian landscape here.

4 **San Luis Obispo County.** Friendly college town San Luis Obispo serves as the hub of a burgeoning wine region that stretches nearly 100 miles from Pismo Beach north to Paso Robles; the 230-plus wineries here have earned reputations for high-quality vintages that rival those of northern California.

5 **The Big Sur Coastline.** Rugged cliffs meet the Pacific for more than 60 miles—one of the most scenic and dramatic drives in the world.

6 **Channel Islands National Park.** Home to 145 species of plants and animals found nowhere else on Earth, this relatively undiscovered gem of a park encompasses five islands and a mile of surrounding ocean.

GETTING ORIENTED

The Central Coast region begins about 60 miles north of Los Angeles, near the seaside city of Ventura. From there the coastline stretches north about 200 miles, winding through the cities of Santa Barbara and San Luis Obispo, then north through the small towns of Morro Bay and Cambria to Carmel. The drive through this region, especially the section of Highway 1 from San Simeon to Big Sur, is one of the most scenic in the state.

```
0               20 miles
0               30 kilometers
```

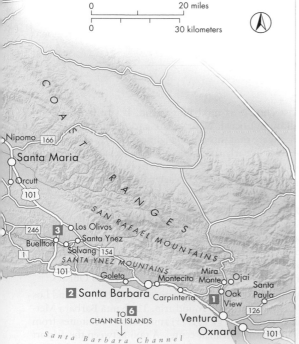

Updated
by Cheryl
Crabtree

Balmy weather, glorious beaches, crystal-clear air, and serene landscapes have lured people to the Central Coast since prehistoric times. It's an ideal place to relax, slow down, and appreciate the good things in life.

Along the Pacific coast, the scenic variety is stunning—everything from dramatic cliffs and grass-tufted bluffs to wildlife estuaries and miles of dunes. Offshore, a pristine national park and a vast marine sanctuary protect the wild, wonderful underwater resources of this incredible corner of the planet. But not all of the Central Coast's top attractions are natural: Ventura, Santa Barbara, and San Luis Obispo are filled with sparkling examples of Spanish-Mediterranean architecture, bustling shopping districts, and first-rate restaurants showcasing regional foods and wines.

PLANNING

WHEN TO GO
The Central Coast climate is mild year-round. If you like to swim in warmer (if still nippy) ocean waters, July and August are the best months to visit. Be aware that this is also high season. Fog often rolls in along the coastal areas in early summer; you'll need a jacket, especially after sunset, close to the shore. It usually rains from December through March. From April to early June and in early fall the weather is almost as fine as in high season, and the pace is less hectic.

GETTING HERE AND AROUND
AIR TRAVEL
Alaska Air, American, Frontier, United, and US Airways fly to Santa Barbara Municipal Airport (SBA), 9 miles from downtown. United Express and US Airways provide service to San Luis Obispo County Regional Airport (SBP), 3 miles from downtown San Luis Obispo.

Santa Barbara Airbus shuttles travelers between Santa Barbara and Los Angeles for $48 one-way and $90 round-trip. The Santa Barbara Metropolitan Transit District Bus 11 ($1.75) runs every 30 minutes from the airport to the downtown transit center. A taxi between the airport and the hotel districts costs between $20 and $38.

Airport Contacts San Luis Obispo County Regional Airport ✉ *903-5 Airport Dr., San Luis Obispo* ☎ *805/781-5205* ⊕ *www.sloairport.com.***Santa Barbara Airport** ✉ *500 Fowler Rd., Santa Barbara* ☎ *805/683-4011* ⊕ *www.flysba. com.* **Santa Barbara Airbus** ☎ *805/964-7759, 800/423-1618* ⊕ *www.sbairbus. com.* **Santa Barbara Metropolitan Transit District** ☎ *805/963-3366* ⊕ *www. sbmtd.gov.*

2

BUS TRAVEL

Greyhound provides service from Los Angeles and San Francisco to San Luis Obispo, Ventura, and Santa Barbara. Local transit companies serve these three cities and several smaller towns. Buses can be useful for visiting some urban sights, particularly in Santa Barbara; they're less so for rural ones.

Bus Contacts Greyhound ☎ *800/231-2222* ⊕ *www.greyhound.com.*

CAR TRAVEL

Driving is the easiest way to experience the Central Coast. U.S. 101 and Highway 1, which run north–south, are the main routes to and through the Central Coast from Los Angeles and San Francisco. Highly scenic Highway 1 hugs the coast, and U.S. 101 runs inland. Between Ventura County and northern Santa Barbara County, the two highways are the same road. Highway 1 again separates from U.S. 101 north of Gaviota, then rejoins the highway at Pismo Beach. Along any stretch where these two highways are separate, U.S. 101 is the quicker route.

The most dramatic section of the Central Coast is the 70 miles between San Simeon and Big Sur. The road is narrow and twisting, with a single lane in each direction. In fog or rain the drive can be downright nerve-racking; in wet seasons mud slides can close portions of the road.

Other routes into the Central Coast include Highway 46 and Highway 33, which head, respectively, west and south from Interstate 5 near Bakersfield.

Contacts Caltrans ☎ *800/427-7623, 888/836-0866 Hwy. 1 Visitor Hotline (Cambria north to Carmel)* ⊕ *www.dot.ca.gov.*

TRAIN TRAVEL

The Amtrak *Coast Starlight,* which runs between Los Angeles and Seattle via Oakland, stops in Paso Robles, San Luis Obispo, Santa Barbara, and Oxnard. Amtrak runs several *Pacific Surfliner* trains daily between San Luis Obispo, Santa Barbara, Los Angeles, and San Diego. Metrolink Regional Rail Service trains connect Ventura and Oxnard with Los Angeles and points between.

Train Contacts Amtrak ☎ *800/872-7245, 805/963-1015 in Santa Barbara, 805/541-0505 in San Luis Obispo* ⊕ *www.amtrakcalifornia.com.* **Metrolink** ☎ *800/371-5465* ⊕ *www.metrolinktrains.com.*

RESTAURANTS

The cuisine in Ventura and Santa Barbara is every bit as eclectic as it is in California's bigger cities; fresh seafood is a standout. A foodie renaissance has overtaken the entire region from Ventura to Paso Robles, spawning dozens of new restaurants touting locavore cuisine made with fresh organic produce and meats. Dining attire on the Central Coast is generally casual, though slightly dressy casual wear is the custom at pricier restaurants. *Prices in the reviews are the average cost of a main course at dinner or, if dinner is not served, at lunch.*

HOTELS

Lodging options abound in the Central Coast, but expect to pay top dollar for rooms along the shore, especially in summer. Moderately priced hotels and motels do exist—most just a short drive inland from their higher-price counterparts. Make your reservations as early as possible and take advantage of midweek specials to get the best rates. It's common for lodgings to require two-day minimum stays on holidays and some weekends, especially in summer, and to double rates during festivals and other events. Hot Spots provides room reservations and tourist information. *Prices in the reviews are the lowest cost of a standard double room in high season. For expanded reviews, facilities, and current deals, visit Fodors.com.*

Hot Spots ☎ *800/793-7666* ⊕ *www.hotspotsusa.com.*

TOUR OPTIONS

Cloud Climbers Jeep and Wine Tours offers four types of daily tours: wine-tasting, mountain, sunset, and a discovery tour for families. These trips to the Santa Barbara/Santa Ynez mountains and Wine Country are conducted in open-air, six-passenger jeeps. Fares range from $89 to $129 per adult. The company also offers a four-hour All Around Ojai Tour ($109) and arranges biking, horseback riding, and trap-shooting tours and Paso Robles wine tours by appointment.

Wine Edventures operates guided wine tours ($110 per person) in the Santa Ynez Valley in vans, minicoaches, and other vehicles. The Grapeline Wine Country Shuttle leads daily wine and vineyard picnic tours ($88 to $138) with flexible itineraries in San Luis Obispo County and the Santa Barbara County Wine Country.

Spencer's Limousine & Tours offers customized tours of Santa Barbara and the Wine Country via sedan, limousine, or van. A five-hour basic tour with at least four participants costs about $90 per person. Sustainable Vine Wine Tours' biodiesel-powered vans can take you on a day of eco-friendly wine touring ($125) in the Santa Ynez Valley. Trips include tastings at green-minded wineries, and a gourmet organic picnic lunch.

Many of the tour companies described above will pick you up at your hotel or central locations; ask about this when booking.

Tour Contacts Cloud Climbers Jeep and Wine Tours ☎ *805/646-3200* ⊕ *www.ccjeeps.com.* **The Grapeline Wine Country Shuttle** ☎ *888/894-6379* ⊕ *www.gogrape.com.* **Spencer's Limousine & Tours** ☎ *805/884-9700* ⊕ *www.spencerslimo.com.* **Sustainable Vine Wine Tours** ☎ *805/698-3911* ⊕ *www.sustainablevine.com.***Wine Edventures** ⊠ *Santa Barbara* ☎ *805/965-9463* ⊕ *www.welovewines.com.*

VISITOR INFORMATION

Contacts Central Coast Tourism Council ⊕ *www.centralcoast-tourism.com.*

VENTURA COUNTY

Ventura County was first settled by the Chumash Indians. Spanish missionaries were the first Europeans to arrive, followed by Americans and other Europeans, who established bustling towns, transportation networks, and highly productive farms. Since the 1920s, though, agriculture has been steadily replaced as the area's main industry—first by the oil business and more recently by tourism.

VENTURA

60 miles north of Los Angeles on U.S. 101.

Like Los Angeles, the city of Ventura enjoys gorgeous weather and sun-kissed beaches—but without the smog and congestion. The miles of beautiful beaches attract athletes—bodysurfers and boogie boarders, runners and bikers—and those who'd rather doze beneath an umbrella all day. Ventura Harbor is home to myriad fishing boats, restaurants, and water-activity centers where you can rent boats and take harbor cruises. Foodies can get their fix all over Ventura—dozens of upscale cafés and wine and tapas bars have opened in recent years. Arts and antiques buffs have long trekked downtown to browse the galleries and shops there.

GETTING HERE AND AROUND

Amtrak and Metrolink trains serve the area from Los Angeles area. Greyhound buses stop in Ventura; Gold Coast Transit serves the city and the rest of Ventura County.

U.S. 101 is the north–south main route into town, but for a scenic drive, take Highway 1 north from Santa Monica. The highway merges with U.S. 101 just south of Ventura. ■TIP➜ Traveling north to Ventura from Los Angeles on weekdays, it's best to depart before 6 am, between 10 and 2, or after 7, or you'll get caught in the extended rush-hour traffic. Coming south from Santa Barbara, depart before 1 or after 6. On weekends, traffic is generally fine except southbound on U.S. 101 between Santa Barbara and Ventura.

ESSENTIALS

Bus Contacts Gold Coast Transit ☎ *805/643–3158* ⊕ *www.goldcoasttransit. org.*

Visitor Information Ventura Visitors and Convention Bureau ✉ *Downtown Visitor Center, 101 S. California St.* ☎ *805/648–2075, 800/483–6214* ⊕ *www. ventura-usa.com.*

EXPLORING

Lake Casitas Recreation Area. Lunker largemouth bass, rainbow trout, crappie, redears, and channel catfish live in the waters at Lake Casitas Recreation Area, an impoundment of the Ventura River. The lake is one of the country's best bass-fishing areas, and anglers come from all over the United States to test their luck. The park, nestled below the Santa Ynez Mountains' Laguna Ridge, is also a beautiful spot for pitching a tent or having a picnic. The Casitas Water Adventure, which has two water playgrounds and a lazy river for tubing and floating, is a great place to take kids in summer ($12 for an all-day pass; $6 from 5 to 7 pm). The park is 13 miles northwest of Ventura. ✉ *11311 Santa Ana Rd., off Hwy. 33* ☎ *805/649–2233, 805/649–1122 campground reservations* 🌐 *www.casitaswater.org* 🎟 *$10–$15 per vehicle, $13 per boat* ⏲ *Daily.*

Mission San Buenaventura. The ninth of the 21 California missions, Mission San Buenaventura was established in 1782 but burned to the ground in the 1790s. It was rebuilt and rededicated in 1809. A self-guided tour takes you through a small museum, a quiet courtyard, and a chapel with 250-year-old paintings. ✉ *211 E. Main St., at Figueroa St.* ☎ *805/643–4318* 🌐 *www.sanbuenaventuramission.org* 🎟 *$2* ⏲ *Weekdays 10–5, Sat. 9–5, Sun. 10–4.*

Ventura Oceanfront. Four miles of gorgeous coastline stretch from the county fairgrounds at the northern border of the city of San Buenaventura, through San Buenaventura State Beach, down to Ventura Harbor in the south. The main attraction here is the San Buenaventura City Pier, a landmark built in 1872 and restored in 1993. Surfers rip the waves just north of the pier, and sunbathers relax on white-sand beaches on either side. The mile-long promenade and the Omer Rains Bike Trail north of the pier attract scores of joggers, surrey cyclers, and bikers throughout the year. ✉ *California St. at ocean's edge.*

WHERE TO EAT

$$$ FRENCH 🍴 **71 Palm Restaurant.** This elegant restaurant occupies a 1910 house, and it still has touches that make it feel like a home: lace curtains, wood floors, a dining patio for good weather, and a fireplace that's often crackling in winter. A standout appetizer is the homemade country pâté with cornichons; for dinner, try the grilled salmon on a potato pancake, the New Zealand rack of lamb Provençal, or the bouillabaise. [$] *Average main: $24* ✉ *71 N. Palm St., at Poli St.* ☎ *805/653–7222* 🌐 *www.71palm.com* ⏲ *Closed Sun.*

$$ SEAFOOD 🍴 **Brophy Bros.** The Ventura outpost of this wildly popular Santa Barbara restaurant provides the same fresh seafood-oriented meals in a spacious second-story setting overlooking the harbor. Feast on everything from fish-and-chips and crab cakes to chowder and delectable fish—often straight from the boats moored below. [$] *Average main: $18* ✉ *1559 Spinnaker Dr., in Ventura Harbor Village* ☎ *805/639–0865* 🌐 *www.brophybros.com* ✍ *Reservations not accepted.*

$ AMERICAN 🍴 **Busy Bee Cafe.** A local favorite for decades, this classic 1950s diner has a jukebox on every table and serves hearty burgers and comfort food (think meat loaf and mashed potatoes, pot roast, and Cobb salad). For breakfast, tuck into a huge omelet; for a snack or dessert, order a shake or hot fudge sundae from the soda fountain. [$] *Average main: $10* ✉ *478 E. Main St., near S. California St.* ☎ *805/643–4864* 🌐 *www.busybeecafe.biz.*

$ AMERICAN 🍴 **Christy's.** You can get breakfast all day—don't miss the breakfast burrito—at this cozy, nautical-theme locals' hangout in the harbor, across the water from the Channel Islands. It also serves burgers, sandwiches, and soup. [$] *Average main: $12* ✉ *1559 Spinnaker Dr., in Ventura Harbor Village* ☎ *805/642–3116.*

Map detail labels:

Morro Bay · Estero Bay · 58 · 1 · Los Osos · San Luis Obispo · Avila Beach · Pismo Beach · Grover Beach · Arroyo Grande · Guadalupe-Nipomo Dunes Preserve · Nipomo · 166 · Guadalupe · Pacific Coast Hwy. · Santa Maria · New Cuyama · 166 · Point Sal · 1 · Orcutt · SANTA MARIA VALLEY · Purisima Point · 101 · Los Alamos · La Purisima Mission State Hist. Park · 246 · Los Olivos · SAN RAFAEL MOUNTAINS · 33 · Lompoc · Buellton · Santa Ynez · Point Arguello · SANTA YNEZ VALLEY · Solvang · 154 · Pacific Coast Hwy. · 1 · SANTA YNEZ MOUNTAINS · Gaviota State Beach · Point Conception · Refugio State Beach · El Capitan State Beach · Goleta · Montecito · Mira Monte · Ojai · 150 · Santa Barbara see detail map · Carpinteria · Oak View · 101 · 33 · 126 · Santa Paula · Ventura · Camarillo · Oxnard · 1 · Santa Barbara Channel · Channel Islands National Park · Anacapa Island · Point Mugu · Santa Monica Mtns. Nat'l. Rec. Area · San Miguel Island · Santa Rosa Island · Santa Cruz Island · CHANNEL ISLANDS · PACIFIC OCEAN · COAST RANGES

Ventura and Santa Barbara Counties

0 — 15 mi
0 — 15 km

$$ ✕ **Peirano's.** In 2012 new owners transformed the historic Peirano's
ECLECTIC building into a colorful, contemporary space filled with art from around
the globe. In keeping with this global perspective, chef Robert Grenner's
seasonal menus incorporate the flavors of California, the Mediterranean
region, and the Middle East. Starters might include braised heirloom
eggplant with sun-dried mint, cardamom, and a rich Middle Eastern
yogurt, or a traditional Caesar salad. Mains might include cioppino or
lamb kebabs marinated in a rosemary-avocado-honey sauce and served
with pearl-barley risotto. $ *Average main: $22* ⬜ *204 E. Main St.,
at Figueroa Street Mall* ☎ *805/648–4853* ⊕ *www.peiranos.com* ⊗ *No
lunch.*

WHERE TO STAY
For expanded reviews, facilities, and current deals, visit Fodors.com.

$$ 🏨 **Crowne Plaza Ventura Beach.** An enviable location is the main draw of
HOTEL this 12-story hotel: it's on the beach, next to a historic pier, and within
walking distance of downtown restaurants and nightlife. **Pros:** on the
beach, near downtown and attractions; steps from waterfront; near
Amtrak. **Cons:** early-morning train noise; waterfront area crowded in
summer; most rooms on the small side. **TripAdvisor:** "a beach treat,"
"clean rooms," "so friendly." $ *Rooms from: $169* ⬜ *450 E. Harbor
Blvd.* ☎ *800/842–0800* ⊕ *cpventura.com* ⇥ *254 rooms, 4 suites.*

$$ RESORT **Four Points by Sheraton Ventura Harbor Resort.** An on-site restaurant, spacious rooms, and a slew of amenities make this 17-acre property (which includes sister hotel Holiday Inn Express) a popular and practical choice for Channel Islands visitors. **Pros:** close to island transportation; mostly quiet; short drive to historic downtown Ventura. **Cons:** not in the heart of downtown; noisy seagulls sometimes congregate nearby. **TripAdvisor:** "staff is the friendliest," "really nice amenities," "super comfy beds." [$] *Rooms from: $145* ✉ *1050 Schooner Dr.* ☎ *805/658–1212* 🌐 *www.fourpoints.com/ventura* 🛏 *102 rooms, 4 suites.*

$$ HOTEL **Holiday Inn Express Ventura Harbor.** A favorite among Channel Islands visitors, this quiet, comfortable, lodge-inspired property sits right at the Ventura Harbor entrance. **Pros:** quiet at night; easy access to harbor restaurants and activities; five-minute drive to downtown sights. **Cons:** busy area on weekends; complaints of erratic service. **TripAdvisor:** "best view and customer service in town," "perfect," "lots of room." [$] *Rooms from: $130* ✉ *1080 Navigator Dr.* ☎ *805/856–9533, 800/315–2621* 🌐 *www.holidayinnexpress.com/venturaca* 🛏 *69 rooms* 🍴 *Breakfast.*

$$$ HOTEL **Ventura Beach Marriott.** Spacious, contemporary rooms, a peaceful location just steps from San Buenaventura State Beach, and easy access to historic downtown Ventura's arts and culture district make the Marriott a popular choice. **Pros:** walk to beach and biking/jogging trails; a block from historic pier; great value for location. **Cons:** close to highway; near busy intersection. **TripAdvisor:** "very comfortable and quiet," "exceptional service," "great place to stay and play." [$] *Rooms from: $189* ✉ *2055 E. Harbor Blvd.* ☎ *805/643–6000, 888/236–2427* 🌐 *www.marriottventurabeach.com* 🛏 *272 rooms, 12 suites.*

SPORTS AND THE OUTDOORS

The most popular outdoor activities in Ventura are beach-going and whale-watching. California gray whales migrate offshore through the Santa Barbara Channel from late December through March; giant blue and humpback whales feed here from mid-June through September. The channel teems with marine life year-round, so tours, which depart from Ventura Harbor, include more than just whale sightings. To learn about the spectacular hiking trails on the five islands that comprise Channel Islands National Park, check out its visitor center, also at the harbor.

Island Packers. A cruise through the Santa Barbara Channel with Island Packers will give you the chance to spot dolphins and seals—and sometimes even whales—throughout the year. ✉ *Ventura Harbor, 1691 Spinnaker Dr.* ☎ *805/642–1393* 🌐 *www.islandpackers.com.*

OJAI

15 miles north of Ventura, U.S. 101 to Hwy. 33.

The Ojai Valley, which director Frank Capra used as a backdrop for his 1936 film *Lost Horizon,* sizzles in the summer when temperatures routinely reach 90°F. The acres of orange and avocado groves here evoke postcard images of long-ago agricultural Southern California. Many artists and celebrities have sought refuge in lush Ojai from life in the fast lane.

GETTING HERE AND AROUND

From northern Ventura, Highway 33 veers east from U.S. 101 and climbs inland to Ojai. From Santa Barbara, exit U.S. 101 at Highway 150 in Carpinteria, then travel east 20 miles on a twisting, two-lane road that is not recommended at night or during poor weather. You can also access Ojai by heading west from Interstate 5 on Highway 126. Exit at Santa Paula and follow Highway 150 north for 16 miles to Ojai. Gold Coast Transit provides service to Ojai from Ventura.

Ojai can be easily explored on foot; you can also hop on the Ojai Trolley ($1), which follows two routes around Ojai and neighboring Miramonte between 7:15 and 5:15 on weekdays, and one route between 9 and 5 on weekends. If you tell the driver you're a visitor, you'll get an informal guided tour.

ESSENTIALS

Bus Contact Gold Coast Transit ☎ *805/643–3158* 🌐 *www.goldcoasttransit.org.* **Ojai Trolley** ☎ *805/646–5581* 🌐 *ojaitrolley.com.*

Visitor Information Ojai Visitors Bureau ✉ *206 N. Signal St.* ☎ *888/652–4669* 🌐 *www.ojaivisitors.com* 🕒 *Weekdays 9–4.*

EXPLORING

Ojai Art Center. California's oldest nonprofit, multipurpose art center exhibits artwork from various disciplines and presents theater, dance, and other performances. ✉ *113 S. Montgomery St.* ☎ *805/646–0117* 🌐 *www.ojaiartcenter.org.*

Ojai Avenue. The work of local artists is displayed in the Spanish-style shopping arcade along Ojai Avenue (Highway 150). Organic and specialty growers sell their produce on Sunday between 9 and 1 at the farmers' market behind the arcade.

Ojai Valley Museum. Housed in a former chapel, the Ojai Valley Museum has exhibits on the valley's history and many Native American artifacts. ✉ *130 W. Ojai Ave.* ☎ *805/640–1390* 🌐 *www.ojaivalleymuseum.org* 🎟 *$4.*

Ojai Valley Trail. The 18-mile Ojai Valley Trail is open to pedestrians, bikers, joggers, equestrians, and nonmotorized vehicles. You can access it anywhere along its route. ✉ *Parallel to Hwy. 33 from Soule Park in Ojai to ocean in Ventura* ☎ *888/652–4669* 🌐 *www.ojaivisitors.com.*

WHERE TO EAT

$$ MEDITERRANEAN 🍴 **Azu.** Delectable tapas, a full bar, slick furnishings, and piped jazz music lure diners to this popular, artsy Mediterranean bistro. You can also order soups, salads, and bistro fare such as tagine roasted chicken and paella. Save room for the homemade gelato. [$] *Average main: $16* ✉ *457 E. Ojai Ave.* ☎ *805/640–7987* 🌐 *www.azuojai.com* 🕒 *No lunch Sun. and Mon., early Sept.–early May.*

$ ITALIAN 🍴 **Boccali's.** Edging a ranch, citrus groves, and a seasonal garden that provides much of the produce for menu items, the modest but cheery Boccali's attracts droves of loyal fans. In the warmer months, you can dine alfresco in the oak-shaded patio and lawn area and sometimes listen to live music. The family-run operation, best known for hand-rolled pizzas and homestyle pastas (don't miss the eggplant lasagna), also serves a highly popular seasonal strawberry shortcake. $ *Average main: $15* ✉ *3277 Ojai Ave., about 2 miles east of downtown* ☎ *805/646–6116* ⊕ *www.boccalis.com* ▭ *No credit cards* ⊗ *No lunch Mon. and Tues.*

$$$
AMERICAN
★

✕ **The Ranch House.** This elegant yet laid-back eatery has been around for decades. Main dishes such as the broiled-and-roasted rack of lamb with pineapple guava chutney, and the grilled diver scallops with curried sweet-corn sauce are not to be missed. The verdant patio is a wonderful place to have Sunday brunch. $ *Average main: $27* ✉ *500 S. Lomita Ave.* ☎ *805/646–2360* ⊕ *www.theranchhouse.com* ⊗ *Closed Mon. No lunch.*

$$$
EUROPEAN

✕ **Suzanne's Cuisine.** Peppered filet mignon, linguine with steamed clams, and pan-roasted salmon with a roasted mango sauce are among the offerings at this European-style restaurant. Game, seafood, and vegetarian dishes dominate the dinner menu, and salads and soups star at lunchtime. All the breads and desserts are made on the premises. $ *Average main: $24* ✉ *502 W. Ojai Ave.* ☎ *805/640–1961* ⊕ *www.suzannescuisine.com* ⊗ *Closed Tues.*

WHERE TO STAY

For expanded reviews, facilities, and current deals, visit Fodors.com.

$$
B&B/INN

⌂ **The Blue Iguana Inn & Suites.** Artists run this Southwestern-style hotel, and their work (which is for sale) decorates the rooms. **Pros:** colorful art everywhere; secluded property. **Cons:** 2 miles from the heart of Ojai; sits on the main highway to Ventura; small. **TripAdvisor:** "lovely getaway spot," "a perfect port in a storm," "has it all." $ *Rooms from: $129* ✉ *11794 N. Ventura Ave., Hwy. 33* ☎ *805/646–5277* ⊕ *www.blueiguanainn.com* ⇆ *4 rooms, 8 suites, 8 cottages* ⑩ *Breakfast.*

$$
RESORT

⌂ **Oaks at Ojai.** Rejuvenation is the name of the game at this comfortable spa resort. **Pros:** great place to get fit; peaceful retreat; healthful meals. **Cons:** rooms are basic; sits on the main highway through town. **TripAdvisor:** "excellent all around fitness resort experience," "amazing spa with terrific results," "great place to get your life back." $ *Rooms from: $199* ✉ *122 E. Ojai Ave.* ☎ *805/646–5573, 800/753–6257* ⊕ *www.oaksspa.com* ⇆ *44 rooms, 2 suites* ⑩ *All meals* ⌁ *2-night minimum stay.*

$$$$
RESORT
★

⌂ **Ojai Valley Inn & Spa.** This outdoorsy, golf-oriented resort and spa is set on beautifully landscaped grounds, with hillside views in nearly all directions. **Pros:** gorgeous grounds; exceptional outdoor activities; romantic yet kid-friendly. **Cons:** expensive; areas near restaurants can be noisy. **TripAdvisor:** "relax in the sun," "idyllic setting," "gorgeous property." $ *Rooms from: $400* ✉ *905 Country Club Rd.* ☎ *805/646–1111, 888/697–8780* ⊕ *www.ojairesort.com* ⇆ *231 rooms, 77 suites.*

$$$
B&B/INN

⌂ **Su Nido Inn.** Just a short walk from downtown Ojai sights and restaurants, this posh Mission revival–style inn is nested in a quiet neighborhood a few blocks from Libbey Park. **Pros:** walking distance from downtown; homey feel. **Cons:** no pool; can get hot during summer. **TripAdvisor:** "more than we could have asked for," "serene," "lovingly appointed." $ *Rooms from: $179* ✉ *301 N. Montgomery St.* ☎ *805/646–7080, 866/646–7080* ⊕ *www.sunidoinn.com* ⇆ *3 rooms, 9 suites.*

SANTA BARBARA

27 miles northwest of Ventura and 29 miles west of Ojai on U.S. 101.
Santa Barbara has long been an oasis for Los Angelenos seeking respite from big-city life. The attractions begin at the ocean and end in the foothills of the Santa Ynez Mountains. A few miles up the coast east and west—but still very much a part of Santa Barbara—are the exclusive residential districts of Montecito and Hope Ranch. Santa Barbara is on a jog in the coastline, so the ocean is actually to the south, instead of the west; for this reason, directions can be confusing. "Up" the coast toward San Francisco is west, "down" toward Los Angeles is east, and the mountains are north.

2

GETTING HERE AND AROUND

U.S. 101 is the main route into Santa Barbara. If you're staying in town, a car is handy but not essential; the beaches and downtown are easily explored by bicycle or on foot. Visit the Santa Barbara Car Free website for bike route and walking-tour maps and car-free vacation packages with substantial lodging, dining, activity, and transportation discounts.

Santa Barbara Metropolitan Transit District's Line 22 bus serves major tourist sights. Several bus lines connect with the very convenient electric shuttles that cruise the downtown and waterfront every 8 to 15 minutes (25¢ each way).

Santa Barbara Trolley Co. operates a motorized San Francisco–style cable car that loops past major hotels, shopping areas, and attractions from 10 to 4. Get off whenever you like, and pick up another trolley (they come every hour) when you're ready to move on. The fare is $19 for the day.

TOURS

Land and Sea Tours. Land and Sea Tours takes visitors on narrated, 90-minute land-and-sea adventures in an amphibious 49-passenger vehicle, nicknamed the Land Shark. Tours begin with a drive through the city and continue with a plunge into the harbor for a cruise along the coast. ⊠ *State St. at Stearns Wharf* ☎ *805/683–7600* ⊕ *www.out2seesb. com* ☞ *$25* ⊙ *Tours May–Oct., daily noon, 2, and 4; Nov.–Apr., daily noon and 2.*

ESSENTIALS

Transportation Contacts Santa Barbara Car Free ⊕ *www.santa-barbaracarfree.org.* **Santa Barbara Metropolitan Transit District** ☎ *805/963–3366* ⊕ *www.sbmtd.gov.* **Santa Barbara Trolley Co.** ☎ *805/965–0353* ⊕ *www.sbtrolley.com.*

Visitor Information Santa Barbara Chamber of Commerce Visitor Information Center ⊠ *1 Garden St., at Cabrillo Blvd.* ☎ *805/965–3021, 805/568–1811* ⊕ *www.sbchamber.org.* **Santa Barbara Conference and Visitors Bureau** ⊠ *1601 Anacapa St.* ☎ *805/966–9222* ⊕ *www.santabarbaraca.com.*

Continued on page 52

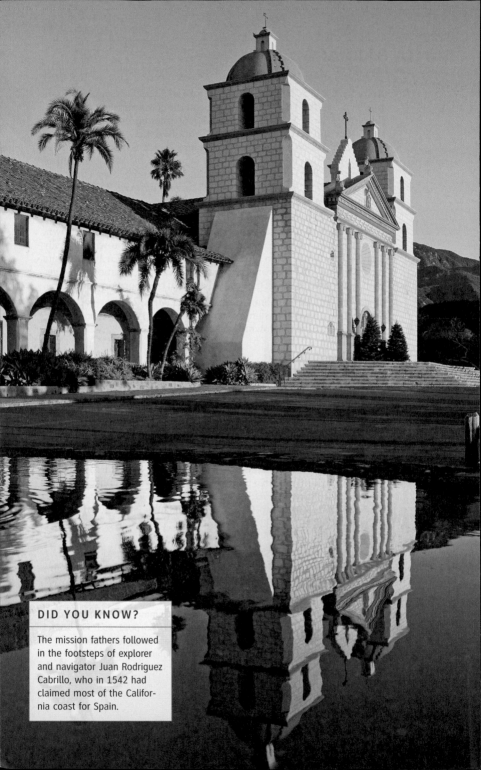

ON A MISSION

Their soul may belong to Spain, their heart to the New World, but the historic missions of California, with their lovely churches, beckon the traveler on a soulful journey back to the very founding of the American West.

by Cheryl Crabtree and Robert I.C. Fisher

California history changed forever in the 18th century when Spanish explorers founded a series of missions along the Pacific coast. Believing they were following God's will, they wanted to spread the gospel and convert as many natives as possible. The process produced a collision between the Hispanic and California Indian cultures, resulting in one of the most striking legacies of Old California: the Spanish mission churches. Rising like mirages in the middle of desert plains and rolling hills, these saintly sites transport you back to the days of the Spanish colonial period.

GOD AND MAN IN CALIFORNIA

The Alta California territory came under pressure in the 1760s when Spain feared foreign advances into the territory explorer Juan Rodríguez Cabrillo had claimed for the Spanish crown back in 1542. But how could Spain create a visible and viable presence halfway around the world? They decided to build on the model that had already worked well in Spain's Mexico colony. The plan involved establishing a series of missions, to be operated by the Catholic Church and protected by four of Spain's *presidios* (military outposts). The native Indians— after quick conversion to Christianity—would provide the labor force necessary to build mission towns.

FATHER OF THE MISSIONS

Father Junípero Serra is an icon of the Spanish colonial period. At the behest of the Spanish government, the diminutive padre—then well into his fifties, and despite a chronic leg infection— started out on foot from Baja California to search for suitable mission sites, with a goal of reaching Monterey. In 1769 he helped establish Alta California's first mission in San Diego and continued his travels until his death, in 1784, by which time he had founded eight more missions.

The system ended about a decade after the Mexican government took control of Alta California in the early 1820s and began to secularize the missions. The church lost horses and cattle, as well as vast tracts of land, which the Mexican government in turn granted to private individuals. They also lost laborers, as the Indians were for the most part free to find work and a life beyond the missions. In 1848, the Americans assumed control of the territory, and California became part of the United States. Today, these missions stand as extraordinary monuments to their colorful past.

Mission Santa Barbara Museum

MISSION ACCOMPLISHED

California's Mission Trail is the best way to follow in the fathers' footsteps. Here, below, are its 21 settlements, north to south.

Amazingly, all 21 Spanish missions in California are still standing—some in their pristine historic state, others with modifications made over the centuries. Many are found on or near the "King's Road"—El Camino Real—which linked these mission outposts. At the height of the mission system the trail was approximately 600 miles long, eventually extending from San Diego to Sonoma. Today the road is commemorated on portions of routes 101 and 82 in the form of roadside bell markers erected by CalTrans every one to two miles between San Diego and San Francisco.

San Francisco Solano, Sonoma (1823; this was the final California mission constructed.)

San Rafael, San Rafael (1817)

San Francisco de Asís (aka Mission Dolores), San Francisco (1776). Situated in the heart of San Francisco,

Mission Santa Clara de Asís

these mission grounds and nearby Arroyo de los Dolores (Creek of Sorrows) are home to the oldest intact building in the city.

Santa Clara de Asís, Santa Clara (1777). On the campus of Santa Clara University, this beautifully restored mission contains original paintings, statues, a bell, and hundreds of artifacts, as well as a spectacular rose garden.

San José, Fremont (1797)

Santa Cruz, Santa Cruz (1791)

San Juan Bautista, San Juan Bautista (1797). Immortalized in Hitchcock's *Vertigo*, this remarkably preserved pueblo contains the largest church of all the California missions, as well as 18th- and 19th-century buildings and a sprawling plaza.

San Carlos Borromeo del Río Carmelo, Carmel (1770). Carmel Mission was head-

quarters for the California mission system under Father Serra and the Father Presidents who succeeded him; the on-site museum includes Serra's tiny sleeping quarters (where he died in 1784).

Nuestra Señora de la Soledad, Soledad (1791)

San Antonio de Padua, Jolon (1771)

San Miguel Arcángel, San Miguel (1797). San Miguel boasts the only intact original interior wall painting in any of the missions, painted in 1821 by Native American converts under the direction of Spanish artist Esteban Muras.

Painting from 1818, San Juan Bautista.

Mission Santa Inés

San Luis Obispo de Tolosa, San Luis Obispo (1772). Bear meat from grizzlies captured here saved the Spaniards from starving, which helped convince Father Serra to establish a mission.

La Purísima Concepción, Lompoc (1787). La Purísima is the nation's most completely restored mission complex. It is

now a living-history museum with a church and nearly forty craft and residence rooms.

Santa Inés, Solvang (1804). Home to one of the most significant pieces of religious art created by a California mission Indian.

Santa Bárbara, Santa Barbara (1786). The "Queen of the Missions" has twin bell towers, gorgeous gardens with heirloom plant varietals, a massive collection of rare artworks and artifacts, and lovely stonework.

San Buenaventura, Ventura (1782). This was the last mission founded by Father Serra; it is still an active parish in the Archdiocese of Los Angeles.

Mission San Fernando Rey de España

San Fernando Rey de España, Mission Hills (1797)

San Gabriel Arcángel, San Gabriel (1771)

San Luis Rey de Francia, Oceanside (1798)

San Juan Capistrano, San Juan Capistrano (1776). This mission is famed for its Saint Joseph's Day (March 19) celebration of the return of swallows in the springtime. The mission's adobe walls enclose acres of lush gardens and historic buildings.

San Diego de Alcalá, San Diego (1769). This was the first California missions constructed, although the original was destroyed in 1775 and rebuilt over a number of years.

KEY

🏠 *Mission*

0   50 mi
0   50 km

MEXICO

SPANISH MISSION STYLE

(left) Mission San Luis Rey de Francia; (right) Mission San Antonio de Padua

The Spanish mission churches derive much of their strength and enduring power from their extraordinary admixture of styles. They are spectacular examples of the combination of races and cultures that bloomed along Father Serra's road through Alta California.

SPIRIT OF THE PLACE

In building the missions, the Franciscan padres had to rely on available resources. Spanish churches back in Europe boasted marble floors and gilded statues. But here, whitewashed adobe walls gleamed in the sun and floors were often merely packed earth.

However simple the structures, the art within the mission confines continued to glorifiy the Church. The padres imported much finery to decorate the churches and perform the mass—silver, silk and lovely paintings to teach the life of Christ to the Indians and soldiers and settlers. Serra himself commissioned fine artists in Mexico to produce custom works using the best materials and according to exact specifications. Sculptures of angels, Mary, Joseph, Jesus and the Franciscan heroes and saints—and of course the Stations of the Cross—adorned all the missions.

AN ENDURING LEGACY

Mission architecture reflects a gorgeous blend of European and New World influences. While naves followed the simple forms of Franciscan Gothic, cloisters (with beautiful arcades) adopted aspects of the Romanesque style, and ornamental touches of the Spanish Renaissance—including red-tiled roofs and wrought-iron grilles—added even more elegance. In the 20th century, the Mission Revival Style had a huge impact on architecture and design in California, as seen in examples ranging from San Diego's Union Station to Stanford University's main quadrangle.

Father Junípero Serra statue at Mission San Gabriel

FOR WHOM THE BELLS TOLLED

Perhaps the most famous architectural motif of the Spanish Mission churches was the belltower. These took the form of either a campanile—a single tower called a campanario—or, more spectacularly, of an open-work espedaña, a perforated adobe wall housing a series of bells (notable examples of this form are at San Miguel Arcángel and San Diego de Alcalá). Bells were essential to maintaining the routines of daily life at the missions.

MISSION LIFE

Morning bells summoned residents to chapel for services; noontime bells introduced the main meal, while the evening bells sounded the alert to gather around 5 pm for mass and dinner. Many of the natives were happy with their new faith, and even enjoyed putting in numerous hours a week working as farmers, soapmakers, weavers, and masons.

Others, however, were less willing to abandon their traditional culture, but were coerced to abide by the new Spanish laws and mission rules. Natives were sometimes mistreated by the friars, who used a system of punishments to enforce submission to the new culture.

NATIVE TRAGEDY

In the end, mission life proved extremely destructive to the Native Californian population. European diseases and contaminated water caused the death of nearly a third, with some tribes—notably the Chumash—being virtually decimated.

Despite these losses, small numbers did survive. After the Mexican government secularized the missions in 1833, a majority of the native population was reduced to poverty. Some stayed at the missions, while others went to live in the pueblos, ranchos, and countryside.

Many Native Californian people today still work and live near the missions that are monuments to their artistry skills.

FOR MORE INFORMATION

California Missions Foundation

✉ 26555 Carmel Rancho Blvd., Ste. 7 Carmel, CA 93923

☎ 831/622-7500

🌐 www.california missionsfoundation.org

Top, Mission San Gabriel Arcángel
Bottom, Mission San Miguel Arcángel

EXPLORING

Santa Barbara's waterfront is beautiful, with palm-studded promenades and plenty of sand. In the few miles between the beaches and the hills are downtown, the old mission, and the botanic gardens.

EXPLORING

TOP ATTRACTIONS

★ **El Presidio State Historic Park.** Founded in 1782, El Presidio was one of four military strongholds established by the Spanish along the coast of California. The park encompasses much of the original site in the heart of downtown. El Cuartel, the adobe guardhouse, is the oldest building in Santa Barbara and the second oldest in California. ⊠ *123 E. Canon Perdido St., at Anacapa St.* ☎ *805/965-0093* ⊕ *www.sbthp.org* ⊠ *$5* ⊙ *Daily 10:30-4:30.*

Fodor's Choice   **Mission Santa Barbara.** Widely referred to as the "Queen of Missions,"
★ this is one of the most beautiful and frequently photographed buildings in coastal California. Dating to 1786, the architecture evolved from adobe-brick buildings with thatch roofs to more permanent edifices as the mission's population burgeoned. An earthquake in 1812 destroyed the third church built on the site. Its replacement, the present structure, is still a functioning Catholic church. Mission Santa Barbara has a splendid Spanish/Mexican colonial art collection, as well as Chumash sculptures and the only Native American–made altar and tabernacle left in the California missions. Docents lead 90-minute tours ($8 adult) Thursday and Friday at 11 and Saturday at 10:30. ⊠ *2201 Laguna St., at E. Los Olivos St.* ☎ *805/682-4149, 805/682-4713* ⊕ *www. santabarbaramission.org* ⊠ *$5* ⊙ *Daily 9-4:30.*

Santa Barbara Botanic Garden. Scenic trails meander through the garden's 78 acres of native plants. The Mission Dam, built in 1806, stands just beyond the redwood grove and above the restored aqueduct that once carried water to Mission Santa Barbara. More than a thousand plant species thrive in various themed sections, including mountains, deserts, meadows, redwoods, and Channel Islands. ⊠ *1212 Mission Canyon Rd., north of Foothill Rd. (Hwy. 192)* ☎ *805/682-4726* ⊕ *www.sbbg. org* ⊠ *$8* ⊙ *Mar.–Oct., daily 9-6; Nov.–Feb., daily 9-5. Guided tours weekends at 11 and 2.*

★ **Santa Barbara County Courthouse.** Hand-painted tiles and a spiral staircase infuse the courthouse with the grandeur of a Moorish palace. This magnificent building was completed in 1929, part of a rebuilding process after a 1925 earthquake destroyed many downtown structures. At the time, Santa Barbara was also in the midst of a cultural awakening, and the trend was toward an architectural style appropriate to the area's climate and history. The result is the harmonious Mediterranean–Spanish look of much of the downtown area, especially the municipal buildings. An elevator rises to an arched observation area in the courthouse tower that provides a panoramic view of the city. The murals in the ceremonial chambers on the courthouse's second floor were painted by an artist who did backdrops for some of Cecil B. DeMille's films. ⊠ *1100 Anacapa St., at E. Anapamu St.* ☎ *805/962-6464* ⊕ *www.santabarbaracourthouse.org* ⊙ *Weekdays 8-4:45, weekends*

2

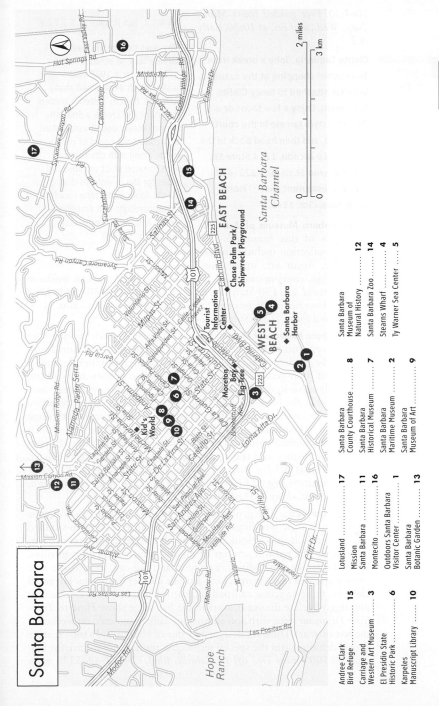

Santa Barbara

EAST BEACH

Santa Barbara Channel

Chase Palm Park/
Shipwreck Playground

Tourist
Information
Center

WEST
BEACH

Santa Barbara
Harbor

Moreton
Bay
Fig Tree

Kid's
World

2 miles

3 km

Hope
Ranch

10–4:30. Free guided tours Mon., Tues., Wed., and Fri. at 10:30, daily at 2.

Cielito Taqueria. Take a break from State Street shopping at the casual taqueria attached to fancy Cielito Restaurant. Enjoy a few tacos or a Oaxacan-style tamale in the courtyard patio, and then head back to the shops. ⊠ *La Arcada, 1114 State St., at E. Figueroa St.* ☎ *805/225–4488* ⊕ *cielitorestaurant.com* ⊗ *Mon. 11–8, Tues.–Sat. 11–6.*

SANTA BARBARA STYLE

Why does downtown Santa Barbara look so scrubbed and uniform? After a 1925 earthquake, which demolished many buildings, the city seized a golden opportunity to create a Spanish-Mediterranean look. It established an architectural board of review, which, along with city commissions, created strict architectural codes for the downtown district: red tile roofs, earth-tone facades, arches, wrought-iron embellishments, and height restrictions (about four stories).

Santa Barbara Museum of Art. The highlights of this museum's permanent collection include ancient sculpture, Asian art, impressionist paintings, contemporary art, photography, and American works in several media. ⊠ *1130 State St., at E. Anapamu St.* ☎ *805/963–4364* ⊕ *www.sbma.net* ⊠ *$9; pay what you wish on Sun.* ⊗ *Tues.–Sun. 11–5. Free guided tours Tues.–Sun. at noon and 1.*

☺ **Santa Barbara Museum of Natural History.** The gigantic skeleton of a blue whale greets you at the entrance of this complex. The major draws include the planetarium, space lab, and a gem and mineral display. A room of dioramas illustrates Chumash Indian history and culture. Startlingly alive-looking stuffed specimens, complete with nests and eggs, roost in the bird diversity room. Many exhibits have interactive components. Outdoors you can stroll on nature trails that wind through the serene oak-studded grounds. Ask about the Nature Pass, which includes discounted unlimited two-day admission to both the Museum of Natural History and the Ty Warner Sea Center on Stearns Wharf. ⊠ *2559 Puesta del Sol Rd., off E. Los Olivos St.* ☎ *805/682–4711* ⊕ *www.sbnature.org* ⊠ *$10 Oct.–Apr., $11 May–Sept.; free 3rd Sun. of month Sept.–May* ⊗ *Daily 10–5.*

☺ **Santa Barbara Zoo.** The grounds of this smallish zoo are so gorgeous people book their weddings here long in advance. The palm-studded lawns on a hilltop overlooking the beach are perfect spots for family picnics. The natural settings of the zoo shelter elephants, gorillas, exotic birds like the California condor, and big cats such as the rare snow leopard, a thick-furred, high-altitude dweller from Asia. For small children, there's a scenic railroad and barnyard petting zoo. Duncan, an amazingly lifelike dinosaur, stars in the live stage show *How to Train Your Dinosaur* (free with zoo admission, daily in summer, on weekends the rest of year). Duncan, designed by one of Hollywood's top creature shops, demonstrates the special techniques trainers use to care for animals. ⊠ *500 Niños Dr., off El Cabrillo Blvd.* ☎ *805/962–5339 main* *line, 805/962–6310 information* ⊕ *www.santabarbarazoo.org* ✉ *Zoo $14, parking $6* ⊙ *Daily 10–5.*

Stearns Wharf. Built in 1872, Stearns Wharf is Santa Barbara's most visited landmark. Expansive views of the mountains, cityscape, and harbor unfold from every vantage point on the three-block-long pier. Although it's a nice walk from the Cabrillo Boulevard parking areas, you can also park on the pier and then wander through the shops or stop for a meal at one of the wharf's restaurants. ⊠ *Cabrillo Blvd. and State St.* ⊕ *www.stearnswharf.org.*

☺ **Ty Warner Sea Center.** A branch of the Santa Barbara Museum of Natural History, the center specializes in Santa Barbara Channel marine life and conservation. Though small compared to aquariums in Monterey and Long Beach, this is a fascinating, hands-on marine science laboratory that lets you participate in experiments, projects, and exhibits, including touch tanks. Two-story glass walls here open to stunning ocean, mountain, and city views. You can purchase a Nature Pass, which includes discounted two-day admission to the natural history museum and the Sea Center. Ty Warner, the Beanie Baby mogul and a local resident, is a major donor. ⊠ *211 Stearns Wharf* ☎ *805/962–2526* ⊕ *www.sbnature. org* ✉ *$8* ⊙ *Daily 10–5.*

WORTH NOTING

Andree Clark Bird Refuge. This peaceful lagoon and its gardens sit north of East Beach. Bike trails and footpaths, punctuated by signs identifying native and migratory birds, skirt the lagoon. ⊠ *1400 E. Cabrillo Blvd., near the zoo* ✉ *Free.*

☺ **Carriage and Western Art Museum.** The country's largest collection of old horse-drawn vehicles—painstakingly restored—is exhibited here, everything from polished hearses to police buggies to old stagecoaches and circus vehicles. In August the Old Spanish Days Fiesta borrows many of the vehicles for a jaunt around town. This is one of the city's hidden gems. ⊠ *Pershing Park, 129 Castillo St.* ☎ *805/962–2353* ⊕ *www. carriagemuseum.org* ✉ *Free* ⊙ *Weekdays 9–3, 3rd Sun. of month 1–4 for docent tours.*

Karpeles Manuscript Library. Ancient political tracts and old Disney cartoons are among the holdings at this facility, which also houses one of the world's largest privately owned collections of rare manuscripts. Fifty display cases contain a sampling of the archive's million-plus documents. ⊠ *21 W. Anapamu St., near Chapala St.* ☎ *805/962–5322* ⊕ *www.karpeles.com* ✉ *Free* ⊙ *Wed.–Sun. noon–4.*

Montecito. Since the late 1800s the tree-studded hills and valleys of this town have attracted the rich and famous (Hollywood icons, business tycoons, dot-commers who divested before the crash, and old-money families who installed themselves here years ago). Shady roads wind through the community, which consists mostly of gated estates. Swank boutiques line Coast Village Road, where well-heeled residents such as Oprah Winfrey sometimes browse for truffle oil, picture frames, and designer jeans. Residents also hang out in the Upper Village, a chic shopping area with restaurants and cafés at the intersection of San

Santa Barbara's downtown is attractive, but be sure also to visit its beautiful—and uncrowded—beaches.

Ysidro and East Valley roads. Montecito is about 3 miles east of Santa Barbara off U.S. 101.

Lotusland. The 37-acre Montecito estate called Lotusland once belonged to Polish opera singer Ganna Walska. Many of the exotic trees and other subtropical flora were planted in 1882 by horticulturist R. Kinton Stevens. On the two-hour guided tour (the only option for visiting unless you're a member), you'll see an outdoor theater, a topiary garden, a huge collection of rare cycads (an unusual plant genus that has been around since the time of the dinosaurs), and a lotus pond. Tours are conducted February 15 through November 15, Wednesday through Saturday at 10 and 1:30. Reservations are required. Child-friendly family tours are available for groups with children under the age of 10; contact Lotusland for scheduling. ⊠ *695 Ashley Rd.* ☎ *805/969–9990* ⊕ *www.lotusland.org* ⊑ *$35*

Outdoors Santa Barbara Visitor Center. The small office provides maps and information about Channel Islands National Park, Channel Islands National Marine Sanctuary, and the Santa Barbara Maritime Museum, which occupies the same harbor building. ⊠ *113 Harbor Way, off Shoreline Dr.* ☎ *805/884–1475* ⊕ *outdoorsb.noaa.gov* ⊑ *Free* ☉ *Daily 11–5.*

Santa Barbara Historical Museum. The historical society's museum exhibits decorative and fine arts, furniture, costumes, and documents from the town's past. Adjacent to it is the Gledhill Library, a collection of books, photographs, maps, and manuscripts. ⊠ *136 E. De La Guerra St., at Santa Barbara St.* ☎ *805/966–1601* ⊕ *www.santabarbaramuseum.com* ⊑ *Museum by donation; library $2–$5 per hr for research* ☉ *Museum*

Tues.–Sat. 10–5, Sun. noon–5, guided tours Sat. at 2; library Tues.–Fri. 10–4, 1st Sat. of month 10–1.

Santa Barbara Maritime Museum. California's seafaring history is the focus here. High-tech, hands-on exhibits, such as a sportfishing activity that lets participants catch a "big one" and a local surfing history retrospective make this a fun stop for families. ⊠ *113 Harbor Way, off Shoreline Dr.* ☎ *805/962–8404* ⊕ *www.sbmm.org* ⊠ *$7* ☉ *June–Aug., Thurs.–Tues. 10–6; Sept.–May, Thurs.–Tues. 10–5.*

Urban Wine Trail. More than a dozen winery tasting rooms form the Urban Wine Trail; most are within walking distance of the waterfront and the lower State Street shopping and restaurant district. **Santa Barbara Winery,** at 202 Anacapa Street, and **Au Bon Climat,** at 813 Anacapa Street, are good places to start your oenological trek. ☎ ⊕ *urbanwinetrailsb.com.*

BEACHES

Santa Barbara's beaches don't have the big surf of the shoreline farther south, but they also don't have the crowds. You can usually find a solitary spot to swim or sunbathe. In June and July, fog often hugs the coast until about noon.

Arroyo Burro County Beach. The usually gentle surf at Arroyo Burro County Beach makes it ideal for families with young children. It's a local favorite, since you can walk for miles in both directions when tides are low. Leashed dogs are allowed on the main stretch of beach and westward; they are allowed to romp off-leash east of the slough at the beach entrance. The parking lots fill early on weekends and throughout the summer, but the park is relatively quiet at other times. Walk along the beach just a few hundreds yards away from the main steps at the entrance to escape crowds on warm-weather days. Surfers, swimmers, standup paddlers, and boogie boarders regularly ply the waves, and photographers come often to catch the vivid sunsets. **Amenities:** food and drink; lifeguard in summer; parking, showers, toilets. **Best For:** sunset; surfing; swimming; walking. ⊠ *Cliff Dr. and Las Positas Rd.*

East Beach. The wide swath of sand at the east end of Cabrillo Boulevard is a great spot for people-watching. East Beach has sand volleyball courts, summertime lifeguard and sports competitions, and arts-and-crafts shows on Sunday and holidays. You can use showers, a weight room, and lockers (bring your own towel) and rent umbrellas and boogie boards at the Cabrillo Bathhouse. Next door, there's an elaborate jungle-gym play area for kids. Hotels line the boulevard across from the beach. **Amenities:** food and drink; lifeguards in summer; parking (fee); showers; toilets; water sports. **Best For:** walking; swimming; surfing. ⊠ *1118 Cabrillo Blvd., at Ninos Dr.* ☎ *805/897–2680.*

WHERE TO EAT

$$

JAPANESE

✕ **Arigato Sushi.** You might have to wait for a table at this trendy, two-story restaurant and sushi bar—locals line up early for the wildly creative combination rolls and other delectables. Fans of authentic

Japanese food sometimes disagree about the quality of the seafood, but all dishes are fresh and artfully presented. The menu includes traditional dishes as well as innovative creations such as sushi pizza on seaweed and Hawaiian sashimi salad. $ *Average main: $20* ⊠ *1225 State St., near W. Victoria St.* ☎ *805/965–6074* ⊕ *www.arigatosantabarbara. com* ⌕ *Reservations not accepted* ⊘ *No lunch.*

$$ **✕ Brophy Bros.** The outdoor tables
SEAFOOD at this casual harborside restaurant have perfect views of the marina and mountains. Staffers serve enormous, exceptionally fresh fish dishes—don't miss the seafood salad and chowder—and provide guests with a pager if there's a long wait for a table. Stroll along the waterfront until the beep lets you know your table's ready. Hugely popular, Brophy Bros. can be crowded and loud, especially on weekend evenings. $ *Average main: $20* ⊠ *119 Harbor Way, off Shoreline Dr.* ☎ *805/966–4418* ⊕ *www.brophybros.com.*

$ **✕ Flavor of India.** Feast on authentic northern Indian dishes like tan-
INDIAN doori chicken, lamb biryani, and a host of curries at this local favorite in a residential neighborhood. Best bets include the combination dinners served in a traditional Indian tray and the all-you-can-eat lunch buffet ($9). $ *Average main: $11* ⊠ *3026 State St., at De La Vina St.* ☎ *805/682–6561* ⊕ *www.flavorofindiasb.com* ⊘ *Closed Sun.*

$$$$ **✕ The Hungry Cat.** The hip Santa Barbara sibling of a famed Hollywood
SEAFOOD eatery, run by chefs David Lentz and his wife Suzanne Goin, dishes up savory seafood in a small but lively nook in the downtown arts district. Feast on sea urchin, addictive peel-and-eat shrimp, and creative cocktails made from farmers' market fruits and veggies. A busy nightspot on weekends, the Cat also awakens for a popular brunch on Sunday. Night or day, come early or be prepared for a wait. $ *Average main: $30* ⊠ *1134 Chapala St., near W. Figueroa St.* ☎ *805/884–4701* ⊕ *www.thehungrycat.com* ⊘ *Closed Mon. Sept.–April.*

$ **✕ La Super-Rica.** Praised by Julia Child, this food stand on the east side
MEXICAN of town serves some of the spiciest and most authentic Mexican dishes
★ between Los Angeles and San Francisco. Fans fill up on the soft tacos served with yummy spicy or mild sauces and legendary beans. Three specials are offered daily. Portions are on the small side; order several dishes and share. $ *Average main: $9* ⊠ *622 N. Milpas St., at Alphonse St.* ☎ *805/963–4940* ▭ *No credit cards* ⊘ *Closed Wed.*

$$$ **✕ Olio e Limone.** Sophisticated Italian cuisine (with an emphasis on Sic-
ITALIAN ily) is served at this restaurant near the Arlington Center. The juicy veal chop is popular, but surprises abound here; be sure to try unusual dishes such as ribbon pasta with quail and sausage in a mushroom ragout, or

the duck ravioli. Tables are placed close together, so this may not be the best spot for intimate conversations. For casual artisanal Italian fare, head next door to the Olio pizzeria/enoteca/bar. [$] *Average main: $29* ✉ *17 W. Victoria St., at State St.* ☎ *805/899–2699* 🌐 *www.olioelimone.com* 🕒 *No lunch Sun.*

BEST VIEWS

Drive along Alameda Padre Serra, a hillside road that begins near the mission and continues to Montecito, to feast your eyes on spectacular views of the city and the Santa Barbara Channel.

$$$ SOUTHERN 🍴 **Palace Grill.** Mardi Gras energy, team-style service, lively music, and great food have made the Palace a Santa Barbara icon. Acclaimed for its Cajun and creole dishes such as blackened redfish and jambalaya with dirty rice, the Palace also serves Caribbean fare, including a delicious coconut-shrimp dish. If you're spice-phobic, you can choose pasta, soft-shell crab, or filet mignon. Be prepared to wait for a table on Friday and Saturday night (when reservations are taken for a 5:30 seating only), though the live entertainment and free appetizers, sent out front when the line is long, will whet your appetite for the feast to come. [$] *Average main: $28* ✉ *8 E. Cota St., at State St.* ☎ *805/963–5000* 🌐 *www.palacegrill.com.*

$$$ ECLECTIC 🍴 **Roy.** Owner-chef Leroy Gandy serves a fixed-price dinner (selections $20, $25, and $30)—a real bargain—that includes a small salad, fresh soup, homemade organic bread, and a rotating selection of contemporary American main courses. If you're lucky, the entrée choices might include grilled local fish with a mandarin beurre blanc, or bacon-wrapped filet mignon. You can also choose from an à la carte menu of inexpensive appetizers and entrées, plus local wines. Roy is a favorite spot for late-night dining—it's open until midnight and has a full bar. [$] *Average main: $25* ✉ *7 W. Carrillo St., near State St.* ☎ *805/966–5636* 🌐 *www.restaurantroy.com* 🕒 *No lunch.*

$$$$ AMERICAN ★ 🍴 **The Stonehouse.** The elegant Stonehouse is inside a century-old granite former farmhouse at the San Ysidro Ranch resort. Executive chef Matt Johnson creates outstanding regional cuisine centered around herbs and veggies from the on-site garden and top-quality local ingredients. The menu changes constantly but typically includes favorites such as crab cake with persimmon relish appetizer and local spiny lobster with mascarpone risotto. Dine on the radiant-heated ocean-view deck with stone fireplace, next to a fountain under a canopy of loquat trees, or in the romantic, candlelit dining room overlooking a creek. The Plow & Angel pub, downstairs, offers more casual bistro fare. [$] *Average main: $47* ✉ *900 San Ysidro La., off San Ysidro Rd., Montecito* ☎ *805/565–1700* 🌐 *www.sanysidroranch.com* ✍ *Reservations essential* 🕒 *No lunch Sun.–Wed.*

$$$ AMERICAN 🍴 **Wine Cask.** A reinvention of a same-named local favorite that closed a few years back, the Wine Cask serves bistro-style meals—many of them made with ingredients from a nearby farmers' market—in a comfortable and classy dining room. The dishes are paired with wines from Santa Barbara's most extensive wine list, not a surprise given co-owner Doug Margerum's main occupation as a winemaker and wine merchant (his wine shop/tasting room is just steps away). The more casual bar-café,

Intermezzo, across the courtyard, serves pizzas, salads, small plates, wines, and cocktails and is open late. [$] *Average main: $29* ✉ *El Paseo, 813 Anacapa St., at E. De La Guerra St.* ☎ *805/966–9463* 🌐 *www.winecask.com* ✍ *Reservations essential.*

$ THAI 🍴 **Zen Yai Thai Cuisine.** As the shingle above the tiny storefront amid lower State Street's club scene states, the food here is "reminiscent of things Thai." That might drive away diners seeking absolute authenticity, but every day a trendy flock of fans packs the room for delectable dishes made from fresh local ingredients. Reserve a table or be prepared for a wait. [$] *Average main: $14* ✉ *425 State St., at W. Haley St.* ☎ *805/957–1102* ⏲ *No lunch Mon. and weekends.*

WHERE TO STAY

For expanded reviews, facilities, and current deals, visit Fodors.com.

$$$$ HOTEL 🏨 **Canary Hotel.** The only full-service hotel in the heart of downtown, the Canary blends a casual, beach-getaway feel with tony urban sophistication. **Pros:** easy stroll to museums, shopping, dining; friendly, attentive service; adjacent fitness center. **Cons:** across from main bus transit center; some rooms feel cramped. **TripAdvisor:** "lovely hotel," "wonderful experience," "helpful staff." [$] *Rooms from: $300* ✉ *31 W. Carrillo St.* ☎ *805/884–0300, 877/468–3515* 🌐 *www.canarysantabarbara.com* 🛏 *77 rooms, 20 suites.*

$$$$ RESORT ★ 🏨 **Four Seasons Resort The Biltmore Santa Barbara.** Surrounded by lush, perfectly manicured gardens and across from the beach, Santa Barbara's grande dame has long been a favorite for quiet, California-style luxury. **Pros:** first-class resort; historic Santa Barbara character; personal service; steps from the beach. **Cons:** back rooms are close to train tracks; expensive. **TripAdvisor:** "gorgeous location," "beautiful hotel with very friendly staff," "well worth it." [$] *Rooms from: $595* ✉ *1260 Channel Dr.* ☎ *805/969–2261, 800/332–3442* 🌐 *www.fourseasons.com/santabarbara* 🛏 *181 rooms, 26 suites.*

$$ HOTEL 🏨 **Franciscan Inn.** Part of this Spanish-Mediterranean motel, a block from the harbor and West Beach, dates back to the 1920s. **Pros:** walking distance from waterfront and harbor; family-friendly; great value. **Cons:** busy lobby; pool can be crowded. **TripAdvisor:** "great staff," "charming," "home away from home." [$] *Rooms from: $160* ✉ *109 Bath St.* ☎ *805/963–8845, 800/663–5288* 🌐 *www.franciscaninn.com* 🛏 *48 rooms, 5 suites* 🍽 *Breakfast.*

$$$ HOTEL 🏨 **Hyatt Santa Barbara.** A complex of four separate buildings on three landscaped acres, Hyatt Santa Barbara provides a wide range of value-laden lodging options in a prime location—right across from East Beach and the Cabrillo Pavilion Bathhouse. **Pros:** steps from the beach; many room types and rates; walk to the zoo and waterfront shuttle. **Cons:** motelish vibe; busy area in summer. **TripAdvisor:** "friendly people make the difference," "excellent customer service and staff," "lovely property." [$] *Rooms from: $229* ✉ *1111 E. Cabrillo Blvd.* ☎ *805/882-1234, 800/643–1994* 🌐 *www.santabarbara.hyatt.com* 🛏 *171 rooms, 3 suites.*

$ HOTEL 🏨 **Motel 6 Santa Barbara Beach.** A half block from East Beach amid fancier hotels sits this basic but comfortable motel, which was the first

2

Motel 6 in existence. **Pros:** less than a minute's walk from the zoo and beach; friendly staff; clean and comfortable. **Cons:** no frills; motel-style rooms; no breakfast. **TripAdvisor:** "great staff," "one of the best Motel 6s," "beautiful room." [$] *Rooms from: $109* ✉ *443 Corona Del Mar Dr.* ☎ *805/564–1392, 800/466–8356* 🌐 *www.motel6.com* 🛏 *51 rooms.*

$$ HOTEL 🏨 **Presidio Motel.** Young globetrotting couple Chris Sewell and Kenny Osehan transformed the Presidio, a formerly funky motel, into a simple yet stylish oasis. **Pros:** great downtown location; friendly staff; hip, artsy vibe. **Cons:** smallish rooms; basic baths; thin walls. **TripAdvisor:** "quirky hidden gem," "California charmer," "really unique place." [$] *Rooms from: $159* ✉ *1620 State St.* ☎ *805/963–1355* 🌐 *www.thepresidiomotel.com* 🛏 *16 rooms.*

$$$$ RESORT ★ 🏨 **San Ysidro Ranch.** At this romantic hideaway on an historic property in the Montecito foothills—where John and Jackie Kennedy spent their honeymoon and Oprah sends her out-of-town visitors—guest cottages are scattered among groves of orange trees and flower beds. **Pros:** ultimate privacy; surrounded by nature; celebrity hangout; pet-friendly. **Cons:** very expensive; too remote for some. **TripAdvisor:** "it doesn't get any better," "outstanding cuisine," "romance and beauty." [$] *Rooms from: $650* ✉ *900 San Ysidro La., Montecito* ☎ *805/565–1700, 800/368–6788* 🌐 *www.sanysidroranch.com* 🛏 *23 rooms, 4 suites, 14 cottages* ☞ *2-day minimum stay on weekends, 3 days on holiday weekends.*

$$$$ B&B/INN ★ 🏨 **Simpson House Inn.** If you're a fan of traditional B&Bs, this property, with its beautifully appointed Victorian main house and acre of lush gardens, is for you. **Pros:** impeccable landscaping; walking distance from everything downtown; ranked among the nation's top B&Bs. **Cons:** some rooms in the main building are small; two-night minimum stay on weekends. **TripAdvisor:** "so beautiful," "charming," "almost perfection." [$] *Rooms from: $250* ✉ *121 E. Arrellaga St.* ☎ *805/963–7067, 800/676–1280* 🌐 *www.simpsonhouseinn.com* 🛏 *11 rooms, 4 cottages* 🍴 *Breakfast.*

$$$$ B&B/INN 🏨 **Spanish Garden Inn.** A half block from the Presidio in the heart of downtown, this elegant Spanish-Mediterranean retreat celebrates Santa Barbara style, from the tile floors, wrought-iron balconies, and exotic plants, to the original art by local plein-air artists. **Pros:** walking distance from downtown; classic Spanish-Mediterranean style; caring staff. **Cons:** far from the beach; not much here for kids. **TripAdvisor:** "lovely small hotel," "perfect oasis of style and quality," "laid back." [$] *Rooms from: $389* ✉ *915 Garden St.* ☎ *805/564–4700, 866/564–4700* 🌐 *www.spanishgardeninn.com* 🛏 *23 rooms* 🍴 *Breakfast.*

NIGHTLIFE AND THE ARTS

Most major hotels present entertainment nightly during the summer and on weekends all year. The town's bar, club, and live-music scene centers on lower State Street, between the 300 and 800 blocks. The thriving arts district, with theaters, restaurants, and cafés, starts around the 900 block of State Street and continues north to the Arlington Center for the Performing Arts, in the 1300 block. The proximity to the University of California at Santa Barbara assures an endless stream of visiting artists and performers. To see what's scheduled around town, pick up a copy of the free weekly *Santa Barbara Independent* newspaper or visit its website ⊕ *www.independent.com.*

NIGHTLIFE

Blue Agave. Leather couches, a crackling fire in chilly weather, a cigar balcony, and pool tables draw a fancy crowd to Blue Agave for good food and designer martinis. ⊠ *20 E. Cota St., near State St.* ☎ *805/899–4694.*

Dargan's. All types of people hang out at Dargan's, a lively pub with four pool tables, great draft beers and Irish whiskeys, and a full menu of traditional Irish dishes. ⊠ *18 E. Ortega St., at Anacapa St.* ☎ *805/568–0702.*

James Joyce. A good place to have a few beers and while away an evening, the James Joyce sometimes hosts folk and rock performers. ⊠ *513 State St., at W. Haley St.* ☎ *805/962–2688.*

Joe's Cafe. Steins of beer accompany hearty bar food at Joe's. It's a fun, if occasionally rowdy, collegiate scene. ⊠ *536 State St., at E. Cota St.* ☎ *805/966–4638.*

Lucky's. A slick sports bar attached to an upscale steak house owned by the maker of Lucky Brand Dungarees, this place attracts hip, fashionably dressed patrons hoping to see and be seen. ⊠ *1279 Coast Village Rd., near Olive Mill Rd., Montecito* ☎ *805/565–7540.*

Milk & Honey. Artfully prepared tapas, coconut-mango mojitos, and exotic cocktails lure trendy crowds to swank M&H, despite high prices and a reputation for inattentive service. ⊠ *30 W. Anapamu St., at State St.* ☎ *805/275–4232.*

SOhO. A hip restaurant, bar, and music club, SOhO books bands, from jazz to blues to rock, every night of the week. ⊠ *1221 State St., at W. Victoria St.* ☎ *805/962–7776.*

THE ARTS

Arlington Center for the Performing Arts. This Moorish-style auditorium hosts major events during the two-week Santa Barbara International Film Festival every winter and presents touring performers and films throughout the year. ⊠ *1317 State St., at Arlington Ave.* ☎ *805/963–4408.*

Center Stage Theatre. This venue hosts plays, music, dance, and readings. ⊠ *Paseo Nuevo Center, Chapala and De la Guerra Sts., 2nd floor* ☎ *805/963–0408.*

Ensemble Theatre Company. The company stages plays by authors ranging from Tennessee Williams and Henrik Ibsen to rising contemporary dramatists. ⊠ *914 Santa Barbara St., at El Canon Perdido St.* ☎ *805/965–5400.*

Granada. A restored and modernized landmark that dates to 1924, the Granada hosts Broadway touring shows and dance, music, and other cultural events. ⊠ *1214 State St., at E. Anapamu St.* ☎ *805/899–2222 box office.*

Lobero Theatre. A state landmark, the Lobero hosts community theater groups and touring professionals. ⊠ *33 E. Canon Perdido St., at Anacapa St.* ☎ *805/963–0761.*

Music Academy of the West. The academy showcases orchestral, chamber, and operatic works every summer. ⊠ *1070 Fairway Rd., off Channel Dr.* ☎ *805/969–4726, 805/969–8787 box office.*

SPORTS AND THE OUTDOORS

BICYCLING **Cabrillo Bike Lane.** The level, two-lane, 3-mile Cabrillo Bike Lane passes the Santa Barbara Zoo, the Andree Clark Bird Refuge, beaches, and the harbor. There are restaurants along the way, and you can stop for a picnic along the palm-lined path looking out on the Pacific.

Wheel Fun Rentals. Wheel Fun Rentals has bikes, quadricycles, and skates; a second outlet around the block rents small electric cars and scooters. ⊠ *23 E. Cabrillo Blvd.* ☎ *805/966–2282.*

BOATS AND CHARTERS **Condor Express.** From SEA Landing, the *Condor Express,* a 75-foot high-speed catamaran, whisks up to 149 passengers toward the Channel Islands on dinner cruises, whale-watching excursions, and pelagic-bird trips. ☎ *805/882–0088, 888/779–4253.*

Santa Barbara Sailing Center. The center offers sailing instruction, rents and charters sailboats, and organizes dinner and sunset champagne cruises, island excursions, and whale-watching trips. ⊠ *Santa Barbara Harbor launching ramp* ☎ *805/962–2826, 800/350–9090.*

🐊 **Santa Barbara Water Taxi.** Children beg to ride *L'il Toot,* a cherry yellow water taxi that cruises from the harbor to Stearns Wharf and back again. ⊠ *Santa Barbara Harbor and Stearns Wharf* ☎ *805/896–6900, 888/316–9363* ⊕ *sbwatertaxi.com* 🎫 *$4 one-way* ⊙ *Departures every ½ hr from noon to 6 in summer, noon to sunset in winter.*

Truth Aquatics. Departing from SEA Landing in the Santa Barbara Harbor, Truth Aquatics ferries passengers on excursions to the National Marine Sanctuary and Channel Islands National Park and takes scuba divers on single-day and multiday trips. ☎ *805/962–1127.*

GOLF **Sandpiper Golf Club.** This 18-hole, par-72 course sits on the ocean bluffs and combines stunning views with a challenging game. Greens fees are $139–$159; a cart (optional) is $16. ⊠ *7925 Hollister Ave., 14 miles north of downtown off U.S. 101* ☎ *805/968–1541.*

Santa Barbara Golf Club. The club has an 18-hole, par-70 course. The greens fees are $48–$58; a cart (optional) costs $15 per rider. ⊠ *3500 McCaw Ave., at Las Positas Rd.* ☎ *805/687–7087.*

BIRTHPLACE OF THE ENVIRONMENTAL MOVEMENT

In 1969, 200,000 gallons of crude oil spilled into the Santa Barbara Channel, causing an immediate outcry from residents, particularly in the UCSB community. The day after the spill, Get Oil Out (GOO) was established; the group helped lead the successful fight for legislation to limit and regulate offshore drilling in California. The Santa Barbara spill also spawned Earth Day, which is still celebrated in communities across the nation today.

TENNIS   Many hotels in Santa Barbara have courts.

City of Santa Barbara Parks and Recreation Department. The City of Santa Barbara Parks and Recreation Department operates public courts with lighted play until 9 pm weekdays. You can purchase day permits ($8) at the courts, or call the department. ☏ 805/564–5473.

Municipal Tennis Center. The 12 hard courts at the Municipal Tennis Center include an enclosed stadium court and three lighted courts open daily. ✉ 1414 Park Pl., near Salinas St. and U.S. 101.

Pershing Park. Pershing Park has eight lighted courts available for public play after 5 pm weekdays and all day on weekends and Santa Barbara City College holidays. ✉ 100 Castillo St., near Cabrillo Blvd.

SHOPPING

SHOPPING   **Brinkerhoff Avenue.** Antiques and gift shops are clustered in restored
AREAS   Victorian buildings on Brinkerhoff Avenue. ✉ 2 blocks west of State St. at W. Cota St.

El Paseo. Shops, art galleries, and studios share the courtyard and gardens of El Paseo, a historic arcade. ✉ Canon Perdido St., between State and Anacapa Sts.

State Street. State Street, roughly between Cabrillo Boulevard and Sola Street, is the commercial hub of Santa Barbara and a shopper's paradise. Chic malls, quirky storefronts, antiques emporia, elegant boutiques, and funky thrift shops abound here. You can do your shopping on foot or by a battery-powered trolley (25¢) that runs between the waterfront and the 1300 block. Nordstrom and Macy's anchor **Paseo Nuevo,** an open-air mall in the 700 block of State that also contains arts institutions such as Center Stage Theater.

Summerland. Serious antiques hunters head southeast of Santa Barbara to Summerland, which is full of shops and markets. Several good ones are along Lillie Avenue and Ortega Hill Road.

CLOTHING   **Channel Islands Surfboards.** Come here for the latest in California beachwear, sandals, and accessories. ✉ 36 Anacapa St., at E. Mason St. ☏ 805/966–7213.

Diani. This upscale, European-style women's boutique dresses clients in designer clothing from around the world. A sibling shoe shop is nearby. ✉ 1324 State St., at Arlington Ave. ☏ 805/966-3114, 805/966-7175 shoe shop ⊕ www.dianiboutique.com.

Santa Barbara Outfitters. Kayakers, climbers, cyclists, runners, hikers, and other active folks shop here for stylish, functional clothing, shoes, and accessories. ✉ 1200 State St., at E. Anapamu St. ☏ 805/564–1007.

Surf 'N Wear's Beach House. This shop carries surf clothing, gear, and collectibles; it's also the home of Santa Barbara Surf Shop and the exclusive local dealer of Surfboards by Yater. ✉ 10 State St., at Cabrillo Blvd. ☏ 805/963–1281.

Territory Ahead. The flagship of the outdoorsy catalog company sells fashionably rugged clothing for men and women. ✉ 515 State St., near W. Haley St. ☏ 805/962-5558.

Wendy Foster. This store sells casual-chic clothing for women. ⊠ *833 State St., at W. Canon Perdido St.* ☎ *805/966–2276.*

EN
ROUTE

If you choose to drive north via U.S. 101 without detouring to the Solvang/Santa Ynez area, you will drive right past some good beaches. In succession from east to west, **El Capitan, Gaviota, and Refugio state beaches** all have campsites, picnic tables, and fire rings.

SANTA BARBARA COUNTY

Residents refer to the glorious 30-mile stretch of coastline from Carpinteria to Gaviota as the South Coast. The Santa Ynez Mountains divide the county geographically; U.S. 101 passes through a mountain tunnel leading inland. Northern Santa Barbara County used to be known for its sprawling ranches and strawberry and broccoli fields. Today its 100-plus wineries and 22,000 acres of vineyards dominate the landscape from the Santa Ynez Valley in the south to Santa Maria in the north. The hit film *Sideways* was filmed almost entirely in the North County Wine Country; when the movie won Golden Globe and Oscar awards in 2005, it sparked national and international interest in visits to the region.

GETTING HERE AND AROUND

Two-lane Highway 154 over San Marcos Pass is the shortest and most scenic route from Santa Barbara into the Santa Ynez Valley. You can also drive along U.S. 101 north 43 miles to Buellton, then 7 miles east through Solvang to Santa Ynez. Santa Ynez Valley Transit shuttle buses serve Santa Ynez, Los Olivos, Ballard, Solvang, and Buellton. COLT Wine Country Express buses connect Lompoc, Buellton, and Solvang weekdays except holidays.

ESSENTIALS

Bus Contacts COLT Wine Country Express ⊠ *Lompoc* ☎ *805/736–7666* ⊕ *www.cityoflompoc.com/transit.* **Santa Ynez Valley Transit** ☎ *805/688–5452* ⊕ *www.syvt.com.*

Visitor Information Santa Barbara County Vintners' Association ☎ *805/688–0881* ⊕ *www.sbcountywines.com.* **The Santa Barbara Conference & Visitors Bureau** ☎ *805/966–9222* ⊕ *www.santabarbaraca.com.*

SANTA YNEZ

31 miles north of Goleta via Hwy. 154.

Founded in 1882, the tiny town of Santa Ynez still has many of its original frontier buildings. You can walk through the three-block downtown area in a few minutes, shop for antiques, and hang around the old-time saloon. At some of the eponymous valley's best restaurants, you just might bump into one of the celebrities who own nearby ranches.

GETTING HERE AND AROUND

Take Highway 154 over San Marcos Pass or U.S. 101 north 43 miles to Buellton, then 7 miles east.

2

ESSENTIALS

Visitor Information **Santa Ynez Valley Visitors Association** ☎ *805/686-0053, 800/742-2843* 🌐 *www.visitthesantaynezvalley.com.*

EXPLORING

Chumash Casino Resort. Just south of Santa Ynez on the Chumash Indian Reservation lies this Las Vegas–style casino with 2,000 slot machines, three restaurants, a spa, and an upscale hotel. ✉ *3400 E. Hwy. 246* ☎ *800/248-6274.*

WHERE TO EAT AND STAY

For expanded reviews, facilities, and current deals, visit Fodors.com.

$$ ITALIAN ★ 🍴 **Trattoria Grappolo.** Authentic Italian fare, an open kitchen, and festive, family-style seating make this trattoria equally popular with celebrities from Hollywood and ranchers from the Santa Ynez Valley. Thin-crust pizza, homemade ravioli, risottos, and seafood linguine are among the menu favorites. The noise level tends to rise in the evening, so this isn't the best spot for a romantic getaway. [$] *Average main: $22* ✉ *3687-C Sagunto St.* ☎ *805/688-6899* 🌐 *www.trattoriagrappolo.com* 🕒 *No lunch Mon.*

$$$ B&B/INN 🏨 **Santa Ynez Inn.** This posh two-story Victorian inn in downtown Santa Ynez was built from scratch in 2002, and the owners have furnished all the rooms with authentic historical pieces. **Pros:** near restaurants; unusual antiques; spacious rooms. **Cons:** high price for location; not a historic building. **TripAdvisor:** "gateway to great hospitality," "comfortable elegance," "every modern luxury." [$] *Rooms from: $245* ✉ *3627 Sagunto St.* ☎ *805/688-5588, 800/643-5774* 🌐 *www.santaynezinn.com* 🛏 *20 rooms, 3 suites* 🍽 *Breakfast.*

LOS OLIVOS

4 miles north of Santa Ynez on Hwy. 154.

This pretty village in the Santa Ynez Valley was once on Spanish-built El Camino Real (Royal Highway) and later a stop on major stagecoach and rail routes. It's so sleepy today, though, that the movie *Return to Mayberry* was filmed here. Tasting rooms, art galleries, antiques stores, and country markets line Grand Avenue and intersecting streets for several blocks.

GETTING HERE AND AROUND

From U.S. 101 north or south, exit at Highway 154 and drive east about 8 miles. From Santa Barbara, travel 30 miles northwest on Highway 154.

EXPLORING

Carhartt Vineyard Tasting Room. At this intimate space, you're likely to meet owners and winemakers Mike and Brooke Carhartt, who pour samples of their small-lot, handcrafted vintages most days. ✉ *2990-A Grand Ave.* ☎ *805/693-5100* 🌐 *www.carharttvineyard.com.*

Daniel Gehrs Tasting Room. Heather Cottage, built in the early 1900s as a doctor's office, houses the Gehrs tasting room, where you can sample various varietals produced in limited small-lot quantities. ✉ *2939 Grand Ave.* ☎ *805/693–9686* 🌐 *www.danielgehrswines.com.*

Firestone Vineyard. This winery has been around since 1972. It has daily tours, grassy picnic areas, and hiking trails in the hills overlooking the valley. The views are fantastic. ✉ *5000 Zaca Station Rd., off U.S. 101* ☎ *805/688–3940* 🌐 *www.firestonewine.com.*

WHERE TO EAT AND STAY

For expanded reviews, facilities, and current deals, visit Fodors.com.

$$ AMERICAN 🍴 **Los Olivos Cafe.** Part wine store and part local social hub, this café that appeared in the film *Sideways* focuses on wine-friendly fish, pasta, and meat dishes, plus salads, pizzas, and burgers. Don't miss the homemade muffuletta and olive tapenade spreads. Other house favorites include an artisanal cheese plate, baked Brie with honey-roasted hazelnuts, and braised pot roast with whipped potatoes. [$] *Average main: $20* ✉ *2879 Grand Ave.* ☎ *805/688–7265, 888/946–3748* 🌐 *www.losolivoscafe.com.*

$$$ AMERICAN ★ 🍴 **Sides Hardware & Shoes: A Brothers Restaurant.** For more than a decade, chef-owners and brothers Matt and Jeff Nichols operated one of the valley's best restaurants at historic Mattei's Tavern. In spring 2012, they renovated and moved to another historic building, Sides Hardware & Shoes. Comfort food, which they prepare with panache, is the focus of their seasonal menu. Popular breakfast dishes include cooked-to-order beignets and eggs Benedict with house-made bacon steak. The Kobe-style burgers make a great lunch, and the dinner favorites include fried chicken and lamb sirloin with herbed gnocchi. [$] *Average main: $24* ✉ *2375 Alamo Pintado Ave.* ☎ *805/688–4820* 🌐 *www.brothersrestaurant.com.*

$$$ B&B/INN 🏨 **The Ballard Inn & Restaurant.** Set among orchards and vineyards in the tiny town of Ballard, 2 miles south of Los Olivos, this inn makes an elegant wine-country escape. **Pros:** exceptional food; attentive staff; secluded. **Cons:** some baths could use updating; several miles from Los Olivos and Santa Ynez. **TripAdvisor:** "beautiful rooms," "fabulous escape," "extremely comfortable." [$] *Rooms from: $225* ✉ *2436 Baseline Ave., Ballard* ☎ *805/688–7770, 800/638–2466* 🌐 *www.ballardinn.com* 🛏 *15 rooms* 🍽 *Breakfast.*

$$$$ B&B/INN 🏨 **Fess Parker's Wine Country Inn and Spa.** This luxury inn includes an elegant, tree-shaded French country–style main building and an equally attractive annex across the street with a pool and day spa. **Pros:** convenient wine-touring base; walking distance from restaurants and galleries; well-appointed rooms. **Cons:** pricey; staff attention is inconsistent. **TripAdvisor:** "beautifully updated hotel with spacious rooms," "homey and relaxing," "simply fabulous." [$] *Rooms from: $395* ✉ *2860 Grand Ave.* ☎ *805/688–7788, 800/446–2455* 🌐 *www.fessparker.com* 🛏 *15 rooms, 4 suites* 🍽 *Breakfast.*

SOLVANG

> *5 miles south of Los Olivos on Alamo Pintado Rd.; 3 miles east of U.S. 101 on Hwy. 246.*

You'll know you've reached the town of Solvang when the architecture suddenly changes to half-timber buildings and windmills. The town was settled in 1911 by a group of Danish educators—the flatlands and rolling green hills reminded them of home—and even today, more than two-thirds of the residents are of Danish descent. Although Solvang has attracted tourists for decades, in recent years it has become more sophisticated, with galleries, upscale restaurants, and wine-tasting rooms. Most shops are locally owned; the city has an ordinance prohibiting chain stores. To get your bearings, park your car in one of the free public lots and stroll around town. You can pick up maps and walking-tour information at the visitor center on Copenhagen Drive. Before you depart, be sure to sample the breads and pastries from the town's excellent bakeries.

GETTING HERE AND AROUND

Highway 246 West (Mission Drive) traverses Solvang, connecting with U.S. 101 to the west and Highway 154 to the east. Alamo Pintado Road connects Solvang with Ballard and Los Olivos to the north. Santa Ynez Valley Transit shuttle buses run between Solvang and nearby towns.

ESSENTIALS

Visitor Information Solvang Conference & Visitors Bureau ⊠ *1639 Copenhagen Dr., at 2nd St.* ☎ *805/688–6144* ⊕ *www.solvangusa.com.*

EXPLORING

Alma Rosa Winery. Richard and Thekla Sanford helped put Santa Barbara County on the international wine map with a 1989 Pinot Noir. In 2005 they started a new winery, Alma Rosa, crafting wines from grapes grown on their 100-plus-acre certified organic vineyards in the Santa Rita Hills. You can taste the current releases—the Pinot Noirs and Chardonnays are exceptional—at one of the most environmentally sensitive tasting rooms and picnic areas in the valley. ⊠ *7250 Santa Rosa Rd., off U.S. 101, Buellton* ☎ *805/688–9090* ⊕ *www.almarosawinery. com.*

Mission Santa Inés. The mission holds an impressive collection of paintings, statuary, vestments, and Chumash and Spanish artifacts in a serene bluff-top setting. Take a self-guided tour through the museum, sanctuary, and tranquil gardens. ⊠ *1760 Mission Dr., at Alisal Rd.* ☎ *805/688–4815* ⊕ *www.missionsantaines.org* 🎟 *$5* ⊙ *Daily 9–4:30.*

Rideau Vineyard. Housed in an 1884 adobe, Rideau's tasting room provides simultaneous blasts from the area's ranching past and from its hand-harvested, Rhône-varietal wine-making present. ⊠ *1562 Alamo Pintado Rd., 2 miles north of Hwy. 246* ☎ *805/688–0717* ⊕ *www. rideauvineyard.com.*

WHERE TO EAT

$$ ✕ **Bit O' Denmark.** Perhaps the most authentic Danish eatery in Solvang, SCANDINAVIAN this restaurant occupies an old-beam building that was a church until 1929. Two specialties of the house are the *Frikadeller* (meatballs with

pickled red cabbage, potatoes, and thick brown gravy) and the *Medisterpølse* (Danish beef and pork sausage with cabbage). [$] *Average main: $18* ✉ *473 Alisal Rd., at Park Way* ☎ *805/688–5426* 🌐 *www.bitodenmark.com.*

$$$ AMERICAN 🍴 **The Hitching Post II.** You'll find everything from grilled artichokes to ostrich at this casual eatery just outside Solvang, but most people come for the wonderful smoky Santa Maria–style barbecue. Be sure to try a glass of owner-chef-winemaker Frank Ostini's signature Highliner Pinot Noir, a star in the film *Sideways.* [$] *Average main: $28* ✉ *406 E. Hwy. 246, off U.S. 101* ☎ *805/688–0676* 🌐 *www.hitchingpost2.com* ⏲ *No lunch.*

$$$ AMERICAN ★ 🍴 **Root 246.** The chefs at this chic restaurant tap local purveyors and shop for organic ingredients at farmers' markets before deciding on the day's menu. Depending on the season, you might feast on local squid with sweet baby prawns, rib-eye steak grilled over an oak fire and served with root vegetable gratin, or rhubarb and polenta upside-down cake. The well-informed wait staff can recommend regional wines from the restaurant's 1,800-bottle selection. Root 246's gorgeous design incorporates wood, stone, tempered glass, and leather elements in several distinct areas, including a slick 47-seat dining room, a more casual bar with sofas and chairs, and a hip lounge. [$] *Average main: $26* ✉ *Hotel Corque, 420 Alisal Rd., at Molle Way* ☎ *805/686–8681* 🌐 *www.root-246.com* ⏲ *Closed Mon. No lunch.*

WHERE TO STAY

For expanded reviews, facilities, and current deals, visit Fodors.com.

$$$$ RESORT ★ 🏨 **Alisal Guest Ranch and Resort.** Since 1946 this 10,000-acre ranch has been popular with celebrities and plain folk alike. **Pros:** Old West atmosphere; tons of activities; ultraprivate. **Cons:** isolated; cut off from the high-tech world; some units are aging. **TripAdvisor:** "the pacing is seductive," "come to have fun," "wonderful horseback riding." [$] *Rooms from: $515* ✉ *1054 Alisal Rd.* ☎ *805/688–6411, 800/425–4725* 🌐 *www.alisal.com* 🛏 *36 rooms, 37 suites* 🍽 *Some meals.*

$$$ HOTEL ★ 🏨 **Hotel Corque.** Sleek, stunning Hotel Corque—the Santa Ynez Valley's largest hotel—provides a full slate of upscale amenities on the edge of town. **Pros:** front desk staff are trained concierges; short walk to shops, tasting rooms and restaurants; smoke-free property. **Cons:** no kitchenettes or laundry facilities; pricey. **TripAdvisor:** "outstanding service and accommodations," "kind and comfy," "beautifully remodeled." [$] *Rooms from: $239* ✉ *400 Alisal Rd.* ☎ *805/688–8000, 800/624–5572* 🌐 *www.hotelcorque.com* 🛏 *122 rooms, 10 suites.*

$ HOTEL 🏨 **King Frederik Inn.** If you want to stay right in Solvang and not spend a fortune, this is a good bet. **Pros:** great value; near main square; spacious rooms; good for families. **Cons:** on main highway; miniature lobby; next to major parking lot. [$] *Rooms from: $109* ✉ *1617 Copenhagen Dr.* ☎ *805/688–5515, 800/549–9955* 🌐 *www.kingfrederikinn.com* 🛏 *45 rooms, 1 suite* 🍽 *Breakfast.*

$$ B&B/INN 🏨 **Petersen Village Inn.** The canopy beds here are plush, the bathrooms small but sparkling, and the rates include a European buffet breakfast. **Pros:** in the heart of Solvang; easy parking; comfy beds. **Cons:**

on highway; some find atmosphere too traditional. **TripAdvisor:** "old-world charm," "delightfully retro," "superb meal and excellent service." [$] *Rooms from: $120* ✉ *1576 Mission Dr.* ☎ *805/688–3121, 800/321–8985* 🌐 *www.petersoninn.com* 🛏 *39 rooms, 1 suite* 🍴 *Breakfast.*

$ B&B/INN 🏨 **Solvang Gardens Lodge.** The lush gardens with fountains and waterfalls and the cheery English-country-theme rooms make for a peaceful retreat just a few blocks—but worlds away—from Solvang's main tourist area. **Pros:** homey; family-friendly; colorful gardens. **Cons:** some rooms are tiny; some need upgrades. **TripAdvisor:** "great location," "quiet," "kitschy and quaint." [$] *Rooms from: $119* ✉ *293 Alisal Rd.* ☎ *805/688–4404, 888/688–4404* 🌐 *www.solvanggardens.com* 🛏 *16 rooms, 8 suites* 🍴 *Breakfast.*

LOMPOC

20 miles west of Solvang on Hwy. 246.

Known as the flower-seed capital of the world, Lompoc is blanketed with vast fields of brightly colored flowers that bloom from May through August.

GETTING HERE AND AROUND

Driving is the easiest way to get to Lompoc. From Santa Barbara, follow U.S. 101 north to Highway 1 exit off Gaviota Pass, or Highway 246 west at Buellton.

EXPLORING

👶 **La Purisima Mission State Historic Park.** The most fully restored mission in the state, Mission La Purisima Concepción, founded in 1787, stands in a stark and still remote location that powerfully evokes the lives and isolation of California's Spanish settlers. Docents lead tours every afternoon, and displays illustrate the secular and religious activities that were part of mission life. From March through October the mission holds special events, including crafts demonstrations by costumed docents. ✉ *2295 Purisima Rd., off Hwy. 246* ☎ *805/733–3713* 🌐 *www.lapurisimamission.org* 🎟 *$6 per vehicle* ⏲ *Daily 9–5; tour daily at 1.*

Lompoc Valley Flower Festival. Around the last weekend of June, Lompoc celebrates its floral heritage with a parade, a carnival, and a crafts show. ☎ *805/735–8511* 🌐 *www.flowerfestival.org.*

EN ROUTE

Guadalupe-Nipomo Dunes Preserve. This spectacular preserve straddles the coast for 18 miles between Santa Barbara and San Luis Obispo counties. The largest and most ecologically diverse dune system in the state, this habitat shelters more than 200 species of birds as well as sea otters, black bears, bobcats, coyotes, and deer. The 1,500-foot Mussel Rock is the highest beach dune in the western states. About two dozen movies have been filmed here, including Cecil B. DeMille's 1923 silent feature *The Ten Commandments*. At the **Dunes Center** (check ahead for hours), in downtown Guadalupe, you can get nature information and view an exhibit about DeMille's movie set. The main Santa Barbara County entrance to the preserve is at the far west end of Highway 166 (Main Street) in Guadalupe. ✉ *Hwy. 166/Main St., 5 miles west of Hwy. 1 and 15 miles west from Santa Maria, off U.S. 101, Guadalupe*

☎ *805/343–2455* ⊕ *www.dunescenter.org* ✉ *Free, donation suggested; dogs not permitted on this section of dunes.*

SAN LUIS OBISPO COUNTY

San Luis Obispo County's pristine landscapes and abundant wildlife areas, especially those around Morro Bay and Montaña de Oro State Park, have long attracted nature lovers. In the south, Pismo Beach and other coastal towns have great sand and surf; inland, a booming wine region stretches from the Edna and Arroyo Grande valleys in the south to Paso Robles in the north. With historical attractions, a photogenic downtown, and busy shops and restaurants, the college town of San Luis Obispo is at the heart of the county.

GETTING HERE AND AROUND

San Luis Obispo Regional Transit Authority operates buses in San Luis Obispo and serves Paso Robles as well as Pismo Beach and other coastal towns.

ESSENTIALS

Transportation Contacts San Luis Obispo Regional Transit Authority ☎ *805/541–2228* ⊕ *www.slorta.org.*

Visitor Information San Luis Obispo County Visitors and Conference Bureau ✉ *811 El Capitan Way, Suite 200, San Luis Obispo* ☎ *805/541–8000* ⊕ *www.sanluisobispocounty.com.*

PISMO BEACH

U.S. 101/Hwy. 1, about 40 miles north of Lompoc.

About 20 miles of sandy shoreline—nicknamed the Bakersfield Riviera for the throngs of vacationers who come here from the Central Valley—begins at the town of Pismo Beach. The southern end of town runs along sand dunes, some of which are open to cars and off-road vehicles. Sheltered by the dunes, a grove of eucalyptus trees attracts thousands of migrating monarch butterflies from November through February. A long, broad beach fronts the center of town, where a municipal pier extends into the sea at the foot of shop-lined Pomeroy Street. To the north, hotels and homes perch atop chalky oceanfront cliffs.

Fewer than 10,000 people live in this quintessential surfer haven, but Pismo Beach has a slew of hotels and restaurants with great views of the Pacific Ocean. Still, rooms can sometimes be hard to come by. Each Father's Day weekend the Pismo Beach Classic, one of the West Coast's largest classic-car and street-rod shows, overruns the town. A Dixieland jazz festival in February also draws crowds.

GETTING HERE AND AROUND

Pismo Beach straddles both sides of U.S. 101. If you're traveling from Santa Barbara and have time for a scenic drive, exit U.S. 101 in Santa Maria and take Highway 166 west for 8 miles to Guadalupe and follow Highway 1 north 16 miles to Pismo Beach. South County Area Transit (SCAT; ⊕ *www.slorta.org*) buses run throughout the city and connects

San Luis Obispo County and Big Sur
Pacific Grove
Salinas
Monterey
Carmel
Carmel Highlands
Gonzales
SALINAS VALLEY
Soledad
SANTA LUCIA RANGE
Point Sur State Historic Park
Big Sur
Pfeiffer Beach
Pfeiffer Big Sur State Park
Central Big Sur
Julia Pfeiffer Burns State Park
Southern Big Sur
Jade Cove
Lopez Point
Lucia
Greenfield
King City
San Lucas
COAST RANGES
Jolon
Lake San Antonio
Gorda
Pacific Coast Hwy.
Hearst San Simeon State Historical Monument
Ragged Point
Piedras Blancas Lighthouse
Point Piedras Blancas
San Simeon
Cambria
Harmony
Lake Nacimiento
San Miguel
Paso Robles
Shandon
Templeton
Atascadero
Cayucos
Morro Bay
Estero Bay
Los Osos
Santa Margarita
California Valley
San Luis Obispo
Montaña de Oro State Park
Avila Beach
Pismo Beach
Arroyo Grande
TO SANTA BARBARA
PACIFIC OCEAN
0 15 mi
0 15 km
101
1
G16
G18
198
46
41
58
227
5

with nearby towns and the city of San Luis Obispo. On summer weekends, the free Avila Trolley extends service to Pismo Beach.

WHERE TO EAT

$$$ SEAFOOD 🍴 **Cracked Crab.** This traditional New England–style crab shack imports fresh seafood daily from Australia, Alaska, and the East Coast. Fish is line-caught, much of the produce is organic, and everything is made from scratch. For a real treat, don a bib and chow through a bucket of steamed shellfish with Cajun sausage, potatoes, and corn on the cob, all dumped right onto your table. [$] *Average main: $23* ✉ *751 Price St., near Main St.* ☎ *805/773–2722* 🌐 *www.crackedcrab.com* ✍ *Reservations not accepted.*

$$ ITALIAN 🍴 **Giuseppe's Cucina Italiana.** The classic flavors of southern Italy are highlighted at this lively downtown spot. Most recipes originate from Bari, a seaport on the Adriatic; the menu includes breads and pizzas baked in the wood-burning oven, hearty dishes such as osso buco and lamb, and homemade pastas. The wait for a table can be long at peak dinner hours, but sometimes an accordion player gets the crowd singing. [$] *Average main: $22* ✉ *891 Price St., at Pismo Ave.* ☎ *805/773–2870* 🌐 *www.giuseppesrestaurant.com* ✍ *Reservations not accepted* 🕓 *No lunch weekends.*

$ SEAFOOD 🍴 **Splash Café.** Folks stand in line down the block for clam chowder served in a sourdough bread bowl at this wildly popular seafood stand. You can also order beach food such as fresh steamed clams, burgers, and fried calamari at the counter (no table service). Many items on the menu cost $8 or less. The grimy, cramped, but cheery hole-in-a-wall is open daily for lunch and dinner (plus a rock-bottom basic breakfast), but closes early on weekday evenings during low season. [$] *Average main: $8* ✉ *197 Pomeroy St., at Cypress St.* ☎ *805/773–4653* 🌐 *www.splashcafe.com.*

VOLCANOES?

Those funny looking, sawed-off peaks along the drive from Pismo Beach to Morro Bay are the Seven Sisters—a series of ancient volcanic plugs. Morro Rock, the northernmost sibling and a state historic monument, is the most famous and photographed of the clan.

WHERE TO STAY

For expanded reviews, facilities, and current deals, visit Fodors.com.

$$$$ RESORT 🏨 **Dolphin Bay.** Perched on grass-covered bluffs overlooking Shell Beach, this luxury resort looks and feels like an exclusive community of villas. **Pros:** lavish apartment units; killer views; walking distance from the beach. **Cons:** hefty price tag; vibe too upper-crust for some. **TripAdvisor:** "wonderful room," "everything was perfect," "great place to relax." [$] *Rooms from: $390* ✉ *2727 Shell Beach Rd.* ☎ *805/773–4300, 800/516–0112 reservations, 805/773–8900 restaurant* 🌐 *www.thedolphinbay.com* 🛏 *62 suites.*

$$$ HOTEL 🏨 **Pismo Lighthouse Suites.** Each of the well-appointed two-room, two-bath suites at this oceanfront resort has a private balcony or patio. **Pros:** lots of space for families and groups; nice pool area. **Cons:** not easy to walk to main attractions; some units are next to busy road. **TripAdvisor:** "home away from home," "could have stayed much longer," "nice property." [$] *Rooms from: $239* ✉ *2411 Price St.* ☎ *805/773–2411, 800/245–2411* 🌐 *www.pismolighthousesuites.com* 🛏 *70 suites* 🍽 *Breakfast.*

$$$ HOTEL 🏨 **Sea Venture Resort.** The bright, homey rooms at this hotel all have fireplaces and featherbeds; most have balconies with private hot tubs, and some have beautiful ocean views. **Pros:** on the beach; excellent food; romantic rooms. **Cons:** touristy area; some rooms and facilities are beginning to age; dark hallways. **TripAdvisor:** "romantic getaway," "can't ask for more," "nice location." [$] *Rooms from: $179* ✉ *100 Ocean View Ave.* ☎ *805/773–4994, 800/662-5545* 🌐 *www.seaventure.com* 🛏 *50 rooms.*

$ HOTEL 🏨 **Shell Beach Inn.** Just 2½ blocks from the beach, this basic but cozy motor court is a great bargain for the area. **Pros:** walking distance from the beach; clean rooms; friendly and dependable service. **Cons:** sits on a busy road; small rooms; tiny pool. **TripAdvisor:** "loved the owners and the rooms," "a hidden gem in a wonderful setting," "great service." [$] *Rooms from: $100* ✉ *653 Shell Beach Rd.* ☎ *805/773–4373, 800/549–4727* 🌐 *www.shellbeachinn.com* 🛏 *10 rooms.*

AVILA BEACH

⏱ *4 miles north of Pismo Beach on U.S. 101/Hwy. 1.*

Because the village of Avila Beach and the sandy, cove-front shoreline for which it's named face south into the Pacific Ocean, they get more sun and less fog than any other stretch of coast in the area. It can be bright and warm here while the surrounding hillside communities shiver under the marine layer. With its fortuitous climate and protected waters, Avila's public beach draws plenty of sunbathers and families; weekends are very busy. Downtown Avila Beach has a lively seaside promenade and some shops and hotels, but for real local color, head to the far end of the cove and watch the commercial fishers offload their catch on the old Port San Luis wharf. A few seafood shacks and fish markets do business on the pier while sea lions congregate below. On Friday from mid-April through mid-September, a fish and farmers' market livens up the beach area with music, fresh local produce and seafood, and children's activities.

GETTING HERE AND AROUND

Exit U.S. 101 at Avila Beach Drive and head 3 miles west to reach the beach. The free Avila Trolley operates weekends year-round, plus Friday afternoon/evenings from April to September. The minibuses connect Avila Beach and Port San Luis to Shell Beach, with multiple stops along the way. Service extends to Pismo Beach in summer.

WHERE TO STAY

For expanded reviews, facilities, and current deals, visit Fodors.com.

$$$$
HOTEL
🏨 **Avila La Fonda.** Modeled after a village in early California's Mexican period, Avila La Fonda surrounds guests with rich jewel tones, fountains, and upscale comfort. **Pros:** one-of-a-kind theme and artwork; flexible room combinations; a block from the beach. **Cons:** pricey; most rooms don't have an ocean view. **TripAdvisor:** "a special getaway," "a hidden gem," "great staff." $ *Rooms from: $300* ✉ *101 San Miguel St.* ☎ *805/595–1700* ⊕ *www.avilalafondahotel.com* ⇲ *28 rooms, 1 suite.*

$$
RESORT
🏨 **Sycamore Mineral Springs Resort.** This wellness resort's hot mineral springs bubble up into private outdoor tubs on an oak-and-sycamore-forest hillside. **Pros:** great place to rejuvenate; nice hiking; incredible spa services. **Cons:** rooms vary in quality; 2½ miles from the beach. **TripAdvisor:** "great place for a relaxing time," "quaint," "a little piece of heaven." $ *Rooms from: $169* ✉ *1215 Avila Beach Dr., San Luis Obispo* ☎ *805/595–7302, 800/234–5831* ⊕ *www.sycamoresprings.com* ⇲ *26 rooms, 50 suites.*

SAN LUIS OBISPO

8 miles north of Avila Beach on U.S. 101/Hwy. 1.

About halfway between San Francisco and Los Angeles, San Luis Obispo—nicknamed SLO—spreads out below gentle hills and rocky extinct volcanoes. Its main appeal lies in its architecturally diverse and commercially lively downtown, especially several blocks of Higuera Street. The pedestrian-friendly district bustles with shoppers, restaurant goers, and students from California Polytechnic State University, known

as Cal Poly. On Thursday from 6 pm to 9 pm a farmers' market fills Higuera Street with local produce, entertainment, and food stalls. SLO is less a vacation destination than a pleasant stopover along Highway 1; it's a nice place to stay while touring the Wine Country south of town.

GETTING HERE AND AROUND

U.S. 101/Highway 1 traverses the city for several miles. From the north, Highway 1 jogs inland from the coast and merges with the interstate when it reaches the city of San Luis Obispo. SLO City Transit buses operate daily; Regional Transit Authority (SLORTA) buses connect with towns throughout the north county. The Downtown Trolley lumbers through the city's hub on Thursday, Friday, and Saturday.

ESSENTIALS

Visitor Information San Luis Obispo Chamber of Commerce ⊠ *1039 Chorro St.* ☎ *805/781-2777* ⊕ *www.visitslo.com.* **San Luis Obispo City Visitor Information** ☎ ⊕ *www.sanluisobispovacations.com.* **San Luis Obispo Vintners Association** ☎ *805/541-5868* ⊕ *www.slowine.com.*

EXPLORING
TOP ATTRACTIONS

Edna Valley/Arroyo Grande Valley wine country. San Luis Obispo is the commercial center of a wine region whose appellations stretch west toward the coast and east toward the inland mountains. Many of the nearly 30 wineries here line Highway 227 and connecting roads. The region is known for Chardonnay and Pinot Noir, although many wineries experiment with other varietals and blends. Wine-touring maps are available around town. Many wineries charge a small tasting fee; most tasting rooms close at 5.

☙ **History Center of San Luis Obispo County.** Across the street from the old Spanish mission, the center presents exhibits that survey topics such as Native American life in the county, the California ranchos, and the impact of railroads. A separate children's room has theme activities for kids. On the center's website are links to free downloadable video-podcast walking tours of historic San Luis Obispo. ⊠ *696 Monterey St., at Broad St.* ☎ *805/543-0638* ⊕ *historycenterslo.org* 🎫 *Free* ☉ *Daily 10-4.*

★ **Mission San Luis Obispo de Tolosa.** Special events often take place on sun-dappled Mission Plaza in front of Mission San Luis Obispo de Tolosa, established in 1772. Its small museum exhibits artifacts of the Chumash Indians and early Spanish settlers, and docents sometimes lead tours of the church and grounds. ⊠ *751 Palm St., at Chorro St.* ☎ *805/543-6850* ⊕ *www.missionsanluisobispo.org* 🎫 *$3 suggested donation* ☉ *Apr.-late-Oct., daily 9-5; late Oct.-Mar., daily 9-4.*

San Luis Obispo Museum of Art. San Luis Obispo Museum of Art displays a mix of traditional work and cutting-edge arts and crafts by Central Coast, national, and international artists. The permanent collection focuses on the artistic legacy of the Central Coast. ⊠ *Mission Plaza, 1010 Broad St., at Monterey St.* ☎ *805/543-8562* ⊕ *www.sloma.org* ☉ *Daily 11-5* ☉ *Closed Tues. early Sept.-late June.*

WORTH NOTING

DEEP ROOTS

Way back in the 1700s, the Spanish padres who accompanied Father Junípero Serra planted grapevines from Mexico along California's Central Coast, and began using European wine-making techniques to turn the grapes into delectable vintages.

Baileyana Winery. A refurbished 1909 schoolhouse serves as tasting room for Baileyana, which produces chardonnays, pinot noirs, and syrahs. Four sister wineries share the tasting facility. ✉ *5828 Orcutt Rd., at Righetti Rd.* ☎ *805/269–8200* 🌐 *www.baileyana.com.*

Claiborne & Churchill. An eco-friendly winery built from straw bales, Claiborne & Churchill makes small lots of exceptional Alsatian-style wines such as dry Riesling and gewürztraminer, plus pinot noir and chardonnay. ✉ *2649 Carpenter Canyon Rd., at Price Canyon Rd.* ☎ *805/544–4066* 🌐 *www.claibornechurchill.com.*

Edna Valley Vineyard. For sweeping views of the Edna Valley while you sample estate-grown chardonnay, go to the modern tasting bar at Edna Valley Vineyard. ✉ *2585 Biddle Ranch Rd., off Edna Rd.* ☎ *805/544–5855* 🌐 *www.ednavalleyvineyard.com.*

Old Edna. While touring Edna Valley wine country, be sure to stop at Old Edna, a peaceful, 2-acre site that once was the town of Edna. Browse local art, peek at the vintage 1908 farmhouse (now a B&B), taste wines, pick up sandwiches at the gourmet deli, and stroll along Old Edna Lane. ✉ *1655 Old Price Canyon Rd., at Hwy. 227* ☎ *805/544–8062, 805/543–0900 deli* 🌐 *www.oldedna.com.*

👶 **San Luis Obispo Children's Museum.** Indoor and outdoor activities at this delightful museum present a kid-friendly version of the city of San Luis Obispo. An "imagination-powered" elevator transports visitors to a series of underground caverns, and simulated lava and steam sputters from an active volcano. Kids can pick rubber fruit at a farmers' market, race in a fire engine to fight a fire, and learn about solar energy from a 15-foot sunflower. The facility is geared to kids under eight; older children may lose interest quickly. ✉ *1010 Nipomo St., at Monterey St.* ☎ *805/545–5874* 🌐 *www.slocm.org* 🎟 *$8* 🕒 *Apr.–Sept., Tues.–Fri. 10–4, Sat. 10–5, Sun. and some Mon. holidays 11–5; Oct.–Mar., Tues. and Wed. 10–3, Thurs.–Sat. 10–5, Sun. and some Mon. holidays 1–5.*

WHERE TO EAT

$$ ECLECTIC ★ 🍴 **Big Sky Café.** A quintessentially Californian, family-friendly (and sometimes noisy) café, Big Sky turns local and organically grown ingredients into global dishes, starting with breakfast. Brazilian churasco chicken breast, Thai catfish, New Mexican *pozole* (hominy stew): just pick your continent. Vegetarians have lots to choose from. [$] *Average main: $17* ✉ *1121 Broad St., at Higuera St.* ☎ *805/545–5401* 🌐 *www.bigskycafe.com* ✍ *Reservations not accepted.*

$$ ITALIAN 🍴 **Buona Tavola.** Homemade pasta with river shrimp in a creamy tomato sauce and porcini-mushroom risotto are among the northern Italian dishes served at this casual spot. Daily fresh fish and salad specials and an impressive wine list attract a steady stream of regulars. In good weather you can dine on the flower-filled patio. The Paso Robles branch

is equally enjoyable. [$] *Average main: $20* ✉ *1037 Monterey St., near Osos St.* ☎ *805/545–8000* 🌐 *www.btslo.com* ⏲ *No lunch weekends.*

$ SOUTHERN 🍴 **Mo's Smokehouse BBQ.** Barbecue joints abound on the Central Coast, but this one excels. Various Southern-style sauces season tender hickory-smoked ribs and shredded-meat sandwiches; sides such as baked beans, coleslaw, homemade potato chips, and garlic bread extend the pleasure. [$] *Average main: $9* ✉ *1005 Monterey St., at Osos St.* ☎ *805/544–6193* 🌐 *www.smokinmosbbq.com.*

$$ ECLECTIC 🍴 **Novo Restaurant & Lounge.** In the colorful dining room or on the large creek-side deck, this animated downtown eatery will take you on a culinary world tour: The salads, small plates, and entrées come from nearly every continent. The wine and beer list also covers the globe and includes local favorites. Many of the decadent desserts are baked at the restaurant's sister property in Cambria, the French Corner Bakery. [$] *Average main: $18* ✉ *726 Higuera St., at Broad St.* ☎ *805/543–3986* 🌐 *www.novorestaurant.com.*

WHERE TO STAY

For expanded reviews, facilities, and current deals, visit Fodors.com.

$$$ HOTEL 🏨 **Apple Farm.** Decorated to the hilt with floral bedspreads and watercolors by local artists, this Victorian country-style hotel is one of the most popular places to stay in San Luis Obispo. **Pros:** flowers everywhere; convenient to Cal Poly and U.S. 101; creek-side setting. **Cons:** hordes of tourists during the day; too floral for some people's tastes. **TripAdvisor:** "a wonderful picture of Americana," "lots of little extras," "charming and restful." [$] *Rooms from: $209* ✉ *2015 Monterey St.* ☎ *800/255–2040, 805/544-2040* 🌐 *www.applefarm.com* 🛏 *104 rooms.*

$$$ B&B/INN 🏨 **Garden Street Inn.** From this fully restored 1887 Italianate Queen Anne, the only lodging in downtown SLO, you can walk to many restaurants and attractions. **Pros:** classic B&B; walking distance from everywhere downtown; nice wine-and-cheese reception. **Cons:** city noise filters through some rooms; not great for families. **TripAdvisor:** "nice location," "close to everything," "incredible charm." [$] *Rooms from: $189* ✉ *1212 Garden St.* ☎ *805/545–9802, 800/488–2045* 🌐 *www.gardenstreetinn.com* 🛏 *9 rooms, 4 suites* 🍽 *Breakfast.*

$$$ HOTEL 🏨 **Madonna Inn.** From its rococo bathrooms to its pink-on-pink frou-frou steak house, the Madonna Inn is fabulous or tacky, depending on your taste. **Pros:** fun, one-of-a-kind experience. **Cons:** rooms vary widely; must appreciate kitsch. **TripAdvisor:** "very fun," "great place for a unique experience," "for something different." [$] *Rooms from: $179* ✉ *100 Madonna Rd.* ☎ *805/543–3000, 800/543–9666* 🌐 *www.madonnainn.com* 🛏 *106 rooms, 4 suites.*

$ HOTEL 🏨 **Peach Tree Inn.** Extra touches such as rose gardens, a porch with rockers, and flower-filled vases turn this modest, family-run motel into a relaxing creek-side haven. **Pros:** bargain rates; cozy rooms; decent breakfast. **Cons:** near a busy intersection and freeway; basic amenities. **TripAdvisor:** "nice personal touch," "very clean rooms," "wonderful staff." [$] *Rooms from: $89* ✉ *2001 Monterey St.* ☎ *805/543–3170, 800/227–6396* 🌐 *www.peachtreeinn.com* 🛏 *37 rooms* 🍽 *Breakfast.*

$$ B&B/INN 🏨 **Petit Soleil.** A cobblestone courtyard, country-French custom furnishings, and Gallic music piped through the halls evoke a Provençal mood

at this cheery inn on upper Monterey Street's motel row. **Pros:** French details throughout; scrumptious breakfasts; cozy rooms. **Cons:** sits on a busy avenue; cramped parking. **TripAdvisor:** "quaint and comfortable," "peaceful and relaxing," "what an unexpected delight." ⓢ *Rooms from: $159* ✉ *1473 Monterey St.* ☎ *805/549–0321, 800/676–1588* ⊕ *www.psslo.com* ↻ *15 rooms, 1 suite* ⦿ *Breakfast.*

NIGHTLIFE AND THE ARTS

NIGHTLIFE

The club scene in this college town is centered on Higuera Street off Monterey Street.

Frog and Peach. This is a decent spot to nurse an English beer and listen to live music. ✉ *728 Higuera St., at Broad St.* ☎ *805/595–3764.*

Koberl at Blue. A trendy crowd hangs out at the slick bar at Koberl at Blue, an upscale restaurant with late-night dining, exotic martinis, and a huge list of local and imported beer and wine. ✉ *998 Monterey St., at Osos St.* ☎ *805/783–1135.*

Linnaea's Cafe. A mellow java joint, Linnaea's sometimes hosts poetry readings, as well as blues, jazz, and folk music performances. ✉ *1110 Garden St., at Higuera St.* ☎ *805/541–5888.*

MoTav. Chicago-style MoTav draws crowds with good pub food and live entertainment in a turn-of-the-20th-century setting (complete with antique U.S. flags and a wall-mounted moose head). ✉ *725 Higuera St., at Broad St.* ☎ *805/541–8733.*

THE ARTS

Festival Mozaic. Held each year in mid-July, the festival celebrates five centuries of classical music. ☎ *805/781–3008* ⊕ *www.festivalmozaic. com.*

Performing Arts Center, San Luis Obispo. The center hosts live theater, dance, and music performances by artists from around the world. ✉ *Cal Poly, 1 Grand Ave., off U.S. 101* ☎ *805/756–7222, 805/756–2787 box office, 888/233–2787 toll-free* ⊕ *www.pacslo.org.*

SPORTS AND THE OUTDOORS

Parks and Recreation Department. Hilly greenbelts with extensive hiking trails surround San Luis Obispo. For information about trailheads, call the parks department or download a trail map on its website. ☎ *805/781–7300* ⊕ *www.slocity.org/parksandrecreation.*

EN ROUTE

Montaña de Oro State Park. Instead of continuing north on U.S. 101/Highway 1 from San Luis Obispo to Morro Bay, consider detouring west along Los Osos Valley Raod past farms and ranches to Montaña de Oro State Park, where miles of nature trails traverse rocky shoreline, wild beaches, and hills that overlook dramatic scenery. Check out the tide pools, watch the waves roll into the bluffs, and picnic in the eucalyptus groves. From Montaña de Oro you can reach Morro Bay by following the coastline along South Bay Boulevard 8 miles through the quaint residential villages of Los Osos and Baywood Park. ✉ *West about 13 miles on Madonna Rd., to Los Osos Valley Rd., to Pecho Valley Rd.; to continue on to Morro Bay, backtrack east to Los Osos*

Valley Rd., then head north on S. Bay Blvd., and west on State Park Rd. ☎ *805/528–0513, 805/772–7434* ⊕ *www.parks.ca.gov.*

MORRO BAY

14 miles north of San Luis Obispo on Hwy. 1.

Commercial fishermen slog around Morro Bay in galoshes, and beat-up fishing boats bob in the bay's protected waters. Nature-oriented activities take center stage here: kayaking, hiking, biking, fishing, and wildlife watching around the bay and national marine estuary and along the state beach.

GETTING HERE AND AROUND

From U.S. 101 south or north, exit at Highway 1 in San Luis Obispo and head west. Scenic Highway 1 passes through the eastern edge of town. From Atascadero, two-lane Highway 41 West treks over the mountains to Morro Bay. San Luis Obispo RTA Route 12 buses travel year-round between Morro Bay, San Luis Obispo, Cayucos, Cambria, San Simeon, and Hearst Castle. The Morro Bay Shuttle picks up riders throughout the town from Friday through Monday in summer ($1.25).

ESSENTIALS

Visitor Information Morro Bay Visitors Center ✉ *845 Embarcadero Rd., near Harbor St.* ☎ *805/772–4467, 800/231–0592* ⊕ *www.morrobay.org* ☉ *Daily 9–5.*

EXPLORING

Embarcadero. The center of the action on land is the Embarcadero, where vacationers pour in and out of souvenir shops and seafood restaurants and stroll or bike along the scenic half-mile Harborwalk to Morro Rock. From here, you can get out on the bay in a kayak or tour boat. ✉ *On waterfront from Beach St. to Tidelands Park.*

Morro Bay State Park Museum of Natural History. The entertaining and educational interactive exhibits at this spiffy museum south of downtown Morro Bay explain the natural environment and how to preserve it—in the bay and estuary and on the rest of the planet. ✉ *State Park Rd.* ☎ *805/772–2694* ⊕ *www.ccnha.org/morrobay* 💲 *$3* ☉ *Daily 10–5.*

Morro Rock. At the mouth of Morro Bay, which is both a state and national estuary, stands 576-foot-high Morro Rock, one of nine such small volcanic peaks, or morros, in the area. A short walk leads to a breakwater, with the harbor on one side and the crashing waves of the Pacific on the other. You may not climb the rock, where endangered falcons and other birds nest. Sea lions and otters often play in the water at the foot of the peak. ✉ *Northern end of Embarcadero.*

WHERE TO EAT

$$
SEAFOOD

✗**Dorn's Original Breakers Cafe.** This seafood restaurant overlooking the harbor has satisfied Morro Bay appetites since 1948. In addition to straight-ahead fish dishes such as petrale sole or calamari steaks sautéed in butter and wine, Dorn's serves breakfast. 💲 *Average main: $18* ✉ *801 Market Ave., at Morro Bay Blvd.* ☎ *805/772–4415* ⊕ *www. dornscafe.com.*

$ SOUTHWESTERN ★ 🍴 **Taco Temple.** The devout stand in line at this family-run diner that serves some of the freshest food around. Seafood anchors a menu of dishes—salmon burritos, superb fish tacos with mango salsa—hailing from somewhere between California and Mexico. Desserts get rave reviews, too. Make an effort to find this gem. It's in a supermarket parking lot on the frontage road parallel to Highway 1, just north of the Highway 41 junction. [$] *Average main: $14* ✉ *2680 Main St., at Elena St.* ☎ *805/772–4965* ✍ *Reservations not accepted* 💳 *No credit cards* 🕒 *Closed Tues.*

$$$ SEAFOOD 🍴 **Windows on the Water.** Diners at this second-floor restaurant view the sunset through giant picture windows. Meanwhile, fresh fish and other dishes based on local ingredients emerge from the wood-fired oven in the open kitchen, and oysters on the half shell beckon from the raw bar. The extensive, California-centric wine list includes about 20 selections poured by the glass. [$] *Average main: $28* ✉ *699 Embarcadero, at Pacific St.* ☎ *805/772–0677* 🌐 *www.windowsmb.com* 🕒 *No lunch.*

WHERE TO STAY

For expanded reviews, facilities, and current deals, visit Fodors.com.

$$$ B&B/INN ★ 🏨 **Anderson Inn.** The innkeepers' friendly, personalized service and an oceanfront setting keep loyal patrons returning to this Embarcadero inn, built from scratch in 2008. **Pros:** walk to restaurants and sights; well-appointed rooms; attentive service. **Cons:** waterfront area gets crowded on weekends and in summer; not low-budget. **TripAdvisor:** "exceptional in every way," "first class," "a lovely retreat with warm hospitality." [$] *Rooms from: $239* ✉ *897 Embarcadero* ☎ *805/772–3434* 🌐 *www.andersoninnmorrobay.com* 🛏 *8 rooms.*

$$$ B&B/INN ★ 🏨 **Cass House.** In tiny Cayucos, an oceanfront enclave about 4 miles north of Morro Bay, the 1867 home of shipping pioneer Captain James Cass is now a luxurious B&B surrounded by rose and other gardens. **Pros:** historic property; some ocean views; excellent meals. **Cons:** not near Morro Bay nightlife or tourist attractions; not designed for families. **TripAdvisor:** "great rooms," "peaceful oasis of comfort," "amazing food." [$] *Rooms from: $200* ✉ *222 N. Ocean Ave., Cayucos* ☎ *805/995–3669* 🌐 *casshouseinn.com* 🛏 *5 rooms* 🍽 *Breakfast.*

$$ HOTEL 🏨 **Embarcadero Inn.** The rooms at this waterfront hotel are cheery and welcoming, and many have fireplaces. **Pros:** right across from the waterfront. **Cons:** tiny lobby; no pool. **TripAdvisor:** "huge first-rate rooms," "great view and great people," "all around awesome." [$] *Rooms from: $145* ✉ *456 Embarcadero* ☎ *805/772–2700, 800/292–7625* 🌐 *www.embarcaderoinn.com* 🛏 *29 rooms, 4 suites* 🍽 *Breakfast.*

SPORTS AND THE OUTDOORS

Kayak Horizons. This outfit rents kayaks and gives lessons and guided tours. ✉ *551 Embarcadero, near Marina St.* ☎ *805/772–6444* 🌐 *www.kayakhorizons.com.*

Lost Isle Adventures. Captain Alan Rackov cruises his Tiki-Boat into the bay and out to Morro Rock every hour starting at 11 am daily (less often in winter). ✉ *Giovanni's Fish Market, 1001 Front St., on the Embarcadero* ☎ *805/440–8170* 🌐 *lostisleadventures.com.*

Sub-Sea Tours. Sub-Sea operates glass-bottom boat and catamaran cruises, and has kayak and canoe rentals and summer whale-watching cruises. ✉ *699 Embarcadero, at Pacific St.* ☎ *805/772–9463* ⊕ *subseatours.com.*

Virg's Landing. Virg's conducts deep-sea fishing and whale-watching trips. ✉ *1215 Embarcadero* ☎ *805/772–1222* ⊕ *www.virgs.com.*

PASO ROBLES

30 miles north of San Luis Obispo on U.S. 101; 25 miles northwest of Morro Bay via Hwy. 41 and U.S. 101.

In the 1860s tourists began flocking to this dusty ranching outpost to "take the cure" in a luxurious bathhouse fed by underground mineral hot springs. An Old West town, complete with opera house, emerged, and grand Victorian homes went up, followed in the 20th century by Craftsman bungalows. A 2003 earthquake demolished or weakened several beloved downtown buildings, but historically faithful reconstruction has helped the district retain its character.

More than 200 wineries and more than 26,000 vineyard acres pepper the wooded hills of Paso Robles west of U.S. 101 and blanket the flatter, more open land on the east side. The region's brutally hot summer days and cool nights yield stellar grapes that make noteworthy wines, particularly robust reds such as Cabernet Sauvignon, Merlot, Zinfandel, and Rhône varietals such as Syrah. Exquisite whites also come out of Paso, including Chardonnay and Rhône varietals such as Viognier. Small-town friendliness prevails at most wineries, especially smaller ones, which tend to treat visitors like neighbors. Pick up a regional wine-touring map at lodgings, wineries, and attractions around town. Most tasting rooms close at 5 pm; many charge a small fee.

But more attracts people to the Paso Robles area than fine wine and fancy tasting rooms. Golfers play the four local courses and spandex-clad bicyclists race along the winding back roads. Down-home and upmarket restaurants, bars, antiques stores, and little shops fill the streets around oak-shaded City Park, where special events of all kinds—custom car shows, an olive festival, Friday-night summer concerts—take place on many weekends. Despite its increasing sophistication, Paso (as the locals call it) more or less remains cowboy country. Each year in late July and early August, the city throws the two-week California Mid-State Fair, complete with livestock auctions, carnival rides, and corn dogs.

GETTING HERE AND AROUND
U.S. 101 runs through the city of Paso Robles. Highway 46 West links Paso Robles to Highway 1 and Cambria on the coast. Highway 46 East connects Paso Robles with Interstate 5 and the San Joaquin Valley. Public transit is not convenient for wine touring and sightseeing.

ESSENTIALS
Visitor Information Paso Robles Wine Country Alliance ☎ *805/239–8463, 800/549–9463* ⊕ *www.pasowine.com.*

EXPLORING

TOP ATTRACTIONS

Eberle Winery. Even if you don't drink wine, stop at Eberle Winery for a fascinating tour of the huge wine caves beneath the east-side Paso Robles vineyard. Gary Eberle, one of Paso wine's founding fathers, is obsessed with Cabernet Sauvignon. ⊠ *3810 E. Hwy. 46, 3½ miles east of U.S. 101* ☎ *805/238–9607* ⊕ *www.eberlewinery.com.*

Firestone Walker Brewing Company. As they say around Paso Robles, it takes a lot of beer to make good wine, and to meet that need the locals turn to Firestone, where you can sample medal-winning craft beers such as Double Barrel Ale. ⊠ *1400 Ramada Dr., east side of U.S. 101; exit at Hwy. 46 W/Cambria exit, but head east* ☎ *805/238–2556* ⊕ *www. firestonebeer.com.*

Justin Vineyards & Winery. At the western end of Paso Robles wine country, swank Justin makes Bordeaux-style blends. This readers' favorite offers winery, vineyard, and barrel-tasting tours ($15 to $400). In the tasting room there's a deli bar; a high-end restaurant and B&B are also part of the complex. ⊠ *11680 Chimney Rock Rd., 15 miles west of U.S. 101's Hwy 46 E exit; take 24th St. west and follow road (name changes along the way) to Chimney Rock Rd.* ☎ *805/238–6932, 800/726–0049* ⊕ *www.justinwine.com.*

Paso Robles Wine Festival. Most local wineries pour at this mid-May outdoor festival that has live bands and diverse food vendors. Winery open houses and winemaker dinners round out the weekend. ⊠ *City Park, Spring St., between 10th and 12th Sts.* ☎ *805/239–8463, 800/549–9463* ⊕ *www.pasowine.com* ▧ *$55 basic admission, designated driver or child $15.*

★ **Pasolivo.** While touring the idyllic west side of Paso Robles, take a break from wine by stopping at Pasolivo. Find out how the artisans here make their Tuscan-style olive oils on a high-tech Italian press, and taste the acclaimed results. ⊠ *8530 Vineyard Dr., west off U.S. 101 (Exit 224) or Hwy. 46 W (Exit 228)* ☎ *805/227–0186* ⊕ *www.pasolivo.com.*

River Oaks Hot Springs & Spa. The lakeside spa, on 240 hilly acres near the intersection of U.S. 101 and Highway 46E, is a great place to relax after wine tasting or festival-going. Soak in a private indoor or outdoor hot tub fed by natural mineral springs, or indulge in a massage or facial. ⊠ *800 Clubhouse Dr., off River Oaks Dr.* ☎ *805/238–4600* ⊕ *www.riveroakshotsprings.com* ▧ *Hot tubs $13 to $24 per person per hr* ⊙ *Tues.–Sun. 9–9.*

Tablas Creek Vineyard. Tucked in the far-west hills of Paso Robles, Tablas Creek Vineyard makes some of the area's finest wine by blending organically grown, hand-harvested Rhône varietals such as Syrah, Grenache, Roussanne, and Viognier. Tours include a chance to graft your own grapevine; call to reserve space. ⊠ *9339 Adelaida Rd., west of Vineyard Dr.* ☎ *805/237–1231* ⊕ *www.tablascreek.com.*

WORTH NOTING

Harris Stage Lines. Former pro rodeo riders and horse trainers Tom and Debby Harris offer stagecoach rides (learn to hitch the team of horses beforehand), riding-and-driving lessons, and various Old

2

West-themed events at their ranch on the north side of town. ✉ *5995 North River Rd., east of U.S. 101, Exit 230* ☎ *805/237–1860* 🌐 *www.harrisstagelines.com.*

Paso Robles Pioneer Museum. The museum's one-room schoolhouse and its displays of ranching paraphernalia, horse-drawn vehicles, hot-springs artifacts, and photos evoke Paso's rural heritage. ✉ *2010 Riverside Ave., at 21st St.* ☎ *805/239–4556* 🌐 *www.pasoroblespioneermuseum.org* 🎟 *Free* 🕓 *Thurs.–Sun. 1–4.*

Paso Wine Centre. Four dozen local wines are available for tasting via enomatic dispensers at this spacious, contemporary space downtown that's furnished with comfy sofas and handhewn oak tables. More than 200 wines are available for purchase. ✉ *1240 Park St., at 13th St.* ☎ *805/239–9156* 🌐 *www.pasowinecentre.com.*

LAID-BACK WINE COUNTRY

Hundreds of vineyards and wineries dot the hillsides from Paso Robles to San Luis Obispo, through the scenic Edna Valley and south to northern Santa Barbara County. The wineries offer much of the variety of northern California's Napa and Sonoma valleys—without the glitz and crowds. Since the early 1980s the region has developed an international reputation for high-quality wines, most notably Pinot Noir, Chardonnay, and Zinfandel. Wineries here tend to be small, but most have tasting rooms (some have tours), and you'll often meet the winemakers themselves.

WHERE TO EAT

$$$ AMERICAN 🍴 **Artisan.** Innovative renditions of traditional American comfort foods, a well-chosen list of regional wines, a stylish full bar, and a sophisticated urban vibe lure winemakers, locals, and tourists to this small, family-run American bistro in an art-deco building near the town square. Chris Kobayashi (Chef Koby, a James Beard award nominee) uses local, organic, wild-caught ingredients to whip up regional favorites, which might include red abalone with fried green tomatoes and pancetta, scallops with laughing bird prawns, mussels, clams, Spanish chorizo, and saffron, or flatiron steak with shallots, fries, and cabernet butter. Ask for a booth facing the open kitchen, and save room for the restaurant's home-style desserts: brownies, peach crumbles, crème brûlée, and the like. [$] *Average main: $28* ✉ *1401 Park St., at 14th St.* ☎ *805/237–8084* 🌐 *www.artisanpasorobles.com.*

$$$ FRENCH ★ 🍴 **Bistro Laurent.** Owner-chef Laurent Grangien has created a handsome, welcoming French bistro in an 1890s brick building across from City Park. He focuses on traditional dishes such as osso buco, cassoulet, rack of lamb, goat-cheese tart, and onion soup, but always offers a few updated dishes as daily specials. Wines, sourced from the adjacent wine shop, come from around the world. [$] *Average main: $28* ✉ *1202 Pine St., at 12th St.* ☎ *805/226–8191* 🌐 *www.bistrolaurent.com* 🕓 *Closed Sun. and Mon.*

$$$ AMERICAN 🍴 **McPhee's Grill.** In an 1860s building in the tiny cow town of Templeton (just south of Paso Robles), this casual chophouse serves sophisticated, contemporary versions of traditional Western fare—such as oak-grilled filet mignon and cedar-planked salmon. House-label wines, made

especially for McPhee's, are quite good. $ Average main: $25 ⊠ 416 S. Main St., at 5th St., Templeton 📞 805/434–3204 ⊕ mcpheesgrill.com.

$ ✗ **Panolivo Family Bistro.** Scrumptious French bistro fare is the draw at
FRENCH   this cheery downtown café, just a block north of the town square. For breakfast, try a fresh pastry or quiche, or build your own omelet. Lunch and dinner choices include traditional French dishes like snails baked in garlic-butter sauce or cassoulet as well as sandwiches, salads, and fresh pastas—including the house-made beef cannelloni. $ Average main: $15 ⊠ 1344 Park St., at 14th St. 📞 805/239–3366 ⊕ www.panolivo.com.

$$ ✗ **Thomas Hill Organics.** In a casual bistro off a tiny alley, Joe and Debbie
AMERICAN Thomas serve delectable locavore cuisine made from regional ingredients; much of the produce comes from their nearby ten-acre organic farm. The menu changes weekly, depending on what's in-season and available, and includes a good selection of Central Coast wines (there's also a wine bar here). Ask for a table in the outdoor courtyard when the weather's fine. $ Average main: $16 ⊠ 1305 Park St., at 13th St., Templeton 📞 805/226–5888 ⊕ thomashillorganics.com ☽ Closed Tues.

$$$ ✗ **Villa Creek.** With a firm nod to the rancho and mission cuisine of
SOUTHWESTERN California's early Spanish settlers, chef Tom Fundero conjures distinctly modern magic with local and sustainable ingredients. The seasonal menu has included butternut-squash enchiladas and braised lamb shank with saffron risotto and classic beef bourguignonne with parsnip and cauliflower purée, but you might also find duck breast with sweet-potato latkes. Central Coast wines dominate the list, with a smattering of Spanish and French selections. All brick and bare wood, the dining room can get loud when winemakers start passing their bottles from table to table, but it's always festive. For lighter appetites or wallets, the bar serves smaller plates—not to mention a killer margarita. $ Average main: $26 ⊠ 1144 Pine St., at 12th St. 📞 805/238–3000 ⊕ www.villacreek.com ☽ No lunch.

WHERE TO STAY
For expanded reviews, facilities, and current deals, visit Fodors.com.

$ 🛏 **Adelaide Inn.** Family-owned and -managed, this clean, friendly oasis
HOTEL   with meticulous landscaping offers spacious rooms and everything you
Fodor's Choice need: coffeemaker, iron, hair dryer, and peace and quiet. **Pros:** great
★   bargain; attractive pool area; ideal for families. **Cons:** not a romantic retreat; near a busy intersection and freeway. **TripAdvisor:** "pride in ownership," "awesome hotel and location," "comfortable bed." $ Rooms from: $99 ⊠ 1215 Ysabel Ave. 📞 805/238–2770, 800/549–7276 ⊕ www.adelaideinn.com ⇆ 109 rooms ◎ Breakfast.

$$$$ 🛏 **Hotel Cheval.** Equestrian themes surface throughout this intimate,
HOTEL   sophisticated, European-style inn just a half-block from the main square and a short walk to some of Paso's best restaurants. **Pros:** walking distance to downtown restaurants; European-style facilities; personal service. **Cons:** views aren't great; no pool or hot tub. **TripAdvisor:** "a bit of Europe," "in a class by itself," "cozy and comfy." $ Rooms from: $315 ⊠ 1021 Pine St. 📞 805/226–9995, 866/522–6999 ⊕ www.hotelcheval.com ⇆ 16 rooms ◎ Breakfast.

$$$ ⊡ **La Bellasera Hotel & Suites.** The swankest full-service hotel for miles
HOTEL around, the La Bellasera, completed in 2008, caters to those looking
for luxurious high-tech amenities and close proximity to major Central Coast roadways. **Pros:** new property; tons of amenities. **Cons:** far
from town square; located at major intersection. **TripAdvisor:** "excellent amenities," "a lovely place to stay," "hidden gem." Ⓢ *Rooms from:
$229* ⊠ *206 Alexa Court* ☎ *805/238–2834, 866/782–9669* ⊕ *www.
labellasera.com* ⇄ *35 rooms, 25 suites.*

$$ ⊡ **Paso Robles Inn.** On the site of a luxurious old spa hotel by the same
HOTEL name, the inn is built around a lush, shady garden with a pool. **Pros:** private spring-fed hot tubs; historic property; across from park and town
square. **Cons:** fronts a busy street; rooms vary in size and quality. **TripAdvisor:** "hospitable taste of classic California," "perfect location,"
"just right." Ⓢ *Rooms from: $150* ⊠ *1103 Spring St.* ☎ *805/238–2660,
800/676–1713* ⊕ *www.pasoroblesinn.com* ⇄ *92 rooms, 6 suites.*

$$$$ ⊡ **Summerwood Inn.** Verdant gardens and vineyards envelop Summerwood Winery's elegant, friendly B&B in tranquility; four-poster and
B&B/INN sleigh beds, lace and floral fabrics, thick robes, and nightly turn-down
service bring comfort to the individually designed rooms. **Pros:** convenient wine touring base; super-friendly staff; delicious breakfast. **Cons:**
across from winery on a main highway; can be noisy during the day.
Ⓢ *Rooms from: $269* ⊠ *2130 Arbor Rd., 1 mile west of U.S. 101,
at Hwy. 46W* ☎ *805/227–1111* ⊕ *www.summerwoodwine.com* ⇄ *9
rooms* ⓘ⊙ *Breakfast.*

CAMBRIA

*28 miles west of Paso Robles on Hwy. 46; 20 miles north of Morro
Bay on Hwy. 1.*

Cambria, set on piney hills above the sea, was settled by Welsh miners
in the 1890s. In the 1970s, the gorgeous, isolated setting attracted artists
and other independent types; the town now caters to tourists, but it still
bears the unmistakable imprint of its bohemian past. Both of Cambria's
downtowns, the original East Village and the newer West Village, are
packed with art and crafts galleries, antiques shops, cafés, restaurants,
and B&Bs. Late-Victorian homes stand along side streets, and the hills
are filled with redwood-and-glass residences. If you're driving north
up Highway 1 from Morro Bay, make a quick stop 7 miles south of
Cambria at the cute former dairy town of Harmony, population 18, to
visit its glassworks, pottery, and other enterprises.

GETTING HERE AND AROUND
Highway 1 leads to Cambria from the north and south. From U.S. 101
at Paso Robles, Highway 246 West curves through the mountains to
Cambria and the coast. San Luis Obispo RTA Route 12 buses ferry
passengers between San Luis Obispo and Hearst Castle, stopping in
Cambria along the way.

ESSENTIALS
Visitor Information Cambria Chamber of Commerce ☎ *805/927–3624*
⊕ *www.cambriachamber.org.*

EXPLORING

Leffingwell's Landing. A state picnic ground, the landing a good place for examining tidal pools and watching otters as they frolic in the surf. ✉ *North end of Moonstone Beach Dr.* ☎ *805/927–2070.*

Moonstone Beach Drive. Lined with low-key motels, the drive runs along a bluff above the ocean. The 2-mile boardwalk that winds along the beach makes for a fine walk and a great photo op. You're apt to glimpse sea lions and even sea otters, and during winter and spring the occasional gray whale. Year-round birds aplenty fly about, and tiny creatures scurry amid the tide pools. ✉ *Off Hwy. 1.*

Nit Wit Ridge. Arthur Beal (aka Captain Nit Wit, Der Tinkerpaw) spent 51 years building Nit Wit Ridge, a home with terraced rock gardens. For building materials, he used all kinds of collected junk: beer cans, rocks, abalone shells, car parts, TV antennas—you name it. The site, above Cambria's West Village, is a State Historic Landmark. You can drive by and peek in—from the 700 block of Main Street, head southeast on Cornwall Street and east on Hillcrest Drive. Better yet, call ahead for a guided tour of the house and grounds. ✉ *881 Hillcrest Dr.* ☎ *805/927–2690* 🎟 *$10 suggested donation* ⏲ *Daily by appointment.*

WHERE TO EAT

$$$ AMERICAN 🍴 **Black Cat Bistro.** Jazz wafts through the several small rooms of this intimate East Village bistro where stylish cushions line the banquettes. Start with an order of the fried olives stuffed with Gorgonzola, accompanied by a glass from the eclectic list of local and imported wines. The daily-changing menu is centered on sustainable ingredients and might include roasted rack of elk rubbed in cocoa or breast of pheasant stuffed with caramelized apples. [$] *Average main: $24* ✉ *1602 Main St.* ☎ *805/927–1600* 🌐 *www.blackcatbistro.com* ✍ *Reservations essential* ⏲ *Closed Tues. and Wed. No lunch.*

$ CAFÉ 🍴 **French Corner Bakery.** Place your order at the counter and then sit outside to watch the passing East Village scene (if the fog has rolled in, take a seat in the tiny deli). The rich aroma of coffee and fresh breakfast pastries makes mouths water in the morning; for lunch, try a quiche with flaky crust or a sandwich on house-baked bread. [$] *Average main: $7* ✉ *2214 Main St.* ☎ *805/927–8227* ✍ *Reservations not accepted* ⏲ *No dinner.*

$$ ECLECTIC 🍴 **Robin's.** A truly multiethnic and vegetarian-friendly dining experience awaits you at this East Village cottage filled with country antiques. At dinner, choose from lobster enchiladas, pork osso buco, Thai green chicken curry, and more. Lunchtime's extensive salad and sandwich menu embraces burgers and tofu alike. Unless it's raining, ask for a table on the secluded (and heated) garden patio. [$] *Average main: $20* ✉ *4095 Burton Dr., at Center St.* ☎ *805/927–5007* 🌐 *www.robinsrestaurant.com.*

$$$ SEAFOOD 🍴 **The Sea Chest.** The best seafood place in town—readers give it a big thumbs-up—this Moonstone Beach restaurant fills soon after it opens at 5:30. Those in the know grab seats at the oyster bar and take in spectacular sunsets while watching the chefs broil fresh halibut and steam garlicky clams. If you can't get here early, play some cribbage

or checkers while you wait for a table. *$ Average main: $25 ✉ 6216 Moonstone Beach Dr., near Weymouth St./Hwy. 1 ☎ 805/927–4514 🌐 www.seachestrestaurant.com Reservations not accepted ▭ No credit cards ⏲ Closed Tues. mid-Sept.–May. No lunch.*

WHERE TO STAY

For expanded reviews, facilities, and current deals, visit Fodors.com.

$ HOTEL **Bluebird Inn.** This sweet motel in Cambria's East Village sits amid beautiful gardens along Santa Rosa Creek; rooms include simply furnished doubles and nicer creek-side suites with patios, fireplaces, and refrigerators. **Pros:** excellent value; well-kept gardens; friendly staff. **Cons:** few frills; basic rooms; on Cambria's main drag; not on beach. **TripAdvisor:** "homey and sweet," "blast from the past," "lovely ambience." *$ Rooms from: $78 ✉ 1880 Main St. ☎ 805/927–4634, 800/552–5434 🌐 bluebirdmotel.com 37 rooms.*

$$ RESORT **Cambria Pines Lodge.** With lots of recreational facilities and a range of accommodations—from basic state park–style cabins to motel-style standard rooms to large fireplace suites—this 25-acre retreat up the hill from the East Village is a good choice for families. **Pros:** short walk from downtown; verdant gardens; spacious grounds. **Cons:** service and housekeeping not always top-quality; some units need updating. **TripAdvisor:** "like living in a garden," "rustic but clean," "large room with great meal." *$ Rooms from: $169 ✉ 2905 Burton Dr. ☎ 805/927–4200, 800/966–6490 🌐 www.cambriapineslodge.com 72 rooms, 18 cabins, 62 suites 🍽 Breakfast.*

$$ B&B/INN **J. Patrick House.** Monterey pines and flower gardens surround this Irish-theme inn, which sits on a hilltop above Cambria's East Village. **Pros:** fantastic breakfasts; friendly innkeepers; quiet neighborhood. **Cons:** few rooms; fills up quickly. **TripAdvisor:** "getaway from the world," "tastefully done," "great price and wonderful service." *$ Rooms from: $165 ✉ 2990 Burton Dr. ☎ 805/927–3812, 800/341–5258 🌐 www.jpatrickhouse.com 8 rooms 🍽 Breakfast.*

$$ HOTEL ★ **Moonstone Landing.** Friendly staff, lots of amenities, and reasonable rates make this up-to-date motel a top pick with readers who like to stay right on Moonstone Beach. **Pros:** sleek furnishings; across from the beach; cheery lounge. **Cons:** narrow property; some rooms overlook a parking lot. **TripAdvisor:** "charm in a beautiful location," "spacious room," "relaxing coastal getaway." *$ Rooms from: $125 ✉ 6240 Moonstone Beach Dr. ☎ 805/927–0012, 800/830–4540 🌐 www.moonstonelanding.com 29 rooms 🍽 Breakfast.*

SAN SIMEON

Hwy. 1, 9 miles north of Cambria and 65 miles south of Big Sur.

Whalers founded San Simeon in the 1850s but had virtually abandoned the town by the time Senator George Hearst reestablished it 20 years later. Hearst bought up most of the surrounding ranch land, built a 1,000-foot wharf, and turned San Simeon into a bustling port. His son, William Randolph Hearst, further developed the area during the construction of Hearst Castle. Today the town, 4 miles south of the entrance to Hearst San Simeon State Historical Monument, is basically a strip of gift shops and mediocre motels along Highway 1.

GETTING HERE AND AROUND
Highway 1 is the only way to reach San Simeon. From northern California, follow Highway 1 from Big Sur south to San Simeon. From U.S. 101 north or south, exit at Highway 1 in San Luis Obispo and follow it northwest 42 miles to San Simeon. Alternative rural routes to reach Highway 1 from the 101 include Highway 41 West (Atascadero to Morro Bay) and Highway 46 West (Paso Robles to Cambria).

EXPLORING

★ **Hearst Castle.** Hearst Castle, officially known as "Hearst San Simeon State Historical Monument," sits in solitary splendor atop La Cuesta Encantada (the Enchanted Hill). Its buildings and gardens spread over 127 acres that were the heart of newspaper magnate William Randolph Hearst's 250,000-acre ranch. Hearst devoted nearly 30 years and about $10 million to building this elaborate estate. He commissioned renowned architect Julia Morgan—who also designed buildings at the University of California at Berkeley—but he was very much involved with the final product, a hodgepodge of Italian, Spanish, Moorish, and French styles. The 115-room main building and three huge "cottages" are connected by terraces and staircases and surrounded by pools, gardens, and statuary. In its heyday the castle was a playground for Hearst and his guests, many of them Hollywood celebrities. Construction began in 1919 and was never officially completed. Work was halted in 1947 when Hearst had to leave San Simeon because of failing health. The Hearst family presented the property to the State of California in 1958.

Access to the castle is through the large visitor center at the foot of the hill, which contains a collection of Hearst memorabilia and a giant-screen theater that shows a 40-minute film giving a sanitized version of Hearst's life and of the castle's construction. Buses from the visitor center zigzag up the hillside to the neoclassical extravaganza, where guides conduct three different daytime tours of various parts of the estate: grand rooms, upstairs suites, and cottages and kitchen. Daytime tours take about two hours and include the movie. In spring and fall, docents in period costume portray Hearst's guests and staff for the slightly longer evening tour, which begins at sunset. All tours include a ½-mile walk and between 150 and 400 stairs. Reservations for the tours are highly recommended. ⊠ *San Simeon State Park, 750 Hearst Castle Rd.* ☎ *800/444–4445* ⊕ *www.hearstcastle.com* ⊑ *Daytime tours $25, evening tours $36* ☉ *Tours daily 9–3:20, later in summer; additional tours take place most Fri. and Sat. evenings Mar.–May and Sept.–Dec.*

Old San Simeon. Turn west from Highway 1 across from the Hearst Castle entrance to see Old San Simeon, an 1850s whaling village that morphed into an outpost for Hearst employees. There's a one-room schoolhouse and Spanish-style buildings; don't miss Sebastian's General Store in an 1852 building. Now a state historic landmark, Sebastian's houses a store, a wine tasting room, and a café that serves excellent sandwiches and salads. ⊠ *West of Hwy. 1, across from Hearst Castle entrance.*

☺ **Piedras Blancas Elephant Seal Rookery.** A large colony of elephant seals (at last count 15,000 members) gathers every year at Piedras Blancas Elephant Seal Rookery, on the beaches near Piedras Blancas Lighthouse. The huge males with their pendulous, trunklike noses typically start appearing on shore in late November, and the females begin to arrive in December to give birth—most babies are born in the last two weeks of January. The newborn pups spend about four weeks nursing before their mothers head out to sea, leaving them on their own; the "weaners" leave the rookery when they are about 3½ months old. The seals return in the spring and summer months to molt or rest, but not en masse as in winter. You can watch them from a boardwalk along the bluffs just a few feet above the beach; do not attempt to approach them, as they are wild animals. Docents are often on hand to give background information and statistics. The nonprofit Friends of the Elephant Seal runs a small visitor center and gift shop at its office, at 250 San Simeon Avenue in San Simeon. ⊠ *Off Hwy. 1, 4½ miles north of Hearst Castle, just south of Piedras Blancas Lighthouse* ☎ *805/924–1628* ⊕ *www.elephantseal.org.*

Piedras Blancas Light Station. If you think traversing craggy, twisting Highway 1 is tough, imagine trying to navigate a boat up the rocky coastline (piedras blancas means "white rocks" in Spanish) near San Simeon before lighthouses were built. Captains must have cheered wildly when the beam began to shine here in 1875. Try to time a visit to include a morning tour (reservations not required). ■ **TIP→ Do not meet at the gate to the lighthouse—you'll miss the tour. Meet your guide instead at the former Piedras Blancas Motel, a mile and a half north of the light station.** ☎ *805/927–7361* ⊕ *piedrasblancas.org* ▰*$10* ⊙ *Tours at 9:45, mid-June–Aug. Mon–Sat.; Sept.–mid-June Tues., Thurs., and Sat.; no tours on national holidays* ☞ *No pets allowed.*

WHERE TO STAY

For expanded reviews, facilities, and current deals, visit Fodors.com.

$$ ⊡ **Best Western Cavalier Oceanfront Resort.** Reasonable rates, an ocean-
HOTEL   front location, evening bonfires, and well-equipped rooms—some with wood-burning fireplaces and private patios—make this motel one of the best choices in San Simeon. **Pros:** on the bluffs; fantastic views; close to Hearst Castle; bluff bonfires. **Cons:** room amenities and sizes vary; pools are small and sometimes crowded. **TripAdvisor:** "nice grounds," "the most relaxing ever," "breathtaking ocean views." ▨ *Rooms from: $159* ⊠ *9415 Hearst Dr.* ☎ *805/927–4688, 800/826–8168* ⊕ *www.cavalierresort.com* ↴ *90 rooms.*

$$ ⊡ **The Morgan San Simeon.** On the ocean side of Highway 1, near San
HOTEL   Simeon restaurants and shops, the Morgan offers motel-style rooming options while paying tribute to Hearst Castle architect Julia Morgan. **Pros:** fascinating artwork; easy access to Hearst Castle and Highway 1; some ocean views. **Cons:** not right on beach; no fitness room or laundry facilities. **TripAdvisor:** "loved it," "big clean rooms," "wonderful stay."

Rooms from: $149 ⊠ *9135 Hearst Dr.* ☎ *805/927–3878, 800/451–9900* ⊕ *www.hotel-morgan.com* ⌁ *54 rooms, 1 suite* ⊚ *Breakfast.*

BIG SUR COASTLINE

Long a retreat of artists and writers, Big Sur is a place of ancient forests and rugged shoreline, stretching 90 miles from San Simeon to Carmel. Residents have protected it from overdevelopment, and much of the region lies within several state parks and the more than 165,000-acre Ventana Wilderness, itself part of the Los Padres National Forest.

ESSENTIALS

Visitor Information Big Sur Chamber of Commerce ☎ *831/667–2100* ⊕ *www.bigsurcalifornia.org.*

SOUTHERN BIG SUR

Hwy. 1 from San Simeon to Julia Pfeiffer Burns State Park.

This especially rugged stretch of oceanfront is a rocky world of mountains, cliffs, and beaches.

GETTING HERE AND AROUND

Highway 1 is the only major access route from north or south. From the south, access Highway 1 from U.S. 101 in San Luis Obispo. From the north, take rural routes Highway 46 West (Paso Robles to Cambria) or Highway 41 West (Atascadero to Morro Bay). Nacimiento-Fergusson Road snakes through mountains and forest from U.S. 101 at Jolon about 25 miles to Highway 1 at Kirk Creek, about 4 miles south of Lucia; this curving, at times precipitous road is a motorcyclist favorite, not recommended for the faint of heart or during inclement weather.

EXPLORING

Fodor'sChoice **Highway 1.** One of California's most spectacular drives, Highway 1 ★ snakes up the coast north of San Simeon. Numerous pullouts along the way offer tremendous views and photo ops. On some of the beaches, huge elephant seals lounge nonchalantly, seemingly oblivious to the attention of rubberneckers—but keep your distance.

CalTrans. In rainy seasons, portions of Highway 1 north and south of Big Sur are sometimes shut down by mud slides. Contact CalTrans for road conditions. ☎ *888/836–0866* ⊕ *www.dot.ca.gov.*

Jade Cove. In Los Padres National Forest just north of the town of Gorda is Jade Cove, a well-known jade-hunting spot. Rock hunting is allowed on the beach, but you may not remove anything from the walls of the cliffs. ⊠ *Hwy. 1, 34 miles north of San Simeon.*

Julia Pfeiffer Burns State Park. Julia Pfeiffer Burns State Park provides some fine hiking, from an easy ½-mile stroll with marvelous coastal views to a strenuous 6-mile trek through the redwoods. The big attraction here, an 80-foot waterfall that drops into the ocean, gets crowded in summer; still, it's an astounding place to sit and contemplate nature. Migrating whales, harbor seals, and sea lions can sometimes be spotted not far from shore. ✉ *Hwy. 1, 53 miles north of San Simeon, 15 miles north of Lucia* ☎ *831/667–2315* 🌐 *www.parks.ca.gov* 🎟 *$10* 🕒 *Daily sunrise–sunset.*

WHERE TO STAY

For expanded reviews, facilities, and current deals, visit Fodors.com.

$$ HOTEL 🏨 **Ragged Point Inn.** At this cliff-top resort—the only inn and restaurant for miles around—glass walls in most rooms open to awesome, unobstructed ocean views. **Pros:** on the cliffs; great food; idyllic views. **Cons:** busy road stop during the day; often booked for weekend weddings. **TripAdvisor:** "very cool," "all about the location and the views," "beautiful place to get away." [$] *Rooms from: $169* ✉ *19019 Hwy. 1, 20 miles north of San Simeon, Ragged Point* ☎ *805/927–4502, 805/927–5708 restaurant* 🌐 *raggedpointinn.com* 🛏 *30 rooms.*

$$$ RESORT 🏨 **Treebones Resort.** Perched on a hilltop, surrounded by national forest and stunning, unobstructed ocean views, this yurt resort opened in 2004. **Pros:** 360-degree views; spacious pool area; comfortable beds. **Cons:** steep paths; no private bathrooms; more than a mile to the nearest store; not good for families with young children. **TripAdvisor:** "perfect way to commune with nature," "great accommodations," "given me vitality." [$] *Rooms from: $189* ✉ *71895 Hwy. 1, Willow Creek Rd., 32 miles north of San Simeon, 1 mile north of Gorda* ☎ *805/927–2390, 877/424–4787* 🌐 *www.treebonesresort.com* 🛏 *16 yurts, 5 campsites, 1 human nest w/campsite* 🍴 *Breakfast.*

CENTRAL BIG SUR

Hwy. 1, from Partington Cove to Bixby Bridge.

The countercultural spirit of Big Sur—which instead of a conventional town is a loose string of coast-hugging properties along Highway 1—is alive and well today. Its few residents include the very wealthy, the enthusiastically outdoorsy, and the thoroughly evolved: since the 1960s the Esalen Institute, a center for alternative education and East–West philosophical study, has attracted seekers of higher consciousness and devotees of the property's hot springs. Today, posh and rustic resorts hidden among the redwoods cater to visitors drawn from near and far by the extraordinary scenery and serene isolation.

GETTING HERE AND AROUND

From the north, follow Highway 1 south from Carmel. From the south, continue the drive north from Julia Pfeiffer Burns State Park *(above)* on Highway 1. Monterey-Salinas Transit operates the Line 22 Big Sur bus from Monterey and Carmel to Central Big Sur (the last top is Nepenthe), daily from late May to early September and weekends only the rest of the year.

Bus Contact Monterey-Salinas Transit ☎ *888/678–2871* 🌐 *www.mst.org.*

EXPLORING

Bixby Creek Bridge. The graceful arc of Bixby Creek Bridge is a photographer's dream. Built in 1932, it spans a deep canyon, more than 100 feet wide at the bottom. From the parking area on the north side you can admire the view or walk across the 550-foot span. ✉ *Hwy. 1, 6 miles north of Point Sur State Historic Park, 13 miles south of Carmel.*

Pfeiffer Big Sur State Park. Among the many hiking trails at Pfeiffer Big Sur State Park, a short route through a redwood-filled valley leads to a waterfall. You can double back or continue on the more difficult trail along the valley wall for views over miles of treetops to the sea. Stop in at the Big Sur Station visitor center, off Highway 1, less than ½ mile south of the park entrance, for information about the entire area; it's open Wednesday to Sunday from 9 to 4. ✉ *47225 Hwy. 1* ☎ *831/667–2315* 🌐 *www.parks.ca.gov* 🎫 *$10 per vehicle* 🕒 *Daily dawn–dusk.*

★ **Point Sur State Historic Park.** An 1889 lighthouse still stands watch from atop a large volcanic rock at this state park. Four lighthouse keepers lived here with their families until 1974, when the light station became automated. Their homes and working spaces are open to the public only on 2½- to 3-hour ranger-led tours. Considerable walking, including up two stairways, is involved. Strollers are not allowed. ✉ *Hwy. 1, 7 miles north of Pfeiffer Big Sur State Park* ☎ *831/625–4419* 🌐 *www.pointsur.org* 🎫 *$10* 🕒 *Tours generally Nov.–Mar., weekends at 10, Wed. at 1; Apr.–Oct., Sat. and Wed. at 10 and 2, Sun. at 10; call to confirm.*

BEACHES

Pfeiffer Beach. Through a hole in one of the gigantic boulders at secluded Pfeiffer Beach, you can watch the waves break first on the sea side and then on the beach side. Keep a sharp eye out for the unsigned, ungated road to the beach: it branches west of Highway 1 between the post office and Pfeiffer Big Sur State Park. The 2-mile, one-lane road descends sharply. **Amenities:** parking (fee); toilets. **Best For:** solitude; sunset. ✉ *Off Hwy. 1, 1 mile south of Pfeiffer Big Sur State Park* 🎫 *$5 per vehicle per day* 🕒 *Daily 9–8.*

WHERE TO EAT

$$$ AMERICAN 🍴 **Deetjen's Big Sur Inn.** The candlelighted, creaky-floor restaurant in the main house at the historic inn of the same name is a Big Sur institution. It serves spicy seafood paella, steak, and rack of lamb for dinner and wonderfully flavorful eggs Benedict for breakfast. The chef procures much of the fish, meats, and produce from purveyors who practice sustainable farming and fishing practices. [$] *Average main: $30* ✉ *Hwy. 1, 3½ mile south of Pfeiffer Big Sur State Park* ☎ *831/667–2377* 🌐 *www.deetjens.com* 🕒 *No lunch.*

$$$ AMERICAN 🍴 **Nepenthe.** It may be that no other restaurant between San Francisco and Los Angeles has a better coastal view than Nepenthe. The food and drink are overpriced but good; there are burgers, sandwiches, and salads for lunch, and fresh fish and hormone-free steaks for dinner. For the real show, settle on the terraced deck in the late afternoon, order a glass from the extensive wine list, and watch the sun slip into the Pacific Ocean. The less expensive, outdoor Café Kevah serves brunch and lunch. [$] *Average main: $26* ✉ *Hwy. 1, 2½ miles south of Big Sur Station* ☎ *831/667–2345* 🌐 *www.nepenthebigsur.com.*

$$$$ AMERICAN 🍴 **The Restaurant at Ventana.** The redwood, copper, and cedar elements at the Ventana Inn's restaurant pay tribute to the historic natural setting,

while gleaming new fixtures and dining accoutrements place the facility firmly in the 21st century. Chef Truman Jones's seasonal menu showcases meat, fish, and produce—such as rabbit loin, California white sea bass, artichokes, and abalone—grown or caught in California. (Much of the produce comes from the restaurant's organic vegetable garden.) A full slate of regional and international wines complements his dishes. The restaurant is also open for lunch. If the day is sunny, ask for a table on the outdoor terrace and take in the ocean views. $ *Average main: $36* ✉ *Hwy. 1, 1½ miles south of Pfeiffer Big Sur State Park* ☎ *831/667–2242* ⊕ *www.ventanainn.com* ⚓ *Reservations essential.*

$$$$
AMERICAN
✕ **Sierra Mar.** Ocean-view dining doesn't get much better than this. Perched at cliff's edge 1,200 feet above the Pacific at the ultra-chic Post Ranch Inn, Sierra Mar serves cutting-edge American food made from mostly organic, seasonal ingredients. The four-course prix-fixe option is stellar. The restaurant's wine list is one of the most extensive in the nation. $ *Average main: $90* ✉ *Hwy. 1, 1½ miles south of Pfeiffer Big Sur State Park* ☎ *831/667–2800* ⚓ *Reservations essential.*

WHERE TO STAY

For expanded reviews, facilities, and current deals, visit Fodors.com.

$$$
HOTEL
🏨 **Big Sur Lodge.** Modern motel-style cottages with Mission-style furnishings and vaulted ceilings sit in a meadow, surrounded by trees and flowering shrubbery. **Pros:** near trailheads; good camping alternative. **Cons:** basic rooms; walk to main lodge. **TripAdvisor:** "Spartan but comfortable," "spectacular setting," "good restaurant." $ *Rooms from: $199* ✉ *Pfeiffer Big Sur State Park, 47225 Hwy. 1* ☎ *831/667–3100, 800/424–4787* ⊕ *www.bigsurlodge.com* ⤳ *61 rooms.*

$
B&B/INN
🏨 **Deetjen's Big Sur Inn.** This historic 1930s Norwegian-style property is endearingly rustic and charming, especially if you're willing to go with a camplike flow. **Pros:** surrounded by Big Sur history; tons of character; wooded grounds. **Cons:** rustic; thin walls; some rooms don't have private baths. **TripAdvisor:** "bucolic charm," "rustic bliss," "so romantic." $ *Rooms from: $105* ✉ *Hwy. 1, 3½ miles south of Pfeiffer Big Sur State Park* ☎ *831/667–2377* ⊕ *www.deetjens.com* ⤳ *20 rooms, 15 with bath.*

$$$$
HOTEL
🏨 **Glen Oaks Big Sur.** At this rustic-modern cluster of adobe-and-redwood buildings in the heart of Big Sur, you can choose between motel-style rooms and cottages in the woods. **Pros:** in the heart of town; walking distance of restaurants. **Cons:** near busy road and parking lot; no TVs. **TripAdvisor:** "contemporary and cozy gem," "relaxing and welcoming," "best little cabin in the woods." $ *Rooms from: $275* ✉ *Hwy. 1, 1 mile north of Pfeiffer Big Sur State Park* ☎ *831/667–2105* ⊕ *www.glenoaksbigsur.com* ⤳ *16 rooms, 2 cottages, 7 cabins.*

$$$$
RESORT
Fodor's Choice
★
🏨 **Post Ranch Inn.** This luxurious retreat, designed exclusively for adult getaways, has remarkably environmentally conscious architecture. **Pros:** world-class resort; spectacular views; gorgeous property with hiking trails. **Cons:** expensive; austere design; not a good choice if you're scared of heights. **TripAdvisor:** "a special retreat," "this is the best," "bliss." $ *Rooms from: $700* ✉ *Hwy. 1, 1½ miles south of Pfeiffer Big*

Sur State Park ☎ *831/667–2200, 888/524–4787* 🌐 *www.postranchinn.com* 🛏 *39 units* 🍴 *Breakfast.*

$$$$ HOTEL Fodor's Choice ★ 🏨 **Ventana Inn & Spa.** Hundreds of celebrities, from Oprah Winfrey to Sir Anthony Hopkins, have escaped to Ventana, a romantic resort on 243 tranquil acres 1,200 feet above the Pacific. **Pros:** nature trails everywhere; great food; secluded. **Cons:** simple breakfast; some rooms have no ocean view. **TripAdvisor:** "really neat place," "absolutely lovely," "beautiful." [$] *Rooms from: $600* ✉ *Hwy. 1, almost 1 mile south of Pfeiffer Big Sur State Park* ☎ *831/667–2331, 800/628–6500* 🌐 *www.ventanainn.com* 🛏 *25 rooms, 31 suites* 🍴 *Breakfast.*

The Monterey Bay Area

FROM CARMEL TO SANTA CRUZ

WORD OF MOUTH

"To be able to see, up close, the wonders of the ocean, is an amazing experience at the wonderful Monterey Bay Aquarium."

—photo by mellifluous, Fodors.com member

WELCOME TO THE MONTEREY BAY AREA

TOP REASONS TO GO

★ **Marine life:** Monterey Bay is the location of the world's third-largest marine sanctuary, home to whales, otters, and other underwater creatures.

★ **Getaway central:** For more than a century, urbanites have come to the Monterey Bay area to unwind, relax, and have fun. It's a great place to browse unique shops and galleries, ride a giant roller coaster, or play a round of golf on a world-class course.

★ **Nature preserves:** More than the sea is protected here—the region boasts nearly 30 state parks, beaches, and preserves, fantastic places for walking, jogging, hiking, and biking.

★ **Wine and dine:** The area's rich agricultural bounty translates to abundant fresh produce, great wines, and fabulous dining. It's no wonder more than 300 culinary events take place here every year.

★ **Small-town vibes:** Even the cities here are friendly, walkable places where you'll feel like a local.

0 ——————— 5 mi

0 ——————— 5 km

Santa Cruz

1 **Carmel and Pacific Grove.** Exclusive Carmel-by-the-Sea and Carmel Valley Village burst with historic charm, fine dining, and unusual boutiques that cater to celebrity residents and well-heeled visitors. Nearby 17-Mile Drive—quite possibly the prettiest stretch of road you'll ever travel—runs between Carmel-by-the-Sea and Victorian-studded Pacific Grove, home to thousands of migrating monarch butterflies between October and February.

2 **Monterey.** A former Spanish military outpost, Monterey's well-preserved historic district is a hands-on history lesson. Cannery Row, the former center of Monterey's once-thriving sardine industry, has been reborn as a tourist attraction with shops, restaurants, hotels, and the Monterey Bay Aquarium.

3 **Around Monterey Bay.** Much of California's lettuce, berries, artichokes, and Brussels sprouts come from Salinas and Watsonville. Salinas is also home of the National Steinbeck Center, and Moss Landing and Watsonville encompass pristine wildlife wetlands. Aptos, Capitola, and Soquel are former lumber towns that became popular seaside resorts more than a century ago. Today they're filled with antiques shops, restaurants, and wine-tasting rooms; you'll also find some of the bay's best beaches along the shore here.

4 **Santa Cruz.** Santa Cruz shows its colors along an old-time beach boardwalk and municipal wharf. A University of California campus imbues the town with arts and culture and a liberal mind-set.

GETTING ORIENTED

3

North of Big Sur the coastline softens into lower bluffs, windswept dunes, pristine estuaries, and long, sandy beaches, bordering one of the world's most amazing marine environments—the Monterey Bay. On the Monterey Peninsula, at the southern end of the bay, are Carmel-by-the-Sea, Pacific Grove, and Monterey; Santa Cruz sits at the northern tip of the crescent. In between, Highway 1 cruises along the coastline, passing windswept beaches piled high with sand dunes. Along the route are wetlands, artichoke and strawberry fields, and workaday towns such as Castroville and Watsonville.

Updated
by Cheryl
Crabtree

Natural beauty is at the heart of this region's enormous appeal—you sense it everywhere, whether you're exploring one of Monterey Bay's attractive coast-side towns, relaxing at a luxurious resort, or touring the coast on the lookout for marine life.

It's been this way for a long time: an abiding current of plenty runs through the region's history. Military buffs see it in centuries' worth of battles for control of the rich territory. John Steinbeck saw it in the success of a community built on the elbow grease of farm laborers in the Salinas Valley and fishermen along Cannery Row. Biologists see it in the ocean's potential as a more sustainable source of food.

Downtown Carmel-by-the-Sea and Monterey are walks through history. The bay itself is protected by the Monterey Bay National Marine Sanctuary, the nation's largest undersea canyon—bigger and deeper than the Grand Canyon. And of course, the backdrop of natural beauty is still everywhere to be seen.

MONTEREY BAY PLANNER

WHEN TO GO

Summer is peak season; mild weather brings in big crowds. In this coastal region, a cool breeze generally blows and fog often rolls in from offshore; you will frequently need a sweater or windbreaker. Off-season, from November through April, fewer people visit and the mood is mellower. Rainfall is heaviest in January and February, but autumn through spring days are crystal clear more often than in summer.

GETTING HERE AND AROUND

AIR TRAVEL

Monterey Peninsula Airport, 3 miles east of downtown Monterey off Highway 68, is served by Alaska, Allegiant, American Eagle, United/ United Express, and US Airways. Taxi service to downtown runs about $15 to $17; to Carmel the fare is $23 to $32. To and from San Jose International Airport and San Francisco International Airport, Monterey Airbus starts at $35 and the Early Bird Airport Shuttle runs $75 to $190.

Airport Contacts Monterey Regional Airport ✉ *200 Fred Kane Dr., at Olmsted Rd., off Hwy. 68, Monterey* ☎ *831/648–7000* ⊕ *www.montereyairport.com.*

Ground Transportation Central Coast Cab Company ☎ *831/626–3333.***Early Bird Airport Shuttle** ☎ *831/462–3933* ⊕ *www.earlybirdairportshuttle.com.* **Monterey Airbus** ☎ *831/373–7777* ⊕ *www.montereyairbus.com.* **Yellow Cab** ☎ *831/646–1234.*

BUS TRAVEL

Greyhound serves Santa Cruz and Salinas from San Francisco and San Jose. The trips take about 3 and 4½ hours, respectively. Monterey-Salinas Transit (MST) provides frequent service in Monterey County (fares $1 to $3; day pass $8), and Santa Cruz METRO ($2; day pass $10) buses operate throughout Santa Cruz County. You can switch between the two lines in Watsonville, in southern Santa Cruz County.

Bus Contacts Greyhound ☎ *800/231–2222* ⊕ *www.greyhound.com.* **Monterey-Salinas Transit** ☎ *888/678–2871* ⊕ *www.mst.org.*

CAR TRAVEL

Highway 1 runs south–north along the coast, linking the towns of Carmel-by-the-Sea, Monterey, and Santa Cruz; some sections have only two lanes. The freeway, U.S. 101, lies to the east, roughly parallel to Highway 1. The two roads are connected by Highway 68 from Pacific Grove to Salinas; Highway 156 from Castroville to Prunedale; Highway 152 from Watsonville to Gilroy; and Highway 17 from Santa Cruz to San Jose. ⚠ Traffic near Santa Cruz can crawl to a standstill during commuter hours. In the morning, avoid traveling between 7 and 9; in the afternoon avoid traveling between 4 and 7.

The drive south from San Francisco to Monterey can be made comfortably in three hours or less. The most scenic way is to follow Highway 1 down the coast past flower, pumpkin, and artichoke fields and small seaside communities. Unless you drive on sunny weekends when locals are heading for the beach, the two-lane coast highway may take no longer than the freeway. A sometimes-faster route is Interstate 280 south from San Francisco to Highway 17, north of San Jose.

From Los Angeles the drive to Monterey can be made in five to six hours by heading north on U.S. 101 to Salinas and then west on Highway 68. You can also follow Highway 1 all or part of the way north from Southern California.

TRAIN TRAVEL

Amtrak's *Coast Starlight* runs between Los Angeles, Oakland, and Seattle. From the train station in Salinas, you can connect with buses serving Carmel, Monterey, and Santa Cruz.

Train Contacts Amtrak ☎ *800/872–7245* ⊕ *www.amtrakcalifornia.com.*

TOUR OPTIONS

California Parlor Car Tours operates motor-coach tours from San Francisco that include one or two days in Monterey and Carmel. Ag Venture Tours runs wine-tasting, sightseeing, and agricultural tours to several towns.

Tour Contacts Ag Venture Tours ☎ *831/761–8463* ⊕ *www.agventuretours. com.* **California Parlor Car Tours** ☎ *415/474–7500, 800/227–4250* ⊕ *www. calpartours.com.*

RESTAURANTS

The Monterey Bay area is a culinary paradise. The surrounding waters are full of fish, wild game roams the foothills, and the inland valleys are some of the most fertile in the country—local chefs draw on this bounty for their fresh, truly Californian cuisine. Except at beachside stands and inexpensive eateries, where anything goes, casual but neat dress is the norm. *Prices in the restaurant reviews are the average cost of a main course at dinner or, if dinner is not served, at lunch (excluding sales tax).*

HOTELS

Accommodations in the Monterey area range from no-frills motels to luxurious hotels. Pacific Grove, amply endowed with ornate Victorian houses, is the region's B&B capital; Carmel also has charming inns. Lavish resorts cluster in exclusive Pebble Beach and pastoral Carmel Valley.

High season runs from April through October. Rates in winter, especially at the larger hotels, may drop by 50% or more, and B&Bs often offer midweek specials. Whatever the month, some properties require a two-night stay on weekends. *Prices in the hotel reviews are the lowest cost of a standard double room in high season. For expanded reviews, facilities, and current deals, visit Fodors.com.* ⚠ Many of the fancier accommodations aren't suitable for children; if you're traveling with kids, ask before you book.

Lodging Contact Bed and Breakfast Inns of Santa Cruz County. This association of innkeepers can help you find a bed-and-breakfast. ⊕ *www. santacruzbnb.com.*

VISITOR INFORMATION

Contacts Monterey County Convention & Visitors Bureau ☎ *877/666–8373* ⊕ *www.seemonterey.com.* **Monterey County Vintners and Growers Association** ☎ *831/375–9400* ⊕ *www.montereywines.org.* **Santa Cruz County Conference and Visitors Council** ✉ *303 Water St., Santa Cruz* ☎ *831/425–1234, 800/833–3494* ⊕ *www.santacruz.org.* **Santa Cruz Mountain Winegrowers Association** ✉ *7605-A Old Dominion Ct., Aptos* ☎ *831/685–8463* ⊕ *www. scmwa.com.*

CARMEL AND PACIFIC GROVE

As Highway 1 swings inland about 30 miles north of Big Sur, historic Carmel-by-the Sea anchors the southern entry to the Monterey Peninsula—a gorgeous promontory at the southern tip of Monterey Bay. Just north of Carmel along the coast, the legendary 17-Mile Drive wends its way through private Pebble Beach and the town of Pacific Grove.

Highway 1 skirts the peninsula to the east with more direct access to Pebble Beach and Pacific Grove.

CARMEL-BY-THE-SEA

26 miles north of Big Sur on Hwy. 1.

Although the community has grown quickly through the years and its population quadruples with tourists on weekends and in summer, Carmel-by-the-Sea, commonly referred to as Carmel, retains its identity as a quaint village. Self-consciously charming, the town is populated by many celebrities, major and minor, and has its share of quirky ordinances. For instance, women wearing high heels do not have the right to pursue legal action if they trip and fall on the cobblestone streets, and drivers who hit a tree and leave the scene are charged with hit-and-run.

Buildings have no street numbers (street names are written on discreet white posts) and consequently no mail delivery (if you want to see the locals, go to the post office). Artists started this community, and their legacy is evident in the numerous galleries.

GETTING HERE AND AROUND

From north or south follow Highway 1 to Carmel. Head west at Ocean Avenue to reach the main village hub. In summer the MST Carmel-by-the-Sea Trolley loops around town to the beach and mission every 30 minutes or so.

TOURS

For insight into Carmel's history and culture, join a guided two-hour Carmel Walks tour through hidden courtyards, gardens, and pathways. Tours ($25) depart from the Pine Inn courtyard on Lincoln Street. Call to reserve a spot.

ESSENTIALS

Tour Contacts Carmel Walks ✉ *Lincoln St. at 6th Ave.* ☎ *831/642–2700* ⊕ *www.carmelwalks.com* ⊗ *Tues.–Fri. at 10, Sat. at 10 and 2.*

Visitor Information Carmel Chamber of Commerce ✉ *Visitor Center, San Carlos, between 5th and 6th* ☎ *831/624 2522, 800/550 4333* ⊕ *www. carmelcalifornia.org* ⊗ *Daily 10–5.*

EXPLORING
TOP ATTRACTIONS

★ **Carmel Mission.** Long before it became a shopping and browsing destination, Carmel was an important religious center during the establishment of Spanish California. That heritage is preserved in the Mission San Carlos Borroméo del Rio Carmelo, more commonly known as the Carmel Mission. Founded in 1771, it served as headquarters for the mission system in California under Father Junípero Serra. Adjoining the stone church is a tranquil garden planted with California poppies. Museum rooms at the mission include an early kitchen, Serra's spartan sleeping quarters, and the first college library in California. ✉ *3080 Rio Rd., at Lasuen Dr.* ☎ *831/624–3600* ⊕ *www.carmelmission.org* 🎟 *$6.50* ⊗ *Mon.–Sat. 9:30–4:30, Sun. 10:30–4:30.*

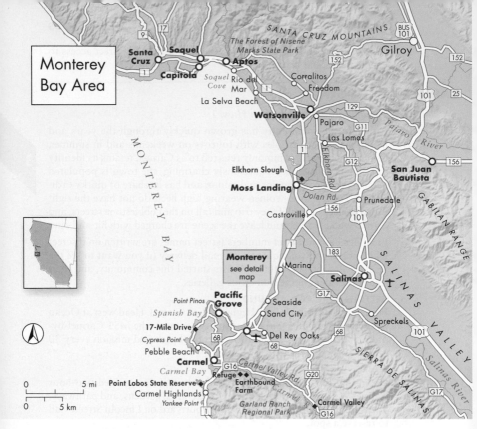

Monterey
Bay Area

★ **Point Lobos State Reserve.** A 350-acre headland harboring a wealth of marine life, this reserve lies a few miles south of Carmel. The best way to explore here is to walk along one of the many trails. The Cypress Grove Trail leads through a forest of Monterey cypress (one of only two natural groves remaining), which clings to the rocks above an emerald-green cove. Sea Lion Point Trail is a good place to view sea lions. From those and other trails you may also spot otters, harbor seals, and (in winter and spring) migrating whales. An additional 750 acres of the reserve is an undersea marine park open to qualified scuba divers. ■TIP→ Arrive early (or in late afternoon) to avoid crowds; the parking lots fill up. No pets are allowed. ⊠ *Hwy. 1* ☎ *831/624–4909, 831/624–8413 for scuba-diving reservations* ⊕ *www.pointlobos.org* 🖃 *$10 per vehicle* ☉ *Daily 8 am–½ hr after sunset in winter, closes 6:30 pm rest of year.*

WORTH NOTING

Carmel Plaza. Carmel Plaza, in the east end of the village proper, holds more than 50 shops and restaurants. ⊠ *Ocean Ave. and Mission St.* ☎ *831/624–1385* ⊕ *www.carmelplaza.com.*

Carmel Wine Walk By-the-Sea. Park the car and sample local wines at tasting rooms and shops in downtown Carmel, all within a few blocks of each other. Purchase a Wine Walk Passport, good for seven tastings within a year; participating venues will stamp it each time you visit. ✉ *Carmel Chamber of Commerce Visitor Center, San Carlos St., between 5th and 6th Aves.* ☎ *831/624–2522, 800/550–4333* 🌐 *www.carmelcalifornia.org* 🎟 *$50.*

WORD OF MOUTH

"The beauty of Point Lobos State Reserve was so stunning, I could not believe it. Here you have a mix of tall cliffs, crashing waves, gorgeous wild flowers, abundant wild life (seals, sea otters, deer), and sheltered emerald-green coves with white sandy beaches."
—Birder

Ocean Avenue. Downtown Carmel's chief lure is shopping, especially along its main street, Ocean Avenue, between Junipero Avenue and Camino Real; the architecture here is a mishmash of ersatz Tudor, Mediterranean, and other styles.

Tor House. Scattered throughout the pines in Carmel-by-the-Sea are houses and cottages originally built for the writers, artists, and photographers who discovered the area decades ago. Among the most impressive dwellings is Tor House, a stone cottage built in 1919 by poet Robinson Jeffers on a craggy knoll overlooking the sea. Portraits, books, and unusual art objects fill the low-ceiling rooms. The highlight of the small estate is Hawk Tower, a detached edifice set with stones from the Carmel coastline—as well as one from the Great Wall of China. The docents who lead tours (six people maximum) are well informed about the poet's work and life. Reservations for tours, via email at ✉ *thf@torhouse.org*, are recommended. ✉ *26304 Ocean View Ave.* ☎ *831/624–1813, 831/624–1840 direct docent office line, available Fri. and Sat. only* 🌐 *www.torhouse.org* 🎟 *$10* 🕒 *Tours on hr Fri. and Sat. 10–3* ☞ *No children under 12.*

BEACHES

Carmel Beach. Carmel-by-the-Sea's greatest attraction is its rugged coastline, with pine and cypress forests and countless inlets. Carmel Beach, an easy walk from downtown shops, has sparkling white sands and magnificent sunsets. ■ **TIP→ Dogs are allowed to romp off-leash here.** **Amenities:** parking (no fee); toilets. **Best For:** sunset; surfing; walking. ✉ *End of Ocean Ave.*

Carmel River State Beach. This sugar-white beach, stretching 106 acres along Carmel Bay, is adjacent to a bird sanctuary, where you might spot pelicans, kingfishers, hawks, and sandpipers. **Amenities:** none. **Best For:** sunrise; sunset; walking. ✉ *Off Scenic Rd. south of Carmel Beach* ☎ *831/624–4909, 831/649–2836* 🌐 *www.parks.ca.gov* 🎟 *Free* 🕒 *Daily 8 am–½ hr after sunset in winter; closes 6:30 pm rest of year.*

WHERE TO EAT

$$$ FRENCH ★ 🍴 **André's Bouchée.** The food here presents an innovative bistro-style take on local ingredients. A Monterey Bay sea scallop reduction adorns pan-seared veal tenderloin; grilled rib-eye steaks are topped with a shallot–cabernet sauvignon sauce. With its copper wine bar, the dining room feels more urban than most of Carmel; perhaps that's why this is the "cool" place in town to dine. The stellar wine list sources the selection at the in-house wineshop. [$] *Average main: $28* ✉ *Mission St.,*

between Ocean and 7th Aves. ☎ *831/626–7880* 🌐 *www.andresbouchee.com* ✍ *Reservations essential* ⏲ *No lunch Mon. and Tues.*

$$$ EUROPEAN 🍴 **Anton and Michel.** Carefully prepared European cuisine is the draw at this airy restaurant. The rack of lamb is carved at the table, the grilled Halloumi cheese and tomatoes are meticulously stacked and served with basil and kalamata olive tapenade, and the desserts are set aflame before your eyes. [$] *Average main: $30* ✉ *Mission St. and 7th Ave.* ☎ *831/624–2406* 🌐 *www.antonandmichel.com* ✍ *Reservations essential.*

$$$ MEDITERRANEAN ★ 🍴 **Casanova.** This cozy restaurant inspires European-style celebration and romance—accordions hang from the walls, and tiny party lights dance along the low ceilings. The food consists of delectable seasonal dishes from southern France and northern Italy. Private dining and a special menu are offered at Van Gogh's Table, a special table imported from France's Auberge Ravoux, the artist's final residence. [$] *Average main: $30* ✉ *5th Ave., between San Carlos and Mission Sts.* ☎ *831/625–0501* 🌐 *www.casanovarestaurant.com* ✍ *Reservations essential.*

$ AMERICAN 🍴 **The Cottage Restaurant.** This family-friendly spot serves sandwiches, pizzas, and homemade soups at lunch and simple entreés at dinner, but the best meal is breakfast (good thing it's served all day). The menu offers six variations on eggs Benedict, and all kinds of sweet and savory crepes. [$] *Average main: $14* ✉ *Lincoln St., between Ocean and 7th Aves.* ☎ *831/625–6260* 🌐 *www.cottagerestaurant.com* ⏲ *No dinner Sun.–Wed.*

$$$ SEAFOOD 🍴 **Flying Fish Grill.** Simple in appearance yet bold with its flavors, this Japanese–California seafood restaurant is one of Carmel's most inventive eateries. Among the best entrées is the almond-crusted sea bass served with Chinese cabbage and rock shrimp stir-fry. The warm, wood-lined dining room is broken up into very private booths. [$] *Average main: $24* ✉ *Mission St., between Ocean and 7th Aves.* ☎ *831/625–1962* 🌐 *flyingfishgrill.com* ⏲ *No lunch.*

$$$ AMERICAN 🍴 **Grasing's Coastal Cuisine.** Chef Kurt Grasing draws from fresh Carmel Coast and Central Valley ingredients to whip up contemporary adaptations of European-provincial and American cooking. Longtime menu favorites include artichoke lasagna in a roasted tomato sauce, duck with fresh cherries and green peppercorns in a port wine sauce, a savory paella, and grilled steaks and chops. [$] *Average main: $30* ✉ *6th Ave. and Mission St.* ☎ *831/624–6562* 🌐 *www.grasings.com* ✍ *Reservations essential.*

$ AMERICAN 🍴 **Jack London's.** This publike local hangout is the only Carmel restaurant to serve food late at night, often until 11 pm or midnight. The menu includes everything from nachos to steaks. [$] *Average main: $15* ✉ *Su Vecino Court on Dolores St., between 5th and 6th Aves.* ☎ *831/624–2336* 🌐 *jacklondons.com.*

$ AMERICAN 🍴 **Katy's Place.** Locals flock to Katy's cozy, country-style eatery to fill up on hearty eggs Benedict dishes. (There are 16 types to choose from, each made with three fresh eggs.) The huge breakfast menu also includes omelets, pancakes, and eight types of Belgian waffles. Salads, sandwiches, and burgers are available for lunch—try the grilled calamari burger with melted Monterey Jack cheese. [$] *Average main: $15*

Point Lobos Reserve State Park is home to one of the only two natural stands of Monterey Cypress in the world.

✉ *Mission St., between 5th and 6th Aves.* ☎ *831/624–0199* 🌐 *www.katysplacecarmel.com* 💳 *No credit cards* 🕒 *No dinner.*

$$$ FRENCH 🍴 **L'Escargot.** Chef-owner Kericos Loutas personally sees to each plate of food served at this romantic, unpretentious French restaurant. Order the pan-roasted duck breast or the bone-in steak in truffle butter; or, if you can't decide, choose the three-course prix-fixe dinner. [$] *Average main: $30* ✉ *Mission St., between 4th and 5th Aves.* ☎ *831/620–1942* 🌐 *www.escargot-carmel.com* ✍ *Reservations essential* 🕒 *No lunch.*

$ AMERICAN 🍴 **Tuck Box.** This bright little restaurant is in a cottage right out of a fairy tale, complete with stone fireplace. Handmade scones, good for breakfast or afternoon tea, are the specialty. [$] *Average main: $12* ✉ *Dolores St., between Ocean and 7th Aves.* ☎ *831/624–6365* 🌐 *www.tuckbox.com* ✍ *Reservations not accepted* 💳 *No credit cards* 🕒 *No dinner.*

$$$ ITALIAN 🍴 **Vesuvio.** Chef and restaurateur Rich Pèpe's heats up the night with his latest venture, a lively trattoria downstairs and a swinging rooftop terrace, Starlight Lounge 65°. Pèpe's elegant take on traditional Italian cuisine yields dishes such as wild-boar Bolognese pappardelle, lobster ravioli, and velvety limoncello mousse cake. Pizzas and small plates are served in the restaurant and two bars. Upstairs, relax in comfy chairs by fire pits and enjoy bird's-eye views of the village and, most nights in summer, take in live music. [$] *Average main: $24* ✉ *6th and Junipero Aves.* ☎ *831/626–7373 ext. 2* 🌐 *pepemag.com* 🕒 *No lunch.*

WHERE TO STAY

For expanded reviews, facilities, and current deals, visit Fodors.com.

$$$$ B&B/INN 🏨 **Cypress Inn.** The decorating style here is luxurious but refreshingly simple. **Pros:** luxury without snobbery; popular lounge; traditional

British-style afternoon tea. **Cons:** not for the pet-phobic. **TripAdvisor:** "consistently great," "best place to go with your pet," "nice atmosphere." [$] *Rooms from: $235* ✉ *Lincoln St. and 7th Ave., Box Y* ☎ *831/624–3871, 800/443–7443* 🌐 *www.cypress-inn.com* 🛏 *39 rooms, 5 suites* 🍴 *Breakfast.*

$$$$ HOTEL ★ 🏨 **Highlands Inn, A Hyatt Hotel.** High on a hill overlooking the Pacific, this place has superb views; accommodations include king rooms with fireplaces, suites with personal Jacuzzis, and full town houses with all the perks. **Pros:** killer views; romantic getaway; great food. **Cons:** thin walls; must drive to Carmel. **TripAdvisor:** "spectacular views," "very good room," "exceptional service." [$] *Rooms from: $439* ✉ *120 Highlands Dr.* ☎ *831/620–1234, 800/233–1234* 🌐 *highlandsinn.hyatt.com* 🛏 *46 rooms, 2 suites.*

$$$$ B&B/INN Fodor's Choice ★ 🏨 **L'Auberge Carmel.** Stepping through the doors of this elegant inn is like being transported to a little European village. **Pros:** in town but off the main drag; four blocks from the beach; full-service luxury. **Cons:** touristy area; not a good choice for families. **TripAdvisor:** "fantastic service and even better food," "perfect location with every luxury," "very captivating." [$] *Rooms from: $385* ✉ *Monte Verde at 7th Ave.* ☎ *831/624–8578* 🌐 *www.laubergecarmel.com* 🛏 *20 rooms* 🍴 *Breakfast.*

$$ HOTEL 🏨 **Mission Ranch.** Movie star Clint Eastwood owns this sprawling property whose accommodations include rooms in a converted barn, and several cottages, some with fireplaces. **Pros:** farm setting; pastoral views; great for tennis buffs. **Cons:** busy parking lot; must drive to the heart of town. **TripAdvisor:** "lovely and quaint," "spectacular setting," "relaxing with a gorgeous view." [$] *Rooms from: $140* ✉ *26270 Dolores St.* ☎ *831/624–6436, 800/538–8221, 831/625–9040 restaurant* 🌐 *www.missionranchcarmel.com* 🛏 *31 rooms* 🍴 *Breakfast.*

$$$ B&B/INN 🏨 **Sea View Inn.** In a residential area a few hundred feet from the beach, this restored 1905 home has a double parlor with two fireplaces, Oriental rugs, canopy beds, and a spacious front porch. **Pros:** quiet; private; close to the beach. **Cons:** small building; uphill trek to the heart of town. **TripAdvisor:** "great location," "excellent staff," "fantastic service." [$] *Rooms from: $180* ✉ *Camino Real, between 11th and 12th Aves.* ☎ *831/624–8778* 🌐 *www.seaviewinncarmel.com* 🛏 *8 rooms, 6 with private bath* 🍴 *Breakfast.*

$$$$ B&B/INN 🏨 **Tickle Pink Inn.** Atop a towering cliff, this inn has views of the Big Sur coastline, which you can contemplate from your private balcony. **Pros:** close to great hiking; intimate; dramatic views. **Cons:** close to a big hotel; lots of traffic during the day. **TripAdvisor:** "divine property," "breathtaking views," "a gem within the cliffs." [$] *Rooms from: $289* ✉ *155 Highland Dr.* ☎ *831/624–1244, 800/635–4774* 🌐 *www.ticklepink.com* 🛏 *23 rooms, 10 suites, 1 cottage* 🍴 *Breakfast.*

$$$ B&B/INN ★ 🏨 **Tradewinds Carmel.** Its sleek decor inspired by the South Seas, this converted motel encircles a courtyard with waterfalls, a meditation garden, and a fire pit. **Pros:** serene; within walking distance of restaurants; friendly service. **Cons:** no pool; long walk to the beach. **TripAdvisor:** "tranquil and plush," "cozy in Carmel," "romantic." [$] *Rooms from: $250* ✉ *Mission St., at 3rd Ave.* ☎ *831/624–2776* 🌐 *www.tradewindscarmel.com* 🛏 *26 rooms, 2 suites* 🍴 *Breakfast.*

SHOPPING

ART GALLERIES **Carmel Art Association.** The association exhibits the original paintings and sculptures of local artists. ⊠ *Dolores St., between 5th and 6th Aves.* ☎ *831/624–6176* ⊕ *www.carmelart.org.*

Galerie Plein Aire. The gallery showcases the oil paintings of a group of local artists. ⊠ *Dolores St., between 5th and 6th Aves.* ☎ *831/625–5686* ⊕ *www.galeriepleinaire.com.*

Weston Gallery. Run by the family of the late Edward Weston, this hands down the best photography gallery around, with contemporary color photography complemented by classic black-and-whites. ⊠ *6th Ave., between Dolores and Lincoln Sts.* ☎ *831/624–4453* ⊕ *www.westongallery.com.*

SPECIALTY **Bittner.** The shop carries a fine selection of collectible and vintage pens
SHOPS from around the world. ⊠ *Ocean Ave., between Mission and San Carlos Sts.* ☎ *831/626–8828* ⊕ *www.bittner.com.*

Intima. Find European lingerie that ranges from lacy to racy here. ⊠ *Mission St., between Ocean and 7th Aves.* ☎ *831/625–0599* ⊕ *www.intimacarmel.com.*

Jan de Luz. This shops monograms and embroiders fine linens (including bathrobes) while you wait. ⊠ *Dolores St., between Ocean and 7th Aves.* ☎ *831/622–7621* ⊕ *www.jandeluz.com.*

Madrigal. Sportswear, sweaters, and accessories for women are the specialties here. ⊠ *Carmel Plaza and Mission St.* ☎ *831/624–3477.*

CARMEL VALLEY

10 miles east of Carmel, Hwy. 1 to Carmel Valley Rd.

Carmel Valley Road, which heads inland from Highway 1 south of Carmel, is the main thoroughfare through this valley, a secluded enclave of horse ranchers and other well-heeled residents who prefer the area's sunny climate to coastal fog and wind. Once thick with dairy farms, the valley has evolved into an esteemed wine appellation. Carmel Valley Village has crafts shops, art galleries, and the tasting rooms of numerous local wineries.

GETTING HERE AND AROUND

From U.S. 101 north or south, exit at Highway 68 and head west toward the coast. Scenic, two-lane Laureles Grade winds west over the mountains to Carmel Valley Road north of the village.

TOURS

The Carmel Valley Grapevine Express, aka MST's Line 24 bus, travels between downtown Monterey and Carmel Valley Village, with stops near wineries, restaurants, and shopping centers. At $8 for a ride-all-day pass, it's an incredible bargain.

Bus Contact Carmel Valley Grapevine Express ☎ *888/678-2871* ⊕ *www.mst.org.*

EXPLORING

Bernardus Tasting Room. At this tasting room you can sample many of Bernardus Winery's offerings, including older vintages and reserve wines. ✉ *5 W. Carmel Valley Rd., at El Caminito Rd.* ☎ *831/298–8021, 800/223–2533* 🌐 *www.bernardus.com* 🕒 *Daily 11–5.*

Château Julien. The expansive winery, recognized internationally for its Chardonnays and Merlots, offers tours by appointment only, but the tasting room is open daily. ✉ *8940 Carmel Valley Rd., at Schetter Rd., Carmel* ☎ *831/624–2600* 🌐 *www.chateaujulien.com* 🕒 *Weekdays 8–5, weekends 11–5; tours weekdays at 10:30 and 2:30, weekends at 12:30 and 2:30, by appointment.*

Earthbound Farm. Pick up fresh veggies, ready-to-eat meals, gourmet groceries, flowers, and gifts at Earthbound Farm, the world's largest grower of organic produce. You can also take a romp in the kid's garden, cut your own herbs, and stroll through the chamomile aromatherapy labyrinth. Special events, on Saturdays from April through December, include bug walks and garlic-braiding workshops. ✉ *7250 Carmel Valley Rd., Carmel* ☎ *831/625–6219* 🌐 *www.ebfarm.com* 🎫 *Free* 🕒 *Mon.–Sat. 8–6:30, Sun. 9–6.*

Garland Ranch Regional Park. Hiking trails stretch across much of this park's 4,500 acres of meadows, forested hillsides, and creeks. ✉ *Carmel Valley Rd., 9 miles east of Carmel-by-the-Sea* ☎ *831/659–4488* 🌐 *www.mprpd.org.*

WHERE TO EAT

$$ ITALIAN 🍴 **Café Rustica.** Italian-inspired country cooking is the focus at this lively roadhouse. Specialties include roasted meats, pastas, and thin-crust pizzas from the wood-fired oven. It can get noisy inside; for a quieter meal, request a table outside. [$] *Average main: $18* ✉ *10 Delfino Pl., at Pilot Rd., off Carmel Valley Rd.* ☎ *831/659–4444* 🌐 *www.caferusticacarmel.com* ✍ *Reservations essential* 🕒 *Closed Mon.*

$ ECLECTIC 🍴 **LokaL.** Slang for "local" in Czech, LokaL infuses Carmel Valley Village with youth and vitality. After stints in Spain and Prague, where he ran a popular bar, local boy and chef Brendan Jones fashioned his hip new restaurant to encourage social interaction. Order Czech-style beer on tap at the 29-foot, recycled-redwood bar and dine on inventive tapas, among them orange-cardamom paella, sardine bocadillo with mojito aioli, and crispy-pig-cheek salad (exotic!), that riff off Jones' Spanish and Czech influences. [$] *Average main: $15* ✉ *13750 Center St., off Village Dr.* ☎ *831/659–5886* 🕒 *Closed Sun. No breakfast or lunch on weekends. No dinner Mon.–Wed.*

$ AMERICAN 🍴 **Wagon Wheel Coffee Shop.** This local hangout decorated with wagon wheels, cowboy hats, and lassos serves up terrific hearty breakfasts, including oatmeal and banana pancakes, eggs Benedict, and biscuits and gravy. The lunch menu includes a dozen different burgers and other sandwiches. [$] *Average main: $11* ✉ *Valley Hill Center, 7156 Carmel Valley Rd., next to Quail Lodge, Carmel* ☎ *831/624–8878* 💳 *No credit cards* 🕒 *No dinner.*

$$$ AMERICAN 🍴 **Will's Fargo.** Around since the 1920s, this restaurant calls itself a "dressed-up saloon." Steer horns and gilt-frame paintings adorn the

walls of the Victorian-style dining room; you can also eat on the patios. The menu is mainly seafood and steaks, including a 20-ounce porterhouse. [$] *Average main: $28* ✉ *16 E. Carmel Valley Rd.* ☎ *831/659–2774* 🌐 *www.bernardus.com* 🕓 *Closed Wed. No lunch Oct.–Mar.*

WHERE TO STAY

For expanded reviews, facilities, and current deals, visit Fodors.com.

$$$$ RESORT Fodor's Choice ★ 🏨 **Bernardus Lodge.** The spacious guest rooms at this luxury spa resort have vaulted ceilings, featherbeds, fireplaces, patios, and bathtubs for two. **Pros:** exceptional personal service; outstanding food and wine. **Cons:** some guests can seem snooty; pricey. **TripAdvisor:** "lovely retreat," "fantastic service," "unbelievable luxury." [$] *Rooms from: $435* ✉ *415 W. Carmel Valley Rd.* ☎ *831/658–3400, 888/648–9463* 🌐 *www.bernardus.com* 🛏 *56 rooms, 1 suite.*

$$$$ RESORT 🏨 **Carmel Valley Ranch.** Hotel scion John Pritzker bought this 500-acre all-suites resort in 2009 and committed more than $30 million to transform the property into an upscale experiential getaway. **Pros:** stunning natural setting; tons of activities; state-of-the-art amenities. **Cons:** must drive several miles to shops and nightlife; pricey. **TripAdvisor:** "quiet getaway," "lovely resort in a spectacular setting," "great place to relax." [$] *Rooms from: $275* ✉ *1 Old Ranch Rd., Carmel* ☎ 📠 *831/626–2510* ☎ *855/687–7262* 🌐 *www.carmelvalleyranch.com* 🛏 *139 suites.*

$$$$ RESORT Fodor's Choice ★ 🏨 **Stonepine Estate Resort.** Set on 330 pastoral acres, this former estate of the Crocker banking family has been converted to a luxurious inn. **Pros:** supremely exclusive. **Cons:** difficult to get a reservation; far from the coast. **TripAdvisor:** "beautiful and over the top," "a special treat," "what a fulfillment of a fantasy." [$] *Rooms from: $300* ✉ *150 E. Carmel Valley Rd.* ☎ *831/659–2245* 🌐 *www.stonepineestate.com* 🛏 *10 rooms, 2 suites, 3 cottages.*

SPAS

Refuge. Relax and recharge in a co-ed, European-style relaxation center on 2 serene acres—without breaking the bank. Heat up in the eucalyptus steam room or cedar sauna, plunge in cold pools, and relax indoors in zero-gravity chairs or outdoors in Adirondack chairs around fire pits. Repeat the cycle a few times, then lounge around the thermal waterfall pools. Talk is limited to whispers, and bathing suits are required. Optional 50-minute massages ($60) are available. ✉ *27300 Rancho San Carlos Rd., south off Carmel Valley Rd., Carmel* ☎ *831/620–7360* 🎟 *$39* 🕓 *Daily 10–10.*

SPORTS AND THE OUTDOORS

GOLF **Quail Lodge Golf Club.** The Quail Lodge Golf Club incorporates several lakes into its course. Depending on the season and day of the week, greens fees range from $75 to $150, including cart rental. ✉ *8000 Valley Greens Dr., Carmel* ☎ *831/624–2888, 831/620–8808 golf shop.*

Rancho Cañada Golf Club. Rancho Cañada Golf Club is a public course with 36 holes, some of them overlooking the Carmel River. Fees range from $40 to $70, plus $19 per rider for cart rental, depending on course and tee time. ✉ *4860 Carmel Valley Rd., 1 mile east of Hwy. 1, Carmel* ☎ *831/624–0111.*

3

17-MILE DRIVE

Fodor's Choice
★

Off North San Antonio Rd. in Carmel-by-the-Sea or off Sunset Dr. in Pacific Grove.

Primordial nature resides in quiet harmony with palatial estates along 17-Mile Drive, which winds through an 8,400-acre microcosm of the Monterey coastal landscape. Dotting the drive are rare Monterey cypress, trees so gnarled and twisted that Robert Louis Stevenson described them as "ghosts fleeing before the wind." The $9.75-per-car fee collected at the gates is well worth the price.

GETTING HERE AND AROUND

If you drive south from Monterey on Highway 1, exit at 17-Mile-Drive/Sunset Drive in Pacific Grove to find the northern entrance gate. Coming from Carmel, exit at Ocean Avenue and follow the road almost to the beach; turn right on North San Antonio Road to the Carmel Gate. You can also enter through the Highway 1 Gate at Scenic Drive/Sunridge Road. Monterey-Salinas Transit buses provide regular service in and around Pebble Beach.

EXPLORING

Bird Rock. Bird Rock, the largest of several islands at the southern end of the Monterey Peninsula Country Club's golf course, teems with harbor seals, sea lions, cormorants, and pelicans.

Crocker Marble Palace. Many of the stately homes along 17-Mile Drive reflect the classic Monterey or Spanish Mission style typical of the region. A standout is the Crocker Marble Palace, about a mile south of the Lone Cypress *(⇨ below)*. It's a private waterfront estate inspired by a Byzantine castle, easily identifiable by its dozens of marble arches.

Lone Cypress. The most-photographed tree along 17-Mile Drive is the weather-sculpted Lone Cypress, which grows out of a precipitous outcropping above the waves about 1½ miles up the road from Pebble Beach Golf Links. You can stop for a view of the Lone Cypress at a parking area, but you can't walk out to the tree.

Seal Rock. Sea creatures and birds—as well as some very friendly ground squirrels—make use of Seal Rock, the largest of a group of islands about 2 miles north of Lone Cypress.

WHERE TO STAY

For expanded reviews, facilities, and current deals, visit Fodors.com.

$$$$
RESORT
★

⬚ **Casa Palmero.** This exclusive spa resort evokes a stately Mediterranean villa. **Pros:** ultimate in pampering; more private than sister resorts; right on the golf course. **Cons:** pricey; may be *too* posh for some. **TripAdvisor:** "lovely hideaway," "pampered luxury," "amazing service in a beautiful place." $ *Rooms from: $875* ⊠ *1518 Cypress Dr.* ☎ *831/622–6650, 800/654–9300* ⊕ *www.pebblebeach.com* ➹ *21 rooms, 3 suites.*

$$$$
RESORT

⬚ **Inn at Spanish Bay.** This resort sprawls across a breathtaking stretch of shoreline, and has lush, 600-square-foot rooms. **Pros:** attentive service; tons of amenities; spectacular views. **Cons:** huge hotel; 4 miles from other Pebble Beach Resort facilities. **TripAdvisor:** "great place to stay for Pebble Beach golf," "beautiful," "simply spectacular." $ *Rooms* *from: $615* ✉ *2700 17-Mile Dr.* ☎ *831/647–7500, 800/654–9300* 🌐 *www.pebblebeach.com* ⇨ *252 rooms, 17 suites.*

$$$$ RESORT ★ 🏨 **Lodge at Pebble Beach.** All rooms have fireplaces and many have wonderful ocean views at this circa-1919 resort. **Pros:** world-class golf; borders the ocean and fairways; fabulous facilities. **Cons:** some rooms are on the small side; very pricey. **TripAdvisor:** "everything we anticipated and more," "stunning," "can't put a price on this." [$] *Rooms from: $715* ✉ *1700 17-Mile Dr.* ☎ *831/624–3811, 800/654–9300* 🌐 *www.pebblebeach.com* ⇨ *142 rooms, 19 suites.*

3

SPORTS AND THE OUTDOORS

GOLF **Links at Spanish Bay.** This course, which hugs a choice stretch of shoreline, is designed in the rugged manner of a traditional Scottish course, with sand dunes and coastal marshes interspersed among the greens. The greens fee is $260, plus $35 per person for cart rental (cart is included for resort guests); nonguests can reserve tee times up to two months in advance. ✉ *17-Mile Dr., north end* ☎ *800/654–9300.*

Pebble Beach Golf Links. Pebble Beach Golf Links attracts golfers from around the world, despite a greens fee of $495, plus $35 per person for an optional cart (complimentary cart for guests of the Pebble Beach and Spanish Bay resorts). The ocean plays a major role in the 18th hole of the famed links. Each February the course is the main site of the AT&T Pebble Beach Pro-Am, where show-business celebrities and golf pros team up for one of the nation's most glamorous tournaments. Tee times are available to guests who book a minimum two-night stay. Nonguests can reserve a tee time only one day in advance on a space-available basis (up to a year for groups); resort guests can reserve up to 18 months in advance. ✉ *17-Mile Dr., near Lodge at Pebble Beach* ☎ *800/654–9300.*

Peter Hay. A 9-hole, par-3 course, Peter Hay charges $30 per person, no reservations necessary. ✉ *17-Mile Dr.* ☎ *831/622–8723.*

Poppy Hills. Poppy Hills, a splendid 18-hole course designed in 1986 by Robert Trent Jones Jr., has a greens fee of $200; an optional cart costs $18 per person. Individuals may reserve up to one month in advance, groups up to a year. ✉ *3200 Lopez Rd., at 17-Mile Dr.* ☎ *831/625–2035* 🌐 *www.poppyhillsgolf.com.*

Spyglass Hill. Spyglass Hill is among the most challenging Pebble Beach courses. With the first five holes bordering on the Pacific and the other 13 reaching deep into the Del Monte Forest, the views offer some consolation. The greens fee is $360, and an optional cart costs $35 (the cart is complimentary for resort guests). Reservations are essential and may be made up to one month in advance (18 months for guests). ✉ *Stevenson Dr. and Spyglass Hill Rd.* ☎ *800/654–9300.*

PACIFIC GROVE

3 miles north of Carmel-by-the-Sea on Hwy. 68.

This picturesque town, which began as a summer retreat for church groups more than a century ago, recalls its prim and proper Victorian heritage in its host of tiny board-and-batten cottages and stately mansions. However, long before the church groups flocked here the area

received thousands of annual pilgrims—in the form of bright orange-and-black monarch butterflies. They still come, migrating south from Canada and the Pacific Northwest to take residence in pine and eucalyptus groves from October through March. In Butterfly Town USA, as Pacific Grove is known, the sight of a mass of butterflies hanging from the branches like a long, fluttering veil is unforgettable.

A prime way to enjoy Pacific Grove is to walk or bicycle the 3 miles of city-owned shoreline along Ocean View Boulevard, a cliff-top area landscaped with native plants and dotted with benches meant for sitting and gazing at the sea. You can spot many types of birds here, including the web-footed cormorants that crowd the massive rocks rising out of the surf. Two Victorians of note along Ocean View are the Queen Anne–style Green Gables, at No. 301—erected in 1888, it's now a B&B—and the 1909 Pryor House, at No. 429, a massive, shingled, private residence with a leaded- and beveled-glass doorway.

GETTING HERE AND AROUND
Reach Pacific Grove via Highway 68 off Highway 1, just south of Monterey. From Cannery Row in Monterey, head north until the road merges with Ocean Boulevard and follow it along the coast. MST buses travel within Pacific Grove and surrounding towns.

EXPLORING

Lovers Point Park. The coastal views are gorgeous from this waterfront park whose sheltered beach has a children's pool and a picnic area. The main lawn has a volleyball court and a snack bar. ⊠ *Ocean View Blvd. northwest of Forest Ave.* ☎ *831/648–5730.*

Monarch Grove Sanctuary. The Monarch Grove Sanctuary is a fairly reliable spot for viewing the butterflies between October and February. ⊠ *1073 Lighthouse Ave., at Ridge Rd.* ⊕ *www.pgmuseum.org.*

Pacific Grove Museum of Natural History. Contact the museum for the latest information about the butterfly population. Year-round, you can view the well-crafted butterfly tree exhibit here. ⊠ *165 Forest Ave., at Central Ave.* ☎ *831/648–5716* ⊕ *www.pgmuseum.org* ⊠ *$3 suggested donation; $5 per family* ☉ *Tues.–Sun. 10–5.*

Point Pinos Lighthouse. At the 1855-vintage Point Pinos Lighthouse, the oldest continuously operating lighthouse on the West Coast, you can learn about the lighting and foghorn operations and wander through a small museum containing U.S. Coast Guard memorabilia. ⊠ *Asilomar Ave., between Lighthouse Ave. and Del Monte Blvd.* ☎ *831/648–3176* ⊕ *www.pgmuseum.org* ⊠ *$2 suggested donation* ☉ *Thurs.–Mon. 1–4.*

BEACHES

Asilomar State Beach. Asilomar State Beach, a beautiful coastal area, stretches between Point Pinos and the Del Monte Forest. The 100 acres of dunes, tidal pools, and pocket-size beaches form one of the region's richest areas for marine life—including surfers, who migrate here most winter mornings. **Amenities:** none. **Best For:** sunrise; sunset; surfing; walking. ⊠ *Sunset Dr. and Asilomar Ave.* ☎ *831/646–6440* ⊕ *www. parks.ca.gov.*

WHERE TO EAT

$$$ ✕ **Fandango.** The menu here is mostly Mediterranean and southern
MEDITERRANEAN   French, with such dishes as calves' liver and onions and paella served
in a skillet. The decor follows suit: stone walls and country furniture
give the restaurant the earthy feel of a European farmhouse. This is
where locals come when they want to have a big dinner with friends,
drink wine, have fun, and generally feel at home. ⓢ *Average main: $25*
✉ *223 17th St., south of Lighthouse Ave.* ☏ *831/372–3456* ⊕ *www.
fandangorestaurant.com.*

$$ ✕ **Fishwife.** Fresh fish with a Latin accent makes this a favorite of locals
SEAFOOD   for lunch or a casual dinner. Standards are the sea garden salads topped
with your choice of fish and the fried seafood plates with fresh veggies.
Diners with large appetites appreciate the fisherman's bowls—fresh
fish served with rice, black beans, spicy cabbage, salsa, vegetables, and
crispy tortilla strips. ⓢ *Average main: $22* ✉ *1996½ Sunset Dr., at Asi-
lomar Blvd.* ☏ *831/375–7107* ⊕ *www.fishwife.com.*

$$$ ✕ **Joe Rombi's La Mia Cucina.** Pastas, fish, steaks, and chops are the spe-
ITALIAN   cialties at this modern trattoria, which is the best in town for Italian
food. The look is spare and clean, with colorful antique wine posters
decorating the white walls. Next door, Joe Rombi's La Piccola Casa
Pizzeria & Coffee House serves breakfast (baked goods), lunch, and
early dinner Wednesday through Sunday. ⓢ *Average main: $23* ✉ *208
17th St., at Lighthouse Ave.* ☏ *831/373–2416* ⊕ *www.joerombi.com*
⊗ *Closed Mon. and Tues. No lunch.*

$$$ ✕ **Passionfish.** South American artwork and artifacts decorate Passion-
MODERN   fish, and Latin and Asian flavors infuse the dishes. Chef Ted Walter
AMERICAN   shops at local farmers' markets several times a week to find the best
★   produce, fish, and meat available, then pairs it with creative sauces.
The menu might include crispy squid with spicy orange-cilantro vinai-
grette. ⓢ *Average main: $23* ✉ *701 Lighthouse Ave., at Congress Ave.*
☏ *831/655–3311* ⊕ *www.passionfish.net* ⊗ *No lunch.*

$ ✕ **Peppers Mexicali Cafe.** This cheerful white-walled storefront serves
MEXICAN   traditional dishes from Mexico and Latin America, with an emphasis
on fresh seafood. Excellent red and green salsas are made throughout
the day, and there's a large selection of beers, along with fresh lime margaritas. ⓢ *Average main: $15* ✉ *170 Forest Ave., between Lighthouse
and Central Aves.* ☏ *831/373–6892* ⊕ *www.peppersmexicalicafe.com*
⊗ *Closed Tues. No lunch Sun.*

$$ ✕ **Red House Café.** When it's nice out, sun pours through the big windows
AMERICAN   of this cozy restaurant and across tables on the porch; when fog rolls in,
the fireplace is lighted. The American menu changes with the seasons,
but typically includes grilled lamb fillets atop mashed potatoes for din-
ner and Dungeness crab cakes over salad for lunch. Breakfast on week-
ends is a local favorite. ⓢ *Average main: $20* ✉ *662 Lighthouse Ave.,
at 19th St.* ☏ *831/643–1060* ⊕ *www.redhousecafe.com* ⊗ *Closed Mon.*

$$ ✕ **Taste Café and Bistro.** Grilled marinated rabbit, roasted half chicken,
AMERICAN   filet mignon, and other meats are the focus at Taste, which serves hearty
European-inspired food in a casual, open-kitchen setting. ⓢ *Average
main: $20* ✉ *1199 Forest Ave.* ☏ *831/655–0324* ⊕ *www.tastecafebistro.
com* ⊗ *Closed Sun. and Mon.*

WHERE TO STAY

For expanded reviews, facilities, and current deals, visit Fodors.com.

$$$
B&B/INN
★
⌨ **Green Gables Inn.** Stained-glass windows and ornate interior details compete with spectacular ocean views at this Queen Anne–style mansion, built by a businessman for his mistress in 1888. **Pros:** exceptional views; impeccable attention to historic detail. **Cons:** some rooms are small; thin walls. **TripAdvisor:** "beautiful ocean views," "wonderful B&B," "great service." Ⓢ *Rooms from: $215 ☒ 301 Ocean View Blvd.* ☎ *831/375–2095, 800/722–1774* ⊕ *www.greengablesinnpg.com* ⤳ *10 rooms, 3 with bath; 1 suite* ⑩ *Breakfast.*

$$$
B&B/INN
⌨ **The Inn at 213 Seventeen Mile Drive.** Set in a residential area just past town, this carefully restored 1920s Craftsman-style home and cottage are surrounded by gardens and redwood, cypress, and eucalyptus trees. **Pros:** killer gourmet breakfast; historic charm; verdant gardens. **Cons:** far from restaurants and shops; few extra amenities. **TripAdvisor:** "great getaway," "great hospitality," "elegant yet cozy Craftsman charm." Ⓢ *Rooms from: $195 ☒ 213 17-Mile Dr., at Lighthouse Dr.* ☎ *831/642–9514, 800/526–5666* ⊕ *www.innat17.com* ⤳ *14 rooms* ⑩ *Breakfast.*

$$
HOTEL
⌨ **Lighthouse Lodge and Suites.** Near the tip of the peninsula, this complex straddles Lighthouse Avenue—the lodge is on one side, the all-suites Lighthouse Resort facility on the other. **Pros:** near lighthouse and 17-Mile Drive; friendly reception; many room options. **Cons:** next to a cemetery; lodge rooms are basic. **TripAdvisor:** "beautiful rooms," "perfect," "a regular guest for 10 years." Ⓢ *Rooms from: $139 ☒ 1150 and 1249 Lighthouse Ave.* ☎ *831/655–2111, 800/858–1249* ⊕ *www. lhls.com* ⤳ *64 rooms, 31 suites* ⑩ *Breakfast.*

$$$
B&B/INN
⌨ **Martine Inn.** The glassed-in parlor and many guest rooms at this 1899 Mediterranean-style villa have stunning ocean views; thoughtful details such as robes, rocking chairs, and nightly turndown create an ambience of luxuriant comfort. **Pros:** romantic; fancy breakfast; ocean views. **Cons:** not child-friendly; sits on a busy thoroughfare. **TripAdvisor:** "beautiful spot," "pure heaven," "friendly hospitable attention to detail." Ⓢ *Rooms from: $199 ☒ 255 Ocean View Blvd.* ☎ *831/373–3388, 800/852–5588* ⊕ *www.martineinn.com* ⤳ *25 rooms* ⑩ *Breakfast.*

MONTEREY

2 miles southeast of Pacific Grove via Lighthouse Ave.; 2 miles north of Carmel-by-the-Sea via Hwy. 1.

Early in the 20th century Carmel Martin, the first mayor of the city of Monterey, saw a bright future for his town: "Monterey Bay is the one place where people can live without being disturbed by manufacturing and big factories. I am certain that the day is coming when this will be the most desirable place in the whole state of California." His Honor was not far off the mark.

GETTING HERE AND AROUND

From San Jose or San Francisco, take U.S. 101 south to Highway 156 West at Prunedale. Head west about 8 miles to Highway 1 and follow it about 15 miles south. From San Luis Obispo, take U.S. 101 north to Salinas and drive west on Highway 68 about 20 miles.

Many MST bus lines connect at the Monterey Transit Center, at Pearl Street and Munras Avenue. In summer (daily from 10 until at least 7), the free MST Monterey Trolley travels from downtown Monterey along Cannery Row to the Aquarium and back.

ESSENTIALS

Visitor Information Monterey County Convention & Visitors Bureau
☎ *877/666–8373* ⊕ *www.seemonterey.com.*

EXPLORING

TOP ATTRACTIONS

Cannery Row. When John Steinbeck published the novel *Cannery Row* in 1945, he immortalized a place of rough-edged working people. The waterfront street, edging a mile of gorgeous coastline, once was crowded with sardine canneries processing, at their peak, nearly 200,000 tons of the smelly silver fish a year. During the mid-1940s, however, the sardines disappeared from the bay, causing the canneries to close. Through the years the old tin-roof canneries have been converted into restaurants, art galleries, and malls with shops selling T-shirts, fudge, and plastic sea otters. Recent tourist development along the row has been more tasteful, however, and includes several stylish inns and hotels, wine tasting rooms, and upscale specialty shops. ⊠ *Cannery Row, between Reeside and David Aves.* ⊕ *www.canneryrow.com.*

Colton Hall. A convention of delegates met here in 1849 to draft the first state constitution. The stone building, which has served as a school, a courthouse, and the county seat, is a city-run museum furnished as it was during the constitutional convention. The extensive grounds outside the hall surround the Old Monterey Jail. ⊠ *570 Pacific St., between Madison and Jefferson Sts.* ☎ *831/646–5640* ⊕ *www.monterey.org/museums* ⊠ *Free* ☉ *Daily 10–4.*

Cooper-Molera Adobe. The restored 2-acre complex includes a house dating from the 1820s, a bookstore, and a large garden enclosed by a high adobe wall. The mostly Victorian-era antiques and memorabilia that fill the house provide a glimpse into the life of a prosperous sea merchant's family. If the house is closed, you can still stop by the visitor center and pick up walking-tour maps and stroll the grounds. ⊠ *Monterey State Historic Park, Polk and Munras Sts.* ☎ *831/649–7111* ⊕ *www.parks. ca.gov/mshp* ⊠ *$5* ☉ *Store open 10–4; tours on weekends, call for hrs.*

Custom House. Built by the Mexican government in 1827 and now California's oldest standing public building, the Custom House was the first stop for sea traders whose goods were subject to duties. In 1846, Commodore John Sloat raised the American flag over this adobe structure and claimed California for the United States. The house is presently closed (state budget cuts), but you can visit the cactus gardens

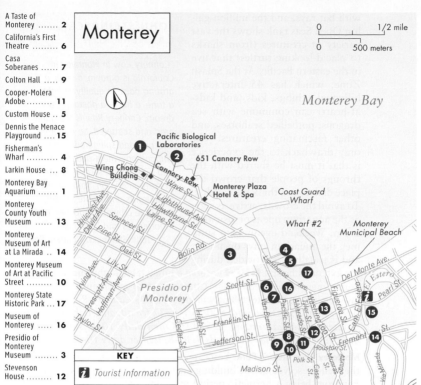

Monterey

0 _____ 1/2 mile
0 _____ 500 meters

Monterey Bay

Pacific Biological Laboratories ❶

❷ 651 Cannery Row

Wing Chong Building

Cannery Row

Wave St.

Monterey Plaza Hotel & Spa

Coast Guard Wharf

Lighthouse Ave.

Hawthorne St.

Laine St.

Wharf #2

Monterey Municipal Beach

Hillcrest Ave.

David Ave.

Spencer St.

Pine St.

Oak St.

Bolio Rd.

❸

❹
❺

Lighthouse Ave.

❶❼

Del Monte Ave.

El Estero

Pearl St.

Lily St.

Irving Ave.

Prescott Ave.

Hoffman Ave.

Presidio of Monterey

Scott St.

❻ ❶❻
❼

Pacific St.

Van Buren St.

Foam St.

Lyndon Ave.

Washington St.

Alvarado St.

Fremont St.

Fidora St.

Calle Principal

El Estero

Taylor Ave.

Cedar St.

High St.

Franklin St.

Jefferson St.

❶❸

❶❷

❷

Houston St.

Abrego St.

Madison St.

Polk St.

❽
❾ ❶❶
❿

Cass St.

Munras Ave.

❶❺

❶❹

Via Mirada

KEY

Tourist information

and stroll the plaza. ✉ *Monterey State Historic Park, 1 Custom House Plaza, across from Fisherman's Wharf* ☎ *831/649–7118* ⊕ *www.parks. ca.gov/mshp* 🎟 *Free.*

🕐 **Fisherman's Wharf.** The mournful barking of sea lions provides a steady sound track all along Monterey's waterfront, but the best way to actu ally view the whiskered marine mammals is to walk along one of the two piers across from Custom House Plaza. Lined with souvenir shops, the wharf is undeniably touristy, but it's lively and entertaining. At Wharf No. 2, a working municipal pier, you can see the day's catch being unloaded from fishing boats on one side, and fishermen casting their lines into the water on the other. The pier has a couple of low-key restaurants, from whose seats lucky customers may spot otters and harbor seals. ✉ *At end of Calle Principal* ⊕ *www.montereywharf.com.*

🕐 **Monterey Bay Aquarium.** The minute you hand over your ticket at this
Fodor's Choice extraordinary aquarium you're surrounded by sea creatures; right at
★ the entrance, you can see dozens of them swimming in a three-story-tall, sunlit kelp forest tank. The beauty of the exhibits here is that they are all designed to give a sense of what it's like to be in the water with the animals—sardines swim around your head in a circular tank, and jellyfish drift in and out of view in dramatically lighted spaces that suggest the ocean depths. A petting pool gives you a hands-on experience

with bat rays, and the million-gallon Open Seas tank shows the vast variety of creatures (from sharks to placid-looking turtles) that live in the eastern Pacific. At the Splash Zone, which has 45 interactive bilingual exhibits, kids (and kids-at-heart) can commune with sea dragons, potbellied seahorses, and other fascinating creatures. The only drawback to the experience is that it must be shared with the throngs of people that crowd the place daily; most think it's worth it. To avoid the crowds, arrive as soon as the aquarium opens or visit after 2 pm. Weekend evenings in summer, the aquarium stays open later and is usually less crowded during the extended hours. ■TIP➔ Reserve a lunch table at the aquarium's restaurant, perched on ocean's edge. Otters and other sea creatures often frolic just outside the floor-to-ceiling windows. ⌂ *886 Cannery Row, at David Ave.* ☎ *800/555–3656 info, 800/756–3737 for advance tickets* ⊕ *www. montereybayaquarium.org* ⌨ *$33* ⊙ *Open daily 10–6; summer/holidays 9:30–6; summer weekends 9:30–8; winter daily 10–5.*

> ## JOHN STEINBECK'S CANNERY ROW
>
> *"Cannery Row in Monterey in California is a poem, a stink, a grating noise, a quality of light, a tone, a habit, a nostalgia, a dream. Cannery Row is the gathered and scattered, tin and iron and rust and splintered wood, chipped pavement and weedy lots and junk heaps, sardine canneries of corrugated iron, honky tonks, restaurants and whore houses, and little crowded groceries, and laboratories and flophouses."*
>
> —John Steinbeck, *Cannery Row*

Monterey State Historic Park. You can glimpse Monterey's early history in the well-preserved adobe buildings scattered along several city blocks. Far from being a hermetic period museum, the park facilities are an integral part of the day-to-day business life of the town—within some of the buildings are a store, a theater, and government offices. At some of the historic houses, the gardens (open daily 10 to 5 in summer, 10 to 4 the rest of the year) are worthy sights themselves. ■TIP➔ At this writing, many buildings are closed and tours on hiatus due to state park budget cuts. Visit the park's website for up-to-date information. ⌂ *20 Custom House Plaza* ☎ *831/649–7118* ⊕ *www.parks.ca.gov/mshp* ⌨ *Free* ⊙ *Call for hrs.*

Museum of Monterey. The former Monterey Maritime Museum still displays maritime artifacts but has expanded its focus to include art, photography, and costumes from Monterey's earliest days to the present. The jewel in the museum's crown remains the enormous Fresnel lens from the Point Sur Light Station. ⌂ *Stanton Center, 5 Custom House Plaza* ☎ *831/372–2608* ⊕ *museumofmonterey.org* ⌨ *$10. Free 1st Tues. of month* ⊙ *Tues.–Sat. 10–5, Sun. noon–5.*

WORTH NOTING

A Taste of Monterey. Without driving the back roads, you can taste the wines of more than 90 area vintners while taking in fantastic bay views. Purchase a few bottles and pick up a map and guide to the county's wineries and vineyards. ⌂ *700 Cannery Row, Suite KK* ☎ *831/646–5446, 888/646–5446* ⊕ *www.tastemonterey.com* ⌨ *Wine tastings $10–$20* ⊙ *Daily 11–6.*

Trained "seals" that perform in circuses are actually California sea lions, intelligent, social animals that live (and sleep) close together in groups.

California's First Theatre. This adobe began its life in 1846 as a saloon and lodging house for sailors. Four years later stage curtains were fashioned from army blankets, and some U.S. officers staged plays to the light of whale oil lamps. As of this writing, the building is not open but you can stroll in the garden. ⊠ *Monterey State Historic Park, Scott and Pacific Sts.* ☎ *831/649–7118* ⊕ *www.parks.ca.gov/mshp* ☎ *Free* ⊙ *Call for hrs.*

Casa Soberanes. A classic low-ceiling adobe structure built in 1842, this was once a Custom House guard's residence. The building is closed, but you can visit the peaceful rear garden and its rose-covered arbor. ⊠ *Monterey State Historic Park, 336 Pacific St., at Del Monte Ave.* ☎ *831/649–7118* ⊕ *www.parks.ca.gov/mshp* ☎ *Free.*

☺ **Dennis the Menace Playground.** This play area was designed by the late cartoonist Hank Ketcham. The equipment is on a grand scale and made for Dennis-like daredevils: there's a roller slide, a clanking suspension bridge, and a real Southern Pacific steam locomotive. You can rent a rowboat or a paddleboat for cruising around U-shaped Lake El Estero, populated with an assortment of ducks, mud hens, and geese. ⊠ *El Estero Park, Pearl St. and Camino El Estero* ☎ *831/646–3866* ⊙ *Daily 10–dusk in summer* ⊙ *Closed Tues., Sept.–May.*

Larkin House. A veranda encircles the second floor of this 1835 adobe, whose design bears witness to the Mexican and New England influences on the Monterey style. Many of the antiques inside were brought from New Hampshire by the building's namesake, Thomas O. Larkin, an early California statesman. The building is closed weekdays, but you can peek in the windows and stroll the gardens. ⊠ *Monterey State Historic Park, 464 Calle Principal, between Jefferson and Pacific Sts.*

☎ *831/649–7118*   ⊕ *www.parks. ca.gov/mshp* ▨*$5* ☉ *Weekends; call for hrs.*

🔥 **Monterey County Youth Museum (MY Museum).** Monterey Bay comes to life from a child's perspective in this fun-filled, interactive indoor exploration center. The seven exhibit galleries showcase the science and nature of the Big Sur coast, theater arts, Pebble Beach golf, and beaches. There's also a live-performance theater, a creation station, a hospital emergency room, and an agriculture corner where kids fol-

MONTEREY: FORMER CAPITAL OF CALIFORNIA

In 1602 Spanish explorer Sebastián Vizcaíno stepped ashore on a remote California peninsula. He named it after the viceroy of New Spain—Count de Monte Rey. Soon the Spanish built a military outpost, and the site was the capital of California until the state came under American rule.

low artichokes, strawberries, and other fruits and veggies on their evolution from sprout to harvest to farmers' markets. ✉ *425 Washington St., between E. Franklin St. and Bonifacio Pl.* ☎ *831/649–6444* ⊕ *www. mymuseum.org* ▨*$7* ☉ *Tues.–Sat. 10–5, Sun. noon–5.*

Monterey Museum of Art at La Mirada. Asian and European antiques fill this 19th-century adobe house. A newer 10,000-square-foot gallery space, designed by Charles Moore, houses Asian and California regional art. Outdoors are magnificent rose and rhododendron gardens. ✉ *720 Via Mirada, at Fremont St.* ☎ *831/372–3689* ⊕ *www.montereyart. org* ▨*$10, also good for admission to museum's Pacific Street facility* ☉ *Wed.–Sat. 11–5, Sun. 1–4.*

Monterey Museum of Art at Pacific Street. Photographs by Ansel Adams and Edward Weston, as well as works by other artists who have spent time on the peninsula, are on display here, along with international folk art, from Kentucky hearth brooms to Tibetan prayer wheels. ✉ *559 Pacific St., across from Colton Hall* ☎ *831/372–5477* ⊕ *www.montereyart. org* ▨*$10, also good for admission to museum's La Mirada facility* ☉ *Wed.–Sat. 11–5, Sun. 1–4.*

Presidio of Monterey Museum. This spot has been significant for centuries. Its first incarnation was as a Native American village for the Rumsien tribe. The Spanish explorer Sebastián Vizcaíno landed here in 1602, and Father Junípero Serra arrived in 1770. Notable battles fought here include the 1818 skirmish in which the corsair Hipólito Bruchard conquered the Spanish garrison that stood on this site and claimed part of California for Argentina. The indoor museum tells the stories; plaques mark the outdoor sites. ✉ *Presidio of Monterey, Corporal Ewing Rd., off Lighthouse Ave.* ☎ *831/646–3456* ⊕ *www.monterey.org/museums* ▨*Free* ☉ *Mon. 10–1, Thurs.–Sat. 10–4, Sun. 1–4.*

Stevenson House. This house was named in honor of author Robert Louis Stevenson, who boarded here briefly in a tiny upstairs room. Items from his family's estate furnish Stevenson's room; period-decorated chambers elsewhere in the house include a gallery of memorabilia and a children's nursery stocked with Victorian toys and games. ✉ *Monterey State His-*

CLOSE UP

The Underwater Kingdom

Although Monterey's coastal landscapes are stunning, their beauty is more than equaled by the wonders that lie offshore. The huge Monterey Bay National Marine Sanctuary—which stretches 276 miles, from north of San Francisco almost all the way down to Santa Barbara—teems with abundant life, and has topography as diverse as that aboveground.

The preserve's 5,322 square miles include vast submarine canyons, which reach down 10,663 feet at their deepest point. They also encompass dense forests of giant kelp—a kind of seaweed that can grow more than a hundred feet from its roots on the ocean floor. These kelp forests are especially robust off Monterey.

The sanctuary was established in 1992 to protect the habitat of the many species that thrive in the bay. Some animals can be seen quite easily from land. In summer and winter you might glimpse the offshore spray of gray whales as they migrate between their summer feeding grounds in Alaska and their breeding grounds in Baja. Clouds of marine birds—including white-faced ibis, three types of albatross, and more than 15 types of gull—skim the waves, or roost in the rock islands along 17-Mile Drive. Sea otters dart and gambol in the calmer waters of the bay; and of course, you can watch the sea lions—and hear their round-the-clock barking—on the wharves in Santa Cruz and Monterey.

The sanctuary supports many other creatures, however, that remain unseen by most on-land visitors. Some of these are enormous, such as the giant blue whales that arrive to feed on plankton in summer; others, like the more than 22 species of red algae in these waters, are microscopic. So whether you choose to visit the Monterey Bay Aquarium, take a whale-watch trip, or look out to sea with your binoculars, remember you're seeing just a small part of a vibrant underwater kingdom.

toric Park, 530 Houston St., near Pearl St. ☎ *831/649–7118* 🌐 *www.parks.ca.gov/mshp* 🎟 *Free* 🕒 *Sat. 1–4 and last Sun. of month 1–4.*

WHERE TO EAT

$ AMERICAN 🍴 **Café Lumiere.** Attached to the lobby of Monterey's art-house cinema, this café shows work by local artists. Eat a light breakfast, lunch, or dinner; order beer on tap; drink coffee; or choose a pot of tea from the extensive selection. The menu includes baked goods, cakes, sandwiches, granola, and other breakfast items. Most patrons bring their laptops for the free Wi-Fi, and most tables are shared. Close to downtown bars, it's open until 10 pm. [$] *Average main: $8* ✉ *365 Calle Principal* ☎ *831/920–2451.*

$$ SEAFOOD 🍴 **Monterey's Fish House.** Casual yet stylish and always packed, this seafood restaurant is removed from the hubbub of the wharf. If the dining room is full, you can wait at the bar and savor deliciously plump oysters on the half shell. The bartenders and waitstaff will gladly advise you on the perfect wine to go with your poached, blackened, or oak-grilled

seafood. [$] *Average main: $21* ✉ *2114 Del Monte Ave., at Dela Vina St.* ☎ *831/373–4647* ✍ *Reservations essential* 🕒 *No lunch weekends.*

$$$ AMERICAN Fodor's Choice ★ 🍴 **Montrio Bistro.** This quirky, converted firehouse, with its rawhide walls and iron indoor trellises, has a wonderfully sophisticated menu. Chef Tony Baker uses organic produce and meats and sustainably sourced seafood to create imaginative dishes that reflect local agriculture, such as baby artichoke risotto fritters, and pesto-rubbed prime sirloin with marinated prawns, spinach, and a red wine–veal reduction sauce. The wine list also draws primarily on California—Monterey-area wineries are well represented—and signature cocktails are infused with local fruits, herbs, and veggies. [$] *Average main: $24* ✉ *414 Calle Principal, at W. Franklin St.* ☎ *831/648–8880* 🌐 *www.montrio.com* ✍ *Reservations essential* 🕒 *No lunch.*

$ AMERICAN 🍴 **Old Monterey Café.** Breakfast here gets constant local raves. The café's fame rests on familiar favorites: a dozen kinds of omelets, and pancakes from blueberry to cinnamon-raisin-pecan. For lunch are good soups, salads, and sandwiches. This is a fine place to relax with an afternoon cappuccino. [$] *Average main: $12* ✉ *489 Alvarado St., at Munras Ave.* ☎ *831/646–1021* 🌐 *www.cafemonterey.com/about.html* ✍ *Reservations not accepted* 🕒 *No dinner.*

$$ AMERICAN 🍴 **Tarpy's Roadhouse.** Fun, dressed-up American favorites—a little something for everyone—are served in this renovated early-1900s stone farmhouse several miles east of town. The kitchen cranks out everything from Cajun-spiced prawns to meat loaf with marsala-mushroom gravy to grilled ribs and steaks. Eat indoors by a fireplace or outdoors in the courtyard. [$] *Average main: $22* ✉ *2999 Monterey–Salinas Hwy., Hwy. 68* ☎ *831/647–1444* 🌐 *www.tarpys.com.*

WHERE TO STAY

For expanded reviews, facilities, and current deals, visit Fodors.com.

$$ RESORT 🏨 **Best Western Beach Resort Monterey.** With a great waterfront location about 2 miles north of Monterey—with views of the bay and the city skyline—and a surprising array of amenities, this hotel is one of the area's best values. **Pros:** on the beach; great value; family-friendly. **Cons:** several miles from major attractions; big-box mall neighborhood. **TripAdvisor:** "can't get any closer to the beach," "great location," "amazing view." [$] *Rooms from: $159* ✉ *2600 Sand Dunes Dr.* ☎ *831/394–3321, 800/242–8627* 🌐 *www.montereybeachresort.com* 🛏 *196 rooms.*

$$$ RESORT 👶 🏨 **InterContinental The Clement Monterey.** Spectacular bay views, assiduous service, a slew of upscale amenities, and a superb waterfront location next to the aquarium propelled this full-service luxury hotel to immediate stardom. **Pros:** a block from the aquarium; fantastic views from some rooms; great for families. **Cons:** a tad formal; not budget-friendly. **TripAdvisor:** "amazing views," "excellent service," "comfortable." [$] *Rooms from: $225* ✉ *750 Cannery Row* ☎ *831/375–4500, 866/781–2406 toll free* 🌐 *www.ictheclementmonterey.com* 🛏 *192 rooms, 16 suites.*

$$ HOTEL ★ 🏨 **Monterey Bay Lodge.** Location (on the edge of Monterey's El Estero Park) and superior amenities give this cheerful facility an edge over

other motels in town. **Pros:** within walking distance of beach and playground; quiet at night; good family choice. **Cons:** near busy boulevard. **TripAdvisor:** "can't be beat," "good value," "great location." [$] *Rooms from: $129* ✉ *55 Camino Aguajito* ☎ *831/372–8057, 800/558–1900* 🌐 *www.montereybaylodge.com* 🛏 *43 rooms, 3 suites.*

THE FIRST ARTICHOKE QUEEN

Castroville, a tiny town off Highway 1 between Monterey and Watsonville, produces about 95% of U.S. artichokes. Back in 1948, the town chose its first queen to preside during its Artichoke Festival—a beautiful young woman named Norma Jean Mortenson, who later changed her name to Marilyn Monroe.

$$$$ HOTEL 🏨 **Monterey Plaza Hotel and Spa.** This hotel commands a waterfront location on Cannery Row, where you can see frolicking sea otters from the wide outdoor patio and many room balconies. **Pros:** on the ocean; lots of amenities; attentive service. **Cons:** touristy area; heavy traffic. **TripAdvisor:** "excellent service," "great experience," "out of this world." [$] *Rooms from: $279* ✉ *400 Cannery Row* ☎ *831/646–1700, 800/334–3999* 🌐 *www.montereyplazahotel.com* 🛏 *280 rooms, 10 suites.*

$$$$ B&B/INN Fodor's Choice ★ 🏨 **Old Monterey Inn.** This three-story manor house was the home of Monterey's first mayor, and today it remains a private enclave within walking distance of downtown. **Pros:** gorgeous gardens; refined luxury; serene. **Cons:** must drive to attractions and sights; fills quickly. **TripAdvisor:** "luxurious retreat," "welcoming and relaxing," "literally the best of the best." [$] *Rooms from: $269* ✉ *500 Martin St.* ☎ *831/375–8284, 800/350–2344* 🌐 *www.oldmontereyinn.com* 🛏 *6 rooms, 3 suites, 1 cottage* 🍴 *Breakfast.*

$ HOTEL 🏨 **Quality Inn Monterey.** This attractive motel has a friendly, country-inn feeling. **Pros:** indoor pool; bargain rates; cheerful innkeepers. **Cons:** street is busy during the day; some rooms are dark. **TripAdvisor:** "exceptional quality," "genuinely awesome staff," "quaint accommodation gem." [$] *Rooms from: $105* ✉ *1058 Munras Ave.* ☎ *831/372–3381* 🌐 *www.qualityinnmonterey.com* 🛏 *55 rooms* 🍴 *Breakfast.*

$$$ HOTEL 🏨 **Spindrift Inn.** This boutique hotel on Cannery Row has beach access and a rooftop garden that overlooks the water. **Pros:** close to aquarium; steps from the beach; friendly staff. **Cons:** throngs of visitors outside; can be noisy; not good for families. **TripAdvisor:** "very romantic," "a heavenly place on the ocean," "nice and cozy." [$] *Rooms from: $200* ✉ *652 Cannery Row* ☎ *831/646–8900, 800/841–1879* 🌐 *www.spindriftinn.com* 🛏 *45 rooms* 🍴 *Breakfast.*

THE ARTS

Bruce Ariss Wharf Theater. American musicals past and present are the focus here, with dramas and comedies also in the mix. ✉ *1 Fisherman's Wharf* ☎ *831/649–2332.*

★ **Dixieland Monterey.** Traditional jazz bands play waterfront venues during this festival, held on the first full weekend of March. ☎ *831/675–0298, 888/349–6879* 🌐 *www.dixieland-monterey.com.*

Monterey Bay Blues Festival. Blues fans flock to the Monterey Fairgrounds for this festival, held the last weekend in June. ☎ *831/394–2652* ⊕ *www. montereyblues.com.*

Monterey Jazz Festival. The world's oldest jazz festival attracts top-name performers to the Monterey Fairgrounds on the third full weekend of September. ☎ *888/248–6499 ticket office, 831/373–3366* ⊕ *www. montereyjazzfestival.org.*

SPORTS AND THE OUTDOORS

Throughout most of the year, the Monterey Bay area is a haven for those who love tennis, golf, surfing, fishing, biking, hiking, scuba diving, and kayaking. In the rainy winter months, when the waves grow larger, adventurous surfers flock to the water.

Monterey Bay National Marine Sanctuary. The sanctuary, home to mammals, seabirds, fishes, invertebrates, and plants, encompasses a 276-mile shoreline and 5,322 square miles of ocean. Ringed by beaches and campgrounds, it's a place for kayaking, whale-watching, scuba diving, and other water sports. ☎ *831/647–4201* ⊕ *montereybay.noaa.gov.*

BICYCLING

Adventures by the Sea, Inc. You can rent surreys and tandem and standard bicycles from Adventures by the Sea, which also offers bike tours. ⊠ *299 Cannery Row* ☎ *831/372–1807, 831/648–7236* ⊕ *adventuresbythesea. com* ⊠ *210 Alvarado Mall* ⊠ *Stillwater Cove, 17-Mile Drive, Pebble Beach* ⊠ *Beach at Lovers Point, Pacific Grove.*

Bay Bikes. For bicycle and surrey rentals and tours, visit Bay Bikes. ⊠ *585 Cannery Row* ☎ *831/655–2453* ⊕ *www.baybikes.com.*

FISHING

Randy's Fishing and Whale Watching Trips. A family-run business, Randy's has been in business since 1949. ⊠ *66 Fisherman's Wharf* ☎ *831/372–7440, 800/251–7440* ⊕ *www.randysfishingtrips.com.*

SCUBA DIVING

Monterey Bay waters never warm to the temperatures of their Southern California counterparts (the warmest they get is the low 60s), but that's one reason why the marine life here is among the world's most diverse.

Aquarius Dive Shop. Staffers at Aquarius give diving lessons and tours, and rent equipment. The diving-conditions information line is updated daily. ⊠ *2040 Del Monte Ave.* ☎ *831/375–1933, 831/657–1020 diving conditions* ⊕ *www.aquariusdivers.com.*

WALKING

Monterey Bay Coastal Trail. From Custom House Plaza, you can walk along the coast in either direction on this 29-mile-long trail for spectacular views of the sea. The trail runs from north of Monterey to Pacific Grove, with sections continuing around Pebble Beach. ☎ *831/372–3196* ⊕ *www.mtycounty.com/pgs-parks/bike-path.html.*

WHALE-WATCHING

Thousands of gray whales pass close by the Monterey Coast on their annual migration between the Bering Sea and Baja California. The gigantic creatures are sometimes visible through binoculars from shore, but a whale-watching cruise is the best way to get a close look at these magnificent mammals. The migration south takes place from December through March; January is prime viewing time. The whales migrate north from March through June. In addition, some 2,000 blue whales and 600 humpbacks pass the coast and are easily spotted in late summer and early fall.

★ **Monterey Bay Whale Watch.** The marine biologists here lead three- to five-hour whale-watching tours. ⊠ *84 Fisherman's Wharf* ☎ *831/375–4658* ⊕ *www.montereybaywhalewatch.com.*

Princess Monterey Whale Watching. Tours are offered daily on a 150-passenger high-speed cruiser and a large 75-foot boat. ⊠ *96 Fisherman's Wharf #1* ☎ *831/372–2203, 800/979–3370* ⊕ *www.montereywhalewatching. com.*

AROUND MONTEREY BAY

As Highway 1 follows the curve of the bay between Monterey and Santa Cruz, it passes through a rich agricultural zone. Opening right onto the bay, where the Salinas and Pajaro rivers drain into the Pacific, a broad valley brings together fertile soil, an ideal climate, and a good water supply to create optimum growing conditions for crops such as strawberries, artichokes, brussels sprouts, and broccoli. Several beautiful beaches line this part of the coast. Salinas and Moss Landing are in Monterey County; the other cities and towns covered here are in Santa Cruz County.

GETTING HERE AND AROUND

All the towns in this area are on or just off Highway 1. MST buses serve Monterey County destinations, connecting in Watsonville with Santa Cruz METRO buses, which operate throughout Santa Cruz County.

SALINAS

17 miles east of Monterey on Hwy. 68.

Salinas, a hard-working city surrounded by vineyards and fruit and vegetable fields, honors the memory and literary legacy of John Steinbeck, its most famous native, with the National Steinbeck Center. The facility spurred the revival of Old Town Salinas, where renovated turn-of-the-20th-century stone buildings house shops and restaurants.

ESSENTIALS

Transportation Information Salinas Amtrak Station ⊠ *30 Railroad Ave., Salinas* ☎ *800/872-7245.*

Visitor Information Salinas Valley Chamber of Commerce ⊠ *119 E. Alisal St., Salinas* ☎ *831/751-7725* ⊕ *www.salinaschamber.com.*

EXPLORING

National Steinbeck Center. The center's exhibits document the life of Pulitzer- and Nobel-prize winner John Steinbeck and the history of the nearby communities that inspired novels such as *East of Eden.* Highlights include reproductions of the green pickup-camper from *Travels with Charley* and of the bunkroom from *Of Mice and Men.* **Steinbeck House,** the author's Victorian birthplace, at 132 Central Avenue, is two blocks from the center in a so-so neighborhood. Now a decent lunch spot, it displays memorabilia. ✉ *1 Main St., at Central Ave.* ☎ *831/775–4721* 🌐 *www.steinbeck.org* 🎟 *$11* 🕒 *Daily 10–5.*

MOSS LANDING

17 miles north of Monterey on Hwy. 1; 12 miles north of Salinas on Highway 183.

Moss Landing is not much more than a couple of blocks of cafés and restaurants, art galleries, and studios plus a busy fishing port, but therein lies its charm. It's a fine place to overnight or stop for a meal and get a dose of nature.

GETTING HERE AND AROUND

From Highway 1 north or south, exit at Moss Landing Road on the ocean side. MST buses serve Moss Landing via Watsonville.

ESSENTIALS

Visitor Information Moss Landing Chamber of Commerce ☎ *831/633–4501* 🌐 *www.mosslandingchamber.com.*

EXPLORING

★ **Elkhorn Slough National Estuarine Research Reserve.** In the Elkhorn Slough National Estuarine Research Reserve, 1,400 acres of tidal flats and salt marshes form a complex environment that supports some 300 species of birds. A walk along the meandering waterways and wetlands can reveal hawks, white-tailed kites, owls, herons, and egrets. Sea otters, sharks, rays, and many other animals also live or visit here. On weekends, guided walks from the visitor center to the heron rookery begin at 10 and 1. ✉ *1700 Elkhorn Rd.* ☎ *831/728–2822* 🌐 *www.elkhornslough.org* 🎟 *$4* 🕒 *Wed.–Sun. 9–5.*

WHERE TO EAT AND STAY

For expanded reviews, facilities, and current deals, visit Fodors.com.

$ SEAFOOD 🍴 **Phil's Fish Market & Eatery.** Exquisitely fresh, simply prepared seafood (try the cioppino) is on the menu at this warehouselike restaurant on the harbor; all kinds of glistening fish are for sale at the market in the front. ■ **TIP→** Phil's Snack Shack, a tiny sandwich-and-smoothie joint, serves quicker meals at the north end of town. [$] *Average main: $15* ✉ *7600 Sandholdt Rd.* ☎ *831/633–2152* 🌐 *www.philsfishmarket.com.*

$$ B&B/INN 🏨 **Captain's Inn.** Commune with nature and pamper yourself with upscale creature comforts at this green-certified getaway in the heart of town. **Pros:** walk to restaurants and shops; tranquil natural setting; homey atmosphere **Cons:** rooms in historic building don't have water views; far from urban amenities; not appropriate for young children. **TripAdvisor:** "beautiful views," "excellent hospitality," "a quiet getaway."

§ *Rooms from: $165* ⊠ *8122 Moss Landing Rd.* ☎ *831/633–5550*
⊕ *www.captainsinn.com* ↶ *10 rooms* ❏ *Breakfast.*

SPORTS AND THE OUTDOORS

Elkhorn Slough Safari. This outfit's naturalists lead two-hour tours of Elkhorn Sough aboard a 27-foot pontoon boat. Reservations are required. ⊠ *Moss Landing Harbor* ☎ *831/633–5555* ⊕ *www.elkhornslough.com* ⬚ *$35.*

WATSONVILLE

3

7 miles north of Moss Landing on Hwy. 1.

If ever a city was built on berries, Watsonville is it. Produce has long driven the economy here, and this is where the Santa Cruz County Fair takes place each September.

GETTING HERE AND AROUND

From Santa Cruz or Monterey, follow Highway 1 to Watsonville. From U.S. 101, take Highway 152 West from Gilroy (a curving but scenic road over the mountains) or Highway 129 West from just north of San Juan Bautista. MST and Santa Cruz METRO buses connect at the Watsonville Transit Center, at Rodriguez Street and West Lake Avenue.

EXPLORING

🜂 **Agricultural History Project.** One feature of the Santa Cruz County Fairgrounds is the Agricultural History Project, which preserves the history of farming in the Pajaro Valley. In the Codiga Center and Museum you can examine antique tractors and milking machines, peruse an exhibit on the era when Watsonville was the "frozen food capital of the West," and watch experts restore farm implements and vehicles. ⊠ *2601 E. Lake Ave., Hwy. 152, at Carlton Rd.* ☎ *831/724–5898* ⊕ *www. aghistoryproject.org* ⬚ *$2 suggested donation* ☉ *Thurs.–Sun. noon–4.*

🜂 **Watsonville Fly-in & Air Show.** Every Labor Day weekend, aerial performers execute elaborate aerobatics at the Watsonville Fly-in & Air Show. More than 300 classic, experimental, and military aircraft are on display; concerts and other events fill three days. ⊠ *Watsonville Municipal Airport, 100 Aviation Way* ☎ *831/763–5600* ⊕ *www.watsonvilleflyin. org* ⬚ *$15.*

APTOS

7 miles north of Watsonville on Hwy. 1.

Backed by a redwood forest and facing the sea, downtown Aptos—known as Aptos Village—is a place of wooden walkways and false-fronted shops. Antiques dealers cluster along Trout Gulch Road, off Soquel Drive east of Highway 1.

GETTING HERE AND AROUND

Use Highway 1 to reach Aptos from Santa Cruz or Monterey. Exit at State Park Drive to reach the main shopping hub and Aptos Village. You can also exit at Freedom Boulevard or Rio del Mar. Soquel Drive is the main artery through town.

SAN JUAN BAUTISTA

About as close to early-19th-century California as you can get, San Juan Bautista (15 miles east of Watsonville on Highway 156) has been protected from development since 1933, when much of it became a state park. Small antiques shops and restaurants occupy the Old West and art-deco buildings that line 3rd Street.

The wide green plaza of San Juan Bautista State Historic Park is ringed by 18th- and 19th-century buildings, many of them open to the public.

The cemetery of the long, low, colonnaded mission church contains the unmarked graves of more than 4,300 Native American converts. Nearby is an adobe home furnished with Spanish-colonial antiques, a hotel frozen in the 1860s, a blacksmith shop, a stable, a pioneer cabin, and a jailhouse.

The first Saturday of each month, costumed volunteers engage in quilting bees, tortilla making, and other frontier activities. 🌐 *www.san-juan-bautista.ca.us.*

ESSENTIALS

Visitor Information **Aptos Chamber of Commerce** ✉ *7605-A Old Dominion Ct.* ☎ *831/688–1467* 🌐 *www.aptoschamber.com.*

BEACHES

Seacliff State Beach. Sandstone bluffs tower above popular Seacliff State Beach. You can fish off the pier, which leads out to a sunken World War I tanker ship built of concrete. **Amenities:** food and drink; lifeguards; parking (fee); showers; toilets. **Best For:** sunset; swimming; walking. ✉ *201 State Park Dr., off Hwy. 1* ☎ *831/685–6442* 🌐 *www.parks.ca.gov* 🎟 *$10 per vehicle.*

WHERE TO EAT AND STAY

For expanded reviews, facilities, and current deals, visit Fodors.com.

$$$ MEDITERRANEAN ★ 🍴 **Bittersweet Bistro.** A large old tavern with cathedral ceilings houses this popular bistro, where chef-owner Thomas Vinolus draws culinary inspiration from the Mediterranean. The menu changes seasonally, but regular highlights include pan-seared Monterey Bay petrale sole, seafood puttanesca (pasta with a spicy sauce of garlic, tomatoes, anchovies, and olives), and fire-roasted pork tenderloin. The decadent chocolate desserts are not to be missed. Breakfast and lunch are available in the casual Bittersweet Café. Pets are welcome on the outdoor patio. [$] *Average main: $25* ✉ *787 Rio Del Mar Blvd., off Hwy. 1* ☎ *831/662–9799* 🌐 *www.bittersweetbistro.com.*

$$$ HOTEL 👶 🏨 **Best Western Seacliff Inn.** Families and business travelers like this 6-acre property near Seacliff State Beach that's more resort than hotel. **Pros:** walking distance to the beach; family-friendly; hot breakfast buffet. **Cons:** close to freeway; occasional nighttime bar noise. **TripAdvisor:** "affordable accommodation," "fun," "choose your room wisely." [$] *Rooms from: $180* ✉ *7500 Old Dominion Ct.* ☎ *831/688–7300, 800/367–2003* 🌐 *www.seacliffinn.com* 🛏 *139 rooms, 10 suites* 🍽 *Breakfast.*

$$$ B&B/INN 🏨 **Flora Vista.** Multicolor fields of flowers, strawberries, and veggies unfold in every direction at this luxury neo-Georgian inn set on 2 serene

acres just south of Aptos. **Pros:** super-private; near Sand Dollar Beach; flowers everywhere. **Cons:** no restaurants or nightlife within walking distance; not a good place for kids. **TripAdvisor:** "warm innkeepers," "excellent food," "beautiful setting." [$] *Rooms from: $195* ✉ *1258 San Andreas Rd., La Selva Beach* ☎ *831/724–8663, 877/753–5672* 🌐 *www.floravistainn.com* 🛏 *5 rooms* 🍴 *Breakfast.*

$$$$ RESORT 👶 🏨 **Seascape Beach Resort.** On a bluff overlooking Monterey Bay, Seascape is a full-fledged resort that makes it easy to unwind. **Pros:** time-share-style apartments; access to miles of beachfront; superb views. **Cons:** far from city life; most bathrooms are small. **TripAdvisor:** "everything you desire," "cool setting," "lovely room and staff." [$] *Rooms from: $300* ✉ *1 Seascape Resort Dr.* ☎ *831/688–6800, 800/929–7727* 🌐 *www.seascaperesort.com* 🛏 *285 suites.*

3

CAPITOLA AND SOQUEL

4 miles northwest of Aptos on Hwy. 1.

On the National Register of Historic places as California's first seaside resort town, the village of Capitola has been in a holiday mood since the late 1800s. Casual eateries, surf shops, and ice cream parlors pack its walkable downtown. Inland, across Highway 1, antiques shops line Soquel Drive in the town of Soquel. Wineries dot the Santa Cruz Mountains beyond.

GETTING HERE AND AROUND

From Santa Cruz or Monterey, follow Highway 1 to the Capitola/Soquel (Bay Avenue) exit about 7 miles south of Santa Cruz and head west to reach Capitola and east to access Soquel Village. On summer weekends, park for free in the lot behind the Crossroads Center, a block west of the freeway, and hop aboard the free Capitola Shuttle to the village.

ESSENTIALS

Visitor Information Capitola-Soquel Chamber of Commerce ✉ *716-G Capitola Ave.* ☎ *831/475–6522, 800/474–6522* 🌐 *www.capitolachamber.com.*

BEACHES

New Brighton State Beach. New Brighton State Beach, once the site of a Chinese fishing village, is now a popular surfing and camping spot. Its Pacific Migrations Visitor Center traces the history of the Chinese and other peoples who settled around Monterey Bay, as well as the migratory patterns of the area's wildlife, such as monarch butterflies and gray whales. **■TIP→ New Brighton Beach connects with Seacliff Beach, and at low tide you can walk or run along this scenic stretch of sand for nearly 16 miles south (you might have to wade through a few creeks). The 1½-mile stroll from New Brighton to Seacliff's cement ship is a local favorite.** **Amenities:** parking (fee); showers; toilets. **Best For:** sunset; swimming; walking. ✉ *1500 State Park Dr., off Hwy. 1* ☎ *831/464–6330* 🌐 *www.parks.ca.gov* 🎟 *$10 per vehicle.*

WHERE TO EAT

$ 🍴 **Carpo's.** Locals love this casual counter. Seafood predominates, but Carpo's also serves burgers, salads, and steaks. Favorites include the baskets of fresh battered snapper, calamari and prawns, seafood kebabs, and homemade olallieberry pie. Nearly everything costs less than $10. Go early to beat the crowds. [$] *Average main: $9* ✉ *2400 Porter St., at Hwy. 1* ☎ *831/476–6260* 🌐 *www.carposrestaurant.com.*
SEAFOOD 👶

CALIFORNIA'S OLDEST RESORT TOWN

As far as anyone knows for certain, Capitola is the oldest seaside resort town on the Pacific Coast. In 1856 a pioneer acquired Soquel Landing, the picturesque lagoon and beach where Soquel Creek empties into the bay, and built a wharf. Another man opened a campground along the shore, and his daughter named it Capitola after a heroine in a novel series. After the train came to town in the 1870s, thousands of vacationers began arriving to bask in the sun on the glorious beach.

$ 🍴 **Gayle's Bakery & Rosticceria.** Whether you're in the mood for an orange-olallieberry muffin, a wild rice and chicken salad, or tri-tip on garlic toast, this bakery-cum-deli's varied menu is likely to satisfy. Munch your chocolate macaroon on the shady patio or dig into the daily blue-plate dinner amid the whirl inside. [$] *Average main: $10* ✉ *504 Bay Ave., at Capitola Ave.* ☎ *831/462–1200* 🌐 *www.gaylesbakery.com.*
CAFÉ 👶

$$ 🍴 **Michael's on Main.** Creative variations on classic comfort food draw lively crowds to this upscale-but-casual creek-side eatery. Chef Michael Clark's menu changes seasonally, but you can always count on finding such home-style dishes as pork osso bucco in red-wine tomato-citrus sauce, as well as unusual entrées like pistachio-crusted salmon with mint vinaigrette. For a quiet conversation spot, ask for a table on the romantic patio overlooking the creek. The busy bar area hosts live music from Wednesday through Saturday. [$] *Average main: $22* ✉ *2591 Main St., at Porter St.* ☎ *831/479–9777* 🌐 *www.michaelsonmain.net* 🕒 *Closed Mon.*
AMERICAN

$$$ 🍴 **Shadowbrook.** To get to this romantic spot overlooking Soquel Creek, you can take a cable car or walk the stairs down a steep, fern-lined bank beside a running waterfall. Dining room options include the rooftop Redwood Room, the wood-paneled Wine Cellar, and the airy, glass-enclosed Garden Room. Prime rib and grilled seafood are the stars of the simple menu. A cheaper menu of light entrées is available in the lounge. [$] *Average main: $28* ✉ *1750 Wharf Rd., at Lincoln Ave.* ☎ *831/475–1511, 800/975–1511* 🌐 *www.shadowbrook-capitola.com* 🕒 *No lunch.*
EUROPEAN

WHERE TO STAY

For expanded reviews, facilities, and current deals, visit Fodors.com.

$$$$ 🏨 **Inn at Depot Hill.** This inventively designed B&B in a former rail depot sees itself as a link to the era of luxury train travel. **Pros:** short walk to beach and village; historic charm; excellent service. **Cons:** fills quickly; hot tub conversation on the patio may irk second-floor guests. **TripAdvisor:** "always lovely," "perfect romantic getaway," "oasis of
B&B/INN

rest." $ *Rooms from: $279* ✉ *250 Monterey Ave.* ☎ *831/462–3376, 800/572–2632* ⊕ *www.innatdepothill.com* ⇆ *12 rooms* ⦿ *Breakfast.*

SANTA CRUZ

5 miles west of Capitola on Hwy. 1; 48 miles north of Monterey on Hwy. 1.

The big city on this stretch of the California coast, Santa Cruz (pop. 57,500) is less manicured than Carmel or Monterey. Long known for its surfing and its amusement-filled beach boardwalk, the town is a mix of grand Victorian-era homes and rinky-dink motels. The opening of the University of California campus in the 1960s swung the town sharply to the left politically, and the counterculture more or less lives on here. At the same time, the revitalized downtown and an insane real-estate market reflect the city's proximity to Silicon Valley and to a growing wine country in the surrounding mountains.

GETTING HERE AND AROUND

From the San Francisco Bay Area, take Highway 17 south over the mountains to Santa Cruz, where it merges with Highway 1. Use Highway 1 to get around the area. The Santa Cruz Transit Center is at 920 Pacific Avenue, at Front Street, a short walk from the Wharf and Boardwalk, with connections to public transit throughout the Monterey Bay and San Francisco Bay areas. You can purchase Santa Cruz METRO bus day passes here.

ESSENTIALS

Transportation Information Santa Cruz METRO ☎ *831/425–8600* ⊕ *www.scmtd.com.*

Visitor Information Santa Cruz County Conference and Visitors Council ✉ *303 Water St.* ☎ *831/425–1234, 800/833–3494* ⊕ *www.santacruz.org.*

EXPLORING

TOP ATTRACTIONS

Pacific Avenue. When you've had your fill of the city's beaches and waters, take a stroll in downtown Santa Cruz, especially on Pacific Avenue between Laurel and Water streets. Vintage boutiques and mountain sports stores, sushi bars and Mexican restaurants, day spas, and nightclubs keep the main drag and the surrounding streets hopping mid-morning until late evening.

Santa Cruz Beach Boardwalk. Santa Cruz has been a seaside resort since the mid-19th century. Along one end of the broad, south-facing beach, the Boardwalk has entertained holidaymakers for more than a century. Its Looff carousel and classic wooden Giant Dipper roller coaster, both dating from the early 1900s, are surrounded by high-tech thrill rides and easygoing kiddie rides with ocean views. Video and arcade games, a mini-golf course, and a laser-tag arena pack one gigantic building, which is open daily even if the rides aren't running. You have to pay to play, but you can wander the entire boardwalk for free while sampling delicacies such as corn dogs and garlic fries. ✉ *Along Beach St.*

☎ *831/426–7433 info line* ⊕ *www.beachboardwalk.com* ⌦ *$30 day pass for unlimited rides, or pay per ride* ☾ *Apr.–early Sept., daily; early Sept.–late May, weekends, weather permitting; call for hrs.*

Ⓒ **Santa Cruz Municipal Wharf.** Jutting half a mile into the ocean near one end of the Boardwalk, the Municipal Wharf is lined with seafood restaurants, a wine bar, souvenir shops, and outfitters offering bay cruises, fishing trips, and boat rentals. A salty sound track drifts up from under the wharf, where barking sea lions lounge in heaps on crossbeams. ⊠ *Beach St. at Pacific Ave.* ☎ *831/420–6025* ⊕ *www.santacruzwharf. com.*

★ **Santa Cruz Surfing Museum.** This museum inside the Mark Abbott Memorial Lighthouse chronicles local surfing history. Photographs show old-time surfers, and a display of boards includes rarities such as a heavy redwood plank predating the fiberglass era and the remains of a modern board chomped by a great white shark. On-site surfer-docents talk about the good old days. ⊠ *Lighthouse Point Park, 701 W. Cliff Dr., near Pelton Ave.* ☎ *831/420–6289* ⊕ *www.santacruzsurfingmuseum. org* ⌦ *$2 suggested donation* ☾ *Sept.–June, Thurs.–Mon. noon–4; July and Aug., Wed.–Mon. 10–5.*

West Cliff Drive. The road that winds along an oceanfront bluff from the municipal wharf to Natural Bridges State Beach makes for a spectacular drive, but it's even more fun to walk, blade, or bike the paved path that parallels the road. Surfers bob and swoosh in Monterey Bay at several points near the foot of the bluff, especially at a break known as Steamer Lane. Named for a surfer who died here in 1965, the nearby Mark Abbott Memorial Lighthouse stands at Point Santa Cruz, the cliff's major promontory. From here you can watch pinnipeds hang out, sunbathe, and frolic on Seal Rock.

WORTH NOTING

Mystery Spot. Hokey tourist trap or genuine scientific enigma? Since 1940, curious throngs baffled by the Mystery Spot have made it one of the most visited attractions in Santa Cruz. The laws of gravity and physics don't appear to apply in this tiny patch of redwood forest, where balls roll uphill and people stand on a slant. Advance online tickets ($6) are recommended for weekend and holiday visits. ⊠ *465 Mystery Spot Rd., off Branciforte Dr. (north off Hwy. 1)* ☎ *831/423–8897* ⊕ *www.mysteryspot.com* ⌦ *$5 on site, $6 in advance, parking $5* ☾ *Late May–early Sept., daily 10–7; early Sept.–late May, weekdays 10–4, weekends 10–5.*

Santa Cruz Mission State Historic Park. On the northern fringes of downtown is the site of California's 12th Spanish mission, built in the 1790s and destroyed by an earthquake in 1857. A museum in a restored 1791 adobe and a half-scale replica of the mission church are part of the complex. ⊠ *144 School St., at Adobe St.* ☎ *831/425–5849* ⊕ *www.parks. ca.gov* ⌦ *Free* ☾ *Thurs.–Sat. 10–4.*

OFF THE BEATEN PATH

Santa Cruz Mountains wineries. Highway 9 heads northeast from Santa Cruz into hills densely timbered with massive coastal redwoods. The road winds through the lush San Lorenzo Valley, past hamlets consisting of a few cafés, antiques shops, and old-style tourist cabins. Residents of the hunting-and-fishing persuasion coexist with hardcore flower-power survivors and wannabes here, and a new generation has joined the pioneers who opened wineries decades ago. Mountain grapes produce some superb Chardonnays, Pinot Noirs, and Cabernet Sauvignons, among other wines. To sample some, you can start a **winery tour** in downtown Santa Cruz at Storrs Winery, at 303 Potrero Street—a

> ## HAWAIIAN ROYALTY SURFS THE BAY
>
> In 1885 relatives of Hawaiian Queen Kapiolani reputedly visited Santa Cruz and surfed near the mouth of the San Lorenzo River. Nearly 20 years later, legendary Hawaiian surfer Duke Kahanamoku also surfed the Santa Cruz swells.

block off River Street, which, heading north from here becomes Highway 9. Drive north to Felton to visit the Organic Wine Works, just west of Highway 9 on Felton Empire Road downtown. Continue north on Highway 9 and east on Bear Creek Road to the classy Byington and David Bruce wineries, both in Los Gatos. ■TIP→ The Santa Cruz Mountains Winegrowers Association (⊕ www.scmwa.com) distributes a wine-touring map at member wineries and many lodgings and attractions around Santa Cruz.

Seymour Marine Discovery Center. Part of Long Marine Laboratory at UCSC's Institute of Marine Sciences, the center looks more like a research facility than a slick aquarium. Interactive exhibits demonstrate how scientists study the ocean, and the aquarium displays creatures of interest to marine biologists. The 87-foot blue whale skeleton is one of the world's largest. Tours (sign up when you arrive) take place at 11, 1, 2, and 3. ✉ *100 Shaffer Rd., off Delaware Ave., west of Natural Bridges State Beach* ☎ *831/459–3800* ⊕ *seymourcenter.ucsc.edu* ✉ *$6* ⊙ *Tues.–Sat. 10–5, Sun. noon–5.*

University of California at Santa Cruz. The 2,000-acre UC Santa Cruz campus nestles in the forested hills above town. Its sylvan setting, sweeping ocean vistas, and redwood architecture make the university worth a visit. Wander about on your own (maps available at the office of admissions) or on a guided tour (reservations required). Either way, the free campus shuttles can help you get around. ✉ *Main entrance at Bay and High Sts.* ☎ *831/459–0111* ⊕ *www.ucsc.edu/visit.*

   UCSC Arboretum. Half a mile beyond the main campus entrance, the arboretum contains a stellar collection of gardens arranged by geography. A walking path leads through areas dedicated to the plants of California, Australia, New Zealand, and South Africa. ✉ *1156 High St.* ☎ *831/427–2998* ⊕ *arboretum.ucsc.edu* ✉ *$5* ⊙ *Daily 9–5, guided tours by appointment*

Wilder Ranch State Park. In the park's Cultural Preserve you can visit the homes, barns, workshops, and bunkhouse of a 19th-century dairy farm. Nature has reclaimed most of the ranch land, and native plants and wildlife have returned to the 7,000 acres of forest, grassland, canyons, estuaries, and beaches. Hike, bike, or ride horseback on miles of ocean-view trails. ✉ *Hwy. 1, 1 mile north of Santa Cruz* ☎ *831/426–0505*

Interpretive Center, 831/423–9703 trail information 🌐 *www.parks.ca.gov* 🎟 *Parking $10* 🕓 *Daily 8 am–sunset.*

BEACHES

👋 **Natural Bridges State Beach.** At the end of West Cliff Drive lies Natural Bridges State Beach, a stretch of soft sand edged with tide pools and sea-sculpted rock bridges. ■**TIP**➔ **From October to early March a colony of monarch butterflies roosts in a eucalyptus grove.** **Amenities:** lifeguards; parking (fee); toilets. **Best For:** sunrise; sunset; surfing; swimming. ✉ *2531 W. Cliff Dr.* ☎ *831/423–4609* 🌐 *www.parks.ca.gov* 🎟 *Beach free, parking $10* 🕓 *Daily 8 am–sunset. Visitor center Oct.–Feb., daily 10–4; Mar.–Sept., weekends 10–4.*

WHERE TO EAT

$$ SEAFOOD ★ 🍴 **Crow's Nest.** This classic California beachside eatery sits right on the water in Santa Cruz Harbor. Vintage surfboards and local surf photography line the walls in the main dining room; nearly every table overlooks the sand and surf. Seafood and steaks, served with local veggies, dominate the menu; favorite appetizers include the chilled shrimp-stuffed artichoke and crispy tempura prawns, served with rice pilaf. No need to pile high on your first trip to the endless salad bar—you can return as often as you like. For sweeping ocean views and more casual fare (think fish tacos and burgers), head upstairs to the Breakwater Bar & Grill. Live entertainment several days a week makes for a dynamic atmosphere year-round. [$] *Average main: $18* ✉ *2218 E. Cliff Dr., west of 7th Ave.* ☎ *831/476–4560* 🌐 *www.crowsnest-santacruz.com.*

$$ ITALIAN 🍴 **Gabriella Café.** The work of local artists hangs on the walls of this petite, romantic café in a tile-roof cottage. Featuring organic produce from area farms, the seasonal Italian menu has included wild-mushroom risotto, roast rabbit tenderloin wrapped in prosciutto, and roasted beet salad with arugula, goat cheese and pistachios. [$] *Average main: $22* ✉ *910 Cedar St., at Church St.* ☎ *831/457–1677* 🌐 *www.gabriellacafe.com.*

$$$ ITALIAN 🍴 **La Posta.** Authentic Italian fare made with fresh local produce lures diners into cozy, modern-rustic La Posta. Nearly everything is house-made, from the pizzas and breads baked in the brick oven to the pasta and the vanilla-bean gelato. The seasonal menu includes flavorful dishes such as fried artichokes, ravioli filled with crab, chicken with brussels sprouts, or sautéed fish from local waters. Come Sunday for the family-style, fixed-price dinner—four courses for just $30. [$] *Average main: $26* ✉ *538 Seabright Ave., at Logan St.* ☎ *831/457–2782* 🌐 *www.lapostarestaurant.com* 🕓 *Closed Mon. No lunch.*

$$$ EUROPEAN ★ 🍴 **Oswald.** Sophisticated yet unpretentious European-inspired California cooking is the order of the day at this intimate and stylish bistro. The menu changes seasonally, but might include such items as perfectly prepared sherry-steamed mussels or sautéed duck breast. Sit at the slick marble bar and order a creative concoction like whiskey mixed with aperol and organic strawberry and lemon juices or tequila with celery juice and lime. [$] *Average main: $25* ✉ *121 Soquel Ave., at Front St.*

☎ *831/423–7427* 🌐 *www.oswaldrestaurant.com* 🕒 *Closed Mon. Lunch Fridays only.*

$ AMERICAN 🍴 **Seabright Brewery.** Great burgers, big salads, and stellar microbrews make this a favorite hangout in the youthful Seabright neighborhood east of downtown. Sit outside on the patio or inside at a comfortable, spacious booth; both are popular with families. [$] *Average main: $12* ✉ *519 Seabright Ave., at Murray St.* ☎ *831/426–2739* 🌐 *www.seabrightbrewery.com.*

$$ MEDITERRANEAN 🍴 **Soif.** Wine reigns at this sleek bistro and wineshop that takes its name from the French word for thirst. The lengthy list includes selections from near and far, many of which you can order by the taste or glass. Infused with the tastes of the Mediterranean, small plates and mains are served at the copper-top bar, the big communal table, and private tables. A jazz combo or solo pianist plays some evenings. [$] *Average main: $22* ✉ *105 Walnut Ave., at Pacific Ave.* ☎ *831/423–2020* 🌐 *www.soifwine.com* 🕒 *No lunch.*

$ AMERICAN 🍴 **Zachary's.** This noisy café filled with students and families defines the funky essence of Santa Cruz. It also dishes up great breakfasts: stay simple with sourdough pancakes, or go for Mike's Mess—eggs scrambled with bacon, mushrooms, and home fries, then topped with sour cream, melted cheese, and fresh tomatoes. **■ TIP→ If you arrive after 9 am, expect a long wait for a table; lunch is a shade calmer (closing time is 2:30 pm).** [$] *Average main: $10* ✉ *819 Pacific Ave.* ☎ *831/427–0646* ✍ *Reservations not accepted* 🕒 *Closed Mon. No dinner.*

WHERE TO STAY

For expanded reviews, facilities, and current deals, visit Fodors.com.

$$$ B&B/INN 🏨 **Babbling Brook Inn.** Though it's smack in the middle of Santa Cruz, this B&B has lush gardens, a running stream, and tall trees that make you feel like you're in a secluded wood. **Pros:** close to UCSC; within walking distance of downtown shops; woodsy feel. **Cons:** near a high school; some rooms close to a busy street. **TripAdvisor:** "beautiful gardens," "serene and friendly," "pristine and cozy rooms." [$] *Rooms from: $219* ✉ *1025 Laurel St.* ☎ *831/427–2437, 800/866–1131* 🌐 *www.babblingbrookinn.com* 🛏 *13 rooms* 🍽 *Breakfast.*

$$$$ RESORT 🏨 **Chaminade Resort & Spa.** A full-on renovation of the entire property, completed in 2009, sharpened this hilltop resort's look, enhanced its amenities, and qualified it for regional green certification. **Pros:** far from city life; spectacular property; ideal spot for romance and rejuvenation. **Cons:** must drive to attractions and sights; near major hospital. **TripAdvisor:** "the hidden jewel," "comfortable and convenient," "beautiful." [$] *Rooms from: $299* ✉ *1 Chaminade La.* ☎ *800/283–6569 reservations, 831/475–5600* 🌐 *www.chaminade.com* 🛏 *112 rooms, 44 suites.*

$ B&B/INN 🏨 **Harbor Inn.** Family-run, friendly, and funky, this basic but sparkling-clean lodge offers exceptional value just a few blocks from Santa Cruz Harbor and Twin Lakes Beach. **Pros:** affordable; free Wi-Fi; park your car and walk to the beach. **Cons:** not fancy; not near downtown. **TripAdvisor:** "nice place with character," "clean and comfortable," "staff is wonderful." [$] *Rooms from: $89* ✉ *645 7th Ave.* ☎ *831/479–9731* 🌐 *www.harborinn.info* 🛏 *17 rooms, 2 suites.*

$$$ B&B/INN 🏨 **Pacific Blue Inn.** Green themes reign in this three-story, eco-friendly B&B, built from scratch in 2009 on a sliver of prime property downtown. **Pros:** free bicycles; five-minute walk to boardwalk and wharf; right in downtown. **Cons:** tiny property; not suitable for children. **TripAdvisor:** "stylish," "wonderfully appointed," "Santa Cruz secret." [$] *Rooms from: $189* ✉ *636 Pacific Ave.* ☎ *831/600–8880* 🌐 *www.pacificblueinn.com* 🛏 *9 rooms* 🍴 *Breakfast.*

$$$$ B&B/INN ★ 🏨 **Santa Cruz Dream Inn.** Just a short stroll from the boardwalk and wharf, this full-service luxury hotel is the only lodging in Santa Cruz directly on the beach. **Pros:** directly on the beach; easy parking; walk to boardwalk and downtown. **Cons:** expensive; area gets congested on busy weekends. **TripAdvisor:** "can't get any closer to the sand," "courtesy and service still exist," "comfortable luxury." [$] *Rooms from: $309* ✉ *175 W. Cliff Dr.* ☎ *831/426–4330, 866/774–7735 reservations* 🌐 *www.dreaminnsantacruz.com* 🛏 *149 rooms, 16 suites.*

$$$ B&B/INN ★ 🏨 **West Cliff Inn.** Perched on the bluffs across from Cowell Beach, this posh nautical-theme inn commands sweeping views of the boardwalk and Monterey Bay. **Pros:** killer views; walking distance of the beach; close to downtown. **Cons:** boardwalk noise; street traffic. **TripAdvisor:** "outstanding accommodations," "diamond in Santa Cruz," "beautifully restored." [$] *Rooms from: $200* ✉ *174 West Cliff Dr.* ☎ *800/979–0910 toll free, 831/457–2200* 🌐 *www.westcliffinn.com* 🛏 *7 rooms, 2 suites, 1 cottage* 🍴 *Breakfast.*

NIGHTLIFE AND THE ARTS

NIGHTLIFE

★ **Catalyst.** Dance with the crowds at this huge, grimy club that regularly features big names, from Neil Young to the Red Hot Chili Peppers. ✉ *1011 Pacific Ave.* ☎ *831/423–1338* 🌐 *www.catalystclub.com.*

Kuumbwa Jazz Center. The renowned center draws top performers such as Herbie Hancock, Pat Metheny, and Charlie Hunter; the café serves meals an hour before most shows. ✉ *320–2 Cedar St.* ☎ *831/427–2227* 🌐 *kuumbwajazz.org.*

Moe's Alley. Blues, salsa, reggae, funk: Moe's has it all (and more), six nights a week. ✉ *1535 Commercial Way* ☎ *831/479–1854* 🌐 *www.moesalley.com.*

THE ARTS

Cabrillo Festival of Contemporary Music. Each August, the Cabrillo Festival of Contemporary Music brings some of the world's finest artists to the Santa Cruz Civic Auditorium to play groundbreaking symphonic music, including major world premieres. ☎ *831/426–6966, 831/420–5260 box office* 🌐 *www.cabrillomusic.org.*

Santa Cruz Baroque Festival. Using period and reproduction instruments, the festival presents classical music at various venues. As the name suggests, the focus is on 17th- and 18th-century composers such as Bach and Handel. ☎ *831/457–9693* 🌐 *www.scbaroque.org.*

Shakespeare Santa Cruz. This six-week festival in July and August occasionally includes a modern dramatic performance. Most performances are outdoors under the redwoods. A holiday program takes place in December. ⊠ *SSC/UCSC Theater Arts Center, 1156 High St.* ☎ *831/459–2121 administration, 831/459–2159 tickets* ⊕ *www. shakespearesantacruz.org.*

SPORTS AND THE OUTDOORS

BICYCLING

Another Bike Shop. Mountain bikers should head here for tips on the best area trails and to browse cutting-edge gear made and tested locally. ⊠ *2361 Mission St., at King St.* ☎ *831/427–2232* ⊕ *www. anotherbikeshop.com.*

BOATS AND CHARTERS

Chardonnay Sailing Charters. The 70-foot *Chardonnay II* departs year-round from Santa Cruz yacht harbor on whale-watching, sunset, and other cruises around Monterey Bay. Most regularly scheduled excursions cost $50; food and drink are served on many of them. Reservations are essential. ☎ *831/423–1213* ⊕ *www.chardonnay.com.*

Stagnaro Sport Fishing. Stagnaro operates salmon, albacore, and rock-cod fishing expeditions; the fees ($50 to $75) include bait. The company also runs whale-watching, dolphin, and sea-life cruises ($45) year-round. ⊠ *June–Aug., Santa Cruz Municipal Wharf; Sept.–May, Santa Cruz West Harbor* ☎ *831/427–2334* ⊕ *www.stagnaros.com.*

GOLF

Pasatiempo Golf Club. Designed by famed golf architect Dr. Alister MacKenzie in 1929, this semiprivate course, set amid undulating hills just above the city, is among the nation's top championship courses. Golfers rave about the spectacular views and challenging terrain. The greens fee is $220; an electric cart is $30 per player. ⊠ *20 Clubhouse Rd.* ☎ *831/459–9155* ⊕ *www.pasatiempo.com.*

KAYAKING

Kayak Connection. In March, April, and May, participants on this outfit's tours mingle with gray whales and their calves on their northward journey to Alaska. Throughout the year, the company rents kayaks and paddle boards and conducts tours of Natural Bridges State Beach, Capitola, and Elkhorn Slough. Most regularly scheduled tours cost between $20 and $55. ⊠ *Santa Cruz Harbor, 413 Lake Ave. #3* ☎ *831/479–1121* ⊕ *www.kayakconnection.com.*

Venture Quest Kayaking. Explore hidden coves and kelp forests on guided nature tours that depart from Santa Cruz Wharf or Harbor, depending on the season. A two-hour kayak nature tour and introductory lesson costs $58. A three-hour kayak rental is $30 and includes wet suit and gear. Venture Quest also arranges tours at other Monterey Bay destinations, including Capitola and Elkhorn Slough. ⊠ *#2 Santa Cruz Wharf* ☎ *831/427–2267 kayak hotline, 831/425–8445 rental office* ⊕ *www. kayaksantacruz.com.*

CLOSE UP

O'Neill: A Santa Cruz Icon

O'Neill wet suits and beachwear weren't exactly born in Santa Cruz, but as far as most of the world is concerned, the O'Neill brand is synonymous with Santa Cruz and surfing legend.

The O'Neill wet-suit story began in 1952, when Jack O'Neill and his brother Robert opened their first Surf Shop in a garage across from San Francisco's Ocean Beach. While shaping balsa surfboards and selling accessories, the O'Neills experimented with solutions to a common surfer problem: frigid waters. Tired of being forced back to shore, blue-lipped and shivering, after just 20 or 30 minutes riding the waves, they played with various materials and eventually designed a neoprene vest.

In 1959 Jack moved his Surf Shop 90 miles south to Cowell Beach in Santa Cruz. It quickly became a popular surf hangout, and O'Neill's new wet suits began to sell like hotcakes. In the early 1960s the company opened a warehouse for manufacturing on a larger scale. Santa Cruz soon became a major surf city, attracting wave-riders to prime breaks at Steamer Lane, Pleasure Point, and The Hook. In 1965 O'Neill pioneered the first wet-suit boots, and in 1971 Jack's son invented the surf leash. By 1980, O'Neill stood at the top of the world wet-suit market.

O'Neill operates two flagship stores, one downtown and one close to Jack O'Neill's home on Pleasure Point, along with a smaller outlet on the Santa Cruz Wharf. Sporting stores all over town also carry the line (it's everywhere). ⊕ www.oneill.com

---

SURFING

Pleasure Point. Surfers gather for the spectacular waves and sunsets here. ⊠ *E. Cliff and Pleasure Point Drs.*

Steamer Lane. This area near the lighthouse on West Cliff Drive has a decent break. Steamer Lane hosts several competitions in summer.

EQUIPMENT AND LESSONS **Club-Ed Surf School and Camps.** Find out what all the fun is about at Club-Ed. Your first private or group lesson ($85 and up) includes all equipment. ⊠ *Cowell Beach, at Santa Cruz Dream Inn* ☎ *831/464–0177* ⊕ *www.club-ed.com.*

Cowell's Beach Surf Shop. This shop sells gear, clothing, and swimwear; rents surfboards, standup paddle boards, and wet suits; and offers lessons. ⊠ *30 Front St.* ☎ *831/427–2355* ⊕ *www.cowellssurfshop.com.*

San Francisco

WORD OF MOUTH

"The part I was really looking forward to was walking down [Telegraph Hill] and looking for parrots. I'd seen the movie *The Wild Parrots of Telegraph Hill*, and the neighborhood was one of the things that meant 'San Francisco' to me. The neighborhood itself was beautiful, and we did indeed see parrots."

—sunny16

WELCOME TO SAN FRANCISCO

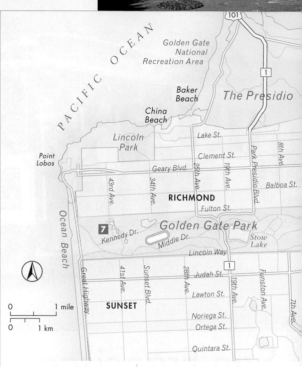

TOP REASONS TO GO

★ **The bay:** It's hard not to gasp as you catch sight of sunlight dancing on the water when you crest a hill, or watch the Golden Gate Bridge vanish and reemerge in the summer fog.

★ **The food:** San Franciscans are serious about what they eat, and with good reason. Home to some of the nation's best chefs, top restaurants, and finest local produce, it's hard not to eat well here.

★ **The shopping:** Shopaholics visiting the city will not be disappointed: San Francisco is packed with browsing destinations, everything from quirky boutiques to massive malls.

★ **The good life:** A laid-back atmosphere, beautiful surroundings, and oodles of cultural, culinary, and aesthetic pleasures . . . if you spend too much time here, you might not leave!

★ **The great outdoors:** From Golden Gate Park to sidewalk cafés in North Beach, San Franciscans relish their outdoor spaces.

1 Union Square and Chinatown. Union Square has hotels, public transportation, and shopping; walking through Chinatown is like visiting another country.

2 SoMa and Civic Center. SoMa is anchored by SFMOMA and Yerba Buena Gardens; the city's performing arts venues are in Civic Center.

3 Nob Hill and Russian Hill. Nob Hill is old money San Francisco; Russian Hill's steep streets have excellent eateries and shopping.

4 North Beach. This small Italian neighborhood is a great place to enjoy an espresso.

5 On the Waterfront. Head here to visit the exquisitely restored Ferry Building, Fisherman's Wharf, Pier 39, and Ghirardelli Square.

6 The Marina and the Presidio. The Marina has trendy boutiques, restaurants, and cafés; the wooded Presidio offers great views of the Golden Gate Bridge.

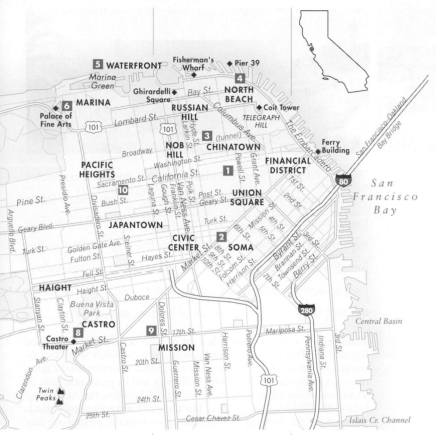

5 WATERFRONT Fisherman's Wharf ◆ Pier 39
Marina Green
4
Ghirardelli ◆ Bay St. NORTH BEACH
6 MARINA Square ◆ Coit Tower
Palace of Fine Arts RUSSIAN HILL TELEGRAPH HILL
Lombard St. 101
Broadway (tunnel) Ferry Building
NOB HILL **3** CHINATOWN
PACIFIC HEIGHTS Washington St. FINANCIAL DISTRICT
Sacramento St. California St. **1**
Bush St. Post St. UNION SQUARE
Pine St. Divisadero St. Geary St. **80**
Geary Blvd. JAPANTOWN Turk St.
Turk St. CIVIC CENTER **2** SOMA
Fulton St. Golden Gate Ave. Hayes St. Market St.
Full St. Harrison St.
HAIGHT Haight St. Duboce
Buena Vista Park **280**
CASTRO Central Basin
Castro **8** **9** 17th St.
Theater Market St. Mariposa St.
Clarendon Ave. MISSION 20th St.
Twin Peaks 24th St. 101
25th St.
Cesar Chavez St. Islais Cr. Channel

San Francisco Bay

4

---

7 **Golden Gate Park and the Western Shoreline.** San Francisco's 1,000-acre backyard has sports fields, windmills, museums, and gardens; the windswept Western Shoreline stretches for miles.

8 **The Haight, the Castro, and Noe Valley.** After you've seen the blockbuster sights, come to these neighborhoods to see where the city's heart beats.

9 **The Mission.** This Latino neighborhood has destination restaurants, bargain ethnic eateries, and a hip bar scene.

10 **Pacific Heights and Japantown.** Pacific Heights has some of the city's most opulent real estate; Japantown is packed with authentic Japanese shops and restaurants.

GETTING ORIENTED

San Francisco is a compact city; just 46½ square miles. Essentially a tightly packed cluster of extremely diverse neighborhoods, the city dearly rewards walking. The areas that most visitors cover are easy (and safe) to reach on foot, but many have steep— make that *steep*—hills.

Updated by
Denise M.
Leto, Michele
Bigley, Marcia
Gagliardi,
Fiona G.
Parrott, Jerry
James Stone

"You could live in San Francisco a month and ask no greater entertainment than walking through it," wrote Inez Hayes Irwin, author of *The Californiacs*, an effusive 1921 homage to the Golden State and the City by the Bay. Follow in her footsteps, and you'll find that her claim still rings true today: simply wandering around this beautiful metropolis on foot is the best way to experience all of its diverse wonders.

Snuggling on a 46½-square-mile strip of land between San Francisco Bay and the Pacific Ocean, San Francisco is a relatively small city of about 750,000 residents. San Franciscans cherish their city for the same reasons visitors do: the proximity to the bay and its pleasures, rows of Victorian homes clinging precariously to the hillsides, the sun setting behind the Golden Gate Bridge. But the city's attraction goes much deeper, from the diversity of its neighborhoods to the progressive free spirit here. Take all these things together, and you'll begin to understand why many San Franciscans can't imagine calling anyplace else home— despite the dizzying cost of living.

San Francisco's charms are great and small. You won't want to miss Golden Gate Park, the Palace of Fine Arts, the Golden Gate Bridge, or a cable car ride over Nob Hill. But a walk down the Filbert Street Steps or through Macondray Lane or an hour gazing at murals in the Mission or the thundering Pacific from the cliffs of Lincoln Park can be equally inspiring.

PLANNING

WHEN TO GO
You can visit San Francisco comfortably any time of year. Possibly the best time to visit San Francisco is September and October, when the city's summerlike weather brings outdoor concerts and festivals. The climate here always feels Mediterranean and moderate—with a foggy, sometimes chilly bite. The temperature rarely drops below 40°F, and anything warmer than 80°F is considered a heat wave. Be prepared for

rain in winter, especially December and January. Winds off the ocean can add to the chill factor. That old joke about summer in SF feeling like winter is true at heart, but once you move inland, it gets warmer. (And some locals swear the thermostat has inched up in recent years.)

GETTING HERE AND AROUND
AIR TRAVEL
The major gateway to San Francisco is San Francisco International Airport (SFO), 15 miles south of the city. It's off U.S. 101 near Millbrae and San Bruno. Oakland International Airport (OAK) is across the bay, not much farther away from downtown San Francisco (via Interstate 80 east and Interstate 880 south), but rush-hour traffic on the Bay Bridge may lengthen travel times considerably. San Jose International Airport (SJC) is about 40 miles south of San Francisco; travel time depends largely on traffic flow, but plan on an hour and a half with moderate traffic.

Airports San Francisco International Airport (*SFO*) ☎ *800/435–9736, 650/821–8211* ⊕ *www.flysfo.com.* **Oakland International Airport** (*OAK*) ☎ *510/563–3300* ⊕ *www.flyoakland.com.* **San Jose International Airport** (*SJC*) ☎ *408/392–3600* ⊕ *www.flysanjose.com.*

Airport Transfers American Airporter ☎ *415/202–0733* ⊕ *www. americanairporter.com.* **BayPorter Express** ☎ *415/467–1800* ⊕ *www. bayporter.com.* **Caltrain** ☎ *800/660–4287* ⊕ *www.caltrain.com.* **East Bay Express Airporter** ☎ *877/526–0304* ⊕ *www.eastbaytransportation.com.* **Lorrie's Airport Service** ☎ *415/334–9000* ⊕ *www.gosfovan.com.* **Marin Airporter** ☎ *415/461–4222* ⊕ *www.marinairporter.com.* **Marin Door to Door** ☎ *415/457–2717* ⊕ *www.marindoortodoor.com.* **SamTrans** ☎ *800/660–4287* ⊕ *www.samtrans.com.* **South & East Bay Airport Shuttle** ☎ *800/548–4664* ⊕ *www.southandeastbayairportshuttle.com.* **SuperShuttle** ☎ *800/258–3826* ⊕ *www.supershuttle.com.* **VIP Airport Shuttle** ☎ *408/986–6000, 800/235–8847* ⊕ *www.viptransportgroup.com.*

BART TRAVEL
Bay Area Rapid Transit (BART) trains, which run until midnight, travel under the bay via tunnel to connect San Francisco with Oakland, Berkeley, Pittsburgh/Bay Point, Richmond, Fremont, Dublin/Pleasanton, and other small cities and towns in between. Within San Francisco, stations are limited to downtown, the Mission, and a couple of outlying neighborhoods.

Trains travel frequently from early morning until evening on weekdays. After 8 pm weekdays and on weekends there's often a 20-minute wait between trains on the same line. Trains also travel south from San Francisco as far as Millbrae. BART trains connect downtown San Francisco to San Francisco International Airport; a ride is $8.10.

Intracity San Francisco fares are $1.75; intercity fares are $2.90 to $5.95. BART bases its ticket prices on miles traveled, and does not offer price breaks by zone. The easy-to-read maps posted in BART stations list fares based on destination, radiating out from your starting point of the current station.

Contact BART. ☎ *415/989–2278 San Francisco/Daly City, 510/465–2278 East Bay* ⊕ *www.bart.gov.*

BOAT AND FERRY TRAVEL

Several ferry lines run out of San Francisco. Blue & Gold Fleet operates a number of routes, including service to Sausalito ($10.50 one-way) and Tiburon ($10.50 one-way). Tickets are sold at Pier 41 (between Fisherman's Wharf and Pier 39), where the boats depart. Alcatraz Cruises, owned by Hornblower Yachts, operates the ferries to Alcatraz Island ($28 including audio tour and National Park Service ranger-led programs) from Pier 33, about a half mile east of Fisherman's Wharf. Boats leave 10 times a day (14 times a day in summer), and the journey itself is 30 minutes. Allow roughly 2½ hours for a round-trip jaunt. Golden Gate Ferry runs daily to and from Sausalito ($9.25 one way) and Larkspur ($8.75 one-way), leaving from Pier 1, behind the San Francisco Ferry Building. The Alameda/Oakland Ferry operates daily between Alameda's Main Street Ferry Building, Oakland's Jack London Square, and San Francisco's Pier 41 and the Ferry Building ($6.25 one-way); some ferries go only to Pier 41 or the Ferry Building, so ask when you board. Purchase tickets onboard.

Ferry Lines Alameda/Oakland Ferry ☎ 510/522–3300 ⊕ www.eastbayferry. com. **Alcatraz Cruises** ☎ 415/981–7625 ⊕ www.alcatrazcruises.com. **Blue & Gold Fleet** ☎ 415/705–8200 ⊕ www.blueandgoldfleet.com. **Golden Gate Ferry** ☎ 415/455–2000 ⊕ www.goldengateferry.org. **San Francisco Ferry Building** ✉ 1 Ferry Bldg., at foot of Market St. on Embarcadero ☎ 415/983–8030.

CABLE CAR TRAVEL

The fare (for one direction) is $6. You can buy tickets on board (exact change isn't necessary) or at the kiosks at the cable car turnarounds at Hyde and Beach streets and at Powell and Market streets.

The heavily traveled Powell–Mason and Powell–Hyde lines begin at Powell and Market streets near Union Square and terminate at Fisherman's Wharf; lines for these routes can be long, especially in summer. The California Street line runs east and west from Market and California streets to Van Ness Avenue; there is often no wait to board this route.

CAR TRAVEL

Driving in San Francisco can be a challenge because of the one-way streets, snarly traffic, and steep hills. The first two elements can be frustrating enough, but those hills are tough for unfamiliar drivers. ■TIP→ Remember to curb your wheels when parking on hills—turn wheels away from the curb when facing uphill, toward the curb when facing downhill. You can get a ticket if you don't do this.

MUNI TRAVEL

The San Francisco Municipal Railway, or Muni, operates light-rail vehicles, the historic F-line streetcars along Fisherman's Wharf and Market Street, trolley buses, and the world-famous cable cars. Light rail travels along Market Street to the Mission District and Noe Valley (J line), the Ingleside District (K line), and the Sunset District (L, M, and N lines); during peak hours (weekdays 6 am–9 am and 3 pm–7 pm) the J line continues around the Embarcadero to the Caltrain station at 4th and King streets. The T line light rail runs from the Castro, down Market Street, around the Embarcadero, and south past Hunters Point and

Candlestick Park to Sunnydale Avenue and Bayshore Boulevard. Muni provides 24-hour service on select lines to all areas of the city.

On buses and streetcars the fare is $2. Exact change is required, and dollar bills are accepted in the fare boxes. For all Muni vehicles other than cable cars, 90-minute transfers are issued free upon request at the time the fare is paid. These are valid for two additional transfers in any direction. Cable cars cost $6 and include no transfers (*see Cable Car Travel, above*).

One-day ($14), three-day ($21), and seven-day ($27) Passports valid on the entire Muni system can be purchased at several outlets, including the cable car ticket booth at Powell and Market streets and the visitor information center downstairs in Hallidie Plaza. A one-day passport can be purchased from cable-car drivers. A monthly ticket, called a Fast Pass, is available for $72, and can be used on all Muni lines (including cable cars) and on BART within city limits. The San Francisco CityPass ($69), a discount ticket booklet to several major city attractions, also covers all Muni travel for seven consecutive days.

4

The San Francisco Municipal Transit and Street Map ($3) is a useful guide to the extensive transportation system. You can buy the map at most bookstores and at the San Francisco Visitor Information Center, on the lower level of Hallidie Plaza at Powell and Market streets.

Outside the city, AC Transit serves the East Bay, and Golden Gate Transit serves Marin and Sonoma counties.

Bus Lines AC Transit ☎ *510/839–2882* ⊕ *www.actransit.org.***Golden Gate Transit** ☎ *511, 415/455–2000* ⊕ *www.goldengate.org.***San Francisco Municipal Railway System** (*Muni*) ☎ *311, 415/701–3000* ⊕ *www.sfmta.com.*

TAXI TRAVEL

Taxi service is notoriously bad in San Francisco, and hailing a cab can be frustratingly difficult in some parts of the city, especially on weekends. Popular nightspots such as the Mission, SoMa, North Beach, the Haight, and the Castro have a lot of cabs but a lot of people looking for taxis, too. Midweek, and during the day, you shouldn't have much of a problem—unless it's raining. In a pinch, hotel taxi stands are an option, as is calling for a pick-up. But be forewarned: taxi companies frequently don't answer the phone in peak periods. The absolute worst time to find a taxi is Friday afternoon and evening; plan well ahead, and if you're going to the airport, make a reservation or book a shuttle instead. Most taxi companies take advance reservations for airport and out-of-town runs but not in-town transfers.

Taxis in San Francisco charge $3.50 for the first 1/5 mile (one of the highest base rates in the United States and rising), 55¢ for each additional 1/5 mile, and 55¢ per minute in stalled traffic. There is no charge for additional passengers; there is no surcharge for luggage. For trips outside city limits, multiply the metered rate by 1.5.

Taxi Companies DeSoto Cab ☎ *415/970–1300.* **Luxor Cab** ☎ *415/282–4141.* **Veteran's Taxicab** ☎ *415/648–1313.* **Yellow Cab** ☎ *415/626–2345.*

Complaints San Francisco Police Department Taxi Complaints ☎ *415/553–1447.*

TRAIN TRAVEL

Amtrak trains travel to the Bay Area from some cities in California and the United States. The *Coast Starlight* travels north from Los Angeles to Seattle, passing the Bay Area along the way, but contrary to its name, the train runs inland through the Central Valley for much of its route through Northern California; the most scenic stretch is in Southern California, between San Luis Obispo and Los Angeles. Amtrak also has several routes between San Jose, Oakland, and Sacramento. The *California Zephyr* travels from Chicago to the Bay Area, and has spectacular alpine vistas as it crosses the Sierra Nevada mountains. San Francisco doesn't have an Amtrak train station but does have an Amtrak bus station, at the Ferry Building, which provides service to trains in Emeryville, just over the Bay Bridge. Shuttle buses also connect the Emeryville train station with downtown Oakland, the Caltrain station, and other points in downtown San Francisco.

Caltrain connects San Francisco to Palo Alto, San Jose, Santa Clara, and many smaller cities en route. In San Francisco, trains leave from the main depot, at 4th and Townsend streets, and a rail-side stop at 22nd and Pennsylvania streets. One-way fares are $2.75 to $12.75, depending on the number of zones through which your travel tickets are valid for four hours after purchase time. A ticket is $6.75 from San Francisco to Palo Alto, at least $8.75 to San Jose. You can also buy a day pass ($5.50–$25.50) for unlimited travel in a 24-hour period. It's worth waiting for an express train for trips that last 1 to 1¾ hours. On weekdays, trains depart three or four times per hour during the morning and evening, twice per hour during daytime non-commute hours, and as little as once per hour in the evening. Weekend trains run once per hour. The system shuts down at midnight. There are no onboard ticket sales. You must buy tickets before boarding the train or risk paying a $250 fine for fare evasion.

Train Contacts **Amtrak** ☎ 800/872–7245 ⊕ *www.amtrak.com.* **Caltrain** ☎ 800/660–4287 ⊕ *www.caltrain.com.* **San Francisco Caltrain station** ⊠ 700 4th St., at King St. ☎ 800/660–4287.

VISITOR INFORMATION

The San Francisco Convention and Visitors Bureau can mail you brochures, maps, and festivals and events listings. Once you're in town, you can stop by their info center near Union Square. Information about the Wine Country, redwood groves, and northwestern California is available at the California Welcome Center on Pier 39.

Contacts **San Francisco Visitor Information Center** ⊠ Hallidie Plaza, lower level, 900 Market St., at Powell St., Union Sq. ☎ 415/391–2000 TDD ⊕ www. onlyinsanfrancisco.com.

EXPLORING SAN FRANCISCO

UNION SQUARE AND CHINATOWN

The Union Square area bristles with big-city bravado, while just a stone's throw away is a place that feels like a city unto itself, Chinatown. The two areas share a strong commercial streak, although manifested very differently. In Union Square the crowds zigzag among international brands, trailing glossy shopping bags. A few blocks north in Chinatown, people dash between small neighborhood stores, their arms draped with plastic totes filled with groceries or souvenirs.

EXPLORING IN UNION SQUARE

Maiden Lane. Known as Morton Street in the raffish Barbary Coast era, this former red-light district reported at least one murder a week during the late 19th century. Things cooled down after the 1906 fire destroyed the brothels, and these days Maiden Lane is a chic, boutique-lined pedestrian mall stretching two blocks, between Stockton and Kearny streets. Wrought-iron gates close the street to traffic most days between 11 and 5, when the lane becomes a patchwork of umbrella-shaded tables.

At **140 Maiden Lane** you can see the only Frank Lloyd Wright building in San Francisco. Walking through the brick archway and recessed entry feels a bit like entering a glowing cave. The interior's graceful, curving ramp and skylights are said to have been his model for the Guggenheim Museum in New York. Xanadu Gallery, which showcases Baltic, Latin American, and African folk art, now occupies the space. ⊠ *Between Stockton and Kearny Sts., Union Sq.*

San Francisco Visitor Information Center. A multilingual staff operates this facility below the cable-car terminus. Staffers answer questions and provide maps and pamphlets. You can also pick up discount coupons—the savings can be significant, especially for families—and hotel brochures here. If you're planning to hit the big-ticket stops like the California Academy of Sciences, the Exploratorium, and SFMOMA, and ride the cable cars, consider picking up a CityPass here (or at any of the attractions it covers). ■ TIP→ The CityPass ($69, $39 ages 5–12), good for nine days including seven days of transit, will save you about 50%. Also buy your Muni Passport here. ⊠ *Hallidie Plaza, lower level, Powell and Market Sts., Union Sq.* ☎ *415/391–2000, 415/283–0177* ⊕ *www.sanfrancisco.travel* ☼ *Weekdays 9–5, Sat. 9–3; also Sun. 9–3 May–Oct.*

Union Square. Ground zero for big-name shopping in the city and within walking distance of most hotels, Union Square is home base for many visitors. The St. Francis and Macy's line two sides of the square, with Saks, Neiman-Marcus, and Tiffany & Co. bordering the other sides, and shopping titan Bloomie's lies just a few blocks down the cable-car tracks. Considered the heart of San Francisco's downtown since 1850, the landscaped, 2½-acre square is about the only place you can sit for free in this part of town. Back in 2002, the public responded to Union Square's redesign with a resounding shrug. With its pretty landscaping, easier street access, and the addition of a café (welcome,

4

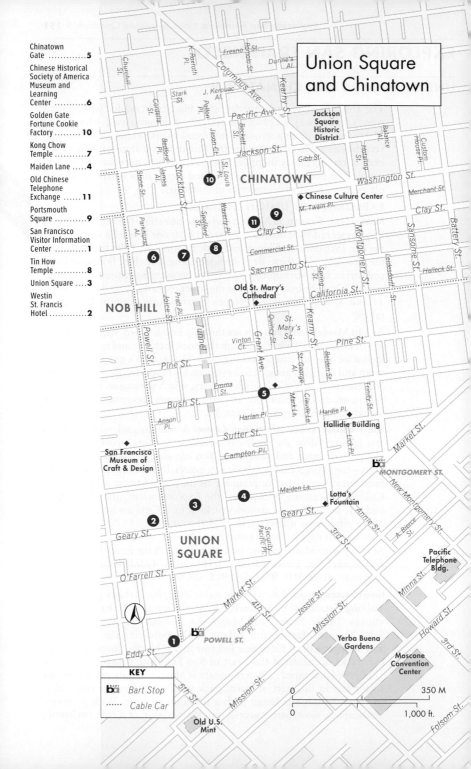

Union Square and Chinatown

Jackson Square Historic District

CHINATOWN

◆ Chinese Culture Center

M. Twain Pl.

Old St. Mary's Cathedral

St. Mary's Sq.

NOB HILL

Old St. Mary's Cathedral

Hallidie Building

San Francisco Museum of Craft & Design

Lotta's Fountain

UNION SQUARE

Pacific Telephone Bldg.

Yerba Buena Gardens

Moscone Convention Center

POWELL ST.

MONTGOMERY ST.

Old U.S. Mint

KEY

🅱 *Bart Stop*

.... *Cable Car*

0   350 M

0   1,000 ft.

but nothing special), it certainly was an improvement over the previous concrete wasteland. Four globular lamp sculptures by the artist R.M. Fischer preside over the space; there's also a café, an open-air stage, a visitor information booth, and a front-row seat to the cable-car tracks. And there's a familiar kaleidoscope of characters: office workers sunning and brown-bagging, street musicians, shoppers taking a rest, kids chasing pigeons, and a fair number of homeless people.

The square takes its name from the violent pro-Union demonstrations staged here before the Civil War. At center stage, Robert Ingersoll Aitken's *Victory Monument* commemorates Commodore George Dewey's victory over the Spanish fleet at Manila in 1898. The 97-foot Corinthian column, topped by a bronze figure symbolizing naval conquest, was dedicated by Theodore Roosevelt in 1903 and withstood the 1906 earthquake. After the earthquake and fire of 1906, the square was dubbed Little St. Francis because of the temporary shelter erected for residents of the St. Francis Hotel. Actor John Barrymore (grandfather of actress Drew Barrymore and a notorious carouser) was among the guests pressed into volunteering to stack bricks in the square. His uncle, thespian John Drew, remarked, "It took an act of God to get John out of bed and the United States Army to get him to work."

On the eastern edge of Union Square, **TIX Bay Area** (☎ *415/433–7827 info only* ⊕ *www.theatrebayarea.org*) provides half-price day-of-performance tickets to all types of performing-arts events, as well as regular full-price box-office services.

Union Square covers a convenient four-level garage, allegedly the first underground garage in the world. ⊠ *Bordered by Powell, Stockton, Post, and Geary Sts., Union Sq.*

Westin St. Francis Hotel. The second-oldest hotel in the city, established in 1904, was conceived by railroad baron and financier Charles Crocker and his associates as a hostelry for their millionaire friends. Swift service and sumptuous surroundings have always been hallmarks of the property. After the hotel was ravaged by the 1906 fire, a larger, more luxurious Italian Renaissance–style residence was opened in 1907 to attract loyal clients from among the world's rich and powerful. The hotel's checkered past includes the ill-fated 1921 bash in the suite of the silent-film comedian Fatty Arbuckle, at which a woman became ill and later died. Arbuckle endured three sensational trials for rape and murder before being acquitted, by which time his career was kaput. In 1975 Sara Jane Moore, standing among a crowd outside the hotel,

CABLE CAR TERMINUS

Two of the three cable car lines begin and end their runs at Powell and Market streets, a couple of blocks south of Union Square. These two lines are the most scenic, and both pass near Fisherman's Wharf, so they're usually clogged with first-time sightseers. The wait to board a cable car at this intersection is longer than at any other stop in the system. If you'd rather avoid the mob, board the less-touristy California line at the bottom of Market Street, at Drumm Street.

4

attempted to shoot then-president Gerald Ford. As might be imagined, no plaques in the lobby commemorate these events. ■**TIP➜** One of the best views in the city is from the glass elevators here—and best of all, a ride is free. Zip up to the 32nd floor for a bird's-eye view; the lights of the nighttime cityscape are particularly lovely. Don't be shy if you're not a guest: some visitors make this a stop every time they're in town.

> **LOOK UP!**
>
> When wandering around Chinatown, don't forget to look up! Above the chintziest souvenir shop might loom an ornate balcony or a curly pagoda roof. The best examples are on the 900 block of Grant Avenue (at Washington Street) and at Waverly Place.

Every November the hotel's pastry chef adds a new touch to his spectacular, rotating 12-foot gingerbread castle, on display in the grand lobby—a fun holiday treat for families. ⊠ *335 Powell St., at Geary St., Union Sq.* ☎ *415/397–7000* ⊕ *www. westinstfrancis.com.*

EXPLORING IN CHINATOWN

Chinatown Gate. This is the official entrance to Chinatown. Stone lions flank the base of the pagoda-topped gate; the lions, dragons, and fish up top symbolize wealth, prosperity, and other good things. The four Chinese characters immediately beneath the pagoda represent the philosophy of Sun Yat-sen (1866–1925), the leader who unified China in the early 20th century. Sun Yat-sen, who lived in exile in San Francisco for a few years, promoted the notion of friendship and peace among all nations based on equality, justice, and goodwill. The vertical characters under the left pagoda read "peace" and "trust," the ones under the right pagoda "respect" and "love." The whole shebang telegraphs the internationally understood message of "photo op." ⊠ *Grant Ave. at Bush St., Chinatown.*

Chinese Historical Society of America Museum and Learning Center. This airy, light-filled gallery has displays about the Chinese-American experience from 19th-century agriculture to 21st-century food and fashion trends, including a moving collection of racist games and toys. A separate room hosts rotating exhibits by contemporary Chinese-American artists. ⊠ *965 Clay St., Chinatown* ☎ *415/391–1188* ⊕ *www.chsa.org* ᐧ *$5, free 1st Thurs. of month* ⊙ *Tues.–Fri. noon–5, Sat. 11–4.*

🔄 **Golden Gate Fortune Cookie Factory.** Follow your nose down Ross Alley to this tiny but fragrant cookie factory. Workers sit at circular motorized griddles and wait for dollops of batter to drop onto a tiny metal plate, which rotates into an oven. A few moments later out comes a cookie that's pliable and ready for folding. It's easy to peek in for a moment, and hard to leave without a few free samples. A bagful of cookies—with mildly racy "adult" fortunes or more benign ones—costs $4.50. You can also purchase the cookies "fortuneless" in their waferlike unfolded state, which makes snacking that much more efficient. Being allowed to photograph the cookie makers at work will set you back 50¢. ⊠ *56 Ross Alley, west of and parallel to Grant Ave., between Washington and Jackson Sts., Chinatown* ☎ *415/781–3956* ᐧ *Free* ⊙ *Daily 9–8.*

Continued on page 161

CHINATOWN

Chinatown's streets flood the senses. Incense and cigarette smoke mingle with the scents of briny fish and sweet vanilla. Rooflines flare outward, pagoda-style. Loud Cantonese bargaining and honking car horns rise above the sharp clack of mah-jongg tiles and the eternally humming cables beneath the street.

Most Chinatown visitors march down Grant Avenue, buy a few trinkets, and call it a day. Do yourself a favor and dig deeper. This is one of the largest Chinese communities outside Asia, and there is far more to it than buying a back-scratcher near Chinatown Gate. To get a real feel for the neighborhood, wander off the main drag. Step into a temple or an herb shop and wander down a flag-draped alley. And don't be shy: residents welcome guests warmly, though rarely in English.

Whatever you do, don't leave without eating something. Noodle houses, bakeries, tea houses, and dim sum shops seem to occupy every other storefront. There's a feast for your eyes as well: in the market windows on Stockton and Grant, you'll see hanging whole roast ducks, fish, and shellfish swimming in tanks, and strips of shiny, pink-glazed Chinese-style barbecued pork.

CHINATOWN'S HISTORY

Sam Brannan's 1848 cry of "Gold!" didn't take long to reach across the world to China. Struggling with famine, drought, and political upheaval at home, thousands of Chinese jumped at the chance to try their luck in California. Most came from the Pearl River Delta region, in the Guangdong province, and spoke Cantonese dialects. From the start, Chinese businesses circled around Portsmouth Square, which was conveniently central. Bachelor rooming houses sprang up, since the vast majority of new arrivals were men. By 1853, the area was called Chinatown.

The Street of Gamblers (Ross Alley), 1898 (top). The first Chinese telephone operator in Chinatown (bottom).

COLD WELCOME

The Chinese faced discrimination from the get-go. Harrassment became outright hostility as first the gold rush, then the work on the Transcontinental Railroad petered out. Special taxes were imposed to shoulder aside competing "coolie labor." Laws forbidding the Chinese from moving outside Chinatown kept the residents packed in like sardines,

with nowhere to go but up and down— thus the many basement establishments in the neighborhood. State and federal laws passed in the 1870s deterred Chinese women from immigrating, deeming them prostitutes. In the late 1870s, looting and arson attacks on Chinatown businesses soared.

The coup de grace, though, was the Chinese Exclusion Act, passed by the U.S.

Chinatown's Grant Avenue.

Women and children flooded into the neighborhood after the Great Quake.

Congress in 1882, which slammed the doors to America for "Asiatics." This was the country's first significant restriction on immigration. The law also prevented the existing Chinese residents, including American-born children, from becoming naturalized citizens. With a society of mostly men (forbidden, of course, from marrying white women), San Francisco hoped that Chinatown would simply die out.

OUT OF THE ASHES

When the devastating 1906 earthquake and fire hit, city fathers thought they'd seize the opportunity to kick the Chinese out of Chinatown and get their hands on that desirable piece of downtown real estate. Then Chinatown businessman Look Tin Eli had a brainstorm of Disneyesque proportions.

He proposed that Chinatown be rebuilt, but in a tourist-friendly, stylized, "Oriental" way. Anglo-American architects would design new buildings with pagoda roofs and dragon-covered columns. Chinatown would attract more tourists—the curious had been visiting on the sly

for decades—and add more tax money to the city's coffers. Ka-ching: the sales pitch worked.

PAPER SONS

For the Chinese, the 1906 earthquake turned the virtual "no entry" sign into a flashing neon "welcome!" All the city's immigration records went up in smoke, and the Chinese quickly began to apply for passports as U.S. citizens, claiming their old ones were lost in the fire. Not only did thousands of Chinese become legal overnight, but so did their sons in China, or "sons," if they weren't really related. Whole families in Chinatown had passports in names that weren't their own; these "paper sons" were not only a windfall but also an uncomfortable neighborhood conspiracy. The city caught on eventually and set up an immigration center on Angel Island in 1910. Immigrants spent weeks or months being inspected and interrogated while their papers were checked. Roughly 250,000 people made it through. With this influx, including women and children, Chinatown finally became a more complete community.

A GREAT WALK THROUGH CHINATOWN

■ Start at the Chinatown Gate and walk ahead on Grant Avenue, entering the souvenir gauntlet. (You'll also pass Old St. Mary's Cathedral.)

■ Make a right on Clay Street and walk to Portsmouth Square. Sometimes it feels like the whole neighborhood's here, playing chess and exercising.

■ Head up Washington Street to the elaborately pago-daed Old Chinese Telephone Exchange building, now the Bank of Canton. Across Grant, look left for Waverly Place. Here Republic of China flags flap over some of the neighborhood's most striking buildings, including Tin How Temple.

■ At the Sacramento Street end of Waverly Place stands the oddly beautiful brick First Chinese Baptist Church of 1908. Just across the way, the Clarion Music Center is chock-full of unusual instruments, as well as exquisite lion-dance sets.

■ Head back to Washington Street and check out the herb shops, like the Superior Trading Company (No. 839) and the Great China Herb Co. (No. 857).

■ Follow the scent of vanilla from Washington Street down Ross Alley (entrance across from Superior Trading Company) to the Golden Gate Fortune Cookie Factory. Then head across the alley to Sam Bo Trading Co., where religious items are stacked chockablock in the narrow space. Tell the friendly owners your troubles and they'll prepare a package of joss papers, joss sticks, and candles, and tell you how and when to offer them up.

■ Turn left on Jackson Street; ahead is the real Chinatown's main artery, Stockton Street. This is where most residents do their grocery shopping; if it's Saturday, get ready for throngs (and their elbows). Look toward the back of stores for Buddhist altars with offerings of oranges and grapefruit. From here you can loop one block east back to Grant.

ALL THE TEA IN CHINATOWN

Preparing a perfect brew at Red Blossom Tea.

San Francisco's close ties to Asia have always made it more tea-conscious than other American burgs, but these days the city is in the throes of a tea renaissance, with new tasting rooms popping up in every neighborhood. Below are our favorite spots for every tea under the sun.

Blest Tea. Chinatown's smallest tea shop is a calm, modern space with a thoughtful selection of teas by the pound. The Taiwane owners sell teas from many Asian countries, but their offerings emphasize Taiwan. Regulars rave about the service. ⊠ *752 Grant Ave.* ☎ *415/951–8516.*

Red Blossom Tea. A light and modern shop—the staff really know their stuff. It's a favorite among younger tea enthusiasts, who swear by its excellent bang-for-the-buck value. While Red Blossom doesn't do formal tastings or sell tea by the cup, they'll gladly brew up perfect samples of the teas you're interested in. ⊠ *831 Grant Ave.* ☎ *415/395–0868.*

Vital Tea Leaf. Tastings here work like those for wine—one of the gregarious, knowledgeable servers chooses the teas and describes them as you sample. It's a great spot for tea newbies to get their feet wet without a hard sell, but local connoisseurs grumble about the high prices and the self-promotion. ⊠ *1044 Grant Ave.* ☎ *415/981–2388.*

Imperial Tea Court. If you want to visit the most respected of traditional tea purveyors, you'll need to venture outside of Chinatown. Imperial Tea Court's serene Powell Street oasis closed unexpectedly in 2007, but you'll find the same great selection and expertise at their fancy new digs in the Ferry Building. ☎ *415/544–9830.*

WAITING FOR CUSTARD

As you're strolling down Grant Avenue, past the plastic Buddhas and yin/yang balls, be sure to stop at the Golden Gate Bakery (No. 1029) for some delicious eggy *dan tat* (custard tarts). These flaky-crusted treats are heaven for just a buck. There's often a line, but it's worth the wait.

DON'T-MISS SHOPS

Locals snap up flowers from an outdoor vendor.

If you're in the market for a pair of chirping metal crickets (oh you'll hear them, trust us), you can duck into any of the obvious souvenir-stuffed storefronts. But if you're looking for something special, head for these tempting sources.
■TIP➜ Fierce neighborhood competition keeps prices within reason, but for popular wares like jade, it pays to shop around before making a serious investment. Many stores accept cash only.

Chinatown Kite Shop. Family-run shop selling bright, fun-shaped kites—dragons, butterflies, sharks—since the 1960s. ⊠ 717 Grant Ave. ☎ 415/989–5182.

Dragon House. A veritable museum: the store sells authentic, centuries-old antiques like ivory carvings. ⊠ 455 Grant Ave. ☎ 415/421–3693.

Old Shanghai. One of the largest selections of hand-painted robes, formal dresses, and jackets in Chinatown, plus chic Asian-inspired pieces. ⊠ 645 Grant Ave. ☎ 415/986–1222.

CHINATOWN WITH KIDS

It can be tough for the little ones to keep their hands to themselves, especially when all sorts of curios spill out onto the sidewalk at just the right height. To burn off some steam (in them) and relieve some stress (in you), take them to the small but spruce playground in St. Mary's Square, across California from Old St. Mary's. If that setting's too tranquil, head to the more boisterous Willie Wong Playground, on Sacramento Street at Waverly Place.

Kong Chow Temple. This ornate temple sets a somber, spiritual tone right away with a sign warning visitors not to touch *anything*. The god to whom the members of this temple pray represents honesty and trust. Chinese stores and restaurants often display his image because he's thought to bring good luck in business. Chinese immigrants established the temple in 1851; its congregation moved to this building in 1977. Take the elevator up to the fourth floor, where incense fills the air. You can show respect by placing a dollar or two in the donation box and by leaving your camera in its case. Amid the statuary, flowers, and richly colored altars (red wards off evil spirits and signifies virility, green symbolizes longevity, and gold connotes majesty), a couple of plaques announce that "Mrs. Harry S. Truman came to this temple in June 1948 for a prediction on the outcome of the election . . . this fortune came true." The temple's balcony has a good view of Chinatown. ⊠ *855 Stockton St., Chinatown* ☷ *Free* ☷ *Mon.–Sat. 9–4.*

Old Chinese Telephone Exchange. After the 1906 earthquake, many Chinatown buildings were rebuilt in Western style with pagoda roof and fancy balconies slapped on. This building—today the Bank of Canton—is the exception, an example of top-to-bottom Chinese architecture. The intricate three-tier pagoda was built in 1909. The exchange's operators were renowned for their prodigious memories, about which the San Francisco Chamber of Commerce boasted in 1914: "These girls respond all day with hardly a mistake to calls that are given (in English or one of five Chinese dialects) by the name of the subscriber instead of by his number—a mental feat that would be practically impossible to most high-schooled American misses." ⊠ *Bank of Canton, 743 Washington St., Chinatown.*

Portsmouth Square. Chinatown's living room buzzes with activity. The square, with its pagoda-shape structures, is a favorite spot for morning tai chi; by noon dozens of men huddle around Chinese chess tables, engaged in not-always-legal competition. Kids scamper about the square's two grungy playgrounds (warning: the bathrooms are sketchy). Back in the late 19th century this land was near the waterfront. The square is named for the U.S.S. *Portsmouth*, the ship helmed by Captain John Montgomery, who in 1846 raised the American flag here and claimed the then-Mexican land for the United States. A couple of years later, Sam Brannan kicked off the gold rush at the square when he waved his loot and proclaimed, "Gold from the American River!" Robert Louis Stevenson, the author of *Treasure Island,* often dropped by, chatting up the sailors who hung out here. Some of the information he gleaned about life at sea found its way into his fiction. A bronze galleon sculpture, a tribute to Stevenson, anchors the square's northwest corner. ⊠ *Bordered by Walter Lum Pl. and Kearny, Washington, and Clay Sts., Chinatown.*

Tin How Temple. Duck into the inconspicuous doorway, climb three flights of stairs—on the second floor is a mah-jongg parlor whose patrons hope the spirits above will favor them—and be assaulted by the aroma of incense in this tiny, altar-filled room. Day Ju, one of the first three Chinese to arrive in San Francisco, dedicated this temple to the Queen of the Heavens and the Goddess of the Seven Seas in 1852. In the temple's entryway, elderly ladies can often be seen preparing "money" to be burned as offerings to various Buddhist gods or as funds for ancestors to use in the afterlife. Hundreds of red-and-gold lanterns cover the ceiling; the larger the lamp, the larger its donor's contribution to the temple. Gifts of oranges, dim sum, and money left by the faithful, who kneel mumbling prayers, rest on altars to various gods. Tin How presides over the middle back of the temple, flanked by one red and one green lesser god. Take a good look around, since taking photographs is not allowed. ⊠ *125 Waverly Pl., Chinatown* ◳ *Free, donations accepted* ⊕ *Daily 9–4.*

SOMA AND CIVIC CENTER

To a newcomer, SoMa (short for "south of Market") and Civic Center may look like cheek-by-jowl neighbors—they're divided by Market Street. To locals, though, these areas are firmly separate entities, especially since Market Street itself is considered such a strong demarcation line. SoMa is less a neighborhood than it is a sprawling area of wide, traffic-heavy boulevards lined with office high-rises and pricey live-work lofts. Across Market Street from the western edge of SoMa is Civic Center, with San Francisco's eye-catching, gold-domed City Hall. Tickets to a show at one of the neighborhood's grand performance halls are the main reason to venture here.

EXPLORING SOMA

California Historical Society. If you're not a history buff, the CHS might seem like an obvious skip—who wants to look at fading old photographs and musty artifacts? If the answer is an indignant "I do!" or if you're just curious, these airy galleries are well worth a stop. A rotating selection draws from the society's vast repository of Californiana—hundreds of thousands of photographs, publications, paintings, and gold-rush paraphernalia. ■ TIP➔ From out front, take a look across the street: this is the best view of the Museum of the African Diaspora's three-story photo mosaic. ⊠ *678 Mission St., SoMa* ☎ *415/357–1848* ⊕ *www.californiahistoricalsociety.org* ◳ *$3* ⊕ *Wed.–Sat. noon–5; galleries close between exhibitions.*

Cartoon Art Museum. Krazy Kat, Zippy the Pinhead, Batman, and other colorful cartoon icons greet you at the Cartoon Art Museum, established with an endowment from cartoonist-icon Charles M. Schulz. The museum's strength is its changing exhibits, which explore such topics as America from the perspective of international political cartoons, and the output of women and African-American cartoonists. Serious fans of cartoons—especially those on the quirky underground side—will likely enjoy the exhibits; those with a casual interest may be disappointed. The museum store carries loads of cool titles to add to your collection. ⊠ *655 Mission St., SoMa* ☎ *415/227–8666* ⊕ *www.cartoonart. org* ◳ *$7, pay what you wish 1st Tues. of month* ⊕ *Tues.–Sun. 11–5.*

Contemporary Jewish Museum. Daniel Liebeskind designed the postmodern CJM, whose impossible-to-ignore diagonal blue cube juts out of a painstakingly restored power substation. A physical manifestation of the Hebrew phrase *l'chaim* (to life), the cube may have obscure

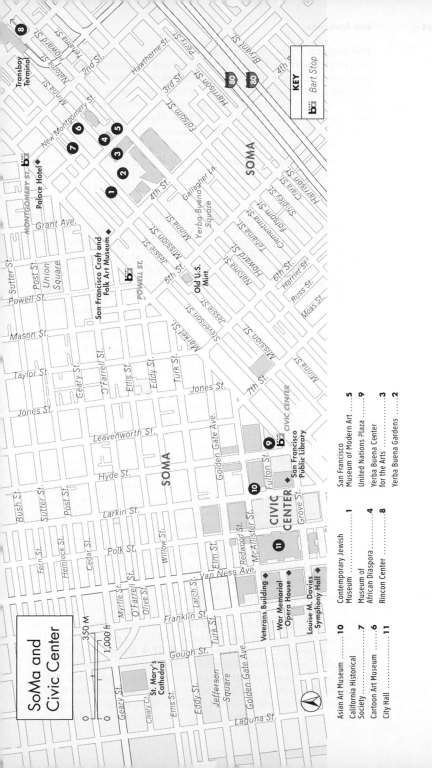

SoMa and Civic Center

KEY

b Bart Stop

St. Mary's Cathedral

Veterans Building ◆ **10**
War Memorial Opera House ◆
Louise M. Davies Symphony Hall ◆

San Francisco Craft and Folk Art Museum ◆

Palace Hotel ◆

Old U.S. Mint

San Francisco Public Library ◆

Asian Art Museum **10**
California Historical Society **7**
Cartoon Art Museum **6**
City Hall **11**
Contemporary Jewish Museum **1**
Museum of African Diaspora **4**
Rincon Center **8**
San Francisco Museum of Modern Art **5**
United Nations Plaza **9**
Yerba Buena Center for the Arts **3**
Yerba Buena Gardens **2**

philosophical origins, but Liebeskind created a unique, light-filled space that merits a stroll through the lobby even if current exhibits don't entice you into the galleries. Be sure to check out the seam where old building meets new. ■TIP➜ At the end of 2012 look for *The Snowy Day and the Art of Ezra Jack Keats*, the first major U.S. exhibit to showcase this award-winning author and illustrator. ⊠ *736 Mission St., between 3rd and 4th Sts., SoMa* ☎ *415/655–7800* ⊕ *www.thecjm.org* 🏷 *$12, $5 Thurs. after 5 pm, free 1st Tues. of the month* ☉ *Thurs. 1–8, Fri.–Tues. 11–5.*

Museum of the African Diaspora (MoAD). Dedicated to the influence that people of African descent have had all over the world, MoAD provokes discussion from the get-go with the question, "When did you discover you are African?" painted on the wall at the entrance. With no permanent collection, the museum is light on displays and heavy on interactive exhibits. For instance, you can sit in a darkened theater and listen to the moving life stories of slaves; hear snippets of music that helped create genres from gospel to hip-hop; and see videos about the Civil Rights movement or the Haitian Revolution. Some grumble that sweeping generalities replace specific information, but almost everyone can appreciate the museum's most striking exhibit in the front window. The three-story mosaic, made from thousands of photographs, forms the image of a little girl's face. Walk up the stairs inside the museum and view the photographs up close—Malcolm X is there, Muhammad Ali, too, along with everyday folks—but the best view is from across the street. ⊠ *685 Mission St., SoMa* ☎ *415/358–7200* ⊕ *www.moadsf. org* 🏷 *$10* ☉ *Wed.–Sat. 11–6, Sun. noon–5.*

Rincon Center. The only reason to visit what is basically a modern office building is the striking Works Project Administration mural by Anton Refregier in the lobby of the streamlined moderne–style former post office on the building's Mission Street side. The 27 panels depict California life from the days when Native Americans were the state's sole inhabitants through World War I. Completion of this significant work was interrupted by World War II (which explains the swastika in the final panel) and political infighting. The latter led to some alteration in Refregier's "radical" historical interpretations; they exuded too much populist sentiment for some of the politicians who opposed the artist. A permanent exhibit below the murals contains photographs and artifacts of life in the Rincon area in the 1800s. A sheer five-story column of water resembling a mini-rainstorm is the centerpiece of the indoor arcade around the corner from the mural. ⊠ *Bordered by Steuart, Spear, Mission, and Howard Sts., SoMa.*

Fodor's Choice ★ **San Francisco Museum of Modern Art (SFMOMA).** With its brick facade and a striped central tower lopped at a lipstick-like angle, architect Mario Botta's SFMOMA building fairly screams "modern-art museum." The stripes continue inside, from the black marble and gray granite of the floors to the wooden slats on the ceiling. ■TIP➜ Taking in all four exhibit floors can be overwhelming, but keep in mind that the heavy hitters are on floors 2 and 3. Floor 2 gets the big-name traveling exhibits and collection highlights such as Matisse's Woman with the Hat, Diego Rivera's The Flower Carrier, and Georgia O'Keeffe's Black Place 1. Photography

Light streams in through the skylight atop the bold striped cylinder of the San Francisco Museum of Modern Art (SFMOMA).

buffs should hustle up to floor 3, with its works by Ansel Adams and Alfred Stieglitz. Large-scale contemporary exhibits unfold on floors 4 and 5. If it's on display, don't miss sculptor Jeff Koons' memorably creepy, life-size gilded porcelain Michael Jackson and Bubbles, on the fifth floor at the end of the Turret Bridge, a vertiginous catwalk dangling under the central tower. (Look down if you dare.) The window at the bridge's other (west) end offers a great view of the Yerba Buena Gardens below. Back on the fifth floor's east side is the garage-top sculpture garden.

SFMOMA highlights in late 2012 and into 2013 include Jasper Johns: Seeing with the Mind's Eye and the documentary photography exhibit South Africa in Apartheid and After.

Caffè Museo, accessible from the street, provides a refuge with reasonably priced drinks and light meals. The museum's large store sells fun gadgets, artsy doodads of all kinds, very modern furniture, and has a superb collection of kids' books. ■TIP→ No ticket is required to visit the lobby, so if it's the architecture you're interested in, you can peek for free.

Note: the SFMOMA will be closed for a massive expansion project starting June 2013 and ending in 2016. The portions of the collection will temporarily move to neighboring museums like the Exploratorium and the Museum of the African Diaspora. See their website for details. ⌧ 151 3rd St., SoMa ☎ 415/357–4000 ⊕ www.sfmoma.org ⌚ $18, free 1st Tues. of month, ½ price Thurs. 6–9 ☉ Labor Day–Memorial Day, Fri.–Tues. 11–5:45, Thurs. 11–8:45; Memorial Day–Labor Day, Fri.–Tues. 10–5:45, Thurs. 10–8:45.

Yerba Buena Center for the Arts. You never know what's going to be on display at this facility in Yerba Buena Gardens, but whether it's an exhibit of Mexican street art (graffiti to laypeople), innovative modern dance, or baffling video installations, it's likely to be memorable. The productions here tend to draw a young, energetic crowd, and lean hard toward the cutting edge. ⊠ *701 Mission St., SoMa* ☎ *415/978–2787* ⊕ *www.ybca.org* 🎟 *Galleries $7, free 1st Tues. of month* ⊙ *Thurs.–Sat. noon–8, Sun. noon–6, 1st Tues. of the month noon–8.*

⟳ ★ **Yerba Buena Gardens.** There's not much south of Market that encourages lingering outdoors, or indeed walking at all, with this notable exception. These two blocks encompass the Center for the Arts, Metreon, Moscone Convention Center, and the convention center's rooftop Children's Creativity Museum, but the gardens themselves are the everyday draw. Office workers escape to the green swath of the East Garden. The memorial to Martin Luther King Jr. is the focal point here. Powerful streams of water surge over large, jagged stone columns, mirroring the enduring force of King's words that are carved on the stone walls and on glass blocks behind the waterfall. Moscone North is behind the memorial, and an overhead walkway leads to Moscone South and its rooftop attractions. ■TIP➜ **The gardens are liveliest during the week and especially during the Yerba Buena Gardens Festival (May through October, ⊕ *www.ybgf.org*),** when free performances run from Latin music to Balinese dance.

Atop the Moscone Convention Center perch a few lures for kids. The historic Looff carousel ($3 for two rides) twirls daily 11 to 6. South of the carousel is the Children's Creativity Museum (☎ *415/820–3320* ⊕ *creativity.org*), a high-tech, interactive arts-and-technology center ($10) geared to children ages eight and over. Kids can make Claymation videos, work in a computer lab, check out new games and apps, and perform and record music videos. The museum is open 10–4 Wednesday through Sunday. Also part of the rooftop complex are gardens, an ice-skating rink, and a bowling alley. ⊠ *Bordered by 3rd, 4th, Mission, and Folsom Sts., SoMa* ⊕ *www.yerbabuenagardens.com* 🎟 *Free* ⊙ *Daily sunrise–10 pm.*

EXPLORING CIVIC CENTER

★ **Asian Art Museum.** Expecting a building full of Buddhas and jade? Well, yeah, you can find plenty of that here. Happily, though, you don't have to be a connoisseur of Asian art to appreciate a visit to this splendidly renovated museum, whose monumental exterior conceals a light, open,

HAYES VALLEY

Hayes Valley, right next door to the Civic Center, is an offbeat neighborhood with terrific eateries, cool watering holes, and great browsing in its funky clothing and home-decor boutiques. Swing down main drag Hayes Street, between Franklin and Laguna, and you can hit the highlights, including two very popular restaurants, Absinthe and Suppenküche. Comfy Place Pigalle (at Hayes and Octavia streets) is also a favorite for its living-room atmosphere, wines, and microbrews. Locals love this quarter, but without any big-name draws it remains off the radar for most visitors.

and welcoming space. The fraction of the museum's items on display (about 2,500 pieces from a 15,000-plus-piece collection) is laid out thematically and by region, making it easy to follow developments. Begin on the third floor, where highlights of Buddhist art in Southeast Asia and early China include a large, jewel-encrusted, exquisitely painted 19th-century Burmese Buddha and clothed rod puppets from Java. On the second floor you can find later Chinese works, as well as pieces from Korea and Japan. Look for a cobalt tiger jauntily smoking a pipe on a whimsical Korean jar and delicate Japanese tea implements. The ground floor displays rotating exhibits, including contemporary and traveling shows. ■TIP➔ If you'd like to attend one of the occasional tea ceremonies and tastings at the Japanese Teahouse, call ahead, since preregistration is required. ⊠ *200 Larkin St., between McAllister and Fulton Sts., Civic Center* ☎ *415/581–3500* ⊕ *www.asianart.org* 🖼 *$12, free 1st Sun. of month; $10 some Thurs. 5–9; tea ceremony $27, includes museum* ☽ *Tues.–Sun. 10–5; Jan.–Oct., Thurs. until 9.*

City Hall. This imposing 1915 structure with its massive gold-leaf dome—higher than the U.S. Capitol's—is about as close to a palace as you're going to get in San Francisco. (Alas, the metal detectors take something away from the grandeur.) The classic granite-and-marble behemoth was modeled after St. Peter's Cathedral in Rome. Architect Arthur Brown Jr., who also designed Coit Tower and the War Memorial Opera House, designed an interior with grand columns and a sweeping central staircase. San Franciscans were thrilled, and probably a bit surprised, when his firm built City Hall in just a few years. The 1899 structure it replaced had taken 27 years to erect, as corrupt builders and politicians lined their pockets with funds earmarked for it. That building collapsed in about 27 seconds during the 1906 earthquake, revealing trash and newspapers mixed into the construction materials.

City Hall was spruced up and seismically retrofitted in the late 1990s, but the sense of history remains palpable. Some noteworthy events that have taken place here include the marriage of Marilyn Monroe and Joe DiMaggio (1954); the hosing—down the central staircase—of civil-rights and freedom-of-speech protesters (1960); the murders of Mayor George Moscone and openly gay supervisor Harvey Milk (1978); the torching of the lobby by angry members of the gay community in response to the light sentence given to the former supervisor who killed both men (1979); and the registrations of scores of gay couples in celebration of the passage of San Francisco's Domestic Partners Act (1991). February 2004 has come to be known as the Winter of Love: thousands of gay and lesbian couples responded to Mayor Gavin Newsom's decision to issue marriage licenses to same-sex partners, turning City Hall into the site of raucous celebration and joyful nuptials for a month before the state Supreme Court ordered the practice stopped. That celebratory scene replayed during 2008, when scores of couples were wed between the court's June ruling that everyone enjoys the civil right to marry and the November passage of California's ballot proposition banning same-sex marriage. (Stay tuned as the issue moves through the courts and perhaps back to the voters.) Free tours are offered weekdays at 10, noon, and 2.

The South Light Court houses a modest, rotating display from the collection of the **Museum of the City of San Francisco** (⊕ *www.sfmuseum. org*), including historical items, maps, and photographs. That enormous, 700-pound iron head once crowned the *Goddess of Progress* statue, which topped the old City Hall building when it crumbled during the 1906 earthquake.

Across Polk Street is **Civic Center Plaza,** with lawns, walkways, seasonal flower beds, a playground, and an underground parking garage. This sprawling space is generally clean but somewhat grim. A large part of the city's homeless population hangs out here, despite frequently being shunted away, so the plaza can feel dodgy. ⊠ *Bordered by Van Ness Ave. and Polk, Grove, and McAllister Sts., Civic Center* ☎ *415/554–6023* ⊕ *www.sfgov.org/site/cityhall* ☜ *Free* ⊙ *Weekdays 8–8.*

United Nations Plaza. Locals know this plaza for two things: its Wednesday and Sunday farmers' market—cheap and earthy to the Ferry Building's pricey and beautiful—and its homeless population, which seems to return no matter how many times the city tries to shunt them aside. Brick pillars listing various nations and the dates of their admittance into the United Nations line the plaza, and its floor is inscribed with the goals and philosophy of the United Nations charter, which was signed at the War Memorial Opera House in 1945. ⊠ *Fulton St. between Hyde and Market Sts., Civic Center.*

NOB HILL AND RUSSIAN HILL

In place of the quirky charm and cultural diversity that mark other San Francisco neighborhoods, Nob Hill exudes history and good breeding. Topped with some of the city's most elegant hotels, Gothic Grace Cathedral, and private blue-blood clubs, it's the pinnacle of privilege. One hill over, across Pacific Avenue, is another old-family bastion, Russian Hill. It may not be quite as wealthy as Nob Hill, but it's no slouch—and it's known for its jaw-dropping views.

Nob Hill was officially dubbed during the 1870s when "the Big Four"— Charles Crocker, Leland Stanford, Mark Hopkins, and Collis Huntington, who were involved in the construction of the transcontinental railroad—built their hilltop estates. The lingo is thick from this era: those on the hilltop were referred to as "nabobs" (originally meaning a provincial governor from India) and "swells," and the hill itself was called Snob Hill, a term that survives to this day. By 1882 so many estates had sprung up on Nob Hill that Robert Louis Stevenson called it "the hill of palaces." But the 1906 earthquake and fire destroyed all the palatial mansions except for portions of the Flood brownstone. History buffs may choose to linger here, but for most visitors, a casual glimpse from a cable car will be enough.

Essentially a tony residential neighborhood of spiffy pieds-à-terre, Victorian flats, Edwardian cottages, and boxlike condos, Russian Hill also has some of the city's loveliest stairway walks, hidden garden ways, and steepest streets—brave drivers can really have some fun here—not to mention those bay views. Several stories explain the origin of Russian Hill's name. One legend has it that Russian farmers raised vegetables

here for Farallon Islands seal hunters; another attributes the name to a Russian sailor of prodigious drinking habits who drowned when he fell into a well on the hill. A plaque at the top of the Vallejo Steps gives credence to the version that says sailors of the Russian-American company were buried here in the 1840s. Be sure to visit the sign for yourself—its location offers perhaps the finest vantage point on the hill.

EXPLORING NOB HILL

Cable Car Museum. The Cable Car Museum is one of the city's best free offerings and an absolute must for kids. (You can even ride a cable car there, since all three lines stop between Russian Hill and Nob Hill.) The museum, which is inside the city's last cable-car barn, takes the top off the system to let you see how it all works. Eternally humming and squealing, the massive powerhouse cable wheels steal the show. You can also climb aboard a vintage car and take the grip, let the kids ring a cable-car bell (briefly), and check out vintage gear dating from 1873.

The gift shop sells cable-car paraphernalia, including an authentic grip-man's bell for $600 (it'll sound like Powell Street in your house every day). For significantly less, you can pick up a key chain made from a piece of worn-out cable. ⊠ *1201 Mason St., at Washington St., Nob Hill* ☎ *415/474–1887* ⊕ *www.cablecarmuseum.com* ⊠ *Free* ⊙ *Oct.–Mar., daily 10–5; Apr.–Sept., daily 10–6.*

Grace Cathedral. Not many churches can boast an altarpiece by Keith Haring and not one but two labyrinths. The seat of the Episcopal Church in San Francisco, this soaring Gothic-style structure, erected on the site of Charles Crocker's mansion, took 53 years to build, wrapping up in 1964. The gilded bronze doors at the east entrance were taken from casts of Lorenzo Ghiberti's incredible Gates of Paradise, which are on the Baptistery in Florence, Italy. A black-and-bronze stone sculpture of St. Francis by Beniamino Bufano greets you as you enter.

The 35-foot-wide limestone labyrinth is a replica of the 13th-century stone maze on the floor of Chartres Cathedral. All are encouraged to walk the ¼-mile-long labyrinth, a ritual based on the tradition of meditative walking. There's also a terrazzo outdoor labyrinth on the church's north side. The AIDS Interfaith Chapel, to the right as you enter Grace, contains a metal triptych by the late artist Keith Haring and panels from the AIDS Memorial Quilt. ■ **TIP→** Especially dramatic times to view the cathedral are during Thursday-night evensong (5:15) and during special holiday programs. ✉ *1100 California St., at Taylor St., Nob Hill* ☎ *415/749–6300* ⊕ *www.gracecathedral.org* ⊙ *Weekdays 7–6, Sat. 8–6, Sun. 8–7.*

Pacific Union Club. The former home of silver baron James Flood cost a whopping $1.5 million in 1886, when even a stylish Victorian like the Haas-Lilienthal House cost less than $20,000. All that cash did buy some structural stability. The Flood residence (to be precise, its shell) was the only Nob Hill mansion to survive the 1906 earthquake and fire. The Pacific Union Club, a bastion of the wealthy and powerful, purchased the house in 1907 and commissioned Willis Polk to redesign it; the architect added the semicircular wings and third floor. (The ornate fence design dates from the mansion's construction.) West of the house, Huntington Park is the site of the Huntington mansion, destroyed in 1906. Mrs. Huntington donated the land to the city for use as a park; the Crockers purchased the Fountain of the Tortoises, based on the original in Rome. ■ **TIP→** The benches around the fountain offer a welcome break after climbing Nob Hill. It's hard to get the skinny on the club itself; its 700 or so members allegedly follow the directive "no women, no Democrats, no reporters." Those who join usually spend years on the waiting list and undergo a stringent vetting process, the rigors of which might embarrass the NSA. Needless to say, the club is closed to the public. ✉ *1000 California St., Nob Hill.*

EXPLORING RUSSIAN HILL

Feusier House. Octagonal houses were once thought to make the best use of space and enhance the physical and mental well-being of their occupants. A brief mid-19th-century craze inspired the construction of several in San Francisco. Only the Feusier House, built in 1857, and the Octagon House in Pacific Heights remain standing. A private residence, the Feusier House is easy to overlook unless you look closely— it's dwarfed by the large-scale apartments around it. Across from the Feusier House is the **1907 Firehouse** (✉ *1088 Green St.*). Louise M. Davies, the local art patron for whom Symphony Hall is named, bought it from the city in 1957. The firehouse is closed to the public, but it's worth taking in the exterior. ✉ *1067 Green St., Russian Hill.*

Continued on page 175

CABLE CARS

The moment it dawns on you that you severely underestimated the steepness of the San Francisco hills will likely be the same moment you look down and realize those tracks aren't just for show—or just for tourists.

Sure, locals rarely use the cable cars for commuting these days. (That's partially due to the $6 fare—hear that, Muni?) So you'll likely be packed in with plenty of fellow sightseers. You may even be approaching cable-car fatigue after seeing its image on so many souvenirs. But if you fear the magic is gone, simply climb on board, and those jaded thoughts will dissolve. Grab the pole and gawk at the view as the car clanks down an insanely steep grade toward the bay. Listen to the humming cable, the clang of the bell, and the occasional quip from the gripman. It's an experience you shouldn't pass up, whether on your first trip or your fiftieth.

HOW CABLE CARS WORK

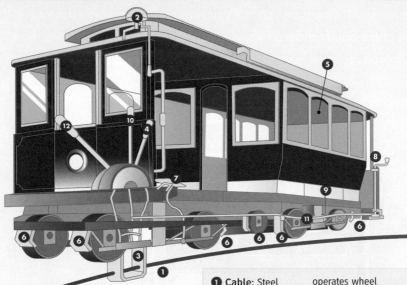

The mechanics are pretty simple: cable cars grab a moving subterranean cable with a "grip" to go. To stop, they release the grip and apply one or more types of brakes. Four cables, totaling 9 miles, power the city's three lines. If the gripman doesn't adjust the grip just right when going up a steep hill, the cable will start to slip and the car will have to back down the hill and try again. This is an extremely rare occurrence—imagine the ribbing the gripman gets back at the cable car barn!

Gripman: Stands in front and operates the grip, brakes, and bell. Favorite joke, especially at the peak of a steep hill: "This is my first day on the job folks..."

Conductor: Moves around the car, deals with tickets, alerts the grip about what's coming up, and operates the rear wheel brakes.

❶ Cable: Steel wrapped around flexible sisal core; 2 inches thick; runs at a constant 9½ mph.

❷ Bells: Used for crew communication; alerts other drivers and pedestrians.

❸ Grip: Vice-like lever extends through the center slot in the track to grab or release the cable.

❹ Grip Lever: Left-hand lever; operates grip.

❺ Car: Entire car weighs 8 tons.

❻ Wheel Brake: Steel brake pads on each wheel.

❼ Wheel Brake Lever: Foot pedal; operates wheel brakes.

❽ Rear Wheel Brake Lever: Applied for extra traction on hills.

❾ Track Brake: 2-foot long sections of Monterey pine push down against the track to help stop the car.

❿ Track Brake Lever: Middle lever; operates track brakes.

⓫ Emergency Brake: 18-inch steel wedge, jams into street slot to bring car to an immediate stop.

⓬ Emergency Brake Lever: Right-hand lever, red; operates emergency brake.

ROUTES

Cars run at least every 15 minutes, from around 6 AM to about 1 AM.

Powell–Hyde line: Most scenic, with classic Bay views. Begins at Powell and Market streets, then crosses Nob Hill and Russian Hill before a white-knuckle descent down Hyde Street, ending near the Hyde Street Pier.

Powell–Mason line: Also begins at Powell and Market streets, but winds through North Beach to Bay and Taylor streets, a few blocks from Fisherman's Wharf.

California line: Runs from the foot of Market Street, at Drumm Street, up Nob Hill and back. Great views (and aromas and sounds) of Chinatown on the way up. Sit in back to catch glimpses of the Bay. ■TIP➜ Take the California line if it's just the cable-car experience you're after—the lines are shorter, and the grips and conductors say it's friendlier and has a slower pace.

RULES OF THE RIDE

Tickets. A whopping $6 each way. There are ticket booths at all three turnarounds, or you can pay the conductor after you board (they can make change). Try not to grumble about the price—they're embarrassed enough as it is.

■TIP➜ If you're planning to use public transit a few times, or if you'd like to ride back and forth on the cable car without worrying about the price, consider a one-day Muni passport ($14). You can get passports online, at the Powell Street turnaround, the TIX booth on Union Square, or the Fisherman's Wharf cable-car ticket booth at Beach and Hyde streets.

All Aboard. You can board on either side of the cable car. It's legal to stand on the running boards and hang on to the pole, but keep your ears open for the gripman's warnings. ■TIP➜ Grab a seat on the outside bench for the best views.

Most people wait (and wait) in line at one of the cable car turnarounds, but you can also hop on along the route. Board wherever you see a white sign showing a figure climbing aboard a brown cable car; wave to the approaching driver, and wait until the car stops.

Riding on the running boards can be part of the thrill.

CABLE CAR HISTORY

HALLIDIE FREES THE HORSES

In the 1850s and '60s, San Francisco's streetcars were drawn by horses. Legend has it that the horrible sight of a car dragging a team of horses downhill to their deaths roused Andrew Smith Hallidie to action. The English immigrant had invented the "Hallidie Ropeway," essentially a cable car for mined ore, and he was convinced that his invention could also move people. In 1873, Hallidie and his intrepid crew prepared to test the first cable car high on Russian Hill. The anxious engineer peered down into the foggy darkness, failed to see the bottom of the hill, and promptly turned the controls over to Hallidie. Needless to say, the thing worked . . . but rides were free for the first two days because people were afraid to get on.

SEE IT FOR YOURSELF

The **Cable Car Museum** is one of the city's best free offerings and an absolute must for kids. (You can even ride a cable car there, since all three lines stop between Russian Hill and Nob Hill.) The museum, which is inside the city's last cable-car barn, takes the top off the system to let you see how it all works.

Eternally humming and squealing, the massive powerhouse cable wheels steal the show. You can also climb aboard a vintage car and take the grip, let the kids ring a cable-car bell (briefly, please!), and check out vintage gear dating from 1873.

✉ *1201 Mason St., at Washington St., Nob Hill* ☎ *415/474–1887* ⊕ *www.cablecarmuseum.com* 🖾 *Free* ☉ *Oct.–Mar., daily 10–5; Apr.–Sept., daily 10–6*

■ **TIP→** The gift shop sells cable car paraphernalia, including an authentic gripman's bell for $600 (it'll sound like Powell Street in your house every day). For significantly less, you can pick up a key chain made from a piece of worn-out cable.

CHAMPION OF THE CABLE CAR BELL

Each June the city's best and brightest come together to crown a bell-ringing champion at Union Square. The crowd cheers gripmen and conductors as they stomp, shake, and riff with the rope. But it's not a popularity contest; the ringers are judged by former bell-ringing champions who take each ping and gong very seriously.

★ **Ina Coolbrith Park.** If you make it all the way up here, you may have the place all to yourself, or at least feel like you do. The park's terraces are carved from a hill so steep that it's difficult to see if anyone else is there or not. Locals love this park because it feels like a secret no one else knows about—one of the city's magic hidden gardens, with a meditative setting and spectacular views of the bay peeking out from among the trees. A poet, Oakland librarian, and niece of Mormon prophet Joseph Smith, Ina Coolbrith (1842–1928) introduced Jack London and Isadora Duncan to the world of books. For years she entertained literary greats in her Macondray Lane home near the park. In 1915 she was named poet laureate of California. ⊠ *Vallejo St. between Mason and Taylor Sts., Russian Hill.*

★ **Lombard Street.** The block-long "Crookedest Street in the World" makes eight switchbacks down the east face of Russian Hill between Hyde and Leavenworth streets. Residents bemoan the traffic jam outside their front doors, but the throngs continue. Join the line of cars waiting to drive down the steep hill, or avoid the whole mess and walk down the steps on either side of Lombard. You take in super views of North Beach and Coit Tower whether you walk or drive—though if you're the one behind the wheel, you'd better keep your eye on the road lest you become yet another of the many folks who ram the garden barriers. ■TIP➔ Can't stand the traffic? Thrill seekers of a different stripe may want to head two blocks south of Lombard to Filbert Street. At a gradient of 31.5%, the hair-raising descent between Hyde and Leavenworth streets is the city's steepest. Go slowly! ⊠ *Lombard St. between Hyde and Leavenworth Sts., Russian Hill.*

Fodor's Choice
★ **Macondray Lane.** San Francisco has no shortage of impressive, grand homes, but it's the tiny fairy-tale lanes that make most folks want to move here, and Macondray Lane is the quintessential hidden garden. Enter under a lovely wooden trellis and proceed down a quiet, cobbled pedestrian lane lined with Edwardian cottages and flowering plants and trees. Watch your step—the cobblestones are quite uneven in spots. A flight of steep wooden stairs at the end of the lane leads to Taylor Street—on the way down you can't miss the bay views. If you've read any of Armistead Maupin's *Tales of the City* books, you may find the lane vaguely familiar. It's the thinly disguised setting for part of the series' action. ⊠ *Between Jones and Taylor Sts., and Union and Green Sts., Russian Hill.*

★ **San Francisco Art Institute.** A Moorish-tile fountain in a tree-shaded courtyard draws the eye as soon as you enter the institute. The number-one reason for a visit is Mexican master Diego Rivera's *Making of a Fresco Showing the Building of a City* (1931), in the student gallery to your immediate left inside the entrance. Rivera himself is in the fresco—his broad behind is to the viewer—and he's surrounded by his assistants. They in turn are surrounded by a construction scene, laborers, and city notables such as sculptor Robert Stackpole and architect Timothy Pfleuger. *The Making of a Fresco* is one of three San Francisco murals painted by Rivera. The number-two reason to come here is the café, or more precisely the eye-popping, panoramic view from the café, which serves surprisingly decent food for a song.

The older portions of the Art Institute, including the lovely Mission-style bell tower, were erected in 1926. To this day, otherwise pragmatic people claim that ghostly footsteps can be heard in the tower at night. Ansel Adams created the school's fine-arts photography department in 1946, and school directors established the country's first fine-arts film program. Notable faculty and alumni have included painter Richard Diebenkorn and photographers Dorothea Lange, Edward Weston, and Annie Leibovitz.

The **Walter & McBean Galleries** (☎ *415/749–4563* ☉ *Tues.–Sat. 11–6*) exhibit the often provocative works of established artists. ✉ *800 Chestnut St., North Beach* ☎ *415/771–7020* ⊕ *www.sfai.edu* ✇ *Galleries free* ☉ *Student gallery daily 8:30–8:30.*

NORTH BEACH

San Francisco novelist Herbert Gold calls North Beach "the longest-running, most glorious American bohemian operetta outside Greenwich Village." Indeed, to anyone who's spent some time in its eccentric old bars and cafés, North Beach evokes everything from the Barbary Coast days to the no-less-rowdy Beatnik era. Italian bakeries appear frozen in time, homages to Jack Kerouac and Allen Ginsberg pop up everywhere, and the modern equivalent of the Barbary Coast's "houses of ill repute," strip joints, do business on Broadway. With its outdoor café tables, throngs of tourists, and holiday vibe, this is probably the part of town Europeans are thinking of when they say San Francisco is the most European city in America.

EXPLORING NORTH BEACH

★ **City Lights Bookstore.** Take a look at the exterior of the store: the replica of a revolutionary mural destroyed in Chiapas, Mexico, by military forces; the poetry in the windows; and the sign that says "Turn your sell [sic] phone off. Be here now." This place isn't just doling out best sellers. Designated a city landmark, the hangout of Beat-era writers— Allen Ginsberg and store founder Lawrence Ferlinghetti among them— remains a vital part of San Francisco's literary scene. Browse the three levels of sometimes haphazardly arranged poetry, philosophy, politics, fiction, history, and local zines, to the tune of creaking wood floors. ■ TIP→ Be sure to check the calendar of literary events.

Back in the day, the basement was a kind of literary living room, where writers like Ginsberg and Jack Kerouac would read and even receive mail. Ferlinghetti cemented City Lights's place in history by publishing Ginsberg's *Howl and Other Poems* in 1956. The small volume was ignored in the mainstream . . . until Ferlinghetti and the bookstore manager were arrested for corruption of youth and obscenity. In the landmark First Amendment trial that followed, the judge exonerated both men, declaring that a work that has "redeeming social significance" can't be obscene. *Howl* went on to become a classic.

Kerouac Alley, branching off Columbus Avenue next to City Lights, was rehabbed in 2007. Embedded in the pavement are quotes from

Ferlinghetti, Maya Angelou, Confucius, John Steinbeck, and the street's namesake. ⊠ *261 Columbus Ave.* ☎ *415/362–8193* ⊕ *www.citylights. com* ⊙ *Daily 10 am–midnight.*

★ **Coit Tower.** Whether or not you agree that it resembles a fire-hose nozzle, this 210-foot tower is among San Francisco's most distinctive skyline sights. Although the monument wasn't intended as a tribute to firemen, it's often considered as such because of the donor's special attachment to the local fire company. As the story goes, a young gold rush–era girl, Lillie Hitchcock Coit (known as Miss Lil), was a fervent admirer of her local fire company—so much so that she once deserted a wedding party and chased down the street after her favorite engine, Knickerbocker No. 5, while clad in her bridesmaid finery. She became the Knickerbocker Company's mascot and always signed her name "Lillie Coit 5." When Lillie died in 1929 she left the city $125,000 to "expend in an appropriate manner . . . to the beauty of San Francisco."

You can ride the elevator to the top of the tower—the only thing you have to pay for here—to enjoy the view of the Bay Bridge and the Golden Gate Bridge; due north is Alcatraz Island. ■**TIP➔** The views from the base of the tower are also expansive—and free. Parking at Coit Tower is limited; in fact, you may have to wait (and wait) for a space. Save yourself some frustration and take the 39 bus, which goes all the way up to the tower's base, or, if you're in good shape, hike up. ⇨ *For more details on the lovely stairway walk, see the Telegraph Hill listing.*

Inside the tower, 19 Depression-era murals depict California's economic and political life. The federal government commissioned the paintings from 25 local artists, and ended up funding a controversy. The radical Mexican painter Diego Rivera inspired the murals' socialist-realist style, with its biting cultural commentary, particularly about the exploitation of workers. At the time the murals were painted, clashes between management and labor along the waterfront and elsewhere in San Francisco were widespread. ⊠ *Telegraph Hill Blvd. at Greenwich St. or Lombard St., North Beach* ☎ *415/362–0808* ⊠ *Free; elevator to top $7* ⊙ *Mar.– Sept., daily 10–5:30; Oct.–Feb., daily 9–4:30.*

Fodor's Choice
★ **Telegraph Hill.** Residents here have some of the city's best views, as well as the most difficult ascents to their aeries. The hill rises from the east end of Lombard Street to a height of 284 feet and is capped by Coit Tower *(see above)*. Imagine lugging your groceries up that! If you brave the slope, though, you can be rewarded with a "secret treasure" SF moment. Filbert Street starts up the hill, then becomes the Filbert Steps when the going gets too steep. You can cut between the Filbert Steps and another flight, the Greenwich Steps, on up to the hilltop. As you climb, you can pass some of the city's oldest houses and be surrounded by beautiful, flowering private gardens. In some places the trees grow over the stairs so it feels like you're walking through a green tunnel; elsewhere, you'll have wide-open views of the bay. And the telegraphic name? It comes from the hill's status as the first Morse code signal station back in 1853. ⊠ *Bordered by Lombard, Filbert, Kearny, and Sansome Sts., North Beach.*

North Beach and On the Waterfront

East Harbor

Mexican Museum

Fort Mason

Aquatic Park

San Francisco Bay

Pier 47

Pier 45

12

13

The Cannery at Del Monte Square

11

Pier 41

NORTH BEACH

14

10

Pier 35

Pier 33

Pier 31

Pier 29

Pier 27

Russian Hill Park

RUSSIAN HILL

Washington Square

7

8

9

Levi Strauss Headquarters

Pier 23

Pier 19

Pier 17

Pier 15

Pier 9

5

Cable Car Museum

6

NOB HILL

4

3

Huntington Park

Pier 7

Pier 5

Pier 3

Pier 1

Wells Fargo Bank History Museum

Union Square

DOWNTOWN

MONTGOMERY ST.

Market St.

EMBARCADERO

Justin Herman Plaza

Hyatt Regency Hotel

2

Jessie St.

Mission St.

1

Yerba Buena Gardens

Minna St.

Natoma St.

Audiffred Building

CITY FRONT

Tehama St.

Clementina St.

Folsom St.

Howard St.

0   350 meters

0   1,000 ft

Taber Pl.

Bryant St.

80

San Francisco - Oakland Bay Bridge

Pier 26

CLOSE UP

The Birds

While on Telegraph Hill, you might be startled by a chorus of piercing squawks and a rushing sound of wings. No, you're not about to have a Hitchcock bird-attack moment. These small, vivid green parrots with cherry-red heads number in the hundreds; they're descendants of former pets that escaped or were released by their owners. (The birds dislike cages and they bite if bothered... must've been some disillusioned owners along the way.)

The parrots like to roost high in the aging cypress trees on the hill, chattering and fluttering, sometimes taking wing en masse. They're not popular with most residents, but they did find a champion in local bohemian Mark Bittner, a former street musician. Bittner began chronicling their habits, publishing a book and battling the homeowners who wanted to cut down the cypresses. A documentary, *The Wild Parrots of Telegraph Hill*, made the issue a cause célèbre. In 2007 City Hall, which recognizes a golden goose when it sees one, stepped in and brokered a solution to keep the celebrity birds in town. The city will cover the homeowners' insurance worries and plant new trees for the next generation of wild parrots.

—Denise M. Leto

Washington Square. Once the daytime social heart of Little Italy, this grassy patch has changed character numerous times over the years. The Beats hung out in the 1950s, hippies camped out in the 1960s and early 70s, and nowadays you're just as likely to see kids of Southeast Asian descent tossing a Frisbee as Italian men or women chatting about their children and the old country. In the morning elderly Asians perform the motions of tai chi, but by mid-morning groups of conservatively dressed Italian men in their seventies and eighties begin to arrive. Any time of day, the park may attract a number of homeless people, who stretch out to rest on the benches and grass, and young locals sunbathing or running their dogs. Lillie Hitchcock Coit, in yet another show of affection for San Francisco's firefighters, donated the statue of two firemen with a child they rescued. ■TIP➔ The North Beach Festival, the city's oldest street fair, celebrates the area's Italian culture here each June. ⊠ *Bordered by Columbus Ave. and Stockton, Filbert, and Union Sts., North Beach.*

ON THE WATERFRONT

San Francisco's waterfront neighborhoods have fabulous views and utterly different personalities. Kitschy, overpriced Fisherman's Wharf struggles to maintain the last shreds of its existence as a working wharf, while Pier 39 is a full-fledged consumer circus. The Ferry Building draws well-heeled locals with its culinary pleasures, firmly reconnecting the Embarcadero to downtown. Between the Ferry Building and Pier 39 a former maritime no-man's-land is filling in with Alcatraz Landing, fashionable waterfront restaurants, restored pedestrian-friendly piers, and in 2013, the new Exploratorium.

Today's shoreline was once Yerba Buena Cove, filled in during the latter half of the 19th century, when San Francisco was a brawling, extravagant gold-rush town. Jackson Square, now a genteel and upscale corner of the inland Financial District, was the heart of the Barbary Coast, bordering some of the roughest wharves in the world. Below Montgomery Street (in today's Financial District), between California Street and Broadway, lies a remnant of these wild days: more than 100 ships abandoned by frantic crews and passengers caught up in gold fever lie under the foundations of buildings here.

EXPLORING THE WATERFRONT

Alcatraz. Thousands of visitors come every day to walk in the footsteps of Alcatraz's notorious criminals. The stories of life and death on "the Rock" may sometimes be exaggerated, but it's almost impossible to resist the chance to wander the cellblock that tamed the country's toughest gangsters and saw daring escape attempts of tremendous desperation. Fewer than 2,000 inmates ever did time on the Rock, and though they weren't the worst criminals, they were definitely the worst prisoners, include Al "Scarface" Capone, Robert "The Birdman" Stroud, and George "Machine Gun" Kelly.

Some tips for escaping to Alcatraz: 1) Buy your ticket in advance. Visit the website for Alcatraz Cruises (*www.alcatrazcruises.com*) to scout out available departure times for the ferry. Prepay by credit card and keep a receipt record; the ticket price covers the boat ride and the audio tour. Pick up your ticket at the "will call" window at Pier 33 up to an hour before sailing. 2) Dress smart. Bring a jacket to ward off the chill from the boat ride and wear comfortable shoes. 3) Go for the evening tour. You'll get even more out of your Alcatraz experience at night. The evening tour has programs not offered during the day, the bridge-to-bridge view of the city twinkles at night, and your "prison experience" will be amplified as darkness falls. 4) Be mindful of scheduled and limited-capacity talks. Some programs are only given once a day (the schedule is posted in the cell house). Certain talks have limited-capacity seating, so keep an eye out for a cell-house staffer handing out passes shortly before the start time.

The boat ride to the island is brief (15 minutes), but affords beautiful views of the city, Marin County, and the East Bay. The audio tour, highly recommended, includes observations by guards and prisoners about life in one of America's most notorious penal colonies. Plan your schedule to allow at least three hours for the visit and boat rides combined. ⊠ *Pier 33, Embarcadero* ☎ *415/981–7625* ⊕ *www.nps.gov/alca* 🎟 *$28, including audio tour; $35 evening tour, including audio* ⊙ *Ferry departs every 30–45 mins Sept.–late May, daily 9:30–2:15, 4:20 for evening tour Thurs.–Mon. only; late May–Aug., daily 9:30–4:15, 6:30 and 7:30 for evening tour.*

☾ **Exploratorium.** Walking into this fascinating "museum of science, art, and
★ human perception" is like visiting a mad scientist's laboratory. Most of the exhibits are supersize, and you can play with everything. After moving into its new, larger digs on the Embarcadero in April 2013, the Exploratorium will have even more space for its signature experiential

Thousands of visitors take ferries to Alcatraz each day to walk in the footsteps of the notorious criminals who were held on "The Rock."

exhibits, including a new Tinkering Studio and a brand-new glass Bay Observatory building, where exhibits inside will help visitors better understand what they see outside. Look for surprises outside the building, too. Quintessential Exploratorium exhibits remain: Get an Alice in Wonderland feeling in the distortion room, where you seem to shrink and grow as you walk across the slanted, checkered floor. In the shadow room, a powerful flash freezes an image of your shadow on the wall; jumping is a favorite pose. "Pushover" demonstrates cow-tipping, but for people: stand on one foot and try to keep your balance while a friend swings a striped panel in front of you (trust us, you're going to fall).

More than 650 other exhibits focus on sea and insect life, computers, electricity, patterns and light, language, the weather, and much more. "Explainers"—usually high-school students on their days off—demonstrate cool scientific tools and procedures, like DNA sample-collection and cow-eye dissection. One surefire hit is the pitch-black, touchy-feely Tactile Dome, newly built in the Embarcadero space. In this geodesic dome strewn with textured objects, you crawl through a course of ladders, slides, and tunnels, relying solely on your sense of touch. Not surprisingly, lovey-dovey couples sometimes linger in the "grope dome," but be forewarned: the staff will turn on the lights if they have to. ■ TIP→ Reservations are required for the Tactile Dome, and will get you 75 minutes of access. You have to be at least seven years old to go through the dome, and the space is not for the claustrophobic. The Exploratorium plans to remain open in its Marina home through January 2013. Call ahead to confirm which location is open when you visit and the hours it's open. ⊠ *Piers 15–17, Embarcadero* ☎ *415/561–0360 general information, 415/561–0362 Tactile Dome reservations ⊕ www.exploratorium.edu* ✉ *$15, free 1st Wed. of month; Tactile Dome $5 extra* ☉ *Tues.–Sun. 10–5.*

Fodor's Choice ★ **Ferry Building.** The jewel of the Embarcadero, erected in 1896, is topped by a 230-foot clock tower modeled after the campanile of the cathedral in Seville, Spain. On the morning of April 18, 1906, the tower's four clock faces, powered by the swinging of a 14-foot pendulum, stopped at 5:17—the moment the great earthquake struck—and stayed still for 12 months.

Today San Franciscans flock to the street-level marketplace, stocking up on supplies from local favorites such as Acme Bread, Scharffen Berger Chocolate, Cowgirl Creamery, and Blue Bottle Coffee. Lucky diners claim a coveted table at Slanted Door, the city's beloved high-end Vietnamese restaurant. The seafood bars at Hog Island Oyster Company and Ferry Plaza Seafood have fantastic city panoramas—or you can take your purchases around to the building's bay side, where benches face views of the Bay Bridge. On Saturday mornings the plazas outside the building buzz with an upscale farmers' market where you can buy exotic sandwiches and other munchables. Extending from the piers on the north side of the building south to the Bay Bridge, the waterfront promenade is a favorite among joggers and picnickers, with a front-row view of the sailboats slipping by. The Ferry Building also serves actual ferries: from behind the building they sail to Sausalito, Larkspur, Tiburon, and the East Bay. ⊠ *Embarcadero at foot of Market St., Embarcadero* ☎ *415/983–8030* ⊕ *www.ferrybuildingmarketplace.com.*

QUICK BITES **Buena Vista Café.** Smack-dab at the end of the Hyde Street cable-car line, the Buena Vista packs 'em in for its famous Irish coffee—which, according to owners, was the first served stateside (in 1952). The place oozes nostalgia, drawing devoted locals as well as out-of-towners relaxing after a day of sightseeing. It's narrow and can get crowded, but this spot is a welcome respite from the overpriced generic tourist joints nearby. ⊠ *2765 Hyde St., at Beach St., Fisherman's Wharf* ☎ *415/474–5044* ⊕ *www.thebuenavista.com.*

☼ **Fisherman's Wharf.** It may be one of the city's best-known attractions, but the Wharf is a no-go zone for most locals, who shy away from the difficult parking, overpriced food, and cheesy shops at third-rate shopping centers like the Cannery at Del Monte Square. If you can't resist a

F-LINE TROLLEYS

F-line. The F-line, the city's system of vintage electric trolleys, gives the cable cars a run for their money as San Francisco's best-loved mode of transportation. These beautifully restored streetcars—some dating from the 19th century—run from the Castro all the way down Market Street to the Embarcadero, then north to Fisherman's Wharf. Each car is unique, restored to the colors of its city of origin, from New Orleans and Philadelphia to Moscow and Milan. Purchase tickets on board; exact change is required. ⊕ *www.streetcar.org* ✉ *$2.*

visit here, come early to avoid the crowds and get a sense of the Wharf's functional role—it's not just an amusement park replica.

Most of the entertainment at the Wharf is schlocky and overpriced, with one notable exception: the splendid **Musée Mécanique** (☎ *415/346–2000* ☾ *Weekdays 10–7, weekends 10–8*), a time-warped arcade with antique mechanical contrivances, including peep shows and nickelodeons. Some favorites are the giant and rather creepy "Laffing Sal," an arm-wrestling machine, the world's only steam-powered motorcycle, and mechanical fortune-telling figures that speak from their curtained boxes. Note the depictions of race that betray the prejudices of the time: stoned Chinese figures in the "Opium-Den" and clown-faced African-Americans eating watermelon in the "Mechanical Farm." Admission is free, but you'll need quarters to bring the machines to life.

Just outside, the USS *Pampanito* (Pier 45, ☎ *415/775–1943* ⊕ *www. maritime.org/pamphome.htm*☾ *Oct.–Memorial Day, Sun.–Thurs. 9–6, Fri. and Sat. 9–8; Memorial Day–Sept., Thurs.–Tues. 9–8, Wed. 9–6*) provides an intriguing if mildly claustrophobic glimpse into life on a submarine during World War II. The sub sank six Japanese warships and damaged four others. Admission is $10; the family pass is a great deal at $20 for two adults and up to four kids.

Among the two floors of exhibits at **Ripley's Believe It or Not! Museum** (✉ 175 Jefferson St., ☎ *415/771–6188* ⊕ *www.ripleysf.com* ✍ *$19.99* ☾ *Late June–Labor Day, Sun.–Thurs. 9 am–11 pm, Fri. and Sat. 9 am–midnight; Labor Day–early June, Sun.–Thurs. 10–10, Fri. and Sat. 10 am–midnight*) is a tribute to San Francisco—an 8-foot-long scale model of a cable car, made entirely of matchsticks.

Notables from local boy Robin Williams to King Tut await at the **Wax Museum** (✉ *145 Jefferson St.* ☎ *415/202–0400, 800/439–4305* ⊕ *www.waxmuseum.com*), open daily 10–9. Admission is $14. ✉ *Jefferson St. between Leavenworth St. and Pier 39, Fisherman's Wharf.*

Ghirardelli Square. Most of the redbrick buildings in this early-20th-century complex were once part of the Ghirardelli factory. Now tourists come here to pick up the famous chocolate, though you can purchase it all over town and save yourself a trip to what is essentially a mall. But this is the only place to watch the cool chocolate manufactory in action. (If you're a chocoholic, this definitely beats the Cannery.) There are no fewer than three Ghirardelli stores here, as well as gift shops and a couple of restaurants—including Ana Mandara—that even locals love. Fairmont recently opened an upscale urban time-share directly on the square. Placards throughout the square describe the factory's history. ✉ *900 N. Point St., Fisherman's Wharf* ☎ *415/775–5500* ⊕ *www. ghirardellisq.com.*

☾ ★ **Hyde Street Pier.** Cotton candy and souvenirs are all well and good, but if you want to get to the heart of the Wharf—boats—there's no better place to do it than at this pier, one of the Wharf area's best bargains. Depending on the time of day, you might see boatbuilders at work or children pretending to man an early-1900s ship.

Don't pass up the centerpiece collection of historic vessels, part of the **San Francisco Maritime National Historic Park,** almost all of which can be boarded. The *Balclutha,* an 1886 full-rigged three-masted sailing vessel that's more than 250 feet long, sailed around Cape Horn 17 times; kids especially love the *Eureka,* a side-wheel passenger and car ferry, for her onboard collection of vintage cars; the *Hercules* is a steam-powered tugboat. The *C.A. Thayer,* a three-masted schooner, recently underwent a painstaking restoration.

Across the street from the pier and almost a museum in itself is the San Francisco Maritime National Historic Park's **Visitor Center** (✉ *499 Jefferson St.* ☎ *415/447–5000* ☯ *June–Aug., daily 9:30–5:30; Sept.– May, daily 9:30–5*), happily free of mind-numbing, text-heavy displays. Instead, fun large-scale exhibits, such as a huge First Order Fresnel lighthouse lens and a shipwrecked boat, make this an engaging and relatively quick stop. ✉ *Hyde and Jefferson Sts., Fisherman's Wharf* ☎ *415/561–7100* ⊕ *www.nps.gov/safr* ⛴ *Ships $5* ☯ *June–Aug., daily 9:30–5:30; Sept.–May, daily 9:30–5.*

Jackson Square. This was the heart of the Barbary Coast of the Gay 90s (the 1890s, that is). Although most of the red-light district was destroyed in the fire that followed the 1906 earthquake, old redbrick buildings and narrow alleys recall the romance and rowdiness of San Francisco's early days. The days of brothels and bar fights are long gone—now Jackson Square is a genteel, quiet corner of the Financial District. It's of interest to the historically inclined and antiques-shop browsers, but otherwise safely skipped.

Some of the city's first business buildings, survivors of the 1906 quake, still stand between Montgomery and Sansome streets. After a few decades of neglect, these old-timers were adopted by preservation-minded interior designers and wholesale furniture dealers for use as showrooms. In 1972 the city officially designated the area—bordered by Columbus Avenue on the west, Broadway and Pacific Avenue on the north, Washington Street on the south, and Sansome Street on the east—San Francisco's first historic district. When property values soared, many of the fabric and furniture outlets fled to Potrero Hill. Advertising agencies, attorneys, and antiques dealers now occupy the Jackson Square–area structures.

It takes a bit of conjuring to evoke the wild Barbary Coast days when checking out the now-gentrified gold rush–era buildings in the 700 block of **Montgomery Street.** But this was an especially colorful block. Author Mark Twain was a reporter for the spunky *Golden Era* newspaper, which occupied No. 732 (now part of the building at No. 744). From 1959 to 1996 the late ambulance-chaser extraordinaire, lawyer Melvin Belli, had his headquarters at Nos. 722 and 728–730. There was never a dull moment in Belli's world; he represented clients from Mae West to Gloria Sykes (who in 1964 claimed that a cable-car accident turned her into a nymphomaniac) to Jim and Tammy Faye Bakker. Whenever he won a case, he fired a cannon and raised the Jolly Roger. Belli was also known for receiving a letter from the never-caught Zodiac killer. It seems fitting that the building sat for years, deteriorating and moldering, while the late attorney's sons fought wife number five (joined with Belli in holy matrimony just three months before his death). She eventually won, but today the dilapidated building is for sale.

Restored 19th-century brick buildings line Hotaling Place, which connects Washington and Jackson streets. The lane is named for the head of the **A.P. Hotaling Company whiskey distillery** (⊠ *451 Jackson St., at Hotaling Pl.*), which was the largest liquor repository on the West Coast in its day. (Hotaling whiskey is still made in the city, by the way; look for their single malts for a sip of truly local flavor.) ⊠ *Jackson Sq. district, bordered by Broadway and Washington, Kearny, and Sansome Sts., Financial District.*

☾ **Pier 39.** The city's most popular waterfront attraction draws millions of visitors each year who come to browse through its shops and concessions hawking every conceivable form of souvenir. The pier can be quite crowded, and the numerous street performers may leave you feeling more harassed than entertained. Arriving early in the morning ensures you a front-row view of the sea lions, but if you're here to shop—and make no mistake about it, Pier 39 wants your money—be aware that most stores don't open until 9:30 or 10 (later in winter).

Pick up a buckwheat hull–filled otter neck wrap or a plush sea lion to snuggle at the **Marine Mammal Center Store** (☎ *415/289–7373*), whose proceeds benefit Sausalito's respected wild-animal hospital, the Marine Mammal Center.

Brilliant colors enliven the double-decker **San Francisco Carousel** ($3 per ride), decorated with images of such city landmarks as the Golden Gate Bridge and Lombard Street.

Follow the sound of barking to the northwest side of the pier to view the sea lions that flop about the floating docks.

At **Aquarium of the Bay** (☎ *415/623–5300 or 888/732–3483* ⊕ *www. aquariumofthebay.org* ⊠ *$16.95* ☾ *June–Sept., daily 9–8; Mar.–May and Oct., Mon.–Thurs. 10–7, Fri.–Sun. 10–8; Nov.–Feb., daily 10–7)* moving walkways transport you through a space surrounded on three sides by water filled with indigenous San Francisco Bay marine life, from fish and plankton to sharks. Many find the aquarium overpriced; if you can, take advantage of the family rate ($46 for two adults and two kids under 12).

The **California Welcome Center** (☎ *415/981–1280* ⊕ *www.visitcwc. com* ☾ *Daily 10–6)*, on Pier 39's second level, can help you reserve tours and plan your time in the city.

Parking (free with validation from a Pier 39 restaurant) is at the Pier 39 Garage, off Powell Street at the Embarcadero. ⊠ *Beach St. at Embarcadero, Fisherman's Wharf* ⊕ *www.pier39.com.*

☾ **San Francisco Railway Museum.** A labor of love brought to you by the same vintage-transit enthusiasts responsible for the F-line's revival, this one-room museum and store celebrates the city's storied streetcars and cable cars with photographs, models, and artifacts. The permanent exhibit includes the replicated end of a streetcar with a working cab—complete with controls and a bell—for kids to explore; the cool, antique Wiley birdcage traffic signal; and models and display cases to view. Right on

4

the F-line track, just across from the Ferry Building, this is a great quick stop. ⊠ *77 Steuart St., Embarcadero* ☎ *415/974–1948* ⊕ *www.streetcar. org* ⌷ *Free* ☉ *Tues.–Sun. 10–6.*

Transamerica Pyramid. It's neither owned by Transamerica nor is it a pyramid, but this 853-foot-tall obelisk *is* the most photographed of the city's high-rises. Excoriated in the design stages as "the world's largest architectural folly," the icon was quickly hailed as a masterpiece when it opened in 1972. Today it's probably the city's most recognized structure after the Golden Gate Bridge. A fragrant redwood grove along the east side of the building, replete with benches and a cheerful fountain, is a placid patch in which to unwind. ⊠ *600 Montgomery St., Financial District* ⊕ *www.transamerica.com.*

THE MARINA AND THE PRESIDIO

Yachts bob at their moorings, satisfied-looking folks jog along the Marina Green, and multimillion-dollar homes overlook the bay in this picturesque, if somewhat sterile, neighborhood. Does it all seem a bit too perfect? Well, it got this way after the hard knock of Loma Prieta—the current pretty face was put on after hundreds of homes collapsed in the 1989 earthquake. Just west of this waterfront area is a more natural beauty: the Presidio. Once a military base, this beautiful, sprawling park is mostly green space, with hills, woods, and the marshlands of Crissy Field.

EXPLORING THE MARINA

Fort Mason Center. Originally a depot for the shipment of supplies to the Pacific during World War II, the fort was converted into a cultural center in 1977. Here you can find the vegetarian restaurant Greens and shops, galleries, and performance spaces, most of which are closed Monday. You have to be seriously into Italian-American culture to appreciate the text- and photograph-heavy exhibits at the **Museo Italo-Americano** (⊠ *Bldg. C* ☎ *415/673–2200* ⊕ *museoitaloamericano.org* ☉ *Tues.–Sun. noon–4*), but depending on the exhibit, it might be worth a glance if you're already at Fort Mason. Plus, it's free. The temporary exhibits downstairs at the free **SFMOMA Artists Gallery** (⊠ *Bldg. A* ☎ *415/441–4777*) can be great, but head upstairs and check out the paintings, sculptures, prints, and photographs for sale and for rent. It's a fun scene, with folks flipping through the works like posters. You won't find a Picasso or a Rembrandt here, but you can find works of high quality by emerging Northern California artists—and where else can you get a $50,000 work of art to hang on your wall for $400 (a month)? It's open Tuesday through Saturday 11:30–5:30. While waiting for its permanent home downtown, the **Mexican Museum** (⊠ *Bldg. D* ☎ *415/202–9700*) hosts temporary exhibits in this small space. It's open Wednesday through Sunday noon to 4 and admission is free. ⊠ *Buchanan St. and Marina Blvd., Marina* ☎ *415/345–7500 event information* ⊕ *www.fortmason.org.*

Fodor's Choice
★

Palace of Fine Arts. At first glance this stunning, rosy rococo palace seems to be from another world, and indeed, it's the sole survivor of the many tinted-plaster structures (a temporary classical city of sorts) built for the 1915 Panama-Pacific International Exposition, the world's fair that celebrated San Francisco's recovery from the 1906 earthquake and fire. The expo buildings originally extended about a mile along the shore. Bernard Maybeck designed this faux–Roman classic beauty, which was reconstructed in concrete and reopened in 1967. A victim of the elements, the Palace required a piece-by-piece renovation that was completed in 2008.

The pseudo-Latin language adorning the Palace's exterior urns continues to stump scholars. The massive columns (each topped with four "weeping maidens"), great rotunda, and swan-filled lagoon have been used in countless fashion layouts, films, and wedding photo shoots. After admiring the lagoon, look across the street to the house at 3460 Baker Street. If the maidens out front look familiar, they should—they're original casts of the lovely "garland ladies" you can see in the Palace's colonnade. ⊠ *3301 Lyon St., at Beach St., Marina* ☎ *415/561–0364 Palace history tours* ⊕ *www.palaceoffinearts.org* ✉ *Free* ☉ *Daily 24 hrs.*

EXPLORING THE PRESIDIO

Fort Point. Dwarfed today by the Golden Gate Bridge, this brick fortress constructed between 1853 and 1861 was designed to protect San Francisco from a Civil War sea attack that never materialized. It was also used as a coastal-defense fortification post during World War II, when soldiers stood watch here. This National Historic Site is now a sprawling museum filled with military memorabilia, surrounding a lonely, windswept courtyard. The building has a gloomy air and is suitably atmospheric. (It's usually chilly and windy, too, so bring a jacket.) On days when Fort Point is staffed, guided group tours and cannon drills take place. The top floor affords a unique angle on the bay. ■TIP→ Take care when walking along the front side of the building, as it's slippery, and the waves have a dizzying effect. Note that the fort is open only Friday through Sunday. The fort's popular guided candlelight tours, available only in winter, sell out in advance, so be sure to book ahead. Southeast of this structure is the **Fort Point Mine Depot,** an army facility that functioned as the headquarters for underwater mining operations throughout World War II. Today it's the Warming Hut, a National Park Service café and bookstore. ⊠ *Marine Dr. off Lincoln Blvd., Presidio* ☎ *415/556–1693* ⊕ *www.nps.gov/fopo* ✉ *Free* ☉ *Fri.–Sun. 10–5.*

Fodor's Choice
★

Golden Gate Bridge. The suspension bridge that connects San Francisco with Marin County has long wowed sightseers with its simple but powerful art-deco design. Completed in 1937 after four years of construction, the 1.7-mile span and its 750-foot towers were built to withstand winds of more than 100 mph. It's also not a bad place to be in an earthquake: designed to sway up to 27.7 feet, the Golden Gate Bridge, unlike the Bay Bridge, was undamaged by the 1989 Loma Prieta quake. (If you're on the bridge when it's windy, stand still and you can feel it swaying a bit.) Though it's frequently gusty and misty—always bring a jacket, no matter what the weather's like—the bridge provides unparalleled views of the Bay Area. Muni buses 28 and 76 make stops at the Golden Gate Bridge toll plaza, on the San Francisco side. However, drive to fully appreciate the bridge from multiple vantage points in and around the Presidio; you'll be able to park at designated areas.

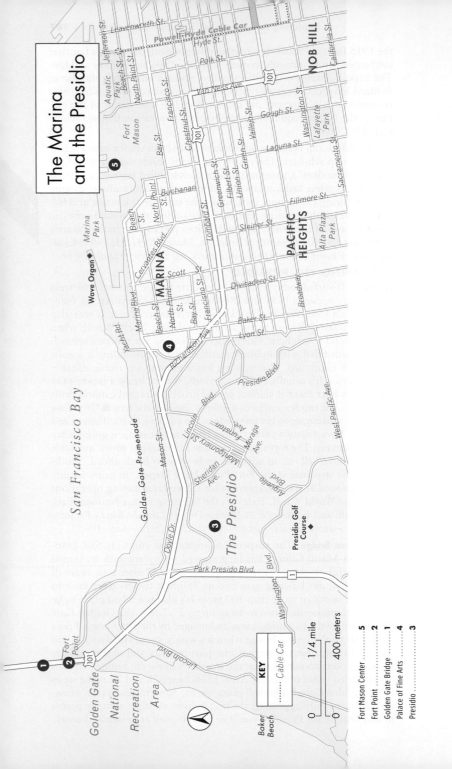

The Marina
and the Presidio

NOB HILL

PACIFIC HEIGHTS

MARINA

The Presidio

Golden Gate National Recreation Area

San Francisco Bay

Golden Gate Promenade

Fort Point

Wave Organ ◆

Marina Park

Fort Mason

Aquatic Park

Marina Blvd.

Yacht Rd.

Cervantes Blvd.

Richardson Ave.

Mason St.

Doyle Dr.

Lincoln Blvd.

Baker Beach

Lincoln Blvd.

Presidio Golf Course ◆

Presidio Blvd.

West Pacific Ave.

Arguello Blvd.

Washington Blvd.

Park Presido Blvd.

Sheridan Ave.

Moraga Ave.

Montgomery St.

Funston Ave.

Leavenworth St.

Jefferson St.

Beach St.

North Point St.

Bay St.

Francisco St.

Chestnut St.

Lombard St.

Greenwich St.

Filbert St.

Union St.

Green St.

Vallejo St.

Broadway

Pacific Ave.

Washington St.

Sacramento St.

California St.

Hyde St.

Polk St.

Van Ness Ave.

Gough St.

Laguna St.

Buchanan St.

Fillmore St.

Steiner St.

Divisadero St.

Broderick St.

Baker St.

Lyon St.

Scott St.

Beach St.

North Point St.

Bay St.

Francisco St.

Powell-Hyde Cable Car

Lafayette Park

Alta Plaza Park

101

101

1

KEY
⬤ Cable Car

0	1/4 mile
0	400 meters

From the bridge's eastern-side walkway—the only side pedestrians are allowed on—you can take in the San Francisco skyline and the bay islands; look west for the wild hills of the Marin Headlands, the curving coast south to Land's End, and the Pacific Ocean. On sunny days sailboats dot the water, and brave windsurfers test the often-treacherous tides beneath the bridge. A vista point on the Marin side gives you a spectacular city panorama.

But there's a well-known, darker side to the bridge's story, too. The bridge is perhaps the world's most popular suicide platform, with an average of about 20 jumpers per year. (The first leaped just three months after the bridge's completion, and the official count was stopped in 1995 as the 1,000th jump approached.) Signs along the bridge read "There is hope. Make the call," referring the disconsolate to the special telephones on the bridge. Bridge officers, who patrol the walkway and watch by security camera to spot potential jumpers, successfully talk down two-thirds to three-quarters of them each year. Documentary filmmaker Eric Steel's controversial 2006 movie *The Bridge* once again put pressure on the Golden Gate Bridge Highway and Transportation District to install a suicide barrier. The unobtrusive net supported by most locals is finally in the design phase, though funding hasn't been secured. ✉ *Lincoln Blvd. near Doyle Dr. and Fort Point, Presidio* ☎ *415/921–5858* ⊕ *www.goldengatebridge.org* ☉ *Pedestrians Mar.–Oct., daily 5 am–9 pm; Nov.–Feb., daily 5 am–6 pm; hrs change with daylight saving time. Bicyclists daily 24 hrs.*

★ **Presidio.** When San Franciscans want to spend a day in the woods, they head here. The Presidio has 1,400 acres of hills and majestic woods, two small beaches, and stunning views of the bay, the Golden Gate Bridge, and Marin County. Famed environmental artist Andy Goldsworthy's sculpture greets visitors at the Arguello Gate entrance. The 100-plus-foot *Spire*, made of 37 cypress logs reclaimed from the Presidio, looks like a rough, natural version of a church spire. ■ **TIP→** The best lookout points lie along Washington Boulevard, which meanders through the park.

Part of the **Golden Gate National Recreation Area,** the Presidio was a military post for more than 200 years. Don Juan Bautista de Anza and a band of Spanish settlers first claimed the area in 1776. It became a Mexican garrison in 1822, when Mexico gained its independence from Spain; U.S. troops forcibly occupied the Presidio in 1846. The U.S. Sixth Army was stationed here until October 1994.

Today the area is being transformed into a self-sustaining national park with a combination of public, commercial, and residential projects. In 2005 Bay Area filmmaker George Lucas opened the **Letterman Digital Arts Center,** his 23-acre digital studio "campus," along the eastern edge of the land. Seventeen of those acres are exquisitely landscaped and open to the public. If you have kids in tow or are a *Star Wars* fan yourself, sidle over to the **Yoda Fountain** (Letterman Dr. and Dewitt Rd.), between two of the ILM buildings.

The battle over the fate of the rest of the Presidio is ongoing. Many older buildings have been reconstructed; the issue now is how to fill them. The original plan described a nexus for arts, education, and environmental

Armed with only helmets, safety harnesses, and painting equipment, a full-time crew of 38 painters keeps the Golden Gate Bridge clad in International Orange.

groups. Since the Presidio's overseeing trust was tasked with making the park financially self-sufficient by 2013, which means generating enough revenue to keep afloat without the federal government's monthly $20 million checks, many fear that money will trump culture. The Asian-theme SenSpa and a new Walt Disney museum have opened, and a lodge at the Main Post is in the planning stages. With old military housing now repurposed as apartments and homes with rents up to $10,000 a month, there's some concern that the Presidio will become an incoherent mix of pricey real estate. Still, the $6 million that Lucas shells out annually for rent does plant a lot of saplings.

The Presidio also has two beaches, a golf course, a visitor center, and picnic sites; the views from the many overlooks are sublime.

Especially popular is **Crissy Field**, a stretch of restored marshland along the sand of the bay. Kids on bikes, folks walking dogs, and joggers share the paved path along the shore, often winding up at the Warming Hut, a combination café and fun gift store at the end of the path, for a hot chocolate in the shadow of the Golden Gate Bridge. Midway along the Golden Gate Promenade that winds along the shore is the Gulf of the Farallones National Marine Sanctuary Visitor Center, where kids can get a close-up view of small sea creatures and learn about the rich ecosystem offshore. Temporarily relocated to East Beach, just across from the Palace of Fine Arts, Crissy Field Center offers great children's programs and has cool science displays; grab lunch at the Beach Hut Café next door. West of the Golden Gate Bridge is sandy **Baker Beach,** beloved for its spectacular views and laid-back vibe (read: you'll see naked people here). This is one of those places that inspires local pride.

✉ *Between Marina and Lincoln Park, Presidio* ⊕ *www.nps.gov/prsf and www.presidio.gov.*

GOLDEN GATE PARK AND THE WESTERN SHORELINE

More than 1,000 acres, stretching from the Haight all the way to the windy Pacific coast, Golden Gate Park is a vast patchwork of woods, trails, lakes, lush gardens, sports facilities, museums—even a herd of buffalo. There's more natural beauty beyond the park's borders, along San Francisco's wild Western Shoreline.

EXPLORING GOLDEN GATE PARK

California Academy of Sciences. With its native plant–covered living roof, retractable ceiling, three-story rain forest, gigantic planetarium, living coral reef, and frolicking penguins, the Cal Academy is one of the city's most spectacular treasures. Dramatically designed by Renzo Piano, it's an eco-friendly, energy-efficient adventure in biodiversity and green architecture. The roof's large mounds and hills mirror the local topography, and Piano's audacious design completes the dramatic transformation of the park's Music Concourse. Moving away from a restrictive role as a backward-looking museum that catalogued natural history, the new academy is all about sustainability and the future, but you'll still find those beloved dioramas in African Hall.

By the time you arrive, hopefully you've decided which shows and programs to attend, looked at the academy's floor plan, and designed a plan to cover it all in the time you have. And if not, here's the quick version: Head left from the entrance to the wooden walkway over otherworldly rays in the Philippine Coral Reef, then continue to the Swamp to see the famous albino alligator. Swing through African Hall and gander at the penguins, take the elevator up to the living roof, then return to the main floor and get in line to explore the Rainforests of the World, ducking free-flying butterflies and watching for other live surprises. You'll end up below ground in the Amazonian Flooded Rainforest, where you can explore the academy's other aquarium exhibits. Phew. ✉ *55 Music Concourse Dr.* ☎ *415/379–8000* ⊕ *www.calacademy.org* 🖭 *$29.95, free one Sun. per quarter* ☉ *Mon.–Sat. 9:30–5, Sun. 11–5.*

Conservatory of Flowers. Whatever you do, be sure to at least drive by the Conservatory of Flowers—it's just too darn pretty to miss. The gorgeous, white-framed 1878 glass structure is topped with a 14-ton glass dome. Stepping inside the giant greenhouse is like taking a quick trip to the rain forest, with its earthy smell and humid warmth. The undeniable highlight is the Aquatic Plants section, where lily pads float and carnivorous plants dine on bugs to the sounds of rushing water. On the east side of the conservatory (to the right as you face the building), cypress, pine, and redwood trees surround the Dahlia Garden, which blooms in summer and fall. To the west is the Rhododendron Dell, which contains 850 varieties, more than any other garden in the country. It's a favorite local Mother's Day picnic spot. ✉ *John F. Kennedy Dr. at Conservatory Dr., Golden Gate Park* ☎ *415/666–7001* ⊕ *www.conservatoryofflowers.org* 🖭 *$7, free 1st Tues. of month* ☉ *Tues.–Sun. 10–4:30.*

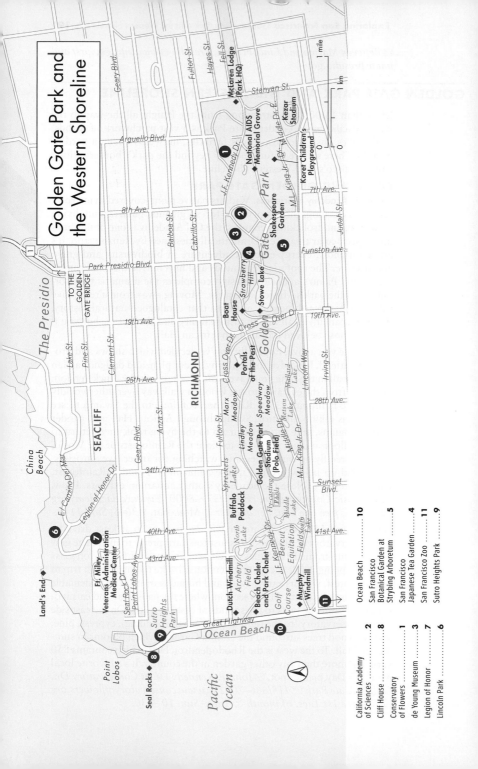

Golden Gate Park and the Western Shoreline

The Presidio

TO THE GOLDEN GATE BRIDGE

SEACLIFF

RICHMOND

Golden Gate Park

Geary Blvd.

Arguello Blvd.

Park Presidio Blvd.

Lake St.

Pine St.

Clement St.

Geary Blvd.

Anza St.

Fulton St.

8th Ave.

19th Ave.

25th Ave.

34th Ave.

40th Ave.

43rd Ave.

41st Ave.

28th Ave.

Balboa St.

Cabrillo St.

El Camino Del Mar

Legion of Honor Dr.

Seal Rock Dr.

Point Lobos Ave.

China Beach

Land's End

Point Lobos

Seal Rocks

Pacific Ocean

Ocean Beach

Great Highway

Sunset Blvd.

Sutro Heights Park

Ft. Miley

Veterans Administration Medical Center

Dutch Windmill

Archery Field

Beach Chalet and Park Chalet

Murphy Windmill

Golf Course

North Lake

Buffalo Paddock

Middle Lake

South Lake

J.F. Kennedy Dr.

Bercut Equitation Field

Fly-casting Pools

Golden Gate Park Stadium (Polo Field)

Spreckels Lake

Lindley Meadow

Marx Meadow

Speedway Meadow

Fulton St.

M.L. King Jr. Dr.

Middle Dr.

Metson Lake

Mallard Lake

Lincoln Way

Irving St.

Judah St.

Funston Ave.

7th Ave.

Stanyan St.

Fulton St.

Hayes St.

Fell St.

McLaren Lodge (Park HQ)

National AIDS Memorial Grove

Kezar Stadium

Koret Children's Playground

M.L. King Jr. Dr.

Middle Dr. E.

Shakespeare Garden

Stowe Lake

Strawberry Hill

Boat House

Portals of the Past

Cross Over Dr.

Over Dr.

J.F. Kennedy Dr.

19th Ave.

1 mile

1 km

de Young Museum. It seems that everyone in town has a strong opinion about the de Young Museum: Some adore its striking copper facade, while others just hope that the green patina of age will mellow the effect. Most maligned is the 144-foot tower, but the view from its ninth-story observation room, ringed by floor-to-ceiling windows and free to the public, is worth a trip here by itself. The building almost overshadows the de Young's respected collection of American, African, and Oceanic art. The museum also plays host to major international exhibits, such as 2010's showing of postimpressionist works on loan from the Musée d'Orsay and 2011's exhibit of 100 works from Paris's Musée National Picasso. ✉ *50 Hagiwara Tea Garden Dr., Golden Gate Park* 🕾 *415/750–3600* ⊕ *deyoung.famsf.org* 💳 *$10, free 1st Tues. of month* 🕙 *Tues.–Sun. 9:30–5:15; mid-Jan.–Nov., Fri. until 8:45.*

San Francisco Japanese Tea Garden. As you amble through the manicured landscape, past Japanese sculptures and perfect miniature pagodas, over ponds of carp that have been here since before the 1906 quake, you may be transported to a more peaceful plane. Or maybe the shrieks of kids clambering over the almost vertical "humpback" bridges will keep you firmly in the here and now. Either way, this garden is one of those tourist spots that's truly worth a stop (a half hour will do). And at 5 acres, it's large enough that you'll always be able to find a bit of serenity, even when the tour buses drop by. The garden is especially lovely in April, when the cherry blossoms are in bloom. ✉ *Hagiwara Tea Garden Dr., off John F. Kennedy Dr., Golden Gate Park* 🕾 *415/752–4227* ⊕ *www. japaneseteagardensf.com* 💳 *$7, free Mon., Wed., and Fri. if you enter by 10 am* 🕙 *Mar.–Oct., daily 9–6; Nov.–Feb., daily 9–4:45.*

San Francisco Botanical Garden at Strybing Arboretum. One of the best picnic spots in a very picnic-friendly park, the 55-acre arboretum specializes in plants from areas with climates similar to that of the Bay Area. Walk the Eastern Australian garden to see tough, pokey shrubs and plants with cartoon-like names, such as the hilly-pilly tree. Kids gravitate toward the large shallow fountain and the pond with ducks, turtles, and egrets. Alas, the city began charging admission to the gardens in 2010, so it's a slightly less alluring picnic spot compared to the free stretches in front of the Conservatory of Flowers and on the Music Concourse between the de Young and the Cal Academy. ✉ *Enter the park at 9th Ave. at Lincoln Way, Golden Gate Park* 🕾 *415/661–1316* ⊕ *www.sfbotanicalgarden.org* 💳 *$7, free 2nd Tues. of month* 🕙 *Apr.– Oct., daily 9–6; Nov.–Mar., daily 10–5.*

EXPLORING THE WESTERN SHORELINE

Cliff House. A meal at the Cliff House isn't about the food—the spectacular ocean view is what brings folks here. The vistas, which include offshore Seal Rock (the barking marine mammals who reside there are actually sea lions), can be 30 miles or more on a clear day—or less than a mile on foggy days. ■ TIP➜ Come for drinks just before sunset; then head back into town for dinner.

Three buildings have occupied this site since 1863. The current building dates from 1909; a 2004 renovation has left a strikingly attractive restaurant and a squat concrete viewing platform out back. The complex, owned by the National Park Service, includes a gift shop.

Sitting on the observation deck is the **Giant Camera,** a camera obscura with its lens pointing skyward housed in a cute yellow-painted wooden shack. Built in the 1940s and threatened many times with demolition, it's now on the National Register of Historic Places. Step into the dark, tiny room inside (for a $3 fee); a fascinating 360-degree image of the surrounding area—which rotates as the "lens" on the roof rotates—is projected on a large, circular table. ■**TIP➜** In winter and spring you may also glimpse migrating gray whales from the observation deck.

To the north of the Cliff House are the ruins of the once-grand glass-roof **Sutro Baths,** which you can explore on your own (they look a bit like water-storage receptacles). Adolf Sutro, eccentric onetime San Francisco mayor and Cliff House owner, built the bath complex, including a train out to the site, in 1896, so that everyday folks could enjoy the benefits of swimming. Six enormous baths (some freshwater and some seawater), more than 500 dressing rooms, and several restaurants covered 3 acres north of the Cliff House and accommodated 25,000 bathers. Likened to Roman baths in a European glass palace, the baths were for decades the favorite destination of San Franciscans in search of entertainment. The complex fell into disuse after World War II, was closed in 1952, and burned down (under officially questionable circumstances, wink wink) during demolition in 1966. ⊠ *1090 Point Lobos Ave., Outer Richmond* ☎ *415/386–3330* ⊕ *www.cliffhouse.com* ⊒ *Free* ⊙ *Weekdays 9 am–9:30 pm, weekends 9 am–10 pm.*

Fodor's Choice   **Legion of Honor.** The old adage of real estate—location, location, loca-
★   tion—is at full force here. You can't beat the site of this museum of European art atop cliffs overlooking the ocean, the Golden Gate Bridge, and the Marin Headlands. A pyramidal glass skylight in the entrance court illuminates the lower-level galleries, which exhibit prints and drawings, English and European porcelain, and ancient Assyrian, Greek, Roman, and Egyptian art. The 20-plus galleries on the upper level display the permanent collection of European art (paintings, sculpture, decorative arts, and tapestries) from the 14th century to the present day.

The noteworthy Auguste Rodin collection includes two galleries devoted to the master and a third with works by Rodin and other 19th-century sculptors. An original cast of Rodin's *The Thinker* welcomes you as you walk through the courtyard. As fine as the museum is, the setting and view outshine the collection and make a trip here worthwhile.

The **Legion Café,** on the lower level, serves tasty light meals (soup, sandwiches, grilled chicken) inside and on a garden terrace. (Unfortunately, there's no view.) Just north of the museum's parking lot is George Segal's *The Holocaust,* a stark white installation that evokes life in concentration camps during World War II. It's haunting at night, when backlighted by lights in the Legion's parking lot. ■**TIP➜** Admission to the Legion also counts as same-day admission to the de Young Museum. ⊠ *34th Ave. at Clement St., Outer Richmond* ☎ *415/750–3600* ⊕ *legionofhonor.famsf.org* ⊒ *$10, $2 off with Muni transfer, free 1st Tues. of month* ⊙ *Tues.–Sun. 9:30–5:15.*

★ **Lincoln Park.** Although many of the city's green spaces are gentle and welcoming, Lincoln Park is a wild 275-acre park with windswept cliffs and panoramic views. The newly renovated Coastal Trail, the park's most dramatic one, leads out to **Lands End;** pick it up west of the Legion of Honor (at the end of El Camino del Mar) or from the parking lot at Point Lobos and El Camino del Mar. Time your hike to hit Mile Rock at low tide, and you might catch a glimpse of two wrecked ships peeking up from their watery graves. ⚠ Do be careful if you hike here; landslides are frequent, and many people have fallen into the sea by standing too close to the edge of a crumbling bluff top.

On the tamer side, large Monterey cypresses line the fairways at Lincoln Park's 18-hole golf course, near the Legion of Honor. At one time this land was the Golden Gate Cemetery, where the dead were segregated by nationality; most were indigent and interred without ceremony in the potter's field. In 1900 the Board of Supervisors voted to ban burials within city limits, and all but two city cemeteries (at Mission Dolores and the Presidio) were moved to Colma, a small town just south of San Francisco. When digging has to be done in the park, bones occasionally surface again. ⊠ *Entrance at 34th Ave. at Clement St, Outer Richmond.*

Ocean Beach. Stretching 3 miles along the western side of the city from the Richmond to the Sunset, this sandy swath of the Pacific coast is good for jogging or walking the dog—but not for swimming. The water is so cold that surfers wear wet suits year-round, and riptides are strong. As for sunbathing, it's rarely warm enough here; think meditative walking instead of sun worshipping.

Paths on both sides of the Great Highway lead from Lincoln Way to Sloat Boulevard (near the zoo); the beachside path winds through landscaped sand dunes, and the paved path across the highway is good for biking and in-line skating. (Though you have to rent bikes elsewhere.) The **Beach Chalet** restaurant and brewpub is across the Great Highway from Ocean Beach, about five blocks south of the Cliff House. ⊠ *Along Great Hwy. from Cliff House to Sloat Blvd. and beyond.*

☺ **San Francisco Zoo.** Ever since one of its tigers escaped its enclosure and killed a visitor on Christmas Day 2007, the city's zoo has concentrated on polishing its image, raising funds to update its habitats, and restoring its reputation with animal welfare organizations. Occupying prime oceanfront property, the zoo is touting its metamorphosis into the "New Zoo," a wildlife-focused recreation center that inspires visitors to become conservationists. Integrated exhibits group different species of animals from the same geographic areas together in enclosures that don't look like cages. More than 250 species reside here, including endangered species such as the snow leopard, Sumatran tiger, grizzly bear, and as of 2011, a new Siberian tiger.

The zoo's superstar exhibit is **Grizzly Gulch,** where orphaned sisters Kachina and Kiona enchant visitors with their frolicking and swimming. When the bears are in the water, the only thing between you and them is (thankfully thick) glass. Grizzly feedings are 11:30 am daily.

The **Lemur Forest** has five varieties of the bug-eyed, long-tailed primates from Madagascar. You can help hoist food into the lemurs' feeding

4

towers and watch the fuzzy creatures climb up to chow down. African Kikuyu grass carpets the circular outer area of **Gorilla Preserve,** one of the largest and most natural gorilla habitats of any zoo in the world. Trees and shrubs create communal play areas.

Ten species of rare monkeys—including black howler monkeys, black-and-white ruffed lemurs, and macaques—live and play at the two-tier **Primate Discovery Center,** which contains 23 interactive learning exhibits on the ground level.

Magellanic penguins waddle about the rather sad concrete **Penguin Island,** splashing and frolicking in its 200-foot pool. Feeding times are 10:15 and 3:30. Koalas peer out from among the trees in **Koala Crossing,** and kangaroos and wallabies headline the **Australian Walkabout** exhibit. The 7-acre **Puente al Sur** (Bridge to the South) re-creates habitats in South America, replete with giant anteaters and capybaras.

An **African Savanna** exhibit mixes giraffes, zebras, kudus, ostriches, and many other species, all living together in a 3-acre section with a central viewing spot accessed by a covered passageway.

The 6-acre **Children's Zoo** has about 300 mammals, birds, and reptiles, plus an insect zoo, a meerkat and prairie-dog exhibit, a nature trail, a nature theater, a restored 1921 Dentzel carousel, and a mini–steam train. A ride on the train costs $4, and you can hop astride one of the carousel's 52 hand-carved menagerie animals for $2. ⊠ *Sloat Blvd. and 47th Ave.(Muni L–Taraval streetcar from downtown), Sunset* ☎ *415/753–7080* ⊕ *www.sfzoo.org* ⊠ *$15, $1 off with Muni transfer* ⊙ *Mid-Mar.–Oct., daily 10–5; Nov.–mid-Mar., daily 10–4.*

Sutro Heights Park. Crows and other large birds battle the heady breezes at this cliff-top park on what were once the grounds of the home of Adolph Sutro, an eccentric mining engineer and former San Francisco mayor. An extremely wealthy man, Sutro may have owned about 10% of San Francisco at one point, but he couldn't buy good taste: a few remnants of his gaudy, faux-classical statue collection still stand (including the lions at what was the main gate). Monterey cypresses and Canary Island palms dot the park, and photos on placards depict what things looked like before the house burned down in 1896, from the greenhouse to the ornate carpet-bed designs.

All that remains of the main house is its foundation. Climb up for a sweeping view of the Pacific Ocean and the Cliff House below (which Sutro owned), and try to imagine what the perspective might have been like from one of the upper floors. San Francisco City Guides (☎ 415/557–4266) runs a free Saturday tour of the park that starts at 2 (meet at the lion statue at 48th and Point Lobos avenues). ⊠ *Point Lobos and 48th Aves., Outer Richmond.*

THE HAIGHT, THE CASTRO, AND NOE VALLEY

Once you've seen the blockbuster sights and you're getting curious about the neighborhoods where the city's soul resides, come out to these three areas. They wear their personalities large and proud, and all are perfect for just strolling around. You can move from the Haight's residue of 1960s counterculture to the Castro's connection to 1970s and '80s gay life to 1990s gentrification in Noe Valley. Although history thrust the Haight and the Castro onto the international stage, both are anything but stagnant—they're still dynamic areas well worth exploring. Noe Valley may lack the headlines, but a mellow morning walk here will make you feel like a local.

EXPLORING THE HAIGHT

Haight-Ashbury Intersection. On October 6, 1967, hippies took over the intersection of Haight and Ashbury streets to proclaim the "Death of Hip." If they thought hip was dead then, they'd find absolute confirmation of it today, what with the only tie-dye in sight on the famed corner being Ben & Jerry's storefront.

Everyone knows the Summer of Love had something to do with free love and LSD, but the drugs and other excesses of that period have tended to obscure the residents' serious attempts to create an America that was more spiritually oriented, more environmentally aware, and less caught up in commercialism. The Diggers, a radical group of actors and populist agitators, for example, operated a free shop a few blocks off Haight Street. Everything really was free at the free shop; people brought in things they didn't need and took things they did. (The group also coined immortal phrases like "Do your own thing.")

Among the folks who hung out in or near the Haight during the late 1960s were writers Richard Brautigan, Allen Ginsberg, Ken Kesey, and Gary Snyder; anarchist Abbie Hoffman; rock performers Marty Balin, Jerry Garcia, Janis Joplin, and Grace Slick; LSD champion Timothy Leary; and filmmaker Kenneth Anger. If you're keen to feel something resembling the hippie spirit these days, there's always Hippie Hill, just inside the Haight Street entrance of Golden Gate Park. Think drum circles, guitar players, and whiffs of pot smoke. ⊠ *Haight.*

EXPLORING THE CASTRO

★ **Castro Theatre.** Here's a classic way to join in the Castro community: grab some popcorn and catch a flick at this gorgeous, 1,500-seat art-deco theater; opened in 1922, it's the grandest of San Francisco's few remaining movie palaces. The neon marquee, which stands at the top of the Castro strip, is the neighborhood's great landmark. The Castro was the fitting host of 2008's red-carpet preview of Gus Van Sant's film *Milk*, starring Sean Penn as openly gay San Francisco supervisor Harvey Milk. The theater's elaborate Spanish baroque interior is fairly well preserved. Before many shows the theater's pipe organ rises from the orchestra pit and an organist plays pop and movie tunes, usually ending with the Jeanette McDonald standard "San Francisco" (go ahead, sing along). The crowd can be enthusiastic and vocal, talking back to the screen as loudly as it talks to them. Classics such as *Who's Afraid of Virginia Woolf?* take on a whole new life, with the assembled beating the actors to the punch and fashioning even snappier comebacks for Elizabeth Taylor. Head here to catch classics, a Fellini film retrospective, or the latest take on same-sex love. ⊠ *429 Castro St., Castro* ☎ *415/621–6120* ⊕ *www.castrotheatre.com.*

The Haight, the Castro, Noe Valley and the Mission District

Balmy Alley **7**
Castro Theatre **2**
Galeria de la Raza **8**
Golden fire hydrant **4**
Haight-Ashbury
intersection **3**

Harvey Milk Plaza **1**
Mission Dolores **5**
Precita Eyes Mural Arts
and Visitors Center **6**

0   350 M
0   1,000 ft

A colorful mosaic mural in the Castro

Harvey Milk Plaza. An 18-foot-long rainbow flag, the symbol of gay pride, flies above this plaza named for the man who electrified the city in 1977 by being elected to its Board of Supervisors as an openly gay candidate. In the early 1970s Milk had opened a camera store on the block of Castro Street between 18th and 19th streets. The store became the center for his campaign to open San Francisco's social and political life to gays and lesbians.

The liberal Milk hadn't served a full year of his term before he and Mayor George Moscone, also a liberal, were shot in November 1978 at City Hall. The murderer was a conservative ex-supervisor named Dan White, who had recently resigned his post and then became enraged when Moscone wouldn't reinstate him. Milk and White had often been at odds on the board, and White thought Milk had been part of a cabal to keep him from returning to his post. Milk's assassination shocked the gay community, which became infuriated when the infamous "Twinkie defense"—that junk food had led to diminished mental capacity—resulted in a manslaughter verdict for White. During the so-called White Night Riot of May 21, 1979, gays and their allies stormed City Hall, torching its lobby and several police cars.

Milk, who had feared assassination, left behind a tape recording in which he urged the community to continue the work he had begun. His legacy is the high visibility of gay people throughout city government; a bust of him was unveiled at City Hall on his birthday in 2008, and the 2008 film *Milk* gives insight into his life. A plaque at the base of the flagpole lists the names of past and present openly gay and lesbian state and local officials. ⊠ *Southwest corner of Castro and Market Sts., Castro.*

EXPLORING NOE VALLEY

Golden fire hydrant. When all the other fire hydrants went dry during the fire that followed the 1906 earthquake, this one kept pumping. Noe Valley and the Mission District were thus spared the devastation wrought elsewhere in the city, which explains the large number of pre-quake homes here. Every year on April 18 (the anniversary of the quake) folks gather here to share stories about the earthquake, and the famous hydrant gets a fresh coat of gold paint. ⊠ *Church and 20th Sts., southeast corner, across from Dolores Park, Noe Valley.*

⌐ CASTRO AND NOE WALK

The Castro and Noe Valley are both neighborhoods that beg to be walked— or ambled through, really, without time pressure or an absolute destination. Hit the Castro first, beginning at **Harvey Milk Plaza** under the gigantic rainbow flag. If you're going on to Noe Valley, first head east down **Market Street** for the cafés, bistros, and shops, then go back to **Castro Street** and head south, past the glorious art-deco **Castro Theatre**, checking out boutiques and cafés along the way (Cliff's Variety, at 479 Castro St., is a must).

To tour Noe Valley, go east down **18th Street** to Church (at Dolores Park), and then either strap on your hiking boots and head south over the hill or hop the J–Church to **24th Street**, the center of this rambling neighborhood.

MISSION DISTRICT

The Mission has a number of distinct personalities: it's the Latino neighborhood, where working-class folks raise their families and where gangs occasionally clash; it's the hipster hood, where tattooed and pierced twenty- and thirtysomethings hold court in the coolest cafés and bars in town; it's a culinary epicenter, with the strongest concentration of destination restaurants and affordable ethnic cuisine in the city; and it's the artists' quarter, where murals adorn literally blocks of walls. It's also the city's equivalent of the Sunshine State—this neighborhood's always the last to succumb to fog.

EXPLORING THE MISSION DISTRICT

Balmy Alley. Mission District artists have transformed the walls of their neighborhood with paintings, and Balmy Alley is one of the best-executed examples. Murals fill the one-block alley, with newer ones continually filling in the blank spaces. Local children working with adults started the project in 1971. Since then dozens of artists have steadily added to it, with the aim of promoting peace in Central America, as well as community spirit and AIDS awareness. ■TIP➜ Be alert here: the 25th Street end of the alley adjoins a somewhat dangerous area. ⊠ *24th St. between and parallel to Harrison and Treat Sts., alley runs south to 25th St., Mission.*

Galería de la Raza. San Francisco's premier showcase for contemporary Latino art, the gallery exhibits the works of mostly local artists. Events include readings and spoken word by local poets and writers, screenings of Latin American and Spanish films, and theater works by local minority theater troupes. Just across the street, amazing art festoons the 24th Street/York Street Minipark, a tiny urban playground. A mosaic-covered

Quetzalcoatl serpent plunges into the ground and rises, creating hills for little ones to clamber over, and mural-covered walls surround the space. ⊠ *2857 24th St., at Bryant St., Mission* ☏ *415/826–8009* ⊕ *www. galeriadelaraza.org* ⊙ *Gallery Tues. 1–7, Wed.–Sat. noon–6.*

★ **Mission Dolores.** Two churches stand side by side at this mission, including the small adobe **Mission San Francisco de Asís,** the oldest standing structure in San Francisco. Completed in 1791, it's the sixth of the 21 California missions founded by Father Junípero Serra in the 18th and early 19th centuries. Its ceiling depicts original Ohlone Indian basket designs, executed in vegetable dyes. The tiny chapel includes frescoes and a hand-painted wooden altar. There's a hidden treasure here, too. In 2004 an archaeologist and an artist crawling along the ceiling's rafters opened a trap door behind the altar and rediscovered the mission's original mural, painted with natural dyes by Native Americans in 1791. The centuries have taken their toll, so the team photographed the 20-by-22-foot mural and began digitally restoring the photographic version. Among the images is a dagger-pierced Sacred Heart of Jesus. There's a small museum covering the mission's founding and history, and the pretty little mission cemetery (made famous by a scene in Alfred Hitchcock's *Vertigo*) maintains the graves of mid-19th-century European immigrants. (The remains of an estimated 5,000 Native Americans lie in unmarked graves.) Services are held in both the Mission San Francisco de Asís and next door in the handsome multi-dome basilica. ⊠ *Dolores and 16th Sts., Mission* ☏ *415/621–8203* ⊕ *www.missiondolores. org* ⊠ *$5 donation, audio tour $7* ⊙ *Nov.–Apr., daily 9–4; May–Oct., daily 9–4:30.*

Precita Eyes Mural Arts and Visitors Center. Founded by muralists, this nonprofit arts organization designs and creates murals. The artists themselves lead informative guided walks of murals in the area. Most tours start with a 45-minute slide presentation. The bike and walking trips, which take between one and three hours, pass several dozen murals. May is Mural Awareness Month, with visits to murals-in-progress and presentations by artists. You can pick up a map of 24th Street's murals at the center and buy art supplies, T-shirts, postcards, and other mural-related items. Bike tours are available by appointment; Saturday's 11 am walking tour meets at Cafe Venice, at 24th and Mission streets. (All other tours meet at the center.) ⊠ *2981 24th St., Mission* ☏ *415/285–2287* ⊕ *www.precitaeyes.org* ⊠ *Center free, tours $12–$15* ⊙ *Center weekdays 10–5, Sat. 10–4, Sun. noon–4; walks weekends at 11 and 1:30 or by appointment.*

PACIFIC HEIGHTS AND JAPANTOWN

Pacific Heights and Japantown are something of an odd couple: privileged, old-school San Francisco and the workaday commercial center of Japanese-American life in the city, stacked virtually on top of each other. The sprawling, extravagant mansions of Pacific Heights gradually give way to the more modest Victorians and unassuming housing tracts of Japantown. The most interesting spots in Japantown huddle in the Japan Center, the neighborhood's two-block centerpiece, and along

Post Street. You can find plenty of authentic Japanese treats in the shops and restaurants, if you have a special interest in these.

■ **TIP→** Japantown is a relatively safe area, but the Western Addition, south of Geary Boulevard, can be dangerous even during the daytime. Avoid going too far west of Fillmore Street on either side of Geary.

EXPLORING PACIFIC HEIGHTS

Ⓒ **Alta Plaza Park.** Golden Gate Park's longtime superintendent, John McLaren, designed Alta Plaza in 1910, modeling its terracing on that of the Grand Casino in Monte Carlo, Monaco. From the top you can see Marin to the north, downtown to the east, Twin Peaks to the south, and Golden Gate Park to the west. Kids love the many play structures at the large, enclosed playground at the top; everywhere else is dog territory. ⊠ *Bordered by Clay, Steiner, Jackson, and Scott Sts., Pacific Heights.*

Franklin Street buildings. What at first looks like a stone facade on the **Golden Gate Church** (1901 Franklin St.) is actually redwood painted white. A Georgian-style residence built in the early 1900s for a coffee merchant sits at 1735 Franklin. On the northeast corner of Franklin and California streets is a **Christian Science church**; built in the Tuscan revival style, it's noteworthy for its terra-cotta detailing. **The Coleman House** (1701 Franklin St.) is an impressive twin-turret Queen Anne mansion that was built for a gold-rush mining and lumber baron. Don't miss the large, brilliant-purple stained-glass window on the house's north side. ⊠ *Franklin St. between Washington and California Sts., Pacific Heights.*

Haas-Lilienthal House. A small display of photographs on the bottom floor of this elaborate, gray 1886 Queen Anne house makes clear that despite its lofty stature and striking, round third-story tower, the house was modest compared with some of the giants that fell victim to the 1906 earthquake and fire. The Foundation for San Francisco's Architectural Heritage operates the home, whose carefully kept rooms provide an intriguing glimpse into late-19th-century life through period furniture, authentic details (antique dishes in the kitchen built-in), and photos of the family who occupied the house until 1972. Volunteers conduct one-hour house tours three days a week and informative two-hour walking tours ($8) of the Civic Center, Broadway, and Union Street areas on Saturday afternoon, and of the eastern portion of Pacific Heights on Sunday afternoon (call or check website for schedule). ⊠ *2007 Franklin St., between Washington and Jackson Sts., Pacific Heights* ☎ *415/441–3004* ⊕ *www.sfheritage.org* ☑ *Entry $8* ☉ *1-hr tour Wed. and Sat. noon–3, Sun. 11–4; 2-hr tour Sun. at 12:30.*

Noteworthy Victorians. Two **Italianate Victorians** (1818 and 1834 California St.) stand out on the 1800 block of California. A block west is the Victorian-era **Atherton House** (1990 California St.), whose mildly daffy design incorporates Queen Anne, Stick-Eastlake, and other architectural elements. Many claim the house—now apartments—is haunted by the ghosts of its 19th-century residents, who regularly whisper, glow, and generally cause a mild fuss. The oft-photographed **Laguna Street Victorians**, on the west side of the 1800 block of Laguna Street, cost between $2,000 and $2,600 when they were built in the 1870s. No

DID YOU KNOW?

These soft-colored Victorian homes in Pacific Heights are closer to the original hues sported back in the 1900s. It wasn't until the 1960s that the bold, electric colors now seen around SF gained popularity. Before that, the most typical house paint color was a standard gray.

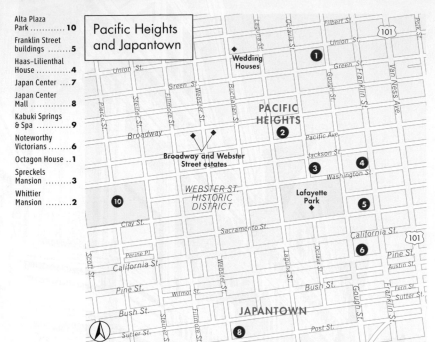

bright colors here though—most of the paint jobs are in soft beiges or pastels. ✉ *California St. between Franklin and Octavia Sts., and Laguna St. between Pine and Bush Sts., Pacific Heights.*

Octagon House. This eight-sided home sits across the street from its original site on Gough Street; it's one of two remaining octagonal houses in the city (the other is on Russian Hill), and the only one open to the public. White quoins accent each of the eight corners of the pretty blue-gray exterior, and a colonial-style garden completes the picture. Inside, it's full of antique American furniture, decorative arts (paintings, silver, rugs), and documents from the 18th and 19th centuries. A deck of Revolutionary-era hand-painted playing cards takes an antimonarchist position: in place of kings, queens, and jacks, the American upstarts substituted American statesmen, Roman goddesses, and Indian chiefs. ✉ *2645 Gough St., Pacific Heights* ☎ *415/441–7512* ✉ *Free, donations encouraged* ☉ *Feb.–Dec., 2nd Sun. and 2nd and 4th Thurs. of month noon–3; group tours weekdays by appointment.*

Spreckels Mansion. Shrouded behind tall juniper hedges at the corner of lovely winding, brick Octavia Street, overlooking Lafayette Park, the estate was built for sugar heir Adolph Spreckels and his wife Alma. Mrs. Spreckels was so pleased with her house that she commissioned George Applegarth to design another building in a similar vein: the

Legion of Honor. One of the city's great iconoclasts, Alma Spreckels was the model for the bronze figure atop the Victory Monument in Union Square. Today this house belongs to prolific romance novelist Danielle Steel. ⊠ *2080 Washington St., at Octavia St., Pacific Heights.*

Whittier Mansion. With a Spanish-tile roof and scrolled bay windows on all four sides, this is one of the most elegant 19th-century houses in the state. Unlike other grand mansions lost in the 1906 quake, the Whittier Mansion was built so solidly that only a chimney toppled over during the disaster. ⊠ *2090 Jackson St., Pacific Heights.*

EXPLORING JAPANTOWN

★ **Japan Center.** Cool and curious trinkets, noodle houses and sushi joints, a destination bookstore, and a peek at Japanese culture high and low await at this 5-acre complex designed in 1968 by noted American architect Minoru Yamasaki. The Japan Center includes the shop- and restaurant-filled Kintetsu and Kinokuniya buildings; the excellent Kabuki Springs & Spa; the Hotel Kabuki; and the Sundance Kabuki, Robert Redford's fancy, reserved-seating cinema/restaurant complex. Unfortunately, the development hasn't aged well, and its Peace Plaza, where seasonal festivals are held, is an unwelcoming sea of cement.

The Kinokuniya Bookstores, in the Kinokuniya Building, have an extensive selection of Japanese-language books, *manga* (graphic novels), books on design, and English-language translations and books on Japanese topics. Just outside, follow the Japanese teenagers to Pika Pika, where you and your friends can step into a photo booth and then use special effects and stickers to decorate your creation. On the bridge connecting the center's two buildings, check out Shige Antiques for *yukata* (lightweight cotton kimonos) for kids and lovely silk kimonos, and Asakichi and its tiny incense shop for tinkling wind chimes and display-worthy teakettles. Continue into the Kintetsu Building for a selection of Japanese restaurants.

Between the Miyako Mall and Kintetsu Building are the five-tier, 100-foot-tall **Peace Pagoda** and the Peace Plaza. The pagoda, which draws on the 1,200-year-old tradition of miniature round pagodas dedicated to eternal peace, was designed in the late 1960s by Yoshiro Taniguchi to convey the "friendship and goodwill" of the Japanese people to the people of the United States. The plaza itself is a shadeless, unwelcoming stretch of cement with little seating. Continue into the Miyako Mall to Ichiban Kan, a Japanese dollar store where you can pick up fun Japanese kitchenware, tote bags decorated with hedgehogs, and erasers shaped like food. ⊠ *Bordered by Geary Blvd. and Fillmore, Post, and Laguna Sts., Japantown.*

Japan Center Mall. The buildings lining this open-air mall are of the shoji school of architecture. The shops are geared more toward locals—travel agencies, electronics shops—but there are some fun Japanese-goods stores. Arrive early in the day and you may score some fabulous mochi (a soft, sweet Japanese rice treat) at Benkyodo (⊠ *1747 Buchanan St.* ☎ *415/922–1244*). It's easy to spend hours among the fabulous origami and craft papers at Paper Tree (⊠ *1743 Buchanan St.* ☎ *415/921–7100*). You can have a seat on local artist Ruth Asawa's twin origami-style fountains, which sit in the middle of the mall; they're squat circular structures made of fieldstone, with three levels for sitting and a brick floor. ✉ *Buchanan St. between Post and Sutter Sts., Japantown.*

★ **Kabuki Springs & Spa.** This serene spa is one Japantown destination that draws locals from all over town, from hipster to grandma, Japanese-American or not. Balinese urns decorate the communal bath area of this house of tranquillity.

The massage menu has also expanded well beyond traditional shiatsu technique. The experience is no less relaxing, however, and the treatment regimen includes facials, salt scrubs, and mud and seaweed wraps. You can take your massage in a private room with a bath or in a curtained-off area.

The communal baths ($22 weekdays, $25 weekends) contain hot and cold tubs, a large Japanese-style bath, a sauna, a steam room, and showers. Bang the gong for quiet if your fellow bathers are speaking too loudly. The clothing-optional baths are open for men only on Monday, Thursday, and Saturday; women bathe on Wednesday, Friday, and Sunday. Bathing suits are required on Tuesday, when the baths are coed.

Men and women can reserve private rooms daily. An 80-minute massage-and-private-bath package costs $120; a package that includes a 50-minute massage and the use of the communal baths costs $100. ✉ *1750 Geary Blvd., Japantown* ☎ *415/922–6000* ⊕ *www.kabukisprings.com* ⊗ *Daily 10–10.*

WHERE TO EAT

San Francisco is a vital culinary crossroads, with nearly every ethnic cuisine represented. Although locals have long headed to the Mission District for Latin food, Chinatown for Asian food, and North Beach for Italian food, they also know that every part of the city offers dining experiences beyond the neighborhood tradition.

Some renowned restaurants are booked weeks or even months in advance. But you can get lucky at the last minute if you're flexible—and friendly. Most restaurants keep a few tables open for walk-ins and VIPs. Show up for dinner early (5:30 pm) or late (after 9 pm) and politely inquire about any last-minute vacancies or cancellations. *Prices in the restaurant reviews are the average cost of a main course at dinner or, if dinner is not served, at lunch (excluding sales tax).*

Use the coordinate (✣ A1) at the end of each listing to locate a site on the corresponding map.

UNION SQUARE

$$$

AMERICAN

✗ **Canteen.** Blink, and you'll miss this place. Chef-owner Dennis Leary has transformed this narrow coffee shop into a popular spot where locals and visiting gourmands rub elbows. The intimate dining room has just 20 seats (7 at a counter and a quartet of booths). But that's all Leary, with a modest open kitchen and a single assistant, can handle. The inspired dinner menu, which changes often, offers only four first courses, four mains, and three or four desserts. A typical meal might start with chestnut soup and rabbit confit, followed by a gratin of chanterelles and tomatoes, or pork tenderloin with braised cranberry beans and fig-olive jus, and then a stellar vanilla soufflé. On Tuesday and Saturday nights a three-course prix-fixe menu is in force (no choices within each course) for $43–$50. Because this is a one-man band, there are set times to dine: 6 pm and 8 pm on Tuesday and 6 pm, 7:30 pm, and 9:15 pm Wednesday through Sunday. Brunch (only on Sunday 8 am until 2 pm) is a popular option; don't miss the eggs Benedict. [$] *Average main: $26* ✉ *817 Sutter St., Union Sq.* ☎ *415/928–8870* 🌐 *www.sfcanteen.com* ✍ *Reservations essential* ⏲ *Closed Mon* ✥ *D4.*

CHINATOWN

$$ CHINESE 👶

🍴 **R&G Lounge.** The name conjures up an image of a dark, smoky bar with a piano player, but this Cantonese restaurant is actually as bright as a new penny. On the lower level (entrance on Kearny Street) is a no-tablecloth dining room that's packed at lunch and dinner. The classy upstairs space (entrance on Commercial Street) is a favorite stop for Chinese businessmen on expense accounts and special-occasion banquets. The street-level room on Kearny is a comfortable spot to wait for an open table. A menu with photographs helps you pick from the many wonderful, sometimes pricey, always authentic dishes, such as the famous salt-and-pepper Dungeness crab, roast squab, and shrimp-stuffed tofu (and much of the seafood is fresh from the tank). [$] *Average main: $20* ✉ *631 Kearny St., Chinatown* ☎ *415/982–7877* 🌐 *www.rnglounge.com* ✥ *F3.*

SOMA

$$$$ MODERN AMERICAN Fodor's Choice ★

🍴 **Benu.** Chef-owner Corey Lee launched his contemporary American restaurant, one of the most high-profile restaurants to open in the city, much to the delight of food-obsessed locals and travelers alike. His pedigree spans 15 years in fine dining (including a position as chef de cuisine at The French Laundry), but Benu is decidedly more relaxed—no jacket required. The dining room is very minimalist, with bare wood tables and high-backed banquettes along the walls. While some guests come early in the week to dine on the à la carte menu, the 17-course tasting menu (mandatory on Friday and Saturday nights) is the way to go if your pocketbook can handle it. Each dish is a marvel, from the meticulous presentation (Lee has had pieces specifically designed for the restaurant and each course) to the sophisticated flavors and textures. Fans of Asian cuisine will be particularly thrilled to see his elegant handling of ingredients like *xiao long bao* dumplings and sea cucumber. He utilizes many modern techniques, but never in an alienating way. You may find dishes like Hokkaido sea cucumber stuffed with shrimp, pork belly, eggplant, fermented pepper or eel, feuille de brick, crème fraiche, and lime. An extremely professional staff is behind the quick pacing and on-point wine pairings. Couples expecting an ultra-romantic environment may be a bit disappointed by the stark atmosphere, but culinary adventurers will be thrilled. [$] *Prix-fixe: $160* ✉ *22 Hawthorne St.,*

SoMa ☎ *415/685–4860* 🌐 *www.benusf.com* ✍ *Reservations essential* 🕒 *Closed Sun. and Mon.* ✥ *G5*

HAYES VALLEY

$$$$ MODERN AMERICAN 🍴 **Jardinière.** A special anniversary? An important business dinner? A fat tax refund? These are the reasons you book a table at Jardinière. The restaurant takes its name from chef-owner Traci Des Jardins, and the sophisticated interior, with its eye-catching oval atrium and curving staircase, fills nightly with locals and out-of-towners alike. An equally sophisticated French-Californian dining room menu, served upstairs in the atrium, changes daily, but regularly includes such high-priced adornments as caviar, foie gras, and truffles. (The tasting menu is available for $120.) Downstairs, the lounge menu, with smaller plates and smaller prices ($8 to $18), is ideal for when you want to eat light while visiting with friends or tame your hunger before or after the nearby opera or symphony. Cheese lovers will appreciate the wide variety of choices—both Old World and New—housed in the glassed-in cheese-aging chamber in the rear of the restaurant. The choice wine selection is worthy of celebration in and of itself. [$] *Average main: $38* ✉ *300 Grove St., Hayes Valley* ☎ *415/861–5555* 🌐 *www.jardiniere.com* ✍ *Reservations essential* 🕒 *No lunch* ✥ *C5.*

$$$ MEDITERRANEAN Fodor's Choice ★ 🍴 **Zuni Café.** After one bite of chef Judy Rodgers's succulent brick-oven-roasted whole chicken with Tuscan bread salad, you'll understand why she's a national star (and why it's the most well-known chicken dish in town). Food is served here on two floors; the rabbit warren of rooms on the second level includes a balcony overlooking the main dining room. Mingle among a disparate mix that reflects the makeup of the city—casual and dressy, young and old, hip and staid—at the long copper bar where trays of briny-fresh oysters on the half shell are dispensed along with cocktails and wine. The southern French–Italian menu changes daily, though the signature chicken, prepared for two, is a fixture (and, alas, its cost reflects its popularity). Rotating dishes are simple but made with excellent ingredients, like house-cured anchovies with Parmigiano-Reggiano, deep-fried squid and lemons, ricotta gnocchi with seasonal vegetables, and brick-oven squab with polenta. Desserts include crumbly crusted tarts and a cream-laced coffee granita. The lunchtime (and late-night) burger on rosemary focaccia with a side of shoestring potatoes is a favorite with locals. [$] *Average main: $28* ✉ *1658 Market St., Hayes Valley* ☎ *415/552–2522* 🌐 *www.zunicafe.com* 🕒 *Closed Mon.* ✥ *C6*

FINANCIAL DISTRICT

$$ SPANISH 🍴 **Bocadillos.** The name means "sandwiches," but that's only half the story here. You'll find 13 bocadillos at lunchtime: plump rolls filled with everything from serrano ham to Catalan sausage with arugula to a memorable lamb burger (pick two for $10). But at night chef-owner Gerald Hirigoyen, who also owns the high-profile Piperade, focuses on tapas, offering some two dozen choices, including a savory octopus carpaccio, an equally superb pig's trotters with chopped egg salad, and

BEST BETS FOR SAN FRANCISCO DINING

With thousands of restaurants to choose from, how will you decide where to eat? Fodor's writers and editors have selected their favorite restaurants by price, cuisine, and experience in the Best Bets lists below. In the first column, Fodor's Choice designations represent the "best of the best" in every price category. You can also search by neighborhood for excellent eats—just peruse the following pages.

Fodor'sChoice★

Acquerello, $$$$, p. 215

Aziza, $$$, p. 224

Benu, $$$$, p. 207

Boulevard, $$$$, p. 218

Coi, $$$$, p. 217

Delfina, $$$, p. 222

Dosa on Fillmore, $$, p. 223

Dosa on Valencia, $$, p. 222

Gary Danko, $$$$, p. 218

L'Osteria del Forno, $, p. 217

Nopalito, $$, p. 221

Quince, $$$$, p. 214

Swan Oyster Depot, $$, p. 217

Zuni Café, $$$, p. 208

By Price

$

Good Noodle, p. 224

L'Osteria del Forno, p. 217

SanJalisco, p. 222

$$

Dosa on Fillmore, p. 223

Dosa on Valencia, p. 222

Nopalito, p. 221

Swan Oyster Depot, p. 217

$$$

A16, p. 220

Aziza, p. 224

Canteen, p. 206

Delfina, p. 222

Zuni Café, p. 208

$$$$

Acquerello, p. 215

Benu, p. 207

Boulevard, p. 218

Coi, p. 217

Gary Danko, p. 218

Quince, p. 214

By Cuisine

AMERICAN

Boulevard, $$$$, p. 218

Canteen, $$$, p. 206

Gary Danko, $$$$, p. 218

Nopa, $$$, p. 221

CHINESE

R&G Lounge, $$, p. 207

Yank Sing, $$, p. 214

INDIAN

Dosa on Fillmore, $$, p. 223

Dosa on Valencia, $$, p. 222

Indian Oven, $$, p. 220

ITALIAN

A16, $$$, p. 220

Delfina, $$$, p. 222

L'Osteria del Forno, $, p. 217

Quince, $$$$, p. 214

MEDITERRANEAN

Zuni Café, $$$, p. 208

MEXICAN

Nopalito, $$, p. 221

SanJalisco, $, p. 222

SEAFOOD

Hog Island Oyster Company, $$, p. 218

Plouf, $$, p. 214

Swan Oyster Depot, $$, p. 217

VIETNAMESE

Good Noodle, $, p. 224

Slanted Door, $$$, p. 219

By Experience

BAY VIEWS

Slanted Door, $$$, p. 219

BRUNCH

Rose's Café, $$, p. 220

CHILD-FRIENDLY

Mifune, $, p. 224

Yank Sing, $$, p. 214

SPECIAL OCCASION

Boulevard, $$$$, p. 218

Gary Danko, $$$$, p. 218

4

THE MISSION, THE CASTRO, AND NOE VALLEY

You'll never go hungry here, in some of San Francisco's most jam-packed restaurant neighborhoods. From dirt-cheap taquerias to hip tapas joints, city dwellers know this sector as the go-to area for a great meal.

The city's best Mexican food can be found in the Mission. A pile of hot, salty chips and fiery salsa often arrives gratis with your meal. A filling super burrito goes for about $8.

Head over to the Mission to dig into Mexican and Latin American menus. In recent years the Latino community has been sharing the neighborhood with legions of twenty- and thirtysomethings who pack the dozens of eateries along Valencia Street, between 16th and 24th streets, and Mission Street from 19th to 24th streets. East of the Mission, Potrero Hill is home to a cluster of casual dining rooms in the blocks around Connecticut and 18th streets.

The Castro neighborhood, the epicenter of the city's gay community, is chockablock with restaurants and bars. Market Street between Church and Castro streets is a great stretch for people-watching and café- or bistro-hopping. Just south, in Noe Valley, everyone seems to be pushing a baby carriage, but they're all eating out too, mostly along 24th Street from Church to Castro streets, and on Church Street from 24th to 30th streets.

WAKE UP

A placard at the door says to sign in and wait to be seated at homey **Chloe's Café** (⊠ 1399 Church St., between 26th and Clipper Sts. ☎ 415/648–4116 ✢ 3:D6). That wait for your croissant French toast or banana-walnut pancakes is bound to be long on weekends—hey, everyone else has the same delicious idea—so come with your patience. Come with cash in your pocket, too, as no credit cards are taken.

MISSION DINING TWO WAYS

	MEXICAN:	ITALIAN:
Grab-and-go	Two **El Tonayense Taco Trucks** (✉ 14th St. and Harrison St. ✛ 3:G4 ✉ 19th St. and Harrison St. ✛ 3:G6) serve up the city's most authentic tacos, stuffed with a variety of meats and spicy salsa.	The no-frills **Arinell** (✉ 509 Valencia St., near 16th St. ☎ 415/255–1303 ✛ 3:E5) is famous for its floppy New York–style slices handed across a walk-up counter, late into the night.
Cheap eats	**Pancho Villa Taqueria** (✉ 3071 16th St., between Mission and Valencia Sts. ☎ 415/864–8840 ✛ 3:E5) is a Mission institution. The bulging burritos, heavy with beans, rice, meat, and salsa, are just $7.	The superbusy **Little Star Pizza** (✉ 400 Valencia St., at 15th St. ☎ 415/551–7827 ✛ 3:F4) doles out cornmeal-crusted pizzas, deep-dish or thin, with toppings like spinach and feta, pesto, and chicken.
Casual chic	**Velvet Cantina** (✉ 3349 23rd St., at Bartlett St. ☎ 415/648–4142 ✛ 3:F6) offers a modern take on Mexican cuisine, in a dimly lighted, bordello-themed room filled with tipsy hipsters. Try the avocado-cactus enchiladas with cilantro pesto, over a pitcher of margaritas.	Stop in at the ever-busy **Pizzeria Delfina** (✉ 3611 18th St., at Guerrero St. ☎ 415/437–6800 ✛ 3:E6), the casual offshoot of upscale Delfina, for top-notch Neapolitan pies, antipasti (eggplant caponata, fresh-stretched mozzarella), and some 20 wines by the glass.

MEXICAN VERSUS ITALIAN

For years the Mission was where San Franciscans went to eat burritos and tacos, enchiladas, and tamales. But in the mid-1990s new Italian eateries began to open up in this Mexican stronghold, with Parmesan and pasta becoming as common as *queso fresco* and *frijoles*. (And the number of Italian places opening just keeps growing.) Thankfully for diners, there are plenty of tasty choices on both sides of the menu.

AND FOR DESSERT

The Mission has ice cream in every flavor imaginable. **Bi-Rite Creamery** (✉ 3692 18th St., near Valencia St. ☎ 415/626–5600 ✛ 3:E6) balances orbs of salted caramel or soft serve in organic cones. And the venerable **Mitchell's** (✉ 668 San Jose St., at 29th St. ☎ 415/648–2300 ✛ 3:E6) has been scooping flavors like toasted almond and Mexican chocolate since 1953. Cult ice-cream shop **Humphry Slocombe** (✉ 2790 Harrison St., near 24th St. ☎ 415/550–6971 ✛ 3:G6) is famous for irreverent flavors like Thai chili lime sorbet. For something baked, wait in line at the ever-busy **Tartine Bakery** (✉ 600 Guerrero St., at 18th St. ☎ 415/487–2600 ✛ 3:E6), where the staff pulls devil's food cakes, banana-cream tarts, éclairs, and brownies from the oven daily. And if doughnuts and coffee are your thing, head to **Dynamo Donut & Coffee** (✉ 2760 24th St., between Potrero and York Sts. ☎ 415/920–1978 ✛ 3:H6), and dunk a chocolate-star anise doughnut in a cup of joe.

4

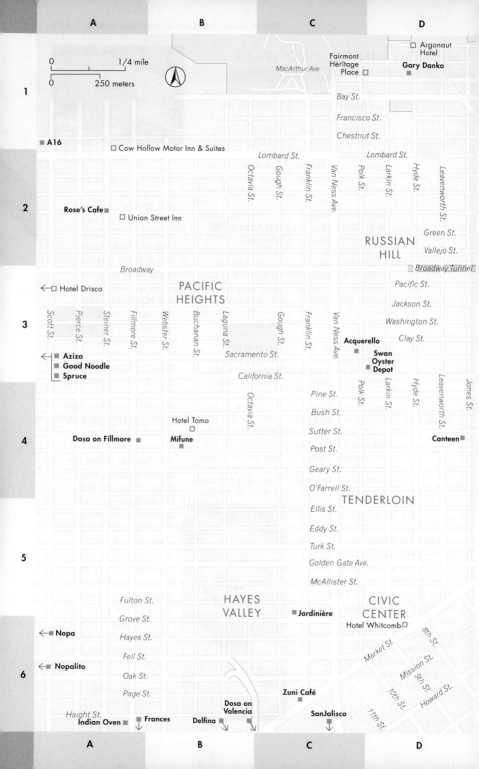

A   **B**   **C**   **D**

0   1/4 mile
0   250 meters

☐ Argonaut Hotel

Fairmont Heritage Place ☐

MacArthur Ave.

■ **Gary Danko**

1

Bay St.

Francisco St.

Chestnut St.

■ **A16**

☐ Cow Hollow Motor Inn & Suites

Lombard St.   Lombard St.

Octavia St.
Gough St.
Franklin St.
Van Ness Ave.
Polk St.
Larkin St.
Hyde St.
Leavenworth St.

2

Rose's Cafe ■

☐ Union Street Inn

Green St.

RUSSIAN HILL

Vallejo St.

Broadway

PACIFIC HEIGHTS

■ Broadway Tunnel

←☐ Hotel Drisco

Pacific St.

Jackson St.

Scott St.
Pierce St.
Steiner St.
Fillmore St.
Webster St.
Buchanan St.
Laguna St.
Gough St.
Franklin St.
Van Ness Ave.

Washington St.

3

Clay St.

■ **Acquerello**

Sacramento St.

■ **Swan Oyster Depot**

←■ **Aziza**
■ **Good Noodle**
■ **Spruce**

California St.

Polk St.
Larkin St.
Hyde St.
Leavenworth St.
Jones St.

Pine St.

Bush St.

Hotel Tomo
☐

Sutter St.

4

Dosa on Fillmore ■

Mifune ■

Octavia St.

Post St.

Canteen ■

Geary St.

O'Farrell St.

TENDERLOIN

Ellis St.

Eddy St.

Turk St.

5

Golden Gate Ave.

McAllister St.

Fulton St.

HAYES VALLEY

CIVIC CENTER

Grove St.

■ **Jardinière**

Hotel Whitcomb ☐

←■ **Nopa**

Hayes St.

Fell St.

Market St.

8th St.

←■ **Nopalito**

Oak St.

Mission St.

9th St.

6

Page St.

Zuni Café

10th St.

Howard St.

Haight St.

Indian Oven ■   ■ **Frances**

Delfina

Dosa on Valencia

SanJalisco ■

11th St.

A   **B**   **C**   **D**

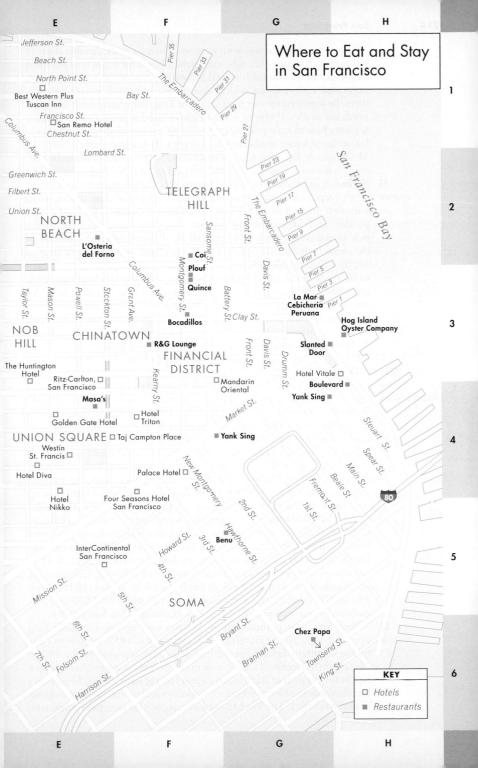

Where to Eat and Stay in San Francisco

patatas bravas (potatoes) with *romesco* sauce (a thick combination of red pepper, tomato, almonds, and garlic). His wine list is well matched to the dishes. A youngish crowd typically piles into the dining space, decorated with redbrick walls, wire chairs, and small square light fixtures. Be prepared to wait for a seat. The large communal table is a good perch for singles. If you're in the neighborhood at breakfast time, there is plenty here to keep you happy, including a scrambled-eggs-and-cheese bocadillo or house-made chorizo and eggs. [$] *Average main: $22* ✉ *710 Montgomery St., Financial District* ☎ *415/982–2622* 🌐 *www.bocasf.com* ✍ *Reservations not accepted* ⏲ *Closed Sun. No lunch Sat.* ✥ *F3*

$$ SEAFOOD 🍴 **Plouf.** A gold mine for mussel lovers, this French-friendly spot offers seven preparations to choose from, plus a variety of clam dishes, all at a modest price. Among the best are *marinière* (white wine, garlic, and parsley) and one combining coconut milk, lime juice, and chili. Add a side of the skinny fries and that's all most appetites need. The rest of the menu includes meaty dishes like lamb shank and New York strip to satisfy any unrepentant carnivores, but many of the presentations seem to be stuck in the last decade (same story with the lackluster desserts, complete with squeeze-bottle squiggles adorning the plates). The tables are clustered together in the lively dining room, so you might overhear neighboring conversations. Solo diners will find a bar where they can dine. On temperate days and nights, try for one of the tables outdoors. [$] *Average main: $22* ✉ *40 Belden Pl., Financial District* ☎ *415/986–6491* 🌐 *www.ploufsf.com* ⏲ *Closed Sun. No lunch Sat.* ✥ *F3*

$$$$ ITALIAN Fodor's Choice ★ 🍴 **Quince.** Previously housed in a small space in Pacific Heights, this smart, wildly praised restaurant has moved and expanded to a much bigger more elegant space in Jackson Square. Chef-owner Michael Tusk, who has cooked at the legendary Chez Panisse and Oliveto, oversees the kitchen, where he uses only the finest local ingredients to turn out his Italian-inspired cuisine. The four-course menu ($95) or chef's tasting menu ($140) changes regularly, featuring a delicious selection of their famed pastas and seasonal dishes, such as tortelloni with robiola and cardoons, quail with cabbage and sausage, suckling pig and sweetbreads, and bosc pear with Medjool date genoise. Don't pass up the cheese course ($16 supplement)—it's one of the city's finer selections. The 800-bottle-strong wine list is top-notch, but can get pricey (a $35 corkage fee means you won't save much by bringing your own bottle), and the seamless service is both refined and welcoming. The lounge is an optimal place to swing by for an excellent cocktail. (You can also slink next door to Quince's new casual offshoot, Cotogna, for an affordable and rustic meal, at either lunch or dinner.) [$] *Prix-fixe: $95* ✉ *470 Pacific Ave., Financial District* ☎ *415/775–8500* 🌐 *www.quincerestaurant.com* ✍ *Reservations essential* ⏲ *No lunch* ✥ *F3.*

$$ CHINESE 👶 🍴 **Yank Sing.** The granddaddy of SF dim sum teahouses, Yank Sing opened in a plain-Jane storefront in Chinatown in 1959, but left its Cantonese neighbors behind for the high-rises of downtown by the 1970s. This brightly decorated location on quiet Stevenson Street (there's also a big, brassy branch in the Rincon Center) serves some of San Francisco's best dim sum to office workers on weekdays and to big, boisterous families on weekends. The kitchen cooks up some 100 varieties of dim sum

on a rotating basis, offering 60 different types daily. These include both the classic (steamed pork buns, shrimp dumplings, egg custard tartlets) and the creative (scallion-skewered prawns tied with bacon, lobster and *tobiko* roe dumplings, basil seafood dumplings). The Shanghai soup dumplings are a classic—and some of the best in the city. The carts will keep whirring up to your table, and the tab can rise quickly, so diners should pace themselves. A take-out counter makes a meal on the run a satisfying and penny-wise compromise when office duties—or touring—won't wait. $ *Average main: $16* ⊠ *49 Stevenson St., Financial District* ☎ *415/541–4949* ⊕ *www.yanksing.com* ☽ *No dinner* ✛ *G4.*

NOB HILL

4

$$$$ ✕ **Masa's.** Although the toque has been passed to several chefs since
FRENCH   the tragic death of founding chef Masataka Kobayashi in 1984, this 25-year-old restaurant, with its chocolate-brown walls, white fabric ceiling, and vermilion-silk-shaded lanterns, remains a noted destination for fine dining in San Francisco. Chef Gregory Short, who worked alongside Thomas Keller at the famed French Laundry for seven years, has been at the helm since 2004. His tasting menus of four or seven courses, including a vegetarian option, all showcase the bounty of the seasons, from winter root vegetables to summer peaches. The California-French cuisine also features Japanese flair (an homage to Masa), and all the dishes are laced with luxe ingredients, from foie gras to Maine lobster to prime beef. In fall, when northern Italy's exquisite white truffles are in season, Short typically puts together a tasting menu that tucks them into every course, which will hopefully include a silky truffle custard whose perfume you can smell before it arrives at the table. The mignardise cart of candies, cookies, and chocolates is a famous component to the dining experience here. Wine drinkers are in excellent hands, with an award-winning list by sommelier Alan Murray that includes many small-production wines from around the globe. The elegant room has a formal atmosphere that is thankfully far from stuffy or suffocating, although a jacket is preferred for gentlemen. $ *Prix-fixe: $98* ⊠ *Hotel Vintage Court, 648 Bush St., Nob Hill* ☎ *415/989–7154* ⊕ *www.masasrestaurant.com* ⌕ *Reservations essential. Jacket required* ☽ *Closed Sun. and Mon. No lunch* ✛ *E4.*

VAN NESS/POLK

$$$$ ✕ **Acquerello.** For years, devotees of chef-owner Suzette Gresham-
ITALIAN   Tognetti's high-end but soulful Italian cooking have been swooning
Fodor's Choice   over her incomparable Parmesan *budino* (pudding), ridged pasta with
★   foie gras and truffles, and veal loin rolled and stuffed with seasonal vegetables. Dishes are complex, refined, and also feature some cutting-edge touches and techniques. Dinners are prix-fixe, with three ($70), four ($82), or five ($96) courses and at least six choices within each course. Tognetti also tempts with a chef's eight-course tasting menu ($195, with wine pairings). The cheese course is definitely worth indulging in since each one has been lovingly selected. Co-owner Giancarlo Paterlini (and his son) oversee the service and the deep list of Italian wines, both of

CLOSE UP

Eating with Kids

Kids can be fussy eaters, but parents can be, too, so picking places that will satisfy both is important. Fortunately, there are plenty of excellent possibilities all over town.

Sears Fine Food. If you're downtown for breakfast, stop at the touristy but venerable Sears Fine Food, home of "the world-famous Swedish pancakes." Eighteen of the silver-dollar-size beauties cost less than a movie ticket. ⊠ *439 Powell St., near Post St.* ☎ *415/986–0700.*

City View Restaurant. Nearby in Chinatown, City View Restaurant serves a varied selection of dim sum, with tasty pork buns for kids and more-exotic fare for adults. ⊠ *662 Commercial St., near Kearny St.* ☎ *415/398–2838.*

Pluto's. Try Pluto's after a visit to Golden Gate Park. Small kids love the chicken nuggets and mac and cheese, whereas bigger kids will likely opt for one of the two-fisted sandwiches or make-your-own salads. Everyone will want a double fudge brownie for dessert. ⊠ *627 Irving St., between 7th and 8th Sts.* ☎ *415/753–8867.*

Barney's Gourmet Burgers. With locations all over the Bay Area, including this one not far from Fort Mason, this chain caters to older kids and their parents with mile-high burgers and giant salads. But Barney's doesn't forget "kids under 8," who have their own menu featuring a burger, an all-beef frank, chicken strips with ranch dressing, and more. ⊠ *3344 Steiner St., near Union St.* ☎ *415/563–0307* ⊕ *www.barneyshamburgers.com.*

The Ferry Building on the Embarcadero has plenty of kid-friendly options, from **Mijita Cocina Mexicana,** which has its own kids' menu,

to **Gott's Roadside Tray Gourmet,** for burgers, shakes, and more. (And the outdoor access can help keep the little ones entertained.)

La Corneta. The Mission has dozens of no-frills taco-and-burrito parlors; especially worthy is bustling La Corneta, which has a baby burrito and well-made quesadillas. ⊠ *2731 Mission St., between 23rd and 24th Sts.* ☎ *415/643–7001.*

St. Francis Fountain. Banana splits and hot-fudge sundaes are what St. Francis Fountain is known for, along with its vintage decor (and popularity with hipsters for weekend brunch). Opened in 1918, it recalls the early 1950s, and the menu, with its burgers, BLTs, grilled-cheese sandwiches, and chili with corn bread, is timeless. ⊠ *2801 24th St., at York St.* ☎ *415/826–4200.*

Rosamunde Sausage Grill. In Lower Haight, the small Rosamunde Sausage Grill serves just that—a slew of different sausages, from Polish to duck to Weisswurst (Bavarian veal). You get your choice of two toppings, like grilled onions, sauerkraut, and chili, and since there are only six stools, plan on takeout. Hint: head to nearby Duboce Park, with its cute playground. ⊠ *545 Haight St., between Steiner and Fillmore Sts.* ☎ *415/437–6851.*

Park Chalet. Finally, both kids and adults love to be by the ocean, and the Park Chalet, hidden behind the two-story Beach Chalet, offers pizza, mac and cheese, sticky ribs, and a big banana split. ⊠ *1000 Great Hwy., at Fulton St.* ☎ *415/386–8439.*

which are superb. The room, with its vaulted ceiling and terra-cotta and pale-ocher palette, suits the refined food. This is a true San Francisco dining gem that is worth every penny. [$] *Prix-fixe: $70* ✉ *1722 Sacramento St., Van Ness/Polk* ☎ *415/567–5432* 🌐 *www.acquerello.com* 🕒 *Closed Sun. and Mon. No lunch* ✥ *C3.*

$$ SEAFOOD Fodor's Choice ★ 🍴 **Swan Oyster Depot.** Half fish market and half diner, this small, slim, family-run seafood operation, open since 1912, has no tables, just a narrow marble counter with about a dozen and a half stools. Most people come in to buy perfectly fresh salmon, halibut, crabs, and other seafood to take home. Everyone else hops onto one of the rickety stools to enjoy a bowl of clam chowder—the only hot food served—a dozen oysters, half a cracked crab, a slice of crusty sourdough, a big shrimp salad, or a smaller shrimp cocktail. And it's all served up with a side of big personality from the jovial folks behind the counter who make you feel like a regular. Come early or late to avoid a long wait. And since this place is notoriously cash only (and seafood is not exactly cheap!), be sure to come with a full wallet. [$] *Average main: $18* ✉ *1517 Polk St., Van Ness/Polk* ☎ *415/673–1101* ✍ *Reservations not accepted* 💳 *No credit cards* 🕒 *Closed Sun. No dinner* ✥ *D3.*

4

NORTH BEACH

$$$$ MODERN AMERICAN Fodor's Choice ★ 🍴 **Coi.** Daniel Patterson, who has made a name for himself internationally both as a chef and as a pundit on contemporary restaurant trends, has created a destination restaurant, an enchanting spot on the gritty end of Broadway. There are two dining rooms: the front room, a bit more casual with rustic wood tables and banquettes with pillows, and the 30-seat formal dining room, with soft lighting, luxe linens, and gold-taupe banquettes along the two walls. On offer is an 11-course tasting menu ($165), full of the bounty of Bay Area produce and ingredients. The highly seasonal and obsessively sourced food (some of it is even foraged by chef Patterson) matches the space in sophistication, with such inspired dishes as Dungeness crab raviolo with sheep sorrel and butter crab broth; aged duck breast with stuffed cabbage, roasted beets, horseradish, and dill; and Monterey Bay abalone with heirloom chicories and shellfish sauce. The kitchen is always tinkering and innovating, so the menu feels like a new and often exciting culinary experience. [$] *Prix-fixe: $165* ✉ *373 Broadway, North Beach* ☎ *415/393–9000* 🌐 *www.coirestaurant.com* 🕒 *Closed Sun., Mon. and Tues. No lunch* ✥ *F2.*

$ ITALIAN 👶 Fodor's Choice ★ 🍴 **L'Osteria del Forno.** Pass through the door of this modest storefront and you'll feel as if you've stumbled into a homey trattoria in Italy, with the staff chattering in Italian and seductive aromas drifting from the open kitchen through the sunny yellow dining room. Each day the kitchen produces small plates of simply cooked vegetables (grilled peppers, roasted potatoes with yams and carrots), a few baked pastas, a daily special or two, lamb skewers, a roast of the day, creamy polenta, and thin-crust pizzas—including a memorable "white" pie topped with porcini mushrooms and mozzarella. (All the hot dishes come out of an oven—no stove here, so don't come expecting a large selection of pastas.) Wine drinkers will find a good match for any dish they order on the all-Italian list, which showcases gems from limited-production vineyards. At lunch try one of North Beach's best focaccia sandwiches. The space is petite, so don't come with a large group, and there can often be a wait for a table. [$] *Average main: $15* ✉ *519 Columbus Ave., North Beach* ☎ *415/982–1124* 🌐 *www.losteriadelforno.com* 💳 *No credit cards* ⏲ *Closed Tues.* ✥ *E2*

FISHERMAN'S WHARF

$$$$ MODERN AMERICAN Fodor's Choice ★

🍴 **Gary Danko.** Be prepared to wait your turn for a table behind chef Gary Danko's legion of loyal fans, who typically keep the reservation book chock-full here (plan on reserving two months in advance). The cost of a meal ($69–$102) is pegged to the number of courses, from three to five. The decadent menu spans a classic yet Californian style that changes seasonally; it may include risotto with lobster and rock shrimp, lemon pepper duck breast with duck hash, and herb-crusted lamb loin. A diet-destroying chocolate soufflé with two sauces is usually among the desserts. So, too, is a "no-cholesterol" Grand Marnier soufflé with raspberry sorbet, perfect for diners with a conscience or a heart problem. But then there's the amazing cheese cart. The wine list is the size of a small-town phone book, and the banquette-lined rooms, with beautiful wood floors and stunning (but restrained) floral arrangements, are as memorable as the food and impeccable service. [$] *Prix-fixe: $69* ✉ *800 N. Point St., Fisherman's Wharf* ☎ *415/749–2060* 🌐 *www.garydanko.com* ✍ *Reservations essential. Jacket required* ⏲ *No lunch* ✥ *D1.*

EMBARCADERO

$$$$ AMERICAN Fodor's Choice ★

🍴 **Boulevard.** Two of San Francisco's top restaurant celebrities—chef Nancy Oakes and designer Pat Kuleto—are responsible for this high-profile, high-priced eatery in the magnificent 1889 Audiffred Building, a Parisian look-alike and one of the few downtown structures to survive the 1906 earthquake. Kuleto's Belle-Époque interior and Oakes's sophisticated-American-food-with-a-French-accent attract well-dressed locals and flush out-of-towners. The menu changes seasonally, but count on standout appetizers and generous portions of dishes like Maine lobster ravioli, grilled king salmon with wild rice and vegetables that include chanterelle mushrooms, and a wood-grilled pork prime rib chop with Kabocha squash gnocchi (all the entrées come with delicious side dishes). Save room (and calories) for one of the dynamite desserts, such as dark chocolate brioche custard. There's counter seating for folks too hungry to wait for a table, and an American Kobe beef burger at lunchtime that lets you eat with the swells without raiding your piggy bank. The well-chosen wine list and excellent service are also hallmarks here. [$] *Average main: $36* ✉ *1 Mission St., Embarcadero* ☎ *415/543–6084* 🌐 *www.boulevardrestaurant.com* ✍ *Reservations essential* ⏲ *No lunch weekends* ✥ *H4.*

$$ SEAFOOD

🍴 **Hog Island Oyster Company.** Hog Island, a thriving oyster farm in Tomales Bay, north of San Francisco, serves up its harvest at this attractive raw bar and retail shop in the busy Ferry Building. The U-shape counter and a handful of tables seat no more than three dozen diners, who come here for impeccably fresh oysters (from Hog Island and elsewhere) or clams (from Hog Island) on the half shell. Other mollusk-centered options include a first-rate oyster stew, baked oysters, clam chowder, and "steamer" clams with Israeli couscous. The bar also turns out what is arguably one of the city's best grilled-cheese sandwiches (with three artisanal cheeses on artisanal bread) this side of Wisconsin. You need to eat early, however, as the bar closes at 8 on weekdays and 6 on weekends. Happy hour, 5 to 7 on Monday and Thursday, is an oyster lover's dream and jam-packed: chef's choice of oysters for a buck apiece and a pint of beer for $4. [$] *Average main: $20* ✉ *Ferry Bldg., Embarcadero at Market St., Embarcadero* ☎ *415/391–7117* 🌐 *www.hogislandoysters.com* ✣ *H3.*

$$$ PERUVIAN 🍴 **La Mar Cebicheria Peruana.** Set right on the water's edge, this casually chic restaurant is divided into three areas: a lounge with a long ceviche bar where diners watch chefs put together their plates; the savvy Pisco Bar facing the Embarcadero, where bartenders make a dozen different cocktails based on Peru's famed Pisco brandy; and a bright blue and whitewashed dining room overlooking an outdoor patio and the bay. Your waiter will start you out with a pile of potato and plantain chips with three dipping sauces, but then you're on your own, choosing from a long list of ceviches, can't-miss *causas* (whipped potatoes topped with a choice of fish, shellfish, or vegetable salads), and everything from crisp, lightly deep-fried fish and shellfish to soups and stews and rice dishes, many spiked with Peruvian chilies. The original La Mar is in Lima, Peru. San Francisco is the first stop in its campaign to open a string of cebicherias across the United States and Latin America. The view of the water is especially enjoyable during lunch or a warm evening. [$] *Average main: $25* ✉ *Pier 1½ between Washington and Jackson Sts., Embarcadero* ☎ *415/397–8880* 🌐 *www.lamarcebicheria.com* ✣ *G3.*

$$$ VIETNAMESE 🍴 **Slanted Door.** If you're looking for homey Vietnamese food served in a down-to-earth dining room at a decent price, *don't* stop here. Celebrated chef-owner Charles Phan has mastered the upmarket, Western-accented Vietnamese menu. To showcase his cuisine, he built a big space with sleek wooden tables and chairs, white marble floors, a cocktail lounge, a bar, and an enviable bay view. Among his popular cult dishes are green papaya salad, daikon rice cakes, cellophane crab noodles, chicken clay pot, and shaking beef (tender beef cubes with garlic and onion)—and they don't come cheap, although the dishes are made with quality ingredients. Alas, the crush of fame means that no one speaking in a normal voice can be heard. To avoid the midday and evening crowds (and to save some bucks), stop in for the afternoon-tea menu (spring rolls, grilled pork over rice noodles), dine at the bar, or visit Out the Door, Phan's take-out counter around the corner from the restaurant. A second Out the Door, complete with table service, is a popular location in the Lower Pacific Heights (and the quality of the food seems to be better). [$] *Average main: $29* ✉ *Ferry Bldg., Embarcadero at Market St., Embarcadero* ☎ *415/861–8032* 🌐 *www.slanteddoor.com* ✍ *Reservations essential* ✣ *G3.*

MARINA

$$$ ITALIAN

🍴 **A16.** Marina residents—and, judging from the crowds, everybody else—gravitate to this lively trattoria, named for the autostrada that winds through Italy's sunny south. The kitchen serves the food of Naples and surrounding Campania, with a twist of seasonal California ingredients. Cult classics on the menu include creamy burrata with olive oil and crostini and crisp-crust pizzas, including a classic Neapolitan Margherita (mozzarella, tomato, and basil). Among the regularly changing pastas are rustic favorites like *maccaronara* with *ragu napoletana* and house-made ricotta salata, and dishes like petrale sole with Monterey squid, sunchokes, and grilled lemon with *salmoriglio* (a southern Italian sauce with garlic and herbs). An expertly chosen wine list of primarily southern Italian with some California wines suits the fare perfectly, along with a newly expanded beer list. The long dining room includes an animated bar scene near the door; ask for a table in the quieter alcove at the far end. Reservations are easier to snag midweek. [$] *Average main: $24* ✉ *2355 Chestnut St., Marina* ☎ *415/771–2216* 🌐 *www.a16sf.com* 🕘 *No lunch Sat.–Tues.* ✥ *A1*

COW HOLLOW

$$ ITALIAN 👶

🍴 **Rose's Café.** Sleepy-headed locals turn up at Rose's for the breakfast pizza of smoked ham, eggs, and fontina; house-baked pastries and breads; poached eggs with Yukon Gold potato and mushroom hash; or soft polenta with mascarpone and jam. Midday is time for a roasted chicken and fontina sandwich; pizza with wild nettles; or linguine with clams. Evening hours find customers eating their way through more pizza and pasta if they are on a budget, and skirt steak and roasted chicken if they aren't. The ingredients are top-notch, the service is friendly, and the seating is in comfortable booths, at tables, and at a counter. At the outside tables, overhead heaters keep you toasty when the temperature dips. Expect long lines for Sunday brunch. [$] *Average main: $22* ✉ *2298 Union St., Cow Hollow* ☎ *415/775–2200* 🌐 *www.rosescafesf.com* ✥ *A2.*

THE HAIGHT

$$ INDIAN

🍴 **Indian Oven.** This white-tablecloth northern Indian restaurant draws diners from all over the city who come for the tandoori specialties—chicken, lamb, breads. Classics like *saag paneer* (spinach with Indian cheese), *aloo gobhi* (potato, cauliflower, and spices), and *bengan bartha* (roasted eggplant with onions and spices) are also excellent. The chef wants to keep his clientele around for the long haul, too, and puts a little "heart healthy" icon next to some of the menu items. On Friday and Saturday nights famished patrons overflow onto the sidewalk as they wait for open tables. If you try to linger over a mango *lassi* or an order of the excellent *kheer* (rice pudding) on one of these nights, you'll probably be hurried along by a waiter. For better service, come on a slower weeknight or for lunch. [$] *Average main: $16* ✉ *233 Fillmore St., Lower Haight* ☎ *415/626–1628* 🌐 *www.indianovensf.com* ✥ *A6.*

$$$

AMERICAN

✕ **Nopa.** In the mid-2000s North of the Panhandle became the city's newest talked-about neighborhood in part because of the big, bustling Nopa, which was cleverly named after it. This casual space, with its high ceilings, concrete floor, long bar, and sea of tables, suits the high-energy crowd of young professionals mixed with stylish neighborhood residents that fill it every night (and since the kitchen doesn't close until 1 am, plenty of restaurant industry types come in and pack the bar late into the night). Diners come primarily for the rustic fare, like an always winning flat bread topped with fennel sausage and caramelized onions; the vegetable tagine with lemon yogurt; smoky, crisp-skinned rotisserie chicken; a juicy grass-fed hamburger with thick-cut fries; one of the city's best pork chops; and for dessert, the donutlike sopapillas. But they also love the lively spirit of the place. Unfortunately, that buzz sometimes means that raised voices are the only way to communicate with fellow diners. A big communal table and the friendly bar ease the way for anyone dining out on his or her own. Wine lovers are happily satisfied here with the excellent list, and weekend brunch is one of the city's best (and most popular—arrive a few minutes before they open at 11 am to score a table). $ *Average main: $24* ⊠ *560 Divisadero St., Haight* ☎ *415/864–8643* ⊕ *www.nopasf.com* ☾ *No lunch* ✛ *A6.*

$$

MEXICAN

☾

Fodor's Choice

★

✕ **Nopalito.** This is one of the more unusual (and delicious) Mexican restaurants in the city—the two chefs here were originally cooks in the kitchen at Nopa around the corner, and their staff/family meals were so delicious that the Nopa owners were inspired to create this restaurant around their cooking. The menu features authentic recipes prepared skillfully with excellent ingredients, from a bright ceviche and seasonal salads to the succulent pork carnitas and a fulfilling posole. All the tortillas are made from an organic house-ground masa (also used in the delicious tortilla chips layering the *chilaquiles* during weekend brunch). It's a casual space with a variety of tables, communal seating, and a counter, quite popular with families and equally pleasing for adult groups perusing its well-selected tequila list. Expect a steady wait in the evening—you'll have to leave your name on a list, but you can call before heading over to get your name on the waitlist in advance. There's also a take-out window if you're feeling impatient. $ *Average main: $15* ⊠ *306 Broderick St., Haight* ☎ *415/437–0303* ⊕ *www. nopalitosf.com* ✛ *A6.*

THE CASTRO

$$$

FRENCH

✕ **Frances.** One of the hottest tickets in town, Frances is located, ironically, on a sleepy residential street in the Castro. Chef-owner Melissa Perello's menu of California and French cuisine is well executed, balanced, and notably affordable for the high quality. Bacon beignets, tender gnocchi, and a savory bavette steak are becoming favorites on the seasonally driven menu, while new entries like baked clams with bacon cream and a duck confit and kale salad are angling to become standbys as well. An apple galette for dessert hits all the right notes. The small space is simply designed and casual, with a limited number of close tables (hence the difficulty in landing a reservation). Service here is both very professional and warm, and there's a small bar area

4

for desperate diners who want to try their luck for a walk-in spot at the counter. $ *Average main: $27* ✉ *3870 17th St., Castro* ☎ *415/621–3870* ⊕ *www.frances-sf.com* ☙ *Reservations essential* ☉ *Closed Mon. No lunch* ✛ *A6.*

THE MISSION

$$$ ✕ **Delfina.** "Irresistible." That's how countless die-hard fans describe
ITALIAN Craig and Anne Stoll's Delfina. Such wild enthusiasm has made patience
Fodor's Choice the critical virtue for anyone wanting a reservation here (although walk-
★ ins can find some success at a counter and in the bar area). The urban interior is comfortable, with hardwood floors, aluminum-top tables, a tile bar, and a casual, friendly atmosphere. The menu changes daily, and among the usual offerings are grilled squid with warm white-bean salad and excellent tripe (they're also known for their spaghetti). If Piemontese fresh white truffles have made their way to San Francisco, you are likely to find hand-cut tagliarini dressed with butter, cream, and the pricey aromatic fungus on the menu alongside dishes built on more-prosaic ingredients. The panna cotta is the best in its class. The storefront next door is home to pint-size Pizzeria Delfina. And for folks who can't get to the Mission, the Stolls have opened a second pizzeria on California Street in lively Lower Pacific Heights. $ *Average main: $25* ✉ *3621 18th St., Mission* ☎ *415/552–4055* ⊕ *www.delfinasf.com* ☙ *Reservations essential* ☉ *No lunch* ✛ *B6.*

$$ ✕ **Dosa on Valencia.** Like Indian food but crave more than chicken tikka
INDIAN masala and naan? Dosa is your answer. This temple of South Indian
Fodor's Choice cuisine, done in cheerful tones of tangerine and turmeric, serves not
★ only the large, thin savory pancake for which it is named, but also cur-
ries, *uttapam* (open-face pancakes), and various starters, breads, rice dishes, and chutneys. You can select from about 10 different dosa fillings, ranging from traditional potatoes, onions, and cashews to spinach and fennel stems. Each comes with tomato and fresh coconut chutneys and *sambar* (lentil curry) for dipping. Tamil lamb curry with fennel and tomatoes and poppy seed prawns are popular, as are starters like Chennai chicken (chicken marinated in yogurt and spices and lightly fried), and the new Indian street-food additions, like *vada pav* (a vegetarian slider). The wine and beer lists are top drawer, and both include some Indian labels; the cocktail list is also very food friendly. Weekend brunch offers a nice change from the usual brunch suspects (the flavorful *pani puri* are a must). Queues for this Mission District spot convinced the owners to open a second, splashier branch on the corner of Fillmore and Post in Japantown. $ *Average main: $15* ✉ *995 Valencia St., at 21st St., Mission* ☎ *415/642–3672* ⊕ *www.dosasf.com* ☉ *No lunch* ✛ *B6.*

$ ✕ **SanJalisco.** This old-time, sun-filled, colorful, family-run restaurant
MEXICAN is a neighborhood gem (and it's not just because it serves breakfast all
☾ day). At brunch, try the hearty *chilaquiles*, made from day-old tortillas cut into strips and cooked with cheese, eggs, chilies, and sauce. Or order eggs scrambled with cactus or with *chicharrones* (crisp pork skins) and served with freshly made tortillas. Soup offerings change daily, with Tuesday's *albondigas* (meatballs) comfort food at its best. On weekends, adventurous eaters may opt for *birria*, a spicy goat stew, or *menudo*, a

tongue-searing soup made from tripe, calf's foot, and hominy. The latter is a time-honored hangover cure—but don't come expecting margaritas here (although you will find beer and sangria). Bring plenty of change for the jukebox loaded with Latin hits. [$] *Average main: $11* ✉ *901 S. Van Ness Ave., Mission* ☎ *415/648–8383* 🌐 *www.sanjalisco.com* ✣ *C6.*

POTRERO HILL

$$$ FRENCH

🍴 **Chez Papa Bistrot.** France arrived on Potrero Hill with this restaurant, which delivers food, waiters, and charm that would be right at home in Provence. The modest corner restaurant, with a Mediterranean blue awning, big windows overlooking the street, and a small heated patio, caters to a lively crowd that can make conversation difficult. Small plates include bistro classics like mussels in pastis, beef tartare, and a leek and tomato tart. Big plates range from duck confit, to grilled flatiron steak and frites, to homey lamb daube. The lavender crème brûlée or chocolate fondant provides a sweet ending. The $34.95 prix-fixe (Sunday through Thursday) is also a good deal for the penny-wise. To accommodate the overflow of Hill residents who have packed this place since day one, the owners opened the tiny (and more casual) Chez Maman (crepes, burgers, salads) a few doors down the block. [$] *Average main: $23* ✉ *1401 18th St., Potrero Hill* ☎ *415/824–8205* 🌐 *www.chezpapasf.com* ⏲ *No lunch Sun.* ✣ *G6*

PACIFIC HEIGHTS

$$$$ MODERN AMERICAN

🍴 **Spruce.** One of the hottest reservations in town from the day it opened, Spruce caters to the city's social set, with the older crowd sliding into oversized faux ostrich chairs in the early hours and the younger set taking their places after 8 (there's also quite the lunch club during the week). The large space, a former 1930s auto barn, shelters a high-style dining room and a more casual bar and library lounge. Charcuterie, bavette steak with bordelaise sauce and duck-fat potatoes, and sweetbreads reflect the French slant of the modern American menu. The wine list is a star here (especially a delight for Riesling fans). If you can't wrangle a table, stop in at the take-out café next door, which carries not only sandwiches, salads, and pastries (like the exquisite palmiers) but also anything from the dining room menu to go. And if you are watching your pocketbook, you can graze off the bar menu (which includes their excellent burger and *boudin blanc*) and watch the swells come and go over a well-crafted cocktail. [$] *Average main: $34* ✉ *3640 Sacramento St., Pacific Heights* ☎ *415/931–5100* 🌐 *www.sprucesf.com* ✍ *Reservations essential* ⏲ *No lunch weekends* ✣ *A3.*

JAPANTOWN

$$ INDIAN Fodor's Choice ★

🍴 **Dosa on Fillmore.** As soon as the large door swings open to this happening two-level space, diners are greeted with a sexy atmosphere with bright colors, vivid artwork, upbeat music, a lively bar scene, and the smell of spices in the air. This is the second location of the popular Dosa on Valencia, but it's definitely the glamorous younger sister, with a full bar, an expanded menu, and much more room. The menu entices with savory fish dishes, fall-off-the-bone pepper chicken, and papery dosas stuffed with a variety of fillings. The restaurant handles group dining often, and has a special menu you can customize. Return for lunch and indulge in the Indian street-food selections, and the famed *pani puri* (little crisp puffs you fill with mint and tamarind water and pop all at once into your mouth). [$] *Average main: $17* ✉ *1700 Fillmore St., Japantown* ☎ *415/441–3672* 🌐 *www.dosasf.com* ⏲ *No lunch Mon. and Tues.* ⊕ *A4*

$ JAPANESE 👍 🍴 **Mifune.** Thin brown soba and thick white udon are the stars at this long-popular North American outpost of an Osaka-based noodle empire. A line regularly snakes out the door, but the house-made noodles, served both hot and cold and with a score of toppings, are worth the wait (and the line moves quickly). Seating is at wooden tables, where diners of every age can be heard slurping down big bowls of such traditional Japanese combinations as *nabeyaki udon,* wheat noodles topped with tempura, chicken, and fish cake; and *tenzaru,* cold noodles and hot tempura with gingery dipping sauce served on lacquered trays. The noodle-phobic can choose from a few rice dishes and sushi. [$] *Average main: $9* ✉ *Japan Center, Kintetsu Bldg., 1737 Post St., Japantown* ☎ *415/922–0337* 🌐 *www.mifune.com* ⊕ *B4.*

RICHMOND

$$$ MOROCCAN Fodor's Choice ★ 🍴 **Aziza.** Chef-owner Mourad Lahlou's California-Moroccan food boasts a healthy dose of modernity that keeps locals coming back for his unique flavors and thoughtfully sourced ingredients. Diners enjoy inspired and gorgeously plated first courses that are always changing with the seasons, like big fin squid with artichoke, citrus, piquillo, and olive, or sweetbreads with winter squash, cornichon, and marash pepper. The main courses are equally elegant, ranging from squab with smoked farro to lamb shank with apricot, turnips, and barley. The basteeya is one delicious holdover from the restaurant's earlier rustic days, although it's now made with duck confit. Desserts here are as sophisticated as the savory dishes. The attractive three-room dining area, done in blue, saffron, and white, is a warm, inviting sea of tiles, arches, and candlelight. The wine list is very food-friendly, with some organic and biodynamic options, while cocktail enthusiasts can pick from more than two dozen inspired drinks that use ingredients like tarragon, Kaffir lime, and cumin. [$] *Average main: $27* ✉ *5800 Geary Blvd., Richmond* ☎ *415/752–2222* 🌐 *www.aziza-sf.com* ⏲ *Closed Tues. No lunch* ⊕ *A3.*

$ VIETNAMESE 👍 🍴 **Good Noodle.** The menu at this no-frills Formica-and-linoleum spot is big and remarkably cheap. You can order everything from Vietnamese salads to rice dishes and noodle plates. But the soups are what take up the most space on the menu, from the two dozen varieties of *pho,* rice noodles in beef broth, to a dozen types of *hu tieu,* seafood and pork noodle soups. All of them are served in three sizes—small, medium, and large—usually separated by just 75¢, and no bowl is skimpy. Regulars, many of whom hail from Southeast Asia, favor the shrimp, fish ball, and pork slices soup with clear noodles and the special combo pho with rare steak, well-done brisket, tendon, and tripe. $ *Average main: $8* ✉ *239 Clement St., Inner Richmond* ☎ *415/379–9008* ✛ *A3.*

WHERE TO STAY

San Francisco is one of the country's best hotel towns, offering a rich selection of properties that satisfy most tastes and budgets. Whether you're seeking a cozy inn, a kitschy motel, a chic boutique, or a grande dame hotel, this city has got the perfect room for you.

Prices in the hotel reviews are the lowest cost of a standard double room in high season. Prices do not include taxes (as high as 14%, depending on the region).

Use the coordinate (✛ A1) at the end of each listing to locate a site on the corresponding map.

4

UNION SQUARE/DOWNTOWN

For expanded reviews, facilities, and current deals, visit Fodors.com.

$

B&B/INN

☺

Fodor's Choice

★

Golden Gate Hotel. Families looking for accommodations in the Union Square area will delight in this homey, family-run B&B. **Pros:** friendly staff; spotless rooms; comfortable bedding; good location if you're a walker. **Cons:** only some of the rooms have private baths. **TripAdvisor:** "very nice," "great location," "wonderful bed and breakfast." $ *Rooms from: $105* ✉ *775 Bush St., Union Sq.* ☎ *415/392–3702, 800/835–1118* ⊕ *www.goldengatehotel.com* ⤳ *25 rooms, 14 with bath* ❑ *Breakfast* ✛ *E4.*

$$

HOTEL

☺

Fodor's Choice

★

Hotel Diva. Entering this hotel requires stepping over footprints, handprints, and autographs embedded into the sidewalk by visiting stars; with two major theaters, the Curran and the American Conservatory Theater, just across the street, this hotel has long been a magnet for actors, musicians, writers, and artists. **Pros:** clean; safe; in the heart of the theater district; accommodating service. **Cons:** no frills; tiny bathrooms. **TripAdvisor:** "excellent location," "friendly staff," "what's not to love." $ *Rooms from: $199* ✉ *440 Geary St., Union Sq.* ☎ *415/885–0200, 800/553–1900* ⊕ *www.hoteldiva.com* ⤳ *115 rooms, 3 suites* ❑ *No meals* ✛ *E4.*

$$$$

HOTEL

☺

Fodor's Choice

★

Hotel Nikko, San Francisco. The vast surfaces of gray-flecked white marble and gurgling fountains in the neoclassical lobby of this business-traveler hotel have the sterility of an airport; however the crisply designed rooms in muted tones, with flat-screen TVs, modern (and newly renovated) bathrooms with sinks that sit on top of granite bases, plus separate showers and tubs, please jet-setters. **Pros:** friendly multilingual staff; large indoor pool; very clean. **Cons:** rooms and antiseptic lobby lack color; some may find the atmosphere cold; expensive parking. **TripAdvisor:** "great room," "comfy beds," "very convenient." $ *Rooms from: $265* ✉ *222 Mason St., Union Sq.* ☎ *415/394–1111, 800/248–3308* ⊕ *www.hotelnikkosf.com* ⤳ *510 rooms, 22 suites* ❑ *No meals* ✛ *E4.*

$$

HOTEL

Fodor's Choice

★

Hotel Triton. The spirit of fun has taken up full-time residence in this Kimpton property, which has a youngish, superfriendly staff; pink-and-blue-neon elevators; and a colorful psychedelic lobby mural depicting the San Francisco art and music scene—think flower power mixed with

Andy Warhol. **Pros:** attentive service; refreshingly funky atmosphere; hip arty environs; good location. **Cons:** rooms and baths are on the small side. **TripAdvisor:** "a triumph over calamity," "quirky," "customer service at its finest."[$] *Rooms from: $179* ✉ *342 Grant Ave., Union Sq.* ☎ *415/394–0500, 800-800-1299* 🌐 *www.hoteltriton.com* 🛏 *133 rooms, 7 suites* 🍴 *No meals* ✥ *F4.*

$$$$ HOTEL Fodor's Choice ★ 🏨 **Taj Campton Place San Francisco.** Beauty and highly attentive service remain the hallmarks of this exquisite jewel-like, top-tier hotel. **Pros:** attentive service; first-class restaurant; abundant natural light; the most lavish robes in town. **Cons:** pricey (but worth it). **TripAdvisor:** "lovely boutique property," "over and above customer service," "luxury on Union Square."[$] *Rooms from: $615* ✉ *340 Stockton St., Union Sq.* ☎ *415/781–5555, 866/332–1670* 🌐 *www.camptonplace.com* 🛏 *101 rooms, 9 suites* 🍴 *No meals* ✥ *E4.*

$$$$ HOTEL 🏨 **Westin St. Francis.** The site of sensational, headline-making scandals, this hotel's past is shrouded as much in infamy as in stardust: This is where Sara Jane Moore tried to assassinate President Gerald Ford and where singer Al Jolson died playing poker—not to mention the tempest that erupted after a booze fest hosted by silent-film comedian Fatty Arbuckle in Suite 1219–21 ended with the death of an aspiring actress. **Pros:** fantastic beds; prime location; spacious rooms, some with great views. **Cons:** some guests comment on the long wait at check-in; rooms in original building can be small; glass elevators are not for the faint of heart. **TripAdvisor:** "perfect location," "we loved it," "gracious service."[$] *Rooms from: $299* ✉ *335 Powell St., Union Sq.* ☎ *415/397–7000, 800/917–7458* 🌐 *www.westinstfrancis.com* 🛏 *1,157 rooms, 38 suites* 🍴 *No meals* ✥ *E4.*

SOMA

$$$$ HOTEL 👶 Fodor's Choice ★ 🏨 **Four Seasons Hotel San Francisco.** Occupying floors 5 through 17 of a skyscraper, this exclusive, award-winning hotel is sandwiched between multimillion-dollar condos, elite shops, and a premier sports-and-fitness complex. **Pros:** near museums, galleries, restaurants, shopping and clubs; terrific fitness facilities; luxurious rooms and amenities. **Cons:** pricey; staff can be uppity. **TripAdvisor:** "luxury," "exceptional experience," "cradle of comfort."[$] *Rooms from: $415* ✉ *757 Market St., SoMa* ☎ *415/633–3000, 800/332–3442, 800/819–5053* 🌐 *www.fourseasons.com/sanfrancisco* 🛏 *231 rooms, 46 suites* 🍴 *No meals* ✥ *F4.*

$$$$ HOTEL 🏨 **InterContinental San Francisco.** The arctic-blue glass exterior and subdued, Zen-like lobby of this sparkling hotel may be as bland as an airport concourse, but they're merely a prelude to the spectacularly light, expansive, thoughtfully laid-out guest rooms, which have all the ultramodern conveniences. **Pros:** a stone's throw from the Moscone Center; well-equipped gym; near hip clubs and edgy eateries. **Cons:** conservative decor is a bit short on character; borders a rough neighborhood; a few blocks off from many major points of interest for tourists. **TripAdvisor:** "excellent service," "amazing views and perfect location," "lovely."[$] *Rooms from: $289* ✉ *888 Howard St., SoMa* ☎ *415/616–*

6500, 866/781–2364 🌐 www.intercontinentalsanfrancisco.com 🛏 536 rooms, 14 suites 🍴 No meals ✣ E5.

$$$$ HOTEL 🏨 **Palace Hotel, San Francisco.** "Majestic" is the word that best sums up this landmark hotel, which was the world's largest and most luxurious when it opened in 1875. **Pros:** gracious service; close to Union Square; near BART. **Cons:** design from another era; smallish rooms with even smaller baths; many nearby establishments closed on weekends; west-facing rooms can be warm and stuffy. **TripAdvisor:** "ideal location and beautiful surroundings," "historic beauty," "old-world elegance." [$] *Rooms from: $599 ✉ 2 New Montgomery St., SoMa ☎ 415/512–1111, 888/627–7196 🌐 www.sfpalace.com 🛏 518 rooms, 34 suites 🍴 No meals ✣ F4.*

4

CIVIC CENTER/VAN NESS

$ HOTEL 🏨 **Hotel Whitcomb.** Built in 1910, this historic hotel was the temporary seat of city government from 1912 to 1915 before becoming a hotel in 1916. **Pros:** good location; rich architectural and historic legacy; opulent lobby; airport shuttle; free Wi-Fi. **Cons:** difficult to find street parking; area can be dodgy at night; rooms are not as flashy as the lobby. **TripAdvisor:** "New York in San Francisco," "outstanding service," "old-time elegance." [$] *Rooms from: $129 ✉ 1231 Market St., Civic Center ☎ 415/626–8000, 800/227–4747 🌐 www.hotelwhitcomb.com 🛏 447 rooms, 13 suites 🍴 No meals ✣ D6.*

FINANCIAL DISTRICT

$$$$ HOTEL 🏨 **Mandarin Oriental, San Francisco.** Two towers connected by glass-enclosed sky bridges compose the top 11 floors of one of San Francisco's tallest buildings, offering spectacular panoramas from every room; the windows open so you can hear that trademark San Francisco sound: the "ding ding" of the cable cars some 40 floors below (and some rooms even include binoculars). **Pros:** spectacular "bridge-to-bridge" views; attentive service; in the running for the most comfy beds in the city. **Cons:** located in a business area that's quiet on weekends; extremely pricey. **TripAdvisor:** "spectacular view," "amazing and magical," "quiet, pretty rooms." [$] *Rooms from: $445 ✉ 222 Sansome St., Financial District ☎ 415/276–9600, 800/622–0404 🌐 www.mandarinoriental.com/sanfrancisco 🛏 151 rooms, 7 suites 🍴 No meals ✣ F3.*

NOB HILL

$$$$ HOTEL Fodor's Choice ★ 🏨 **The Huntington Hotel.** The venerable ivy-covered hotel, a family-owned property for three generations, has provided gracious personal service to everyone from Bogart and Bacall to Picasso and Pavarotti. **Pros:** personal service; an aura of old San Francisco; guests have access to the primo spa with city views; cable car passes by right out front. **Cons:** up a steep hill from downtown. **TripAdvisor:** "classic San Francisco hotel," "large rooms," "the bar and spa are the highlights." [$] *Rooms from: $410 ✉ 1075 California St., Nob Hill ☎ 415/474–5400, 800/227–4683 🌐 www.huntingtonhotel.com 🛏 96 rooms, 40 suites 🍴 No meals ✣ E4.*

Fairmont Heritage Place, Ghirardelli Square

The Huntington Hotel

Argonaut Hotel

Hotel Vitale

Ritz-Carlton, San Francisco.

Hotel Drisco

Hotel Tomo

Union Street Inn

BEST BETS FOR SAN FRANCISCO LODGING

Fodor's offers a selective listing of quality lodging experiences at every price range, from the city's best budget motel to its most sophisticated luxury hotel. Here we've compiled our top recommendations by price and experience. The very best properties—in other words, those that provide a particularly remarkable experience in their price range—are designated in the listings with the Fodor's Choice logo.

Fodor'sChoice★

Argonaut Hotel, $$$$, p. 231
Cow Hollow Motor Inn and Suites, $, p. 232
Fairmont Heritage Place, Ghirardelli Square, $$$$, p. 232
Four Seasons Hotel San Francisco, $$$$, p. 226
Golden Gate Hotel, $, p. 225
Hotel Diva, $$, p. 225
Hotel Drisco, $$$$, p. 233
Hotel Nikko, San Francisco, $$$$, p. 225
Hotel Tomo, $, p. 232

Hotel Triton, $$, p. 225
Hotel Vitale, $$$$, p. 232
Huntington Hotel, $$$$, p. 227
Ritz-Carlton, San Francisco, $$$$, p. 231
San Remo Hotel, $, p. 231
Taj Campton Place San Francisco, $$$$, p. 226
Union Street Inn, $$$, p. 233

By Price

$

Cow Hollow Motor Inn and Suites, p. 232
Golden Gate Hotel, p. 225
Hotel Tomo, p. 232
San Remo Hotel, p. 231

$$

Hotel Triton, p. 225
Hotel Diva, p. 225

$$$

Union Street Inn, p. 233

$$$$

Argonaut Hotel, p. 231
Fairmont Heritage Place, Ghirardelli Square, p. 232
Four Seasons Hotel San Francisco, p. 226
Hotel Drisco, p. 233
Hotel Nikko, San Francisco, p. 225
Hotel Vitale, p. 232
Huntington Hotel, p. 227
Ritz-Carlton, San Francisco, p. 231
Taj Campton Place San Francisco, p. 226

By Experience

BUSINESS TRAVELERS

Four Seasons Hotel San Francisco, $$$$, p. 226
Hotel Nikko, San Francisco, $$$$, p. 225

GREAT CONCIERGE

Ritz-Carlton, San Francisco, $$$$, p. 231

HISTORICAL FLAVOR

Hotel Whitcomb, $, p. 227
Palace Hotel, San Francisco, $$$$, p. 227
Westin St. Francis, $$$$, p. 226

MOST KID-FRIENDLY

Argonaut Hotel, $$$$, p. 231
Four Seasons Hotel San Francisco, $$$$, p. 226
Hotel Tomo, $, p. 232

MOST ROMANTIC

Hotel Drisco, $$$$, p. 233
Huntington Hotel, $$$$, p. 227
Palace Hotel, San Francisco, $$$$, p. 227
Union Street Inn, $$$, p. 233

TOP B&BS

Hotel Drisco, $$$$, p. 233

TOP SPAS

Huntington Hotel, $$$$, p. 227
Mandarin Oriental San Francisco, $$$$, p. 227

$$$$ HOTEL Fodor's Choice ★ **Ritz-Carlton, San Francisco.** A preferred destination for travel-industry honchos, movie stars, and visitors alike, this hotel—a stunning tribute to beauty and attentive, professional service—is completing a $12.5-million renovation to offer a modern luxurious experience with Ritz style. **Pros:** terrific service; all-day food service on Club Level; beautiful surroundings; fantastic new restaurant and lobby lounge; renovated fitness center. **Cons:** expensive; hilly location; no pool. **TripAdvisor:** "as good as it gets," "excellent service," "definitely lovely." [$] *Rooms from: $399* ✉ *600 Stockton St., at California St., Nob Hill* ☎ *415/296–7465* 🌐 *www.ritzcarlton.com* 🛏 *276 rooms, 60 suites* 🍴 *No meals* ✣ *E4.*

NORTH BEACH

$ HOTEL Fodor's Choice ★ **San Remo Hotel.** A few blocks from Fisherman's Wharf, this three-story 1906 Italianate Victorian—once home to longshoremen and Beat poets—has a narrow stairway from the street leading to the front desk and labyrinthine hallways; rooms are small but charming, with lace curtains, forest-green-painted wood floors, and brass beds and other antique furnishings. **Pros:** inexpensive; historic; cozy. **Cons:** some rooms are dark; no private bath; spartan amenities. **TripAdvisor:** "an authentic taste of old San Francisco," "clean and beautiful," "excellent hotel in a quiet area." [$] *Rooms from: $65* ✉ *2237 Mason St., North Beach* ☎ *415/776–8688, 800/352–7366* 🌐 *www.sanremohotel.com* 🛏 *64 rooms with shared baths, 1 suite* 🍴 *No meals* ✣ *E1.*

FISHERMAN'S WHARF

$$$$ HOTEL Fodor's Choice ★ **Argonaut Hotel.** When the four-story Haslett Warehouse was a fruit-and-vegetable canning complex in 1907, boats docked right up against the building; today it's a hotel with a nautical decor—think anchors, ropes, compasses, and a row of cruise-ship deck chairs in the lobby—that makes perfect sense given the fact that the Argonaut is part of the San Francisco Maritime National Historical Park (whose visitors center occupies the ground floor). **Pros:** bay views; near Hyde Street cable car; sofa beds; toys for the kids. **Cons:** nautical theme isn't for everyone; cramped public areas; service can be hit or miss; location is a bit of a trek from other parts of town. **TripAdvisor:** "can't get a better location," "a brilliant experience," "very pleased." [$] *Rooms from: $319* ✉ *495 Jefferson St., at Hyde St., Fisherman's Wharf* ☎ *415/563–0800, 866/415–0704* 🌐 *www.argonauthotel.com* 🛏 *239 rooms, 13 suites* 🍴 *No meals* ✣ *D1.*

$$$ HOTEL **Best Western Plus Tuscan Inn.** Described by some Fodors.com users as a "hidden treasure," this hotel's redbrick facade barely hints at the Tuscan country villa that lies within. **Pros:** wine and beer hour; down-home feeling; great location near Fisherman's Wharf. **Cons:** congested touristy area; small rooms. **TripAdvisor:** "great location," "excellent service," "nice comfortable hotel." [$] *Rooms from: $249* ✉ *425 N. Point St., at Mason St., Fisherman's Wharf* ☎ *415/561–1100, 800/648–4626* 🌐 *www.tuscaninn.com* 🛏 *212 rooms, 12 suites* 🍴 *No meals* ✣ *E1.*

$$$$
RENTAL
☾
Fodor'sChoice
★

⊡ **Fairmont Heritage Place, Ghirardelli Square.** Housed in the former Ghirardelli chocolate factory, these one-to-three-bedroom serviced apartments might possibly be the most luxurious accommodations in San Francisco. **Pros:** luxury at its finest; gigantic apartments with heaps of amenities; bay views from most apartments; free hotel car to deliver you within a 2-mile radius. **Cons:** a bit of a trek from downtown; expensive. **TripAdvisor:** "the only way to travel," "comfort and style," "great rooms." $ *Rooms from: $599* ⊠ *950 North Point St., Fisherman's Wharf* ☎ *415/268–9900* ⊕ *www.fairmont.com/ghirardelli* ¶⊙*Breakfast* ✛ *D1.*

EMBARCADERO

$$$$
HOTEL
☾
Fodor'sChoice
★

⊡ **Hotel Vitale.** "Luxury, naturally," the theme of this eight-story terraced bay-front hotel, is apparent in every thoughtful detail: little vases of aromatic herbs mounted outside each room; the penthouse day spa with soaking tubs set in a rooftop bamboo forest; and the aromatherapy garden off the patio of restaurant Americano, whose outdoor terrace is packed with hip jet-setters. **Pros:** family-friendly studios; great views; fanciful spa; luxurious amenities throughout. **Cons:** cramped rooms can be noisy; some guests report inconsistent service from staff and find the hotel pricey. **TripAdvisor:** "great staff and pleasant views," "truly dog friendly," "a comfortable relaxing stay." $ *Rooms from: $399* ⊠ *8 Mission St., Embarcadero* ☎ *415/278-3700, 888/890–8688* ⊕ *www. hotelvitale.com* ↩ *190 rooms, 9 suites* ¶⊙*No meals* ✛ *H3.*

JAPANTOWN

$
HOTEL
☾
Fodor'sChoice
★

⊡ **Hotel Tomo.** Japanese Pop, or J-Pop as it is known across the pond, comes alive in this Japantown boutique hotel, located just a couple of blocks from the chic Fillmore district, Yoshi's, and the famous Fillmore concert venue. **Pros:** J-Pop style; anime playing on the lobby TV and manga in your room; great price in a fun neighborhood. **Cons:** tight quarters; a trek from downtown. **TripAdvisor:** "charming refuge from the typical SFO hotel," "nice rooms," "fun and modern." $ *Rooms from: $149* ⊠ *1800 Sutter St., Japantown* ☎ *415/921–4000* ⊕ *www. hoteltomo.com* ↩ *125 rooms, 1 suite* ¶⊙*No meals* ✛ *B4.*

PACIFIC HEIGHTS/COW HOLLOW

$
RENTAL
Fodor'sChoice
★

⊡ **Cow Hollow Motor Inn and Suites.** Newly refreshed suites at this large, family-owned modern motel are more spacious than average, featuring one or two bedrooms, hardwood floors, sitting and dining areas, Oriental rugs, marble wood-burning fireplaces, big living rooms, and fully equipped kitchens. **Pros:** suites are the size of apartments; good for families; covered parking in building. **Cons:** congested neighborhood has a frat-boy feel; standard rooms are on a loud street. **TripAdvisor:** "comfortable and conveniently located," "great base for San Francisco," "clean with great service." $ *Rooms from: $140* ⊠ *2190 Lombard St., Marina* ☎ *415/921–5800* ⊕ *www.cowhollowmotorinn. com* ↩ *117 rooms, 12 suites* ¶⊙*No meals* ✛ *A1.*

$$$$ B&B/INN Fodor's Choice ★ 🏨 **Hotel Drisco.** Pretend you're a resident of one of the wealthiest and most beautiful residential neighborhoods in San Francisco at this understated, elegant 1903 Edwardian hotel. **Pros:** great service; comfortable rooms; quiet residential retreat. **Cons:** small rooms; far from downtown. **TripAdvisor:** "traditional charm and warmth," "everyone was friendly and helpful," "live like a tycoon." [$] *Rooms from: $335* ✉ *2901 Pacific Ave., Pacific Heights* ☎ *415/346–2880, 800/634–7277* 🌐 *www.hoteldrisco.com* 🛏 *29 rooms, 19 suites* 🍴 *Breakfast* ✣ *A3.*

$$$ B&B/INN Fodor's Choice ★ 🏨 **Union Street Inn.** Precious family antiques and unique artwork helped British innkeepers Jane Bertorelli and David Coyle (former chef for the Duke and Duchess of Bedford) transform this green-and-cream 1902 Edwardian into a delightful B&B. **Pros:** personal service; Jane's excellent full breakfast; romantic setting. **Cons:** parking in the neighborhood is tricky; no air-conditioning; no elevator. **TripAdvisor:** "a wonderful retreat," "a relaxing garden," "Victorian beauty." [$] *Rooms from: $219* ✉ *2229 Union St., Cow Hollow* ☎ *415/346–0424* 🌐 *www.unionstreetinn.com* 🛏 *6 rooms* 🍴 *Breakfast* ✣ *A2.*

4

NIGHTLIFE

This small city packs the punch of a much larger metropolis after dark. Downtown cool, trendy, relaxed, quirky, and downright outrageous could all be used to describe San Francisco's diverse and vibrant collection of bars, clubs, and performance venues.

THE 4-1-1

Entertainment information is printed in the pink Sunday "Datebook" section (🌐 *www.sfgate.com/datebook*) and the more calendar-based Thursday "96 Hours" section (🌐 *www.sfgate.com/96hours*) in the *San Francisco Chronicle.* Also consult any of the free alternative weeklies, notably the *SF Weekly* (🌐 *www.sfweekly.com*), which blurbs nightclubs and music, and the *San Francisco Bay Guardian* (🌐 *www.sfbg.com*), which lists neighborhood, avant-garde, and budget events. SF Station (🌐 *www.sfstation.com*; online only) has an up-to-date calendar of entertainment goings-on.

BARS AND LOUNGES

Bourbon & Branch. The address and phone are unlisted, the black outer door unmarked, and when you make your reservation (required), you get a password for entry. In short, Bourbon & Branch reeks of Prohibition-era speakeasy cool. It's not exclusive, though: everyone is granted a password. The place has sex appeal, with tin ceilings, bordello-red silk wallpaper, intimate booths, and low lighting; loud conversations and cell phones are not allowed. The menu of expertly mixed cocktails and quality bourbon and whiskey is substantial, but the servers aren't always authorities. ■ **TIP→ This place is small, so couples or groups of four or fewer are ideal.** Your reservation dictates your exit time, which is strictly enforced. ✉ *501 Jones St., at O'Farrell St., Tenderloin* 🌐 *www.bourbonandbranch.com.*

★ **Cliff House.** Classier than the nearby Beach Chalet, with a more impressive view of Ocean Beach, the Cliff House is our pick if you must choose just one oceanfront restaurant/bar. Sure, it's the site of many high-school prom dates, and you could argue that the food and drinks are overpriced, and some say the sleek facade looks like a mausoleum—but the views are terrific. The best window seats are reserved for diners, but there's a small upstairs lounge where you can watch gulls sail high above the vast blue Pacific. Come before sunset. ⊠ *1090 Point Lobos, at Great Hwy., Lincoln Park* ☎ *415/386–3330* ⊕ *www.cliffhouse.com.*

★ **Hôtel Biron.** Sharing an alleylike block with the backs of Market Street restaurants, this tiny, cavelike (in a good way) spot displays rotating artwork of the Mission School aesthetic on its brick walls. The clientele is well-behaved twenty- to thirtysomethings who enjoy the cramped quarters, good range of wines and prices, off-the-beaten path location, soft lighting, and hip music. ⊠ *45 Rose St., off Market St. near Gough St., Hayes Valley* ☎ *415/703–0403* ⊕ *www.hotelbiron.com.*

Redwood Room. Opened in 1933 and updated by designer Philippe Starck in 2001, the Redwood Room at the Clift Hotel is a San Francisco icon. The entire room, floor to ceiling, is paneled with the wood from a single redwood tree, giving the place a rich, monochromatic look. The gorgeous original art-deco sconces and chandeliers still hang, but bizarre video installations on plasma screens also adorn the walls. It's packed on weekend evenings after 10, when young scenesters swarm the hotel; for maximum glamour, visit on a weeknight. ⊠ *Clift Hotel, 495 Geary St., at Taylor St., Union Sq.* ☎ *415/929–2372 for table reservations, 415/775–4700 for hotel* ⊕ *www.clifthotel.com.*

Smuggler's Cove. With the decor of a pirate ship and a slew of rum-based cocktails, you half expect Captain Jack Sparrow to sidle up next to you at this offbeat, Disney-esque hangout. But don't let the kitschy ambience fool you. The folks at Smuggler's Cove take rum so seriously that they even make their own, which you can sample along with more than 200 other offerings, some of them vintage and very hard to find. A punch card is provided so you can try all 70 cocktails and remember where you left off without getting shipwrecked. The small space has won numerous awards and fills up quickly, so arrive early. ⊠ *650 Gough St., at McAllister St., Hayes Valley* ☎ *415/869–1900* ⊕ *www.smugglerscovesf.com.*

Tonga Room. Since 1947 the Tonga Room has given San Francisco a taste of high Polynesian kitsch. Fake palm trees, grass huts, a lagoon (three-piece combos play pop standards on a floating barge), and faux monsoons—courtesy of sprinkler-system rain and simulated thunder and lightning—grow more surreal as you quaff fruity cocktails. ⊠ *Fairmont San Francisco, 950 Mason St., at California St., Nob Hill* ☎ *415/772–5278* ⊕ *www.tongaroom.com.*

★ **Vesuvio Café.** If you're only hitting one bar in North Beach, it should be this one. The low-ceiling second floor of this raucous boho hangout, little altered since its 1960s heyday (when Jack Kerouac frequented the place), is a fine vantage point for watching the colorful Broadway and Columbus Avenue intersection. Another part of Vesuvio's appeal is its diverse clientele (twenties to sixties), from neighborhood regulars and young couples to Bacchanalian posses of friends. ⊠ *255 Columbus Ave., at Broadway, North Beach* ☎ *415/362–3370* ⊕ *www.vesuvio.com.*

GAY AND LESBIAN NIGHTLIFE

Bay Area Reporter. The *Bay Area Reporter*, a weekly newspaper, lists gay and lesbian events in its calendar and has a special nightlife site (⊕ *www. bartabsf.com).* ☎ *415/861–5019* ⊕ *www.ebar.com.*

San Francisco Bay Times. The biweekly *San Francisco Bay Times* is aimed at gay and lesbian readers. ☎ *415/626–0260* ⊕ *www.sfbaytimes.com.*

Lexington Club. According to its slogan, "every night is ladies' night" at this all-girl club geared to urban alterna-dykes in their twenties and thirties (think piercings and tattoos, not lipstick). ■ **TIP➔** The women's room has awesome graffiti. ⊠ *3464 19th St., at Valencia, Mission* ☎ *415/863–2052* ⊕ *www.lexingtonclub.com.*

★ **Martuni's.** A mixed crowd enjoys cocktails in the semirefined environment of this elegant bar at the intersection of the Castro, the Mission, and Hayes Valley; variations on the martini are a specialty. ■ **TIP➔** The Godiva Chocolate Martini is a crowd favorite. In the intimate back room a pianist plays nightly, and patrons take turns boisterously singing show tunes. It's a favorite post-theater spot—especially after the symphony or opera, which are within walking distance. ⊠ *4 Valencia St., at Market St., Mission* ☎ *415/241–0205.*

★ **The Mint Karaoke Lounge.** A mixed gay-straight crowd that's drop-dead serious about its karaoke—to the point where you'd think an *American Idol* casting agent was in attendance—comes here seven nights a week. Regulars sing everything from Simon and Garfunkel songs to disco classics in front of an attentive audience. Do *not* walk onstage unprepared! Check out the songbook online to perfect your debut before you attempt to take the mike. ⊠ *1942 Market St., between Duboce Ave. and Laguna St., Hayes Valley* ☎ *415/626–4726* ⊕ *www.themint.net.*

★ **The Stud.** Open since 1966, the Stud is the bar for glam trannies, bears, tight-teed pretty boys, ladies and their ladies, and a handful of straight onlookers who dance to the live DJ and watch world-class drag performers on the small stage. The entertainment is often campy, pee-your-pants funny, and downright fantastic. At Frolic, the Stud's most outrageous party, club-goers dance the night away dressed as bunnies, kittens, and even stranger creatures. Each night's music is different—from funk, soul, and hip-hop to 80s tunes and disco favorites. ⊠ *1284 Harrison St., at 9th St., SoMa* ☎ *415/863–6623* ⊕ *www.studsf.com.*

JAZZ CLUBS

★ **Yoshi's.** The legendary Oakland club that has pulled in some of the world's best jazz musicians—Pat Martino, Branford Marsalis, Betty Carter, and Dizzy Gillespie, to name just a few—opened a San Francisco location in 2007. The new club has terrific acoustics, a 9-foot Steinway grand piano (broken in by Chick Corea), and seating for 411; it's been hailed as "simply the best jazz club in the city." Yoshi's serves Japanese food in an adjoining restaurant set in a soaring two-story space, decorated with blond wood and hanging paper lanterns (you can also order food at café tables in the club). And yes, the coupling of sushi and jazz *is* as elegant as it sounds. Sightlines are good from just about any vantage point, including the back balcony. Yoshi's is in the Fillmore District, which was known as the "Harlem of the West" in its 1940s and '50s heyday. The club is on a tough block in an even tougher neighborhood, so take advantage of the valet parking. ⊠ *1330 Fillmore St., at Eddy St., Japantown* ☎ *415/655–5600* ⊕ *www.yoshis.com.*

ROCK, POP, HIP-HOP, FOLK, AND BLUES CLUBS

★ **Bimbo's 365 Club.** The plush main room and adjacent lounge of this club, here since 1951, retain a retro vibe perfect for the "Cocktail Nation" programming that keeps the crowds entertained. For a taste of the old-school San Francisco nightclub scene, you can't beat this place. Indie low-fi and pop bands like Stephen Malkmus and the Jicks and Camera Obscura fill the bill. ⊠ *1025 Columbus Ave., at Chestnut St., North Beach* ☎ *415/474–0365* ⊕ *www.bimbos365club.com.*

Fodor's Choice ★ **BooM BooM RooM.** John Lee Hooker's old haunt has been an old-school blues haven for years, attracting top-notch acts from all around the country. Luck out with legendary masters like James "Super Chikan" Johnson, or discover new blues and funk artists. ⊠ *1601 Fillmore St., at Geary Blvd., Japantown* ☎ *415/673–8000* ⊕ *www.boomboomblues. com.*

★ **Bottom of the Hill.** This is a great live-music dive—in the best sense of the word—and truly the epicenter for independent rock in the Bay Area. The club has hosted some great acts over the years, including the Strokes and the Throwing Muses. Rap and hip-hop acts occasionally make it to the stage. ⊠ *1233 17th St., at Texas St., Potrero Hill* ☎ *415/621–4455* ⊕ *www.bottomofthehill.com.*

★ **The Fillmore.** This is *the* club that all the big names, from Coldplay to Clapton, want to play. San Francisco's most famous rock-music hall serves up a varied menu of national and local acts: rock, reggae, grunge, jazz, folk, acid house, and more. Most tickets cost $20–$30, and some shows are open to all ages. ■**TIP→** Avoid steep service charges by purchasing tickets at the Fillmore box office on Sunday (10–4). At the end of each show, apples are set near the door and free for the taking, and staffers hand out collectible posters that at the very least will sell well on eBay. ⊠ *1805 Geary Blvd., at Fillmore St., Western Addition* ☎ *415/346–6000* ⊕ *www.thefillmore.com.*

Fodor's Choice ★ **Great American Music Hall.** You can find top-drawer entertainment at this eclectic nightclub. Acts range from the best in blues, folk, and jazz to up-and-coming college-radio and American-roots artists to of-the-moment indie rock stars (OK Go, Mates of State) and the establishment (Cowboy Junkies). The colorful marble-pillared emporium (built in 1907 as a bordello) also accommodates dancing at some shows. Pub grub is available most nights. ⊠ *859 O'Farrell St., between Polk and Larkin Sts., Tenderloin* ☎ *415/885–0750* ⊕ *www.slimspresents.com.*

THE ARTS

San Francisco's symphony, opera, and ballet all perform in the Civic Center area, also home to the 928-seat Herbst Theatre, which hosts many fine soloists and ensembles.

TICKETS

City Box Office. This charge-by-phone service, sells tickets for many performances and lectures. You can buy tickets in person at its downtown location weekdays 9:30–5:30. ✉ *180 Redwood St., Suite 100, off Van Ness Ave. between Golden Gate Ave. and McAllister St., Civic Center* ☎ *415/392–4400* ⊕ *www.cityboxoffice.com.*

San Francisco Performances. SFP brings an eclectic array of top-flight global music and dance talents to various venues—mostly the Yerba Buena Center for the Arts, Davies Symphony Hall, and Herbst Theatre. Artists have included the Los Angeles Guitar Quartet, Edgar Meyer, the Paul Taylor Dance Company, and Midori. Tickets can be purchased in person, online, or by phone. ✉ *500 Sutter St., Suite 710* ☎ *415/392–2545* ⊕ *www.performances.org.*

Tickets.com. You can charge tickets for everything from jazz concerts to Giants games by phone or online through **Tickets.com.** ☎ *800/955–5566* ⊕ *www.tickets.com.*

TIX Bay Area. Half-price, same-day tickets for many local and touring stage shows go on sale (cash only) at 11 am Tuesday through Saturday at the Union Square booth of **TIX Bay Area.** TIX is also a full-service ticket agency for theater and music events around the Bay Area, open Tuesday through Friday 11–6, Saturday 10–6, and Sunday 10–3. ✉ *Powell St. between Geary and Post Sts., Union Sq.* ☎ *415/433–7827* ⊕ *www.tixbayarea.com.*

THE 4-1-1

The best guide to the arts is the Sunday "Datebook" section (⊕ *www. sfgate.com/datebook*), printed on pink paper, in the *San Francisco Chronicle.* The four-day entertainment supplement "96 Hours" (⊕ *www.sfgate.com/96hours*) is in the Thursday *Chronicle.* Also be sure to check out the city's free alternative weeklies, including *SF Weekly* (⊕ *www.sfweekly.com*) and the more avant-garde *San Francisco Bay Guardian* (⊕ *www.sfbg.com*).

Online, SF Station (⊕ *www.sfstation.com*) has a frequently updated arts and nightlife calendar. San Francisco Arts Monthly (⊕ *www.sfarts.org*), which is published at the end of the month, has arts features and events, plus a helpful "Visiting San Francisco?" section. For offbeat, emerging artist performances, consult CounterPULSE (⊕ *www.counterpulse.org*).

DANCE

Fodor's Choice ★ **San Francisco Ballet.** For ballet-lovers, this company is reason alone to visit the Bay Area. Under artistic director Helgi Tomasson, the San Francisco Ballet's works—both classical and contemporary—have won critical raves. The primary season runs from February through May. The repertoire includes full-length ballets such as *Don Quixote* and

Built as a bordello in 1907, the Great American Music Hall now pulls in top-tier performers.

Sleeping Beauty; the December presentation of *The Nutcracker* is truly spectacular. The company also performs bold new dances from star choreographers such as William Forsythe and Mark Morris, alongside modern classics by George Balanchine and Jerome Robbins. Tickets and information are available at the **War Memorial Opera House.** ✉ *War Memorial Opera House, 301 Van Ness Ave., at Grove St., Civic Center* ☎ *415/865–2000* ⊕ *www.sfballet.org* ☉ *Weekdays 10–4.*

MUSIC

FodorsChoice
★

San Francisco Symphony. One of America's top orchestras, the San Francisco Symphony performs from September through May, with additional summer performances of light classical music and show tunes; visiting artists perform here the rest of the year. The orchestra and its charismatic music director, Michael Tilson Thomas, who is known for his daring programming of 20th-century American works (most notably his Grammy Award–winning Mahler cycle), often perform with soloists of the caliber of Andre Watts, Gil Shaham, and Renée Fleming. The adventuresome side of the organization is amply illustrated by this symphony's collaboration with the heavy-metal group Metallica. David Byrne has performed here, as well. Tickets run from $15 to $100. ✉ *Davies Symphony Hall, 201 Van Ness Ave., at Grove St., Civic Center* ☎ *415/864–6000* ⊕ *www.sfsymphony.org.*

Summer in the City. Many members of the San Francisco Symphony perform in the Summer in the City concert series, held in the 2,400-seat Davies Symphony Hall. The schedule includes light classics and Broadway, country, and movie music. ☎ *415/864–6000* ⊕ *www.sfsymphony. org*

MUSIC FESTIVALS

Stern Grove Festival. The nation's oldest continual free summer music festival hosts Sunday-afternoon performances of symphony, opera, jazz, pop music, and dance. The amphitheater is in a beautiful eucalyptus grove below street level, perfect for picnicking before the show. (Dress for cool weather.) ✉ *Sloat Blvd. at 19th Ave., Sunset* ☎ *415/252–6252* ⊕ *www.sterngrove.org.*

OPERA

Fodor'sChoice
★ **San Francisco Opera.** Founded in 1923, this world-renowned company has resided at the Civic Center's War Memorial Opera House since the building's completion in 1932. Over its split season—September through January and June through July—the opera presents about 70 performances of 10 to 12 operas. Translations are projected above the stage during almost all non-English operas. Long considered a major international company and the most important operatic organization in the United States outside New York, the opera frequently embarks on productions with European opera companies and unconventional projects, some with a popular cultural edge designed to attract younger audiences. Ticket prices can range from $25 to $195. The full-time box office (Monday 10–5, Tuesday through Friday 10–6) is at 199 Grove Street, at Van Ness Avenue. ✉ *War Memorial Opera House, 301 Van Ness Ave., at Grove St., Civic Center* ☎ *415/864–3330 tickets* ⊕ *www. sfopera.com.*

THEATER

★ **American Conservatory Theater.** Not long after its founding in the mid-1960s, the city's major nonprofit theater company became one of the nation's leading regional theaters. During its season, which runs from early fall to late spring, ACT presents approximately eight plays, from classics to contemporary works, often in rotating repertory. In December ACT stages a much-loved version of Charles Dickens's *A Christmas Carol.* ✉ *415 Geary St., Union Sq.* ☎ *415/749-2228* ⊕ *www.act-sf.org.*

ACT ticket office. The **ACT ticket office** is next door to the American Conservatory Theater. ✉ *405 Geary St., Union Sq.* ☎ *415/749–2228*

Fodor'sChoice
★ **Teatro ZinZanni.** Contortionists, chanteuses, jugglers, illusionists, and circus performers entertain the audiences who dine on a surprisingly good five-course dinner in a fabulous antique Belgian traveling-dance-hall tent (slated for a permanent relocation to Broadway and the Embarcadero in late 2012). Be ready to laugh, and arrive early for a front-and-center table. Reservations are essential; tickets are $125 to $150; call or check the website for prices. And dress fancy. ✉ *Broadway and the Embarcadero, Northern Waterfront* ☎ *415/438–2668* ⊕ *www. zinzanni.org.*

SPORTS AND THE OUTDOORS

BASEBALL

🕲 **San Francisco Giants.** The National League's New York Giants became the
Fodor's Choice San Francisco Giants when they moved to California in 1958, the same
★ year that the Brooklyn Dodgers moved to Los Angeles. Today the classic
design of the Giants' AT&T Park and the team's 2010 World Series title
have created a new legion of fans. Buy your tickets in advance—nearly
every game sells out. ⊠ *AT&T Park, 24 Willie Mays Plaza, between
2nd and 3rd Sts., SoMa* ☎ *415/972–2000, 800/734–4268* ⊕ *sanfran-
cisco.giants.mlb.com.*

Tickets.com. Tickets.com sells game tickets over the phone and charges
a per-ticket fee of $5–$24, plus a per-call processing fee of up to $3.50.
☎ *877/473–4849* ⊕ *www.tickets.com.*

Giants Dugout. The team sells tickets at the ballpark and numerous Dugout locations, among them Embarcadero Center and Union Square. A
surcharge is added except at the ballpark. ⊠ *AT&T Park, 24 Willie
Mays Plaza, at 3rd St., SoMa* ☎ *415/972–2000, 800/734–4268* ⊕ *san-
francisco.giants.mlb.com/sf/ballpark/dugout_stores.jsp* ⊠ *4 Embarcadero Center, Embarcadero* ☎ *415/951–8888.*

BICYCLING

San Francisco Bicycle Coalition. The San Francisco Bicycle Coalition has
extensive information about the policies and politics of riding and lists
local events for cyclists on its website. You can download (but not print)
a PDF version of the *San Francisco Bike Map and Walking Guide.*
☎ *415/431–2453* ⊕ *www.sfbike.org.*

WHERE TO RENT

Bike and Roll. You can rent bikes at this operator's locations for $8 per
hour or $32 per day; discounted weekly rates are available, and com-
plimentary maps are provided. ⊠ *899 Columbus Ave., at Lombard
St., North Beach* ☎ *415/229–2000* ⊕ *www.bicyclerental.com* ⊠ *353
Jefferson St., between Jones and Leavenworth Sts., Fisherman's Wharf*
⊠ *2800 Leavenworth St., at Beach St., Fisherman's Wharf.*

Blazing Saddles. This outfitter rents bikes for $8 to $9 an hour, depending
on the type of bike, or $32 to $88 a day, and shares tips on sights to
see along the paths. ⊠ *2715 Hyde St., at Beach St., Fisherman's Wharf*
☎ *415/202–8888* ⊕ *www.blazingsaddles.com* ⊠ *433 Mason St., at Post
St., Union Sq.* ⊠ *Pier 41, Fisherman's Wharf* ⊠ *465 Jefferson St., at
Hyde St., Fisherman's Wharf* ⊠ *2555 Powell St., at the Embarcadero,
Fisherman's Wharf* ⊠ *1095 Columbus, at Francisco St., North Beach*
⊠ *721 Beach St., at Hyde St., North Beach.*

The beat movement of the 1950s was born in San Francisco's most famous bookstore, City Lights.

SHOPPING

UNION SQUARE

Fodor'sChoice **Diptyque.** The original Diptyque boutique in Paris has long attracted a
★ following of celebrities. You can find the full line of scented candles and
fragrances in this chic shop that would be at home on the Boulevard
St-Germain. Trademark black-and-white labels adorn the popular L'eau
toilet water, scented with geranium and sandalwood. Candles come in
both traditional and esoteric scents, including lavender, basil, leather,
and fig tree. Also available is a collection of French Mariage Frères
teas. ⊠ *171 Maiden La., between Grant Ave. and Stockton St., Union
Sq.* ☎ *415/402–0600.*

★ **Gump's.** It's a San Francisco institution, dating to the 19th century,
and it's a strikingly luxurious one. The airy store exudes a museum-
like vibe, with its large decorative vases, sumptuous housewares, and
a gobsmacking Tahitian pearl display. Locals line up to register for
weddings here. But it's also a great place to pick up gifts, such as the
Golden Gate Bridge note cards or the silver-plated butter spreaders in a
signature Gump's box. ⊠ *135 Post St., between Grant Ave. and Kearny
St., Union Sq.* ☎ *415/982–1616.*

Fodor'sChoice **Hang Art.** A spirit of fun imbues this inviting second-floor space that
★ showcases emerging artists. Prices range from a few hundred dollars to
several thousand, making it an ideal place for novice art collectors to
get their feet wet. A rental program lets you take a piece home before

buying it. ⊠ *567 Sutter St., between Mason and Powell Sts., Union Sq.* ☎ *415/434–4264.*

Fodor's Choice ★ **Lang Antiques and Estate Jewelry.** Dozens of diamond bracelets in the window attract shoppers to one of the city's best vintage jewelry shops, where rings, brooches, and other glittering items represent various eras and styles, from Victorian and Edwardian to art nouveau and Arts and Crafts. The shop has been selling fine jewelry, including engagement rings and a small number of vintage watches, since 1969. ⊠ *323 Sutter St., at Grant Ave., Union Sq.* ☎ *415/982–2213.*

Fodor's Choice ★ **Margaret O'Leary.** If you can only buy one piece of clothing in San Francisco, make it a hand-loomed, locally made cashmere sweater by this Irish-born local legend. The perfect antidote to the city's wind and fog, the sweaters are so beloved by San Franciscans that some people literally never wear anything else. Pick up an airplane wrap for your trip home and a media cozy to keep your iPod toasty, too. Another store is located in Pacific Heights on Fillmore Street. ⊠ *1 Claude La., at Sutter St., Union Sq.* ☎ *415/391–1010.*

★ **Nordstrom.** Somehow Nordstrom manages to be all things to all people, and this location, with spiral escalators circling a four-story atrium, is no exception. Whether you're an elegant lady of a certain age shopping for a new mink coat or a teen on the hunt for a Roxy hoodie, the salespeople are known for being happy to help. Nordstrom carries the best selections in town of new designers like Tory Burch, but its own brands have loyal followings, too. The café upstairs is a superb choice for a ladies-who-lunch shopping break. ⊠ *San Francisco Shopping Centre, 865 Market St., at 5th St., Union Sq.* ☎ *415/243–8500.*

CHINATOWN

Chinatown Kite Shop. Kites at this family-owned business range from basic diamond shapes to box- and animal-shape configurations. Colorful dragon kites make great Chinatown souvenirs. ⊠ *717 Grant Ave., between Clay and Sacramento Sts., Chinatown* ☎ *415/989–5182.*

SOMA

★ **K&L Wine Merchants.** More than any other wine store, this one has an ardent cult following around town. The friendly staffers promise not to sell what they don't taste themselves, and weekly events (Thursday from 5 pm and 6:30 pm and Saturday from noon to 3 pm) open the tastings to customers. The best-seller list for varietals and regions for both the under- and over-$30 categories appeals to the wine lover in everyone. ⊠ *638 4th St., between Brannan and Townsend Sts., SoMa* ☎ *415/896–1734.*

HAYES VALLEY

★ **Miette Confiserie.** There is truly nothing sweeter than a cellophane bag tied with blue-and-white twine and filled with malt balls or chocolate sardines from this European-style apothecary. The lovely pastel-color cake stands make even window-shopping a treat. ⊠ *449 Octavia Blvd., between Hayes and Fell Sts., Hayes Valley* ☎ *415/626–6221.*

NORTH BEACH

Fodor's Choice
★ **City Lights Bookstore.** The city's most famous bookstore is where the Beat movement of the 1950s was born. Neal Cassady and Jack Kerouac hung out in the basement, and now regulars and tourists while hours away in this well-worn space. The upstairs room highlights impressive poetry and Beat literature collections. Poet Lawrence Ferlinghetti, the owner, remains active in the workings of this three-story shop. City Lights Publishers, which issued the poet Allen Ginsberg's *Howl* in 1956, publishes a dozen new titles each year. ⊠ *261 Columbus Ave., at Broadway, North Beach* ☎ *415/362–8193.*

Fodor's Choice
★ **Molinari Delicatessen.** Billing itself as the oldest delicatessen west of the Rockies, the store has been making its own salami, sausages, and cold cuts since 1896. Other homemade specialties include meat and cheese ravioli, tomato sauces, and fresh pastas. ■ **TIP→** Do like the locals: grab a made-to-order sandwich for lunch and eat it at one of the sidewalk tables. ⊠ *373 Columbus Ave., at Vallejo St., North Beach* ☎ *415/421–2337.*

EMBARCADERO

Fodor's Choice
★ **Ferry Plaza Farmers' Market.** The most upscale and expensive of the city's farmers' markets, in front of the restored Ferry Building, places baked goods and fancy pots of jam alongside organic basil and heirloom tomatoes. The Saturday market is the grandest, with about 100 vendors packed along three sides of the building. The Tuesday and Thursday markets are smaller. At the Sunday garden market, vegetable and ornamental plants crop up next to a small selection of food items. (The Thursday and Sunday markets don't operate in winter, generally December or January through March.) ■ **TIP→** On Saturday, don't miss the coffee at Blue Bottle—and yes, the line is worth it. ⊠ *Ferry Plaza, The Embarcadero at Market St., Embarcadero* ☎ *415/291–3276* ☉ *Tues. and Sun. 10–2, Thurs. 4–8, Sat. 8–2.*

THE HAIGHT

Fodor's Choice
★ **Amoeba Music.** With more than 2.5 million new and used CDs, DVDs, and records, this warehouselike store (and the original Berkeley location) carries titles you can't find on Amazon at bargain prices. No niche is ignored—from electronica and hip-hop to jazz and classical— and the stock changes daily. Weekly in-store performances attract large crowds. ⊠ *1855 Haight St., between Stanyan and Shrader Sts., Haight* ☎ *415/831–1200.*

THE MISSION

Fodor's Choice
★ **Paxton Gate.** Elevating gardening to an art, this serene shop offers beautiful earthenware pots, amaryllis and narcissus bulbs, decorative garden items, and coffee-table books such as *An Inordinate Fondness for*

Beetles. The collection of taxidermy and preserved bugs provides more unusual gift ideas. ✉ *824 Valencia St., between 19th and 20th Sts., Mission* ☎ *415/824–1872.*

PACIFIC HEIGHTS

★ **BeneFit.** You can find the locally based BeneFit line of cosmetics and skincare products at Macy's and Sephora, but it's much more fun to come to one of the eponymous boutiques. No-pressure salespeople dab you with whimsical makeup such as Ooh La Lift concealer and Tinted Love, a stain for lips and cheeks. ✉ *2117 Fillmore St., between California and Sacramento Sts., Pacific Heights* ☎ *415/567–0242.*

JAPANTOWN

★ **Kinokuniya Bookstore.** The selection of English-language books about Japanese culture—everything from medieval history to origami instructions—is one of the finest in the country. Kinokuniya is the city's biggest seller of Japanese-language books. Dozens of glossy Asian fashion magazines attract the young and trendy, and books and DVDs related to the Japanese anime director Hayao Miyazaki are the latest trend. ✉ *Kinokuniya Bldg., 1581 Webster St., at Geary Blvd., Japantown* ☎ *415/567–7625.*

The Bay Area

WITH MARIN COUNTY, BERKELEY, OAKLAND, AND THE COASTAL PENINSULA

WORD OF MOUTH

"We . . . caught the ferry over to Sausalito. A stroll along the sheltered waterfront and a close-quarters view of Alcatraz on the way back rounded out a perfect stay in the City by the Bay."

—kiwi_rob

WELCOME TO THE BAY AREA

TOP REASONS TO GO

★ **Walk among giants:** Walking into Muir Woods, a mere 12 miles north of the Golden Gate Bridge, is like entering a cathedral built by God.

★ **Sip some coffee:** Lytton Square in downtown Mill Valley is a tranquil place to soak up some sun, caffeine, and a real local "hanging out" kind of vibe.

★ **Bite into the "Gourmet Ghetto":** Eat your way through this area of Berkeley, starting with a slice of pizza from the Cheese Board.

★ **Sit on a dock by the bay:** Admire the beauty of the Bay Area from the rocky, picturesque shores of Sausalito.

★ **Find solitude at Point Reyes National Seashore:** Head here to hike beautifully rugged—and deserted—beaches.

1 Marin County. Marin is considered the prettiest of the Bay Area counties, primarily because of its wealth of open space. Anchored by water on three sides, the county is mostly parkland, including long stretches of undeveloped coastline. The picturesque small towns here—Sausalito, Tiburon, Mill Valley, and Bolinas among them—may sometimes look rustic, but they're mostly in a dizzyingly high tax bracket. There's a reason why people call BMWs "basic Marin wheels."

2 Oakland. Life in this harbor-front city is strongly defined by a turbulent history. But the up-and-coming downtown scene and rejuvenated waterfront are signals of good things ahead.

3 **Berkeley.** This college town has long been known for its liberal ethos, stimulating university community (and perhaps even more stimulating coffee shops), and activist streak. But these days the booming restaurant and arts scenes are luring even those who wouldn't be caught dead in Birkenstocks.

4 **The Coastal Peninsula.** The coastal towns between Santa Cruz and San Francisco have long been agricultural outposts, supplying food for the missions and towns. Today, artichokes and grapes still grow in the fields, but the big attraction here is the beaches.

GETTING ORIENTED

Cross the Golden Gate Bridge and head north to reach Marin County's rolling hills and green expanses, where residents enjoy an haute-suburban lifestyle. Farther afield, the wild landscapes of the Marin Headlands, Muir Woods, Mt. Tamalpais, Stinson Beach, and Point Reyes National Seashore await.
East of the city, across the San Francisco Bay, are Berkeley and Oakland, which most Bay Area residents refer to as the East Bay. These two towns have distinct personalities, but life here feels more relaxed than in the city—though every bit as vibrant.

5

Updated by
Fiona G.
Parrott

It's rare for a metropolis to compete with its suburbs for visitors, but the view from any of San Francisco's hilltops shows that the Bay Area's temptations extend far beyond the city limits. To the north is Marin County, the beauty queen, with small but chic villages like Tiburon and Mill Valley, plus dramatic coastal scenery. East of town are two energetic urban centers, Berkeley and Oakland. Formerly radical Berkeley is getting more glam, while Oakland is shaking off its image as San Francisco's ugly stepsister and developing its own brand of hipness.

Up in Marin, the birthplace of mountain biking, trail-veined Mt. Tamalpais and the woods below draw hikers and cyclists. Beaches lure families and thrill seekers, while little towns offer respite to harried urbanites. In the mid-1960s and '70s alternative lifestyle seekers established Marin's reputation as ground zero for gurus, granola, and redwood hot tubs. Despite the influx of stock-market millionaires and chic boutiques, the counterculture identity still sticks. Immediately after crossing the Golden Gate Bridge on U.S. 101 northbound, you'll pass through a tunnel whose archway is painted with a rainbow that welcomes you to magical Marin, "Land of Oz."

Meanwhile, the town often referred to as the People's Republic of Berkeley retains its liberal image, though it's drastically tamer than it was in the late 1960s. It's now as famous for chef and food activist Alice Waters (and her pricey restaurant Chez Panisse) as it is for its role as the birthplace of the Free Speech movement. Oakland is polishing some of its rough edges, too, with a successful port and a revitalized downtown, an alternative arts scene, and hipster cafés and boutiques.

PLANNING

WHEN TO GO

Berkeley is a university town, and the rhythm of the school year might affect your visit. It's easier to navigate the streets and find parking near the university between semesters, but there's also less buzz around town. Surprisingly, summer is chock-full of students attending the many summer sessions on campus. Moving-in weeks, before the fall semester starts, bring a massive influx of students *and* parents and other family members—definitely not the best time to take a campus tour.

BART trains can be packed during the morning and evening rush hours, but things are less congested at other times. BART can get you from downtown San Francisco to a coffee shop in Rockridge in about 25 minutes. (It's closer to 30 minutes for farther points in Berkeley.)

It'll take about the same amount of time by car to reach Tiburon if traffic is clear on the Golden Gate Bridge (also depending, of course, on what part of the city you're departing from).

GETTING HERE AND AROUND

BART TRAVEL

Using public transportation to reach Berkeley or Oakland is ideal. The under- and above-ground BART (Bay Area Rapid Transit) trains make stops in both towns. Trips to either take 30 to 45 minutes one way from the center of San Francisco.

Contacts BART ☎ *510/465–2278* ⊕ *www.bart.gov.*

BOAT AND FERRY TRAVEL

For sheer romance, nothing beats the ferry; there's service from San Francisco to Sausalito and Tiburon in Marin County, and to Alameda and Oakland in the East Bay.

The Golden Gate Ferry crosses the bay to Sausalito from San Francisco's Ferry Building (⊠ *Market St. and the Embarcadero*). Blue & Gold Fleet ferries depart daily for Sausalito and Tiburon from Pier 41 at Fisherman's Wharf; weekday commuter ferries leave from the Ferry Building for Tiburon. The trip to Sausalito takes 30 minutes; to Tiburon, it takes 20 minutes.

The Angel Island–Tiburon Ferry sails to the island daily April through September and weekends the rest of the year.

The Alameda/Oakland Ferry runs several times daily between San Francisco's Ferry Building or Pier 39, Alameda, and the Clay Street dock near Oakland's Jack London Square; one-way tickets are $6.25. The trip lasts 30 to 45 minutes, depending on your departure point, and leads to Oakland's waterfront shopping and restaurant district. Purchase tickets on board.

Boat and Ferry Lines Alameda/Oakland Ferry ☎ *510/522–3300* ⊕ *www. eastbayferry.com.* **Angel Island–Tiburon Ferry** ☎ *415/435–2131* ⊕ *www. angelislandferry.com.* **Blue & Gold Fleet** ☎ *415/705–8200* ⊕ *www. blueandgoldfleet.com.* **Golden Gate Ferry** ☎ *415/923–2000* ⊕ *www. goldengateferry.org.*

5

BUS TRAVEL

Golden Gate Transit buses travel to Sausalito, Tiburon, and Mill Valley from 1st and Mission streets and from other points in San Francisco. For Mt. Tamalpais State Park and West Marin (e.g., Stinson Beach, Bolinas, and Point Reyes Station), take Bus 10, 70, or 80 to Marin City; in Marin City transfer to the West Marin Stagecoach (schedules vary). San Francisco MuniBus 76 runs hourly from 4th and Townsend streets to the Marin Headlands Visitor Center on Sunday and major holidays only. The trip takes roughly 45 minutes.

Though much less convenient than BART, AC Transit buses run between San Francisco's Transbay Temporary Terminal (on the block bordered by Main, Folsom, Beale and Howard streets) and the East Bay. AC Transit's F and FS lines stop near the university and 4th Street shopping in Berkeley. Lines C and P travel to Piedmont in Oakland. The O bus stops at the edge of Chinatown near downtown Oakland.

Bus Lines AC Transit ☏ *511* ⊕ *www.actransit.org.* **Golden Gate Transit** ☏ *415/455–2000* ⊕ *www.goldengate.org.* **San Francisco Muni** ☏ *415/701–2311* ⊕ *www.sfmuni.com.* **West Marin Stagecoach** ☏ *415/526–3239* ⊕ *www. marintransit.org/stage.html.*

CAR TRAVEL

Head north on U.S.101 and cross the Golden Gate Bridge to reach all points in Marin by car, which is essential to visit the outer reaches unless you want to spend all day on the bus. From San Francisco, the towns of Sausalito and Tiburon and the Marin Headlands and Point Reyes National Seashore are accessed off U.S. 101. The coastal route, Highway 1, also known as Shoreline Highway, can be accessed off U.S. 101 as well. Follow this road to Mill Valley, Muir Woods, Mt. Tamalpais State Park, Stinson Beach, and Bolinas. From Bolinas, you can continue north on Highway 1 to Point Reyes. Depending on traffic, it takes from 20 to 45 minutes to get to Sausalito, Tiburon, and the Marin Headlands; driving directly to Point Reyes from San Francisco takes about 90 minutes in moderate traffic if you drive north on U.S. 101 and west on Sir Francis Drake Boulevard. Trips to Muir Woods take from 35 minutes to an hour from San Francisco. Add another 30 minutes for the drive to Stinson Beach (the curving roads make the going slower), 10 more if you continue on to Bolinas. The drive from Bolinas to Point Reyes takes an additional half hour.

To reach the East Bay from San Francisco, take Interstate 80 East across the Bay Bridge. For most of Berkeley, take the University Avenue exit through downtown Berkeley to the campus or take the Ashby Avenue exit and turn left on Telegraph Avenue; there's a parking garage on Channing Way near the campus. For Oakland, take Interstate 580 off the Bay Bridge to the Grand Avenue exit for Lake Merritt. To reach downtown and the waterfront, take Interstate 980 from Interstate 580 and exit at 12th Street. Both trips take about 30 minutes unless it's rush hour or a weekend afternoon, when you should count on an hour.

SIGHTSEEING GUIDES

Blue & Gold Fleet has a 3½-hour narrated tour of the San Francisco Bay, for $46, with frequent daily departures from Pier 39 in San Francisco. Super Sightseeing offers a 4-hour bus tour of Muir Woods. The tour, which stops in Sausalito en route, leaves at 9 am and 2 pm daily from North Point and Taylor Street at Fisherman's Wharf and costs $52 ($50 senior citizens, $27 ages 5–11); 24-hour advance reservations are recommended. Great Pacific Tour Co. runs 4-hour morning and afternoon tours of Muir Woods and Sausalito for $55 ($53 senior citizens, $43 ages 5–11), with hotel pickup, in 14-passenger vans with excellent interpretation.

By Bus and Van Blue & Gold Fleet ☎ 415/705–8200 ⊕ www.blueandgoldfleet. com. **Great Pacific Tour Co.** ☎ 415/626–4499 ⊕ www.greatpacifictour.com. **Super Sightseeing** ☎ 415/353–5310 ⊕ www.supersightseeing.com.

RESTAURANTS

The Bay Area is home to some of the most popular and innovative restaurants in the country, including Chez Panisse Café & Restaurant, in Berkeley, and the Buckeye, in Mill Valley—for which reservations must be made well in advance. Expect an emphasis on locally grown produce, hormone-free meats, and California wine. Keep in mind that many Marin cafés don't serve dinner, and when dinner it is offered, service ends on the early side. (No 10 pm reservations in this neck of the woods.)

Prices in the restaurant reviews are the average cost of a main course at dinner or, if dinner is not served, at lunch (excluding sales tax).

HOTELS

Hotels in Berkeley or Oakland tend to be standard issue, but many Marin hotels package themselves as cozy retreats. Summer is often booked well in advance, despite weather that is sometimes downright chilly. Check for special packages during this season.

Prices in the hotel reviews are the lowest cost of a standard double room in high season. Prices do not include taxes (as high as 14%, depending on the region).

Hotel reviews have been condensed for this book. For expanded reviews, facilities, and current deals, visit Fodors.com.

VISITOR INFORMATION

Contact Marin Convention & Visitors Bureau ✉ 1 Mitchell Blvd., Suite B, San Rafael ☎ 415/925–2060 ⊕ www.visitmarin.org.

MARIN COUNTY

Marin is quite simply a knockout—some go so far as to call it spectacular and wild. This isn't an extravagant claim, since more than 40% of the county (180,000 acres), including the majority of the coastline, is parkland. The territory ranges from chaparral, grassland, and coastal scrub to broadleaf and evergreen forest, redwood, salt marsh, and rocky shoreline.

Regardless of its natural beauty, what gave the county its reputation was Cyra McFadden's 1977 book *The Serial,* a literary soap opera that depicted the county as a bastion of hot-tubbing and "open" marriages. Indeed old-time bohemian, but also increasingly jet-set, Marinites still spend a lot of time outdoors, and surfing, cycling, and hiking are common after-work and weekend activities. Adrenaline junkies mountain bike down Mt. Tamalpais, and those who want solitude take a walk on one of Point Reyes's many empty beaches. The hot tub remains a popular destination, but things have changed since the boho days. Artists and musicians who arrived in the 1960s have set the tone for mellow country towns, but Marin is now undeniably chic, with BMWs supplanting VW buses as the cars of choice.

Most cosmopolitan is Sausalito, the town just over the Golden Gate Bridge from San Francisco. Across the inlet from Sausalito, Tiburon and Belvedere are lined with grand homes that regularly appear on fund-raising circuits, and to the north, landlocked Mill Valley is a hub of wining and dining and tony boutiques. The next town, Corte Madera, hosts regular readings by top-notch authors and Larkspur, San Anselmo, and Fairfax beyond have walkable downtown areas, each a bit folksier than the next but all with good restaurants and shops and a distinct sense of place.

In general, the farther you get from the Golden Gate Bridge the more country things become, and West Marin is about as far as you can get from the big city, both physically and ideologically. Separated from the inland county by the slopes and ridges of giant Mt. Tamalpais, this territory beckons to mavericks, artists, ocean lovers, and other free spirits. Stinson Beach has tempered its isolationist attitude to accommodate out-of-towners, as have Inverness and Point Reyes Station. Bolinas, on the other hand, would prefer you not know its location.

SAUSALITO

2 miles north of Golden Gate Bridge.

Bougainvillea-covered hillsides and an expansive yacht harbor give Sausalito the feel of an Adriatic resort. The town sits on the northwestern edge of San Francisco Bay, where it's sheltered from the ocean by the Marin Headlands; the mostly mild weather here is perfect for strolling and outdoor dining. Nevertheless, morning fog and afternoon winds can roll over the hills without warning, funneling through the central part of Sausalito once known as Hurricane Gulch.

South on Bridgeway (toward San Francisco), which snakes between the bay and the hills, a waterside esplanade is lined with restaurants on piers that lure diners with good seafood and even better views. Stairs along the west side of Bridgeway climb the hill to wooded neighborhoods filled with both rustic and opulent homes. As you amble along Bridgeway past shops and galleries, you'll notice the absence of basic services. If you need an aspirin or some groceries (or if you want to see the locals), you'll have to head to Caledonia Street, which runs parallel to Bridgeway, north of the ferry terminus and inland a couple of blocks. The streets closest to the ferry landing flaunt their fair share of

The crowded piers and rolling hillside of the Sausalito waterfront

shops selling T-shirts and kitschy souvenirs. Venture into some of the side streets or narrow alleyways to catch a bit more of the town's taste for eccentric jewelry and handmade crafts.

■TIP→ The ferry is the best way to get to Sausalito from San Francisco; you get more romance (and less traffic) and disembark in the heart of downtown.

Sausalito had a raffish reputation before it went upscale. Discovered in 1775 by Spanish explorers and named Sausalito (Little Willow) for the trees growing around its springs, the town served as a port for whaling ships during the 19th century. By the mid-1800s wealthy San Franciscans were making Sausalito their getaway across the bay. They built lavish Victorian summer homes in the hills, many of which still stand. In 1875 the railroad from the north connected with ferryboats to San Francisco, bringing the merchant and working classes with it. This influx of hardworking, fun-loving folk polarized the town into "wharf rats" and "hill snobs," and the waterfront area grew thick with saloons, gambling dens, and bordellos. Bootleggers flourished during Prohibition, and shipyard workers swelled the town's population in the 1940s.

Sausalito developed its bohemian flair in the 1950s and '60s, when creative types, led by a charismatic Greek portraitist named Varda, established an artists' colony and a houseboat community here. Today more than 450 houseboats are docked in Sausalito, which has since also become a major yachting center. Some of the houseboats are ragged, others deluxe, but all are quirky (one, a miniature replica of a Persian castle, even has an elevator inside). For a close-up view of the community, head north on Bridgeway—Sausalito's main thoroughfare—from downtown, turn right on Gate Six Road, and park where it dead-ends

Marin
County

0   5 mi

0   5 km

at the public shore. Keep a respectful distance; these are homes, after all, and the residents become a bit prickly from too much ogling.

ESSENTIALS

Visitor Information Sausalito Chamber of Commerce ✉ *780 Bridgeway* ☎ *415/332–0505, 415/331–7262* ⊕ *www.sausalito.org.*

GETTING HERE AND AROUND

From San Francisco by car or bike, follow U.S. 101 north across the Golden Gate Bridge and take the first exit, Alexander Avenue, just past Vista Point; continue down the winding hill to the water to where the road becomes Bridgeway. Buses 10 and 22 will drop you off in downtown Sausalito, and the ferries dock downtown as well. The center of town is flat, with plenty of sidewalks and bay views. It's a pleasure and a must to explore on foot.

EXPLORING

☉ **Bay Area Discovery Museum.** Sitting at the base of the Golden Gate Bridge, this indoor-outdoor museum offers entertaining and enlightening hands-on exhibits for children under eight. Kids can fish from a boat at the indoor wharf, imagine themselves as marine biologists in the Wave Workshop, and play outdoors at Lookout Cove (made up of scaled-down sea caves, tidal pools, and even a re-created shipwreck). At Tot Zone, toddlers and preschoolers dress up in animal costumes and crawl through miniature tunnels. From San Francisco, take U.S. 101's Alexander Avenue exit and follow signs to East Fort Baker. ⊠ *557 McReynolds Rd., at East Rd. off Alexander Ave.* ☎ *415/339–3900* ⊕ *www.baykidsmuseum.org* ✉ *$11; children under 6 months free* ⊙ *Tues.–Fri. 9–4, weekends 10–5.*

☾ **Bay Model.** An anonymous-looking World War II shipyard building holds a great treasure: the sprawling (more than 1½ acres) Bay Model of the entire San Francisco Bay and the San Joaquin–Sacramento River delta, complete with flowing water. The U.S. Army Corps of Engineers uses the model to reproduce the rise and fall of tides, the flow of currents, and the other physical forces at work on the bay. Science becomes tangible as interactive displays draw children in and adults also learn more about some real California flow. ⊠ *2100 Bridgeway, at Marinship Way* ☎ *415/332–3870 recorded information, 415/332–3871 operator assistance* ⊕ *www.spn.usace.army.mil/bmvc* ✉ *Free* ⊙ *Memorial Day–Labor Day, Tues.–Fri. 9–4, weekends 10–5; Labor Day–Memorial Day, Tues.–Sat. 9–4.*

Drinking Fountain. On the waterfront between the Hotel Sausalito and the Sausalito Yacht Club is an unusual historic landmark—a drinking fountain. It's inscribed with "Have a drink on Sally" in remembrance of Sally Stanford, the former San Francisco madam who later became the town's mayor in the 1970s. Sassy Sally, as they called her, would have appreciated the fountain's eccentric custom attachment: a knee-level basin that reads "Have a drink on Leland," in memory of her beloved dog.

QUICK BITES

Hamburgers. Judging by the crowds gathered outside Hamburgers, you'd think someone was juggling flaming torches out front. They're really gaping at the juicy hand-formed beef patties sizzling on a rotating grill. Brave the line (it moves fast), get your food to go, and head for the esplanade to enjoy the sweeping views. Hours are 11 am–5 pm. ⊠ *737 Bridgeway, at Humboldt Ave.* ☎ *415/332–9471.*

Plaza Viña del Mar. The landmark Plaza Viña del Mar, named for Sausalito's sister city in Chile, marks the center of town. Flanked by two 14-foot-tall elephant statues (created in 1915 for the Panama-Pacific International Exposition), the fountain is a great setting for snapshots and people-watching. ⊠ *Bridgeway and Park St.*

Sausalito Visitors Center and Historical Exhibit. Get your bearings and find out what's happening in town at the Sausalito Visitors Center and Historical Exhibit, operated by the town's historical society. The center is closed Monday. ⊠ *780 Bridgeway, at Bay St.* ☎ *415/332–0505.*

WHERE TO EAT

$$
ITALIAN
✕ **Bar Bocce.** Few Bay Area eateries can boast of having a beach adjoining the outdoor dining area. And when you play a game of bocce here, it's framed by Richardson Bay. Modern Californian cuisine is served, including pizzas, salads, and signature dishes such as the meatball sliders and the fire-roasted game hen. Reservations aren't taken, so be prepared to wait for a table—time you can spend sipping local beer

and wine by the outdoor fire pit. [$] *Average main: $17* ✉ *1250 Bridgeway, between Pine and Turney Sts.* ☎ *415/331–0555* 🌐 *barbocce.com* ✍ *Reservations not accepted.*

$$ SEAFOOD Fodor's Choice ★ ✌ 🍴 **Fish.** When locals want fresh seafood, they head to this gleaming dockside fish house a mile north of downtown. Order at the counter and then grab a seat by the floor-to-ceiling windows or at a picnic table on the pier, overlooking the yachts and fishing boats. Most of the sustainably caught fish is hauled in from the owner's boats, docked right outside. Try the ceviche, crab Louis, cioppino, barbecue oysters, or anything fresh that's being grilled over the oak-wood fire. Outside, kids can doodle with sidewalk chalk on the pier. [$] *Average main: $22* ✉ *350 Harbor Dr., off Bridgeway* ☎ *415/331–3474* 🌐 *www.331fish.com* ✍ *Reservations not accepted* 💳 *No credit cards.*

$$$ BISTRO ★ 🍴 **Le Garage.** Brittany-born Olivier Souvestre serves traditional French bistro fare in a relaxed, sidewalk café–style bayside setting. The menu is small, but the dishes are substantial in flavor and presentation. Standouts include frisée salad with poached egg, bacon, croutons, and pancetta vinaigrette; steak frites with a shallot confit and crispy fries; and a chef's selection of cheese or charcuterie with soup and mixed greens. The restaurant only seats 35 inside and 15 outside, so to avoid a long wait for lunch, arrive before 11:30 or after 1:30. [$] *Average main: $23* ✉ *85 Liberty Ship Way, off Marinship Way* ☎ *415/332–5625* 🌐 *www.legaragebistrosausalito.com* ✍ *Reservations essential* ⏲ *No dinner Sun.*

$ SCANDINAVIAN 🍴 **Lighthouse Cafe.** A cozy spot with a long coffee bar and dose of Scandinavian flair, this local establishment has been a favorite brunch destination for nearly two decades. The hearty Norwegian salmon omelet with spinach and cream cheese or fruit pancakes, as well as the grilled burgers, sandwiches, and Danish specials like meatballs with potato salad always hit the spot, especially on chilly days. Expect a wait on weekends and at lunch hour. [$] *Average main: $12* ✉ *1311 Bridgeway, near Turney St.* ☎ *415/331–3034* 🌐 *www.lighthouse-restaurants.com* ✍ *Reservations not accepted* ⏲ *No dinner.*

$$$ MODERN AMERICAN 🍴 **Plate Shop.** Sausalito's newest shrine to farm-to-table organic, sustainable, and seriously local cuisine sits tucked neatly away from traffic. The seasonal menu is ever-changing, but the bar favorites include the grilled Monterey squid and the smoked trout; for dinner entrées, if they're offered, consider the fried chicken with fingerling potatoes or the rabbit braised in mustard sauce. The bar scene's fun here, too. [$] *Average main: $23* ✉ *39 Caledonia St., between Pine and Johnson Sts.* ☎ *415/887–9047.*

$$ ITALIAN ★ 🍴 **Poggio.** One of the few restaurants in Sausalito to attract both food-savvy locals and tourists, Poggio serves modern Tuscan cuisine in a handsome, open-wall space that spills onto the street. Expect dishes such as grilled lamb chops with roasted eggplant, braised artichokes with polenta, feather-light gnocchi, and pizzas from the open kitchen's wood-fired oven. [$] *Average main: $21* ✉ *777 Bridgeway, at Bay St.* ☎ *415/332–7771* ✍ *Reservations essential.*

$$ SUSHI ★ 🍴 **Sushi Ran.** Sushi aficionados swear that this is the Bay Area's best option for raw fish, but don't overlook the excellent Pacific Rim fusions, a melding of Japanese ingredients and French cooking techniques,

served up in unusual presentations. Because Sushi Ran is so highly ranked among area foodies, book two to seven days in advance for dinner. Otherwise, expect a long wait, which you can soften by sipping one of the 45 by-the-glass sakes from the outstanding wine-and-sake bar. ■ **TIP→ If you arrive without a reservation and can't get a table, you can sometimes dine in the noisy bar.** [$] *Average main: $18* ✉ *107 Caledonia St., at Pine St.* ☎ *415/332–3620* ✍ *Reservations essential* ⏲ *No lunch weekends.*

$ WINE BAR 🍴 **Wellingtons Wine Bar.** British memorabilia decorates the walls of this establishment that celebrates English and Californian liquid culture. The space is bright, warm, and welcoming with hardwood floors, leather sofas, and actual Wellington boots mounted beside the big glass windows. When the weather is nice, you can sit on the boat dock and drink your pint of lager or sip a glass of wine while scooping up hummus with garlic pita chips. The menu is as big as a book—no one leaves this place hungry (or thirsty). [$] *Average main: $10* ✉ *1306 Bridgeway, at Turney St.* ☎ *415/331–9463* 🌐 *www.wellingtonswinebar.com* ✍ *Reservations not accepted.*

5

WHERE TO STAY

For expanded reviews, facilities, and current deals, visit Fodors.com.

$$$$ HOTEL 🏨 **Cavallo Point.** Set in Golden Gate National Park, this luxury hotel and resort's location is truly one of a kind, featuring turn-of-the-20th-century buildings converted into well-appointed yet eco-friendly rooms. **Pros:** stunning views and numerous activities: a cooking school, yoga classes, and nature walks; spa with a tea bar; art gallery. **Cons:** landscaping feels incomplete; isolated from urban amenities. **TripAdvisor:** "hidden gem in the Bay area," "fantastic stay," "wonderful place to bring a toddler." [$] *Rooms from: $310* ✉ *601 Murray Circle, Fort Baker* ☎ *415/339–4700* 🌐 *www.cavallopoint.com* 🛏 *68 historic and 74 contemporary guest rooms.*

$$ B&B/INN 🏨 **Hotel Sausalito.** Handmade furniture and tasteful original art and reproductions give this well-run inn the feel of a small European hotel. **Pros:** great staff; excellent central location; feels like home away from home. **Cons:** no room service; some rooms feel cramped. **TripAdvisor:** "best of Sausalito," "great location," "delightful." [$] *Rooms from: $170* ✉ *16 El Portal* ☎ *415/332–0700, 888/442–0700* 🌐 *www.hotelsausalito.com* 🛏 *14 rooms, 2 suites.*

$$$$ B&B/INN 🏨 **The Inn Above Tide.** This is the only hotel in the Bay Area with balconies literally hanging over the water, and each of its rooms has a perfect-10 view that takes in wild Angel Island as well as the city lights across the bay. **Pros:** great complimentary breakfast; minutes from restaurants/attractions; free in-room binoculars let you indulge in the incredible views. **Cons:** costly parking; some rooms are on the small side. **TripAdvisor:** "what a view," "sweet and stunning," "comfortable luxury." [$] *Rooms from: $340* ✉ *30 El Portal* ☎ *415/332–9535, 800/893–8433* 🌐 *www.innabovetide.com* 🛏 *29 rooms, 3 suites.*

SPORTS AND THE OUTDOORS

Sea Trek Ocean Kayaking Center. The center offers guided half-day sea-kayaking trips underneath the Golden Gate Bridge and full- and half-day trips to Angel Island, both for beginners. Starlight and full-moon paddles are particularly popular. Trips for experienced kayakers, classes, and rentals are also available. Prices start at $20 per hour for rentals; $65 for a three-hour guided trip. ✉ *Schoonmaker Point Marina, off Libertyship Way* ☎ *415/488–1000* ⊕ *www.seatrekkayak.com.*

SF Bay Adventures. This outfit's expert skippers conduct sunset and full-moon sails around the bay, as well as fascinating eco and great-white-shark tours. If you're interested, they can arrange for you to spend the night in a lighthouse or even barbecue on Angel Island. ✉ *60 Liberty Ship Way, Suite 4* ☎ *415/331–0444* ⊕ *www.sfbayadventures.com.*

THE ARTS

Sausalito Art Festival. The annual festival, held over Labor Day weekend, attracts more than 50,000 people to the northern waterfront area; Blue & Gold Fleet ferries from San Francisco dock at the pier adjacent to the festival. Tickets are $25. ☎ *415/332–3555, 415/331–3757* ⊕ *www. sausalitoartfestival.org.*

SHOPPING

☺ **Sausalito Ferry Co.** Eccentric and fun, this shop is a great place to buy trendy T-shirts, wallets, and clocks—not to mention solar-powered bobbleheads, outrageous cocktail napkins, even one-of-a-kind key chains. ✉ *688 Bridgeway, near Princess St.* ☎ *415/332–9590* ⊕ *www. sausalitoferry.com.*

Something/Anything Gallery. Where Bridgeway ends and curves toward the dock, this gallery with a friendly staff carries jewelry and gifts, from unique watches to humorous pendants. It's a good spot to pick up your Sausalito memento. ✉ *20 Princess St., at Broadway* ☎ *415/339–8831.*

TIBURON

2 miles north of Sausalito, 7 miles north of Golden Gate Bridge.

On a peninsula that was called Punta de Tiburon (Shark Point) by the Spanish explorers, this beautiful Marin County community retains the feel of a village—it's more low-key than Sausalito—despite the encroachment of commercial establishments from the downtown area. The harbor faces Angel Island across Raccoon Strait, and San Francisco is directly south across the bay—which makes the views from the decks of harbor restaurants a major attraction. Since its incarnation, in 1884, when ferries from San Francisco connected the point with a railroad to San Rafael, the town has centered on the waterfront. ■TIP➔ The ferry is the most relaxing (and fastest) way to get here, particularly in summer, allowing you to skip traffic and parking problems. If visiting midweek, keep in mind that many shops close either Tuesday or Wednesday, or both.

ESSENTIALS

Visitor Information Tiburon Peninsula Chamber of Commerce ✉ *96-B Main St.* ☎ *415/435–5633* ⊕ *www.tiburonchamber.org.*

GETTING HERE AND AROUND

By car, head north from San Francisco on U.S. 101 and get off at CA 131/Tiburon Boulevard/East Blithedale Avenue (Exit 447). Turn right onto Tiburon Boulevard and drive just over 4 miles to downtown. Golden Gate Transit buses 8 and 19 serve downtown Tiburon from San Francisco, as does the Blue & Gold Fleet Ferry service. Tiburon's Main Street is made for wandering, as are the footpaths that frame the water's edge.

EXPLORING

Ark Row. Past the pink-brick bank building, Main Street is known as Ark Row, and has a tree-shaded walk lined with antiques and specialty stores. Some of the buildings are actually old houseboats. They floated in Belvedere Cove before being beached and transformed into stores. If you're curious about architectural history, the Tiburon Heritage & Arts Commission prints a self-guided walking-tour map, available at local businesses. ⊠ *Ark Row, parallel to Main St.* ⊕ *www.landmarks-society.org.*

Old St. Hilary's Landmark and Wildflower Preserve. The stark-white Old St. Hilary's Landmark and Wildflower Preserve, an 1886 Carpenter Gothic church barged over from Strawberry Point in 1957, overlooks the town and the bay from its hillside perch. ■TIP➔ The church is surrounded by a wildflower preserve that's spectacular in May and June, when the rare black jewel flower blooms. Expect a steep walk uphill to reach the preserve. The hiking trails behind the landmark wind up to a peak that has 360-degree views of the entire Bay Area (great photo op). ⊠ *201 Esperanza St., off Mar West St.* ☎ *415/435–1853* ⊕ *www.landmarks-society.org* ⊠ *$3 suggested donation* ☉ *Apr.–Oct., Wed. and Sun. 1–4 and by appointment.*

WHERE TO EAT

$$$
AMERICAN

✕ The Caprice. For more than 50 years this Tiburon landmark, perched on a cliff overlooking the bay, has been the place to come to mark special occasions. The views are spectacular, and soft-yellow walls and starched white tablecloths help to make the space bright and light. Elegant comfort food is the premise, with choices like seared day boat scallops or pan-roasted filet mignon. Polishing off the warm chocolate cake with almond ice cream while gazing out at the sunset and porpoises bobbing in the waves below is a near perfect end to the evening. $ *Average main: $27* ⊠ *2000 Paradise Dr.* ☎ *415/435–3400* ⊕ *www.thecaprice.com* ☉ *Closed Mon. No lunch.*

$$
MODERN
MEXICAN

✕ Guaymas. The festive Guaymas restaurant at the ferry terminal claims a knockout view of the bay, handsome whitewashed adobe walls, tile floors, and a heated terrace bar—and it serves a top-notch margarita. A large open kitchen churns out fairly authentic Mexican dishes such as ceviche, *carnitas uruapan* (slow-roasted pork with salsa and black beans), mesquite-grilled fish, tamales, and a long list of others. ■TIP➔ Sunday lunch is very popular, so make a reservation. $ *Average main: $19* ⊠ *5 Main St.* ☎ *415/435–6300.*

$
AMERICAN

✕ New Morning Cafe. Omelets and scrambles are served all day long at this homey café. If you're past morning treats, choose from the many soups, salads, and sandwiches. New Morning is open 6:30 am–2:30 pm weekdays and 6:30 am–4 pm weekends. [$] *Average main: $11* ✉ *1696 Tiburon Blvd.* ☎ *415/435–4315* ⏲ *No dinner.*

$$ AMERICAN ★ 🍴 **Sam's Anchor Cafe.** Open since 1921, this casual dockside restaurant with mahogany wainscoting is the town's most famous eatery. Today most people flock here for the deck, where out-of-towners and old salts sit shoulder to shoulder for bay views, beer, seafood, and Ramos fizzes. The lunch menu has the usual suspects—burgers, sandwiches, salads, fried fish with tartar sauce—and you'll sit on plastic chairs at tables covered with blue-and-white-checked oilcloths. At night you can find standard seafood dishes with vegetarian and meat options. Expect a wait for outside tables on sunny summer days or weekends (there are no reservations for deck seating or weekend lunch). Mind the seagulls; they know no restraint. [$] *Average main: $22* ✉ *27 Main St.* ☎ *415/435–4527.*

$$ PIZZA 🍴 **Waypoint Pizza.** A nautical decor theme and a tasty "between the sheets" pizza-style sandwich are signatures of this creative pizzeria that also serves slices and whole gourmet pies. Booths are brightened with blue-checked tablecloths, and a playful air is added by indoor deck chairs, a picnic table complete with umbrella, and lighthouse salt-and-pepper shakers. [$] *Average main: $15* ✉ *15 Main St.* ☎ *415/435–3440.*

WHERE TO STAY

For expanded reviews, facilities, and current deals, visit Fodors.com.

$$ HOTEL 🏨 **The Lodge at Tiburon.** A block from Main Street and framed by stone pillars and sloped rooftops, the Lodge at Tiburon has the feel of a winter ski chalet, though the outdoor pool and its cabanas provide a summery counterpoint. **Pros:** spacious work desks in each room; plush bathrobes; L'Occitane bath products; room service from the Tiburon Grill. **Cons:** breakfast for a fee; some rooms have a few too many mirrors; no bay views. **TripAdvisor:** "clean modern rooms," "beautiful common areas," "perfect spot for a quiet romantic evening." [$] *Rooms from: $170* ✉ *1651 Tiburon Blvd., at Beach St.* ☎ *415/435–3133* 🌐 *lodgeattiburon.com* 🛏 *102 rooms.*

$$$ B&B/INN ★ 🏨 **Waters Edge Hotel.** Checking into this elegant hotel feels like tucking away into a inviting retreat by the water—the views are stunning and the lighting is perfect. **Pros:** complimentary wine and cheese for guests every evening; restaurants/sights are minutes away; free bike rentals for guests. **Cons:** except for breakfast delivery, no room service; fitness center is off-site; not a great place to bring small children. **TripAdvisor:** "just about perfect," "a beautiful haven," "comfortable and relaxing." [$] *Rooms from: $209* ✉ *25 Main St., off Tiburon Blvd.* ☎ *415/789–5999, 877/789–5999* 🌐 *www.marinhotels.com* 🛏 *23 rooms.*

SHOPPING

🦢 **The Candy Store on Main Street.** This store is every child's (and many adults') dream come true, with rows of fresh homemade fudge, barrels of rainbow-colored jelly beans, and neat boxes of truffles with pin-striped ribbons. A train in the window drives figure eights through chocolate mountains and around M&M houses. ✉ *7 Main St., at Tiburon Blvd.* ☎ *415/435–0434.*

Nasimiyu. The beaded jewelry sold here—necklaces, earrings, and bracelets—is big, vibrant, and very colorful. The shop's namesake owner, Nasimiyu Wekesa, who greets all customers with her warm smile, draws inspiration from her African heritage, making her crafts not just something to wear but also to be proud of. ⊠ *80D Main St.* ☎ *415/435–3429.*

Ruth Livingston Studio. The namesake owner of this design showcase and walk-in shop will greet you and explain the concepts behind her neomodern pieces. Find everything from striking vases to one-of-a-kind furniture. ⊠ *74 Main St.* ☎ *415/435–5264.*

Schoenberg Guitars. Small, narrow, and chockablock with handmade guitars, this shop is a treat even for those who don't play music. Dozens, if not hundreds, of guitars varying in size, shape, and color hang from the walls and stand against the polished wood floor. There is an organized beauty to the layout of this place and a comforting sense of musical harmony. ⊠ *106 Main St.* ☎ *415/789–0846.*

5

MILL VALLEY

2 miles north of Sausalito, 4 miles north of Golden Gate Bridge.

Chic and woodsy Mill Valley has a dual personality. Here, as elsewhere in the county, the foundation is a superb natural setting. Virtually surrounded by parkland, the town lies at the base of Mt. Tamalpais and contains dense redwood groves traversed by countless creeks. But this is no lumber camp. Smart restaurants and chichi boutiques line the streets, and more rock stars than one might suspect live here.

The rustic village flavor is not a modern conceit but a holdover from the town's early days as a logging camp. In 1896 the Mill Valley and Mt. Tamalpais Scenic Railroad—called "the crookedest railroad in the world" because of its curvy tracks—began transporting visitors from Mill Valley to the top of Mt. Tam and down to Muir Woods, and the town soon became a vacation retreat for city slickers. The trains stopped running in the 1940s, but you can see the old railway depot: the 1924 building has been transformed into the popular Depot Bookstore & Cafe, at 87 Throckmorton Avenue.

The small downtown area has the constant bustle of a leisure community; even at noon on a Tuesday, people are out shopping for fancy cookware and lacy pajamas.

ESSENTIALS
Visitor Information Mill Valley Chamber of Commerce ⊠ *85 Throckmorton Ave.* ☎ *415/388–9700* ⊕ *www.millvalley.org.*

GETTING HERE AND AROUND
By car, from San Francisco head north on U.S. 101 and get off at CA 131/Tiburon Boulevard/East Blithedale Avenue (Exit 447). Turn left onto East Blithedale and continue west to Throckmorton Avenue; turn left to reach Lytton Square, then park. Golden Gate Transit bus 4 leaves for Mill Valley from 8th and Folsom streets in San Francisco every 30 minutes during commute hours. Once here, explore the town on foot; it's great for strolling.

EXPLORING

Ⓒ **Lytton Square.** Mill Valley locals congregate on weekends to socialize in the many coffeehouses near the town's central square, but it bustles most any time of day. Shops, restaurants, and cultural venues line the nearby streets. ⊠ *Miller and Throckmorton Aves.*

OFF THE BEATEN PATH

Marin County Civic Center. This wonder of arches, circles, and skylights was Frank Lloyd Wright's last major architectural undertaking. You can wander about on your own or take a docent-led tour of the complex. Tours ($5) leave from the gift shop, on the second floor, on Wednesday mornings at 10:30. If you can't make it on a Wednesday, pick up the self-guided tour map for 50¢ at the gift shop. Don't miss the photographs on the first floor, which show Marin County homes designed by Wright. There's also an excellent California library here for bibliophiles and oral-history buffs. ⊠ *3501 Civic Center Dr., off N. San Pedro Rd., San Rafael* ☎ *415/499–7009* 🖅 *Free* ☉ *Weekdays 8–5.*

Ⓒ **Old Mill Park.** To see one of the numerous outdoor oases that make Mill Valley so appealing, follow Throckmorton Avenue ¼ mile west from Lytton Square to Old Mill Park, a shady patch of redwoods that shelters a playground and reconstructed sawmill. From the park, Cascade Way winds its way past creek-side homes to the trailheads of several forest paths. ⊠ *Throckmorton Ave. and Cascade Dr.*

WHERE TO EAT

$$$
AMERICAN

✕ **The Balboa Café.** With intimate lighting, rich wood accents, and fresh-pressed white linens, this café offers an upscale dining experience. The bar is so busy that you'll be lucky if your elbow gets anywhere near it. Although the cocktails aren't as stiff as their price tags, the food is creative, local, and beautifully presented. Try the Black Angus rib eye, wild-mushroom risotto, or seared sea scallops—and be sure to save room for the blueberry brioche bread pudding. The extensive wine list includes a few wines from Marin County. 🖇 *Average main: $26* ⊠ *38 Miller Ave., at Sunnyside Ave.* ☎ *415/381–7321* ⌔ *Reservations essential.*

$$$
AMERICAN

✕ **Buckeye Roadhouse.** This is Mill Valley's secret den of decadence, where house-smoked meats and fish, grilled steaks, and old-fashioned dishes such as brisket bring the locals coming back for more. The restaurant also serves beautiful organic, locally grown salads and desserts so heavenly—like the rich but light crème brûlée—you'll just about melt into the floor. The look of the 1937 roadhouse is decidedly hunting-lodge chic, with trophy heads and a river-rock fireplace dominating one wall. Marin County's Jaguar-driving bon vivants pack the place every night. The busy but cozy bar with elegant mahogany paneling and soft lighting is a good place to quench your thirst for a Marin martini or Californian Merlot. 🖇 *Average main: $23* ⊠ *15 Shoreline Hwy., off U.S. 101* ☎ *415/331–2600* ⌔ *Reservations essential.*

$$
MODERN
AMERICAN

✕ **Bungalow 44.** Banana plants and tropical lighting set the mood at this glowing space that serves Californian comfort and glistening cocktails (the restaurant is as popular for its bar as it is for its food). The dance of flames is everywhere—in the crackling dining-room fireplace, and the kitchen's wood oven. House specialties include goat-cheese ravioli in a tomato vodka sauce, fried chicken with local-honey coleslaw, and braised short ribs with horseradish cream. In nice weather, you can eat outdoors. [$] *Average main: $21* ✉ *44 E. Blithedale Ave., at Sunnyside Ave.* ☎ *415/381–2500* 🌐 *www.bungalow44.com.*

$ FRENCH 🍴 **Champagne.** This adorable little bakery/café on Mill Valley's main shopping street is a nice place to pop into for breakfast, a light lunch, dinner, or afternoon pick-me-up. Filled with light, authentic French decor and only a dozen tables, Champagne serves amazing crepes with roasted chicken, creamed spinach, and Swiss cheese, as well as an assortment of savory flat breads—try the pesto-and-tomato version. It's a popular place for breakfast, too. The perennial favorite: brioche French toast with bacon. The afternoon crowd chats over cappuccinos, raspberry-almond croissants, and meringue cookies. [$] *Average main: $11* ✉ *41 Throckmorton Ave., at Miller Ave.* ☎ *415/380–0410.*

$$ AMERICAN 👶 🍴 **The Dipsea Cafe.** There is no better place for breakfast than the Dipsea, which is named after the gorgeous trail that stretches from Mill Valley to Stinson Beach. Locals crowd its cozy interior most mornings, but weekends are especially popular. Choose from huge plates of French toast, eggs Benedict, and huevos rancheros; the homemade fries and jam that accompany the breakfast entrées are to die for. The café also serves hearty lunches and dinners, like the Chinese salad with seared salmon and the enormous BLTs. After 4 pm you can order from the Greek-influenced menu. This is a great spot to fuel up on your way to or from Muir Woods and Stinson Beach. [$] *Average main: $14* ✉ *200 Shoreline Hwy., west of Tennessee Valley Rd.* ☎ *415/381–0298* 🕓 *No dinner Mon. and Tues.*

$$$ CONTEMPORARY Fodor's Choice ★ 🍴 **El Paseo House of Chops.** Chef Tyler Florence and rocker Sammy Hagar teamed up to restore El Paseo, which was established in 1947 and remains *the* place for a romantic and culinary night out. You'll feel as if you're on one of Spain's tiny cobbled lanes as you enter the secluded brick walkway that wraps around a candlelit dining room. If you reserve well in advance you can sit in the bougainvillea-framed courtyard, but the dining room casts its own atmospheric charms, with soft leather chairs, white tablecloths, and dark wooden walls. And then there's Tyler Florence's famous seasonal Californian cuisine. The spinach-and-artichoke dip is rich and full of fresh flavors, as is the bacon-wrapped pork tenderloin with spiced-apple pulp and glazed turnips. Don't overlook the decadent desserts. [$] *Average main: $30* ✉ *17 Throckmorton Ave., at E. Blithedale Ave.* ☎ *415/388–0741* ✍ *Reservations essential* 🕓 *No lunch.*

$ MEXICAN 👶 🍴 **Joe's Taco Lounge.** A funky, bright lounge (and it really does feel like someone's lounge), this is a fun place to go for a casual, cheap, and delicious Mexican meal. There are all sorts of colorful relics on the walls, and chili-pepper lights adorn the windows. The signature dishes are fish tacos and snapper burritos—which are generous in both size and flavor. The organic burger with spicy fries and the fire-grilled corn on the cob are also yummy. Choose from a wide selection of Mexican beers, or go for a refreshing wine-based margarita. Between 5 and 7 pm, this place is popular with families. [$] *Average main: $11* ✉ *382 Miller Ave., and Montford Ave.* ☎ *415/383–8164.*

5

$$ ✕ **La Ginestra.** In business since 1964, La Ginestra is a Mill Valley institu-
ITALIAN tion renowned for its no-pretense, family-style Italian meals—the great-
est hits include thin-crusted pizzas, homemade pastas, breaded veal, and
chicken with artichokes—and impressive wine list. An adorable little
bar sits off to the side of the dining room, just right for a martini or two
and a plate of antipasto. Ⓢ *Average main: $19* ✉ *127 Throckmorton
Ave., at Miller Ave.* ☎ *415/388–0224* ⊘ *Closed Mon. No lunch.*

$ ✕ **Pearl's Phat Burgers.** Families, couples, and teenagers flock to Pearl's
BURGER for juicy, grass-fed organic burgers stacked high with tomatoes, lettuce,
bacon, and cheese; sweet-potato fries that are not too crispy and not
too soft; and thick, creamy milk shakes. The food here is among the
freshest, biggest, and fastest in town. No wonder there's always a line
out the door. Ⓢ *Average main: $9* ✉ *8 E. Blithedale Ave., at Sunnyside
Ave.* ☎ *415/381–6010* ⊕ *www.pearlsdeluxe.com.*

$$ ✕ **Piazza D'Angelo.** In the heart of downtown, busy D'Angelo's is known
ITALIAN for its osso buco and veal saltimbocca, as well as pastas and delicious
crème brûlée. The food is authentic and fresh, but another draw is the
scene, especially in the lounge area, which hosts a lively cocktail hour
packed with beautiful people and serves food until 10 or 11 pm—late
for Mill Valley. The sprawling space encompasses a bright front room,
romantic booths, and a warm patio. Ⓢ *Average main: $21* ✉ *22 Miller
Ave., near Sunnyside Ave.* ☎ *415/388–2000* ⊕ *www.piazzadangelo.
com.*

WHERE TO STAY

For expanded reviews, facilities, and current deals, visit Fodors.com.

$$ ⊟ **Acqua Hotel.** Astride Richardson Bay, this boutique hotel has modern,
HOTEL elegant rooms decorated in deep purples and classic golds. **Pros:** eve-
ning cookie hour; complimentary bikes; hearty breakfast. **Cons:** next
to freeway; traffic audible in rooms facing east. **TripAdvisor:** "beauti-
ful view and walking path," "nice amenities," "well located and clean
design." Ⓢ *Rooms from: $189* ✉ *555 Redwood Hwy., off U.S. 101*
☎ *415/388–9353* ⊕ *www.marinhotels.com* ⤳ *49 rooms* ⦙◯⦙ *Breakfast.*

$ ⊟ **Larkspur Hotel.** In the shadow of Mt. Tamalpais and practically sur-
HOTEL rounded by water, the Larkspur Hotel is central to Marin's attractions.
Pros: central location; complimentary breakfast; popular restaurant
(Frantoio) next door. **Cons:** hallway is disorienting; lobby is cold;
new-carpet smell lingers in the air. **TripAdvisor:** "pleasant staff,"
"nice rooms," "an oasis of quiet." Ⓢ *Rooms from: $149* ✉ *160 Shore-
line Hwy, at U.S. 101* ☎ *415/332–5700* ⊕ *www.larkspurhotels.com/
larkspur-hotels/mill-valley* ⤳ *100 rooms* ⦙◯⦙ *Breakfast.*

$$$ ⊟ **Mill Valley Inn.** The only hotel in downtown Mill Valley has smart-
B&B/INN looking rooms done up in Tuscan colors of ocher and olive, with hand-
crafted beds, armoires, and lamps by local artisans. **Pros:** minutes from
local shops and restaurants; great complimentary Continental breakfast. **Cons:** dark in winter because of surrounding trees; some rooms
are not accessible via elevator; no in-room coffeemakers. **TripAdvisor:**
"awesome gem in Mill Valley," "personal service with care," "nice hotel
in a gorgeous area." Ⓢ *Rooms from: $239* ✉ *165 Throckmorton Ave.,
near Miller Ave.* ☎ *415/389–6608, 800/595–2100* ⊕ *www.marinhotels.
com* ⤳ *25 rooms, 1 suite, 2 cottages* ⦙◯⦙ *Breakfast.*

$$$$ B&B/INN **Fodor's Choice** ★ **Mountain Home Inn.** Abutting 40,000 acres of state and national parks, the inn sits on the skirt of Mt. Tamalpais, where you can follow hiking trails all the way to Stinson Beach. **Pros:** amazing deck and views; peaceful, remote setting. **Cons:** nearest town is a 20-minute drive away; restaurant can get crowded on sunny weekend days. **TripAdvisor:** "brilliant location and restaurant," "stunning view and tranquil setting," "outstanding service." [$] *Rooms from: $279* ✉ *810 Panoramic Hwy., at Edgewood Ave.* ☎ *415/381–9000* 🌐 *www.mtnhomeinn.com* 🛏 *10 rooms* 🍴 *Breakfast.*

NIGHTLIFE AND THE ARTS

142 Throckmorton Theatre. This ultra-quirky venue presents plays, musical acts, and comedy shows, along with visual and related arts. Top events include the DjangoFest Mill Valley, celebrating the gypsy-jazz artist Django Reinhardt; a film series hosted by comedian Mort Sahl; and the annual Writers with Attitude festival of short-play readings. Stunning murals cover the theater's ceiling, and the foyer has on old-fashioned popcorn maker. ✉ *142 Throckmorton Ave., at Madrona St.* ☎ *415/383–9600* 🌐 *www.142throckmortontheatre.com.*

Beerworks. A fine place to rest your feet after shopping or hiking, Beerworks serves more than 100 local, national, and international beers, from ale to port to lager. For food, you'll find cheese plates, olives, homemade pretzels, and sandwiches. ✉ *173 Throckmorton Ave., at Madrona St.* ☎ *415/336–3596* 🌐 *millvalleybeerworks.com.*

★ **Sweetwater Saloon.** With the help of part-owner Bob Weir of the Grateful Dead, this renowned club reopened in an old Masonic Hall. The location may be new, but the Sweetwater's reputation as the best music club and bar in Marin remains. In its former life it hosted the likes of John Lee Hooker and Jerry Garcia. Today, famous as well as up-and-coming bands play nightly, and local stars such as Bonnie Raitt and Huey Lewis have been known to stop in for a pickup session. ✉ *19 Corte Madera Ave., between Throckmorton and Lovell Aves.* ☎ *415/388–3850.*

SHOPPING

The area around Throckmorton Avenue downtown brims with stylish and quirky stores, indies as well as chains.

Book Passage. This sprawling independent bookstore north of Mill Valley in Corte Madera is beloved for its many author events, with readings by notables like Alice Walker, Val McDermid, Michael Connelly, and Peter Mayle. Coffee and snacks are available at the in-store café. ✉ *The Marketplace, 51 Tamal Vista Blvd., between Madera Blvd. and Wornum Dr., Corte Madera* ☎ *415/927–0960, 800/999–7909.*

Jaylina's. Budget fashionistas flock to this chic consignment store, where Prada dresses, Seven jeans, even Chanel bags sell for reasonable prices. The items are carefully selected and easy to find; no need to rummage through crowded racks. ✉ *19 E. Blithedale Ave., at Throckmorton Ave.* ☎ *415/388–4682.*

Summer House. All sorts of surprises pile up here. For the home: furniture, lavish pillows, and decorative objects. For the body: scented potions and soaps. To decorate both: stunning jewelry, tableware, and tempting shirts. ⊠ *21 Throckmorton Ave., at W. Blithedale Ave.* ☎ *415/383–6695.*

Tyler Florence Shop. Stock up here on everything you need for cooking—the celebrity chef's shop has the works, from chicken-shape hard-boiled-egg holders to copper frying pans. If you want to escape into one of Florence's many cookbooks, there's a library in back with leather sofas. ⊠ *59 Throckmorton Ave., at Corte Madera Ave.* ☎ *415/380–9200.*

THE MARIN HEADLANDS

Due west of the Golden Gate Bridge's northern end.

★ The term "Golden Gate" may now be synonymous with the world-famous bridge, but it originally referred to the grassy, poppy-strewn hills flanking the passageway into San Francisco Bay. To the north of the gate lie the Marin Headlands, part of the Golden Gate National Recreation Area (GGNRA) and the most dramatic scenery in these parts. Windswept hills plunge down to the ocean, and creek-fed thickets shelter swaying wildflowers.

The headlands stretch from the Golden Gate Bridge to Muir Beach. Photographers perch on the southern headlands for shots of the city, with the bridge in the foreground and the skyline on the horizon. Equally remarkable are the views north along the coast and out to sea, where the Farallon Islands are visible on clear days. ■TIP➔ Almost any of the roads, all very windy, offer great coast views, especially as you drive at higher elevations.

The headlands' strategic position at the mouth of San Francisco Bay made them a logical site for World War II military installations. Today you can explore the crumbling concrete batteries where naval guns protected the approaches from the sea. The headlands' main attractions are centered on Forts Barry and Cronkhite, which lie just across Rodeo Lagoon from each other. Fronting the lagoon is Rodeo Beach, a dark stretch of sand that attracts sand-castle builders and dog owners.

⚠ Note: The beaches at the Marin Headlands are not safe for swimming. The giant cliffs are steep and unstable, so hiking down them can be dangerous. Stay on trails.

GETTING HERE AND AROUND
Driving from San Francisco, head north on U.S. 101. Just after you cross the Golden Gate Bridge, take the Alexander Avenue exit. From there take the first left (signs read "San Francisco/U.S. 101 South"), go through the tunnel under the freeway, and turn right up the hill where the sign reads: "Forts Barry and Cronkhite." The MuniBus 76 runs hourly from 4th and Townsend streets to the Marin Headlands Visitor Center on Sunday and major holidays only. Once here, you can explore this beautiful countryside on foot.

EXPLORING
Green Gulch Zen Center. Giant eucalyptus trees frame the long winding road that leads to this tranquil retreat. There are mediation programs on Sunday, workshops, and events, as well as an extensive organic garden. Visitors are welcome to roam freely through the acres of gardens

Shutterbugs rejoice in catching a scenic Muir Beach sunset.

that reach down toward Muir Beach. If you follow the main dirt road it will take you to a walking path that brings you to the beach. It's a peaceful walk surrounded by trees, birds, and the ocean breeze. ⊠ *1601 Shoreline Hwy., at Green Gulch Rd., Muir Beach* ☏ *415/383–3134* ⊕ *www.sfzc.org* ✉ *Free* ☉ *Tues.–Sat. 9–noon and 2–4, Sun. 9–10 am.*

Headlands Center for the Arts. The center's main building, formerly the barracks, exhibits contemporary art in a rustic natural setting; the downstairs "archive room" contains objects found and created by residents, such as natural rocks, interesting glass bottles filled with collected items, and unusual masks. Stop by the industrial gallery space, two flights up, to see what the resident visual artists are up to—most of the work is quite contemporary. ⊠ *Fort Barry, Field and Bunker Rds., Bldg. 944* ☏ *415/331–2787* ⊕ *www.headlands.org* ☉ *Weekdays 10–5, Sun. noon–5.*

☞ **Marin Headlands Visitor Center.** Open daily 9:30–4:30, the center sells a guide to historic sites and wildlife and has exhibits on the area's history and ecology. Pick up the park newspaper for a schedule of guided walks. Kids will enjoy the "please touch" educational sites and small play area inside. ⊠ *Fort Barry, Field and Bunker Rds., Bldg. 948* ☏ *415/331–1540* ⊕ *www.nps.gov/goga/marin-headlands.htm.*

★ **Muir Beach.** Small but scenic, this beach—a rocky patch of shoreline off
☞ Highway 1 in the northern headlands—is a good place to stretch your legs and gaze out at the Pacific. Locals often walk their dogs here; families and cuddling couples come for picnicking and sunbathing. At one end of the sand is a cluster of waterfront homes, and at the other are the bluffs of Golden Gate National Recreation Area. The beach itself

has an interesting history. Janis Joplin's ashes were scattered here among the sands, and this is where author Ken Kesey hosted the second of his famed Acid Tests. ✉ *190 Pacific Way, off Shoreline Highway, Muir Beach* 🌐 *www.parksconservancy.org/visit/park-sites/muir-beach.html.*

★ ☺ **Point Bonita Lighthouse.** At the end of Conzelman Road, in the southern headlands, is the Point Bonita Lighthouse, a restored beauty that still guides ships to safety with its original 1855 refractory lens. Half the fun of a visit is the steep ½-mile walk from the parking area down to the lighthouse, which takes you through a rock tunnel and across a suspension bridge. Signposts along the way detail the bravado of surfmen, as the early lifeguards were called, and the tenacity of the "wickies," the first keepers of the light. ✉ *End of Conzelman Rd.* 🎟 *Free* ⏲ *Sat.–Mon. 12:30–3:30.*

WHERE TO STAY

For expanded reviews, facilities, and current deals, visit Fodors.com.

$$$ B&B/INN ★ 🏨 **Pelican Inn.** From its slate roof to its whitewashed plaster walls, this inn looks so Tudor that it's hard to believe it was built in the 1970s. **Pros:** five-minute walk to beach; great bar and restaurant; peaceful setting. **Cons:** 20-minute drive to nearby attractions; no Wi-Fi or wheelchair access to bedrooms. **TripAdvisor:** "quaint inn with lots of charm," "very British," "fantastic getaway." [$] *Rooms from: $210* ✉ *10 Pacific Way, off Hwy. 1, Muir Beach* ☎ *415/383–6000* 🌐 *www.pelicaninn.com* 🛏 *7 rooms* 🍴 *Breakfast.*

MUIR WOODS NATIONAL MONUMENT

12 miles northwest of the Golden Gate Bridge.

GETTING HERE AND AROUND

To get here from San Francisco by car, take U.S. 101 north across the Golden Gate Bridge to the Mill Valley/Stinson Beach exit, then follow signs to Highway 1 north. On weekends and holidays, Memorial Day through Labor Day, Golden Gate Transit operates a shuttle ($3 round-trip) from Mill Valley every half hour. Park in Marin City at the Gateway Shopping Center (look for lighted signs directing you from U.S. 101) or at the Manzanita Park-and-Ride, at the Highway 1 exit off U.S. 101 (look for the lot under the elevated freeway), or take connecting bus service from San Francisco with Golden Gate Transit. Once here, you can wander by foot through this pristine patch of nature.

EXPLORING

☺ Fodor's Choice ★ **Muir Woods National Monument.** One hundred fifty million years ago, ancestors of redwood and sequoia trees grew throughout the United States. Today the *Sequoia sempervirens* can be found only in a narrow, cool coastal belt from Monterey to Oregon. The 550 acres of Muir Woods National Monument contain some of the most majestic redwoods in the world—some nearly 250 feet tall and 1,000 years old. The stand was saved from destruction in 1905, when it was purchased by a couple who donated it to the federal government. Three years later it was named after naturalist John Muir, whose environmental campaigns helped to establish the national park system. His response: "Saving

these woods from the ax and saw is in many ways the most notable service to God and man I have heard of since my forest wandering began."

Muir Woods, part of the Golden Gate National Recreation Area, is a pedestrian's park. The trails vary in difficulty and length. Beginning from the park headquarters, a 2-mile, wheelchair-accessible **loop trail** crosses streams and passes ferns and azaleas, as well as magnificent redwood groves. Among the most famous are **Bohemian Grove** and the circular formation called **Cathedral Grove.** On summer weekends, visitors oohing and aahing in a dozen languages line the trail. If you prefer a little serenity, consider the challenging **Dipsea Trail,** which climbs west from the forest floor to soothing views of the ocean and the Golden Gate Bridge. For a complete list of trails, check with rangers, who can also help you pick the best one for your ability level.

■ **TIP→** The weather in Muir Woods is usually cool and often wet, so wear warm clothes and shoes appropriate for damp trails. Picnicking and camping aren't allowed, and pets aren't permitted. Parking can be difficult here—the lots are small and the crowds are large—so try to come early in the morning or late in the afternoon. The fine **Muir Woods Visitor Center** has books and exhibits about redwood trees and the woods' history. ⊠ *1 Muir Woods Trail, off Panoramic Hwy., Mill Valley* ☎ *415/388–2595 park information, 415/925–4501 shuttle information* ⊕ *www.nps.gov/muwo* ⊠ *$7* ☉ *Daily 8 am–sunset.*

MT. TAMALPAIS STATE PARK

16 miles northwest of Golden Gate Bridge.

GETTING HERE AND AROUND

By car, take the Highway 1–Stinson Beach exit off U.S. 101 and follow the road west and then north. From San Francisco the trip can take from 30 minutes up to an hour, depending on traffic. By bus, take the 10, 70 or 80 to Marin City; in Marin City transfer to the West Marin Stagecoach (☎ *415/226–0855* ⊕ *www.marintransit.org/stage.html*). Once here, the only way to explore is on foot or by bike.

EXPLORING

Mt. Tamalpais State Park. Although the summit of Mt. Tamalpais is only 2,571 feet high, the mountain rises practically from sea level, dominating the topography of Marin County. Adjacent to Muir Woods National Monument, Mt. Tamalpais State Park affords views of the entire Bay Area and the Pacific Ocean to the west. The mountain was sacred to Native Americans, who saw in its profile—as you can see today—the silhouette of a sleeping Indian maiden. Locals fondly refer to it as the "Sleeping Lady." For years the 6,300-acre park has been a favorite destination for hikers. There are more than 200 miles of trails, some rugged but many developed for easy walking through meadows, grasslands, and forests and along creeks. Mt. Tam, as it's called by locals, is also the birthplace (in the 1970s) of mountain biking, and today many spandex-clad bikers whiz down the park's winding roads.

The park's major thoroughfare, the Panoramic Highway, snakes its way up from U.S. 101 to the **Pantoll Ranger Station** (⊠ *Pantoll Rd.*). The office is staffed sporadically, depending on funding. From the ranger station, the Panoramic Highway drops down to the town of Stinson Beach. Pantoll Road branches off the highway at the station, connecting up with Ridgecrest Boulevard. Along these roads are numerous parking areas, picnic spots, scenic overlooks, and trailheads. Parking is free along the roadside, but there's a fee at the ranger station and at some of the other parking lots.

The **Mountain Theater** (⊠ *Richardson Blvd. off Panoramic Hwy.*), also known as the Cushing Memorial Amphitheatre, is a natural amphitheater with terraced stone seats (for nearly 4,000 people) constructed in its current form by the Civilian Conservation Corps in the 1930s.

The **Rock Spring Trail** starts at the Mountain Theater and gently climbs about 1¾ mile to the **West Point Inn,** once a stop on the Mt. Tam railroad route. Relax at a picnic table and stock up on water before forging ahead, via Old Railroad Grade Fire Road and the Miller Trail, to Mt. Tam's Middle Peak, about 2 miles uphill.

Starting from the Pan Toll Ranger Station, the precipitous **Steep Ravine Trail** brings you past stands of coastal redwoods and, in the springtime, numerous small waterfalls. Take the connecting **Dipsea Trail** to reach the town of Stinson Beach and its swath of golden sand. If you're too weary to make the 3½-mile trek back up, Golden Gate Transit Bus 63 (Saturday, Sunday, and holidays from mid-March through early December) takes you from Stinson Beach back to the ranger station. ⊠ *Pantoll Ranger Station, 3801 Panoramic Hwy., at Pantoll Rd.* ☎ *415/388–2070* ⊕ *www.parks.ca.gov.*

NIGHTLIFE AND THE ARTS

☺ **Mountain Play.** Every May and June, locals tote overstuffed picnic baskets to the Mountain Theater to see the Mountain Play, popular musicals such as *The Music Man* and *My Fair Lady*. Depending on the play, this can be a great family activity. Summer 2013 marks the 100th anniversary of this Bay Area tradition. ⊠ *Richardson Blvd. off Panoramic Hwy.* ☎ *415/383–1100* ⊕ *www.mountainplay.org* 🎟 *$40.*

STINSON BEACH

20 miles northwest of Golden Gate Bridge.

GETTING HERE AND AROUND

If you're driving, take the Highway 1–Stinson Beach exit off U.S. 101 and follow the road west and then north. The journey from San Francisco can take from 35 minutes to more than an hour, depending on traffic. By bus, take the 10, 70, or 80 to Marin City; in Marin City transfer to the West Marin Stagecoach. The intimate town is perfect for casual walking.

EXPLORING

☺ **Stinson Beach.** Stinson Beach is the most expansive stretch of sand in Marin County. It's as close (when the fog hasn't rolled in) as you can get to the stereotypical feel of a Southern California beach. ⚠ Swimming here is recommended only from early May through September, when lifeguards are on duty, because the undertow can be strong and shark sightings, although infrequent, aren't unusual. There are several clothing-optional areas (such as Red Rock Beach). On any hot summer weekend, every road to Stinson Beach is jam-packed, so factor this into your plans. The town itself is down to earth—like tonier Mill Valley, but more relaxed. ⊠ *1 Calle Del Sierra, off Shoreline Hwy. 1.*

WHERE TO EAT AND STAY

For expanded reviews, facilities, and current deals, visit Fodors.com.

$$
AMERICAN

✕ **Parkside Cafe.** The Parkside is popular for its beachfront snack bar (cash only), but inside is Stinson's best restaurant, with classic Cal-cuisine offerings such as the day-boat-scallop and ceviche appetizers, and mains like the lamb with goat-cheese-stuffed red peppers. Breakfast is served until 2 pm. Creeping vines on the sunny patio shelter diners from the wind; for a cozier atmosphere eat by the fire in the dining room. $ *Average main: $20* ⊠ *43 Arenal Ave., off Shoreline Hwy. 1* ☎ *415/868–1272.*

$
AMERICAN

✕ **Sand Dollar.** The town's oldest restaurant still attracts all the old salts from Muir Beach to Bolinas, but these days they sip whiskey over an up-to-date bar or beneath market umbrellas on the spiffy deck. The food is good—try the panfried sand dabs (small flatfish) and pear salad with blue cheese—but the big draw is the lively atmosphere. Musicians play on weekends in summer, and on sunny afternoons the deck gets so packed that people sit on the fence rails sipping beer. $ *Average main: $13* ⊠ *3458 Shoreline Hwy.* ☎ *415/868–0434* ☯ *No lunch Tues. Nov.–Mar.*

$$
B&B/INN

⊡ **The Sandpiper.** Recharge, rest, and enjoy the local scenery at this ultra-popular lodging that books up months, even years, in advance. **Pros:** bright rooms; lush gardens; minutes from the beach. **Cons:** not exactly on the beach; walls are thin. **TripAdvisor:** "hospitable," "ideal spot for quiet beach vacation," "peaceful getaway." $ *Rooms from: $180* ⊠ *1 Marine Way, at Arenal Ave.* ☎ *415/868–1632* ⊕ *www. sandpiperstinsonbeach.com* ⤳ *10 rooms.*

BOLINAS

7 miles north of Stinson Beach.

The tiny town of Bolinas wears its 1960s idealism on its sleeve, attract-ing potters, poets, and peace lovers to its quiet streets. With a funky gallery, a general store selling organic produce, a café, and an offbeat saloon, the main thoroughfare, Wharf Road, looks like a hippie-fied version of Main Street, USA.

GETTING HERE AND AROUND

Bolinas isn't difficult to find: heading north from Stinson Beach follow Highway 1 west and then north. Make a left at the first road just past the Bolinas Lagoon (⊠ *Olema–Bolinas Rd.*), and then turn left at the stop sign. The road dead-ends smack-dab in the middle of town. By bus, take the 10, 70, or 80 to Marin City; in Marin City transfer to the West Marin Stagecoach. Walking is the only way to see this small town.

WHERE TO EAT

$$ AMERICAN 🍴 **Coast Cafe.** Decked out in a nautical theme with surfboards and buoys, the dining room at the Coast serves dependably good American fare, including specials such as shepherd's pie, pot roast, local fresh fish, grass-fed steaks, and gorgeous salads. The café is open for breakfast on weekends. [$] *Average main: $16* ✉ *46 Wharf Rd., off Olema–Bolinas Rd.* ☎ *415/868–2298* 🌐 *www.bolinascafe.com.*

POINT REYES NATIONAL SEASHORE

Bear Valley Visitor Center is 12 miles northwest of Bolinas.

GETTING HERE AND AROUND

From San Francisco, take U.S. 101 north, head west at Sir Francis Drake Boulevard (Exit 450B), and follow the road just under 20 miles to Bear Valley Road. From Stinson Beach or Bolinas, drive north on Highway 1 and turn left on Bear Valley Road. If you're going by bus, take the 10, 70, or 80 to Marin City; in Marin City transfer to the West Marin Stagecoach. Once at the visitor center, the best way to get around is on foot.

5

EXPLORING

Fodor's Choice ★ **Point Reyes National Seashore.** One of the Bay Area's most spectacular treasures and the only national seashore on the West Coast, the 66,500-acre Point Reyes National Seashore encompasses hiking trails, secluded beaches, and rugged grasslands as well as Point Reyes itself, a triangular peninsula that juts into the Pacific. The town of **Point Reyes Station** is a quaint, one-main-drag affair, with a charming bakery, some good gift shops with locally made and imported goods, and a few places to eat. It's nothing fancy, but that's part of its relaxed charm.

When explorer Sir Francis Drake sailed along the California coast in 1579, he missed the Golden Gate and San Francisco Bay, but he did land at what he described as a convenient harbor, now thought to be Drake's Bay, which flanks the point on the east. Today Point Reyes's hills and dramatic cliffs attract other kinds of explorers: hikers, whale-watchers, and solitude seekers.

The infamous San Andreas Fault runs along the eastern edge of the park and up the center of Tomales Bay; take the short **Earthquake Trail** from the visitor center to see the impact near the epicenter of the 1906 earthquake that devastated San Francisco. A ½-mile path from the visitor center leads to **Kule Loklo,** a brilliantly reconstructed Miwok village that sheds light on the daily lives of the region's first inhabitants. From here, trails also lead to the park's free campgrounds (camping permits are required).

■ TIP→ In late winter and spring, take the short walk at Chimney Rock, just before the lighthouse, to the Elephant Seal Overlook. Even from the cliff, the male seals look enormous as they spar for resident females.

You can experience the diversity of Point Reyes's ecosystems on the scenic **Coast Trail,** which starts at the Palomarin Trailhead, just outside Bolinas. From here it's a 3-mile trek through eucalyptus groves and pine forests and along seaside cliffs to beautiful and tiny Bass Lake. To reach the Palomarin Trailhead, take Olema–Bolinas Road toward Bolinas, follow signs to the Point Reyes Bird Observatory, and then continue until the road dead-ends.

The 4.7-mile-long (one-way) **Tomales Point Trail** follows the spine of the park's northernmost finger of land through a Tule Elk Preserve, providing spectacular ocean views from the high bluffs. Expect to see elk, but keep your distance from the animals. To reach the fairly easy hiking trail, look for the Pierce Point Road turnoff on the right, just north of the town of Inverness; park at the end of the road by the old ranch buildings. ⊕ *www.nps.gov/pore*.

Bear Valley Visitor Center. The center's informative exhibits explain the park's wildlife and history. Rangers here dispense information about beaches, whale-watching, hiking trails, and camping. ⊠ *Bear Valley Visitor Center Access Rd., west of Hwy. 1* ☎ *415/464–5100* ⊕ *www. nps.gov/pore/planyourvisit* ☉ *Weekdays 9–5, weekends 8–5*.

Duxbury Reef. Mile-long Duxbury Reef is the largest shale intertidal reef in North America. Look for starfish, barnacles, sea anemones, purple urchins, limpets, sea mussels, and the occasional abalone. But check a tide table (⊕ *www.wrh.noaa.gov/mtr/marine.php*) or the local papers if you plan to explore the reef—it's accessible only at low tide. To get here, take Mesa Road and turn left onto Overlook Drive and then right on Elm Avenue.

Point Reyes Bird Observatory. Birders adore the observatory, which lies in the southernmost part of Point Reyes National Seashore and is accessed through Bolinas. (Those not interested in birds might find it ho-hum.) The compact visitor center has excellent interpretive exhibits, including a comparative display of real birds' talons, and the surrounding woods, well worth a visit, harbor more than 200 bird species. As you hike the quiet trails through forest and along ocean cliffs, you're likely to see biologists banding birds to aid in the study of their life cycles. ⊠ *Mesa Rd., Bolinas* ☎ *415/868–0655* ⊕ *www.prbo.org* ☐ *Free* ☉ *Daily 9–5*.

★ **Point Reyes Lighthouse.** In operation since December 1, 1870, this light-
☾ house is one of the premier attractions of the Point Reyes National Seashore. It occupies the tip of Point Reyes, 22 miles from the Bear Valley Visitor Center, a scenic 45-minute drive over hills scattered with longtime cattle ranches. The lighthouse originally cast a rotating beam lighted by four wicks that burned lard oil. Keeping the wicks lighted and the lens soot-free in Point Reyes's perpetually foggy climate was a constant struggle that reputedly drove the early attendants to alcoholism and insanity. On busy whale-watching weekends (late December through mid-April), parking at the forged-iron-plate lighthouse may be restricted by park staff; on these days buses shuttle visitors from the Drakes Beach lot to the top of the stairs leading down to the lighthouse (bus $5, admission free). Once there, consider whether you have it in you to walk down—and up—the 308 steps to the lighthouse. The view from the bottom is worth the effort, but the whales are visible from the cliffs above the lighthouse. ⊠ *Western end of Sir Francis Drake Blvd.* ☎ *415/669–1534* ☉ *Thurs.–Mon. 10–4:30; weather lens room 2:30–4, except during very windy weather*.

WHERE TO EAT

$ AMERICAN 👶 🍴 **Pine Cone Diner.** A block off the main drag, this oh-so-cute diner serves great traditional breakfasts as well as Mexican specialties such as huevos rancheros. At lunch expect hearty homemade soups, fresh salads, and thick sandwiches, all made with local, organic ingredients. ■ **TIP→ Kids love the outdoor picnic tables.** [$] *Average main: $11* ✉ *60 4th St., at B St., Point Reyes Station* ☎ *415/663–1536* 🌐 *www.pineconediner.com* ⏲ *No dinner.*

$$ AMERICAN 🍴 **Station House Cafe.** In good weather, hikers fresh from the park fill the Station House's garden to enjoy alfresco dining, and on weekends there's not a spare seat on the banquettes in the dining room. The focus is on local, seasonal, and sustainable food: oyster shooters, Niman Ranch braised lamb, Californian white sea bass, and sweet bread pudding are the standbys. The place is also open for breakfast, and there's a full bar. [$] *Average main: $22* ✉ *11180 Hwy. 1, Point Reyes Station* ☎ *415/663–1515* 🌐 *www.stationhousecafe.com* ⏲ *Closed Wed.*

$$$ AMERICAN ★ 🍴 **Tomales Bay Foods.** A renovated hay barn off the main drag houses this collection of food shops, a favorite stopover among Bay Area foodies. Watch workers making Cowgirl Creamery cheese; then buy some at a counter that sells exquisite artisanal cheeses from around the world. Tomales Bay Foods showcases local organic fruits and vegetables and premium packaged foods, and the kitchen turns the best ingredients into creative sandwiches, salads, and soups. You can eat at a small café table or on the lawn. The shops are open until 6 pm. [$] *Average main: $23* ✉ *80 4th St., at B. St., Point Reyes Station* ☎ *415/663–9335 cheese shop, 415/663–8478 deli* ⏲ *Closed Mon. and Tues.*

WHERE TO STAY

For expanded reviews, facilities, and current deals, visit Fodors.com.

$$$$ B&B/INN Fodor's Choice ★ 🏨 **Manka's Inverness Lodge.** Chef-owner Margaret Grade takes rustic fantasy to extravagant heights in her 1917 hunting lodge and cabins, where mica-shaded lamps cast an amber glow, and bearskin rugs warm wide-planked floors. **Pros:** extremely romantic, remote and quiet. **Cons:** no on-site restaurant; sounds from neighboring room are easily heard. **TripAdvisor:** "pristine oasis in Inverness," "rustic luxury," "relaxed setting." [$] *Rooms from: $450* ✉ *30 Callendar Way, at Argyle Way, Inverness* ☎ *415/669–1034* 🌐 *www.mankas.com* 🛏 *8 rooms, 1 boathouse, 4 cabins.*

$$$$ B&B/INN 🏨 **Olema Druids Hall.** Set on a quiet hill beneath towering eucalyptus trees, the inn, built in 1885 as a meeting hall for the Ancient Order of Druids, now holds gorgeously appointed rooms, each of which seems like a designer showcase. **Pros:** heated hardwood floors; wood-burning fireplaces. **Cons:** not much to do at night; some traffic noise. **TripAdvisor:** "comfortable luxury," "old-world heaven," "casual and comfortable." [$] *Rooms from: $325* ✉ *9870 Shoreline Hwy., Box 96, Olema* ☎ *415/663–8727, 866/554–4255* 🌐 *www.olemadruidshall.com* 🛏 *3 rooms, 1 suite, 1 cottage* 🍽 *Breakfast.*

$$$ B&B/INN 🏨 **Olema Inn & Restaurant.** Built in 1876, this inn retains all of its 19th-century architectural charm but has been decorated in a sophisticated, uncluttered style. **Pros:** great restaurant; magnificent scenery. **Cons:** no elevator means carrying your luggage up the stairs; the carpets need to

DID YOU KNOW?

The majestic Point Reyes
National Seashore offers
many attractions for nature
lovers: hiking, bird-watching,
camping, or whale-watching
depending on the season.
But flower picking isn't an
approved activity; the wild
flowers here are protected.

be replaced. **TripAdvisor:** "clean and quiet," "amazing hospitality," "largely very nice." $ *Rooms from: $222* ✉ *10000 Sir Francis Drake Blvd., Olema* ☎ *415/663–9559* ⊕ *www.theolemainn.com* ↻ *6 rooms* ⊗ *Closed Tues. No lunch weekdays.*

$$

B&B/INN

🛏 **Ten Inverness Way.** This is the kind of down-to-earth place where you sit around after breakfast and share tips for hiking Point Reyes or linger around the living room with its stone fireplace and library. **Pros:** great base for exploring nearby wilderness; peaceful garden and friendly staff. **Cons:** overly folksy decor; some rooms on the small side; poor cell-phone reception. **TripAdvisor:** "romantic," "great host," "lovely setting." $ *Rooms from: $182* ✉ *10 Inverness Way, Inverness* ☎ *415/669–1648* ⊕ *www.teninvernessway.com* ↻ *4 rooms, 1 suite.*

SPORTS AND THE OUTDOORS

Blue Waters Kayaking. This outfit rents kayaks and offers tours and lessons. ✉ *12938 Sir Francis Drake Blvd., Inverness* ☎ *415/669–2600* ⊕ *www.bwkayak.com.*

Five Brooks Stable. Tour guides here lead horse rides lasting from one to six hours; trails from the stable wind through Point Reyes National Seashore and along the beaches. ✉ *8001 Hwy. 1, north of town, Olema* ☎ *415/663–1570* ⊕ *www.fivebrooks.com* 💲 *$40–$240.*

THE EAST BAY

When San Franciscans refer to it, the East Bay often means nothing more than what you can see across the bay from the city—mainly Oakland and Berkeley, both of which are in Alameda County. In fact, the East Bay stretches north and east of Alameda to Contra Costa County, which itself has emerged as a powerful business nexus.

OAKLAND

Directly east of Bay Bridge.

Often overshadowed by San Francisco's beauty and Berkeley's storied counterculture, Oakland's allure lies in its amazing diversity. Here you can find a Nigerian clothing store, a beautifully renovated Victorian home, a Buddhist meditation center, and a lively salsa club, all within the same block. Oakland's multifaceted nature reflects its colorful and often tumultuous history. Once a cluster of Mediterranean-style homes and gardens that served as a bedroom community for San Francisco, the city became a hub of shipbuilding and industry almost overnight when the United States entered World War II. New jobs in the city's shipyards and factories attracted thousands of workers, including some of the first female welders, and the city's neighborhoods were imbued with a proud but gritty spirit. In the 1960s and '70s this intense community pride gave rise to such militant groups as the Black Panther Party and the Symbionese Liberation Army, but they were little match for the economic hardships and racial tensions that plagued Oakland. In many neighborhoods the reality was widespread poverty and gang violence—subjects that dominated the songs of such Oakland-bred rappers as the late Tupac Shakur. The highly publicized protests of the Occupy Oakland movement in 2011 and 2012 illustrated just how much Oakland remains a mosaic of its past.

The affluent reside in the city's hillside homes, which provide a warmer, more spacious, and more affordable alternative to San Francisco, and a constant flow of newcomers—many from Central America and Asia—ensures continued diversity, vitality, and growing pains. Many neighborhoods to the west and south of the city center remain rundown and unsafe, but a renovated downtown area—sparking a vibrant arts scene—and the thriving though sterile Jack London Square have injected new energy into the city.

Everyday life here revolves around the neighborhood, with a main business strip attracting both shoppers and strollers. In some areas, such as high-end Piedmont and Rockridge, you'd swear you were in Berkeley or San Francisco's Noe Valley or Cow Hollow. These are perfect places for browsing, eating, or just relaxing between sightseeing trips to Oakland's architectural gems, rejuvenated waterfront, and numerous green spaces. Between Rockridge and Piedmont and to the west, you can find the Temescal District, along Telegraph Avenue just south of 51st Street, where interesting eateries and shops are beginning to congregate.

ESSENTIALS
Visitor Information **Oakland Convention and Visitors Bureau** ⊠ *463 11th St.* ☎ *510/839–9000* ⊕ *www.oaklandcvb.com.*

GETTING HERE AND AROUND
Driving from San Francisco, take Interstate 80 East across the Bay Bridge, then take Interstate 580 to the Grand Avenue exit for Lake Merritt. To reach downtown and the waterfront, take Interstate 980 from Interstate 580 and exit at 12th Street.

By BART, use the Lake Merritt Station for the Oakland Museum and southern Lake Merritt; the Oakland City Center–12th Street Station for downtown, Chinatown, and Old Oakland; and the 19th Street Station for the Paramount Theatre and the north side of Lake Merritt.

By bus, take the AC Transit's C and P lines to get to Piedmont in Oakland. The O bus stops at the edge of Chinatown near downtown Oakland. Once you arrive, be aware of how quickly neighborhoods can change. Walking is safe and advised downtown as well as in the Piedmont and Rockridge areas, but avoid walking west and south of downtown.

EXPLORING
Chinatown. Across Broadway from Old Oakland but worlds apart, Chinatown is a densely packed, bustling neighborhood. Unlike its San Francisco counterpart, Oakland's Chinatown makes no concessions to tourists; you won't find baskets of trinkets lining the sidewalk and souvenir displays in the shop windows. But supermarkets such as **Yuen Hop Noodle Company and Asian Food Products** (⊠ *824 Webster St.*), open since 1931, overflow with goodies. And the line for sweets, breads, and towering cakes snakes out the door of **Napoleon Super Bakery** (⊠ *810 Franklin St.*).

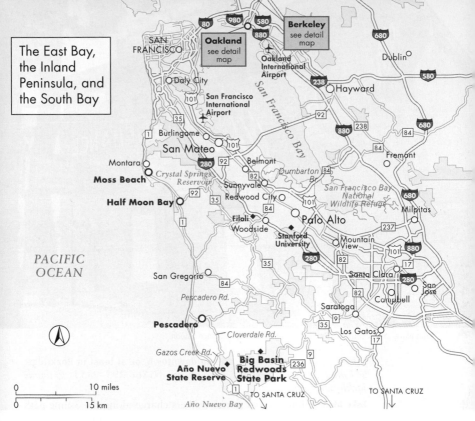

The East Bay, the Inland Peninsula, and the South Bay

Fox Theater. The Fox Theater, an art-deco movie palace built in 1928, sat decaying and mostly unused for decades until the last of several redevelopment schemes culminated in a stunning renovation. The Mediterranean Moorish–style Fox and its attached buildings contain the main theater, these days used for music concerts; a charter arts school; and a restaurant space. The theater's restoration helped revive what's known as the Uptown neighborhood. ⊠ *1807 Telegraph Ave., at 18th St., Uptown* ⊕ *www.thefoxoakland.com.*

Jack London Square. Shops, restaurants, small museums, and historic sites line Jack London Square, which is named after one of California's best-known authors; London wrote *The Call of the Wild* and *The Sea Wolf,* among many other books. When he lived in Oakland, he spent many a day boozing and brawling in the waterfront area, most notably at the tiny, wonderful **Heinold's First and Last Chance Saloon** (⊠ *48 Webster St., at Embarcadero West* ☎ *510/839–6761*). The saloon has been serving since 1883, although it's a little worse for wear since the 1906 earthquake. Next door is the Klondike cabin in which London spent a summer in the late 1890s. The cabin was moved from Alaska and reassembled here in 1970.

■**TIP**➜ The square is an obvious spot for tourists to visit and it's worth a peek if you take a ferry that docks here; to really get a feel for Oakland,

A fun place to wet your whistle, Heinold's First and Last Chance Saloon

though, you're better off browsing downtown, or at least in Rockridge. ✉ *Embarcadero West at Broadway* ☎ *866/295–9853* ⊕ *www.jacklondonsquare.com.*

Lake Merritt. Joggers and power-walkers charge along the 3-mile path that encircles this 155-acre natural saltwater lake in downtown Oakland. Crew teams often glide across the water, and boatmen guide snuggling couples in authentic Venetian gondolas. **Lakeside Park,** which surrounds the north side of Lake Merritt, has several outdoor attractions, including a cute children's park and a waterfowl refuge. Herons, egrets, geese, and ducks nest here in spring and summer, and migrating birds pass through from September through February. Year-round, you can watch birds being fed daily at 3:30 pm. Look for the sign that says "Sailboat House, Gondola Servizio." Gondola fares start at $40 per couple for 30 minutes. ✉ *Lakeside Park, Bellevue and Grand Aves.*

★ **Oakland Museum of California.** One of Oakland's top attractions, the
Ⓢ museum showcases the state's art, history, and natural wonders in absorbing, detailed exhibits. You can travel through myriad ecosystems in the Natural Sciences Gallery, from the sand dunes of the Pacific to the coyotes and brush of the Nevada border. Kids love the lifelike wild-animal exhibits, especially the snarling wolverine, big-eyed harbor seal, and trove of hidden creatures. The rambling Cowell Hall of California History includes everything from Spanish-era armor to a small but impressive collection of vintage vehicles, including a gorgeous, candy-apple-red "Mystery" car from the 1960s and a gleaming red, gold, and silver fire engine that battled the flames in San Francisco in 1906. The Gallery of California Art holds an eclectic collection of modern works

and early landscapes. Of particular interest are paintings by Richard Diebenkorn, Joan Brown, Elmer Bischoff, and David Park, all members of the Bay Area Figurative School, which flourished here after World War II. Fans of Dorothea Lange won't want to miss the gallery's comprehensive collection of her work. The museum also has a sculpture garden with a view of the Oakland and Berkeley hills in the distance. ✉ *1000 Oak St., at 10th St.* ☎ *510/238–2200* ⊕ *www.museumca.org* ✉ *$12, free 1st Sun. of month* ☿ *Wed.–Sun. 11–5.*

Old Oakland. In the shadow of the convention center and towering downtown hotels, Old Oakland was once a booming business district. Today the restored Victorian storefronts lining four historic blocks house restaurants, cafés, shops, galleries, and a lively three-block farmers' market, which takes place Friday morning. Architectural consistency distinguishes the area from surrounding streets and lends it a distinct neighborhood feel. The Italian grocer **Ratto's International Market** (✉ *827 Washington St.* ☎ *510/832–6503*) has been in business for more than a century. Stop in for a deli sandwich there, or head over to the genial **Pacific Coast Brewing Company** (✉ *906 Washington St.* ☎ *510/836–2739*) for a microbrew on the patio.

★ **Paramount Theatre.** Some truly stunning examples of late art-deco architecture can be found in the Uptown (but still downtown) neighborhood around the 19th Street BART station. Some of these buildings have fallen into disrepair, but the Paramount Theatre, perhaps the most glorious art-deco specimen in the city, if not the entire Bay Area, still operates as a venue for concerts and performances of all kinds, from the Oakland East Bay Symphony to Tom Waits and Elvis Costello. You can take a two-hour tour of the building, which starts near the box office on 21st Street at 10 am on the first and third Saturday of each month. ✉ *2025 Broadway, at 20th St., Uptown* ☎ *510/465–6400* 🌐 *www.paramounttheatre.com* 🎟 *Tour $5.*

Rockridge. The upscale neighborhood of Rockridge is one of Oakland's most desirable places to live. Explore the tree-lined streets that radiate out from **College Avenue** just north and south of the Rockridge BART station for a look at California bungalow architecture at its finest. By day College Avenue between Broadway and Alcatraz Avenue is crowded with shoppers buying fresh flowers, used books, and clothing; by night the same folks are back for dinner and locally brewed ales in the numerous restaurants and pubs. With its pricey specialty-food shops, **Market Hall,** an airy European-style marketplace at Shafter Avenue, is a hub of culinary activity.

WHERE TO EAT

$$ MEDITERRANEAN

🍴 **À Côté.** This place for Mediterranean food is all about small plates, cozy tables, family-style eating—and truly excellent food. The butternut-squash ravioli, Alsatian goose sausage, and pear-and-walnut flat bread are all lovely choices. And you won't find a better plate of pommes frites anywhere. The restaurant offers more than 40 wines by the glass. Desserts here are tempting: try the warm crème-fraîche pound cake with apple confit, vanilla ice cream, and huckleberry sauce or a tangy pomegranate sorbet. The heavy wooden tables, cool tiles, and natural light make this a coveted destination for students, families, couples, and after-work crowds. [$] *Average main: $18* ✉ *5478 College Ave., at Taft Ave., Rockridge* ☎ *510/655–6469* ✍ *Reservations not accepted* 🕒 *No lunch.*

$ AMERICAN

🍴 **Brown Sugar Kitchen.** Chef and owner Tanya Holland uses local, organic, and seasonal products to craft meals influenced by her African-American heritage and her culinary education in France. Holland blends sweet and savory flavors like no one else, and pairs her dishes with well-chosen wines. The dining room is fresh and bright, with a long, sleek counter, red-leather stools, and spacious booths and tables. This is *the* place to come for chicken and waffles. [$] *Average main: $13* ✉ *2534 Mandela Pkwy., at 26th St., West Oakland* ☎ *510/839–7685* 🌐 *www.brownsugarkitchen.com* 🕒 *Closed Mon. No dinner.*

$$$ AMERICAN

🍴 **Camino.** The first solo venture of chef-owner Russell Moore (a Chez Panisse alum of 21 years) and co-owner Allison Hopelain focuses on simple, seasonal, and straightforward dishes cooked in the enormous, crackling *camino* (Italian for "fireplace"). Everything is made with top-notch ingredients, including local sardines; grilled lamb and sausage with shell beans; and grilled white sea bass with green beans and new potatoes. The menu changes nightly and includes vegetarian options such as eggplant gratin. The restaurant is decorated in a Craftsman-meets-refectory style, with brick walls and two long redwood communal tables. Seasonally inspired cocktails from the small bar are not to be missed; the gin-based drink with house-made cherry and hibiscus bitters is notably delicious. [$] *Average main: $24* ✉ *3917 Grand Ave., at Boulevard Way, Lake Merritt* ☎ *510/547–5035* ⏲ *Closed Tues. No lunch (weekend brunch 10–2).*

$$ MEXICAN 🍴 **Doña Tomás.** A neighborhood favorite, this spot in Oakland's up-and-coming Temescal District serves seasonal Mexican fare to a hip but low-key crowd. Mexican textiles and art adorn walls in two long rooms; there's also a vine-covered patio. Banish all images of taquería grub and tuck into starters such as quesadillas filled with butternut squash and goat cheese and entrées such as *albondigas en sopa de zanahoria* (pork-and-beef meatballs in carrot puree). A fine selection of tequilas rounds out the offerings. [$] *Average main: $18* ✉ *5004 Telegraph Ave., near 51st St.* ☎ *510/450–0522* ⏲ *Closed Sun. and Mon. No lunch.*

$ CAFÉ 🍴 **L'Amyx Tea Bar.** Light through the large windows bathes the blond-wood tables, comfy chairs, and long bar, all filled with absorbed students, chatting friends, and tired shoppers in need of a boost. A small area in the back sells first-rate tea accoutrements, but sink into a couch or private nook to bask in much more than the usual cuppa. Try a tea smoothie or an herbal remedy such as Tealaxation. [$] *Average main: $4* ✉ *4179 Piedmont Ave., at Linda Ave., Piedmont* ☎ *510/594–8322.*

$ VIETNAMESE 🍴 **Le Cheval Restaurant.** This is a good place to sample *pho*, Hanoi-style beef noodle soup fragrant with star anise. Other entrées include lemon chicken, cubed beef steak, clay-pot snapper, and shark in coconut milk. It's hard to spend more than $20 for an entire meal unless you order the special crab (about $30). The complementary mini-bowls of soup that are placed on the table as soon as you sit down are a great balm to hungry diners although service is lightning-quick anyway. [$] *Average main: $12* ✉ *1019 Clay St., at 11th St., Downtown* ☎ *510/763–8495* ⏲ *No lunch Sun.*

$$ BELGIAN 🍴 **Luka's Taproom & Lounge.** Luka's is a real taste of downtown Oakland: hip and urban, with an unpretentious vibe. Diners nibble on *frites* any Belgian would embrace and entrées like *choucroute garni* (sauerkraut with duck confit, ham hock, and pork shoulder). The brews draw 'em in, too—you'd be hard-pressed to find a larger selection of Belgian beer this side of the pond—and the DJs in the adjacent lounge keep the scene going late. [$] *Average main: $22* ✉ *2221 Broadway, at West Grand Ave., Lake Merritt* ☎ *510/451–4677* ⏲ *No lunch Sat.*

$$$ MEDITERRANEAN 🍴 **Oliveto Cafe & Restaurant.** Respected chef Jonah Rhodehamel is at the helm of this locally renowned eatery that anchors Market Hall in the Rockridge neighborhood. The first-class dining room upstairs serves straightforward Italian cuisine; the menu changes daily, but might include house-made duck prosciutto, pan-seared swordfish, or spit-roasted leg of lamb. Downstairs, in the less pricey café ($–$$), everything from a morning espresso to pizza to a full-blown Italian meal (at half the upstairs price) can be enjoyed at one of the small tables or at the bar. [$] *Average main: $26* ✉ *5655 College Ave., at Keith Ave., Rockridge* ☎ *510/547–5356* ⏲ *No lunch weekends in restaurant.*

WHERE TO STAY

For expanded reviews, facilities, and current deals, visit Fodors.com.

5

$$ ⊡ **Waterfront Hotel.** One of Oakland's more appealing neighborhoods is
HOTEL home to this thoroughly modern waterfront hotel. **Pros:** great location;
dog-friendly. **Cons:** passing trains can be noisy; parking is pricey. **Trip-**
Advisor: "stylish remodel," "great customer service," "warm friendly
charm." $ Rooms from: $159 ⊠ 10 Washington St., Jack London
Square ☎ 510/836–3800, 800/729–3638 ⊕ www.waterfrontplaza.com
↩ 143 rooms.

NIGHTLIFE AND THE ARTS

Artists have found cheap rent and loft spaces in Oakland, giving rise to
an underground cultural scene—visual arts, indie music, spoken word,
film—that is definitely buzzing, especially in Uptown (which is pretty
much downtown). Trendy bars and clubs have also emerged—every-
thing from artisan breweries to all-out retro dives. The nightlife scene
here is less crowded and more intimate than what you'll find in San
Francisco. Music is just about everywhere, though the most popular
venues are downtown.

Fodor'sChoice **Café van Kleef.** Dutch artist Peter van Kleef's candle-strewn, funky café-
★ bar crackles with creative energy. Van Kleef has a lot to do with the
convivial atmosphere; the garrulous owner loves sharing tales about
his quirky, floor-to-ceiling collection of mementos, including what he
claims are Cassius Clay's boxing gloves and Dorothy's ruby slippers.
The café also has a consistently solid calendar of live music, heavy on
the jazz side. The drinks are quite possibly the stiffest in town. ⊠ 1621
Telegraph Ave., between 16th and 17th Sts., Lake Merritt ☎ 510/763–
7711 ⊕ www.cafevankleef.com.

Fox Theater. Willie Nelson, Counting Crows, Rebelution, and Rodrigo Y
Gabriela and their band C.U.B.A. have all been booked at this recently
renovated art-deco stunner that has good sight lines, a state-of-the-
art sound system and acoustics, and bars and other amenities aplenty.
⊠ 1807 Telegraph Ave., at 18th St., Uptown ☎ 510/548–3010 ⊕ www.
thefoxoakland.com.

The Layover Music Bar and Lounge. Bright, bold, and very hip, this hangout
filled with recycled furniture is constantly evolving because everything is
for sale, from the artwork to the pillows, rugs, and lamps. The busy bar
serves up organic cocktails, and depending on the night, the entertain-
ment might include comedy or live or DJ music. ⊠ 1517 Franklin St.,
near 15th St., Uptown ☎ 510/763–7711 ⊕ www.oaklandlayover.com.

Mua. Cuisine, cocktails, and culture—Mua puts it all together in a bright
and airy former garage: The chefs serve up beautifully crafted meals like
softshell crab and duck confit; the bartenders shake up elegant cocktails;
and the rich cultural offerings include poetry readings, art shows, DJ
music, and more. ⊠ 2442a Webster St., between 16th and 17th Sts.,
Uptown ☎ 510/238–1100 ⊕ www.muaoakland.com.

Paramount Theatre. The art-deco movie palace is home to the Oakland
East Bay Symphony and also presents ballet, comedy (Cedric, Sinbad,
Bill Cosby), well-known rock and other musical acts, and the occasional
classic film. ⊠ 2025 Broadway, at 20th St., Uptown ☎ 510/465–6400
⊕ www.paramounttheatre.com.

The Trappist. Grand pillars, brick walls, soft lighting, and the buzz of conversation set a warm and mellow tone inside this Victorian space that's been renovated to resemble a traditional Belgian pub. The setting is definitely a draw, but the real stars are the artisan beers: more than a hundred Belgian, Dutch, and North American ones. The light fare includes panini made with organic ingredients. ✉ *460 8th St., at Broadway, Old Oakland* ☎ *510/238–8900* ⊕ *www.thetrappist.com.*

Fodor's Choice **Yoshi's.** Oma Sosa and Charlie Hunter are among the musicians who
★ play at Yoshi's, one of the area's best jazz venues. Monday through Saturday shows start at 8 pm and 10 pm; Sunday shows usually start at 2 pm and 8 pm. The cover runs from $16 to $30. ✉ *510 Embarcadero St., between Washington and Clay Sts., Jack London Square* ☎ *510/238–9200* ⊕ *www.yoshis.com.*

SPORTS AND THE OUTDOORS

BASEBALL

Oakland A's. Billy Beane of *Moneyball* fame is the general manager of the American League baseball team. Same-day tickets can usually be purchased at the **O.co Coliseum** box office (Gate D). To get to the game, take a BART train to the Coliseum/Oakland Airport Station. ✉ *O.co Coliseum, 7000 Coliseum Way, off I–880, north of Hegenberger Rd.* ☎ *510/638–4900* ⊕ *oakland.athletics.mlb.com.*

BASKETBALL

Golden State Warriors. The National Basketball Association's Golden State Warriors play at the **Oracle Arena** from November through April. You can take a BART train to the game. Get off at the Coliseum/Oakland Airport Station. Warriors tickets are available through **Ticketmaster** (☎ *800/653-8000* ⊕ *www.ticketmaster.com*). ✉ *Oracle Arena, 7000 Coliseum Way, off I–880, north of Hegenberger Rd.* ☎ *510/986–2200, 888/479–4667* ⊕ *www.nba.com/warriors.*

FOOTBALL

Oakland Raiders. The National Football League's brawling Oakland Raiders play at **O.co Coliseum.** Purchase Raiders tickets through **Tickets.com** (☎ *800/653–8000* ⊕ *www.tickets.com*); except for high-profile games, they're easy to come by. ✉ *O.co Coliseum, 7000 Coliseum Way, off I–880, north of Hegenberger Rd.* ☎ *510/864–5000* ⊕ *www.raiders. com.*

SHOPPING

College Avenue is great for upscale strolling, shopping, and people-watching. The more casual streets around Lake Merritt and Grand Lake have smaller, less fancy boutiques.

Diesel. Wandering bibliophiles collect armfuls of the latest fiction and nonfiction here. The loftlike space, with its high ceilings and spare design, encourages airy contemplation, and on chilly days (a rarity) there's a fire going in the hearth. Keep an eye out for the excellent reading series. ✉ *5433 College Ave., at Kales Ave., Rockridge* ☎ *510/653–9965.*

Maison d'Etre. Close to the Rockridge BART station, this store epitomizes the Rockridge neighborhood's funky-chic shopping scene. Look for impulse buys like whimsical watches, imported fruit-tea blends, and a basket of funky slippers near the back. ⊠ *5640 College Ave., at Keith Ave., Rockridge* ☎ *510/658–2801.*

BERKELEY

2 miles northeast of Bay Bridge.

The birthplace of the Free Speech Movement, the radical hub of the 1960s, the home of arguably the nation's top public university, and the city whose government condemned the bombing of Afghanistan— Berkeley is all of those things. The city of 100,000 facing San Francisco across the bay is also culturally diverse, a breeding ground for social trends, a bastion of the counterculture, and an important center for Bay Area writers, artists, and musicians. Berkeley residents, students, and faculty spend hours nursing various coffee concoctions while they read, discuss, and debate at any of the dozens of cafés that surround the campus. Oakland may have Berkeley beat when it comes to cutting-edge arts, and the city may have forfeited some of its renegade 1960s spirit, as some residents say, but unless a guy in a hot-pink satin body suit, skullcap, and cape rides a unicycle around *your* town, you'll likely find that Berkeley remains plenty offbeat.

It's the quintessential university town, and many who graduated years ago still bask in daily intellectual conversation, great weather, and good food. Residents will walk out of their way to go to the perfect bread shop or consult with their favorite wine merchant. And every September, residents gently lampoon themselves during the annual "How Berkeley Can You Be?" parade and festival where they celebrate their tie-dyed past and consider its new incarnations.

ESSENTIALS

Visitor Information Berkeley Convention and Visitors Bureau ⊠ *2030 Addison St., #102* ☎ *510/549–7040* ⊕ *www.visitberkeley.com.*

GETTING HERE AND AROUND

BART is the easiest way to get to Berkeley from San Francisco. Alight at the Berkeley (not North Berkeley) Station, and walk a block up Center Street to get to the western edge of campus. AC Transit buses F and FS lines stop near the university and 4th Street shopping. By car, take Interstate 80 east across the Bay Bridge then take the University Avenue exit through downtown Berkeley to the campus or take the Ashby Avenue exit and turn left on Telegraph Avenue to the traditional campus entrance. Once you arrive, explore on foot. Berkeley is very pedestrian friendly.

EXPLORING

4th Street. An industrial area on 4th Street north of University Avenue has been converted into a pleasant shopping stretch, with popular eateries and shops selling handcrafted and eco-conscious goods. About six blocks long, this compact area (the action has spilled onto neighboring streets) is busiest on bright weekend afternoons. Stained Glass Garden, Hear Music, and the Crate and Barrel Outlet are among shoppers'

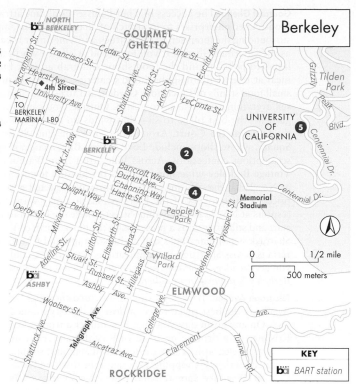

favorites, along with a mini-slew of upscale boutiques and wonderful paper stores. ✉ *4th St., between University Ave. and Delaware Sts.*

QUICK
BITES

Cheese Board Pizzeria. With a jazz combo playing in the storefront and a long line snaking down the block, Cheese Board taps into the pulse of the Gourmet Ghetto. The cooperatively owned takeout spot draws devoted customers with the smell of just-baked garlic, fresh vegetables, and perfect sauces. For just a nibble, bakery–cheese shop next door sells cookies, muffins, scones, bialys—you name it, they bake it. ✉ *1504–1512 Shattuck Ave., at Vine St.* ☎ *510/549-3055* ⊗ *Tues.–Fri. 11:30–2 and 4:30–7, Sat. 11:30–3.*

Elmwood. Shops and cafés pack two pleasant blocks of College Avenue in the Elmwood neighborhood south of the U.C. campus. You'll know you're here when you see the logo for the beloved art-house cinema and performance space, the **Elmwood theater,** near College and Ashby avenues, though you're just as apt to see a line snaking outside nearby **Ici Ice Cream,** at 2948 College. All the treats here are made on the premises. While you're waiting, check out the architectural details of the nearby pre–World War II storefronts. Century-old shingled houses line the tree-shaded streets nearby. ✉ *College Ave. between Russell and Webster Sts., Elmwood.*

Gourmet Ghetto. The success of Chez Panisse restaurant attracted other food-related enterprises to its stretch of Shattuck Avenue, and the area surrounding the intersection of Shattuck and Vine Street became known as the Gourmet Ghetto. If you love food at all, it's worth a couple of hours to poke around the food shops and grab a quick bite or a full meal at one of the neighborhood's eateries. Of special note are the small food stands of **Epicurious Garden,** at 1509–1513 Shattuck, which sell everything from sushi to gelato. Outside, you can find a terraced garden—the best place to sit—that winds up four levels and ends at the **Imperial Tea Court.** Around the corner on Vine Street is **Walnut Square,** whose shops include **Love at First Bite,** a cupcakery that sells scrumptious confections. Across Vine Street from Walnut Square, the **Vintage Berkeley** wineshop occupies the historic former pump house at No. 2113; the offerings here are shrewdly selected and reasonably priced. Coffee lovers of the Peet's persuasion may want to pay brief respects at No. 2124, at Walnut Street, where the famed roaster got its start and still maintains a presence. In the block north of Vine Street on Shattuck is popular **Saul's** deli and restaurant, and **Cheese Board Pizzeria** is across Shattuck from Epicurious Garden. We could go on, but you get the idea. ⊠ *Shattuck Ave. between Cedar and Rose Sts., North Berkeley* ⊕ *www.gourmetghetto.org.*

Telegraph Avenue. Berkeley's student-oriented thoroughfare, Telegraph Avenue is the best place to get a dose of the city's famed counterculture. On any given day you might encounter a troop of chanting Hare Krishnas or a drumming band of Rastafarians. First and foremost, however, Telegraph is a place for socializing and shopping, the only uniquely Berkeley shopping experience in town and a definite don't-miss. ■TIP➔ Take care at night, as things get edgier on Telegraph. The nearby People's Park, mostly harmless by day, is best avoided after sunset. Cafés, bookstores, poster shops, and street vendors line the avenue. T-shirt vendors and tarot-card readers come and go on a whim, but a few establishments—**Rasputin Music** (No. 2401), **Amoeba Music** (No. 2455), and **Moe's Books** (No. 2476)—are neighborhood landmarks. Allen Ginsberg wrote his acclaimed poem "Howl" at **Caffe Mediterraneum** (No. 2475), a relic of 1960s-era café culture that also lays claim to inventing the café latte.

★ **Tilden Regional Park.** The **Regional Parks Botanic Garden** is the star of
☼ this beautiful 2,000-acre park to the east of the Cal campus. Botanically speaking, a stroll through the garden, which focuses on native plants of California, provides a whirlwind tour of the entire state. You can pick up information about Tilden's other attractions, including its picnic spots, Lake Anza swimming site, golf course, and hiking trails (the paved **Nimitz Way** is a popular hike with wonderful views) at the garden's visitors center. Children love Tilden Park's miniature steam trains; Little Farm, where kids can feed the animals; and the vintage carousel with wooden animals. ⊠ *Regional Parks Botanic Garden, Wildcat Canyon Rd. and South Park Dr., Tilden Park* 🕾 *510/544–2747* ⊕ *www. ebparks.org/parks/tilden* 🎟 *Free to park and botanic garden* ⊙ *Daily 8 am–10 pm.*

University of California. The founding campus of California's university system, chartered in 1868, sits on a rising plain of oak trees split by Strawberry Creek. Frederick Law Olmsted, who designed New York City's Central Park, proposed the first campus plan. University architects over the years have included Bernard Maybeck as well as Julia Morgan, who designed Hearst Castle at San Simeon. The central campus occupies 178 acres, bounded by Bancroft Way to the south, Hearst Avenue to the north, Oxford Street to the west, and Gayley Road to the east. With more than 30,000 students and a full-time faculty of 1,400, the university, known simply as "Cal," is one of the leading intellectual centers in the United States and a major site for scientific research.

The **Berkeley Visitor Information Center** (⊠ *University Hall, Room 101, 2200 University Ave., at Oxford St.* ☎ *510/642–5215* ☉ *Weekdays 8:30–4:30*) is the starting point for the free, student-guided tours of the campus, which last 1½ hours and start at 10 on weekdays. (Weekend tours depart from Sather Tower.)

Student-guided campus tours leave from **Sather Tower** (⊠ *South of University Dr.* ▱*$2* ☉ *Weekdays 10–4, Sat. 10–5, Sun. 10–1:30 and 3–5*), the campus landmark popularly known as the Campanile, at 10 on Saturday and 1 on Sunday. The 307-foot structure, modeled on St. Mark's Tower in Venice and completed in 1914, can be seen for miles. The carillon is played daily at 7:50 am, noon, and 6 pm and for an extended 45-minute concert Sunday at 2. Take the elevator up 175 feet; then walk another 38 steps to the observation deck for a view of the campus and a close-up look at the iron bells, each of which weighs up to 10,500 pounds.

Sproul Plaza (⊠ *Telegraph Ave. and Bancroft Way*), just inside the U.C. Berkeley campus border on Bancroft Way, was the site of several free-speech and civil-rights protests in the 1960s. Today a lively panorama of political and social activists, musicians, and students show off Berkeley's flair for the bizarre. Preachers orate atop milk crates, amateur entertainers bang on makeshift drum sets, and protesters distribute leaflets about everything from marijuana to the Middle East. No matter what the combination, on weekdays when school is in swing, it always feels like a carnival. ■**TIP→** Walk through at noon for the liveliest show of student spirit.

The collection at the **University of California, Berkeley Art Museum & Pacific Film Archive** (⊠ *2626 Bancroft Way, between College Ave. and Bowditch St.* ☎ *510/642–0808, 510/642–1124 film-program information* ⊕ *www.bampfa.berkeley.edu* ▱*$10, free 1st Thurs. of month* ☉ *Wed.–Sun. 11–5, Fri. 11–9*) spans five centuries. Look for Jonathan Borofsky's enormous orange-red *Hammering Man* sculpture, which can be seen from the outside through the museum's floor-to-ceiling windows. Among the other noteworthy holdings here are a series of vibrant paintings by abstract expressionist Hans Hofmann. The downstairs galleries, which house rotating exhibits, are always free. The museum's raw foods café is famous, and you can also find some cooked options, too. The Pacific Film Archive, on the ground floor, has a library and hosts programs about historic and contemporary films, but its main theater sits across the street at 2575 Bancroft Way, near Bowditch Street.

> ### A TASTING TOUR
>
> For an unforgettable foodie experience, take Lisa Rogovin's **Culinary Walking Tour** (☎ *510/540–6444* 🌐 *www.gourmetghetto.org*). You'll taste your way through the Gourmet Ghetto, learn some culinary history, and meet the chefs behind the food. Tours run Thursday 11 am–2:15 pm and cost $75 per person.

Thanks to Berkeley's temperate climate, about 13,500 species of plants from all over the world flourish in the 34-acre **University of California Botanical Garden** (✉ *200 Centennial Dr.* ☎ *510/643–2755* 🌐 *botanicalgarden.berkeley.edu* 🎟 *$9, free 1st Thurs. of month* 🕒 *Daily 9–5. Closed 1st Tues. of month*). Free garden tours are given Thursday, Saturday, and Sunday at 1:30. Benches and shady picnic tables make this a relaxing place to take in breathtaking views.

At this dazzling hands-on **Lawrence Hall of Science** (✉ *Centennial Dr. near Grizzly Peak Blvd.* ☎ *510/642–5132* 🌐 *www.lawrencehallofscience.org* 🎟 *$12* 🕒 *Daily 10–5*), kids can look at insects under microscopes, solve crimes using chemical forensics, and explore the physics of baseball. On weekends there are special lectures, demonstrations, and planetarium shows. Popular (and free) stargazing sessions take place on the first and third Saturday of each month, weather permitting.

🌐 *www.berkeley.edu.*

WHERE TO EAT

Dining in Berkeley is a low-key affair; even in the finest restaurants, most folks dress casually. Late diners be forewarned: Berkeley is an "early to bed" kind of town.

$ SOUTHERN 🍴 **Angeline's Louisana Kitchen.** There's always a line winding out the door for the delicious food at Angeline's. The brick walls, maps of Louisana, ceiling fans, and true New Orleans music create a festive atmosphere that is both welcoming and exciting. Specialties include Voo Doo shrimp with blue lake beans, crawfish étouffée, and buttermilk fried chicken. A lot of love goes into the food here and the Creole pecan pie is so good, you'll be coming back for more. [$] *Average main: $14* ✉ *2261 Shattuck Ave* ☎ *510/548-6900.*

$ AMERICAN 🍴 **Bette's Oceanview Diner.** Buttermilk pancakes are just one of the specialties at this 1930s-inspired diner complete with checkered floors and burgundy booths. Huevos rancheros and lox and eggs are other breakfast options; kosher franks, generous slices of pizza, and a slew of sandwiches are available for lunch. The wait for a seat can be quite long; thankfully, 4th Street was made for strolling. **■ TIP→ If you're starving, head to Bette's to Go, next door, for takeout.** [$] *Average main: $10* ✉ *1807 4th St., near Delaware St., 4th Street* ☎ *510/644–3230* ✍ *Reservations not accepted* 🕒 *No dinner.*

$$ MEDITERRANEAN 🍴 **Café Rouge.** You can recover from 4th Street shopping in this spacious two-story bistro complete with zinc bar, skylights, and festive lanterns. The short, seasonal menu ranges from the sophisticated, such as rack of lamb and juniper-berry-cured pork chops, to the homey, like spit-roasted chicken or pork loin, or cheddar-topped burgers. If you visit

by day, be certain to peek at the meat market in the back. $ *Average main: $21 ⊠ 1782 4th St., at Delaware St., 4th Street ☎ 510/525–1440 ☽ No dinner Mon.*

$ ✕ **César.** In true Spanish style, dinners are served late at César, whose
SPANISH kitchen closes at 11:30 pm on Friday and Saturday and at 11 pm the rest of the week. Couples spill out from its street-level windows on warm nights, or rub shoulders at the polished bar or center communal table. Founded by a trio of former Chez Panisse chefs, César is like a first cousin to Chez Panisse, each restaurant recommending the other if there's a long wait ahead. For tapas and perfectly grilled *bocadillos* (small sandwiches), there's no better choice. The bar also makes a mean martini and has an impressive wine list. ■TIP→ Come early to get seated quickly and also to hear your tablemates; the room gets loud when the bar is in full swing. $ *Average main: $10 ⊠ 1515 Shattuck Ave., at Vine St., North Berkeley ☎ 510/883–0222 ⚐ Reservations not accepted.*

$$$$ ✕ **Chez Panisse Café & Restaurant.** At Chez Panisse even humble pizza is
AMERICAN reincarnated, with innovative toppings of the freshest local ingredients.
Fodor's Choice The downstairs portion of Alice Waters's legendary eatery is noted
★ for its formality and personal service. The daily-changing multicourse dinners are prix-fixe ($$$$), with the cost slightly lower on weekdays. Upstairs, in the informal café, the crowd is livelier, the prices are lower ($$–$$$), and the ever-changing menu is à la carte. The food is simpler, too: penne with new potatoes, arugula, and sheep's-milk cheese; fresh figs with Parmigiano-Reggiano cheese and arugula; and grilled tuna with Savoy cabbage, for example. Legions of loyal fans insist that Chez Panisse lives up to its reputation and delivers a dining experience well worth the price. Visiting foodies won't want to miss a meal here; be sure to make reservations a few weeks ahead of time. $ *Prix-fixe: $95 ⊠ 1517 Shattuck Ave., at Vine St., North Berkeley ☎ 510/548–5525 restaurant, 510/548–5049 café ⊕ www.chezpanisse.com ⚐ Reservations essential ☽ Closed Sun. No lunch in the restaurant.*

$ ✕ **Freehouse.** High ceilings, a warm fireplace, worn leather sofas, and a
MODERN BRITISH snooker table lend this restaurant the feel of a British country pub. The bar is bright, busy, and well stocked with whiskies and local beers on tap. The food, from sustainable sources, includes items like pot pies, cider-brined pork chops, and Loch Duart salmon burgers. There's a spacious patio outside. $ *Average main: $14 ⊠ 2700 Brancroft Way, at College Ave. ☎ 510/647–2300 ⊕ berkeleyfreehouse.com ⚐ Reservations not accepted.*

$$ ✕ **Gather.** Here organic, sustainable and all things Berkeley reside har-
MODERN moniously beneath one tasty roof. This vibrant, well-lighted eatery
AMERICAN boasts an inviting patio, comfy leather chairs, and a variety of shiny wood furnishings. Everything feels contemporary and local, especially the food. The stinging nettles pizza is refreshing and the grilled chicken with beluga lentils is oh so juicy. This is a haven for vegetarian, vegan, and gluten-free eaters, but there's plenty for meat eaters to choose from, too. And the desserts don't get much better than the chocolate budino with braised cherries and Sonoma salt. Yum, yum. $ *Average main: $20 ⊠ 2200 Oxford St. ☎ 510/809-0400.*

The pioneer restaurant Chez Panisse focuses on seasonal local ingredients.

$$ MEDITERRANEAN ★ 🍴 **Lalime's.** Inside a charming, flower-covered house, this restaurant serves dishes that reflect the entire Mediterranean region. The menu, constantly changing and unfailingly great, depends on the availability of fresh seasonal ingredients. Choices might include grilled ahi tuna or creamy Italian risotto. Light colors used in the dining room, which has two levels, help to create a cheerful mood. A star in its own right, Lalime's is a good second choice if Chez Panisse is booked. [$] *Average main: $22* ✉ *1329 Gilman St., at Tevlin St., North Berkeley* ☎ *510/527–9838* ✍ *Reservations essential* ⏲ *No lunch.*

$ MEXICAN 🍴 **Picante.** A barnlike space full of cheerful Mexican tiles and folk-art masks, Picante is a find for anyone seeking good Mexican food for a song. The *masa* (flour) is freshly ground for the tortillas and tamales, the salsas are complex, and the flavor combinations are inventive. Try tamales filled with butternut squash and chilies or a simple taco of roasted poblanos and sautéed onions; we challenge you to finish a plate of supernachos. [$] *Average main: $11* ✉ *1328 6th St., North Berkeley* ☎ *510/525–3121* ✍ *Reservations not accepted.*

$ AMERICAN 🍴 **Rick & Ann's.** Haute comfort food is the focus here. The brunches are legendary for quality and value, and customers line up outside the door before the restaurant opens on the weekend. If you come during prime brunch hours, expect a long wait, but the soft-style eggs are worth it. Pancakes, waffles, and French toast are more flavorful than usual, with variations such as potato-cheese and orange-rice pancakes. Lunch and dinner offer burgers, favorites such as Mom's macaroni and cheese, and chicken potpie, but always with a festive twist. Reservations are accepted 48 hours in advance for dinner and for lunch parties of six or more, but, alas, you can't reserve a table for brunch. [$] *Average* *main: $14 ✉ 2922 Domingo Ave., Claremont ☎ 510/649–8538 ⏲ No dinner Mon.*

$ AMERICAN 🍴 **Saul's.** Well known for its homemade sodas and enormous sandwiches, the Saul's of today also uses sustainably sourced seafood, grass-fed beef, and organic eggs. The restaurant is a Berkeley institution, and has a loyal clientele that swears by the pastrami sandwiches, stuffed cabbage rolls, and tuna melts. For breakfast, the challah French toast is so thick it's almost too big to bite and the deli omelets are served pancake style. The high ceilings and red-leather booths add to the friendly atmosphere. Don't overlook the glass deli case where you can order food to go. [$] *Average main: $13 ✉ 1475 Shattuck Ave., near Vine St., North Berkeley ☎ 510/848–3354 🌐 www.saulsdeli.com ✍ Reservations not accepted ⏲ Closed Thanksgiving and Yom Kippur.*

WHERE TO STAY

For inexpensive lodging, investigate University Avenue, west of campus. The area is noisy, congested, and somewhat dilapidated, but does include a few decent motels and chain properties. All Berkeley lodgings, except for the swanky Claremont, are strictly midrange.

For expanded reviews, facilities, and current deals, visit Fodors.com.

$ HOTEL 🏨 **The Bancroft Hotel.** Lovingly remodeled in 2012, this new green hotel is fresh, stylish and completely eco-friendly. **Pros:** heating under the floorboards; great rooftop deck; closest hotel in Berkeley to campus. **Cons:** some of the rooms are on the small side; bathrooms could be freshened up. **TripAdvisor:** "great staff," "beautiful but noisy," "great breakfast." [$] *Rooms from: $120 ✉ 2680 Bancroft Way ☎ 510/549-1000 🛏 22 rooms 🍽 Breakfast.*

$$$ HOTEL Fodor's Choice ★ 🏨 **Claremont Resort and Spa.** Straddling the Oakland–Berkeley border, the hotel beckons like a gleaming white castle in the hills, luring traveling executives that come for the business amenities, including T-1 Internet connections, guest email addresses, and oversize desks. **Pros:** amazing spa; supervised child care; some rooms have great views of the bay. **Cons:** parking is pricey; additional facilities charge for use of spa, tennis courts, pool, gym etc.; no Wi-Fi in rooms; breakfast is an additional fee. **TripAdvisor:** "excellent gym and good food," "Claremont bliss," "great facilities." [$] *Rooms from: $249 ✉ 41 Tunnel Rd., at Ashby and Domingo Aves., Claremont ☎ 510/843–3000, 800/551–7266 🌐 www.claremontresort.com 🛏 249 rooms, 30 suites.*

$$ HOTEL ★ 🏨 **Hotel Shattuck Plaza.** In 2009 this elegant boutique hotel in the heart of Berkeley underwent a major multimillion-dollar renovation, which successfully combined turn-of-the-20th-century glamour (the hotel was built in 1910) with all the contemporary amenities. **Pros:** central location; modern facilities; good views; great restaurant. **Cons:** pricey parking; limited fitness center. **TripAdvisor:** "very comfortable," "nice staff," "charming original Berkeley hotel." [$] *Rooms from: $185 ✉ 2086 Allston Way, at Shattuck Ave. ☎ 510/845–7300 🌐 www.hotelshattuckplaza.com 🛏 199 rooms, 17 suites.*

NIGHTLIFE AND THE ARTS

Berkeley Repertory Theatre. One of the region's highly respected resident professional companies and a Tony Award winner for Outstanding Regional Theatre (in 1997), the theater performs classic and contemporary plays from autumn to spring. Well-known pieces such as *Mother Courage* and *Oliver Twist* mix with edgier fare. The theater's complex is near BART's Downtown Berkeley Station. ⊠ *2025 Addison St.* ☎ *510/647–2949* ⊕ *www.berkeleyrep.org.*

Berkeley Symphony Orchestra. The works of 20th-century composers are a focus of this prominent orchestra, but traditional pieces are also performed. BSO plays a handful of concerts each year, in Zellerbach Hall and other locations. ⊠ *1942 University Ave., Suite 207* ☎ *510/841– 2800* ⊕ *www.berkeleysymphony.org.*

★ **Cal Performances.** The series, running from September through May at Zellerbach Hall and various other U.C. Berkeley venues, offers the Bay Area's most varied bill of internationally acclaimed artists in all disciplines, from classical soloists to the latest jazz, world-music, theater, and dance ensembles. Look for frequent campus colloquiums or preshow talks featuring Berkeley's professors. ⊠ *Zellerbach Hall, Telegraph Ave. and Bancroft Way* ☎ *510/642–9988* ⊕ *calperformances.org.*

Fodor's Choice **Freight & Salvage Coffeehouse.** Some of the most talented practitioners of
★ folk, blues, Cajun, and bluegrass perform in this alcohol-free space, one of the finest folk houses in the country. Most tickets are less than $20. ⊠ *2020 Addison St., between Shattuck and Milvia Sts.* ☎ *510/644–2020* ⊕ *www.thefreight.org.*

SHOPPING

Fodor's Choice **Amoeba Music.** Heaven for audiophiles, this legendary Berkeley favor-
★ ite is *the* place to head for new and used CDs, records, cassettes, and DVDs. The dazzling stock includes thousands of titles for all music tastes. The store even has its own record label. There are now branches in San Francisco and Hollywood, but this is the original. ⊠ *2455 Telegraph Ave., at Haste St.* ☎ *510/549–1125.*

Body Time. Founded in Berkeley in 1970, this local chain emphasizes the premium-quality ingredients it uses in its natural perfumes and skin-care and aromatherapy products. Sustainably harvested essential oils that you can combine and dilute to create your own personal fragrances are the specialty. Its distinct Citrus, Lavender-Mint, and China Rain scents are all popular. ⊠ *1942 Shattuck Ave., at Berkeley Way* ☎ *510/841–5818.*

Kermit Lynch Wine Merchant. Lynch's newsletters describing his finds are legendary, as is his friendship with Alice Waters of Chez Panisse. Credited with taking American appreciation of French wine to another level, this shop is a great place to peruse as you educate your palate. The friendly salespeople can direct you to the latest French bargains. ⊠ *1605 San Pablo Ave., at Dwight Way* ☎ *510/524–1524.*

★ **Moe's Books.** The spirit of Moe—the cantankerous, cigar-smoking late proprietor—lives on in this four-story house of books. Students and professors come here for used books, including large sections of literary and cultural criticism, art books, and literature in foreign languages. ✉ *2476 Telegraph Ave., near Haste St.* ☎ *510/849–2087.*

THE COASTAL PENINSULA

Bookended by San Francisco and Silicon Valley are some surprisingly low-key and unspoiled natural treasures. The vistas here are the Pacific and rolling hills, making it easy to forget the hustle and bustle that's just out of sight.

MOSS BEACH

20 miles south of San Francisco on Hwy. 1.

Moss Beach was a busy outpost during Prohibition, when regular shipments of liquid contraband from Canada were unloaded at the secluded beach and hauled off to San Francisco. The town stayed under the radar out of necessity, with only one local hotel and bar (now the Distillery) where Bay Area politicians and gangsters could go for a drink while waiting for their shipments. Today, although it has grown into a cheerful surfing town with charming inns and restaurants, it is still all but invisible from the highway—a good hideaway for those allergic to crowds.

GETTING HERE AND AROUND

To get to Moss Beach from San Francisco, take Highway 1, also known as the Coast Highway, south along the San Mateo coast.

Fitzgerald Marine Reserve. Arguably, the biggest Moss Beach attraction is this 3-mile stretch of bluffs and tide pools. Since the reserve was protected in 1969, scientists have discovered 25 new aquatic species here; depending on the tide, you'll most likely find shells, anemones, or starfish. ✉ *California and North Lake Sts.* ☎ *650/728–3584*

Mavericks. Just off the coast at Moss Beach is one of the biggest surfing breaks in the world. Waves here have reportedly reached 60 feet in height, and surfers get towed out to them by Jet Skis. The break is a mile offshore, so seeing it from the coast can be tough and requires a challenging hike.

WHERE TO EAT

$$ SEAFOOD

🍴 **Sam's Chowder House.** An East Coast–style seafood joint in the Bay Area? This waterfront restaurant isn't textbook Cape Cod, but that's OK—dine here, and you'll get the best of both coasts: true New England–style clam chowder and lump crab cakes and ahi tuna poke with sesame oil and scallions or local halibut with mango salsa. Indoor seats are in one of several long dining rooms; outdoor seats are warmed by gas fire pits and heaters on chilly days; and every seat in the house looks out to the water. The attached market sells fresh fish and picnic food. [$] *Average main: $22* ✉ *4210 N. Hwy. 1* ☎ *650/712–0245* 🌐 *www.samschowderhouse.com.*

HALF MOON BAY

7 miles south of Moss Beach on Hwy. 1.

It may be the largest and most visited of the coastal communities, but Half Moon Bay is still by all measures a small town. Looking from the highway you'd hardly even know it was there. Turn onto Main Street, though, and you'll find five blocks of galleries, shops, and cafés, many of which occupy renovated 19th-century buildings. While traditionally this was an agricultural center for local growers of artichokes and other coastal crops, in recent years it has also come to be a haven for Bay Area retirees.

GETTING HERE AND AROUND

To get to Half Moon Bay from San Francisco, take Highway 1, also known as the Coast Highway, south along the length of the San Mateo coast.

Half Moon Bay Art and Pumpkin Festival The town comes to life on the third weekend in October, when 250,000 people gather for this festival. Highlights include a parade, pie-eating contests, street performers, and a "weigh-off" of giant pumpkins, some as big as 1,200 pounds.

Half Moon Bay State Beach. This 4-mile stretch of is perfect for long walks, kite flying, and picnic lunches, though the 50°F water and dangerous currents make swimming inadvisable. There are three access points, one in Half Moon Bay and two south of town off the highway. To find them, look for road signs that have a picture of footsteps. ✉ *Hwy. 1, west of Main St.* ☎ *650/726–8819.*

WHERE TO EAT

$$$ ITALIAN ★ 🍴 **Pasta Moon.** As one of the best restaurants on the coast between San Francisco and Monterey, Pasta Moon boasts a friendly, laid-back staff and fun, jovial crowd. Local produce flavors the seasonal menu, which includes such highlights as wood-fired pizzas and braised lamb shank. Beware: the dining room can get slightly noisy on weekend nights, when live music plays in the bar and lounge. [$] *Average main: $24* ✉ *315 Main St.* ☎ *650/726–5125* 🌐 *www.pastamoon.com.*

WHERE TO STAY

$$$$ ★ 🏨 **The Ritz-Carlton.** With its enormous and elegantly decorated rooms, secluded oceanfront property, and a staff that waits on guests hand and foot, this golf and spa resort defines opulence. **Pros:** four-star service; total luxury; ocean views. **Cons:** formal; not within walking distance of anything. [$] *Rooms from: $475* ✉ *1 Miramontes Point Rd.* ☎ *650/712–7000 or 800/241–3333* 🌐 *www.ritzcarlton.com* 🛏 *239 rooms, 22 suites.*

PESCADERO

17 miles south of Half Moon Bay on Hwy. 1.

As you walk down Stage Road, Pescadero's main street, it's hard to believe you're only 30 minutes from Silicon Valley. If you could block out the throngs of weekend cyclists, the downtown area could almost serve as the backdrop for a western movie.

GETTING HERE AND AROUND

Pescadero is 2 miles inland from Highway 1 on Pescadero Creek Road.

Harley Farms. There's cuteness overload at this farm, a restored 1910 farm with 200 alpine goats on 12 acres of pasture. It's a fully operational dairy, renowned for its delicious cheeses: chevre, fromage blanc, ricotta, and feta. A two-hour tour follows the milk trail as it moves from goat to dairy, then from curd to cheese. During the week you can walk around the yard and read detailed signage describing the buildings and operations. Purchase a ticket for the tour and you may get to hold a newborn kid. The Harley Farms Shop sells cheese (samples available), lotions, soaps, and gift items. Monthly dinners in the old hay loft showcase local, in-season produce. ⊠ *205 North St.* ☎ *650/879–0480* ⊕ *www.harleyfarms.com* ✉ *Tours $20* ⊙ *Shop daily 11 to 5; tours weekends at 11 and 1.*

Pescadero State Beach. If a quarantine is not in effect (watch for signs), from November through April you can look for mussels amid tidal pools and rocky outcroppings at this beach, then roast them at the barbecue pits. Any time of year is good for exploring the beach, the north side of which has several secluded spots along sandstone cliffs. Across U.S. 101, the **Pescadero Marsh Natural Preserve** has hiking trails that cover 600 acres of marshland. Early spring and fall are the best times to come, when there are lots of migrating birds and other wildlife to see. ⊠ *14½ miles south of Half Moon Bay on Hwy. 1* ☎ *650/879–2170* ✉ *Free, parking $8* ⊙ *Daily 8 am–sunset.*

AÑO NUEVO STATE RESERVE

13 miles south of Pescadero on Hwy. 1.

GETTING HERE AND AROUND

You need your own vehicle to get here. The reserve is on Highway 1, 13 miles south of Pescadero and 21 miles north of Santa Cruz.

Año Nuevo State Reserve. At the height of mating season, upward of 4,000 elephant seals congregate at Año Nuevo, one of the world's only approachable mainland rookeries. The seals are both vocal and spectacularly big (especially the males, which can weigh up to 2½ tons), and some are in residence year-round. An easy, 1½-hour round-trip walk takes you to the dunes, from which you can look down onto the animals lounging on the shoreline. Note that during mating season (mid-December through March), visitors may do the hike only as part of a 2½-hour guided tour, for which reservations must be made well in advance. The area's visitor center has a fascinating film about the seals and some natural-history exhibits (including a sea otter's pelt that you can touch). Dogs are not allowed, even in cars in the parking lot. ⊠ *Hwy. 1, 13 miles south of Pescadero* ☎ *650/879–2025, 800/444–4445 for tour reservations* ✉ *Tour $7, parking $10* ⊙ *Guided tours leave every 15 mins, mid-Dec.–Mar., daily 8:45–3.*

BIG BASIN REDWOODS STATE PARK

17 miles north of Santa Cruz on Hwy. 1.

GETTING HERE AND AROUND

You need your own vehicle to get here. Coming from the coast, access the park at Waddell Creek (off Highway 1, 17 miles north of Santa Cruz), where a confluence of waterways pours out of the redwoods and into the ocean.

Big Basin Redwoods State Park. California's oldest state park is the best place to see old-growth redwoods without going north of San Francisco (and it's far less crowded than Muir Woods and other famous spots). The parkland ranges from sea level up to 2,000 feet in elevation, which means the landscape changes often, from dark redwood groves to oak pastures that are deep green in winter and bleached nearly white in summer. The mountain setting also makes for countless waterfalls, most visible during the winter rains. The visitor center is inland, at park headquarters in Boulder Creek. Staffing at the park's coastal entrance is spotty, but there are always park information and camping check-in available at a self-service kiosk.

A short walk on the Marsh Trail leads to the **Rancho Del Oso Nature Center** (☎ *831/427–2288* ☉ *Weekends noon–4*), which has natural-history exhibits and is the starting point for several self-guided nature walks.

Mountain bikers, horseback riders, and hikers can take the nearly level Canyon Road (a dirt fire road) back up the creek and into the woods. Hikers looking for solitude might consider a more strenuous, uphill climb on Clark Connection to Westridge Trail, which rewards hard work with spectacular views of the ocean. Those who don't want to go anywhere can just stay on the windswept beach, where the main attraction is watching kite surfers get huge air on the windy shoreline waves. ✉ *21600 Big Basin Way, Boulder Creek* ☎ *831/338–8860* ☑ *$10 parking fee.*

The Wine Country

WORD OF MOUTH

"The entire Napa Valley is much smaller than the Sonoma County Wine Country area. The farther north you go, the more expensive it is for hotels . . . Calistoga is at the north end, the city of Napa is at the south end. From there it's about a 30-minute drive through the Alexander Valley to Healdsburg."

—elnap29

WELCOME TO WINE COUNTRY

TOP REASONS TO GO

★ **Biking:** Cycling is one of the best ways to see the Wine Country—the Russian River and Dry Creek valleys, in Sonoma County, are particularly beautiful.

★ **Browsing the farmers' markets:** Many towns in Napa and Sonoma have seasonal farmers' markets, each rounding up an amazing variety of local produce.

★ **Wandering di Rosa:** Though this art and nature preserve is just off the busy Carneros Highway, it's a relatively unknown treasure. The galleries and gardens are filled with hundreds of pieces of art.

★ **Canoeing on the Russian River:** Trade in your car keys for a paddle and glide down the Russian River in Sonoma County. May through October is the best time to be on the water.

★ **Touring Wineries:** Let's face it: this is the reason you're here, and the range of excellent sips to sample would make any oeno-phile (or novice drinker, for that matter) giddy.

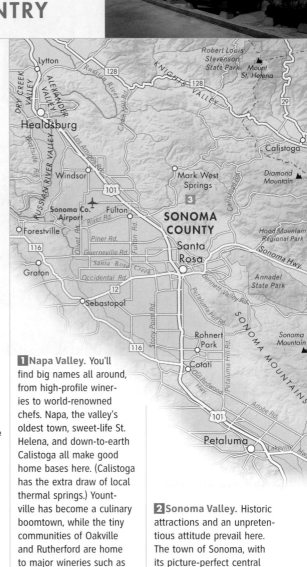

1 Napa Valley. You'll find big names all around, from high-profile wineries to world-renowned chefs. Napa, the valley's oldest town, sweet-life St. Helena, and down-to-earth Calistoga all make good home bases here. (Calistoga has the extra draw of local thermal springs.) Yountville has become a culinary boomtown, while the tiny communities of Oakville and Rutherford are home to major wineries such as Robert Mondavi and Grgich Hills. Rutherford in particular is the source for outstanding Cabernet Sauvignon.

2 Sonoma Valley. Historic attractions and an unpretentious attitude prevail here. The town of Sonoma, with its picture-perfect central plaza, is rich with 19th-century buildings. Glen Ellen, meanwhile, has a special connection with author Jack London.

GETTING ORIENTED

The Napa and Sonoma valleys run roughly parallel, northwest to southeast, and are separated by the Mayacamas Mountains. Northwest of the Sonoma Valley are several more important viticultural areas in Sonoma County, including the Dry Creek, Alexander, and Russian River valleys. The Carneros region, which spans southern Sonoma and Napa counties, is just north of San Pablo Bay. Coombsville, recently recognized as a discrete wine region, sits in the southeastern corner of Napa Valley and is the closest of all local wine regions to San Francisco.

6

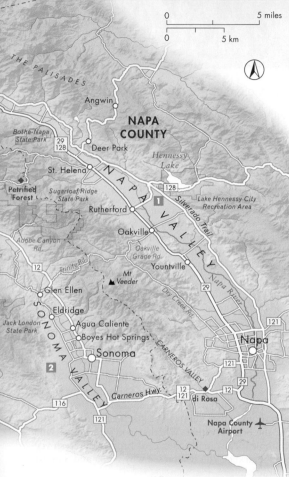

3 Elsewhere in Sonoma. The winding, rural roads here feel a world away from Napa's main drag. The lovely Russian River, Dry Creek, and Alexander valleys are all excellent places to seek out Pinot Noir, Zinfandel, and Sauvignon Blanc. The small town of Healdsburg gets lots of attention, thanks to its terrific restaurants, bed-and-breakfasts, and chic boutiques.

Updated by
Matt Villano

Life is lived well in the California Wine Country. Eating and drinking are cultivated as high arts. If you've been day-dreaming about driving through vineyards, stopping for a wine tasting or a picnic, well, that fantasy is just everyday life here.

It's little wonder that so many visitors to San Francisco take a day or two—or five or six—to unwind in the Napa and Sonoma valleys. They join the locals in the tasting rooms, from serious wine collectors making their annual pilgrimages to wine newbies who don't know the difference between a Merlot and Mourvèdre but are eager to learn.

The state's wine industry is booming, and the Napa and Sonoma valleys have long led the field. For instance, in 1975 Napa Valley had no more than 20 wineries; today there are nearly 400. A recent up-and-comer is the Carneros region, which overlaps Napa and Sonoma counties at the head of the San Francisco Bay. Another exciting area: Coombsville, in southeastern Napa, which recently received an official AVA (American Viticultural Area) designation recognizing its unique characteristics.

Great dining and wine go hand in hand, and the local viticulture has naturally encouraged a robust passion for food. Several outstanding chefs have taken root here, sealing the area's reputation as one of the best restaurant destinations in the country. The lust for fine food doesn't stop at the doors of the bistros, either. Whether you visit an artisanal olive-oil producer, nibble locally made cheese, or browse the fresh vegetables in the farmers' markets, you'll soon see why Napa and Sonoma are a food-lover's paradise.

Napa and Sonoma counties are also rich in history. In the town of Sonoma, for example, you can explore buildings from California's Spanish and Mexican past. Some wineries, such as Napa Valley's Beringer, have cellars or tasting rooms dating to the late 1800s. The town of Calistoga is a flurry of Steamboat Gothic architecture, gussied up with the fretwork favored by late-19th-century spa goers. Modern architecture is the exception rather than the rule, but one standout example is the postmodern extravaganza of Clos Pegase winery in Calistoga.

Binding all these temptations together is the sheer scenic beauty of the place. Much of Napa Valley's landscape unspools in orderly, densely planted rows of vines. Sonoma's vistas are broken by rolling hills or stands of ancient oak and madrone trees. Even the climate cooperates, as the warm summer days and refreshingly cool evenings that make the area one of the world's best grape-growing regions make perfect weather for traveling, too. If you're inspired to dig further into the Wine Country, grab a copy of *Fodor's InFocus Napa & Sonoma* or the in-depth *Compass American Guide: California Wine Country*.

PLANNING

WHEN TO GO

"Crush," the term used to indicate the season when grapes are picked and crushed, usually takes place in September or October, depending on the weather. From September until November the entire Wine Country celebrates its bounty with street fairs and festivals. The Sonoma County Harvest Fair, with its famous grape stomp, is held the first weekend in October. Golf tournaments, wine auctions, and art and food fairs occur throughout fall.

In season (April through November), Napa Valley draws crowds of tourists, and traffic along Highway 29 from St. Helena to Calistoga is often backed up on weekends. The Sonoma Valley, Santa Rosa, and Healdsburg are less crowded (though even that is changing). In season and over holiday weekends it's best to book lodging, restaurant, and winery reservations at least a month in advance. Many wineries give tours at specified times and require appointments.

To avoid crowds, visit the Wine Country during the week and get an early start (most wineries open around 10). Because many wineries close as early as 4 or 4:30—and few are open past 5—you'll need to get a reasonably early start if you want to fit in more than one or two, especially if you're going to enjoy the leisurely lunch customary in the Wine Country. Summer is usually hot and dry, and autumn can be even hotter, so dress appropriately if you go during these times.

GETTING HERE AND AROUND

AIR TRAVEL

If you'd like to bypass San Francisco or Oakland, you can fly directly to the small Charles M. Schulz Sonoma County Airport (STS) in Santa Rosa on Horizon Air, which has direct flights from Los Angeles, Portland, Las Vegas, and Seattle. Rental cars are available from Avis, Budget, Enterprise, and Hertz at the airport.

BUS TRAVEL

Bus travel is an inconvenient way to explore the Wine Country. Service is infrequent and buses from San Francisco can only get you to Santa Rosa or the town of Vallejo, south of Napa—neither of which is close to the vineyards. Sonoma County Transit offers daily bus service to points all over the county. VINE (Valley Intracity Neighborhood Express) provides bus service within the city of Napa and between other Napa Valley towns.

304 <   **The Wine Country**

Bus Lines Greyhound ☎ *800/231-2222* ⊕ *www.greyhound.com*. **Sonoma County Transit** ☎ *707/576-7433, 800/345-7433* ⊕ *www.sctransit.com*. **VINE** ☎ *707/251-2800, 800/696-6443* ⊕ *www.nctpa.net/routes-schedules/vine.html*.

CAR TRAVEL

Driving your own car is by far the best way to explore the Wine Country. Well-maintained roads zip through the centers of the Napa and Sonoma valleys, while scenic routes thread through the backcountry. Distances between towns are fairly short, and you can often drive from one end of the Napa or Sonoma valley to the other in less than an hour—if there's no significant traffic. This may be a relatively rural area, but the usual rush hours still apply, and high-season weekend traffic can be excruciatingly slow, especially on Highway 29.

Five major roads cut through the Napa and Sonoma valleys. U.S. 101 and Highways 12 and 121 travel through Sonoma County. Highway 29 heads north from Napa. The 25-mile Silverado Trail, which runs parallel to Highway 29 north from Napa to Calistoga, is Napa Valley's more scenic, less-crowded alternative to Highway 29.

■**TIP→** If you're wine tasting, either select a designated driver or be careful of your wine intake. (When you're taking just a sip or two of any given wine, it can be hard to keep track of how much you're drinking.) Also, keep in mind that you'll likely be sharing the road with cyclists and joggers; keep a close eye on the shoulder.

When calculating the time it will take you to drive between the Napa and Sonoma valleys, remember that the Mayacamas Mountains are between the two. If it's not too far out of your way, you might want to travel between the two valleys along Highway 12/121 to the south, or along Highway 128 to the north, to avoid the slow, winding drive on the Oakville Grade, which connects Oakville, in Napa, and Glen Ellen, in Sonoma.

From San Francisco to Napa: Cross the Golden Gate Bridge, then go north on U.S. 101. Next go east on Highway 37 toward Vallejo, then north on Highway 121, also called the Carneros Highway. Turn left (north) when Highway 121 runs into Highway 29. This should take about 1½ hours when traffic is light.

From San Francisco to Sonoma: Cross the Golden Gate Bridge, then go north on U.S. 101, east on Highway 37 toward Vallejo, and north on Highway 121, aka the Carneros Highway. When you reach Highway 12, take it north. If you're going to any of the Sonoma County destinations north of the valley, take U.S. 101 all the way north through Santa Rosa to Healdsburg. This should take about an hour, not counting substantial traffic.

From Berkeley and other East Bay towns: Take Interstate 80 north to Highway 37 west, then on to Highway 29 north. To head up the Napa Valley, continue on Highway 29; to reach Sonoma County, turn off Highway 29 onto Highway 121 heading north. Getting from Berkeley to Napa will take at least 45 minutes, from Berkeley to Sonoma at least an hour.

RESTAURANTS

Star chefs from around the world have come into the Wine Country's orbit, drawn by the area's phenomenal produce, artisanal foods, and wines. These days, many visitors come to Napa and Sonoma as much for the restaurants' tasting menus as for the wineries' tasting rooms.

Although excellent meals can be found virtually everywhere in the region, the small town of Yountville has become a culinary crossroads under the influence of chef Thomas Keller. If a table at Keller's famed French Laundry is out of reach, keep in mind that he's also behind a number of more modest restaurants in town. In St. Helena the elegant Restaurant at Meadowood has achieved almost as much critical acclaim as the French Laundry, yet is considerably easier to get into. And the buzzed-about restaurants in Sonoma County, including Cyrus and Farmhouse Inn, offer plenty of mouthwatering options.

Inexpensive eateries include high-end delis that serve superb picnic fare, and brunch is a cost-effective strategy at pricey restaurants, as is sitting at the bar and ordering a few appetizers instead of sitting down to a full-blown meal.

With few exceptions (*which are noted in individual restaurant listings*), dress is informal. Where reservations are indicated as essential, you may need to make them a week or more ahead. In summer and early fall you may need to book several weeks ahead.

Prices in the restaurant reviews are the average cost of a main course at dinner or, if dinner is not served, at lunch (excluding sales tax).

HOTELS

Napa and Sonoma know the tourism ropes well; their inns and hotels range from low-key to utterly luxurious, and generally maintain high standards. Most of the bed-and-breakfasts are in historic Victorian and Spanish buildings, and the breakfast part of the equation often involves fresh local produce. The newer hotels tend to have a more modern, streamlined aesthetic and elaborate, spa-like bathrooms. Many hotels and B&Bs have excellent restaurants on their grounds, and those that don't are still just a short drive away from gastronomic bliss.

However, all of this comes with a hefty price tag. As the cost of vineyards and grapes has risen, so have lodging rates. Santa Rosa, the largest population center in the area, has the widest selection of moderately priced rooms. Try there if you've failed to reserve in advance or have a limited budget. In general, all accommodations in the area often have lower rates on weeknights, and prices are about 20% lower in winter.

On weekends, two- or even three-night minimum stays are commonly required, especially at smaller inns and B&Bs. If you'd prefer to stay a single night, though, innkeepers are usually more flexible in winter. Many B&Bs book up long in advance of the summer and fall seasons. Many B&Bs and small inns also discourage the presence of children though fall short of actually prohibiting them. If you're traveling with children, be sure to ask about them when booking to make sure they will receive a warm welcome.

Prices in the hotel reviews are the lowest cost of a standard double room in high season. Prices do not include taxes (as high as 14%, depending on the region).

Hotel reviews have been condensed for this book. Please go to Fodors. com for expanded reviews of each property.

BED-AND-BREAKFAST ASSOCIATIONS

Contacts **Bed & Breakfast Association of Sonoma Valley** ☎ 800/969–4667 ⊕ www.sonomabb.com. **The Wine Country Inns of Sonoma County** ☎ 800/946–3268 ⊕ www.winecountryinns.com.

TOURS

Full-day guided tours of the Wine Country generally include lunch, and cost about $60–$100 per person. Reservations are usually required.

Beau Wine Tours. Based in downtown Sonoma, this outfitter organizes personalized tours of Napa and Sonoma in limos, vans, and shuttle buses. ✉ *21707 8th St. E, Sonoma* ☎ *707/938–8001, 800/387–2328* ⊕ *www.beauwinetours.com.*

Gray Line. The national outfitter offers a tour that covers the southern Napa and Sonoma valleys in a single day, with stops for shopping and sightseeing at Sonoma Plaza and lunch in Yountville. ✉ *Pier 43½, Embarcadero, San Francisco* ☎ *415/434–8687, 888/428–6937* ⊕ *www. grayline.com.*

Great Pacific Tour Co. This friendly outfitter operates full-day tours of Napa and Sonoma, including a restaurant lunch and a tour at Domaine Chandon. Tours are offered in passenger vans that seat 14. ✉ *518 Octavia St., Hayes Valley, San Francisco* ☎ *415/626–4499* ⊕ *www. greatpacifictour.com.*

Wine Country Bikes. This family-owned Healdsburg outfitter rents bikes by the day and organizes one-day and multi-day trips throughout Sonoma County. ✉ *61 Front St., Healdsburg* ☎ *707/473–0610, 866/922–4537* ⊕ *www.winecountrybikes.com.*

VISITOR INFORMATION

Napa Valley Welcome Center. Visitors love the Napa Valley Wecome Center, a downtown storefront offering everything from baked goods to information about winery tours and recreation. ✉ *600 Main St., Napa* ☎ *707/251–5895* ⊕ *www.legendarynapavalley.com.*

THE NAPA VALLEY

When it comes to wine production in the United States, Napa Valley rules the roost, with nearly 400 wineries and many of the biggest brands in the business. Vastly diverse soils and microclimates give Napa winemakers the chance to make a tremendous variety of wines. But what's the area like beyond the glossy advertising and boldface names?

The small towns strung along Highway 29 are where wine-industry workers live, and they're also where most of the area lodging is. Napa—the valley's largest town—lures with its growing cultural attractions and accommodations that are (relatively) reasonably priced. A few miles

Continued on page 316

Napa Valley

WINE TASTING *in* NAPA *and* SONOMA

VISITING WINERIES

Napa and Sonoma are outstanding destinations for both wine newcomers and serious wine buffs. Tasting rooms range from modest to swanky, offering everything from a casual conversation over a few sips of wine to in-depth tours of winemaking facilities and vineyards. And there's a tremendous variety of wines to taste. The one constant is a deep, shared pleasure in the experience of wine tasting.

Wineries in Napa and Sonoma range from faux châteaux with vast gift shops to rustic converted barns where you might have to step over the vintner's dog in the doorway. Many are regularly open to the public, usually daily from around 10 am to 5 pm. Others require advance reservations to visit, and still others are closed to the public entirely. When in doubt, call ahead.

There are many, many more wineries in Napa and Sonoma than we could possibly include here. Free maps pinpointing most of them are widely available, though; ask the staff at the tasting rooms you visit or look for the ubiquitous free tourist magazines.

Pick a designated driver before setting out for the day. Although wineries rarely advertise it, many will provide a free nonalcoholic drink for the designated driver; it never hurts to ask.

Fees. In the past few years, tasting fees have skyrocketed. Most Napa wineries charge $10 to $20 to taste four or so wines, though $30, $40 or even $50 fees aren't unheard of. Sonoma wineries are often a bit cheaper, in the $5 to $15 range, and you'll still find the occasional freebie.

Some winery tours are free, in which case you're usually required to pay a separate fee if you want to taste the wine. If you've paid a fee for the tour—often $15 to $30—your wine tasting is usually included in that price.

The tantalizing pop of a cork. Roads unspooling through hypnotically even rows of vines. Sun glinting through a glass of sparkling wine or ruby colored cabernet. If these are your daydreams, you won't be disappointed when you get to Napa and Sonoma. The vineyard-blanketed hills, shady town squares, and ivy-draped wineries—not to mention the luxurious restaurants, hotels, and spas— really *are* that captivating.

(opposite page) Carneros vineyards in autumn, Napa Valley. (top) Pinot Gris grapes (bottom) Bottles from Far Niente winery.

MAKING THE MOST OF YOUR TIME

■**Call ahead.** Some wineries require reservations to visit or tour. If you have your heart set on visiting a specific place, double-check their availability.

■**Come on weekdays**, especially if you're visiting during high season (May to November), to avoid traffic-clogged roads and crowded tasting rooms. For more info on the best times of year to visit, see this chapter's Planner.

■**Get an early start.** Tasting rooms are often deserted before 11 am or so, when most visitors are still lingering over a second cup of coffee. If you come early, you'll have the staff's undivided attention. You'll usually encounter the largest crowds between 3 and 5 pm.

■**Consider skipping Napa.** If you've got less than two days to spend in the Wine Country, dip into the Carneros area or the Sonoma Valley rather than Napa Valley or northern Sonoma County. Though you might find fewer big-name wineries and critically acclaimed

(top) Sipping and swirling in the De Loach tasting room. (bottom) Learning about barrel aging at Robert Mondavi Winery.

restaurants, these regions are only about an hour and half away from the city . . . if you don't hit traffic.

■**Divide your attention.** If you're lucky enough to have three nights or more here, split your overnights between Napa and Sonoma to easily see the best that both counties have to offer.

Domaine Carneros.

AT THE BAR

In most tasting rooms, you'll be handed a list of the wines available that day. The wines will be listed in a suggested tasting order, starting with the lightest-bodied whites, progressing to the most intense reds, and ending with dessert wines. If you can't decide which wines to choose, tell the server what types of wines you usually like and ask for a recommendation.

The server will pour you an ounce or so of each wine you select. As you taste it, feel free to take notes or ask questions. Don't be shy—the staff are there to educate you about their wine. If you don't like a wine, or you've simply tasted enough, feel free to pour the rest into one of the dump buckets on the bar.

TOURS

Tours tend to be the most exciting (and the most crowded) in September and October, when the harvest and crush-

ing are underway. Tours typically last from 30 minutes to an hour and give you a brief overview of the winemaking process. At some of the older wineries, the tour guide might focus on the history of the property.

■ TIP→ If you plan to take any tours, wear comfortable shoes, since you might be walking on wet floors or dirt or gravel pathways or stepping over hoses or other equipment.

MONEY-SAVING TIPS

■ Many hotels and B&Bs distribute coupons for free or discounted tastings to their guests—don't forget to ask.

■ If you and your travel partner don't mind sharing a glass, servers are happy to let you split a tasting.

■ Some wineries will refund all or part of the tasting fee if you buy a bottle, making it so much easier to rationalize buying that $80 bottle of cabernet.

■ Almost all wineries will also waive the fee if you join their wine club program. However, this typically commits you to buying a certain number of bottles of their wine for a period of time, so be sure you really like their wines before signing up.

Preston Vineyards bottles only estate-grown grapes.

TOP 2-DAY ITINERARIES

First-Timer's Napa Tour

Start: Oxbow Public market, Napa. Get underway by browsing the shops selling wines, spices, locally grown produce, and other fine foods, for a taste of what the Wine Country has to offer.

Inglenook, Rutherford. The tour here is a particularly fun way to learn about the history

of Napa winemaking—and you can see the old, atmospheric, ivy-covered château.

Frog's Leap, Rutherford. Friendly, unpretentious, and knowledgeable staff makes this place great for wine newbies. (Make sure you get that advance reservation lined up.)

Dinner and Overnight: St. Helena. Spluge at Meadowood Resort and you won't need to leave the property for an

Domaine Carneros

di Rosa Preserve

Old Sonoma Rd.

121
12

Oxbow Public Market
Napa
29

NAPA COUNTY

Robert Mondavi

Far Niente

Yountville
Oakville

KEY

First-Timer's Napa Tour
Wine Buff's Tour

Silverado Trail

Stag's Leap Wine Cellars

Wine Buff's Tour

Start: Stag's Leap Wine Cellars, Yountville. Famed for its cabernet sauvignon and Bordeaux blends.

Beaulieu Vineyard, Rutherford. Pony up the extra fee to visit the reserve tasting room to try their flagship cabernet sauvignon.

Mumm Napa, Rutherford. Come for the bubbly— which is available in a variety of tastings— stay for the photography exhibits.

Dinner and Overnight: Yountville. Have dinner at one of the Thomas Keller restaurants. Splurge at Bardessono; save at

Maison Fleurie.

Next Day: Robert Mondavi, Oakville. Spring for the reserve room tasting so you can sip the top-of-the-line wines, especially the stellar cabernet. Head across Highway 29 to the Oakville Grocery to pick up a picnic lunch.

extravagant dinner at their restaurant. Save at El Bonita Motel with dinner at Gott's.

Next Day: Poke around St. Helena's shops, then drive to Yountville for lunch.

di Rosa, Napa. Call ahead to book a one- or two-hour tour of the acres of gardens and galleries, which

are chock-full of thousands of works of art.

Domaine Carneros, Napa. Toast your trip with a glass of outstanding bubbly.

Far Niente, Oakville. You have to reserve in advance and the fee for the tasting and tour is steep, but the

payoff is an especially intimate winery experience. You'll taste excellent cabernet and chardonnay, then end your trip on a sweet note with a dessert wine.

Sonoma Backroads

Start: Iron Horse Vineyards, Russian River Valley.
Soak up a view of vine-covered hills and Mount St. Helena while sipping a sparkling wine or pinot noir at this beautifully rustic spot.

Hartford Family Winery, Russian River Valley.
A terrific source for pinot noir and chardonnay, the stars of this valley.

Dinner and Overnight: Forestville. Go all out with a stay at the Farmhouse Inn, whose award-winning restaurant is one of the best in all of Sonoma.

Next Day: Westside Road, Russian River Valley.
This scenic route, which follows the river, is crowded with worthwhile wineries like Gary Farrell and Rochioli—but it's not crowded with visitors. Pinot fans will find a lot to love. Picnic at Rochioli and enjoy the lovely view.

Matanzas Creek Winery, near Santa Rosa.
End on an especially relaxed note with a walk through their lavender fields (best in June).

WINE TASTING 101

TAKE A GOOD LOOK.
Hold your glass by the stem, raise it to the light, and take a close look at the wine. Check for clarity and color. (This is easiest to do if you can hold the glass in front of a white background.) Any tinge of brown usually means that the wine is over the hill or has gone bad.

Swirl

BREATHE DEEP.
1. Sniff the wine once or twice to see if you can identify any smells.

2. Swirl the wine gently in the glass. Aerating the wine this way releases more of its aromas. (It's called "volatilizing the esters," if you're trying to impress someone.)

3. Take another long sniff. You might notice that experienced wine tasters spend more time sniffing the wine than drinking it. This is because this step is where the magic happens. The number of scents you might detect is almost endless, from berries, apricots, honey, and wildflowers to leather, cedar, or even tar. Does the wine smell good to you? Do you detect any "off" flavors, like wet dog or sulfur?

Sniff

AT LAST! TAKE A SIP.
1. Swirl the wine around your mouth so that it makes contact with all your taste buds and releases more of its aromas. Think about the way the wine feels in your mouth. Is it watery or rich? Is it crisp or silky? Does it have a bold flavor, or is it subtle? The weight and intensity of a wine are called its body.

Sip

2. Hold the wine in your mouth for a few seconds and see if you can identify any developing flavors. More complex wines will reveal many different flavors as you drink them.

SPIT OR SWALLOW.
The pros typically spit, since they want to preserve their palate (and sobriety!) for the wines to come, but you'll find that swallowers far outnumber the spitters in the winery tasting rooms. Whether you spit or swallow, notice the flavor that remains after the wine is gone (the finish).

DODGE THE CROWDS

To avoid bumping elbows in the tasting rooms, look for wineries off the main drags of Highway 29 in Napa and Highway 12 in Sonoma. The back roads of the Russian River, Dry Creek, and Alexander valleys, all in Sonoma, are excellent places to explore. In Napa, try the northern end. Also look for wineries that are open by appointment only; they tend to schedule visitors carefully to avoid a big crush at any one time.

HOW WINE IS MADE

1. CRUSHING
Harvested grapes go into a stemmer-crusher, which separates stems from fruit and crushes the grapes to release "free-run" juice.

2. PRESSING
Remaining juice is gently extracted from grapes. Usually done by pressing grapes against the walls of a tank with an inflatable bladder.

3. FERMENTING
Extracted juice (and also grape skins and pulp, when making red wine) goes into stainless-steel tanks or oak barrels to ferment. During fermentation, sugars convert to alcohol.

4. AGING
Wine is stored in stainless-steel or oak casks or barrels to develop flavors.

5. RACKING
Wine is transferred to clean barrels; sediment is removed. Wine may be filtered and fined (clarified) to improve its clarity, color, and sometimes flavor.

6. BOTTLING
Wine is bottled either at the winery or at a special facility, then stored again for bottle-aging.

WHAT'S AN APPELLATION?

A specific region with a particular set of grape-growing conditions, such as soil type, climate, and elevation, is called an appellation. What makes things a little confusing is that appellations, which are defined by the Alcohol and Tobacco Tax and Trade Bureau, often overlap. California is an appellation, for example, but so is the Napa Valley. Napa and Sonoma counties are each county appellations, but they, too, are divided into even smaller regions, usually called subappellations or AVAs (American Viticultural Areas). You'll hear a lot about these AVAs from the staff in the tasting rooms; they might explain, for example, why the Russian River Valley AVA is such an excellent place to grow pinot noir grapes.

By law, if the label on a bottle of wine lists the name of an appellation, then at least 85% of the grapes in that wine must come from that appellation.

Wine and contemporary art find a home at di Rosa.

farther north, compact Yountville is a culinary boomtown, densely packed with top-notch restaurants and hotels, including a few luxury properties. Continuing north, St. Helena teems with elegant boutiques and restaurants; mellow Calistoga, known for spas and hot springs, feels a bit like an Old West frontier town, and has a more casual attitude.

ESSENTIALS

Contacts Napa Valley Destination Council ☎ *707/226–5813, 707/251-5895* ⊕ *www.legendarynapavalley.com.*

NAPA

46 miles from San Francisco via I–80 east and north, Hwy. 37 west, and Hwy. 29 north.

The town of Napa is the valley's largest, and visitors who get a glimpse of the strip malls and big-box stores from Highway 29 often speed right past on the way to smaller and more seductive Yountville or St. Helena. But Napa is changing. After many years as a blue-collar town that more or less turned its back on the Wine Country scene, Napa has spent the last few years attempting to increase its appeal to visitors. A walkway that follows the river through town, completed in 2008, makes the city more pedestrian-friendly, and in the last two years a surprising number of high-profile new restaurants have popped up. Of course there's also the Oxbow Public Market, a klatch of high-end food purveyors. At night, catch a show at either the circa-1880 Napa Valley Opera House, or the recently renovated Uptown Theatre.

Many visitors choose to stay in Napa after experiencing hotel sticker shock; prices in Napa are marginally more reasonable than elsewhere. If you set up your home base here, you'll undoubtedly want to spend some time getting out of town and into the beautiful countryside, but don't neglect taking a stroll to see what the valley's least pretentious town has to offer, or checking out the ever-changing culinary landscape.

GETTING HERE AND AROUND

To get to downtown Napa from Highway 29, take the 1st Street exit and follow the signs for Central Napa less than a mile through town until you reach the corner of 2nd Street and Main Street. Most of the town's sights and many of its restaurants are clustered in an easily walkable area near this intersection.

EXPLORING

Artesa Vineyards & Winery. With its modern, minimalist look in the tasting room, which is dug into a Carneros hilltop, and contemporary sculptures and fountains on the property, Artesa Vineyards & Winery is a far cry from the many faux French châteaus and rustic Italian-style villas in the region. Although the Spanish owners once made only sparkling wines, now they also produce still wines, mostly Chardonnay and Pinot Noir, but also Cabernet Sauvignon and a smattering of other limited-release wines such as Syrah and Albariño. Call ahead to reserve a spot on one of the specialty tours, such as a wine-and-cheese pairing, a wine-and-chocolate pairing, or the walk through the vineyard ($45). ⊠ *1345 Henry Rd., north off Old Sonoma Rd. and Dealy La.* ☎ *707/224–1668* ⊕ *www.artesawinery.com* 🍷 *Tasting $10–$15, tour $20* ⊗ *Daily 10–5; tour daily at 11 and 2.*

Clos du Val. Although this austere winery doesn't seduce you with dramatic architecture or lush grounds, it doesn't have to: the wines, crafted by winemaker John Clews, have a wide following, especially among those who are patient enough to cellar the wines for a number of years. Though Clews and his team make great Pinot Noir and Chardonnay (grown in the nearby Carneros region), the real claim to fame is the intense reserve Cabernet, made with fruit from the Stags Leap District. The few picnic tables (in a peaceful olive grove) fill up early on summer weekends, and anyone is welcome to try a hand at the boccie-style French game of pétanque. ⊠ *5330 Silverado Trail* ☎ *707/261–5251, 800/993–9463* ⊕ *www.closduval.com* 🍷 *Tasting $15–$25* ⊗ *Daily 10–5; tour by appointment.*

Fodor's Choice
★
di Rosa. While you're driving along the Carneros Highway on your way to Napa from San Francisco, it would be easy to zip by one of the region's best-kept secrets: di Rosa. Metal sculptures of sheep grazing in the grass mark the entrance to this sprawling, art-stuffed property. Thousands of 20th-century artworks by hundreds of Northern California artists crop up everywhere—in galleries, in the former di Rosa residence, on every lawn, in every courtyard, and even on the lake. Some of the works were commissioned especially for the preserve, such as Paul Kos's meditative *Chartres Bleu,* a video installation in a chapel-like setting that replicates a stained-glass window of the cathedral in Chartres, France. If you stop by without a reservation, you'll only gain

access to the Gatehouse Gallery, where there's a small collection of riotously colorful figurative and abstract sculpture and painting, as well as rotating modern-art exhibits throughout the year. ■TIP➔ To see the rest of the property and artwork, you'll have to sign up for one of the various tours of the grounds (from 1 to 2½ hours). Tour reservations are recommended, but walk-ins are sometimes accommodated. ⊠ *5200 Sonoma Hwy./Carneros Hwy.* ☎ *707/226–5991* ⊕ *www.dirosaart.org* ⊟ *Suggested donation $5, tour $10–$15* ⊙ *Wed.–Sat. 9–3; tours 10–3.*

★ **Domaine Carneros.** The majestic château here looks for all the world like it belongs in France, and in fact it does: it's modeled after the Château de la Marquetterie, an 18th-century mansion owned by the Taittinger family near Epernay, France. Carved into the hillside beneath the winery, Domaine Carneros's cellars produce delicate sparkling wines reminiscent of those made by Taittinger, using only grapes grown locally in the Carneros wine district. The winery sells full glasses, flights, and bottles of their wines, which also include still wines like Pinot Noir, Merlot, and Chardonnay, and serves them with cheese plates, charcuterie plates, caviar, or smoked salmon. Seating is in the Louis XV–inspired salon or on the terrace overlooking the vineyards. Though this makes a visit here a tad more expensive than some stops on a winery tour, it's also one of the most opulent ways to enjoy the Carneros District, especially on fair days, when the views over the vineyards are spectacular. ⊠ *1240 Duhig Rd., at Carneros Hwy.* ☎ *707/257–0101, 800/716–2788* ⊕ *www. domainecarneros.com* ⊟ *Tasting $6.50–$85, tour $25* ⊙ *Daily 10–6; tour daily at 11, 1, and 3.*

Fodor'sChoice
★ **Hess Collection Winery.** Nine miles northwest of the city of Napa, up a winding road ascending Mt. Veeder, this winery is a delightful discovery. The simple limestone structure, rustic from the outside but modern and airy within, contains Swiss owner Donald Hess's personal art collection, including mostly large-scale works by such contemporary European and American artists as Robert Motherwell, Andy Goldsworthy, and Frank Stella. Cabernet Sauvignon is the real strength here, though Hess also produces some fine Chardonnays. A number of wine-and-food pairings also are available. Self-guided tours of the art collection and guided tours of the winery's production facilities are both free. On weekdays, ask to borrow an iPod for the free audio tour, which includes commentary by Donald Hess and some of the artists featured in the collection. ⊠ *4411 Redwood Rd., west of Hwy. 29* ☎ *707/255–1144* ⊕ *www. hesscollection.com* ⊟ *Tasting $10–$50* ⊙ *Daily 10–5:30; guided tours daily, usually hourly 10:30–3:30.*

★ **Oxbow Public Market.** Though not terribly large, this collection of about 25 small shops, wine bars, and artisanal food producers is a fun place to begin your introduction to the wealth of food and wine available in the Napa Valley. Swoon over the decadent charcuterie at the Fatted Calf, slurp down some oysters on the half shell at Hog Island Oyster Company, chow down on tacos with homemade tortillas at C Casa, or get a whiff of the hard-to-find seasonings at the Whole Spice Company before sitting down to a glass of wine at the Oxbow Wine Merchant & Wine Bar. A branch of the retro fast-food joint Gott's Roadside tempts those who prefer hamburgers (or egg-and-cheese breakfast sandwiches)

Climbing ivy and lily pads decorate the Hess Collection's rustic exterior.

to duck-liver mousse. ✉ *610 and 644 1st St., at McKinstry St.* ☎ *No phone* ⊕ *www.oxbowpublicmarket.com* ✉ *Free* ⊙ *Generally weekdays 9–9, weekends 10–9; hrs of some merchants vary.*

Sodaro Estate Winery. Upscale-yet-modest Sodaro is a great introduction to Coombsville, Napa's newest AVA. Tours start on the crush pad, with a view of rolling vineyards, then head inside the wine cave, to a marble banquet table, for a seated tasting of the winery's signature wines: a Cabernet Sauvignon and a Bordeaux-style blend. You might also taste a special limited release, perhaps a Malbec or a Cabernet Franc. All wines are paired with local cheese and breadsticks. The tour concludes with a walk through the wine cave itself. It's no surprise the vibe here is so luxurious: owners Don and Deedee Sodaro also own the Hanford Hotels chain. ✉ *24 Blue Oak La., off 3rd Ave.* ☎ *707/251–8216* ⊕ *www.sodarowines.com* ✉ *Tour and tasting $30* ⊙ *Open by appointment only.*

WHERE TO EAT

$$$ ✕ **Angèle.** An 1890s boathouse with a vaulted wood-beam ceiling sets
FRENCH the scene for romance at this cozy French bistro. Though the style is casual—tables are close together, and the warm, crusty bread is plunked right down on the paper-top tables—the food is always well executed. Look for classic French dishes like duck breast accompanied with confit, guinea hen wrapped in house-cured pancetta, or a starter of *ris de veau* (veal sweetbreads). Save room for the homemade desserts. In fair weather, ask for one of the charming outdoor tables. Ⓢ *Average main: $30* ✉ *540 Main St., at 5th St.* ☎ *707/252–8115* ⊕ *www. angelerestaurant.com.*

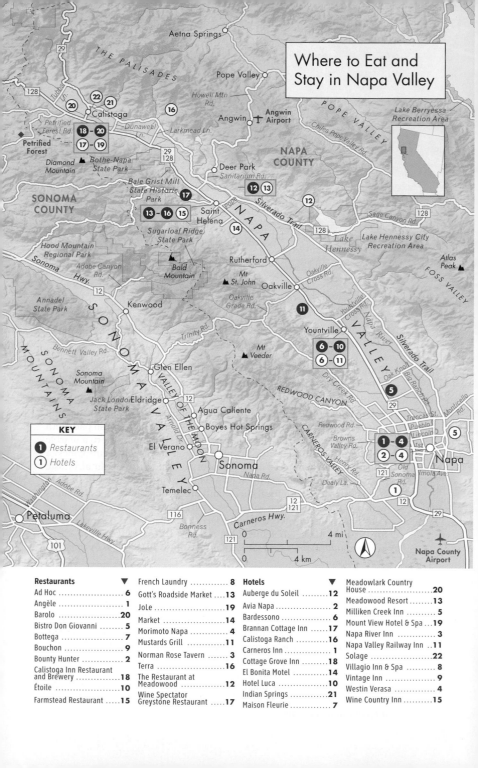

Where to Eat and Stay in Napa Valley

$$$ ITALIAN ★ 🍴 **Bistro Don Giovanni.** Co-owner and host Giovanni Scala might be around to warmly welcome you to this lively bistro, where you can peek past the copper pots hanging in the open kitchen to see the 750-degree wood-burning oven. The Cal-Italian food is simultaneously inventive and comforting: an excellent fritto misto usually comprised of onions, fennel, calamari, and plump rock shrimp; pizza with Brussels sprouts and garlic; and whole roasted fish. Children are unusually welcome here, catered to with crayons and paper-topped tables and a menu with items like pizza topped with cheese, french fries, and "no green stuff." Fodors.com Forum users suggest angling for a table on the covered patio for a "more intimate and quiet" experience. [$] *Average main: $27* ✉ *4110 Howard La. /Hwy. 29* ☎ *707/224–3300* 🌐 *www.bistrodongiovanni.com.*

$$$ SOUTHERN ★ 🍴 **Bounty Hunter.** A triple threat, Bounty Hunter is a wine store, a wine bar, and a restaurant in one. You can stop by for just wine—about 40 choices available by the glass in both 2- and 5-ounce pours, and 400 by the bottle—but it's best to come with an appetite. A miniscule kitchen means the menu is also small, but every dish is a standout, including the pulled-pork and beef brisket sandwiches served with three types of barbecue sauce, the signature beer-can chicken, and meltingly tender St. Louis–style ribs. The space is whimsically rustic, with stuffed game trophies mounted on the wall and leather saddles standing in for seats at a couple of tables. ■ **TIP→** The restaurant remains open until midnight on Friday and Saturday, making it a popular spot for a late-night bite. [$] *Average main: $24* ✉ *975 1st St., at Main St.* ☎ *707/226–3976* 🌐 *www.bountyhunterwinebar.com* ✍ *Reservations not accepted.*

$$$$ JAPANESE 🍴 **Morimoto Napa.** Masuharu Morimoto, known to many as the star of Iron Chef but also well regarded for his eponymous restaurants around the world, is the big name behind this hot restaurant in downtown Napa. Organic materials like twisting grapevines above the bar and rough-hewn wooden tables seem simultaneously earthy and modern, which seems a fitting setting for the gorgeously plated Japanese fare, from super-fresh sashimi served with grated fresh wasabi to more-elaborate concoctions like sea-urchin carbonara, made with udon noodles. For the full experience, consider the omakase menu ($120). If no tables are available, you can still order many dishes in the lounge, where a young and lively crowd drinks specialty cocktails along with appetizers like a tempura calamari salad and pork gyoza. [$] *Average main: $44* ✉ *610 Main St., at 5th St.* ☎ *707/252–1600* 🌐 *www.morimotonapa.com.*

$$ AMERICAN 🍴 **Norman Rose Tavern.** If downtown Napa has its own version of the bar in *Cheers*, the Norman Rose Tavern is it. Casual and family-friendly, "The Rose," as locals call it, serves up classic American fare such as hamburgers, sandwiches, and fish-and-chips, and proudly pours local wines and regional beers until 9 or 10 pm. Happy Hour, held weeknights from 3 to 6 pm, is particularly rollicking, with $4 draft beers, $6 glasses of wine, $6 hot wings (by the pound), and $2.50 sliders. On warm days, arrive early for a spot on the open-air patio. [$] *Average main: $17* ✉ *1401 1st St., at Franklin St.* ☎ *707/258–1516.*

WHERE TO STAY

For expanded reviews, facilities, and current deals, visit Fodors.com.

$ HOTEL **Avia Napa.** Hands down, this boutique hotel, now part of the Hyatt family, is the hippest place to stay in Napa; the rooms, most of them suites, are modern but welcomingly so. **Pros:** proximity to restaurants, theaters, and tasting rooms downtown; modern fitness center. **Cons:** on-site restaurant and bar lack identity; parking can be a challenge on popular weekends. **TripAdvisor:** "beautiful and comfortable," "modern," "great breakfast." [$] *Rooms from: $189* ✉ *1450 1st St.* ☎ *707/224–3900* 🌐 *avianapa.hyatt.com/hyatt/hotels* ⇨ *50 rooms, 91 suites.*

$$$$ RESORT Fodor's Choice ★ **Carneros Inn.** Freestanding board-and-batten cottages with rocking chairs on each porch are simultaneously rustic and chic at this luxurious property. **Pros:** cottages have lots of privacy; beautiful views from the hilltop pool and hot tub; heaters on each private patio encourage lounging outside in the evening. **Cons:** a long drive from destinations up-valley; smallish rooms with limited seating options. **TripAdvisor:** "everything you need," "great vistas," "beautiful location and relaxing accommodation." [$] *Rooms from: $550* ✉ *4048 Sonoma Hwy.(Hwy. 121)* ☎ *707/299–4900, 888/400–9000* 🌐 *www.thecarnerosinn.com* ⇨ *76 cottages, 10 suites.*

$$$ B&B/INN **Milliken Creek Inn.** Wine and cheese at sunset set a romantic mood in the intimate lobby, with its terrace overlooking the Napa River and a lush lawn. **Pros:** soft-as-clouds beds; serene hotel-guests-only spa; breakfast delivered to your room (or wherever you'd like to eat on the grounds); gratuities are not accepted (except at the spa). **Cons:** expensive; road noise can be heard from the admittedly beautiful outdoor areas. **TripAdvisor:** "very friendly attentive staff," "romantic getaway," "consistent elegance." [$] *Rooms from: $350* ✉ *1815 Silverado Trail* ☎ *707/255–1197, 800/835–6112* 🌐 *www.millikencreekinn.com* ⇨ *12 rooms.*

$$ B&B/INN **Napa River Inn.** Almost everything's close here: this waterfront inn is part of a complex of restaurants, shops, a gallery, and a spa, all within easy walking distance of downtown Napa. **Pros:** a pedestrian walkway connects the hotel to downtown Napa; unusual pet-friendly policy; wide range of room sizes and prices. **Cons:** river views could be more scenic; some rooms get noise from nearby restaurants. **TripAdvisor:** "first class," "great location," "clean and comfortable." [$] *Rooms from: $300* ✉ *500 Main St.* ☎ *707/251–8500, 877/251–8500* 🌐 *www.napariverinn.com* ⇨ *65 rooms, 1 suite.*

$ HOTEL **Westin Verasa.** Across the street from the Wine Train depot and just behind the Oxbow Public Market, this spacious hotel-condo complex, opened in 2008, is sophisticated and soothing, with pristine white bedding and furniture in warm earth tones. **Pros:** pool is heated year-round; most rooms have well-equipped kitchenettes; spacious double-headed showers. **Cons:** $20 "amenities fee" charged in addition to room rate. **TripAdvisor:** "wonderful property," "needs a few extra touches," "great food on-site." [$] *Rooms from: $239* ✉ *1314 McKinstry St.* ☎ *707/257–1800, 800/937–8461* 🌐 *www.westinnapa.com* ⇨ *130 rooms, 50 suites.*

NIGHTLIFE AND THE ARTS

Napa Valley Opera House. The interior of the 1879 Italianate Victorian Napa Valley Opera House isn't quite as majestic as the facade, but the intimate 500-seat venue is still an excellent place to see all sorts of performances, from Pat Metheny and Mandy Patinkin to the Napa Valley Film Festival and, yes, even the occasional opera. ⊠ *1030 Main St., at 1st St.* ☎ *707/226-7372* ⊕ *www.nvoh.org.*

Uptown Theatre. This Napa icon opened as a movie house in 1937. After years in disrepair, it was renovated and in 2010 reopened as a live-music venue that has attracted the likes of Lucinda Williams and Devo. ⊠ *1350 3rd St., at Franklin St.* ☎ *707/259-0123* ⊕ *www. uptowntheatrenapa.com.*

MAKING TRACKS IN NAPA

Napa Valley Wine Train. Turn the driving over to someone else—a train conductor. The Napa Valley Wine Train runs a scenic route between Napa and St. Helena with several restored 1915-17 Pullman railroad cars. The ride often includes a meal, such as brunch or dinner. While it's no bargain (starting at around $99 for lunch, $109 for dinner) and can feel a bit hokey, the train gives you a chance to enjoy the vineyard views without any driving worries. ⊠ *1275 McKinstry St., off 1st St.* ☎ *707/253-2111, 800/427-4124* ⊕ *www.winetrain.com.*

SPORTS AND THE OUTDOORS

Thanks to the scenic country roads that wind through the region, bicycling is a practically perfect way to get around the Wine Country. And whether you're interested in an easy spin to a few wineries or a strenuous haul up a mountainside, there's a way to make it happen. Another fine way to take in the scenery is by kayak. ■TIP➔ There are almost no designated bike lanes in the Wine Country, though, so be sure to pay attention to traffic.

Napa Valley Adventure Tours. Operating out of the Oxbow Public Market in downtown Napa, this outfitter offers a variety of half- and full-day outdoor trips, including kayaking along the Napa River in the southern part of the valley. ⊠ *610 1st St., at McKinstry St.* ☎ *707/259-1833, 877/548-6877.*

Napa Valley Bike Tours. Napa Valley Bike Tours will deliver the bikes, which go for $39 to $78 a day, to many hotels in the Napa Valley if you're renting at least two bikes for a full day. In addition to hourly rentals, guided and self-guided winery tours are available. ⊠ *6795 Washington St., at Madison St., Yountville* ☎ *707/944-2953* ⊕ *www. napavalleybiketours.com.*

YOUNTVILLE

13 miles north of the town of Napa on Hwy. 29.

These days Yountville is something like Disneyland for food lovers. It all started with Thomas Keller's French Laundry, simply one of the best restaurants in the United States. Now Keller is also behind two more-casual restaurants a few blocks from his mother ship—and that's only the tip of the iceberg. You could stay here for a week and not exhaust all the options in this tiny town with a big culinary reputation.

Yountville is full of small inns and high-end hotels that cater to those who prefer to walk (not drive) after an extravagant meal. It's also well located for excursions to many big-name Napa wineries, especially those in the Stags Leap District, from which big, bold Cabernet Sauvignons helped put the Napa Valley on the wine-making map.

GETTING HERE AND AROUND

To get to Yountville from Highway 29 traveling north, take the Yountville exit and then take the first left, onto Washington Street. Almost all of Yountville's business and restaurants are clustered along Washington Street in the first half mile. Yountville Cross Road connects tiny downtown Yountville to the Silverado Trail, along which many of the area's best wineries are located.

EXPLORING

Domaine Chandon. On a knoll west of downtown dotted with whimsical sculptures and shaded with ancient oak trees, this French-owned winery claims one of Yountville's prime pieces of real estate. Basic tours of the sleek, modern facilities are available for $12 (not including a tasting), but other tours ($32 each), which focus on various topics (food-and-wine pairing or Pinot production, for example), end with a seated tasting. The top-quality sparklers are made using the laborious *méthode champenoise*. For the complete experience, order hors d'oeuvres to accompany the wines in the tasting room; although Chandon is best known for its bubblies, still wines like the Chardonnay, Pinot Noir, and Pinot Meunier are also worth a try. Only wine club members are welcome to bring young children. ⊠ *1 California Dr., west of Hwy. 29* ☎ *707/944–2280, 888/242–6366* ⊕ *www.chandon.com* ◪ *Tasting $8–$22 by the glass, $18–$25 by the flight* ⊙ *Daily 10–5; tours daily at 11:30, 3:30.*

Napa Valley Museum. Although it's not worth a long detour, this small museum, next to Domaine Chandon on the grounds of the town's Veterans Home, is a great respite from a day of wine tasting. Downstairs, the permanent exhibit, The Land and People of Napa Valley, focuses on the geology and history of the area, from the Native Americans who once lived here through the pioneer period to the modern winemakers who made it famous. The rotating fine-arts shows upstairs feature the work of Napa Valley artists. The museum also hosts regular Family Fun Days, which include arts-and-crafts projects for young kids. ⊠ *55 Presidents Circle, at California Dr.* ☎ *707/944–0500* ⊕ *www.napavalleymuseum. org* ◪ *$10* ⊙ *Wed.–Mon. 10–5.*

Robert Sinskey Vineyards. Although the winemaker here produces well-regarded Cabernet blends and a variety of aromatic white wines from all-organic, certified biodynamic vineyards, Sinskey is best known for its intense, brambly Pinot Noirs, grown in the cooler Carneros District, where the grape thrives. The influence of Rob's wife, Maria Helm Sinskey—a chef and cookbook author and the winery's culinary director—is evident during the tastings, which come with a few bites of food paired with each wine (her books and other culinary items are also available in the gift shop, next to the open kitchen). But for the best sense of how Sinskey wines pair with food, reserve a spot on the ($75) culinary tour, which takes you through the winery's gardens and ends with a seated pairing of foods and wine. ✉ *6320 Silverado Trail, at Yountville Cross Rd., Napa* ☎ *707/944–9090* ⊕ *www.robertsinskey.com* ⊒ *Tasting $25; tour $75* ⊘ *Daily 10–4:30; tours daily at 11 (by appointment).*

Stag's Leap Wine Cellars. The 1973 Cabernet Sauvignon produced by Stag's Leap Wine Cellars put the winery—and the Napa Valley—on the map by placing first in the famous Paris tasting of 1976. Today, a visit to the winery is a no-frills affair. Visitors in the tasting room are clearly serious about tasting wine, and aren't interested in distractions like a gift shop. It costs $30 to taste the top-of-the-line wines, including the limited-production estate-grown Cabernets, a few of which sell for well over $100. If you're interested in more-modestly priced wines, try the $15 tasting, which usually includes a Sauvignon Blanc, Chardonnay, Merlot, and Cabernet. (Note: Don't conflate this winery with Stag's Leap; that's a different operation entirely.) ✉ *5766 Silverado Trail, at Wappo Hill Rd., Napa* ☎ *707/944–2020, 866/422–7523* ⊕ *www. cask23.com* ⊒ *Tasting $15–$30, tour $40* ⊘ *Daily 10–4:30; tours by appointment.*

V Marketplace. In between bouts of eating and drinking, you might stop by V Marketplace. The vine-covered brick complex, which once housed a winery, a livery stable, and a brandy distillery, contains a smattering of clothing boutiques, art galleries, and gift stores. NapaStyle, a large store, deli, and wine bar, sells cookbooks, luxury food items, and kitchenware, as well as an assortment of prepared foods perfect for picnics. The complex's signature restaurant, Bottega, features the food of celebrity chef Michael Chiarello (⇨ *see Bottega*). ✉ *6525 Washington St., near Mulberry St.* ☎ *707/944–2451* ⊕ *www.vmarketplace.com.*

WHERE TO EAT

$$$$
MODERN
AMERICAN
Fodor's Choice
★

✕ **Ad Hoc.** When superstar chef Thomas Keller opened this relatively casual spot in 2006, he meant to run it for only six months until he opened a burger joint in the same space, but locals were so charmed by the homey food that they clamored for the stopgap to stay. Now a single, seasonal, fixed-price menu ($52) is served nightly, with a small menu of decadent brunch items served on Sunday. The selection might include a juicy pork loin and buttery polenta, served family style, or a delicate *panna cotta* with a citrus glaze. The dining room is warmly low-key, with zinc-top tables, wine served in tumblers, and rock and jazz on the stereo. If you just can't wait to know what's going be served before you visit, you can call a day in advance for the menu or sign up for daily email blasts. Ⓢ *Prix-fixe: $52* ✉ *6476 Washington St., at Oak Circle* ☎ *707/944–2487* ⊕ *www.adhocrestaurant.com* ⊘ *No lunch Mon.–Sat. No dinner Tues. and Wed.*

$$$$
ITALIAN

✕ **Bottega.** The food at this lively trattoria is simultaneously soulful and inventive, transforming local ingredients into regional Italian dishes with a twist. The antipasti in particular shine: you can order olives grown on chef Michael Chiarello's own property in St. Helena, house-made charcuterie, or an incredibly fresh fish crudo. Potato gnocchi might be served with duck and a chestnut ragu, and hearty main courses like braised short ribs could come on a bed of spinach prepared with preserved lemons. The vibe is more festival than formal, with exposed brick walls, an open kitchen, and paper-topped tables, but service is spot on, and the reasonably priced wine list offers lots of interesting choices from both Italy and California. $ *Average main: $35* ⊠ *6525 Washington St., near Mulberry St.* ☎ *707/945–1050* ⊕ *www.botteganapavalley. com* ⊙ *No lunch Mon.*

$$$
FRENCH

✕ **Bouchon.** The team that brought French Laundry to its current pinnacle is also behind this place, where everything—the lively and crowded zinc bar, the elbow-to-elbow seating, the traditional French onion soup—could have come straight from a Parisian bistro. Roast chicken with mustard greens and fingerling potatoes and steamed mussels served with crispy, addictive *frites* (french fries) are among the hearty dishes served in the high-ceilinged room. ■TIP→ Late-night meals from a limited menu are served until midnight—a rarity in the Wine Country, where it's often difficult to find a place to eat after 10. $ *Average main: $25* ⊠ *6534 Washington St., near Humboldt St.* ☎ *707/944–8037* ⊕ *www. bouchonbistro.com.*

$$$$
AMERICAN

✕ **Étoile.** Housed at Domaine Chandon, this quietly elegant stunner seems built for romance, with delicate orchids on each table and views of the wooded winery grounds from the large windows. The restaurant's young chef Perry Hoffman turns out sophisticated California cuisine. Starters such as lobster carpaccio with pickled carrots play with a variety of textures, and luxe ingredients like shavings of black truffle dress up pappardelle with maitake mushrooms. Four- and six-course tasting menus can be ordered with or without wine pairings. The wine list naturally features plenty of Domaine Chandon sparklers, but it's strong in wines from throughout other regions of California as well. $ *Average main: $34* ⊠ *1 California Dr., at Hwy. 29* ☎ *888/242–6366* ⊕ *www. chandon.com/etoile-restaurant* ⊙ *Closed Tues. and Wed.*

$$$$
AMERICAN
Fodor's Choice
★

✕ **French Laundry.** An old stone building laced with ivy houses the most acclaimed restaurant in Napa Valley—and, indeed, one of the most highly regarded in the country. The restaurant's two nine-course prix-fixe menus (both $270), one of which is vegetarian, vary, but "oysters and pearls," a silky dish of pearl tapioca with oysters and white sturgeon caviar, is a signature starter. Some courses rely on luxe ingredients like foie gras, while others take humble foods like fava beans and elevate them to art. Many courses also offer the option of "supplements," such as sea urchin or black truffles. Reservations at French Laundry are hard-won, and not accepted more than two months in advance. ■TIP→ Call two months ahead to the day at 10 am, on the dot. Didn't get a reservation? Call on the day you'd like to dine here to be considered if there's a cancellation. $ *Prix-fixe: $270* ⊠ *6640 Washington St., at Creek St.* ☎ *707/944–2380* ⊕ *www.frenchlaundry.com* ⌂ *Reservations essential* 🏛 *Jacket required* ⊙ *No lunch Mon.–Thurs.*

$$$
AMERICAN

✕ **Mustards Grill.** There's not an ounce of pretension at Cindy Pawlcyn's longtime Napa favorite, despite the fact that it's filled every day and night with fans of her hearty cuisine. The menu mixes updated renditions of traditional American dishes (what the restaurant likes to call "deluxe truck-stop classics"), such as barbecued baby back pork ribs and a lemon-lime tart piled high with browned meringue, with a handful of more innovative choices such as sweet corn tamales with tomatillo-avocado salsa and wild mushrooms. A black-and-white marble tile floor and upbeat artwork set a scene that one Fodors.com reader describes as "pure fun, if not fancy." $ *Average main: $25* ✉ *7399 St. Helena Hwy. (Hwy. 29), 1 mile north of town* ☎ *707/944–2424* ⊕ *www. mustardsgrill.com.*

WHERE TO STAY
For expanded reviews, facilities, and current deals, visit Fodors.com.

$$$$
RESORT

:: **Bardessono.** Although Bardessono bills itself as the "greenest luxury hotel in America," there's nothing spartan about its large, sparce rooms. **Pros:** large rooftop lap pool; exciting restaurant on-site; polished service. **Cons:** expensive; the view from many rooms is uninspiring. **TripAdvisor:** "long weekend in paradise," "an exquisite favorite," "heavenly beds." $ *Rooms from: $500* ✉ *6526 Yount St.* ☎ *707/204–6000* ⊕ *www.bardessono.com* ⤳ *50 rooms, 12 suites.*

$$$
B&B/INN

:: **Hotel Luca.** This 20-room Yountville inn that opened in 2009 embodies a rustic Tuscan style, with dark-wood furniture and soothing decor in brown and sage. **Pros:** extremely comfortable beds; attentive service; breakfast, included in rates, is served in the restaurant or delivered to your room. **Cons:** rooms are soundproofed, but outdoor areas get some traffic noise. **TripAdvisor:** "most comfortable bed in the world," "impeccable service," "laid-back luxury." $ *Rooms from: $350* ✉ *6757 Washington St.* ☎ *707/944–8080* ⊕ *www.hotellucanapa.com* ⤳ *20 rooms* ⦿ *Breakfast.*

$
B&B/INN
★

:: **Maison Fleurie.** If you'd like to be within easy walking distance of most of Yountville's best restaurants, and possibly score a great bargain, look into this casual, comfortable inn. **Pros:** smallest rooms are some of the most affordable in town; free bike rental; refrigerator stocked with free bottled water and soda. **Cons:** breakfast room can be crowded at peak times; bedding could be nicer. **TripAdvisor:** "very cozy and romantic," "very relaxing," "charming." $ *Rooms from: $175* ✉ *6529 Yount St.* ☎ *707/944–2056, 800/788–0369* ⊕ *www.maisonfleurienapa.com* ⤳ *13 rooms* ⦿ *Breakfast.*

$
HOTEL

:: **Napa Valley Railway Inn.** Budget-minded travelers and those with kids appreciate these very basic accommodations—inside actual railcars—just steps away from most of Yountville's best restaurants. **Pros:** central Yountville location; guests have access to adjacent gym. **Cons:** minimal service, since the office is often unstaffed; rooms on the parking-lot side get some noise. **TripAdvisor:** "a gem in Yountville," "great carriages," "great location." $ *Rooms from: $175* ✉ *6523 Washington St.* ☎ *707/944–2000* ⊕ *www.napavalleyrailwayinn.com* ⤳ *9 rooms.*

$$$
RESORT
★

:: **Villagio Inn & Spa.** The luxury here is quiet and refined: streamlined furnishings, subdued color schemes, and high ceilings create a sense of spaciousness in the guest rooms, each of which has a fireplace and, beyond louvered doors, a balcony or a patio. **Pros:** amazing buffet breakfast; no extra charge for hotel guests to use the spa facilities; steps away from Yountville's best restaurants. **Cons:** can be bustling with large groups; you can hear highway noise from many of the rooms' balconies or patios. **TripAdvisor:** "perfect place for wine and food lovers,"

6

"extra perks," "heaven in Yountville." Ⓢ *Rooms from: $375* ✉ *6481 Washington St.* ☎ *707/944–8877, 800/351–1133* ⊕ *www.villagio.com* ↯ *86 rooms, 26 suites* ⦿l *Breakfast.*

$$$
RESORT

⊞ **Vintage Inn.** Rooms in this lavish inn are housed in two-story villas scattered around a lush, landscaped 3½-acre property. **Pros:** spacious bathrooms with spa tubs; lavish breakfast buffet; luscious bedding. **Cons:** highway noise is audible in some exterior rooms; pool area is smaller than the one at its sister property, the Villagio Inn & Spa. **TripAdvisor:** "lovely grounds," "well located hotel with comfortable amenities," "quiet place to stay." Ⓢ *Rooms from: $350* ✉ *6541 Washington St.* ☎ *707/944–1112* ⊕ *www.vintageinn.com* ↯ *68 rooms, 12 suites* ⦿l *Breakfast.*

OAKVILLE

2 miles west of Yountville on Hwy. 29.

There are three reasons to visit the town of Oakville: its gourmet grocery store; its scenic mountain road; and its magnificent, highly exclusive wineries.

GETTING HERE AND AROUND

Those driving along Highway 29 will know they've reached Oakville when they see the Oakville Grocery on the east side of the road. Here the Oakville Cross Road provides access to the Silverado Trail, which runs parallel to Highway 29. Oakville wineries are scattered along Highway 29, Oakville Cross Road, and the Silverado Trail in roughly equal measure.

You can reach Oakville from the town of Glen Ellen in Sonoma County by heading east on Trinity Road from Highway 12. The twisting route, along the mountain range that divides Napa and Sonoma, eventually becomes the Oakville Grade. The views of both valleys on this drive are breathtaking, though the continual curves make it unsuitable for those who suffer from motion sickness.

EXPLORING

Fodor's Choice
★

Far Niente. Though the fee for the combined tour and tasting is at the high end, Far Niente is especially worth visiting if you're tired of elbowing your way through crowded tasting rooms and are looking for a more personal experience. Here you're welcomed by name and treated to a glimpse of one of the most beautiful Napa properties. Small groups are shepherded through the historic 1885 stone winery, including some of the 40,000 square feet of caves, for a lesson on the labor-intensive method for making Far Niente's two wines, a Cabernet blend and a Chardonnay. (The latter is made without undergoing malolactic fermentation, so it doesn't have that buttery taste that's characteristic of many California Chards.) The next stop is the Carriage House, where you can see the founder's gleaming collection of classic cars. The tour zips by the property's floating solar panel installation upon request, and ends back in the tasting room with a seated tasting of wines and cheeses. ✉ *1350 Acacia Dr., off Oakville Grade Rd.* ☎ *707/944–2861, 800/363–6523* ⊕ *www.farniente.com* 🖃 *$50* ⊘ *Tasting and tour by appointment.*

Far Niente's wine cellars have a touch of ballroom elegance.

Oakville Grocery. Built in 1881 as a general store, this popular spot carries unusual and high-end groceries and prepared foods. Unbearable crowds pack the narrow aisles on weekends, but it's still a fine place to sit on a bench out front and sip an espresso between winery visits. ✉ *7856 St. Helena Hwy. (Hwy. 29)* ☎ *707/944–8802.*

Opus One. The combined venture of the late California winemaker Robert Mondavi and the late French Baron Philippe de Rothschild, Opus One produces only one wine: a big, inky Bordeaux blend that was the first of Napa's ultra-premium wines, fetching unheard-of prices before it was overtaken by cult wines like Screaming Eagle. The winery's futuristic limestone-clad structure, built into the hillside, seems to be pushing itself out of the earth. Although the tours, which focus on why it costs so much to produce this exceptional wine, can come off as "stuffy" (in the words of one Fodors.com reader), the facilities are undoubtedly impressive, with gilded mirrors, exotic orchids, and a large semicircular cellar modeled on the Château Mouton Rothschild winery in France. You can also taste the current vintage without the tour ($35), as long as you've called ahead for a reservation. ■ **TIP→** Take your glass up to the rooftop terrace if you want to appreciate the views out over the vineyards. ✉ *7900 St. Helena Hwy. (Hwy. 29)* ☎ *707/944–9442, 800/292–6787* ⊕ *www.opusonewinery.com* ✉ *Tours $50-$70; tastings $35* ☉ *Daily 10–4; tasting and tour by appointment.*

PlumpJack. If Opus One is the Rolls-Royce of the Oakville District—expensive, refined, and a little snooty—then PlumpJack is the Mini Cooper: fun, casual, and sporty. With its metal chandelier and wall hangings, the tasting room looks like it could be the stage set for a modern Shakespeare production. (The name "PlumpJack" is a nod to Shakespeare's Falstaff.) The reserve Chardonnay has a good balance of baked fruit and fresh citrus flavors, while a Merlot is blended with a bit of Cabernet Sauvignon, giving the wine enough tannins to ensure it can be aged for another five years or more. Visitors also can taste wines from the sister winery, Cade Estate. If the tasting room is crowded, take a breather under the shady arbor on the back patio, where you can enjoy a close-up view of the vines. ⊠ *620 Oakville Cross Rd., off Hwy 29* ☎ *707/945–1220* ⊕ *www.plumpjack.com* ▧ *Tastings $15* ⊙ *Daily 10–4.*

Robert Mondavi. The arch at the center of the sprawling Mission-style building here perfectly frames the lawn and the vineyard behind, inviting a stroll under the lovely arcades. You can head straight for one of the two tasting rooms, but if you've never taken a winery tour before, the comprehensive Signature Tour and Tasting ($25), which concludes with a seated tasting, is a good way to learn about enology, as well as the late Robert Mondavi's role in California wine making. Those new to tasting and mystified by all that swirling and sniffing should consider the 45-minute Wine Tasting Basics experience ($20). Serious wine lovers should consider springing for the one-hour $55 Exclusive Cellar tasting, where a well-informed server pours and explains limited-production, reserve, and older-vintage wines. Concerts, mostly jazz and R&B, take place in summer on the lawn; call ahead for tickets. ⊠ *7801 St. Helena Hwy.(Hwy. 29)* ☎ *888/766–6328* ⊕ *www.robertmondaviwinery.com* ▧ *Tours and tastings $20–$55* ⊙ *Daily 10–5; tour times vary.*

RUTHERFORD

2 miles northwest of Oakville on Hwy. 29.

From a fast-moving car, Rutherford is a quick blur of vineyards and a rustic barn or two, but don't speed by this tiny hamlet. With its singular microclimate and soil, this is an important viticultural center, with more big-name wineries than you can shake a corkscrew at. Cabernet Sauvignon is king here. The well-drained, loamy soil is ideal for those vines, and since this part of the valley gets plenty of sun, the grapes develop exceptionally intense flavors. The late, great winemaker André Tchelistcheff claimed that "it takes Rutherford dust to grow great Cabernet."

GETTING HERE AND AROUND
Wineries around Rutherford are dotted along Highway 29 and the parallel Silverado Trail just north and south of Rutherford Road/Conn Creek Road, which connect these two major thoroughfares.

EXPLORING
Beaulieu Vineyard. The Cabernet Sauvignon produced at the ivy-covered Beaulieu Vineyard is a benchmark of the Napa Valley. The legendary André Tchelistcheff, who helped define the California style of wine making, worked his magic here from 1938 until his death in 1973. This helps explain why Beaulieu's flagship, the Georges de Latour Private Reserve Cabernet Sauvignon, still garners high marks from major wine publications. The wines being poured in the main tasting room, which might include anything from a zesty Gewürztraminer to a lush Petite

Syrah, are notably good. Still, it's worth the $50 fee to taste that special Cabernet in the less-crowded reserve tasting room. ⊠ *1960 St. Helena Hwy.(Hwy. 29)* ☎ *707/967–5200, 800/373–5896* ⊕ *www.bvwines.com* 🖃 *Tasting $15–$50, tour $20* ⊙ *Daily 10–5.*

Cakebread Cellars. Jack and Dolores Cakebread snapped up the property at Cakebread Cellars in 1973, after Jack fell in love with the area while visiting on a photography assignment. Since then, they've been making luscious Chardonnays, as well as Merlot, a great Sauvignon Blanc, and a beautifully complex Cabernet Sauvignon. You must make an appointment for a tasting, for which there are several different options. The most basic usually involves a stroll through the winery's barrel room and crush pad and past Dolores's kitchen garden before ending in a taste of current releases. Other options focus on red, reserve, or library wines, and might take place in the winery's modern wing, where an elevator is crafted out of a stainless-steel fermentation tank and the ceiling is lined with thousands of corks. ⊠ *8300 St. Helena Hwy.(Hwy 29)* ☎ *707/963–5222, 800/588–0298* ⊕ *www.cakebread.com* 🖃 *Tastings $15–$45, tour $25* ⊙ *Daily 10–4; tasting and tour by appointment.*

Ⓒ **Frog's Leap.** The owner, John Williams, maintains a goofy sense of humor
Fodor's Choice about wine that translates into an entertaining yet informative experi-
★ ence, making Frog's Leap the perfect place for wine novices to begin their education. You'll also find some fine Zinfandel, Cabernet Sauvignon, Merlot, Chardonnay, Sauvignon Blanc, Rosé, and also the German dessert wine Trockenbeerenauslese. The winery includes a red barn built in 1884, 5 acres of organic gardens, an eco-friendly visitor center, and, naturally, a frog pond topped with lily pads. The fun tour ($20) is highly recommended, but you can also just do a seated tasting that takes place on a porch overlooking the garden. ⊠ *8815 Conn Creek Rd.* ☎ *707/963–4704, 800/959–4704* ⊕ *www.frogsleap.com* 🖃 *Tasting $20, tour $20* ⊙ *Daily 10–4; tour by appointment.*

Ⓒ **Honig Vineyard and Winery.** Sustainable farming is the big story at this small, family-run winery in the heart of Rutherford. Michael Honig, the grandson of founder Louis Honig, helped write the code of Sustainable Practices for the Wine Institute, and was a key player in developing the first certification programs for wineries across California. Some of the modern applications of this mind-set: solar panels that generate a majority of the winery's power and an on-site bee colony that helps with pollination. Four wines, including a stellar Cabernet Sauvignon and a renowned Sauvignon Blanc, reflect this commitment to excellence. Because the Honigs have three young children, the winery is incredibly family-friendly, with a special area for toddlers to play. ⊠ *850 Rutherford Rd.* ☎ *800/929–2217* ⊕ *www.honigwine.com* 🖃 *Tasting $10* ⊙ *Daily 10–4:30; tastings by appointment only.*

Inglenook. It's the house *The Godfather* built. Literally. Filmmaker Francis Ford Coppola began his wine-making career in 1975, when he bought part of the historic, renowned Inglenook estate. He eventually reunited the original Inglenook land and purchased the ivy-covered 19th-century château to boot. In 2006 he renamed the property Rubicon Estate, intending to focus on his premium wines, including the

6

Frog's Leap's picturesque country charm extends all the way to the white picket fence.

namesake Cabernet Sauvignon–based blend. (The less expensive wines are showcased at the Francis Ford Coppola Winery in Sonoma County's Geyserville.) Then, in 2011, he renamed the place Inglenook. Various tours cover topics that include the estate's history, the Rutherford climate and geology, and the sensory evaluation of wine. Two distinctly different tastings are held in an opulent, high-ceilinged tasting room. The Bistro, an on-site bistro, has seating in a picturesque courtyard. ⊠ *1991 St. Helena Hwy. (Hwy. 29)* ☎ *707/968–1100, 800/782–4266* ⊕ *www.inglenook.com* ▣ *Tastings $25–$50, tours free–$95* ⊗ *Daily 10–5; call for tour times.*

Mumm Napa. Although this is one of California's best-known sparkling-wine producers, enjoying the bubbly from the light-filled tasting room—available in either single flutes or by the flight—isn't the only reason to visit Mumm. There's also an excellent photography gallery with 30 Ansel Adams prints and rotating exhibits that feature local photographers. You can even take that glass of wonderfully crisp Brut Rosé with you as you wander. For a leisurely tasting of a flight of library wines while seated on their outdoor terrace ($30), reserve in advance. ⊠ *8445 Silverado Trail* ☎ *707/967–7700* ⊕ *www.mummnapa.com* ▣ *Tasting $7–$65, tour free–$20* ⊗ *Daily 10–4:45; tour daily at 10 (free; tasting not included), 11, 1, and 3 ($20, tasting included).*

★ **Round Pond.** This winery makes Cabernet Sauvignon, Sauvignon Blanc and a host of other wines, but it's not all grapevines here—you can switch your focus to olives at will. The small farm grows five varieties of Italian olives and three types of Spanish olives. Within an hour of being handpicked, the olives are crushed in the mill on the property to produce pungent, peppery oils that are later blended and sold. Call at least a day or two in advance to arrange a tour of the mill, followed by an informative tasting, during which you can sample several types of oil, both alone and with Round Pond's own red-wine vinegars and other tasty foods. ■ **TIP→ If you visit between mid-November and the end of December, you might be lucky enough to see the mill in action.** ✉ *875 Rutherford Rd.* ☎ *707/302–2575, 888/302–2575* 🌐 *www.roundpond.com* 🎫 *Tour $30* 🕓 *Tour by appointment.*

Rutherford Hill Winery. A Merlot lover's paradise in a Cabernet Sauvignon world. When the winery's founders were deciding what grapes to plant, they discovered that the climate and soil conditions of their vineyards resembled those of Pomerol, a region of Bordeaux where Merlot is king. The wine caves here are some of the most extensive of any California winery—nearly a mile of tunnels and passageways. You can get a glimpse of the tunnels and the 5,000 barrels inside on the tours, then cap your visit with a picnic in their oak or olive groves. With views over the valley from a perch high on a hill, the picnic grounds are more charming than many others in Napa, which tend to be rather close to one of the busy thoroughfares. ✉ *200 Rutherford Hill Rd., east of Silverado Trail* ☎ *707/963–1871* 🌐 *www.rutherfordhill.com* 🎫 *Tasting $15–$30, tour $25–$40* 🕓 *Daily 10–5; tours daily at 11:30, 1:30, and 3:30.*

6

St. Supéry. Major renovations in 2012 transformed the tasting experience at this Rutherford hotspot from exclusive to ultra-exclusive. The winery now offers several small venues and patios for private tastings of library Cabernet Sauvignon wines. At other, more traditional, sampling sessions, the pours might include Sauvignon Blanc, Merlot, Chardonnay, and even Cabernet Franc or Petit Verdot wines. The tours here provide behind-the-scenes perspectives; the tour that ends with a tasting in the 1882 Queen Anne Victorian is worth the $50 admission. Outside, a small demonstration vineyard allows you to contemplate the variations among grape types and even taste the grapes when they're in season. ✉ *8440 St. Helena Hwy. (Hwy. 29)* ☎ *707/963–4507, 800/942–0809* 🌐 *www.stsupery.com* 🎫 *Tastings $15–$25, tours $25–$50* 🕓 *Daily 10–5.*

WHERE TO STAY

For expanded reviews, facilities, and current deals, visit Fodors.com.

$$$$ RESORT ★ 🏨 **Auberge du Soleil.** Taking a cue from the olive-tree-studded landscape, this hotel with a renowned restaurant and spa cultivates a luxurious Mediterranean look—earth-tone tile floors, heavy wood furniture, and terra-cotta colors—and backs it up with lavish amenities such as flat-screen TVs (in both the rooms and bathrooms), private terraces, jetted soaking tubs, and extra-large showers. **Pros:** stunning views over the valley; spectacular pool and spa areas; the most expensive suites are fit for a superstar. **Cons:** stratospheric prices; the two least expensive rooms (in the main house) get some noise from the bar and restaurant. **TripAdvisor:** "exceeded our expectations," "beautiful property," "absolutely amazing." [$] *Rooms from: $650* ✉ *180 Rutherford Hill Rd., off Silverado Trail north of Hwy. 128* ☎ *707/963–1211, 800/348–5406* 🌐 *www.aubergedusoleil.com* 🛏 *31 rooms, 21 suites* 🍴 *Breakfast.*

ST. HELENA

2 miles northwest of Oakville on Hwy. 29.

Downtown St. Helena is a symbol of how well life can be lived in the Wine Country. Sycamore trees arch over Main Street (Highway 29), a funnel of outstanding restaurants and tempting boutiques. At the north end of town looms the hulking stone building of the Culinary Institute of America. Weathered stone and brick buildings from the late 1800s give off that gratifying whiff of history.

By the time pioneering winemaker Charles Krug planted grapes in St. Helena around 1860, vineyards already existed in the area. Today the town is hemmed in by wineries, and you could easily spend days visiting vintners within a few miles.

GETTING HERE AND AROUND

Downtown St. Helena stretches along Highway 29, which is called Main Street here. Many of the shops and restaurants are clustered on two pedestrian-friendly blocks of Main Street, between Pope Street and Adams Street. Wineries in the area are found both north and south of downtown along both Highway 29 and the Silverado Trail, but some of the less touristed and more scenic spots are on the slopes of Spring Mountain, which rises southwest of town.

EXPLORING

Beringer Vineyards. Arguably the Napa Valley's most beautiful winery, the 1876 Beringer Vineyards is also the oldest continuously operating property. In 1884 Frederick and Jacob Beringer built the Rhine House Mansion to serve as Frederick's family home. Today it serves as the reserve tasting room, where you can sample wines surrounded by Belgian art-nouveau hand-carved oak and walnut furniture and stained-glass windows. The assortment includes a limited-release Chardonnay, a few big Cabernets, and a luscious white dessert wine named Nightingale. Another, less expensive tasting takes place in the original stone winery. ∎TIP➜ If you're looking for an undiscovered gem, pass this one by, but first-time visitors to the valley will learn a lot about the region's winemaking history on the introductory tour. Longer tours, which might pass through a demonstration vineyard or end with a seated tasting in the Rhine House, are also offered. ⊠ *2000 Main St.(Hwy. 29)* ☎ *707/963–4812* ⊕ *www.beringer.com* 🖾 *Tastings $15–$40, tour $20–$30* ⊙ *May 29–Oct. 22, daily 10–6; Oct. 23–May 28, daily 10–5; call for tour times.*

Charles Krug Winery. The first winery founded in the Napa Valley, Charles Krug Winery, opened in 1861 when Count Haraszthy lent Krug a small cider press. Today the family of Peter Mondavi (Robert's brother) runs it. Though the tasting room is modest, the knowledgeable and friendly servers ensure a relaxed visit. The winery is best known for its lush red Bordeaux blends, but its Zinfandel is also good—or go for something unusual with the New Zealand–style Sauvignon Blanc. Its zingy flavor of citrus and tropical fruit is rare in wines from this area. The picnic area behind the tasting room has a view of the redwood cellar (not open to the public), where the wines are aged. ⊠ *2800 N. Main*

St. *(Hwy. 29)* ☎ *707/967–2200* ⊕ *www.charleskrug.com* ◪ *Tastings $15–$25* ⊙ *Daily 10:30–5.*

Culinary Institute of America. The West Coast headquarters of the Culinary Institute of America, the country's leading school for chefs, are in the **Greystone Winery,** an imposing building that was the largest stone winery in the world when it was built in 1889. On the ground floor you can check out the quirky corkscrew display and shop at a well-stocked culinary store that tempts aspiring chefs with gleaming gadgets and an impressive selection of cookbooks. Attached to the store, at the Flavor Bar, you can experience a guided tasting ($10 to $15) of certain types of ingredients (for example, chocolate or olive oil) to gain a greater understanding of them. Upstairs, if no special events are taking place, you can browse the Vintners Hall of Fame, where plaques fastened to 2,200-gallon redwood wine barrels commemorate winemakers past and present. One-hour cooking demonstrations ($20; reservations required) take place on Saturday and Sunday. ⊠ *2555 Main St. (Hwy. 29)* ☎ *707/967–1100* ⊕ *www.ciachef.edu/california* ◪ *Free* ⊙ *Restaurant Sun.–Thurs. 11:30–9, Fri. and Sat. 11:30–10; store and museum daily 10:30–6.*

Fodor's Choice ★ **Joseph Phelps Vineyards.** Although an appointment is required to taste here, it's worth the trouble. In fair weather the casual, self-paced wine tastings are held on the terrace of a huge, modern barnlike building with stunning views down the slopes over oak trees and orderly vines. Though the Sauvignon Blanc and Viognier are good, the blockbuster wines are reds. The 2002 vintage of the flagship wine, a Bordeaux-style blend called Insignia, was selected as *Wine Spectator*'s wine of the year, immediately pushing up prices and demand. Luckily, you'll get a taste of the current vintage of Insignia (which goes for around $200 a bottle). Ninety-minute tasting seminars, available by appointment, are $40. The popular blending seminar, during which you get to try your hand at mixing the various varietals that go into their Insignia blend, is $60. ⊠ *200 Taplin Rd., off Silverado Trail* ☎ *707/963–2745, 800/707–5789* ⊕ *www.jpvwines.com* ◪ *Tastings $25–$60* ⊙ *Weekdays 9–5, weekends 10–4; tastings by appointment only.*

★ **Spring Mountain Vineyard.** Hidden off a winding road behind a security gate, Spring Mountain Vineyard has the feeling of a private estate in the countryside, even though it's only a few miles from downtown St. Helena. Though Sauvignon Blanc, Pinot Noir, and Syrah are produced, the calling card here is Cabernet—big, chewy wines that demand some time in the bottle but promise great things. A tasting of current releases ($25) gives you a good sense of the wines' charms, but consider opting for the estate ($40) or reserve tasting ($50), either of which includes a meander through the beautiful property, from the cellars to the beautifully preserved 1885 mansion. ⊠ *2805 Spring Mountain Rd., off Madrona Ave.* ☎ *707/967–4188, 877/769–4637* ⊕ *www.springmountainvineyard.com* ◪ *Tastings $25–$50* ⊙ *Daily 10–4; tastings by appointment only.*

WHERE TO EAT

$$$$ MODERN AMERICAN 🍴 **Farmstead.** Housed in a former nursery barn, Farmstead revolves around an open kitchen where chef Stephen Barber cooks with as many local and organic ingredients as possible. Many of them—including grass-fed beef, vegetables, extra-virgin olive oil, and honey—come from the property of parent company Long Meadow Ranch. Others are sourced from within a 30-mile radius. On Tuesday, two-course meals ($35) include comfort food such as chicken-fried steak, ribs, or fried chicken and dessert. In warm weather, you can dine on an open-air patio beneath apple trees. Instead of charging a corkage fee, Farmstead collects $2 per bottle to donate to a local non-profit organization. [$] *Average main: $35* ✉ *738 Main St., at Charter Oak Ave.* ☎ *707/963–4555, 877/627–2645* 🌐 *www.longmeadowranch.com/Farmstead-Restaurant.*

$$ AMERICAN ★ 🍴 **Gott's Roadside.** A slick 1950s-style outdoor hamburger stand (formerly known as Taylor's Refresher) goes upscale at this hugely popular spot, where locals are willing to brave long lines to order breakfast sandwiches, juicy burgers, root-beer floats, and garlic fries. You'll also find plenty of choices not available a half century ago, such as the ahi tuna burger and the chicken club with pesto mayo. Try to arrive early or late for lunch, or all the shaded picnic tables on the lawn might be filled. [$] *Average main: $15* ✉ *933 Main St. (Hwy. 29)* ☎ *707/963–3486* 🌐 *www.gotts.com.*

$$ AMERICAN 🍴 **Market.** Comfort reigns at this understated-yet-modern eatery. Executive chef and owner Eduardo Martinez spruces up American classics such as crab Louis, made with local Dungeness crab, and fried chicken served with jalapeño corn bread. Sunday brunch is popular, with locals frequently lining up outside the door. For the most relaxed experience, stroll in at lunchtime midweek and linger over local wine from the extensive list. [$] *Average main: $18* ✉ *1347 Main St., Hunt and Adams Sts.* ☎ *707/963–3799* 🌐 *marketsthelena.com.*

$$$$ AMERICAN Fodor's Choice ★ 🍴 **The Restaurant at Meadowood.** Chef Christopher Kostow has garnered rave reviews for transforming seasonal local products (some grown right on the property) into elaborate, elegant fare. The "composition of carrots," constructed of the tiniest carrots imaginable accompanied by delicate shavings of chocolate, foie gras, and candied tangerine (it sounds odd, but it works) is just one example of Kostow's inventiveness and playfulness. Other dishes, such as slow-cooked black cod with chorizo and lamb, demonstrate an earthier approach. The chef's menu ($225, $430 with wine pairings), composed of (roughly) seven courses, is the best way to appreciate the experience, but the gracious and well-trained servers provide some of the best service in the valley even if you're ordering a less extravagant four- or five-course menu (prices here start at $125, $230 with wine). The warm lighting and well-spaced tables in the dining room, which was renovated in early 2012, makes it a top choice for a romantic tête-à-tête. [$] *Prix-fixe: $125* ✉ *900 Meadowood La.* ☎ *707/967–1205, 800/458–8080* 🌐 *www.meadowood.com* 🕒 *Closed Sun. No lunch.*

$$$$ MEDITERRANEAN ★ 🍴 **Terra.** St. Helena may have newer, flashier, and more dramatic restaurants, but for old-school romance and service, many diners return year after year to this quiet favorite in an 1884 fieldstone building. Since

1988, chef Hiro Sone has been giving unexpected twists to Italian and southern French cuisine in dishes such as the mussel soup with caramelized onions and garlic croutons, heavily perfumed with the scent of saffron. A few, like the signature sake-marinated black cod in a *shiso* broth, draw on Sone's Japanese background. Homey yet elegant desserts, courtesy of Sone's wife, Lissa Doumani, might include a chocolate caramel tart topped with fleur de sel. Next door, Bar Terra serves inventive cocktails and local wines. $ *Average main: $35 ⊠ 1345 Railroad Ave., off Hunt Ave. ☎ 707/963–8931 ⊕ www.terrarestaurant.com ☾ Closed Tues. No lunch.*

$$$

MEDITERRANEAN

✕ **Wine Spectator Greystone Restaurant.** The Culinary Institute of America runs this place in the **Greystone Winery**, which also once served as the Christian Brothers Winery. Century-old stone walls encase a spacious restaurant that bustles at both lunch and dinner, with several cooking stations in full view. On busy nights you may find the hard-at-work chefs more entertaining than your dining companions. The tables on the terrace, shaded by red umbrellas, are away from the action, but on fair days they're even more appealing, providing a panoramic view down the hillside. The menu has a Mediterranean spirit and emphasizes locally grown produce. Typical main courses include prosciutto-wrapped cod and house-made pasta with trumpet mushrooms and a sherry cream sauce. $ *Average main: $25 ⊠ 2555 Main St. (Hwy. 29) ☎ 707/967–1010 ⊕ www.ciachef.edu/restaurants/wsgr/.*

6

WHERE TO STAY
For expanded reviews, facilities, and current deals, visit Fodors.com.

$

HOTEL

⬚ **El Bonita Motel.** Only in St. Helena would a basic room in a roadside motel cost around $200 a night in high season, but for budget-minded travelers the tidy rooms here are pleasant enough, and the landscaped grounds and picnic tables elevate this property over similar places. **Pros:** cheerful rooms; hot tub; microwaves and mini-refrigerators. **Cons:** road noise is a problem in some rooms. **TripAdvisor:** "wonderful budget bargain," "comfortable place to stay," "great location." $ *Rooms from: $149 ⊠ 195 Main St. (Hwy. 29) ☎ 707/963–3216, 800/541–3284 ⊕ www.elbonita.com ⬅ 38 rooms, 4 suites ⧾ Breakfast.*

$$$$

RESORT

Fodor's Choice

★

⬚ **Meadowood Resort.** A rambling lodge and several gray clapboard bungalows are scattered across this sprawling property, giving it an exclusive New England feel, and every unit runs seamlessly—starting with the gatehouse staff, who alert the front desk to arrivals. **Pros:** site of one of Napa's best restaurants; lovely hiking trails on the property; the most gracious service in all of Napa. **Cons:** very expensive; far from shops in downtown St. Helena. **TripAdvisor:** "wonderful property in a great location," "very quiet and romantic," "over-the-top service." $ *Rooms from: $525 ⊠ 900 Meadowood La. ☎ 707/963–3646, 800/458–8080 ⊕ www.meadowood.com ⬅ 85 rooms, suites and cottages.*

$

B&B/INN

⬚ **Wine Country Inn & Gardens.** A pastoral landscape of vine-covered hills surrounds this retreat, which was styled after the traditional New England inns its owners liked to visit in the 1970s—rooms are decorated with homey furniture like four-poster beds, and most have a wood-burning or gas fireplace, a large jetted tub, and a patio or balcony overlooking the vineyards. **Pros:** free shuttle to some restaurants (reserve early); lovely grounds; swimming pool is heated year-round. **Cons:** some rooms let in noise from neighbors; some areas could use updating. **TripAdvisor:** "helpful staff," "quiet cozy country inn," "rustic feel." [$] *Rooms from: $250* ✉ *1152 Lodi La., east of Hwy. 29* ☎ *707/963–7077, 888/465–4608* 🌐 *www.winecountryinn.com* ➪ *24 rooms, 5 cottages* 🍴 *Breakfast.*

SHOPPING

Baksheesh. A member of the Fair Trade Federation, this funky store sells imported art, crafts, textiles, and other items from countries in Africa, Asia, and South America. ✉ *1327 Main St., at Hunt Ave.* ☎ *707/968–9182.*

Spice Islands Marketplace. This fun store inside the Culinary Institute of America at Greystone is the place to shop for cookbooks, kitchenware, and everything else related to cooking and preparing food. ✉ *Culinary Institute of America, 2555 Main St. (Hwy. 29)* ☎ *888/424–2433, 707/967–2309.*

Woodhouse Chocolate. Elaborate confections handmade on the premises are displayed like miniature works of art at this lovely shop that resembles an 18th-century Parisian salon. ✉ *1367 Main St. (Hwy. 29)* ☎ *707/963–8413, 800/966–3468.*

CALISTOGA

3 miles northwest of St. Helena on Hwy. 29.

With false-fronted, Old West–style shops, 19th-century hotels, and unpretentious cafés lining Lincoln Avenue, the town's main drag, Calistoga has a slightly rough-and-tumble feel that's unique in the Napa Valley. It comes across as more down-to-earth than some of the polished towns to the south. And it's easier to find a bargain here, making it a handy home base for exploring the surrounding vineyards and back roads.

Ironically, Calistoga was developed as a swell, tourist-oriented getaway. In 1859 maverick entrepreneur Sam Brannan snapped up 2,000 acres of prime property and laid out a resort, intending to use the area's natural hot springs as the main attraction. Brannan's gamble didn't pay off as he'd hoped, but the hotels and bathhouses won a local following. Many of them are still going, and you can come for an old-school experience of a mud bath or a dip in a warm spring-fed pool.

GETTING HERE AND AROUND

To get to downtown Calistoga from anywhere farther south in the valley, take Highway 29 north and then turn right on Lincoln Avenue. Most of the town's sights are found along a five-block stretch of Lincoln Avenue, or just off one of the side streets that intersect it. After about a mile, Lincoln Avenue (which changes names to Lake County Highway) intersects with the Silverado Trail.

EXPLORING

★ **Castello di Amorosa.** Possibly the most astounding sight in Napa Valley is your first glimpse of the Castello di Amorosa, which looks like a medieval castle, complete with drawbridge and moat, chapel, stables, and secret passageways. Some of the 107 rooms contain replicas of 13th-century frescoes, and the dungeon has an actual iron maiden from Nuremberg, Germany. You must pay for the tour ($33 or $43, depending on the wine you taste) to see the most of the extensive eight-level property, though basic tastings ($18 or $28) include access to a small portion of the astounding complex. All experiences include a sample of several Italian-style wines, including a "super Tuscan," a blend of Sangiovese and Merlot with Cabernet Sauvignon that has more heft than your average Italian red. ⊠ *4045 N. Saint Helena Hwy. (Hwy. 29)* ☎ *707/967–6272* ⊕ *www.castellodiamorosa.com* ✉ *Tasting $18–$28, tour $33–$44* ☉ *Mar.–Oct., daily 9:30–6; Nov.–Feb., daily 9:30–5; tour by appointment.*

Chateau Montelena. This modest winery in northern Calistoga helped establish the Napa Valley's reputation for quality wine making when its 1973 Chardonnay took first place at a blind tasting in Paris, shocking the international wine critics in attendance. The 2008 movie *Bottle Shock* immortalized the event, and the winery milks its cinematic fame with a special tour ($25) that includes a tasting of Chardonnays and a souvenir. More traditional tastings ($20) occur in the circa-1882 château. These five-wine tastings include two stellar Cabernet Sauvignons and a limited-release Riesling. ⊠ *1429 Tubbs La., off Hwy. 29* ☎ *707/942–5105* ⊕ *www.montelena.com* ✉ *Tastings $20–$20, tours $25–$30* ☉ *Daily 9:30–4; tours vary.*

Clos Pegase. Designed by postmodern architect Michael Graves, the Clos Pegase winery is a one-of-a-kind "temple to wine and art" packed with unusual art objects from the collection of owner and publishing entrepreneur Jan Shrem. After tasting the wines, which include a bright Sauvignon Blanc, fruity Chardonnays, and mellow Pinot Noirs, Merlots, and Cabernets (they're made in a soft, approachable style and meant to be drunk somewhat young), be sure to check out the surrealist paintings near the main tasting room, which include a Jean Dubuffet painting you may have seen on a Clos Pegase label. Better yet, bring a picnic and have lunch in the courtyard, where a curvaceous Henry Moore sculpture is one of about two dozen works of art. ⊠ *1060 Dunaweal La., off Hwy. 29* ☎ *707/942–4981* ⊕ *www.clospegase.com* ✉ *Tasting $10–$35, tour $20* ☉ *Daily 10:30–5; tour daily at 11:30 and 2.*

Robert Louis Stevenson State Park. Encompassing the summit of Mt. St. Helena, this mostly undeveloped park is home to the area where Stevenson and his bride, Fanny Osbourne, spent their honeymoon in an abandoned bunkhouse of the Silverado Mine. This stay in 1880 inspired the writer's travel memoir *The Silverado Squatters*, and Spyglass Hill in *Treasure Island* is thought to be a portrait of Mt. St. Helena. A marble memorial marks the site of the bunkhouse. ■**TIP**→ The hike to the summit is 10 miles round-trip; bring water and dress appropriately. The trail is steep and lacks shade in spots, but the summit is often cool and breezy. ⊠ *Hwy. 29, 7 miles north of Calistoga* ☎ *707/942–4575* ⊕ *www.parks. ca.gov/?page_id=472* ✉ *Free* ☉ *Daily sunrise–sunset.*

Fodor's Choice ★ **Schramsberg.** Founded in the 1860s, Schramsberg, one of Napa's oldest wineries, produces bubblies made using the traditional *méthode*

6

Floor-to-ceiling stacked bottles are no exaggeration in Schramsberg's cellars.

champenoise (which means, among other things, that the wine undergoes a second fermentation in the bottle before being "riddled," or turned every few days over a period of weeks, to nudge the sediment into the neck of the bottle). To taste, you must tour first, but what a tour: in addition to glimpsing the winery's historic architecture, you get to tour the underground cellars dug in the late 19th century by Chinese laborers. Down in the caves, a mind-boggling 2 million bottles are stacked in gravity-defying configurations. The tour fee ($45) includes generous pours of several very different sparkling wines, as well as tiny snacks to enhance the experience. ⊠ *1400 Schramsberg Rd., off Hwy. 29* ☎ *707/942–4558, 800/877–3623* ⊕ *www.schramsberg.com* ✉ *Tasting and tour $45* ⊘ *Tasting and tour by appointment.*

Storybook Mountain Vineyards. Tucked into a rock face in the Mayacamas range, Storybook Mountain Vineyards occupies a picture-perfect site, with vines rising steeply from the winery in dramatic tiers. Zinfandel is king here, and there's even a Zin Gris, an unusual dry rosé of Zinfandel grapes. (In Burgundy, *Vin Gris*—pale rosé—is made from Pinot Noir grapes.) Tastings are preceded by a low-key tour, during which you take a short walk up the hillside and then visit the atmospheric tunnels, parts of which have the same rough-hewn look as they did when Chinese laborers painstakingly dug them around 1888. ⊠ *3835 Hwy. 128, 4 miles northwest of town* ☎ *707/942–5310* ⊕ *www.storybookwines.com* ✉ *Free* ⊘ *Mon.–Sat.; tour and tasting by appointment.*

WHERE TO EAT

$$
ITALIAN
✗ **Barolo.** With red-leather seats, artsy light fixtures, and a marble bar indoors and café seating out, this Italian-inflected wine bar inside the Mount View Hotel is a stylish, modern spot for a glass of wine, with many from small producers you probably haven't heard of. Small plates that could have come straight from Tuscany—fried calamari, risotto croquettes, a selection of *salumi*—are great for sharing. A handful of well-executed large plates, like the pappardelle with shrimp and braised short ribs, round out the menu. $ *Average main: $20* ✉ *1457 Lincoln Ave.* ☎ *707/942–9900* ⊕ *www.barolocalistoga.com* ☾ *No lunch.*

$$$
AMERICAN
✗ **Calistoga Inn Restaurant and Brewery.** On pleasant days this riverside restaurant and its sprawling, tree-shaded patio come into their own. At lunchtime, casual plates like a grilled-turkey-and-Brie sandwich or a vegetarian black-bean chili are light enough to leave some energy for an afternoon of wine tasting. And at night, when there's often live jazz played on the patio during the warm months, you'll find heartier dishes such as braised lamb shank or Sonoma duck breast with a fennel-and-Parmesan stuffing. Service can be a bit lackadaisical, so order one of the house-made brews and enjoy the atmosphere while you're waiting. $ *Average main: $25* ✉ *1250 Lincoln Ave., at Cedar St.* ☎ *707/942–4101* ⊕ *www.calistogainn.com/restaurant.html.*

$$$$
MODERN
AMERICAN
✗ **JoLe.** Local produce plays a starring role at this modern American restaurant inside the Mount View Hotel, not surprising as chef Matt Spector is one of the area's biggest proponents of farm-to-table dining. Depending on when you visit, you might enjoy Mendocino-caught squid with crab stuffing; Forni, Brown & Welsh mixed greens with fresh Asian pears; and chicken-fried quail with fig jam. The menu is available à la carte, and there are four-, five- and six-course prix-fixe options. No visit is complete without a slice of coconut cream pie. Pastry chef Sonjia Spector also makes scrumptious cupcakes for patrons to buy and take home. $ *Average main: $45* ✉ *1457 Lincoln Ave., near Fair Way* ☎ *707/942–9538* ⊕ *jolerestaurant.com* ☾ *No Lunch.*

WHERE TO STAY

For expanded reviews, facilities, and current deals, visit Fodors.com.

$
B&B/INN
⌂ **Brannan Cottage Inn.** Housed inside the only one of Sam Brannan's 1860 resort cottages still standing on its original site, this inn, a pristine Victorian house with lacy white fretwork, large windows, and a shady porch, is on the National Register of Historic Places. **Pros:** innkeepers go the extra mile; most rooms have fireplaces; a five-minute walk from most of Calistoga's restaurants. **Cons:** owners' dog may be a problem for those with allergies; beds may be too firm for some. **TripAdvisor:** "friendly and helpful operators," "authentic and unique," "lovely peaceful getaway." $ *Rooms from: $180* ✉ *109 Wapoo Ave.* ☎ *707/942–4200* ⊕ *www.brannancottageinn.com* ⤙ *6 rooms* ⊙ *Breakfast.*

$$$$
RESORT
★
⌂ **Calistoga Ranch.** Spacious free-standing cedar-shingle bungalows throughout this posh, wooded property have outdoor living areas, and even the restaurant, spa, and reception space have outdoor seating areas and fireplaces. **Pros:** almost half the cottages have private hot tubs on the deck; lovely hiking trails on the property; guests have reciprocal

6

All it needs is a fair maiden: Castello di Amorosa's re-created castle.

privileges at Auberge du Soleil. **Cons:** innovative indoor-outdoor organization works better in fair weather than in rain or cold; staff, though friendly, sometimes seems inexperienced compared to similarly priced places. **TripAdvisor:** "escape to serenity," "romantic," "unbelievable property." [$] *Rooms from: $750* ✉ *580 Lommel Rd.* ☎ *707/254–2800, 800/942–4220* 🌐 *www.calistogaranch.com* 🛏 *48 rooms.*

$$ B&B/INN 🏨 **Cottage Grove Inn.** A long driveway lined with 16 freestanding cottages, each shaded by elm trees and with rocking chairs on the porch, looks a bit like Main Street, U.S.A., but inside the skylighted buildings are all the perks needed for a romantic weekend away. **Pros:** bicycles available for loan; freestanding cottages offer privacy; huge bathtubs. **Cons:** no pool; decor may seem a bit frumpy for some. **TripAdvisor:** "terrific property," "cozy romantic wine retreat," "charming and beautiful." [$] *Rooms from: $300* ✉ *1711 Lincoln Ave.* ☎ *707/942–8400, 800/799–2284* 🌐 *www.cottagegrove.com* 🛏 *16 cottages* 🍴 *Breakfast.*

$ RESORT ★ 🏨 **Indian Springs.** Since 1861, this old-time spa has welcomed clients to its mud baths, mineral pool, and steam room, all of them supplied with mineral water from its four geysers. **Pros:** lovely grounds with outdoor seating areas; stylish for the price; enormous mineral pool. **Cons:** lodge rooms are small; service could be more polished. **TripAdvisor:** "indulgent and revitalizing," "heaven on Earth," "perfect place to stay." [$] *Rooms from: $240* ✉ *1712 Lincoln Ave.* ☎ *707/942–4913* 🌐 *www.indianspringscalistoga.com* 🛏 *24 rooms, 17 suites.*

$ B&B/INN Fodor's Choice ★ 🏨 **Meadowlark Country House.** Twenty hillside acres just north of downtown Calistoga surround this decidedly laid-back but sophisticated inn, and each of the rooms in the main house and guest wing has its own charms: one has a deep whirlpool tub looking onto a green hillside, and

Best Wine Country Spas

Spas in Napa and Sonoma have two special angles. First, there are the local mud baths and mineral-water sources, concentrated particularly around Calistoga. Admittedly, it can seem really strange to lower yourself into a vat of thick, muddy paste, but once you've had a few minutes to get used to the intense heat and peaty smell, you may never want to leave your cocoon. Second, there are all those grapes: their seeds, skins, and vines are credited with all sorts of antioxidant and other healthful properties by those who use them in scrubs, lotions, and other spa products.

Below are some of the best spas of the bunch.

Dr. Wilkinson's. The oldest spa in Calistoga, this kitschy spot is well loved for its reasonable prices and its unpretentious vibe. Their mud baths are a mix of volcanic ash and peat moss. ⊠ *1507 Lincoln Ave., at Fair Way, Calistoga* ☎ *707/942–4102* ⊕ *www.drwilkinson.com.*

Fairmont Sonoma Mission Inn & Spa. The largest spa of its type in the Wine Country, the vast complex covers every amenity you could want in a spa, including several pools and Jacuzzis fed by local thermal mineral springs. ⊠ *100 Boyes Blvd./Hwy. 12,* *Boyes Hot Springs* ☎ *707/938–9000* ⊕ *www.fairmont.com/sonoma.*

Kenwood Inn & Spa. Hands down, this is the prettiest spa setting in the Wine Country. The "wine wrap" body treatment is finished off with a slathering of lotion made from various grape-seed oils and red-wine extract. ⊠ *10400 Sonoma Hwy./Hwy. 12, Kenwood* ☎ *707/833–1293, 800/353–6966* ⊕ *www.kenwoodinn.com.*

Spa Solage. This eco-conscious spa has reinvented the traditional Calistoga mud and mineral water therapies. Case in point: the hour-long "Mudslide," a three-part treatment that includes a mud body mask (in a heated lounge), a soak in a geothermal bath, and a power nap in a comfy sound/vibration chair. Traditional spa services are available as well. ⊠ *755 Silverado Trail, at Rosedale Rd., Calistoga* ☎ *866/942–7442.*

Spa Villagio. This 13,000-square-foot spa with fieldstone walls and a Mediterranean theme has all the latest gadgets, including men's and women's outdoor hot tubs and showers with an extravagant number of showerheads. Huge spa suites—complete with flat-panel TV screens and wet bars—are perfect for couples and groups. ⊠ *6481 Washington St., Yountville* ☎ *707/948–5050, 800/351–1133.*

6

others have a deck with a view of the mountains. **Pros:** sauna next to the pool and hot tub; welcoming vibe attracts diverse guests; some of the most gracious innkeepers in Napa. **Cons:** clothing-optional pool policy isn't for everyone. **TripAdvisor:** "amazing owners," "great stay with fantastic breakfast," "we've become regulars." [$] *Rooms from: $250* ⊠ *601 Petrified Forest Rd.* ☎ *707/942–5651, 800/942–5651* ⊕ *www.meadowlarkinn.com* ⤳ *5 rooms, 5 suites* ⏣ *Breakfast.*

$
B&B/INN   ⬚ **Mount View Hotel & Spa.** A National Historic Landmark built in 1917 in the Mission revival style, the Mount View nevertheless feels up-to-date, with freshly painted rooms (some are a dramatic red and

black), feather duvets, and high-tech touches like iPod alarm clocks. **Pros:** convenient location; excellent spa treatments. **Cons:** ground-floor rooms dark; mediocre Continental breakfast; some bathrooms could use updating. **TripAdvisor:** "luxury and history," "super relaxing amenities and spa," "great service and location." [$] *Rooms from: $249* ✉ *1457 Lincoln Ave.* ☎ *707/942–6877, 800/816–6877* 🌐 *www.mountviewhotel.com* *18 rooms, 13 suites and cottages* 🍴 *Breakfast.*

$$$$ RESORT **Solage.** The cottages at this resort, which spreads over 22 acres, don't look particularly luxurious from the outside, but inside the aesthetic is Napa Valley barn meets San Francisco loft, with high ceilings, polished concrete floors, recycled walnut furniture, and all-natural fabrics in soothing muted colors. **Pros:** great service; complimentary bike cruisers available; separate pools for kids and adults. **Cons:** ascetic vibe; some rooms don't have tubs. **TripAdvisor:** "modern touches in a traditional setting," "unparalleled concierge and service," "all around perfection." [$] *Rooms from: $425* ✉ *755 Silverado Trail* ☎ *866/942–7442, 707/226–0800* 🌐 *www.solagecalistoga.com* *83 rooms, 6 suites.*

SPORTS AND THE OUTDOORS

Calistoga Bikeshop. This bike-shop-turned-outfitter currently offers a self-guided Calistoga Cool Wine Tour package ($80), which includes free tastings at small wineries. Best of all, the shop will pick up any wine you purchase along the way if you've bought more than will fit in the handy bottle carrier on your bike. ✉ *1318 Lincoln Ave.* ☎ *707/942–9687.*

SHOPPING

Mudd Hens. Stock up on bath amenities and soaking salts at this eclectic shop on downtown Calistoga's main drag. The store also sells candles and handmade soaps, including some made from carrot seeds. ✉ *1348C Lincoln Ave., at Washington St.* ☎ *707/942–0210, 800/793–9220.*

Wine Garage. Bargain hunters love this garage-turned-wine-shop, where all the bottles go for $25 or less. It's a great way to discover the work of smaller wineries producing undervalued wines. ✉ *1020 Foothill Blvd., at Hwy. 29* ☎ *707/942–5332, 888/690–9463.*

THE SONOMA VALLEY

Although the Sonoma Valley may not have the cachet of the neighboring Napa Valley, wineries here entice with an unpretentious attitude and smaller crowds. The Napa-style glitzy tasting rooms with enormous gift shops and $25 tasting fees are the exception here. Sonoma's landscape seduces, too, its roads gently climbing and descending on their way to wineries hidden from the road by trees.

The scenic valley, bounded by the Mayacamas Mountains on the east and Sonoma Mountain on the west, extends north from San Pablo Bay nearly 20 miles to the eastern outskirts of Santa Rosa. The varied terrain, soils, and climate (cooler in the south because of the bay influence and hotter toward the north) allow grape growers to raise cool-weather varietals such as Chardonnay and Pinot Noir as well as Merlot, Cabernet Sauvignon, and other heat-seeking vines. The valley is home to dozens of wineries, many of them on or near Highway 12, which runs the length of the valley.

ESSENTIALS

Contacts Sonoma County Tourism Bureau ⊠ *3637 Westwind Blvd., Santa Rosa* 🕾 *707/522–5800, 800/576–6662* ⊕ *www.sonomacounty.com.* **Sonoma Valley Visitors Bureau** ⊠ *453 1st St., E, Sonoma* 🕾 *866/996–1090* ⊕ *www. sonomavalley.com.*

SONOMA

14 miles west of Napa on Hwy. 12; 45 miles from San Francisco, north on U.S. 101, east on Hwy. 37, and north on Hwy. 121/12.

Founded in the early 1800s, Sonoma is the oldest town in the Wine Country. The central Sonoma Plaza dates from the Mission era; surrounding it are 19th-century adobes, atmospheric hotels, and the swooping marquee of the 1930s Sebastiani Theatre. On summer days the plaza is a hive of activity, with children blowing off steam in the playground while their folks stock up on picnic supplies and browse the boutiques surrounding the square.

On your way into town from the south, you pass through the Carneros wine district, which straddles the southern sections of Sonoma and Napa counties.

GETTING HERE AND AROUND

To get to the town of Sonoma from San Francisco, cross the Golden Gate Bridge, then go north on U.S. 101, east on Highway 37 toward Vallejo, and north on Highway 121, aka the Carneros Highway. When you reach Highway 12, turn left and take it north. It turns into Broadway, which dead-ends at Sonoma's Central Plaza. If you park here, a pleasant stroll around the plaza will take you by many of the town's restaurants and shops. Interesting wineries can be found a mile or so east of the plaza; signs on East Spain Street or East Napa Street will direct you to most of them.

EXPLORING

FodorsChoice
★
Bartholomew Park Winery. Although this certified organic winery was founded only in 1994, grapes were grown in some of its vineyards as early as the 1830s. The emphasis here is on handcrafted, single-varietal wines—Cabernet, Merlot, Zinfandel, Syrah, and Sauvignon Blanc. The wines themselves, available only at the winery, make a stop worth it, but another reason to visit is its small museum, with vivid exhibits about the history of the winery and the Sonoma region. Another plus is the beautiful, slightly off-the-beaten-path location in a 375-acre private park about 2 miles from downtown Sonoma (head east on East Napa Street and follow the signs). Pack a lunch to enjoy on the woodsy grounds, one of the prettier picnic spots in Sonoma. ⊠ *1000 Vineyard La., off Castle Rd.* 🕾 *707/935–9511* ⊕ *www.bartpark.com* 🖃 *Tasting $10, tour $20* ⊙ *Daily 11–4:30; tour Fri. and Sat. at 11:30 by reservation.*

Buena Vista Winery. It was here in 1857, at California's oldest premium winery, that Count Agoston Haraszthy de Mokcsa laid the basis for modern California wine making, bucking the conventional wisdom that

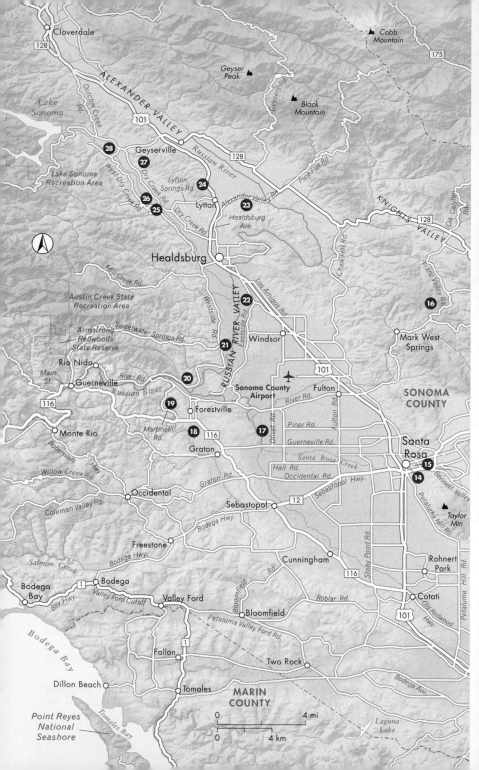

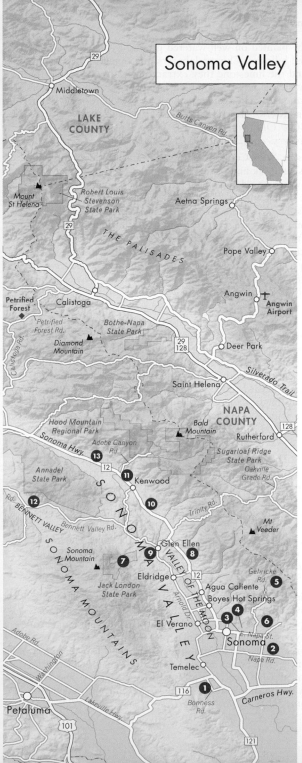

Sonoma Valley

vines should be planted on well-watered ground by instead planting on well-drained hillsides. Chinese laborers dug tunnels 100 feet into the hillside, and the limestone they extracted was used to build the main house, which is now surrounded by redwood and eucalyptus trees and a picnic area. The best wines here are the Chardonnay, Pinot Noir, Syrah, and Merlot grown in the Ramal Vineyard in the Carneros District. ⊠ *18000 Old Winery Rd., off Napa Rd.* ☎ *800/926–1266* ⊕ *buenavistawinery.com* ⊠ *Tasting $10* ⊘ *Daily 10–5.*

Gundlach Bundschu. Wine Country visitors may mispronounce this winery's name (it's gund-lak bund-shoe), but still they flock here to sample ultrapremium wines served by some of the friendliest pourers in Sonoma County. Most of the winery's land has been in the Bundlach family since the 1850s. The Cabernet Sauvignon, Cabernet Franc, Tempranillo, and Chardonnay wines are worth trying, and all are included in the standard $10 tasting. For a more comprehensive experience that also includes a tasting, consider the cave tour ($20) or the vineyard excursion ($40; only available between May and October). ⊠ *2000 Denmark St., at Bundschu Rd, off 8th St. E* ☎ *707/938–5277* ⊕ *www.gunbun.com* ⊠ *Tasting $10, tours $20–$40* ⊘ *Daily 11–4:30.*

Robledo Family Winery. Reynaldo Robledo Sr., a former migrant worker from Michoacán, Mexico, founded this winery that remains a family affair. You're likely to encounter one of the charming Robledo sons in the tasting room, where he'll proudly tell you the story of the immigrant family while pouring tastes of Sauvignon Blanc, Pinot Noir, Merlot, Cabernet Sauvignon, and other wines, including a Chardonnay that comes from the vineyard right outside the door. All seven Robledo sons and two Robledo daughters, as well as matriarch Maria, are involved in the winery operations. ⊠ *21901 Bonness Rd., off Hwy. 116* ☎ *707/939–6903, 888/939–6903* ⊕ *www.robledofamilywinery.com* ⊠ *Tasting $5–$20* ⊘ *Mon.–Sat. 10–5, Sun. 11–4, by appointment.*

Sonoma Mission. The centerpiece of Sonoma State Historic Park, this circa-1823 structure sits just north of Sonoma Plaza. Formally known as the Mission San Francisco Solano, this is the the northernmost of the 21 missions established by Franciscan friars in California. Budget cuts have led to reduced hours, but the facility, worth a peek if you're a history buff, is open daily except Monday between at least 11 and 3. On weekends, docents lead tours every hour on the hour. The modest museum contains exhibits about the California mission network. ⊠ *114 E. Spain St., at 1st St. E* ☎ *707/938–9560* ⊕ *www.parks.ca.gov/?page_id=479* ⊠ *$3* ⊘ *Tues.–Sun. at least 11–3.*

Two Amigos Wines. This tiny winery, just off Sonoma Plaza, has a cultish connection to stardom: Co-owner Squire Fridell was television's Ronald McDonald from 1984 to 1991, and was the spokesman for Toyota for 33 years. Vestiges of Fridell's former life abound in the tasting room—you can't miss the big red shoes on the wall. To some extent, the clown has never left; Fridell and co-owner Bob Briner don Groucho Marx glasses on all wine labels (the glasses also are for sale). The wines here, especially the Bordeaux-style Cuvée Classico, are pretty good, too. ⊠ *Sonoma Court Shops, 25 E. Napa St., at 1st St. E* ☎ *707/799–7146*

⊕ *twoamigoswines.com* ◻*Tasting $10* ⊗ *Thurs.–Mon. 11–6, Tues. and Wed. 1–5.*

WHERE TO EAT

$$$ ✕ **Cafe La Haye.** In a postage-stamp-size open kitchen, skillful chefs turn
AMERICAN out main courses that star on a small but worthwhile seasonal menu
★ emphasizing local ingredients. Chicken, beef, pasta, and fish get deluxe
treatment without fuss or fanfare. The daily roasted chicken and the
risotto specials are always good. Butterscotch pudding is a homey sig-
nature dessert. The dining room is compact, but the friendly owner,
who is often there to greet diners, gives it a particularly welcoming vibe.
ⓢ *Average main: $25* ⊠ *140 E. Napa St., at 1st. St. E* ☎ *707/935–5994*
⊕ *www.cafelahaye.com* ⊗ *Closed Sun. and Mon. No lunch.*

$$ ✕ **Della Santina's.** This longtime favorite, with a charming heated brick
ITALIAN patio out back, serves the most authentic Italian food in town. (The
Della Santina family, which has been running the restaurant since 1990,
hails from Lucca, Italy.) Daily fish and veal specials join classic northern
Italian pastas such as linguine with pesto and lasagna Bolognese. Of
special note are the roasted meat dishes and, when available, petrale sole
and sand dabs. ⓢ *Average main: $18* ⊠ *133 E. Napa St.* ☎ *707/935–
0576* ⊕ *www.dellasantinas.com.*

$$$ ✕ **The Girl & the Fig.** Chef Sondra Bernstein has turned the historic bar-
FRENCH room of the Sonoma Hotel into a hot spot for inventive French cook-
ing. You can always find something with the signature figs in it here,
whether it's a fig-and-arugula salad or an aperitif of sparkling wine with
a fig liqueur. Also look for duck confit with French lentils, a burger
with matchstick fries, or braised pork shank with soft polenta. The
wine list is notable for its emphasis on Rhône varietals, and a counter
in the bar area sells artisanal cheese platters for eating here as well as
cheese by the pound to go. Sunday brunch brings rib-sticking dishes
such as steak and eggs and a Basque frittata with potatoes, onions, and
tomatoes. On weekend nights, the kitchen serves until 11. ⓢ *Average
main: $28* ⊠ *Sonoma Hotel, Sonoma Plaza, 110 W. Spain St., at 1st St.
W* ☎ *707/938–3634* ⊕ *www.thegirlandthefig.com.*

$$ ✕ **Harvest Moon Cafe.** It's easy to feel like one of the family at this little
AMERICAN restaurant with an odd, zigzagging layout. Diners seated at one of the
★ two tiny bars chat with the servers like old friends, but the husband-
and-wife team in the kitchen is serious about the food, much of which
relies on local produce. The daily menu sticks to homey dishes like half
a grilled chicken served with polenta and tapenade, rib-eye steak with
a red-wine sauce, and a marinated-beet-and-frisée salad. Everything is
so perfectly executed and the vibe so genuinely warm that a visit here
is deeply satisfying. In fair weather a spacious back patio, with seats
arranged around a fountain, more than doubles the number of seats.
ⓢ *Average main: $22* ⊠ *487 1st St. W, at W. Napa St.* ☎ *707/933–
8160* ⊕ *www.harvestmooncafesonoma.com* ⊗ *Closed Tues. No lunch
Mon.–Sat.*

$$ ✕ **LaSalette.** Chef-owner Manuel Azevedo, born in the Azores and raised
PORTUGUESE in Sonoma, serves dishes inspired by his native Portugal in this warmly
decorated spot, where the best seats are on the patio, along a pedes-
trian alleyway off Sonoma Plaza. Boldly flavored dishes such as pork

tenderloin *recheado*, stuffed with olives and almonds and topped with a port sauce, or one of the daily seafood specials might be followed by a dish of rice pudding with Madeira-braised figs or a port from the varied list. $ *Average main: $22* ✉ *452 E. 1st St., between E. Spain and E. Napa Sts.* ☎ *707/938–1927* ⊕ *www.lasalette-restaurant.com.*

$$$$

AMERICAN

Fodor'sChoice

★

✕ **Santé.** This elegant dining room has gained a reputation as a destination restaurant through its focus on seasonal and locally sourced ingredients. The room is understated, with drapes in rich earth tones and softly lighted chandeliers, but the food is anything but. Dishes such as the roasted Sonoma duck breast with braised Swiss chard and duck confit are complex without being fussy, while others, like the butter-poached Maine lobster with flageolet beans and lardons, are pure decadence. The restaurant offers a seasonal tasting menu ($125). Brunch is served in summer. $ *Average main: $55* ✉ *Fairmont Sonoma Mission Inn & Spa, 100 Boyes Blvd., off Hwy. 12), 2 miles north of Sonoma, Boyes Hot Springs* ☎ *707/938–9000* ⊕ *www.fairmont.com/ sonoma/GuestServices/Restaurants/SanteRestaurant.htm* ☾ *No lunch.*

$$

AMERICAN

✕ **Sunflower Caffé.** This casual café has one of Sonoma's prettiest patios. Equipped with both heating lamps and plenty of shade, it's comfortable in all but the most inclement weather. On dreary days, cheerful artworks brighten up the interior, where locals hunker over their computers and take advantage of the free Wi-Fi. The menu, composed mostly of salads and sandwiches (as well as omelets and waffles for breakfast), is simple but satisfying, and it relies largely on local ingredients. $ *Average main: $15* ✉ *421 W. 1st St., at W. Spain St.* ☎ *707/996–6645* ⊕ *www. sonomasunflower.com* ☾ *No dinner.*

WHERE TO STAY

For expanded reviews, facilities, and current deals, visit Fodors.com.

$

B&B/INN

🛏 **El Dorado Hotel.** Rooms in this remodeled 1843 building strike a spare, modern pose, with rectilinear four-poster beds and pristine white bedding, but the Mexican-tile floors hint at Sonoma's mission-era past. **Pros:** stylish for the price; hip restaurant downstairs; central location. **Cons:** rooms are small; lighting could be better; noisy. **TripAdvisor:** "awesome food," "rustic chic," "cute place with lots of charm." $ *Rooms from: $175* ✉ *405 1stt St. W, at W. Spain St.* ☎ *707/996–3220* ⊕ *eldoradosonoma.com/el_dorado_hotel.html* ⟿ *27 rooms.*

$$$

RESORT

🛏 **Fairmont Sonoma Mission Inn & Spa.** The real draw at this Mission-style resort is the extensive, swanky spa, easily the biggest in Sonoma, with a vast array of massages and treatments, some using locally sourced grape and lavender products. **Pros:** enormous spa; excellent, well-reviewed restaurant on-site; free shuttle to downtown. **Cons:** standard rooms on the smaller side; not as intimate as some similarly priced places. **TripAdvisor:** "very relaxing," "top notch," "serenity with some fun thrown in." $ *Rooms from: $329* ✉ *100 Boyes Blvd., off Hwy. 12, 2 miles north of Sonoma, Boyes Hot Springs* ☎ *707/938–9000* ⊕ *www. fairmont.com/sonoma* ⟿ *166 rooms, 60 suites.*

$

B&B/INN

☺

🛏 **Sonoma Creek Inn.** The small but cheerful rooms at this roadside inn with a sunny yellow exterior are individually decorated with painted wooden armoires, cozy quilts, and brightly colored contemporary artwork, elevating this bargain option well above your average motel.

Pros: clean, well-lighted bathrooms; a lot of charm for the low price. **Cons:** office not staffed 24 hours a day; slightly out-of-the-way location (about a 10-minute drive from Sonoma Plaza). **TripAdvisor:** "1930's charm with today's comfort," "clean and great value," "sweet and comfy." [$] *Rooms from: $129* ✉ *239 Boyes Blvd., off Hwy. 12* ☎ *707/939–9463, 888/712–1289* 🌐 *www.sonomacreekinn.com* 🛏 *16 rooms.*

NIGHTLIFE AND THE ARTS

Sebastiani Theatre. This theatre, built on Sonoma Plaza in 1934 by Italian immigrant and entrepreneur Samuele Sebastiani, schedules first-run films, as well as occasional musical and theatrical performances. ✉ *476 1st St. E, near W. Spain St.* ☎ *707/996–2020.*

Swiss Hotel. The bar here serves up Glariffee, a cold and potent cousin to Irish coffee, as well as rollicking good times (especially during football season). ✉ *18 W. Spain St., at 1st St. W* ☎ *707/938–2884.*

SHOPPING

Sonoma Plaza is the town's main shopping magnet, with tempting boutiques and specialty food purveyors facing the square or just a block or two away.

Sign of the Bear. This modest and locally owned shop sells the latest and greatest in kitchenware and cookware, as well as a few Wine Country–themed items, such as lazy Susans made from wine barrels. ✉ *435 1st St. W* ☎ *707/996–3722.*

Sonoma Cheese Factory. The town's popular cheese shop offers samples of many local cheeses, though the Sonoma Jack cheese and tangy Sonoma Teleme are no longer made on the premises. The store has everything you need for a picnic, from sandwiches to wine to homemade fudge. ✉ *2 E. Spain St.* ☎ *707/996–1931, 800/535–2855.*

Vella Cheese Company. A block east of Sonoma Plaza, this old-world Italian cheese shop has been making superb cheeses, such as raw-milk cheddars and several varieties of jack, since 1931. ✉ *315 2nd St. E* ☎ *707/938–3232, 800/848–0505.*

GLEN ELLEN

7 miles north of Sonoma on Hwy. 12.

Unlike its flashier Napa Valley counterparts, craggy Glen Ellen eschews well-groomed sidewalks lined with upscale boutiques and restaurants, preferring instead its crooked streets, some with no sidewalks at all, shaded with stands of old oak trees. Jack London, who represents Glen Ellen's rugged spirit, lived in the area for many years; the town commemorates him with place-names and nostalgic establishments. Hidden among sometimes ramshackle buildings abutting Sonoma and Calabasas creeks are low-key shops and galleries worth poking through, and several fine dining establishments.

Where to Eat and Stay in Sonoma Valley

GETTING HERE AND AROUND

To get to Glen Ellen from Sonoma Plaza, drive west on East Spain Street. After about a mile, turn right onto Highway 12. Drive about 7 miles, then take the Arnold Drive exit and turn left. Many of Glen Ellen's restaurants and inns are along a half-mile stretch of Arnold Drive.

EXPLORING

Arrowood Vineyards & Winery. Although it's neither as famous or as old as some of its neighbors, Arrowood produces well-regarded wines, especially the Chardonnays, Syrahs, and age-worthy Cabernets. A wraparound porch with wicker chairs invites you to linger outside the tasting room, built to resemble a New England farmhouse. In fact, if you're more interesting in lounging than a full-on tasting ($10–$15), you can buy a glass of wine to enjoy outside. Tours ($20), offered daily at 10:30 and 2 by appointment, conclude with a seated tasting. ■TIP→ If you're doing a reserve tasting on a weekend and are interested in discovering what Arrowood wines taste like after several years in the bottle, ask if any library wines are available for tasting. ⊠ *14347 Sonoma Hwy. (Hwy. 12)* ☎ *707/935–2600, 800/938–5170* ⊕ *www.arrowoodwinery. com* ⊠ *Tasting $10–$15, tour $20* ☼ *Daily 10–4:30; tours daily 10:30 and 2.*

★ **Benziger Family Winery.** One of the best-known local wineries sits on a sprawling estate in a bowl with 360-degree sun exposure. Benziger is noted for its Merlot, Pinot Noir, Cabernet Sauvignon, Chardonnay, and Sauvignon Blanc. The tram tours here are especially interesting (they're first come, first served). On a ride through the vineyards, guides explain the regional microclimates and geography and provide a glimpse of the extensive cave system. Tours depart several times a day, weather permitting. Reservations are needed for smaller tours that conclude with a seated tasting ($40). ■TIP→ Arrive before lunch for the best shot at joining a tour (they do fill up), and bring a picnic. The grounds here are lovely. ⊠ *1883 London Ranch Rd., off Arnold Dr.* ☎ *707/935–3000, 888/490–2739* ⊕ *www.benziger.com* ⊠ *Tastings $10–$20, tours $20–$40* ☼ *Daily 10–5; tours daily at 11:15, 12:45, and 2:15.*

Jack London State Historic Park. In the hills above Glen Ellen—known as the Valley of the Moon—lies Jack London State Historic Park, where you could easily spend the afternoon hiking along the edge of vineyards and through stands of oak trees. Several of the author's manuscripts and a handful of personal effects are on view at the House of Happy Walls museum, once the home of London's widow. A short hike away from Happy Walls are the ruins of Wolf House. Designed by London, it mysteriously burned down just before he was to move in. Also open to the public are a few restored farm outbuildings, and on weekends you can visit the Cottage, a restored wood-framed building where he wrote many of his later works. London is buried on the property. Budget

FARMERS' MARKET

The **Sonoma Farmers' Market** overflows with locally farmed produce, artisanal cheeses, and baked goods. It's held year-round at Depot Park, just north of Sonoma Plaza, on Friday 9 am–noon. From April through October, it gets extra play on Tuesday evenings, 5:30 pm–sundown, on the plaza itself.

Horseback riding tours loop around Jack London State Historic Park.

cuts may result in reduced hours of operation; be sure to check before you visit. ✉ *2400 London Ranch Rd.* ☎ *707/938–5216* 🎫 *Parking $8, admission to buildings free* 🕘 *Park and museum Fri.–Mon. 10–5, cottage weekends 10–4.*

WHERE TO EAT

$$ FRENCH Fodor's Choice ★ 🍴 **The Fig Cafe.** Pale sage walls, a high, sloping ceiling, and casual but very warm service set a sunny mood in this little bistro that's run by the same team behind Sonoma's The Girl & the Fig. The restaurant's eponymous fruit shows up in all sorts of places, from salads to the wintertime apple-and-fig bread pudding. The small menu focuses on California and French comfort food, like steamed mussels served with terrific crispy fries, and a roast quail served with faro and olives. ■ **TIP→ The unusual no-corkage-fee policy makes it a great place to drink the wine you just discovered down the road.** [$] *Average main: $20* ✉ *13690 Arnold Dr., at O'Donnell La.* ☎ *707/938–2130* 🌐 *www.thefigcafe.com* 🕘 *No lunch weekdays.*

$$$ ECLECTIC 🍴 **Glen Ellen Inn Oyster Grill & Martini Bar.** Tucked inside a creekside 1940s cottage, this cozy restaurant exudes romance, especially if you sit in the shady garden or on the patio strung with tiny lights. After taking the edge off your hunger with some oysters on the half shell and an ice-cold martini, order from a menu that plucks elements from California, French, and occasionally Asian cuisines. You might find ginger tempura calamari with mango salsa or grilled rib-eye steak with Gorgonzola mashed potatoes. Desserts tend toward the indulgent; witness the warm pecan bread pudding with a chocolate center that sits in a puddle of

Hitching a ride on the Benziger Family Winery tram tour

brandy sauce. $ *Average main: $25* ✉ *13670 Arnold Dr., at O'Donnell La.* ☎ *707/996–6409* ⊕ *www.glenelleninn.com* ⊗ *No lunch Wed.*

WHERE TO STAY
For expanded reviews, facilities, and current deals, visit Fodors.com.

$
B&B/INN
★
🖼 **Beltane Ranch.** On a slope of the Mayacamas range a few miles from Glen Ellen, this 1892 ranch house, shaded by magnificent oak trees, contains charmingly old-fashioned rooms, each individually decorated with antiques and thick old-fashioned bedcovers. **Pros:** casual, friendly atmosphere; reasonably priced; beautiful grounds with ancient oak trees. **Cons:** downstairs rooms get some noise from upstairs rooms; cooled with ceiling fans instead of air-conditioning. **TripAdvisor:** "the beauty is in the details," "beautiful and relaxing," "straight out of Gone with the Wind." $ *Rooms from: $175* ✉ *11775 Sonoma Hwy. (Hwy. 12)* ☎ *707/996–6501* ⊕ *www.beltaneranch.com* ⌇ *3 rooms, 2 suites, 1 cottage* ⍩ *Breakfast.*

$$$$
RENTAL
🖼 **The Chauvet.** Originally built in 1906 as a hotel, this yellow-brick property in downtown Glen Ellen is listed on the National Registry of Historic Places and was renovated in 2007 as six upscale condominium rentals. **Pros:** spacious accommodations offer room to spread out; local artwork adorns exposed-brick walls; short (uphill) walk to Jack London State Historic Park. **Cons:** no services on-site; long drive to downtown Sonoma. **TripAdvisor:** "lovely weekend," "true luxury condominiums," "unforgettable." $ *Rooms from: $600* ✉ *13756 Arnold Dr.* ☎ *415/823–4570, 855/242–8838* ⊕ *www.chauvetcondominium.com* ⌇ *6 units.*

$$ B&B/INN Fodor's Choice ★ **Gaige House.** Gorgeous Asian objets d'art and leather club chairs cozied up to the fireplace in the lobby are just a few of the graceful touches in this luxurious but understated B&B. **Pros:** beautiful lounge areas; cottages are very private; excellent service. **Cons:** sound carries in the main house; the least expensive rooms are on the small side. **TripAdvisor:** "amazing boutique hotel," "laid-back Sonoma at its best," "outstanding stay in serenity." [$] *Rooms from: $275* ✉ *13540 Arnold Dr.* ☎ *707/935–0237, 800/935–0237* 🌐 *www.gaige.com* *10 rooms, 13 suites* 🍴 *Breakfast.*

KENWOOD

3 miles north of Glen Ellen on Hwy. 12.

Blink and you might miss tiny Kenwood, which consists of little more than a few restaurants and shops and a historic train depot. But hidden in this pretty landscape of meadows and woods at the north end of Sonoma Valley are several good wineries, most just off the Sonoma Highway.

GETTING HERE AND AROUND

To get to Kenwood from Glen Ellen, drive 3 miles north on Highway 12.

EXPLORING

Deerfield Ranch Winery. Visitors to this fun Kenwood winery arrive already in the middle of the action; from the parking lot, you walk across the crush pad, past a row of barrels, and straight into the wine cave. About halfway back, owners Robert and P.J. Rex have fashioned a makeshift living room, complete with comfy couches, tables, candles and tasting bars. Robert, who is also the winemaker, likes Super Tuscan-style and Bordeaux-style blends and makes them with gusto (the 2002 DRX is a blend to be reckoned with). Standard tastings ($15) include five wines; for an additional $5, you can taste all seven in the portfolio. ✉ *10200 Sonoma Hwy. (Hwy. 12)* ☎ *707/833–5215* 🌐 *www.deerfieldranch.com* 🎫 *Tastings $15–$20* 🕒 *Daily 10:30–4:30.*

Kunde Estate Winery & Vineyards. On your way into Kunde Estate Winery & Vineyards you pass a terrace flanked with fountains, virtually coaxing you to stay for a picnic with views over the vineyard. Kunde is perhaps best known for its toasty Chardonnays, although tastings might include Sauvignon Blanc, Cabernet Sauvignon, and Zinfandel as well. For insight into the winery's approach to sustainable winemaking, take a few minutes to wander around the demonstration vineyard outside the tasting room. The (free) basic tour of the grounds includes the extensive caves, some of which stretch 175 feet below a Syrah vineyard. Reserve in advance if you want to take advantage of the Mountain Top Tasting, a tour that ends with a sampling of reserve wines at the highest point on the property ($30). ✉ *9825 Sonoma Hwy. (Hwy. 12)* ☎ *707/833–5501* 🌐 *www.kunde.com* 🎫 *Tastings $10–$40, tours free–$30* 🕒 *Daily 10:30–5; tours daily at various times.*

★ **St. Francis Winery.** Named for St. Francis of Assisi, founder of the Franciscan order, which established missions and vineyards throughout California, St. Francis Winery has one of the most scenic locations in

6

Sonoma, nestled at the foot of Mt. Hood. The visitor center beautifully replicates the California Mission style, with its red-tile roof and dramatic bell tower. The charm of the surroundings is matched by the wines, most of them red, including rich, earthy Zinfandels from both the Russian River and Sonoma valleys. In addition to the usual wine tastings, food and wine pairings are available ($20 to $35). ✉ *100 Pythian Rd., off Hwy. 12* ☎ *888/675–9463, 707/833–6146* 🌐 *www.stfranciswine.com* 🎫 *Tastings $10–35, tour $30* 🕒 *Daily 10–5; tours by appointment (call for times).*

WHERE TO EAT AND STAY

For expanded reviews, facilities, and current deals, visit Fodors.com.

$$ ITALIAN 🍴 **Café Citti.** Classical music in the background and a friendly staff (as well as a roaring fire when the weather's cold) keep this no-frills roadside café from feeling too spartan. Order dishes such as roast chicken and slabs of tiramisu from the counter and they're delivered to your table, a few of which are on an outdoor patio. The array of prepared salads and sandwiches means the café does a brisk business in takeout for picnic packers, but you can also choose pasta made to order. [$] *Average main: $15* ✉ *9049 Sonoma Hwy. (Hwy. 12)* ☎ *707/833–2690* 🌐 *www.cafecitti.com.*

$$$$ B&B/INN ★ 🏨 **Kenwood Inn and Spa.** Buildings resembling graceful old haciendas and the mature fruit trees that shade the courtyards make it seem like this inn has been here for more than a century (it was actually built in 1990). **Pros:** large rooms; lavish furnishings; extremely romantic. **Cons:** Wi-Fi can be spotty in some areas; expensive. **TripAdvisor:** "Italian getaway in Sonoma," "perfect place," "pure 5-star relaxation." [$] *Rooms from: $499* ✉ *10400 Sonoma Hwy. (Hwy. 12)* ☎ *707/833–1293, 800/353–6966* 🌐 *www.kenwoodinn.com* 🛏 *25 rooms, 4 suites* 🍽 *Breakfast.*

ELSEWHERE IN SONOMA COUNTY

At nearly 1,598 square miles, there's more to Sonoma County than the day-tripper favorites of Sonoma, Glen Ellen, and Kenwood. To the north is Healdsburg, a small town with killer shopping. The national media have latched onto it for its swank hotels and remarkable restaurants, and many Fodors.com readers recommend it as an ideal home base for wine tasting in northern Sonoma County.

Within easy striking distance of Healdsburg are the scenic vineyards of the Alexander, Dry Creek, and Russian River valleys. These lookers produce some of the country's best Pinot Noir, Cabernet Sauvignon, Zinfandel, and Sauvignon Blanc. Though these regions are hardly unknown names, their quiet, narrow roads feel a world away from Highway 29 in Napa. The western stretches of Sonoma County are sparsely populated in comparison to the above destinations and have fewer wineries. River Road heading west from U.S. 101—the exit is about 4 miles north of Santa Rosa—intersects Westside Road, which passes through Pinot Noir paradise on its way to Healdsburg.

SANTA ROSA

8 miles northwest of Kenwood on Hwy. 12.

Santa Rosa, the Wine Country's largest city, isn't likely to charm you with its office buildings, department stores, and frequent snarls of traffic along U.S. 101. It is, however, home to a couple of interesting cultural offerings. Its moderately priced chain lodgings can be handy, especially since Santa Rosa is roughly equidistant from Sonoma, Healdsburg, and the Russian River valley, three of the most popular wine-tasting destinations.

GETTING HERE AND AROUND

To get to Santa Rosa from San Francisco, drive north over the Golden Gate Bridge and continue north on U.S. 101 to the downtown Santa Rosa exit. To get to Santa Rosa from Sonoma Valley, take Highway 12 north. Santa Rosa's hotels, restaurants, and wineries are spread over a wide area; factor in extra time when driving around Santa Rosa, especially during morning and evening commute hours.

EXPLORING

Charles M. Schulz Museum. Fans of Snoopy and Charlie Brown will love the Charles M. Schulz Museum, dedicated to the cartoonist who lived in Santa Rosa for the last 30 years of his life, until his death in 2000. Permanent installations such as a re-creation of the artist's studio share the space with temporary exhibits, which often focus on a particular theme in Schulz's work. Children and adults can take a stab at creating cartoons in the Education Room or wander through the labyrinth in the form of Snoopy's head. ✉ *2301 Hardies La., at W. Steele La.* ☎ *707/579–4452* ⊕ *www.schulzmuseum.org* 🎫 *$10* ⊘ *Labor Day–Memorial Day, Wed.–Fri. and Mon. 11–5, weekends 10–5; Memorial Day–Labor Day, weekdays 11–5, weekends 10–5.*

★ **De Loach Vineyards.** Just far enough off the beaten track to feel like a real find, this winery produces old-vine Zinfandels, Chardonnays, and a handful of other varietals, but it is best for known for its Pinot Noir, some of which is made using open-top wood fermentation vats that are uncommon in Sonoma but have been used in France for centuries. (Some think they intensify a wine's flavor.) Tours focus on the estate vineyards, where you can learn about the labor-intensive biodynamic and organic farming methods used, and take you through the culinary garden. Call a day or two in advance if you want to taste wines paired with regional cheeses ($25) or purchase a picnic basket ($30) to enjoy in their attractive picnic area. ✉ *1791 Olivet Rd.* ☎ *707/526–9111, 800/441–9298* ⊕ *www.deloachvineyards.com* 🎫 *Tasting $10–$25, tour $15* ⊘ *Daily 10–5; tours daily at 11 (or by appointment).*

Luther Burbank Home and Gardens. The Luther Burbank Home and Gardens commemorates the great botanist who lived and worked on these grounds and single-handedly developed the modern techniques of hybridization. The 1.6-acre garden and a greenhouse show the results of some of Burbank's experiments to develop spineless cactus, fruit trees, and flowers such as the Shasta daisy. Instructions for accessing the free self-guided garden tour using visitors' own cell phones is posted near the

6

carriage house. In the music room of his house, a modified Greek revival structure that was Burbank's home from 1884 to 1906, a dictionary lies open to a page on which the verb "burbank" is defined as "to modify and improve plant life." To see the house, you'll need to join one of the docent-led tours, which leave from the gift shop every half hour or so. ✉ *204 Santa Rosa Ave., at Sonoma Ave.* ☎ *707/524–5445* 🌐 *www.lutherburbank.org* 🎟 *Gardens free, tour $7* 🕒 *Gardens daily 8–dusk; museum and gift shop Apr.–Oct., Tues.–Sun. 10–4.*

Fodor's Choice ★ **Matanzas Creek Winery.** The visitor center at this beautiful winery sets itself apart with an understated Japanese aesthetic, extending to a tranquil fountain and a koi pond. Best of all, huge windows overlook a vast field of lavender plants. ■ **TIP→ The ideal time to visit is in May and June, when the lavender blooms and perfumes the air.** The winery specializes in Sauvignon Blanc, Merlot, and Chardonnay, although it also produces a popular dry rosé as well as some Syrah, Pinot Noir, and Cabernet. Guided tours range from an hour-long intro to the Bennett Valley, the tiny AVA where the winery is located ($10), to a more expensive one ($35) that concludes with a taste of limited-production and library wines paired with artisanal cheeses. If you'd like to go it on your own, ask for a printed vineyard-tour guide. ✉ *6097 Bennett Valley Rd.* ☎ *707/528–6464, 800/590–6464* 🌐 *www.matanzascreek.com* 🎟 *Tasting $5, tours $10–$35* 🕒 *Daily 10–4:30; tour by appointment.*

👶 **Safari West.** An unexpected bit of wilderness in the Wine Country, this African wildlife preserve covers 400 acres on the outskirts of Santa Rosa. Set aside an entire morning or afternoon for a visit, which begins with a stroll around enclosures housing lemurs, cheetahs, giraffes, and many varieties of rare birds, like the brightly colored scarlet ibis. Next, guests climb onto open-air vehicles that spend about two hours driving around the expansive property, where more than 80 species, such as African cape buffalo, gazelles, wildebeests, and zebras make their home on the hillsides. All the while you're accompanied by a staff member who informs you about the animals, their behavior, and the threats they face in the wild. Note that the admission price for children ages 3 to 12 is $30–$32. If you'd like to extend your stay, lodging in well-equipped tent cabins ($–$$) is available. ✉ *3115 Porter Creek Rd.* ☎ *707/579–2551, 800/616–2695* 🌐 *www.safariwest.com* 🎟 *$68–$78.*

WHERE TO EAT

$$$ ITALIAN Fodor's Choice ★ 🍴 **Zazu.** A low wooden ceiling, rustic copper tables, and rock music on the stereo create a casual vibe at this roadhouse. It's a few miles west of downtown Santa Rosa, but the hearty, soulful cooking of owners Duskie Estes and John Stewart lures passionate fans from all over the Wine Country. About 30% of the produce comes from their own garden, and the meats are house-cured, so the antipasto plate or a pizza with house-made pepperoni are both excellent choices. The small seasonal menu—a mix of Italian-influenced dishes and updated American classics—tends toward rich flavors, with choices like rabbit braised in red wine and served with a mushroom risotto. On Mondays in summer, try the three-course family-style "farm supper" for $39 per person. Sunday brunch, featuring cornmeal waffles (among other great choices), is worthwhile, too. [$] *Average main: $30* ✉ *3535 Guerneville Rd., at*

Willowside Rd. ☎ *707/523–4814* ⊕ *www.zazurestaurant.com* ◷ *Closed Tues. No lunch.*

WHERE TO STAY

For expanded reviews, facilities, and current deals, visit Fodors.com.

$ **Flamingo Conference Resort & Spa.** If Don Draper from the hit show RESORT *Mad Men* popped into Santa Rosa, he'd probably park himself in this kitschy, 1950s-style resort just beyond downtown; the rooms have been updated since the property opened in 1957, but they've still got high ceilings and that old-school flair. **TripAdvisor:** "great customer service," "well-appointed room," "neat retro atmosphere." [$] *Rooms from: $119* ⊠ *2777 4th St.* ☎ *707/545–8530, 800/848–8300* ⊕ *www. flamingoresort.com* ⇆ *170 rooms.*

RUSSIAN RIVER VALLEY

10 miles northwest of Santa Rosa.

The Russian River flows from Mendocino to the Pacific Ocean, but in terms of wine making, the Russian River valley is centered on a triangle with points at Healdsburg, Guerneville, and Sebastopol. Tall redwoods shade many of the two-lane roads that access this scenic area, where, thanks to the cooling marine influence, Pinot Noir and Chardonnay are the king and queen of grapes.

ESSENTIALS

Contacts Russian River Wine Road ⊠ *498 Moore La., Healdsburg* ☎ *707/433–4335, 800/723–6336* ⊕ *www.wineroad.com.*

GETTING HERE AND AROUND

Many people visit the Russian River valley while based in nearby Healdsburg. To get to the wineries along Westside Road from Healdsburg's central plaza, head south on Center Street and turn right at Mill Street, which turns into Westside Road after it crosses U.S. 101. From Westside Road turn left on Wohler Road and left again on Eastside Road to loop back to U.S. 101 just south of Healdsburg. Wineries are somewhat more widely spaced in this rural area than in other parts of the Wine Country, and you should plan on spending some leisurely time driving along the winding roads. This is also a particularly scenic area for biking and jogging.

EXPLORING

Gary Farrell Winery. Pass through an impressive metal gate and wind your way up a steep hill to reach Gary Farrell, a spot with knockout views over the rolling hills and vineyards below. Although the winery has changed hands a few times since Farrell sold it in 2004, it's managed to continue producing well-regarded bottles under Susan Reed, who worked alongside him. Though its earthy, full-bodied Zinfandels and Carneros and Russian River Chardonnays are winners, the winery has built its reputation on its Pinot Noirs. ⊠ *10701 Westside Rd., Healdsburg* ☎ *707/473–2900* ⊕ *www.garyfarrellwines.com* ⌸ *Tasting $10–$15, tour $25* ◷ *Daily 10:30–4:30; tour by appointment.*

DID YOU KNOW?

People often refer to the Wine Country as having a Mediterranean climate. The temperature year-around and precipitation patterns are very similar to those found in Italy and Greece. But there are also a number of micro-climates that provide the prime conditions for a variety of wines.

Annual barrel tasting along Russian River's wine road

Hartford Family Winery. Pinot Noir fans flock to this opulent winery that sits off a meandering country road. The winemakers here turn grapes from the cooler areas of the Russian River valley, Sonoma coast, and other regions into crisp Chardonnays, old-vine Zinfandels, and Pinots, many of which are single-vineyard wines. Tours of the barrel room ($10, not including tasting) and a seated tasting of library wines ($25) are offered (call ahead). ⊠ *8075 Martinelli Rd., off Hwy. 116 or River Rd., Forestville* ☎ *707/887–1756, 800/588–0234* ⊕ *www. hartfordwines.com* 🍷 *Tastings $15–$25, tour $10* ☉ *Daily 10–4:30; tours by appointment.*

Fodor's Choice
★

Iron Horse Vineyards. A one-lane country road leads to Iron Horse Vineyards, known for its sparkling wines, from the bright and austere to the rich and toasty, as well as estate Chardonnays and Pinot Noirs. Three hundred acres of rolling, vine-covered hills, barnlike buildings, and a rustic outdoor tasting area with a view of Mt. St. Helena set this winery apart from stuffier spots. Tours (by appointment) take place weekdays at 10 am. Winemaker David Munksgard leads the Friday tour. ⊠ *9786 Ross Station Rd., off Hwy. 116, Sebastopol* ☎ *707/887–1507* ⊕ *www. ironhorsevineyards.com* 🍷 *Tasting $10, tour $20* ☉ *Daily 10–4:30; tour weekdays at 10 by appointment.*

J Vineyards and Winery. The dry sparkling wines made here, all from Pinot Noir and Chardonnay grapes planted in Russian River vineyards, have wonderfully complex fruit and floral aromas and good acidity. Best known for its sparklers, J also makes fine still wines, often from Pinot and Chardonnay grapes, as well as brandy-fortified dessert wine and a pear eau-de-vie. You can sample just the wines at the tasting bar, or indulge yourself in the Bubble Room (reservations required), where top-end still and sparkling wines are paired with food. Free, 30-minute tours take place twice daily. ✉ *11447 Old Redwood Hwy., at Eastside Rd., Healdsburg* ☎ *707/431–3646* 🌐 *www.jwine.com* 🎟 *Tasting $20–$65, tours free* 🕒 *Daily 11–5; Bubble Room hrs vary; tours daily 11 and 2:30.*

Rochioli Vineyards and Winery. Claiming one of the prettiest picnic sites in the area, with tables overlooking vineyards, this winery also has an airy little tasting room hung with modern artwork. Production is small—about 12,000 cases annually—and fans on the winery's mailing list snap up most of the bottles, but the wines are still worth a stop. Because of the cool growing conditions in the Russian River valley, the flavors of the Chardonnay and Sauvignon Blanc are intense and complex. It's the Pinot, though, that is largely responsible for the winery's stellar reputation; it helped cement the Russian River's status as a Pinot powerhouse. ■ **TIP→** Though Rochioli typically pours only a couple of wines for visitors, it's one of the few wineries of its stature that still doesn't charge for a tasting. ✉ *6192 Westside Rd., Healdsburg* ☎ *707/433–2305* 🌐 *www.rochioliwinery.com* 🎟 *Tasting free* 🕒 *Thurs.–Mon. 11–4, Tues. and Wed. by appointment; closed mid-Dec.–early Jan.*

6

WHERE TO EAT

$$$$ FRENCH Fodor's Choice ★

🍴 **The Farmhouse Inn.** From the personable sommelier who assists you with wine choices to the servers who describe the provenance of the black truffles shaved over your intricate pasta dish, the staff matches the quality of this restaurant's outstanding French-inspired cuisine. The signature dish, "rabbit, rabbit, rabbit," a rich trio of confit of leg, rabbit loin wrapped in applewood-smoked bacon, and roasted rack of rabbit with a whole-grain mustard sauce, is typical of the preparations that are both rustic and refined, and the starters often include a seared Sonoma foie gras served with an apple cider sauce. The restaurant offers three-course, prix-fixe dinners every Monday for $49 per person. ■ **TIP→** The inn is a favorite of wine-industry foodies, so reserve well in advance; if you haven't done so, you might still be able to dine in the small lounge area. [$] *Prix-fixe: $52* ✉ *7871 River Rd., at Wohler Rd., Forestville* ☎ *707/887–3300, 800/464–6642* 🌐 *www.farmhouseinn.com* ✍ *Reservations essential* 🕒 *Closed Tues. and Wed. No lunch.*

WHERE TO STAY

For expanded reviews, facilities, and current deals, visit Fodors.com.

$$$ B&B/INN Fodor's Choice ★

🏨 **The Farmhouse Inn.** Inside a pale yellow 1873 farmhouse and its adjacent cottages, this hotel maintains individually decorated guest rooms with comfortable touches such as down comforters and whirlpool tubs. **Pros:** one of Sonoma's best restaurants is on-site; free snacks, games, movies, and luxury bath products available; full-service spa uses many products made from local ingredients. **Cons:** rooms closest to the street get a bit of road noise. **TripAdvisor:** "in a different world," "the perfect wine country experience," "wonderful place with fantastic service." [$] *Rooms from: $350* ✉ *7871 River Rd., Forestville* ☎ *707/887–3300, 800/464–6642* 🌐 *www.farmhouseinn.com* 🛏 *12 rooms, 6 suites* 🍽 *Breakfast.*

$ HOTEL [Family] 🏨 **Sebastopol Inn.** Simple but cheerful rooms, freshly painted a sunny yellow and equipped with blue-and-white striped curtains, have a spare California country style at this reasonably priced inn. **Pros:** friendly staff; just steps from a café, wine bar, and spa. **Cons:** 30-minute drive from most Russian River wineries; some will find the beds too firm. **TripAdvisor:** "clean and convenient," "well tended," "big room." [$] *Rooms from: $135* ✉ *6751 Sebastopol Ave., Sebastopol* ☎ *707/829–2500* 🌐 *www.sebastopolinn.com* 🛏 *29 rooms, 2 suites.*

SPORTS AND THE OUTDOORS

Burke's Canoe Trips. This friendly Forestville-based outfitter rents canoes ($60 per day) for a leisurely paddle 10 miles downstream to Guerneville. A shuttle bus will return you to your car at the end of the journey. From late May through mid-October is the best time for canoeing. ✉ *River and Mirabel Rds., 1 mile north of Forestville* ☎ *707/887–1222* 🌐 *www.burkescanoetrips.com.*

HEALDSBURG

17 miles north of Santa Rosa on U.S. 101.

Just when it seems that the buzz about Healdsburg couldn't get any more intense, there's another article published in a glossy food or wine magazine about the restaurant Cyrus or the spanking new h2hotel. The good news: You don't have to be a tycoon to stay here and enjoy the town. For every ritzy restaurant there's a great bakery or relatively modest B&B. A tin-roofed bandstand on Healdsburg's plaza hosts free summer concerts, where you might hear anything from bluegrass to Sousa marches. Add to that the fragrant magnolia trees shading the square and the bright flower beds, and the whole thing is as pretty as a Norman Rockwell painting.

The setting is no less idyllic in the nearby countryside, where stores straddling the relatively untrafficked roads sell just-plucked fruits and vine-ripened tomatoes. Winery buildings here are barely visible, since they're tucked behind groves of eucalyptus or hidden high on fog-shrouded hills.

GETTING HERE AND AROUND

To get to Healdsburg from San Francisco, cross the Golden Gate Bridge and continue north on U.S. 101. About 65 miles from San Francisco, take the Central Healdsburg exit and follow Healdsburg Avenue a few blocks to the town's central plaza. Many of the town's hotels and restaurants ring the scenic town square and the few blocks radiating out from here.

WHERE TO EAT

$$$$ AMERICAN 🍴 **Barndiva.** This hip joint abandons the homey vibe of so many Wine Country spots for a younger, more urban feel. Electronic music plays quietly in the background while hipster servers ferry inventive seasonal cocktails. The food is as stylish as the well-dressed couples cozying up next to one another on the banquette seats. Make a light meal out of starters like goat-cheese croquettes or "The Artisan," a bountiful plate of cheeses and charcuterie, or settle in for the evening with dishes such

as pork tenderloin with potato puree or lobster risotto. During warm weather the open-air patio is the place to be. [$] *Average main: $32* ✉ *231 Center St., at Matheson St.* ☎ *707/431–0100* 🌐 *www.barndiva.com* 🕒 *Closed Mon. and Tues.*

$$ ITALIAN 🍴 **Bovolo.** Husband-and-wife team John Stewart and Duskie Estes—they of Zazu fame—opened this restaurant on the Healdsburg Plaza to serve what they call "slow food . . . fast." The stars of the show: house-cured meats that are featured in pizzas, pastas, and sandwiches. For instance, the Salumist's Salad mixes a variety of cured meats with greens, white beans, and a tangy vinaigrette; and a thin-crust pizza might come topped with house-made Italian pork sausage and roasted peppers. House-made gelato served with a dark chocolate sauce or *zeppole* (Italian donuts) provide a perfect ending to a meal. On summer weekends, the restaurant serves breakfast at 9 am. Closing hours vary according to season, so call ahead if planning an evening visit. [$] *Average main: $18* ✉ *106 Matheson St., at Healdsburg Ave.* ☎ *707/431–2962* 🌐 *www.bovolorestaurant.com* ✍ *Reservations not accepted* 🕒 *Often no dinner Tues. and Wed.; no dinner Sun.–Thurs. fall–spring.*

$$ FRENCH 🍴 **Costeaux.** This French-style bakery in downtown Healdsburg has won numerous awards for its bread, and the croissants and Epi breads are the best in all of Sonoma County. Also worth sampling: savory breakfast and lunch dishes, such as the homemade quiche or the omelet with sun-dried tomatoes, bacon, and Brie. Arrive early on weekends to grab a seat on the open-air patio. [$] *Average main: $15* ✉ *417 Healdsburg Ave., at North St.* ☎ *707/433–1913* 🌐 *www.costeaux.com* 🕒 *No dinner.*

$$$$ AMERICAN Fodor's Choice ★ 🍴 **Cyrus.** Hailed as the best thing to hit the Wine Country since French Laundry, Cyrus has collected lots of awards and many raves from guests. From the moment you're seated to the minute your dessert plates are whisked away, you'll be carefully tended by gracious servers and an expert sommelier. The formal dining room, with its vaulted Venetian-plaster ceiling, is a suitably plush setting for chef Douglas Keane's creative, subtle cuisine. Each night, diners have their choice of four set menus: five- and eight-course extravaganzas ($108 and $135, respectively), for both omnivores and vegetarians. Wine pairings are available for both (also $108 and $135). Set aside three hours to work your way from savory starters such as a terrine of foie gras with curried apple compote, through fragrant dishes such as a truffled wine risotto with Parmesan broth. Desserts are otherworldly, and every guest receives a box of tiny sweets to take home. If you've failed to make reservations, you can order à la carte at the bar, which has one of the best collection of cocktails and spirits in all of the Wine Country. [$] *Prix-fixe: $108* ✉ *29 North St., near Healdsburg Ave.* ☎ *707/433–3311* 🌐 *www.cyrusrestaurant.com* ✍ *Reservations essential* 🕒 *Closed Tues. and Wed. in winter. No lunch.*

$$$ ITALIAN 🍴 **Scopa.** At this tiny eatery chef Ari Rosen cooks up rustic Italian specialties such as house-made ravioli stuffed with ricotta cheese, braised chicken with greens and polenta, and *polpette Calabrese* (spicy meatballs served with smoked mozzarella in a tomato sauce). Simple thin-crust pizzas are worth ordering, too. Locals love the restaurant for its lack of pretension: wine is served in juice glasses, and the friendly

6

hostess visits guests frequently to make sure all are satisfied. You'll be packed in elbow-to-elbow with your fellow diners, but for a convivial evening over a bottle of Nebbiolo, there's no better choice. [$] *Average main: $25* ✉ *109A Plaza St., near Healdsburg Ave.* ☎ *707/433–5282* 🌐 *www.scopahealdsburg.com* 🕓 *No lunch.*

$$$ MEDITERRANEAN 🍴 **Spoonbar.** Cantina doors that open wide onto Healdsburg Avenue make this trendy eatery especially appealing in summer, when the warm breeze wafts into the stylish space. Inside, concrete walls, mid-century modern chairs, and a long communal table fashioned from rough-hewn acacia wood create an urbane setting for the modern Mediterranean fare. "Small bites" like the marinated quail eggs, spicy lamb meatballs, and house-cured olives are standouts, while several of the entrée-sized dishes demonstrate a Moroccan flair (the Moorish-style chicken with grilled lemon and couscous is especially popular). The perpetually packed bar, where celebrity bartender Scott Beattie and his staff mix inventive seasonal cocktails, is the real draw for many locals. [$] *Average main: $29* ✉ *h2hotel, 219 Healdsburg Ave., at Vine St.* ☎ *707/433–7222* 🌐 *www.h2hotel.com/spoonbar* 🕓 *No lunch Mon.–Thurs. in winter.*

$$$ AMERICAN 🍴 **Zin Restaurant and Wine Bar.** Concrete walls and floors and large canvases on the walls lend the restaurant a casual, industrial, and slightly artsy feel. The American cuisine—such as the grilled pork chop with homemade applesauce or the wine-braised lamb shank—is hearty and highly seasoned. Portions are large, so consider sharing if you hope to save room for desserts such as the brownie sundae with house-made ice cream. As you might have guessed from the name, Zinfandel is the drink of choice here: the varietal makes up roughly half of the 100 or so bottles on the wine list. From Sunday through Thursday, blue-plate specials featuring homey fare (like pot roast and chicken and dumplings) make this place a bargain. [$] *Average main: $25* ✉ *344 Center St., at North St.* ☎ *707/473–0946* 🌐 *zinrestaurant.com* 🕓 *No lunch weekends.*

WHERE TO STAY

For expanded reviews, facilities, and current deals, visit Fodors.com.

$ B&B/INN 🏨 **Camellia Inn.** In a well-preserved Italianate Victorian constructed in 1869, this colorful B&B is on a quiet residential street a block from the town's main square. **Pros:** reasonable rates; a rare family-friendly inn; within easy walking distance of restaurants. **Cons:** a few rooms have a shower but no bath; all rooms lack TVs. **TripAdvisor:** "a truly wonderful inn," "make yourself at home," "helpful staff." [$] *Rooms from: $230* ✉ *211 North St.* ☎ *707/433–8182, 800/727–8182* 🌐 *www.camelliainn.com* 🛏 *8 rooms, 1 suite* 🍽 *Breakfast.*

$ B&B/INN 🏨 **h2hotel.** Eco-friendly touches abound at this LEED-certified newcomer, from the undulating plant-covered "green roof" to wooden decks made from salvaged lumber. **Pros:** stylish modern design; Healdsburg's most popular bar; king beds can be converted to two twins. **Cons:** least expensive rooms lack bathtubs; no fitness facilities on-site. **TripAdvisor:** "unique property," "great small touches," "modern hotel." [$] *Rooms from: $200* ✉ *219 Healdsburg Ave.* ☎ *707/922–5251* 🌐 *www.h2hotel.com* 🛏 *34 rooms, 2 suites* 🍽 *Breakfast.*

$$$ B&B/INN ★ **The Honor Mansion.** An 1883 Italianate Victorian houses this photogenic hotel, and rooms in the main house preserve a sense of the building's heritage, while the larger suites are comparatively understated. **Pros:** spacious grounds with boccie and tennis courts, a putting green, and half-court for basketball; homemade sweets available at all hours; spa pavilions by pool available for massages in fair weather. **Cons:** almost a mile from Healdsburg's plaza; walls can seem thin. **TripAdvisor:** "beautiful and relaxing," "simply the best," "Honor Mansion defines service." [$] *Rooms from: $315* ✉ *891 Grove St.* ☎ *707/433–4277, 800/554–4667* 🌐 *www.honormansion.com* 🛏 *5 rooms, 7 suites, 1 cottage* ⏲ *Closed 2 wks around Christmas* 🍴 *Breakfast.*

FARMERS' MARKET

During two weekly **Healdsburg farmers' markets** you can buy locally made goat cheese, fragrant lavender, and olive oil in addition to the usual produce. On Saturday from May through November the market takes place one block west of the town plaza, at the corner of North and Vine streets, 9 am–noon. The smaller Tuesday market, which runs from June through October, takes place two blocks northwest of the plaza, in a parking lot off North Street, 4–7 pm.

$$$ RESORT **Hotel Healdsburg.** Across the street from Healdsburg's tidy town plaza, this spare, sophisticated hotel caters to travelers with an urban sensibility. **Pros:** several rooms overlook the town plaza; comfortable lobby with a small attached bar; extremely comfortable beds. **Cons:** exterior rooms get some street noise; rooms could use better lighting. **TripAdvisor:** "casual luxury at its best," "really comfortable," "refreshing hotel with world-class staff." [$] *Rooms from: $375* ✉ *25 Matheson St.* ☎ *707/431–2800, 800/889–7188* 🌐 *www.hotelhealdsburg.com* 🛏 *46 rooms, 10 suites* 🍴 *Breakfast.*

$$$$ HOTEL **Hôtel Les Mars.** This Relais & Châteaux property takes the prize for opulence with guest rooms spacious and elegant enough for French nobility, with 18th- and 19th-century antiques and reproductions, canopied beds, and gas-burning fireplaces. **Pros:** large rooms; just off Healdsburg's plaza; Bulgari bath products. **Cons:** very expensive. **TripAdvisor:** "absolutely first class," "luxurious weekend getaway destination," "finest hotel in the Sonoma wine country." [$] *Rooms from: $600* ✉ *27 North St.* ☎ *707/433–4211* 🌐 *www.hotellesmars.com* 🛏 *16 rooms* 🍴 *Breakfast.*

$$ B&B/INN **Madrona Manor.** The flagship 1881 Victorian mansion here is surrounded by 8 acres of wooded and landscaped grounds, and rooms in the three-story mansion, the carriage house, and the three separate cottages are splendidly ornate, with mirrors in gilt frames and paintings covering every wall. **Pros:** old-fashioned and romantic; pretty veranda perfect for a cocktail. **Cons:** pool heated May through October only; some might find decor too fussy. **TripAdvisor:** "romantic and relaxation," "beautiful grounds," "European style hotel with great service." [$] *Rooms from: $300* ✉ *1001 Westside Rd.* ☎ *707/433–4231, 800/258–4003* 🌐 *www.madronamanor.com* 🛏 *18 rooms, 5 suites* 🍴 *Breakfast.*

6

SHOPPING

M Clothing. A high-end women's-clothing boutique, M carries dresses, skirts, sweaters, and accessories from Diane von Furstenberg, Nanette Lapore, and other top designers. The shop sometimes hosts fashion shows at local hotels. ⊠ *333 Healdsburg Ave., at Plaza St.* ☎ *707/431–8738* ⊕ *www.martymclothing.com.*

Moustache Baked Goods. This shop specializes in sweets incorporating local, organic ingredients: cupcakes (try the one with locally sourced bacon), whoopie pies, macaroons, and Oreos. Wash everything down with Blue Bottle Coffee. ⊠ *381 Healdsburg Ave., at North St.* ☎ *707/395–4111.*

DRY CREEK AND ALEXANDER VALLEYS

On the west side of U.S. 101, Dry Creek Valley remains one of the least-developed appellations in Sonoma. Zinfandel grapes flourish on the benchlands, whereas the gravelly, well-drained soil of the valley floor is better known for Chardonnay and, in the north, Sauvignon Blanc. The wineries in this region tend to be smaller, which makes them a good bet on summer weekends, when larger spots and those along the main thoroughfares fill up with tourists.

The Alexander Valley, which lies northeast of Healdsburg, is similarly rustic. The largely family-owned wineries often produce Zinfandel and Chardonnay, while the winding Highway 128 through Knights Valley is a popular destination for cyclists and joggers alike.

GETTING HERE AND AROUND

The Dry Creek Valley sits west of downtown Healdsburg, across U.S. 101. If you drive north on Healdsburg Avenue and turn left on Dry Creek Road you'll slip under the freeway and soon see signs pointing the way to wineries on that road and West Dry Creek Road, which runs roughly parallel about a mile to the west, accessible by the cross streets Lambert Bridge Road and Yoakim Bridge Road.

The Alexander Valley is just northeast of Healdsburg. To get here from the plaza, drive north on Healdsburg Avenue and veer right on Alexander Valley Road. Although there are a few wineries on Alexander Valley Road itself, most of them on are on Highway 128, which intersects after 3.3. miles.

EXPLORING

Dry Creek Vineyard. Fumé Blanc is king at Dry Creek, where the refreshing white wine is made in the style of those made in Sancerre, France. The winery also makes well-regarded Zinfandels, a zesty dry Chenin Blanc, a Pinot Noir, and a handful of Cabernet Sauvignon blends. Since many wines are priced at less than $30 a bottle (some less than $20), it's a popular stop for wine lovers looking to stock their cellars for a reasonable price. You can picnic on the lawn here next to a flowering magnolia tree. Conveniently, a general store and deli is close by. ⊠ *3770 Lambert Bridge Rd., off Dry Creek Rd., Dry Creek* ☎ *707/433–1000, 800/864–9463* ⊕ *www.drycreekvineyard.com* 🍷 *Tasting $5* ☉ *Daily 10:30–4:30.*

CLOSE UP

Best Wine Country Festivals

■ **March: Wine Road Barrel Tasting weekends.** For two weekends in March, more than 100 wineries in the Russian River, Dry Creek, and Alexander valleys open their cellars to visitors who want to taste the wine as it ages in barrels, getting previews of what's to come. (☎ 707/433–4335 or 800/723–6336 ⊕ www.wineroad.com)

■ **Early April: Napa Valley Arts in April.** Dozens of wineries have amassed stunning art collections, and many promote the valley's artistic bounty with seminars, parties, and tasting specials. (☎ 707/260–0107 ⊕ www.legendarynapavalley.com/artsinapril)

■ **Late May: Sonoma Jazz + festival.** Headlining jazz, rock, and world music performers play in a large tent in downtown Sonoma, and smaller music, food, and wine events take

place around town. (☎ 866/468–8355 ⊕ www.sonomajazz.org)

■ **Early June: Auction Napa Valley.** One of Napa's glitziest gatherings culminates in a dramatic auction followed by an opulent dinner and party. (☎ 707/963–3388 ⊕ www.napavintners.com)

■ **Early October: Sonoma County Harvest Fair.** This festival celebrates agriculture in Sonoma County, with wine tastings, cooking demos, livestock shows, crafts, carnival rides, and local entertainers filling the Sonoma County Fairgrounds in Santa Rosa. (⊕ www.harvestfair.org)

■ **Mid-November: Napa Valley Film Festival.** Film premieres, pre-movie wine tastings, and food- and wine-related events take place in downtown Napa and St. Helena. (⊕ www.napavalleyfilmfest.org)

6

☺ **Francis Ford Coppola Winery.** The famous film director showcases his less-expensive wines at this majestic French-style château that he transformed into an impressive fantasyland. (Coppola's Napa winery, Inglenook, focuses on the high-end vintages.) In addition to tasting wines or ordering cocktails at the full bar, you can select from tours that include a vineyard walk and the opportunity to watch the bottling facility in action. Scattered throughout the facility are mementos of Coppola's film career, among them his Oscars and Don Corleone's desk in *The Godfather.* Kids (and some adults), though, will be most excited by the large pool. Guests rent small cabanas to shower and change into their swimsuits before spending the afternoon lounging under the striped umbrellas, perhaps even ordering food from the poolside café. The winery's restaurant, Rustic, serves a more elaborate menu from a spacious dining room and a terrace overlooking the vineyards. Prices, pool hours, and tour times change seasonally, so check before coming. ✉ *300 Via Archimedes, at Fulton Rd., Geyserville* ☎ *707/857–1400* ⊕ *www.franciscoppolawinery.com* 🍷 *Tasting free–$7; tour $20–$55; pool pass $15* ☉ *Tasting room daily 11–6, restaurant daily 11–9; pool hrs vary seasonally.*

Jordan Vineyard and Winery. A visit to this sprawling property north of Healdsburg revolves around an impressive estate built in the early 1970s to replicate a French château. Seated tastings of Cabernet Sauvignon and Chardonnay are held in the château itself, in a secluded room that once served as a private cellar. Basic tastings ($20) last 45 minutes and include food and cheese prepared by executive chef Todd Knoll. Tours ($30), which last 75 minutes and include a tasting, wind from the château past a garden and through vineyards shaded by century-old oak trees. The wines alone are worth a visit here, but don't leave without sampling the olive oil grown and milled on the estate. ⊠ *1474 Alexander Valley Rd., on Greco Rd., Alexander Valley* ☎ *800/654–1213, 707/431–5250* ⊕ *www.jordanwinery.com* 🖃 *Tastings and tour $20–$30* ⊙ *Weekdays 8–4:30, weekends 9–3:30; tours and tastings daily by appointment* ⊙ *Closed Sun. Nov.–Apr.*

Papapietro Perry. Pinot Noir and Zinfandel are the only wines on the tasting list at this small winery in the heart of the Dry Creek Valley, but wine lovers hail them as some of the region's best. Most of the grapes come from the Russian River valley, though Zin made from locally sourced fruit is available as well. Standard tastings at the copper-topped bar include five pours, and it always pays to ask what else is open in the back (the 777 Clone Pinot is particularly delicious). For a break in the action, peruse the winery shop for witty T-shirts, or call for Ruby, the winery dog, who always is eager for a gentle pet. ⊠ *4791 Dry Creek Rd., at Wine Creek Rd., Dry Creek* ☎ *707/433–0422, 877/467–4668* ⊕ *www.papapietro-perry.com* 🖃 *Tasting $10* ⊙ *Daily 11–4:30.*

Fodor'sChoice   **Preston Vineyards.** The long driveway at Preston, flanked by vineyards
★   and punctuated by the occasional olive tree, winds down to some farmhouses encircling a shady yard. In summer a small selection of organic produce grown in the winery's gardens is sold from an impromptu stand on the front porch, and house-made bread and olive oil are available year-round. The down-home style is particularly in evidence on Sunday, the only day of the week that tasting-room staffers sell a 3-liter bottle of Guadagni Red, a primarily Zinfandel blend filled from the barrel right in front of you. Owners Lou and Susan Preston are committed to organic growing techniques, and use only estate-grown grapes in their wines, like Sauvignon Blanc, and Rhône varietals such as Syrah and Viognier. ⊠ *Tasting Room, 9206 W. Dry Creek Rd., at Hartsock Rd. No. 1, Dry Creek* ☎ *707/433–3372* ⊕ *www.prestonvineyards.com* 🖃 *Tasting $10* ⊙ *Daily 11–4:30.*

Quivira. An unassuming winery in a modern wooden barn topped by solar panels, Quivira produces some of the most interesting wines in Dry Creek Valley. It's known for its dangerously drinkable reds, including a petite Syrah, and a few hearty Zinfandel blends. The excellent tour provides information about the winery's biodynamic and organic farming practices and offers a glimpse of the beautiful garden and the pigs, chickens, and beehives kept on the property. Visitors also can take a free self-guided tour through the garden. ⊠ *4900 W. Dry Creek Rd., near Wine Creek Rd., Healdsburg* ☎ *707/431–8333, 800/292–8339* ⊕ *www.quivirawine.com* 🖃 *Tasting $10, tours $20–$30* ⊙ *Daily 11–5; tours by appointment.*

The North Coast

FROM THE SONOMA COAST TO REDWOOD NATIONAL PARK

WORD OF MOUTH

"You may be surprised by how (1) Small and (2) Beautiful Trinidad is! I was there for the first time a couple of months ago and it's now one of my favorite places for scenery on the whole North coast."
— roundthebend

WELCOME TO THE NORTH COAST

TOP REASONS TO GO

★ **Scenic coastal drives:** There's hardly a road here that *isn't* scenic.

★ **Wild beaches:** This stretch of California is one of nature's masterpieces. Revel in the unbridled, rugged coastline, without a building in sight.

★ **Dinnertime:** When you're done hiking the beach, refuel with delectable food; you'll find everything from burritos to bouillabaisse.

★ **Romance:** Here you can end almost every day with a perfect sunset.

★ **Wildlife:** Sea lions and otters and deer, oh my!

1 The Sonoma Coast. Heading up through northwestern Marin into Sonoma County, Highway 1 traverses gently rolling pastureland. North of Bodega Bay dramatic shoreline scenery takes over. The road snakes up, down, and around sheer cliffs and steep inclines—some without guardrails—where cows seem to cling precariously. Stunning vistas (or cottony fog) and hairpin turns make this one of the most exhilarating drives north of San Francisco.

2 The Mendocino Coast. The timber industry gave birth to most of the small towns strung along this stretch of the California coastline. Although tourism now drives the economy, the region has retained much of its old-fashioned charm. The beauty of the coastal landscape, of course, has not changed.

3 Redwood Country. There's a different state of mind in Humboldt County. Here, instead of spas, there are old-time hotels. Instead of wineries, there are breweries. The landscape is primarily thick redwood forest, which gets snow in winter and sizzles in summer while the coast sits covered in fog. Until as late as 1924, there was no road that went north of Willits; the coastal towns were reachable only by sea. That legacy is apparent in the communities here today: Eureka and Arcata, both former ports, are sizeable, but otherwise towns are tiny and nestled in the woods, and people have an independent spirit that recalls the original homesteaders. Coming from the south, Garberville is a good place to stop for picnic provisions and stretch your legs.

4 Redwood National Park. For a pristine encounter with giant redwoods, make the trek to this seldom-visited park where even casual visitors have easy access to the trees. *(See Chapter 8, Redwood National Park.)*

GETTING ORIENTED

It's all but impossible to explore the northern California coast without a car. Indeed, you wouldn't want to—driving here is half the fun. The main road is Highway 1, two lanes that twist and turn (sometimes 180 degrees) up cliffs and down through valleys. Towns appear every so often, but this is mostly a land of green pasture, dense forest, and natural, undeveloped coastline. ■TIP→ Pace yourself: Most drivers stop frequently to appreciate the views (and you can't drive faster than 20–40 mph on many portions of the highway), so don't plan to drive too far in one day.

7

Updated by Christine Vovakes

The spectacular coastline between Marin County and the Oregon border defies expectations. The landscape is defined by the Pacific Ocean, but instead of boardwalks and bikinis there are ragged cliffs and pounding waves— and the sunbathers are mostly sea lions.

Instead of strip malls and freeways, there are small towns that retire around sundown and a single-lane road that follows the fickle shoreline. And that's exactly why many Californians, especially those from the Bay Area, come here to escape the Sturm und Drang of daily life.

This stretch of Highway 1 is made up of numerous little worlds, each different from the next. From Point Reyes toward Bodega Bay, the land spreads out into green, rolling pastures and sandy beaches. The road climbs higher and higher as it heads north through Sonoma County, where cows graze on precipitous cliffs and the ocean views are breathtaking. In Mendocino the coastline follows the ins and outs of lush valleys where rivers pour down from the forests and into the ocean. At Humboldt County the highway heads inland to the redwoods, then returns to the shoreline at the tidal flats surrounding the ports of Eureka and Arcata. Heading north to the Oregon border, the coast is increasingly wild and lined with redwood trees.

Although the towns along the way vary from deluxe spa retreat to hippie hideaway, all are reliably sleepy. Most communities have fewer than 1,000 inhabitants, with main streets shuttered by 9 pm. Exceptions are Mendocino and Eureka, but even they are loved best by those who would rather cozy up in bed than paint the town.

NORTH COAST PLANNER

WHEN TO GO

The North Coast is a year-round destination, though when you go determines what you will see. The migration of the Pacific gray whales is a wintertime phenomenon, which lasts roughly from mid-December to early April. Wildflowers follow the winter rain, as early as January in southern areas through June and July farther north. Summer is the high season for tourists, but spring, fall, and even winter are arguably better times to visit when the pace is slower, towns are quieter, and lodging is cheaper.

The coastal climate is quite similar to San Francisco's, although winter nights are colder than in the city. In July and August thick fog can drop temperatures to the high 50s. If you do get caught in the summer fog, fear not! You need only drive inland to find temperatures that are often 20 degrees higher.

GETTING HERE AND AROUND

AIR TRAVEL

The only North Coast airport with commercial air service, Arcata/ Eureka Airport (ACV) receives flights on United Express. The airport is in McKinleyville, which is 16 miles from Eureka.

A taxi to Eureka costs about $50 and takes roughly 25 minutes. Door-to-door airport shuttles cost $20 to Arcata and Trinidad, $24 to Eureka, and $50 to Ferndale. All prices are for the first person, and go up only $5 total for each additional person.

Airport Contact Arcata/Eureka Airport ⊠ *3561 Boeing Ave., McKinleyville* ☎ *707/839–5401.*

Shuttle Contact Door to Door Airport Shuttle ☎ *888/338–5497, 707/839–4186* ⊕ *www.doortodoorairporter.com.*

BUS TRAVEL

Greyhound buses travel along U.S. 101 from San Francisco to Eureka and Arcata. Bus drivers will stop in other towns along the route if you specify your destination when you board. You can also take Greyhound to Seattle, but you must first travel from Eureka to Oakland, with another transfer in Sacramento before continuing north on I-5. Humboldt Transit Authority connects Eureka, Arcata, and Trinidad.

Bus Contacts Greyhound ☎ *800/231–2222* ⊕ *www.greyhound.com.* **Humboldt Transit Authority** ☎ *707/443–0826* ⊕ *www.hta.org.*

CAR TRAVEL

Although there are excellent services along U.S. 101, long, lonesome stretches separate towns (with their resident gas stations and mechanics) along Highway 1, and services are even fewer and farther between on the smaller roads. ■ TIP➔ If you're running low on fuel and see a gas station, stop for a refill. Driving directly to Mendocino from San Francisco is quicker if, instead of driving up the coast on Highway 1, you take U.S. 101 north to Highway 128 west (from Cloverdale) to Highway 1 north. The quickest way to the far North Coast from the Bay Area is a straight shot up U.S. 101, which runs inland all way until Eureka. Weather sometimes forces closure of parts of Highway 1, but it's rare. For information on the condition of roads in Northern California, call the Caltrans Highway Information Network's voice-activated system.

Road Conditions Caltrans Highway Information Network ☎ *800/427–7623* ⊕ *www.dot.ca.gov.*

HEALTH AND SAFETY

In an emergency, dial 911. In state and national parks, park rangers serve as police officers and will help you in any emergency. Bigger towns along the coast have hospitals, but for major medical emergencies you will need to go to San Francisco. Note that cell phones don't work along large swaths of the North Coast.

RESTAURANTS

A few restaurants with national reputations, plus several more of regional note, entice palates on the North Coast. Even the workaday local spots take advantage of the abundant fresh seafood and locally grown vegetables and herbs. Attire is usually informal, though at the pricier establishments dressy casual (somewhere between flip-flops and high heels) is the norm. As in many rural areas, plan to dine early: the majority of kitchens close at 8 or 8:30 and virtually no one serves past 9:30. Also note that many restaurants in the northern part of this region close for a winter break in January. *Prices in the reviews are the average cost of a main course at dinner or, if dinner is not served, at lunch.*

HOTELS

Restored Victorians, rustic lodges, country inns, and vintage motels are among the accommodations available here. Hardly any have air-conditioning (the ocean breezes make it unnecessary), and many have no phones or TVs in the rooms. Although several towns have only one or two places to spend the night, some of these lodgings are destinations in themselves. Budget accommodations are rare, but in winter you're likely to find reduced rates and nearly empty inns and B&Bs. In summer and on the weekends, though, make bed-and-breakfast reservations as far ahead as possible—rooms at the best inns often sell out months in advance. *Prices in the reviews are the lowest cost of a standard double room in high season. For expanded reviews, facilities, and current deals, visit Fodors.com.*

VISITOR INFORMATION

Contacts Humboldt County Convention and Visitors Bureau ⊠ 1034 2nd St., Eureka ☎ 707/443–5097, 800/346–3482 ⊕ www.redwoods.info. **Mendocino Coast Chamber of Commerce** ⊠ 217 S. Main St., Fort Bragg ☎ 707/961–6300 ⊕ www.mendocinocoast.com. **Redwood Coast Chamber: Sonoma to Mendocino** ⊠ 39150 S. Hwy. 1, Gualala ☎ 707/884–1080, 800/778–5252 ⊕ www. redwoodcoastchamber.com. **Sonoma County Tourism Bureau** ⊠ 3637 Westwind Blvd., Santa Rosa ☎ 707/522–5800, 800/576–6662 ⊕ www.sonomacounty. com. **Visit Mendocino County** ⊠ 120 S. Franklin St., Ft. Bragg ☎ 707/462–7417, 866/466–3636 ⊕ www.visitmendocino.com.

THE SONOMA COAST

BODEGA BAY

21 miles north of Marshall on Hwy. 1.

From the busy harbor here, commercial boats pursue fish and Dungeness crab. There's nothing quaint about this working town without a center—it's just a string of businesses along several miles of Highway 1. But some tourists still come to see where Alfred Hitchcock shot *The Birds* in 1962. The Tides Wharf complex, an important location used for the movie, has been expanded and remodeled several times and is no longer recognizable. But a few miles inland, in Bodega, you can find Potter Schoolhouse, which is now a private residence.

GETTING HERE AND AROUND

Reach Bodega Bay from Highway 101 north or south to Santa Rosa, then Highway 12 west (Bodega Highway west of Sebastopol) 23 miles to the coast. From San Francisco you can also take Valley Ford Road (Highway 1) northwest about 27 miles from Petaluma. Mendocino Transit Authority (🌐 *www.4mta.org*) Route 95 buses connect Bodega Bay with coastal towns and Santa Rosa.

WHERE TO EAT AND STAY

For expanded reviews, facilities, and current deals, visit Fodors.com.

$$ SEAFOOD 🍴 **Sandpiper Restaurant.** A local favorite for breakfast, this friendly café on the marina does a good job for a fair price. Peruse the board for the day's fresh catch or order a menu regular such as crab stew or steak and prawns; clam chowder is the house specialty. [$] *Average main: $21* ✉ *1400 N. Hwy. 1* ☎ *707/875–2278* 🌐 *www.sandpiperrestaurant.com.*

$$$$ HOTEL 🏨 **Bodega Bay Lodge.** Looking out to the ocean across a wetland, a group of shingle-and-river-rock buildings houses Bodega Bay's finest accommodations. **Pros:** pampering; ocean views. **Cons:** on the highway. **TripAdvisor:** "peaceful," "pretty place," "a perfect romantic getaway." [$] *Rooms from: $295* ✉ *103 Coast Hwy. 1* ☎ *707/875–3525, 888/875–2250* 🌐 *www.bodegabaylodge.com* 🛏 *78 rooms, 5 suites* 🍽 *No meals.*

SPORTS AND THE OUTDOORS

Bodega Bay Sportfishing. This outfitter charters ocean-fishing boats and rents equipment; they also offer whale-watching trips mid-winter through spring. ✉ *1410 B Bay Flat Rd.* ☎ *707/875–3344* 🌐 *www.bodegabaysportfishing.com.*

Horse N Around Trail Rides. Saddle up at this ranch for guided horseback trail rides, some along the beach. Reservations are required. ✉ *2660 N. Hwy. 1* ☎ *707/875–8849* 🌐 *www.horsenaroundtrailrides.com.*

Links at Bodega Harbour. At the incredibly scenic oceanfront Links at Bodega Harbour you can play an 18-hole Robert Trent Jones–designed course. ✉ *21301 Heron Dr.* ☎ *707/875–3538, 800/503–8158* 🌐 *www.bodegaharbourgolf.com.*

OCCIDENTAL

14 miles northeast of Bodega Bay on Bohemian Hwy.

A village surrounded by redwood forests, orchards, and vineyards, Occidental is a former logging hub with a bohemian vibe. The 19th-century downtown offers a top-notch B&B, good food, and a handful of art galleries and boutiques. The neighboring town of Freestone offers much of the same, but on a smaller scale.

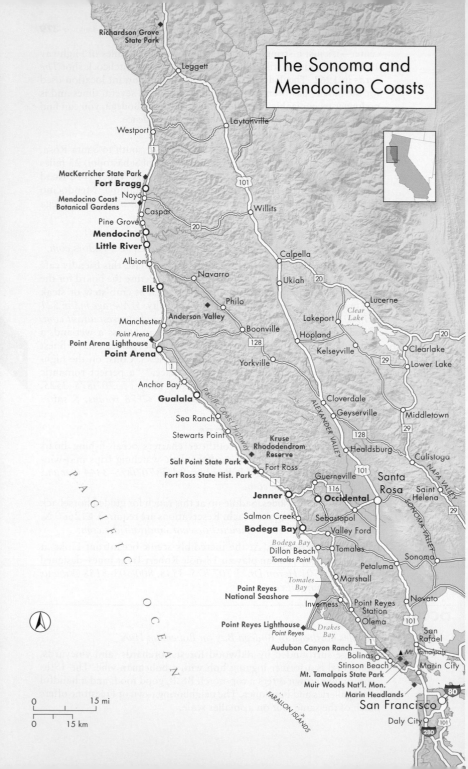

The Sonoma and Mendocino Coasts

Richardson Grove
State Park

Leggett

Westport

Laytonville

MacKerricher State Park
Fort Bragg
Noyo
Mendocino Coast
Botanical Gardens
Caspar
Pine Grove
Mendocino
Little River
Albion

Willits

101

20

Navarro

Elk

Philo

Anderson Valley

Manchester
Point Arena
Point Arena Lighthouse
Point Arena

Boonville

128

Yorkville

Calpella

Ukiah

20

Lucerne

*Clear
Lake*

Lakeport

Hopland

Kelseyville

Clearlake

29

Lower Lake

20

Anchor Bay

Gualala

Sea Ranch

Stewarts Point

Kruse
Rhododendron
Reserve

Salt Point State Park
Fort Ross State Hist. Park

Fort Ross

Pacific Coast Highway

Cloverdale

Geyserville

ALEXANDER VALLEY

128

Healdsburg

Middletown

29

Calistoga

Guerneville

Jenner

116

Salmon Creek

Bodega Bay

Occidental

Sebastopol

Valley Ford

Bodega Bay
Dillon Beach
Tomales Point

Tomales

Petaluma

Marshall

Point Reyes
National Seashore

*Tomales
Bay*

Inverness

Point Reyes Lighthouse
Point Reyes

*Drakes
Bay*

Point Reyes
Station
Olema

101

**Santa
Rosa**

Saint
Helena

NAPA VALLEY

29

SONOMA VALLEY

Sonoma

Novato

San
Rafael

Audubon Canyon Ranch
Bolinas
Stinson Beach
Mt. Tamalpais State Park
Muir Woods Nat'l. Mon.
Marin Headlands

▲ *Mt. Tamalpais*

Marin City

San Francisco

Daly City

101

80

280

PACIFIC OCEAN

FARALLON ISLANDS

0   15 mi

0   15 km

GETTING HERE AND AROUND

To reach Occidental, take Highway 12 (Bodega Highway) east 5 miles from Highway 1. Take a left onto Bohemian Highway, where you'll find Freestone; another 3½ miles and you'll be in Occidental. From Highway 101 north or south take Highway 12 west from Santa Rosa about 13 miles, then head north on Bohemian Highway about 3½ miles to the village.

EXPLORING

Occidental Center for the Arts. From September through May, the Redwood Arts Council presents nine concerts featuring world-class musicians performing with passion in an intimate space. ✉ *3850 Doris Murphy Ct.* ☎ *707/874–1124* 🌐 *www.redwoodarts.org.*

Osmosis–The Enzyme Bath Spa. A traditional Japanese detoxifying treatment awaits you at this spa, which claims to be the only such facility in America. Your bath is a deep redwood tub of damp cedar shavings and rice bran, naturally heated to 140°F by the action of enzymes. Serene attendants bury you up to the neck and during the 20-minute treatment bring you sips of water and place cool cloths on your forehead. After a shower, lie down and listen to brain-balancing music through headphones or have a massage, perhaps in one of the creek-side pagodas. A treatment and access to the gardens costs $85 per person (less for parties of two or more people); reservations are recommended. ✉ *209 Bohemian Hwy., Freestone* ☎ *707/823–8231* 🌐 *www.osmosis.com* 🕒 *Daily 9–8.*

7

WHERE TO EAT AND STAY

For expanded reviews, facilities, and current deals, visit Fodors.com.

$ CAFÉ 🍴 **Wild Flour Bread.** Customers at this bakery in a renovated barn line up early for delectable breads both savory and sweet, plus scones and biscotti, all baked in a wood-fired brick oven. [$] *Average main: $5* ✉ *140 Bohemian Hwy., Freestone* ☎ *707/874–2938* 🌐 *www.wildflourbread.com* 💳 *No credit cards* 🕒 *Closed Tues.–Thurs.*

$$$ B&B/INN ★ 🏨 **The Inn at Occidental.** Quilts, folk art, and original paintings and photographs fill this colorful and friendly inn. **Pros:** colorful; luxurious; friendly. **Cons:** not for those with minimalist tastes; not for kids. **TripAdvisor:** "delightful quiet hidden secret," "first-class service and character," "cute and cozy." [$] *Rooms from: $229* ✉ *3657 Church St. 707/874–1047, 800/522–6324* 🌐 *www.innatoccidental.com* 🛏 *13 rooms, 3 suites, 1 cottage* 🍽 *Breakfast.*

JENNER

10 miles north of Bodega Bay on Hwy. 1.

The broad, lazy Russian River empties into the Pacific Ocean at Jenner, a wide spot in the road where houses dot a mountainside high above the sea. Facing south, the village looks across the river's mouth to Goat Rock State Beach, home to a colony of sea lions for most of the year; pupping season is March through June. The beach, accessed for free off Highway 1 a couple of miles south of town, is open daily from 8 am to sunset. Bring binoculars and walk north from the parking lot to view the sea lions.

GETTING HERE AND AROUND

From Highway 101 in Santa Rosa head west on Highway 12 (Bodega Highway west of Sebastopol) 23 miles to the coast, then travel 10 miles north on Highway 1 to Jenner. From Santa Rosa you can also use Highway 116 west through Guerneville (about 31 miles to Jenner). Mendocino Transit Authority (🌐 *www.4mta.org*) Route 95 buses stop in Jenner and connect with Bodega Bay, Santa Rosa, and other coastal towns.

WHERE TO EAT

$$$$ MODERN AMERICAN

🍴 **River's End.** A magnificent ocean view makes lunch or an evening here memorable. Come for cocktails and Hog Island oysters on the half shell and hope for a splashy sunset. If you stay for dinner, choose from elaborate entrées such as chimichurri lamb or applewood smoked filet mignon with Gorgonzola walnut butter. The execution may not always justify the prices and the dining room is plain-Jane, but just look at that view. Open hours sometimes vary, so call to confirm; reservations are essential on weekends. River's End also rents out a few ocean-view rooms and cabins ($$–$$$). [$] *Average main: $31* ✉ *11048 Hwy. 1* ☎ *707/865–2484* 🌐 *www.ilovesunsets.com* ✍ *Reservations essential* ⏲ *Closed Tues. and Wed. and fall–spring.*

FORT ROSS STATE HISTORIC PARK

12 miles north of Jenner on Hwy. 1.

GETTING HERE AND AROUND

From Santa Rosa, head west on Highway 116 about 31 miles to Jenner, then north 12 miles on Highway 1 to the park entrance. Mendocino Transit Authority (🌐 *www.4mta.org*) Route 95 provides service between Fort Ross and other coastal towns and cities.

EXPLORING

👶 **Fort Ross State Historic Park.** Established in 1812, Fort Ross became Russia's major outpost in California, meant to produce crops and other supplies for northerly fur-trading operations. The Russians brought Aleut sea-otter hunters down from Alaska. By 1841 the area was depleted of seals and otters, and the Russians sold their post to John Sutter, later of gold-rush fame. After a local Anglo rebellion against the Mexicans, the land fell under U.S. domain, becoming part of California in 1850. The state park service has reconstructed Fort Ross, including its Russian Orthodox chapel, a redwood stockade, the officers' barracks, and a blockhouse. The excellent museum here documents the history of the fort and this part of the North Coast. ✉ *19005 Hwy. 1* ☎ *707/847–3286* 🎫 *$8 per vehicle* ⏲ *Weekends 10–4:30* ☞ *No dogs allowed past parking lot and picnic area.*

Surfers check out the waves near Bodega Bay on the Sonoma Coast.

SALT POINT STATE PARK

6 miles north of Fort Ross on Hwy. 1.

GETTING HERE AND AROUND

Exit U.S. 101 in Santa Rosa and travel west on Highway 116 about 31 miles to Jenner, then north 18 miles on Highway 1 to reach the park. Mendocino Transit Authority (⊕ *www.4mta.org*) Route 95 buses stop at Salt Point and connect with other North Coast towns.

EXPLORING

Salt Point State Park. For 5 mi, Highway 1 winds through this park, 6,000 acres of forest, meadows, and rocky shoreline. Heading north, the first park entrance (on the right) leads to forest hiking trails and several campgrounds. The next entrance—the park's main road—winds through meadows and along the wave-splashed coastline (a great place to stop so the kids can let off steam). This is also the route to the visitor center and Gerstle Cove, a favorite spot for abalone divers and sunbathing seals. Next along the highway is Stump Beach Cove, with picnic tables, toilets, and a ¼-mile walk to the sandy beach. The park's final entrance is at Fisk Mill Cove, where centuries of wind and rain erosion have carved unusual honeycomb patterns in the sandstone called "tafonis." A five-minute walk uphill from the parking lot leads to a dramatic view of Sentinel Rock, an excellent spot for sunsets. ⊠ *25050 Hwy. 1* ☎ *707/847-3221* 🖾 *$8 per vehicle* ☉ *Daily sunrise–sunset.*

Kruse Rhododendron State Reserve. Just up the highway, narrow, unpaved Kruse Ranch Road leads to the Kruse Rhododendron State Reserve, where each May thousands of rhododendrons bloom within

a quiet forest of redwoods and tan oaks. ☎ *707/847–3221* ⚏ *Free*
⊘ *Daily sunrise–sunset*

BEACHES

Sonoma Coast State Beach. The gorgeous sandy coves of Sonoma Coast State Beach stretch for 17 miles along the Highway 1 shoreline from Bodega Head to 4 miles north of Jenner, encompassing numerous beaches. Rock Point, Duncan's Landing, and Wright's Beach, clustered at about the halfway mark, have picnic areas, as do several others. A long road leads from the highway to Goat Rock, near the mouth of the Russian River at Jenner, with parking areas at different stops for views of the ocean and the long beach where harbor seals lounge. Shell Beach, 2.5 miles south of Goat Rock, is known for beachcombing, tidepooling, and fishing. Duncan's Landing, about 2 miles south of Shell Beach, is the most dangerous spot on the coast because of unpredictable surf; rogue waves have come up to the parking lot and have also swept people off rocks. If you're lucky you'll catch sight of migrating whales from any of the beaches, but Bodega Head is an especially popular perch for patient gazers. During summer months a few lifeguards are on duty at different spots, but strong rip currents and heavy surf are a treacherous combination that keep would-be swimmers on shore at all the beaches. Wright's Beach and Bodega Dunes have developed campsites. Pick up information about the beaches at state park headquarters at Highway 1 and Salmon Creek, about 2 miles north of Bodega Bay. **Amenities:** parking; toilets. **Best For:** solitude; sunset; walking. ☎ *707/865–2391* ⚏ *$8 per vehicle.*

THE MENDOCINO COAST

GUALALA

16 miles north of Salt Point State Park on Hwy. 1.

This former lumber port on the Gualala River has become a headquarters for exploring the coast. The busiest town between Bodega Bay and Mendocino, it has all the basic services plus a number of galleries and gift shops.

GETTING HERE AND AROUND

From San Francisco exit Highway 101 at Cloverdale and follow Highway 128 northwest 28 miles to Boonville. From Ukiah, take Highway 253 west about 17 miles to Boonville/Highway 128. From Boonville, turn west on Mountain View Road and travel 24 miles to Highway 1, then head south 18½ miles to Gualala. South Mendocino Coast Bus routes 75 and 95 (⊕ *www.4mta.org*) connect Gualala with coastal and inland towns.

EXPLORING

Gualala Point Regional Park. This park has a long, sandy beach, picnic areas ($6 day-use fee), and is an excellent whale-watching spot December through April. Along the river, shaded by redwoods, are two dozen campsites. ✉ *Hwy. 1, 1 mile south of Gualala* ☎ *707/785–2377* 🕒 *Daily 8 am–sunset.*

WHERE TO EAT AND STAY

For expanded reviews, facilities, and current deals, visit Fodors.com.

$$$$ AMERICAN 🍴 **St. Orres.** Resembling a traditional Russian dacha with two onion-dome towers, this intriguing lodge stands on 42 acres of redwood forest and meadow. In one of the towers is a spectacular atrium dining room. Here, locally farmed and foraged ingredients appear in dishes such as garlic flan with black chanterelles and rack of venison medallions with wild huckleberries. The prix-fixe menu ($45) includes soup and salad but no appetizer or dessert (available à la carte). [$] *Average main: $45* ✉ *36601 Hwy. 1, 3 miles north of Gualala* ☎ *707/884–3303* 🌐 *www.saintorres.com* ✍ *Reservations essential* 🕒 *Closed Tues. and Wed. Dec.–May. No lunch weekdays.*

$$ HOTEL 🏨 **Mar Vista Cottages.** The thoughtfully appointed, sparkling clean refurbished 1930s cottages at Mar Vista are intentionally slim on modern gadgetry (no TV, phone, radio, or even a clock) and big on retro charm. **Pros:** charming, peaceful retreat. **Cons:** no other businesses in walking distance. **TripAdvisor:** "pampering for the pros," "charming and relaxing country cottages," "retro relaxation." [$] *Rooms from: $160* ✉ *35101 S. Hwy 1, 5 miles north of Gualala* ☎ *707/884–3522, 877/855–3522* 🌐 *www.marvistamendocino.com* 🛏 *8 1-bedroom cottages, 4 2-bedroom cottages* 🍽 *No meals.*

$$ HOTEL 🏨 **Seacliff on the Bluff.** This motel hugs a bluff overlooking where the Gualala River joins the sea. **Pros:** budget choice; great views. **Cons:** less-than-scenic setting. **TripAdvisor:** "perfect relaxation," "great view," "a lovely surprise." [$] *Rooms from: $140* ✉ *39140 S. Hwy. 1* ☎ *707/884–1213, 800/400–5053* 🌐 *www.seacliffmotel.com* 🛏 *16 rooms* 🍽 *No meals.*

POINT ARENA

★ *14 miles north of Gualala on Hwy. 1.*

Occupied by an eclectic mix of long-time locals and long-haired surfers, this former timber town is part New Age, part rowdy—and always laid back. The one road going west out of downtown will lead you to the harbor, where fishing boats unload urchins and salmon and there's almost always someone riding the waves.

GETTING HERE AND AROUND

From the south, exit Highway 101 at Cloverdale and follow Highway 128 northwest 28 miles to Boonville. From Ukiah, take Highway 253 west about 17 miles to Boonville/Highway 128. From Boonville, Mountain View Road dead-ends after 25 miles at Highway 1; travel south 4 miles to reach Point Arena. South Mendocino Coast Bus Routes 75 and 95 (🌐 *www.4mta.org*) stop in Point Arena and travel to most towns in the region.

EXPLORING

Point Arena Lighthouse. For an outstanding view of the ocean and, in winter, migrating whales, take the marked road off Highway 1 north of town to the 115-foot Point Arena Lighthouse. The lighthouse is open for tours daily from 10 until 3:30, and until 4:30 from Memorial Day until Labor Day weekends; admission is $7.50. It's possible to stay out here, in one of four rental units ($$), all of which have full kitchens. (On weekends there's a two-night minimum.) ✉ *45500 Lighthouse Rd., off Hwy. 1* ☎ *707/882–2777, 877/725–4448* 🌐 *www.pointarenalighthouse.com.*

BEACHES

Manchester State Park. As you head north on Highway 1 from Point Arena toward Elk, you'll pass several beaches. Most notable is the one at Manchester State Park, 3 miles north of Point Arena, which has 5 miles of sandy, usually empty shoreline and lots of trails through the dunes. There's excellent seasonal steelhead fishing in the park's two streams, and you'll see beautiful coastal wildflowers beginning in early spring. Tundra swans overwinter here, and migrating whales are often spotted close to shore. Swimming and water sports are too dangerous because of strong undertows; hiking, bird-watching, and beach strolling are the popular activities. The northernmost segment of the San Andreas Fault cuts through the park and slips into the sea. Dogs are not allowed on the beach. **Amenities:** parking. **Best For:** solitude; sunset; walking. ✉ *44500 Kinney La., off Hwy. 1, about 1½ miles north of Manchester, Manchester* ☎ *707/937–5804* 🌐 *www.parks.ca.gov.*

WHERE TO EAT AND STAY

For expanded reviews, facilities, and current deals, visit Fodors.com.

$ CAFÉ 🍴 **Arena Market.** The simple café at this all-organic grocery store offers hot soups, good sandwiches, and an ample salad bar. Picnickers can stock up on cheese, bread, and other good stuff in the market, which specializes in food from local farms. [$] *Average main: $7* ✉ *185 Main St.* ☎ *707/882–3663.*

$ CAFÉ ★ 🍴 **Franny's Cup and Saucer.** Aided by her mother, Barbara, a former pastry chef at Chez Panisse, Franny turns out baked goods that are sophisticated and inventive. Take the coffee crunch cake: vanilla chiffon cake layered with coffee whipped cream, topped with chocolate ganache and puffs of coffee caramel "seafoam." More familiar options include berry tarts and a strawberry-apricot crisp, plus a mouthwatering assortment of cookies, candy, jams, and jellies. Open Wednesday through Saturday, this delightful bakery in the blue building on Main Street is definitely worth a visit. [$] *Average main: $5* ✉ *213 Main St.* ☎ *707/882–2500* 🌐 *www.frannyscupandsaucer.com* 💳 *No credit cards* ⏲ *Closed Sun.–Tues. No dinner.*

$$$$ B&B/INN ★ 🏨 **Inn at Victorian Gardens.** Set amid 92 acres of meadows and trees, this exquisite Victorian house dates to 1904, but owner-architect Pauline Zamboni has updated and expanded it seamlessly over the past 18 years—skylights open up bathrooms with original hardwood floors, and peaked alcoves frame windows that look out onto lush gardens, open meadows, and the sea. **Pros:** total relaxation; total quiet; total elegance.

Cons: 6 miles from the nearest town. [$] *Rooms from: $255* ✉ *14409 S. Hwy. 1, Manchester* ☎ *707/882–3606* 🌐 *www.innatvictoriangardens.com* 🛏 *4 rooms* 🍴 *Breakfast.*

ELK

33 miles north of Gualala on Hwy. 1.

This quiet town is arranged on the cliff above Greenwood Cove, and just about every spot has a view of the rocky coastline and stunning Pacific sunsets. Beyond walking the beach there's little here for visitors, aside from a handful of restaurants and inns—and that's exactly why people come. Families don't tend to stay here, perhaps because it's such a romantic place.

GETTING HERE AND AROUND

From Ukiah, take Highway 253 west about 17 miles to Boonville/Highway 128, then follow Highway 128 northwest 29 miles until it ends at Highway 1; you'll find Elk about 6 miles south. From San Francisco, travel north on Highway 101 and exit at Cloverdale/Highway 128 West. Follow the road northwest about 56 miles to Highway 1, then head south 6 miles to Elk. South Mendocino Coast Bus Route 75 (🌐 *www.4mta.org*) stops in town.

WHERE TO EAT AND STAY

For expanded reviews, facilities, and current deals, visit Fodors.com.

$ AMERICAN
🍴 **Queenie's Roadhouse Cafe.** The chrome-and-patent-leather diner-style chairs here are usually occupied by locals, as it's a good bet for big breakfasts (served all day) and casual lunches (the cheeseburgers are highly recommended). The wide windows give you a view of the Pacific to go with your coffee. Or, if the day is sunny, grab one of the two picnic tables out front. [$] *Average main: $11* ✉ *6061 S. Hwy. 1* ☎ *707/877–3285* ⏲ *Closed Jan. and Tues. and Wed. No dinner.*

$$ B&B/INN
🏨 **Elk Cove Inn & Spa.** Perched on a bluff above pounding surf and a driftwood-strewn beach, this property has stunning views from most rooms. **Pros:** steps to the beach; gorgeous views; great breakfast. **Cons:** rooms in main house are smallish and within earshot of common TV. **TripAdvisor:** "exceeded all expectations," "beautiful," "simply perfect getaway." [$] *Rooms from: $135* ✉ *6300 S. Hwy. 1* ☎ *707/877–3321, 800/275–2967* 🌐 *www.elkcoveinn.com* 🛏 *7 rooms, 4 suites, 4 cottages* 🍴 *Breakfast.*

$$$$ B&B/INN
🏨 **Harbor House.** Constructed in 1916, this redwood Craftsman-style house is as elegant as its location is rugged. **Pros:** luxurious; romantic. **Cons:** not a place for kids. **TripAdvisor:** "a beautiful place," "divine food and location," "attentive and gracious staff." [$] *Rooms from: $315* ✉ *5600 S. Hwy. 1* ☎ *707/877–3203, 800/720–7474* 🌐 *www.theharborhouseinn.com* 🛏 *6 rooms, 4 cottages* 🍴 *Some meals.*

ANDERSON VALLEY

6 miles north of Elk on Hwy. 101, then 22 miles southeast on Hwy. 128.

At the town of Albion, Highway 128 leads southeast into the Anderson Valley, whose hot summer weather might lure those weary of persistent coastal fog. Most of the first 13 miles wind through redwood forest along the Navarro River, then the road opens up to reveal farms and vineyards. While the community here is anchored in ranching, in the past few decades a progressive, gourmet-minded counterculture has taken root and that is what defines most visitors' experience. In the towns of Philo and Boonville you'll find B&Bs with classic Victorian style as well as small eateries.

Anderson Valley is best known to outsiders for its wineries. Tasting rooms here are more low-key than in Napa; most are in farmhouses and are more likely to play reggae than classical music. That said, Anderson Valley wineries produce world-class wines, particularly Pinot Noirs and Gewürztraminers, whose grapes thrive in the cool, coastal climate. All the wineries are along Highway 128, mostly in Philo with a few east of Boonville. The following are our favorites and are listed here from west to east.

GETTING HERE AND AROUND

Highway 128 West travels through the Anderson Valley; access it from Highway 101 from Cloverdale, or from Ukiah take Highway 253 west about 17 miles. The South Mendocino Coast Bus Route 75 offers limited service in the Anderson Valley between the coast and Ukiah.

EXPLORING

Greenwood Ridge Vineyards. White Riesling is the specialty here. Awards line the walls of the tasting room (built from a single redwood), and you can picnic at tables on an island in the middle of a pond. ⊠ *5501 Hwy. 128, Philo* 🕾 *707/895–2002* ⊕ *www.greenwoodridge.com* ☉ *Tasting room daily 10–5.*

Husch Vineyards. Anderson Valley's oldest winery has a cozy tasting room next to sheep pastures and picnic tables under a grapevine-covered arbor. ⊠ *4400 Hwy. 128, Philo* 🕾 *800/554–8724* ⊕ *www. huschvineyards.com* ☉ *Tasting room daily 10–5.*

Navarro River Redwoods State Park. Known by locals as the "11-mile-long redwood tunnel to the sea," this park just off Highway 128 is great for walks in the second-growth redwood forest and for summer swimming in the gentle Navarro River. There's also fishing, canoeing, and kayaking in the late winter and spring, when the river is higher. The two campgrounds (one on the river "beach") are quiet and clean. ⊠ *Hwy. 128, Navarro* 🕾 *707/937–5804.*

★ **Navarro Vineyards.** A visit to this family-run winery is a classic Anderson Valley experience. Make time if you can for a vineyard tour (conducted daily by appointment at 10:30 and 3); guides draw from years of hands-on experience to explain every aspect of production, from sustainable farming techniques to the choices made in aging and blending. They're best known for their Alsatian varietals, but Navarro offers a wide range of other wines as well, with up to 15 at a time open for tasting. The

You'll find excellent vintages and great places to taste wine in the Anderson Valley—but it's much more laid back than Napa.

tasting room sells cheese and charcuterie for picnickers. ✉ *5601 Hwy. 128, Philo* ☎ *707/895–3686* 🌐 *www.navarrowine.com* 🕓 *Apr.–Oct. daily 9–6; Nov.–Mar. daily 9–5.*

Roederer Estate. To experience the more polished side of Anderson Valley wine production, stop in at Roederer to sample one of their delicious sparkling wines and take in the beautiful view from the patio. ✉ *4501 Hwy. 128, Philo* ☎ *707/895–2288* 🌐 *www.roedererestate.com* 🕓 *Tasting room daily 11–5.*

WHERE TO EAT AND STAY

For expanded reviews, facilities, and current deals, visit Fodors.com.

$ CAFÉ 🍴 **The Boonville General Store.** The café menu here is nothing surprising, but the exacting attention paid to ingredients elevates each dish above the ordinary. Sandwiches are served on fresh-baked bread, the beet salad comes with roasted pecans and local blue cheese. Even the macaroni and cheese—freshly made—is noteworthy. For breakfast there are granola and pastries, made in-house. [$] *Average main: $10* ✉ *14077A Hwy. 128, Boonville* ☎ *707/895–9477* 🕓 *No dinner.*

$$$$ AMERICAN 🍴 **Table 128.** The restaurant at the Boonville Hotel takes small-town dining into the 21st century. Proprietor Johnny Schmitt and his kitchen prepare one prix fixe meal per night ($40 for three courses, $50 for four) and serve it up family-style, with platters of food brought to the table to be shared. Expect an expertly grilled or roasted meat (such as pork chops or flank steak), a sophisticated side (raddichio with polenta; heirloom bean ragout with salsa verde), and a soulful dessert (rhubarb galette; panna cotta with fresh berries). The lack of choices may feel limiting (menus are posted on the Web a few days in advance), but

this is essentially home cooking done at a high level with the freshest ingredients, and it's likely to satisfy most diners. $ *Average main: $40* ✉ *14050 Hwy. 128, Boonville* ☎ *707/895–2210* ⊕ *www.boonvillehotel. com* ⊙ *Closed Mon.–Thurs. Nov.–Apr; closed Tues. and Wed. May–mid-June; closed Tues. mid-June–mid-Oct. No lunch.*

$$$ 🔒 **Boonville Hotel.** From the street this looks like a fairly standard small-
HOTEL town hotel, but once you cross the threshold you start picking up on the laid-back sophistication that captures a lot of what's most appealing about Anderson Valley. **Pros:** stylish but homey; building is the town's main hub. **Cons:** service is friendly but not overly attentive—don't expect to be pampered; two-night stay required most weekends. **TripAdvisor:** "aesthetically pleasing slow down," "country charm," "warm and welcoming." $ *Rooms from: $185* ✉ *14050 Hwy. 128, Boonville* ☎ *707/895–2210* ⊕ *www.boonvillehotel.com* ⟿ *8 rooms, 7 suites* ⦿❙ *Breakfast.*

$$$ 🔒 **The Philo Apple Farm.** Set in an orchard of organic, heirloom apples, the
HOTEL three cottages and one guest room here are tasteful, spare, and inspired by the surrounding landscape. **Pros:** pretty; quiet; country feel. **Cons:** occasionally hot in summer. **TripAdvisor:** "it does not get any nicer," "pure paradise," "best apple juice and jams anywhere." $ *Rooms from: $200* ✉ *18501 Greenwood Rd., Philo* ☎ *707/895–2333* ⊕ *www. philoapplefarm.com* ⟿ *1 room, 3 cottages* ⦿❙ *Breakfast.*

LITTLE RIVER

14 miles north of Elk on Hwy. 1.

The town of Little River is not much more than a post office and a convenience store; Albion, its neighbor to the south, is even smaller. Along the winding road, though, you'll find numerous inns and restaurants, all of them quiet and situated to take advantage of the breathtaking ocean.

GETTING HERE AND AROUND

To reach Little River from San Francisco, exit Highway 101 at Cloverdale and follow Highway 128 northwest about 56 miles until it merges with Highway 1, then head north 7 miles. From the north, exit Highway 101 in Ukiah at Highway 253 West and follow it 17 miles to Boonville/Highway 128. Then travel along Highway 128 northwest 29 miles and Highway 1 north 7 miles to town. South Mendocino Coast Bus Route 75 (⊕ *www.4mta.org*) provides public transit.

EXPLORING

Van Damme State Park. Best known for its beach, this park is a prime abalone diving spot. Upland trails lead through lush riparian habitat and the bizarre **Pygmy Forest,** where acidic soil and poor drainage have produced mature cypress and pine trees that are no taller than a person. The visitor center has displays on ocean life and the historical significance of the redwood lumber industry along the coast. ✉ *Hwy. 1, 3 miles south of Mendocino* ☎ *707/937–5804* ⊕ *www.parks.ca.gov.*

WHERE TO EAT AND STAY

For expanded reviews, facilities, and current deals, visit Fodors.com.

$$$ FRENCH ★ 🍴 **Ledford House.** The only thing separating this bluff-top wood-and-glass restaurant from the Pacific Ocean is a great view. Entrées evoke the flavors of southern France and include hearty bistro dishes—stews, cassoulets, and pastas—and large portions of grilled meats and freshly caught fish (though it also is vegetarian friendly). The long bar, with its unobstructed water view, is a scenic spot for a sunset aperitif. [$] *Average main: $24* ✉ *3000 N. Hwy. 1, Albion* ☎ *707/937–0282* 🌐 *www.ledfordhouse.com* ⏱ *Closed Mon. and Tues. No lunch.*

$$$ B&B/INN 🏨 **Albion River Inn.** Contemporary New England–style cottages at this inn overlook the dramatic bridge and seascape where the Albion River empties into the Pacific. **Pros:** great views; great bathtubs. **Cons:** newer buildings aren't as quaint as they could be. **TripAdvisor:** "absolutely perfect setting and views," "great dining," "beautiful welcoming to California." [$] *Rooms from: $195* ✉ *3790 N. Hwy. 1, Albion* ☎ *707/937–1919, 800/479–7944* 🌐 *www.albionriverinn.com* 🛏 *18 rooms, 4 cottages* 🍽 *Breakfast.*

$$$ B&B/INN ★ 🏨 **Glendeven Inn.** If Mendocino is the New England village of the West Coast, then Glendeven is the local country manor. **Pros:** picture-book pretty; elegant; romantic. **Cons:** not within walking distance of town; on the main drag. **TripAdvisor:** "better than you can imagine," "beautiful place," "a magical experience." [$] *Rooms from: $165* ✉ *8205 N. Hwy. 1 707/937–0083, 800/822–4536* 🌐 *www.glendeven.com* 🛏 *6 rooms, 4 suites* 🍽 *Breakfast.*

MENDOCINO

3 miles north of Little River on Hwy. 1; 153 miles from San Francisco, north on U.S. 101, west on Hwy. 128, and north on Hwy. 1.

Many of Mendocino's original settlers came from the Northeast and built houses in the New England style. Thanks to the logging boom, the town flourished for most of the second half of the 19th century. As the timber industry declined, many residents left, but the town's setting was too beautiful to be ignored. Artists and craftspeople began flocking here in the 1950s, and Elia Kazan chose Mendocino as the backdrop for his 1955 film adaptation of John Steinbeck's *East of Eden*, starring James Dean. As the arts community thrived, restaurants, cafés, and inns sprung up. Today, the small downtown area consists almost entirely of places to eat and shop.

GETTING HERE AND AROUND

From San Francisco, exit Highway 101 at Cloverdale and follow Highway 128 northwest about 56 miles and Highway 1 north 10 miles. You can also exit at Willits and head west on Highway 20 about 33 miles to Highway 1, then head south 8 miles to Mendocino. From Ukiah, use Highway 253 West 17 miles to Boonville, Highway 128 northwest 29 miles and Highway 1 north 7 miles. South Mendocino Coast Bus Route 75 (🌐 *www.4mta.org*) provides public transit.

EXPLORING

Ford House. The restored Ford House, built in 1854, serves as the visitor center for Mendocino Headlands State Park and the town. The house has a scale model of Mendocino as it looked in 1890, when it had 34 water towers and a 12-seat public outhouse. From the museum, you can head out on a 3-mile trail across the spectacular seaside cliffs that border the town. ✉ *735 Main St., West of Lansing St.* ☎ *707/937–5397* 🌐 *www.mendoparks.org* 🎟 *$2 suggested donation* ⏲ *Daily 11–4.*

Kelley House Museum. An 1861 structure holds this museum, whose artifacts include Victorian-era furniture and historical photographs of Mendocino coast's logging days. ✉ *45007 Albion St.* ☎ *707/937–5791* 🌐 *www.kelleyhousemuseum.org* 🎟 *$2* ⏲ *June–Sept., Thurs.–Tues. 11–3; Oct.–May, Fri.–Mon. 11–3.*

Mendocino Art Center. This art center has an extensive program of workshops, mounts rotating exhibits in its galleries, and is the home of the Mendocino Theatre Company. ✉ *45200 Little Lake St.* ☎ *707/937–5818, 800/653–3328* 🌐 *www.mendocinoartcenter.org.*

WHERE TO EAT AND STAY

For expanded reviews, facilities, and current deals, visit Fodors.com.

$$$ AMERICAN
🍴 **Cafe Beaujolais.** The yellow Victorian cottage that houses this popular restaurant is surrounded by a garden of heirloom and exotic plantings. A commitment to the freshest possible organic and local ingredients guides the chef here. The menu is eclectic and ever-evolving, but often includes free-range fowl, line-caught fish, and Niman Ranch beef. The bakery turns out several delicious varieties of bread from a wood-fired oven. [$] *Average main: $30* ✉ *961 Ukiah St.* ☎ *707/937–5614* 🌐 *www.cafebeaujolais.com* ⏲ *No lunch Mon. and Tues.*

$$$$ B&B/INN ★
🏨 **Brewery Gulch Inn.** This tasteful inn gives a modern twist to the elegance of Mendocino. **Pros:** stylish; peaceful; intimate. **Cons:** must drive to town. **TripAdvisor:** "beautiful ocean views with a romantic feel," "the very best," "great service." [$] *Rooms from: $330* ✉ *9401 N. Hwy. 1, 1 mile south of Mendocino* ☎ *707/937–4752, 800/578–4454* 🌐 *www.brewerygulchinn.com* 🛏 *10 rooms, 1 suite* 🍽 *Breakfast.*

$$$ B&B/INN Fodor's Choice ★
🏨 **MacCallum House.** Set on 2 flower-filled acres in the middle of town, this inn is a perfect mix of Victorian charm and modern luxury. **Pros:** best B&B around; excellent breakfast; great in-town location. **Cons:** new luxury suites on a separate property are less charming. **TripAdvisor:** "great restaurant," "perfect getaway," "lovely and romantic." [$] *Rooms from: $179* ✉ *45020 Albion St.* ☎ *707/937–0289, 800/609–0492* 🌐 *www.maccallumhouse.com* 🛏 *11 rooms, 13 suites, 7 cottages* 🍽 *Breakfast.*

NIGHTLIFE AND THE ARTS

Mendocino Theatre Company. The repertoire of this well-established company ranges all over the contemporary map, including works by David Mamet, Arthur Miller, Neil Simon, and local playwrights. Performances take place Thursday through Saturday evenings, with some weekend matinees. ✉ *Mendocino Art Center, 45200 Little Lake St.* ☎ *707/937–4477* 🌐 *www.mendocinotheatre.org.*

The North Coast is famous for its locally caught Dungeness crab; be sure to try some during your visit.

SPORTS AND THE OUTDOORS
Catch-A-Canoe and Bicycles Too. Rent kayaks and regular and outrigger canoes here, as well as mountain and suspension bicycles. ⊠ *Stanford Inn by the Sea, Comptche-Ukiah Rd., off Hwy. 1* ☎ *707/937–0273* ⊕ *www.catchacanoe.com.*

FORT BRAGG

10 miles north of Mendocino on Hwy. 1.

The commercial center of Mendocino County, Fort Bragg is a working-class town that many feel is the most authentic place around; it's certainly less expensive than its neighbors to the south. The declining timber industry has been steadily replaced by booming tourism, but the city maintains a local feel since most people who work at the area hotels and restaurants also live here, as do many local artists. A stroll down Franklin Street (one block east of Highway 1) takes you past numerous bookstores, antiques shops, and boutiques.

GETTING HERE AND AROUND
From Highway 101 at Willits follow Highway 20 west about 33 miles to Highway 1 and go north 2 miles. South Mendocino Coast Bus Route 75 (⊕ *www.4mta.org*) buses service the town and region.

EXPLORING
★ **Mendocino Coast Botanical Gardens.** The gardens have something for nature lovers in every season. Even in winter, heather and camellias bloom. Along 3½ miles of trails, including pathways with ocean views and observation points for whale-watching, is a splendid profusion of

flowers. The rhododendrons are at their peak from April through June; the dahlias begin their spectacular show in August and last until October. ⊠ *18220 N. Hwy. 1, 2 miles south of Fort Bragg* ☎ *707/964–4352* ⊕ *www.gardenbythesea.org* ⌨ *$14* ☉ *Mar.–Oct., daily 9–5; Nov.–Feb., daily 9–4.*

Museum in the Triangle Tattoo Parlor. At the top of a steep staircase, this museum is an unexpected nod to Fort Bragg's rough-and-tumble past. The two-room display shows a wonderful collection of tattoo memorabilia, including pictures of astonishing tattoos from around the world, early 20th-century Burmese tattooing instruments, and a small shrine to sword-swallowing sideshow king Captain Don Leslie. ⊠ *356-B N. Main St.* ☎ *707/964–8814* ⌨ *Free* ☉ *Daily noon–6.*

⊙ **The Skunk Train.** Back in the 1920s, a fume-spewing gas-powered train car shuttled passengers along a rail line dating from the logging days of the 1880s. Nicknamed the Skunk Train, it traversed redwood forests inaccessible to automobiles. The reproduction that you can ride today travels the same route, making a 3½- to 4-hour round-trip between Fort Bragg and the town of Northspur, 21 miles inland. The schedule varies depending on the season and in summer includes evening barbecue excursions and wine parties. ⊠ *Foot of Laurel St., west of Main St.* ☎ *707/964–6371, 866/457–5865* ⊕ *www.skunktrain.com* ⌨ *$49–$70.*

BEACHES

Glass Beach. The ocean is not visible from most of Fort Bragg, but go three blocks west of Main Street on Elm Street, and a gravel path leads to wild coastline where you can walk for miles along the bluffs. The sandy coves in the area you first reach from the road are called Glass Beach because this used to be the dumping ground for the city. That history is still apparent, although the pounding surf has pulverized the trash into a sparkling treasure. Look closely at the sand and you'll find the top layer is comprised almost entirely of sea glass, likely more than you've ever seen in one place before. You can gaze at the dazzling colors, but don't take any glass with you; it's now against the law. No swimming at this beach either, for safety's sake. **Amenities:** parking; toilets. **Best For:** sunset; walking. ⊠ *Elm St. and Old Haul Rd.*

MacKerricher State Park. This park begins at Glass Beach and stretches north for 9 miles, beginning with rocky headlands that taper into dunes and sandy beaches. The headland is a good place for whale-watching from December to mid-April. Fishing at Lake Cleone (a freshwater lake stocked with trout), canoeing, hiking, tide-pooling, jogging, bicycling, beachcombing, camping, and harbor seal watching at Laguna Point are among the popular activities, many of which are accessible to the mobility-impaired. Rangers, who lead nature hikes in summer, discourage swimming in the treacherous surf and remind those on shore to be vigilant for rogue waves and to never turn their backs on the sea. Dogs must be leashed. **Amenities:** parking; toilets. **Best For:** solitude; sunset; walking. ⊠ *Hwy. 1, 3 miles north of Fort Bragg* ☎ *707/937–5804* ⌨ *$8 per vehicle.*

WHERE TO EAT AND STAY

For expanded reviews, facilities, and current deals, visit Fodors.com.

$ ITALIAN 🍴 **Piaci.** The seats are stools and your elbows might bang a neighbor's, but nobody seems to mind at this cozy little spot—this is hands down the most popular casual restaurant around. The food is simple, mostly pizza and calzones, but everything is given careful attention and comes out tasty. Alongside the selective list of wines is a distinctive beer list that has been given equal respect; noted are the origin, brewmaster, and alcohol content for each brew. Dogs and their owners are welcome at the tables outside. [$] *Average main: $13* ✉ *120 W. Redwood Ave.* ☎ *707/961–1133* 🌐 *www.piacipizza.com* ⏲ *No lunch Sun.*

$$$ B&B/INN 🏨 **Weller House Inn.** It's hard to believe that this house was abandoned and slated for demolition when it was purchased in 1994 and then carefully restored into the loveliest Victorian in Fort Bragg. **Pros:** handcrafted details; radiant heat in the wood floors; friendly innkeepers. **Cons:** some may find it too old-fashioned. **TripAdvisor:** "great room," "quiet and accommodating," "charming." [$] *Rooms from: $180* ✉ *524 Stewart St.* ☎ *707/964–4415, 877/893–5537* 🌐 *www.wellerhouse.com* 🛏 *9 rooms* 🍽 *Breakfast.*

SPORTS AND THE OUTDOORS

All Aboard Adventures. From late December through April All Aboard Adventures operates whale-watching trips; they also offer fishing excursions all year out of Noyo Harbor. ✉ *32410 N. Harbor Dr.* ☎ *707/964–1881* 🌐 *www.allaboardadventures.com.*

Ricochet Ridge Ranch. Come here for private and group trail rides through redwood forest and on the beach. ✉ *24201 N. Hwy. 1* ☎ *707/964–7669, 888/873–5777* 🌐 *www.horse-vacation.com.*

7

REDWOOD COUNTRY

HUMBOLDT REDWOODS STATE PARK

20 miles north of Garberville on U.S. 101.

GETTING HERE AND AROUND

Access the park right off U.S. 101, about 43 miles south of Eureka and 20 miles north of Garberville. Contact Humboldt Transit Authority (🌐 *www.hta.org*) for public transportation details.

EXPLORING

🐤 **Avenue of the Giants.** Also known as State Highway 254, this route traverses Humbolt Redwoods State Park south–north, branching off U.S. 101 about 7 miles north of Garberville and more or less paralleling that road for 32 miles north to Pepperwood. Some of the tallest trees on the planet tower over the stretch of two-lane blacktop that follows the south fork of the Eel River.

Humboldt Redwoods State Park Visitor Center. At the visitor center you can pick up information about the redwoods, waterways, and recreational activities in the 53,000-acre park. One brochure describes a self-guided auto tour of the park, with short and long hikes into redwood groves. ✉ *Ave. of the Giants, 2 miles south of Weott* ☎ *707/946–2263 visitor center* 🌐 *www.humboldtredwoods.org* 🎟 *Free; $8 day-use fee*

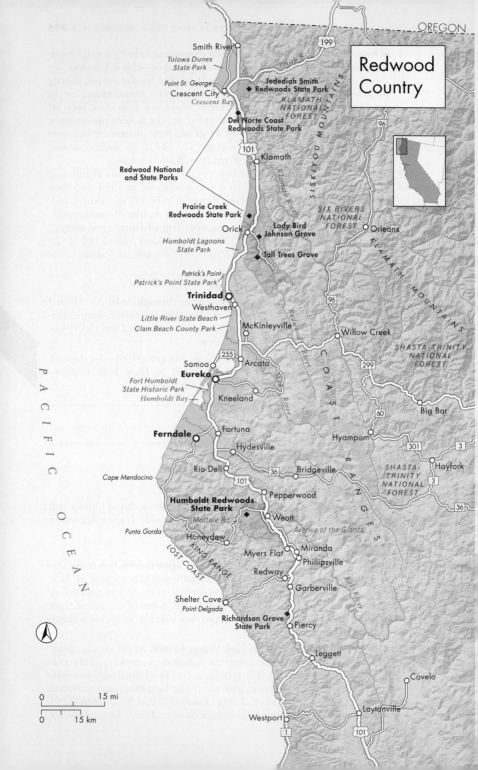

Redwood Country

OREGON

199

Smith River
Tolowa Dunes State Park
Point St. George
Crescent City
Crescent Bay

Jedediah Smith Redwoods State Park

KLAMATH NATIONAL FOREST

96

Del Norte Coast Redwoods State Park

101

Klamath

Klamath River

SISKIYOU MOUNTAINS

SIX RIVERS NATIONAL FOREST

Redwood National and State Parks

Prairie Creek Redwoods State Park

Orick

Lady Bird Johnson Grove

Orleans

Humboldt Lagoons State Park

Tall Trees Grove

KLAMATH MOUNTAINS

Patrick's Point
Patrick's Point State Park

Trinidad
Westhaven
Little River State Beach
Clam Beach County Park

McKinleyville

Redwood River

96

Willow Creek

C O A S T

SHASTA-TRINITY NATIONAL FOREST

Samoa
Eureka
Fort Humboldt State Historic Park
Humboldt Bay

255

Arcata

299

60

Kneeland

Mad River

Big Bar

Ferndale

Fortuna

R A N G E S

Hyampom

301

3

Hydesville

Cape Mendocino

Rio Dell

36

Bridgeville

Hayfork

3

SHASTA-TRINITY NATIONAL FOREST

101

Pepperwood

36

Humboldt Redwoods State Park

Mottole Rd.

Weott

Avenue of the Giants

Punta Gorda

Honeydew

LOST COAST

KING RANGE

Myers Flat

Miranda

Phillipsville

Redway

El River

Shelter Cove
Point Delgada

Garberville

Richardson Grove State Park

Piercy

Leggett

Covelo

P A C I F I C   O C E A N

1

Westport

101

Laytonville

0   15 mi

0   15 km

for parking and facilities in Williams Grove ⊙ Park daily; visitor center
Apr.–Sept., daily 9–5; Oct.–Mar., daily 10–4

Founders Grove. One of the most impressive trees here—the 362-foot-
long Dyerville Giant—fell to the ground in 1991; its root base points
skyward 35 feet. You reach the grove via a ½-mile trail off Avenue of
the Giants. ⊠ *Hwy. 254, 4 miles north of Humboldt Redwoods State
Park Visitor Center*

Rockefeller Forest. The largest remaining old-growth coast redwood
forest contains 40 of the 100 tallest trees in the world. ⊠ *Mattole Rd.,
6 miles north of Humboldt Redwoods State Park Visitor Center*

FERNDALE

*35 miles northwest of Weott; 57 miles northwest of Garberville via U.S.
101 north to Hwy. 211 west.*

Though gift shops and ice-cream stores comprise a fair share of the businesses here, Ferndale remains a fully functioning small town. There's
a butcher, a small grocery, and a local saloon (the westernmost in the
contiguous United States), and descendants of the Portuguese and Scandinavian dairy farmers who settled this town continue to raise dairy
cows in the surrounding pastures. Ferndale is best known for its colorful
Victorian architecture; many shops carry a self-guided tour map that
highlights the town's most interesting historical buildings.

7

GETTING HERE AND AROUND
Ferndale is about 15 miles south of Eureka and 35 miles northwest of
Weott. Exit U.S. 101 at Highway 211 and follow it southwest 5 miles.

EXPLORING
Eel River Delta Tours. Two-hour boat trips examine the wildlife and history of the Eel River's estuary and salt marsh. (Don't be surprised if you
get an informal answering machine when you inquire—this is laid-back
Humboldt, and you will get a call back.) ⊠ *285 Morgan Slough Rd.*
☎ 707/786–4902.

Ferndale Historic Cemetery. A walk through the cemetery on the east side
of town gives interesting insight into the hard, often short lives of the
European immigrants who cultivated this area of California in the mid-
18th century. The gravestones are worn, lovely, and sometimes imagina-
tive (one is in the shape of a nubbly redwood log). The cemetery is lined
by forest, and from the top of the hill there's a nice view of town, the
surrounding farms, and the ocean. ⊠ *Bluff St. and Craig St.*

Ferndale Museum. The main building of this museum exhibits Victoriana
and historical photographs and has a display of an old-style barbershop
and another of Wiyot Indian baskets. In the annex are a horse-drawn
buggy, a re-created blacksmith's shop, and antique farming, fishing,
and dairy equipment. Don't miss the historic Bosch-Omori seismo-
graph, installed in 1933 in Ferndale; it's still checked daily for record-
ings of earthquake activity. ⊠ *515 Shaw Ave.* ☎ 707/786–4466 ⊕ *www.
ferndale-museum.org* 🗷 $1 ⊙ June–Sept., Tues.–Sat. 11–4, Sun. 1–4;
Oct.–Dec. and Feb.–May, Wed.–Sat. 11–4, Sun. 1–4.

The Kinetic Sculpture Race. Memorial Day weekend's annual Kinetic Sculpture Race has artists and engineers (and plenty of hacks) building moving sculptures from used bicycle parts and other scraps, which they race from Arcata to the finish line in Ferndale. Contestants are judged as much on their creativity as on their ability to cross the finish line, and as a result sculptures have included the Albino Rhino and a 93-foot-long fish. ⊕ www.kineticgrandchampionship.com.

Ferndale Kinetic Museum. Stop by here to see a display of "vehicles, costumes, awards, and bribes" from past races. ⊠ 580 Main St. ☎ No phone ⊠ Free, donation encouraged ⊙ Daily 10–5

EUREKA

18 miles north of Ferndale; 66 miles north of Garberville on U.S. 101.

With a population of 28,606, Eureka is the North Coast's largest city. Over the past century, it has cycled through several periods of boom and bust—first with mining and later with timber and fishing—but these days, tourism is developing into a healthy sustaining industry. The town's nearly 100 Victorian buildings have inspired some to dub it "the Williamsburg of the West." Shops draw people to the renovated downtown, and a walking pier extends into the harbor.

GETTING HERE AND AROUND

U.S. 101 travels through Eureka. From Redding and U.S. 5, travel west along Highway 299 about 138 miles to U.S. 101; Eureka is 9 miles south. Eureka Transit buses (⊕ www.eurekatransit.org) travel on regular routes throughout town and connect with regional transit.

EXPLORING

Blue Ox Millworks. Blue Ox is one of only a handful of wood shops in the country that specialize in Victorian-era architecture, but what makes it truly unique is that it uses antique tools to do the work. The most modern tool here is a 1948 band saw. Lucky for curious craftspeople and history buffs, the shop doubles as a dusty historical park. Visitors can watch craftsmen use printing presses, lathes, and even a mill that pares down whole redwood logs into the ornate fixtures for Victorians like those around town. The museum is less interesting on Saturday, when the craftspeople mostly take the day off. ⊠ 1 X St. ☎ 707/444–3437, 800/248–4259 ⊕ www.blueoxmill.com ⊠ $7.50 ⊙ Weekdays 9–5, Sat. 9–4.

Clarke Historical Museum. The Native American Wing of the Clarke Historical Museum contains a beautiful collection of northwestern California basketry. Artifacts from Eureka's Victorian, logging, and maritime eras fill the rest of the museum. ⊠ 240 E St. ☎ 707/443–1947 ⊕ www.clarkemuseum.org ⊠ Donations accepted ⊙ Wed.–Sat. 11–4.

Eureka Chamber of Commerce. You can pick up maps here with self-guided driving tours of Eureka's Victorian architecture, and also learn about organized tours. ⊠ 2112 Broadway ☎ 707/442–3738, 800/356–6381 ⊕ www.eurekachamber.com ⊙ June–Aug., Mon.–Thurs. 8:30–5, Fri. 8:30–4, Sat. 10–3; Sept.–May, Mon.–Thurs. 8:30–5, Fri. 8:30–4.

☺ **Fort Humboldt State Historic Park.** The structure that gives this park its name was built in response to conflicts between white settlers and Native Americans. It no longer stands, but on its grounds are some reconstructed buildings, fort and logging museums, and old logging locomotives. At this writing the museums are closed due to earthquake damage, but the park, which is a good place for a picnic, remains open. ✉ *3431 Fort Ave.* ☎ *707/445–6547* 🌐 *www.parks.ca.gov* 🎟 *Free* 🕐 *Daily 8–5.*

QUICK BITES

Lost Coast Brewery & Cafe. This bustling microbrewery is the best place in town to relax with a pint of ale or porter. Soups, salads, and light meals are served for lunch and dinner. ✉ ***617 4th St.*** ☎ ***707/445–4480*** 🌐 ***www.lostcoast.com.***

WHERE TO EAT AND STAY

For expanded reviews, facilities, and current deals, visit Fodors.com.

$$$ AMERICAN Fodor's Choice ★

🍴 **Restaurant 301.** Eureka's most elegant restaurant, housed in the lovely Carter House, uses ingredients selected from the farmers' market, local cheese makers and ranchers, and the on-site gardens. Dishes are prepared with a delicate hand and a sensuous imagination—the ever-changing menu features a fresh fish offering daily, plus a fixed-price Discovery Menu with optional wine pairing from the restaurant's award-winning wine cellar (which has more than 3,500 bottles). [$] *Average main: $28* ✉ *301 L St.* ☎ *707/444–8062, 800/404–1390* 🌐 *www.carterhouse.com* 🕐 *No lunch.*

$ AMERICAN ☺

🍴 **Samoa Cookhouse.** Originally a cafeteria that fed 500 local mill workers, the cookhouse became a public restaurant in the 1950s—though not much but the clientele has changed. Take a seat at one of the long, communal tables, and waiters will bring bottomless, family-style bowls of whatever is being served at that meal. For breakfast that means eggs, sausage, biscuits and gravy, and the like. Lunch and dinner usually feature soup, potatoes, salad, and pie, plus daily changing entrées such as pot roast and pork loin. A back room contains a museum of logging culture, but really the whole place is a tribute to the rough-and-tumble life and hard work that tamed this wild land. Dieters and vegetarians should look elsewhere for sustenance. [$] *Average main: $16* ✉ *908 Vance Ave., near Cookhouse Rd., Samoa* ☎ *707/442–1659* 🌐 *www.samoacookhouse.net.*

$$ HOTEL

🏨 **Abigail's Elegant Victorian Mansion.** Innkeepers Doug and Lily Vieyra have devoted themselves to honoring this National Historic Landmark (once home to the town's millionaire real-estate sultan) by decorating it with authentic, Victorian-era opulence. **Pros:** unique; lots of character; fun innkeepers. **Cons:** downtown is not within walking distance; bedrooms are a bit worn. **TripAdvisor:** "very nice visit," "a trip back in time," "a genuinely memorable experience." [$] *Rooms from: $105* ✉ *1406 C St.* ☎ *707/444–3144* 🌐 *www.eureka-california.com* 🛏 *4 rooms, 2 with shared bath* 🍽 *No meals.*

$$$ HOTEL Fodor's Choice ★

🏨 **Carter House.** According to owner Mark Carter, his staff has been trained always to say yes; whether it's breakfast in bed or an in-room massage, someone here will make sure you get what you want. **Pros:** elegant; every detail in place; excellent dining at Restaurant 301,

7

bar off the lobby. **Cons:** while kids are allowed, it's better suited for grown-ups. **TripAdvisor:** "beautiful cottage," "a historic property," "helpful staff." $ *Rooms from: $159* ✉ *301 L St.* ☎ *707/444–8062, 800/404–1390* 🌐 *www.carterhouse.com* 🛏 *22 rooms, 8 suites, 2 cottages* 🍴 *Breakfast.*

SHOPPING

Eureka has several art galleries and numerous antiques stores in the district running from C to I streets between 2nd and 3rd streets.

Eureka Books. Along with classics and bestsellers, this bibliophile's haven has an exceptional collection of used books on all topics. ✉ *426 2nd St.* ☎ *707/444–9593* 🌐 *www.eurekabooksellers.com.*

First Street Gallery. Run by Humboldt State University, this is the best spot for contemporary art by local and regional artists, with some national and international representation. ✉ *422 1st St.* ☎ *707/443–6363* 🌐 *www.humboldt.edu/first.*

SPORTS AND THE OUTDOORS

Hum-Boats. Kayak rental and lessons are available here, along with a variety of group kayak tours, including popular whale-watching trips ($75, December–June) that get you close enough to get good photos of migrating gray whales and resident humpback whales. ✉ *Dock A, Woodley Island Marina* ☎ *707/443–5157* 🌐 *www.humboats.com.*

TRINIDAD

21 miles north of Eureka on U.S. 101.

Trinidad got its name from the Spanish mariners who entered the bay on Trinity Sunday, June 9, 1775. The town became a principal trading post for the mining camps along the Klamath and Trinity rivers. Mining and whaling have faded from the scene, and now Trinidad is a quiet and genuinely charming community with ample sights and activities to entertain low-key visitors.

GETTING HERE AND AROUND

Access Trinidad via U.S. 101. If you're driving on Highway 5 south from Oregon, exit at Grants Pass and take U.S. 199 southwest to Crescent City (about 78 miles), then U.S. 101 south to Trinidad (another 66 miles). Redwood Transit System (🌐 *www.redwoodtransit.org*) provides bus service to Trinidad, Eureka, and nearby towns.

EXPLORING

Patrick's Point State Park. On a forested plateau almost 200 feet above the surf, Patrick's Point State Park has stunning views of the Pacific, great whale- and sea lion–watching in season, picnic areas, bike paths, and hiking trails through old-growth spruce forest. There are also tidal pools at Agate Beach, a re-created Yurok Indian village, and a small museum with natural-history exhibits. Because the park is far from major tourist hubs, there are few visitors (most are local surfers), which leaves the land sublimely quiet. In spruce and alder forest above the ocean, the park's three campgrounds have all amenities except RV hookups. In summer it's best to reserve in advance. Dogs are not allowed on trails or the beach. ✉ *U.S. 101, 5 miles north of Trinidad* ☎ *707/677–3570* 🌐 *www.parks.ca.gov* 🎫 *$8 per vehicle.*

BEACHES

👶 **Clam Beach County Park and Little River State Beach.** Together these make a park that stretches from Trinidad to as far south as one can see. The sandy beach here is exceptionally wide, perfect for kids who need to get out of the car and burn off some energy. Beachcombing and clamming are favored activities, as well as savoring fabulous sunsets. The two parks share day use facilities. **Amenities:** parking; toilets. **Best for:** solitude; sunset; walking. ✉ *Hwy. 1, 6½ miles south of Trinidad* ☎ *707/445–7651* 🕑 *Daily 5 am–midnight.*

WHERE TO EAT AND STAY

For expanded reviews, facilities, and current deals, visit Fodors.com.

$ SEAFOOD 🍴 **Katy's Smokehouse.** Purchase delectable picnic fixings at this tiny deli that has been doing things the same way since the 1940s, curing day-boat, line-caught fish with its original smokers. Salmon cured with brown sugar, albacore jerky, and smoked scallops are popular. Buy bread and drinks in town and walk to the waterside for alfresco snacking. Katy's closes at 6 pm. [$] *Average main: $10* ✉ *740 Edwards St.* ☎ *707/677–0151* 🌐 *www.katyssmokehouse.com.*

$$$ AMERICAN 🍴 **Larrupin' Cafe.** Locals consider this restaurant one of the best places to eat on the North Coast. Set in a two-story house on a quiet country road north of town, it's often thronged with people enjoying fresh seafood, Cornish game hen, or mesquite-grilled ribs. While the garden setting and candlelight stir thoughts of romance, service is sometimes rather rushed. [$] *Average main: $30* ✉ *1658 Patrick's Point Dr.* ☎ *707/677–0230* 🌐 *www.larrupin.com* ✍ *Reservations essential* 🕑 *Closed Thurs. in winter. No lunch.*

$$$ B&B/INN 🏨 **Trinidad Bay Bed and Breakfast Inn.** Staying at this small Cape Cod–style inn perched above Trinidad Bay is like spending the weekend at a friend's vacation house. **Pros:** great location above bay; lots of light. **Cons:** if all rooms are full, the main house can feel a bit crowded. **TripAdvisor:** "beautiful rooms," "amazing views," "a special place." [$] *Rooms from: $200* ✉ *560 Edwards St., Box 849* ☎ *707/677–0840* 🌐 *www.trinidadbaybnb.com* 🛏 *4 rooms* 🍽 *Breakfast.*

$$$$ B&B/INN 🏨 **Turtle Rocks Oceanfront Inn.** This comfortable inn has the best view in Trinidad, and the builders have made the most of it. **Pros:** great ocean views; comfy king beds. **Cons:** no businesses within walking distance; not as deluxe as you might expect for the price. **TripAdvisor:** "service was awesome," "breathtaking view," "great breakfast." [$] *Rooms from: $275* ✉ *3392 Patrick's Point Dr., 4½ miles north of town* ☎ *707/677–3707* 🌐 *www.turtlerocksinn.com* 🛏 *5 rooms, 1 suite* 🍽 *Breakfast.*

7

Redwood National Park

WORD OF MOUTH

"Roosevelt elk were easy to find. Whenever we saw an odd collection of cars by the side of the road (or sometimes in the middle of the road!) and a lot of people with cameras, we knew we would see elk."

—Elnap29

WELCOME TO REDWOOD NATIONAL PARK

TOP REASONS TO GO

★ **Giant trees:** These mature coastal redwoods are the tallest trees in the world.

★ **Hiking to the sea:** The park's trails wind through majestic redwood groves, and many connect to the Coastal Trail running along the western edge of the park.

★ **Rare wildlife:** Mighty Roosevelt elk favor the park's flat prairie and open lands; seldom-seen black bears roam the backcountry; trout and salmon leap through streams, and Pacific gray whales swim along the coast during their biannual migrations.

★ **Stepping back in time:** Hike Fern Canyon Trail and explore a prehistoric scene of lush vegetation and giant ferns.

★ **Cheeps, not beeps:** Amid the majestic redwoods you're out of range for cell-phone service—and in range for the soothing sounds of warblers and burbling creeks.

1 Del Norte Coast Redwoods State Park. The rugged terrain of this far northwest corner of California combines stretches of treacherous surf, steep cliffs, and forested ridges. On a clear day it's postcard-perfect; with fog, it's mysteriously mesmerizing.

2 Jedediah Smith Redwoods State Park. Gargantuan old-growth redwoods dominate the scenery here. The Smith River cuts through canyons and splits across boulders, carrying salmon to the inland creeks where they spawn.

3 Prairie Creek Redwoods State Park. The forests here give way to spacious, grassy plains where abundant wildlife thrives. Roosevelt elk are a common sight in the meadows and down to Gold Bluffs Beach.

4 Orick Area. The highlight of the southern portion of Redwood National Park is the Tall Trees Grove. It's difficult to reach and requires a special pass, but it's worth the hassle—this section has the tallest coast redwood trees, with a new record holder discovered in 2006.

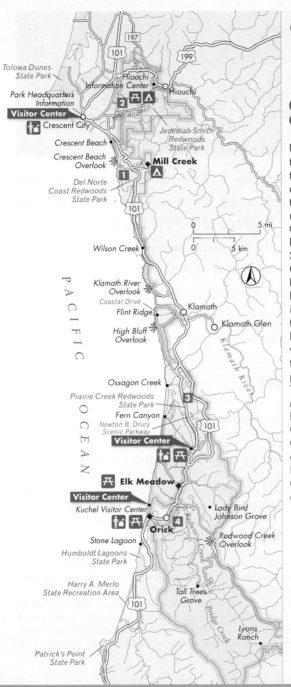

CALIFORNIA

GETTING ORIENTED

U.S. 101 weaves through the southern portion of the park, skirts around the center, and then slips back through redwoods in the north and on to Crescent City. Kuchel Visitor Center, Prairie Creek Redwoods State Park and Visitor Center, Tall Trees Grove, Fern Canyon, and Lady Bird Johnson Grove are all in the park's southern section. The graveled Coastal Drive curves along ocean vistas and dips down to the Klamath River in the park's central section. To the north you'll find Mill Creek Trail, Enderts Beach, and Crescent Beach Overlook in Del Norte Coast Redwoods State Park as well as Jedediah Smith Redwoods State Park, Stout Grove, Little Bald Hills, and Simpson-Reed Grove.

8

Updated
by Christine
Vovakes

Soaring to more than 300 feet, the coastal redwoods that give this park its name are miracles of efficiency—some have survived hundreds of years (a few live for more than 2,000 years). These massive trees glean nutrients from the rich alluvial flats at their feet and from the moisture and nitrogen trapped in their uneven canopy. Their huge, thick-barked trunks can hold thousands of gallons of water, reservoirs that have helped them withstand centuries of firestorms.

REDWOOD PLANNER

WHEN TO GO

Campers and hikers flock to the park from mid-June to early September. Crowds disappear in winter, but you'll have to contend with frequent rains and nasty potholes on side roads. Temperatures fluctuate widely throughout the park: the foggy coastal lowland is much cooler than the higher-altitude interior.

The average annual rainfall here is 90 to 100 inches, and during dry summer months thick fog rolling in from the Pacific veils the forests, giving redwoods a large portion of their moisture intake.

GETTING HERE AND AROUND

CAR TRAVEL

U.S. 101 runs north–south along the park, and Highway 199 cuts east–west through its northern portion. Access routes off 101 include Bald Hills Road, Davison Road, Newton B. Drury Scenic Parkway, Coastal Drive, Requa Road, and Enderts Beach Road. From 199 take South Fork Road to Howland Hill Road. Many of the park's roads aren't paved, and winter rains can turn them into obstacle courses; sometimes they're closed completely. RVs and trailers aren't permitted on some routes.

PARK ESSENTIALS
PARK FEES AND PERMITS
Admission to Redwood National Park is free. There's an $8 day-use fee to enter one or all of Redwood's state parks; for camping at these state parks it's an additional $35. To visit Tall Trees Grove, you must get a free permit at the Kuchel Information Center in Orick. Permits also are needed to camp in Redwood Creek backcountry.

PARK HOURS
The park is open year-round, 24 hours a day.

VISITOR INFORMATION
PARK CONTACT INFORMATION
Redwood National Park ✉ *1111 2nd St., Crescent City* ☎ *707/465-7335* ⊕ *www.nps.gov/redw.*

VISITOR CENTERS
Crescent City Information Center. As the park's headquarters, this center is the main information stop if you're approaching the redwoods from the north. A gift shop and picnic area are here. ✉ *Off U.S. 101 at 2nd and K Sts., 1111 2nd St, Crescent City* ☎ *707/465-7335* ⊕ *www.nps.gov/ redw* ☉ *Mid-May–mid-Oct., daily 9–6; mid-Oct.–mid-May, daily 9–4.*

Hiouchi Information Center. Located in Jedediah Smith Redwoods State Park, 2 miles west of Hiouchi and 9 miles east of Crescent City off U.S. 199, this center has a bookstore, film, and exhibits about the flora and fauna in the park. It's also a starting point for seasonal ranger programs. ✉ *Hiouchi Information Center, Hwy. 199* ☎ *707/458-3294* ⊕ *www. nps.gov/redw* ☉ *Late May–mid-Sept., daily 9–6.*

Jedediah Smith Visitor Center. Located off U.S. 199, this center has information about ranger-led walks and evening campfire programs in the summer in Jedediah Smith Redwoods State Park. Also here are nature and history exhibits, a gift shop, a pay phone, and a picnic area. ✉ *Off U.S. 199* ☎ *707/458-3496* ⊕ *www.parks.ca.gov* ☉ *Late May–mid-Sept., daily 9–6; closed late Sept.–mid-May.*

★ **Prairie Creek Visitor Center.** This center, housed in a redwood lodge, has wildlife displays and a massive stone fireplace that was built in 1933. Several trailheads begin here. Stretch your legs with an easy stroll along Revelation Trail, a short loop behind the lodge. Pick up information about summer programs in Prairie Creek Redwoods State Park. There's a pay phone, nature museum, gift shop, picnic area, and exhibits on flora and fauna. ✉ *Off southern end of Newton B. Drury Scenic Pkwy., Orick* ☎ *707/488-2039* ⊕ *www.parks.ca.gov* ☉ *Daily 9–5.*

★ **Thomas H. Kuchel Visitor Center.** Here you can get brochures, advice, and a free permit to drive up the access road to Tall Trees Grove. Whale-watchers will find the deck of the visitor center an excellent observation point, and bird-watchers will enjoy the nearby Freshwater Lagoon, a popular layover for migrating waterfowl. ✉ *Off U.S. 101, Orick* ☎ *707/465-7765* ⊕ *www.nps.gov/redw* ☉ *Daily 9–5.*

8

Plants and Wildlife in Redwood

Coast redwoods, the world's tallest trees (a new record holder, topping out at 379 feet, was found within the park in 2006) grow in the moist, temperate climate of California's North Coast. These ancient giants thrive in an environment that exists in only a few hundred coastal miles along the Pacific Ocean. They commonly live 600 years—though some have been around for 2,000 years.

A healthy redwood forest is diverse and includes Douglas firs, western hemlocks, tan oaks, and madrone trees. The complex soils of the forest floor support a verdant profusion of ferns, mosses, and fungi, along with numerous shrubs and berry bushes. In spring, California rhododendron bloom throughout the forest, providing a daz- zling purple and pink contrast to the dense greenery.

Redwood National Park holds 45% of all California's old-growth redwood forests. Of the original 3,125 square miles (2 million acres) in the Red- woods Historic Range, only 4% remain following the logging that began in 1850; 1% is privately owned and man- aged, and 3% is on public land.

In the park's backcountry, you might spot mountain lions, black bears, black-tailed deer, river otters, beavers, and minks. Roosevelt elk roam the flatlands, and the rivers and streams teem with salmon and trout. Gray whales, seals, and sea lions cavort near the coastline. And thanks to the area's location along the Pacific Fly- way, an amazing 402 species of birds have been sighted here.

EXPLORING

SCENIC DRIVES

★ **Coastal Drive.** This 8-mile, partially paved road is closed to trailers and RVs and takes about one hour to drive one way. The slow pace along- side stands of redwoods offers close-up views of the Klamath River and expansive panoramas of the Pacific. From here you'll find access to the Flint Ridge section of the Coastal Trail.

SCENIC STOPS

Crescent Beach Overlook. The scenery here includes ocean views and, in the distance, Crescent City and its working harbor; in balmy weather this is a great place for a picnic. From the overlook you can spot migrat- ing gray whales November through December and March through April. ⊠ *2 miles south of Crescent City off Enderts Beach Rd.*

★ **Fern Canyon.** Enter another world and be surrounded by 30-foot canyon walls covered with sword, maidenhair, and five-finger ferns. Allow an hour to explore the 0.25-mile-long vertical garden along a 0.7-mile loop. From the north end of Gold Bluffs Beach it's an easy walk, although you'll have to wade across a small stream several times (in addition to driving across streams on the way to the parking area). But the lush surroundings are otherworldly, and worth a visit when creeks aren't running too high. Be aware that RVs longer than 24 feet and all trailers are not allowed here. ⊠ *10 miles northwest of Prairie Creek Visitor Center, via Davison Rd. off U.S. 101.*

Lady Bird Johnson Grove. This section of the park was dedicated by, and named for, the former first lady. A 1-mile, wheelchair-accessible nature loop follows an old logging road through a mature redwood forest. Allow 45 minutes to complete the trail. ⊠ *5 miles east of Kuchel Visitor Center, along U.S. 101 and Bald Hills Rd.*

★ **Tall Trees Grove.** From the Kuchel Visitor Center, you can get a free permit to make the drive up the steep 14-mile Tall Trees Access Road (the last 6 miles are gravel) to the grove's trailhead (trailers and RVs not allowed). Access to the popular grove is first-come, first-served, and a maximum of 50 permits are handed out each day. ⊠ *Access road is 10-mile drive east of Kuchel Visitor Center, via U.S. 101; turn right at Bald Hills Rd. and follow it to access road.*

SPORTS AND THE OUTDOORS

HIKING

MODERATE

★ **Coastal Trail.** Although this easy-to-difficult trail runs along most of the park's length, smaller sections—of varying degrees of difficulty—are accessible via frequent, well-marked trailheads. The moderate to difficult DeMartin section leads past 5 miles of old-growth redwoods and through prairie. If you're up for a real workout, you'll be well rewarded with the brutally difficult but stunning Flint Ridge section, a 4.5-mile stretch of steep grades and numerous switchbacks that leads past redwoods and Marshall Pond. The moderate 4-mile-long Hidden Beach section connects the Lagoon Creek picnic area with Klamath Overlook and provides coastal views and whale-watching opportunities. *Moderate.* ⊠ *Flint Ridge trailhead: Douglas Bridge parking area, north end of Coastal Dr.*

KAYAKING

With many miles of often-shallow rivers and streams in the area, kayaking is a popular pastime in the park.

OUTFITTERS

Adventure's Edge. You can rent hard-shell kayaks here for $40 a day. In business since 1970, this Arcata outfitter also rents camping equipment and tents. ⊠ *650 10th St., Arcata* ☎ *707/822–4673* ⊗ *Mon.–Sat. 9–6, Sun. 10–5.*

8

CLOSE UP

Best Campgrounds in Redwood

Within a 30-minute drive of Redwood National and State parks there are nearly 60 public and private camping facilities. None of the four primitive areas in Redwood—DeMartin, Flint Ridge, Little Bald Hills, and Nickel Creek—is a drive-in site. Although you don't need a permit at these four hike-in sites, stop at a ranger station to inquire about availability. You will need to get a permit from a ranger station for camping along Redwood Creek in the backcountry. Bring your own water, since drinking water isn't available in any of these sites.

If you'd rather drive than hike in, Redwood has four developed campgrounds—Elk Prairie, Gold Bluffs Beach, Jedediah Smith, and Mill Creek—that are within the state-park boundaries. None has RV hookups, and some length restrictions apply. Fees are $35 in state park campgrounds. For details and reservations, call ☎ 800/444-7275 or check ⊕ www.reserveamerica.com.

Elk Prairie Campground. Adjacent to a prairie and old-growth redwoods, this campground is popular with Roosevelt elk. ⊠ 6 miles north of Orick

on Newton B. Drury Scenic Pkwy. in Prairie Creek Redwoods State Park ☎ 800/444-7275.

Gold Bluffs Beach Campground. You can camp in tents or RVs right on the beach at this Prairie Creek Redwoods State Park campground near Fern Canyon. ⊠ At end of Davison Rd., which is 5 miles south of Redwood Information Center off U.S. 101 ☎ 707/488-2039.

Jedediah Smith Campground. This is one of the few places to camp—in tents or RVs—within groves of old-growth redwood forest. ⊠ 8 miles east of Crescent City on U.S. 199 ☎ 800/444-7275.

Mill Creek Campground. Mill Creek is the largest of the state-park campgrounds. ⊠ East of U.S. 101, 7 miles southeast of Crescent City ☎ 800/444-7275.

Nickel Creek Campground. An easy hike gets you to this primitive site, which is near tide pools and has great ocean views. ⊠ On Coastal Trail ½ mile from end of Enderts Beach Rd. ☎ 707/465-7335.

WHALE-WATCHING

Good vantage points for whale-watching include Crescent Beach Overlook, the Kuchel Visitor Center in Orick, points along the Coastal Drive, and the Klamath River Overlook. Late November through January are the best months to see their southward migrations; February through April they return and generally pass closer to shore.

The Southern Sierra

AROUND SEQUOIA, KINGS CANYON, AND YOSEMITE NATIONAL PARKS

WORD OF MOUTH

"Mono Lake is an ancient saline lake. It is home to trillions of brine shrimp and alkali flies. You can see many limestone formations known as Tufa Towers, such as this, rising from the water's surface. Mono Lake is visited by millions of migratory birds each year."
                    —photo by Randall Pugh, Fodors.com member

WELCOME TO THE SOUTHERN SIERRA

TOP REASONS TO GO

★ **Strap 'em on:** Whether you walk the paved loops in the national parks (⇨ Chapter 10, Yosemite National Park, and Chapter 11, Sequoia and Kings Canyon National Parks) or head off the beaten path into the backcountry, a hike through groves and meadows or alongside streams and waterfalls will allow you to see, smell, and feel nature up close.

★ **Down you go:** Famous for its incredible snow-pack—some of the deepest in the North American continent—the Sierra Nevada has something for every winter-sports fan.

★ **Live it up:** Mammoth Lakes is eastern California's most exciting resort area.

★ **Pamper yourself:** Tucked in the hills south of Oakhurst, the elegant Château du Sureau will make you feel as if you've stepped into a fairy tale.

★ **Go with the flow:** Three Rivers, the gateway to Sequoia National Park, is the launching pad for white-water trips down the Kaweah River.

1 South of Yosemite National Park. Several gateway towns to the south and west of Yosemite National Park (⇨ Chapter 10), most within an hour's drive of Yosemite Valley, have food, lodging, and other services.

2 Mammoth Lakes. A jewel in the vast Eastern Sierra Nevada, the Mammoth Lakes area lies just east of the Sierra crest, on the backside of Yosemite and the Ansel Adams Wilderness. It's a place of rugged beauty, where giant sawtooth mountains drop into the vast deserts of the Great Basin. In winter, 11,053-foot-high Mammoth Mountain provides the finest skiing and snowboarding in California—sometimes as late as June or even July. Once the snows melt, Mammoth transforms itself into a warm-weather playground, with fishing, mountain biking, golfing, hiking, and horseback riding. Nine deep-blue lakes are spread through the Mammoth Lakes Basin, and another 100 lakes dot the surrounding countryside.

3 East of Yosemite National Park. The area to the east of Yosemite National Park (⇨ Chapter 10) includes some ruggedly handsome, albeit desolate, terrain, most notably around Mono Lake. The area is best visited by car, as distances are great and public transportation is negligible. U.S. 395 is the main north–south road on the eastern side of the Sierra Nevada, at the western edge of the Great Basin. It's one of California's most beautiful highways; plan to snap pictures at roadside pullouts.

GETTING ORIENTED

The transition between the Central Valley and the rugged Southern Sierra may be the most dramatic in California sightseeing; as you head into the mountains, your temptation to stop the car and gawk will increase with every foot gained in elevation. Although you should spend most of your time here in the national parks (⇨ *Chapter 10, Yosemite National Park, and Chapter 11, Sequoia and Kings Canyon National Parks*), be sure to check out some of the mountain towns on the parks' fringes—in addition to being great places to stock up on supplies, they have worthy attractions, restaurants, and lodging options.

9

4 South of Sequoia and Kings Canyon: Three Rivers. Scenic Three Rivers is the main gateway for Sequoia and Kings Canyon National Parks (⇨ *Chapter 11*).

Updated by
Reed Parsell

Vast granite peaks and giant sequoias are among the Southern Sierra's mind-boggling natural wonders, many of which are protected in three national parks. Mother Nature goes so far over the top in this region that it might wow you even more than California's more famous urban attractions.

Outside the national parks (⇨ *Chapter 20, Yosemite National Park, and Chapter 21, Sequoia and Kings Canyon National Parks*), pristine lakes, superb skiing, rolling hills, and small towns complete the picture of the Southern Sierra. Heading up U.S. 395 on the Sierra's eastern side, you'll be rewarded with outstanding vistas of dramatic mountain peaks, including Mt. Whitney, the highest point in the contiguous United States, and Mono Lake, a vast expanse of deep blue—one of the most-photographed natural attractions in California—that is struggling to survive.

PLANNING

GETTING HERE AND AROUND

AIR TRAVEL

Fresno Yosemite International Airport (FYI) is the nearest airport to the national parks; Reno–Tahoe is the closest major airport to Mammoth Lakes.

Airports Fresno Yosemite International Airport ⊠ *5175 E. Clinton Ave., Fresno* 📞 *559/621–4500, 559/498–4095* ⊕ *www.flyfresno.org.* **Reno–Tahoe International Airport** ⊠ *U.S. 395, Exit 65B, Reno, Nevada* 📞 *775/328–6400* ⊕ *www.renoairport.com.*

CAR TRAVEL

From San Francisco, heading east on Interstate 80 to 580 to 205E is the most efficient connecting route to Interstate 5 and Highway 99, which straddle the western side of the Sierra Nevada. To best reach the eastern side from the Bay Area, take Interstate 80 to U.S. 395, then head south.

To get to Mammoth Lakes in summer and early fall (or whenever snows aren't blocking Tioga Road), you can travel via Highway 120 (to U.S.

395 south) through the Yosemite high country; the quickest route in winter is Interstate 80 to U.S. 50 to Highway 207 (Kingsbury Grade) to U.S. 395 south; either route takes about seven hours.

■**TIP→** Watch your gas gauge. Gas stations are few and far between in the Sierra, so fill your tank when you can. If you're traveling between October and May, heavy snow may cover mountain roads. Carry tire chains, know how to put them on (on Interstate 80 and U.S. 50 you can pay a chain installer $35 to do it for you, but on other routes you'll have to do it yourself), and always check road conditions before you leave.

Travel Reports Caltrans Current Highway Conditions ☎ *800/427–7623* ⊕ *www.dot.ca.gov.*

BUS TRAVEL

Greyhound serves Fresno, Madera, and other Central Valley towns west of the Sierra. Madera County Connection buses travel between Madera and Oakhurst (and Bass Lake). Eastern Sierra Transit Authority buses serve Mammoth Lakes, Bishop, and other eastern Sierra towns.

Bus Contacts Eastern Sierra Transit Authority ☎ *800/922–1930* ⊕ *www. easternsierratransitauthority.com.* **Greyhound** ⊠ *Fresno* ☎ *800/231–2222* ⊕ *www.greyhound.com.* **Madera County Connection** ⊠ *Madera* ☎ *559/661– 3040* ⊕ *www.maderactc.com/pubtrans.html.*

RESTAURANTS

Most small towns in the Sierra Nevada have at least one restaurant; with few exceptions, dress is casual. You'll most likely be spending a lot of time in the car while you're exploring the area, so pick up snacks and drinks to keep with you. With picnic supplies on hand, you'll be able to enjoy an impromptu meal under giant trees or in one of the eastern Sierra towns' municipal parks. *Prices in the reviews are the average cost of a main course at dinner or, if dinner is not served, at lunch.*

HOTELS

For visits to the Sierra Nevada's western side, book your hotel in advance—especially in summer—or you may wind up far from the action in the Central Valley. Booking in advance is less crucial for travel to the Eastern Sierra. In either area, keep in mind that rural and rustic does not always mean inexpensive. *Prices in the reviews are the lowest cost of a standard double room in high season. For expanded reviews, facilities, and current deals, visit Fodors.com.*

Hotel Contacts Mammoth Lakes Visitors Bureau Lodging Referral ☎ *760/934–2712, 888/466–2666* ⊕ *www.visitmammoth.com.* **Mammoth Reservations** ☎ *800/223–3032* ⊕ *www.mammothreservations.com.*

9

SOUTH OF YOSEMITE NATIONAL PARK

People heading to Yosemite National Park, especially those interested in seeing the giant redwoods on the park's south side, pass through Oakhurst and Fish Camp on Highway 41.

OAKHURST

40 miles north of Fresno on Hwy. 41.

Motels, restaurants, gas stations, and small businesses line Highway 41 in Oakhurst, the last sizeable community before Yosemite (⇨ *Chapter 10)*—the south entrance is 23 miles north of town—and a good spot to find provisions. Continue north on Highway 41 to get to Yosemite. Three miles north of town on Highway 41, then 6 miles east, lies honky-tonk Bass Lake, a popular spot in summer with motorboaters, Jet Skiers, and families looking to cool off in the reservoir.

GETTING HERE AND AROUND

At the junction of Highways 41 and 49, Oakhurst is a solid hour's drive north of Fresno. It's the southern gateway to Yosemite, so many people fly to Fresno and rent a car to get here and beyond. In town, there's no public transportation system of any consequence.

ESSENTIALS

Visitor Information Yosemite Sierra Visitors Bureau ☎ *559/683–4636* 🌐 *www.yosemitethisyear.com.*

WHERE TO EAT

$$$$ EUROPEAN Fodor's Choice ★ 🍴 **Erna's Elderberry House.** Erna Kubin-Clanin, the grande dame of Château du Sureau, created this culinary oasis, stunning for its understated elegance, gorgeous setting, and impeccable service. Red walls and wood beams accent the dining room's high ceilings, and arched windows reflect the glow of candles. The seasonal six-course prix-fixe dinner can be paired with superb wines, with every course delivered in perfect synchronicity by the elite waitstaff. A short bistro menu is served in the former wine cellar. [$] *Average main: $95* ✉ *Château du Sureau, 48688 Victoria La., off Hwy. 41* ☎ *559/683–6800* 🌐 *www.elderberryhouse.com* ✍ *Reservations essential* ⏲ *No lunch Mon.–Sat.*

WHERE TO STAY

For expanded reviews, facilities, and current deals, visit Fodors.com.

$ HOTEL 👶 🏨 **Best Western Yosemite Gateway Inn.** Oakhurst's best motel has carefully tended landscaping and rooms with attractive colonial–style furniture and slightly kitschy hand-painted wall murals of Yosemite. **Pros:** reasonably close to Yosemite; clean; two pools, one heated; comfortable. **Cons:** chain property; some walls seem thin. **TripAdvisor:** "beautiful grounds," "great location," "nice clean room." [$] *Rooms from: $115* ✉ *40530 Hwy. 41* ☎ *800/545–5462, 559/683–2378* 🌐 *www.yosemitegatewayinn.com* 🛏 *121 rooms, 16 suites.*

$$$$ RESORT Fodor's Choice ★ 🏨 **Château du Sureau.** You'll feel pampered from the moment you drive through the wrought-iron gates of this fairy-tale castle. **Pros:** luxurious; you'll feel pampered; great views. **Cons:** expensive; if you're not really into spas, it might not be worth your while. **TripAdvisor:** "a wonderful world away," "elegant," "beyond 5-star accommodations." [$] *Rooms from: $365* ✉ *48688 Victoria La.* ☎ *559/683–6860* 🌐 *www.chateausureau.com* 🛏 *10 rooms, 1 villa* 🍴 *Breakfast.*

$$ B&B/INN ★ 🏨 **Homestead Cottages.** Set on 160 acres of rolling hills that once held a Miwok village, these cottages (the largest sleeps six) have gas fireplaces, fully equipped kitchens, and queen-size beds. **Pros:** remote location;

quiet setting; friendly owners. **Cons:** might be a little *too* quiet for some. **TripAdvisor:** "awesome lodging," "lovely accommodations," "comfortable stay and kind hosts." [$] *Rooms from: $155* ✉ *41110 Rd. 600, 2½ miles off Hwy. 49, Ahwahnee* ☎ *559/683–0495, 800/483–0495* 🌐 *www.homesteadcottages.com* 🛏 *5 cottages, 1 loft.*

FISH CAMP

57 miles north of Fresno and 4 miles south of Yosemite National Park's south entrance.

As you climb in elevation along Highway 41 northbound, you see nothing but trees until you get to the small settlement of Fish Camp, where there's a post office and general store, but no gasoline (for gas, head 10 miles north to Wawona, in the park, or 17 miles south to Oakhurst).

GETTING HERE AND AROUND

Arrive here by car via Highway 41, from Yosemite National Park a few miles to the north, or from Oakhurst (and, farther down the road, Fresno) to the south. Unless you're on foot or a bicycle, a car is your only option.

EXPLORING

👶 **Yosemite Mountain Sugar Pine Railroad.** Travel back to a time when powerful steam locomotives hauled massive log trains through the Sierra. This 4-mile, narrow-gauge railroad excursion takes you near Yosemite's south gate; there's also a moonlight special, with dinner and entertainment ($48). Take Highway 41 south from Yosemite about 8 miles to the departure point. ✉ *56001 Hwy. 41* ☎ *559/683–7273* 🌐 *www.ymsprr.com* 🎫 *$19* 🕐 *Mar.–Oct., daily.*

WHERE TO STAY

$$ B&B/INN ★ 🏨 **Narrow Gauge Inn.** The well-tended rooms at this family-owned property have balconies with great views of the surrounding woods and mountains. **Pros:** close to Yosemite's south entrance; nicely appointed rooms; wonderful balconies. **Cons:** rooms can be a bit dark; dining options are limited, especially for vegetarians. **TripAdvisor:** "quaint little find," "charming," "excellent restaurant." [$] *Rooms from: $145* ✉ *48571 Hwy. 41* ☎ *559/683–7720, 888/644–9050* 🌐 *www.narrowgaugeinn.com* 🛏 *26 rooms, 1 suite* 🍴 *Breakfast.*

$$$$ HOTEL 🏨 **Tenaya Lodge.** One of the region's largest hotels, Tenaya Lodge is ideal for people who enjoy wilderness treks by day but prefer creature comforts at night. **Pros:** rustic setting with modern comforts; good off-season deals; very close to Yosemite National Park. **Cons:** so big it can seem impersonal; pricey during summer; few dining options. **TripAdvisor:** "I want to go back," "Yosemite luxury," "well maintained." [$] *Rooms from: $325* ✉ *1122 Hwy. 41* ☎ *559/683–6555, 888/514–2167* 🌐 *www.tenayalodge.com* 🛏 *244 rooms, 6 suites.*

EL PORTAL

14 miles west of Yosemite Valley on Hwy. 140.

The market in town is a good place to pick up provisions before you get to Yosemite (⇨ *Chapter 10*). You'll find a post office and a gas station, but not much else.

9

GETTING HERE AND AROUND

The drive here on Highway 140 from Mariposa and, farther west, Merced, is the prettiest and gentlest (in terms of steep uphill and downhill portions) route to Yosemite National Park. Much of the road follows the Merced River in a rugged canyon. The Yosemite Area Regional Transportation System (YARTS; ⊕ *www.yarts.com*) is a cheap and dependable way to go between Merced and Yosemite Valley; all buses stop in El Portal, where many park employees reside.

WHERE TO STAY

For expanded reviews, facilities, and current deals, visit Fodors.com.

$$

RESORT

ⓒ

⚏ Evergreen Lodge at Yosemite. Near Hetch Hetchy on Yosemite National Park's northwest side, this sprawling property set in the woods is perfect for families: The 90-cabin complex includes a playground, an amphitheater, a movie room, a restaurant, a gift shop, and an activities desk. **Pros:** near the underrated Hetch Hetchy; family atmosphere; clean cabins. **Cons:** about an hour's drive from Yosemite Valley. **TripAdvisor:** "unexpected delight," "restaurant is the best," "the great outdoors in style."⑤ *Rooms from: $170* ⊠ *33160 Evergreen Rd.* ☎ *209/379–2606, 888/935–6343* ⊕ *www.evergreenlodge.com* ↪ *90 cabins.*

$$$

B&B/INN

⚏ Yosemite View Lodge. Just 2 miles outside the park's Arch Rock entrance, this modern property is the most convenient place to spend the night if you are unable to secure lodgings in the Valley. **Pros:** great location; good views; lots of on-site amenities. **Cons:** somewhat pricey for what you get. **TripAdvisor:** "lovely spot," "great location," "gorgeous view."⑤ *Rooms from: $229* ⊠ *11136 Hwy. 140* ☎ *209/379–2681, 888/742–4371* ⊕ *www.yosemite-motels.com* ↪ *279 rooms.*

MAMMOTH LAKES

30 miles south of eastern edge of Yosemite National Park on U.S. 395.

International real-estate developers joined forces with Mammoth Mountain Ski Area to transform the once sleepy town of Mammoth Lakes (elevation 7,800 feet) into an upscale ski destination. The Village at Mammoth is the epicenter of the recent development. Much of the architecture here is of the faux-alpine variety, but you'll find relatively sophisticated dining and lodging options. Winter is high season; in summer, room rates plummet.

GETTING HERE AND AROUND

The best way to get to Mammoth Lakes is by car. The town is a couple of miles west of U.S. 395. The Yosemite Area Regional Transportation System (YARTS; ⊕ *www.yarts.com*) provides once-a-day service between here and Yosemite Valley. The shuttle buses of Eastern Sierra Transit Authority (☎ 800/922–1930 ⊕ *www.estransit.com*) serve Mammoth Lakes, Bishop, and nearby tourist sites.

Highway 203 heads west from U.S. 395, becoming Main Street as it passes through the town of Mammoth Lakes, and later Minaret Road (which makes a right turn) as it continues west to the Mammoth Mountain ski area and Devils Postpile National Monument.

Twin Lakes, in the Mammoth Lakes region, is a great place to unwind.

ESSENTIALS

Visitor Information Mammoth Lakes Visitors Bureau ✉ *Welcome Center, 2510 Main St., near Sawmill Cutoff Rd.* ☎ *760/934–2712* ⊕ *www.visitmammoth. com.*

EXPLORING

Mammoth Lakes Basin. The lakes, reached by Lake Mary Road off Highway 203 southwest of town, are popular for fishing and boating in summer. First comes Twin Lakes, at the far end of which is Twin Falls, where water cascades 300 feet over a shelf of volcanic rock. Also popular are Lake Mary, the largest lake in the basin; Lake Mamie; and Lake George. Horseshoe Lake is the only lake in which you can swim.

Minaret Vista. The glacier-carved sawtooth spires of the Minarets, the remains of an ancient lava flow, are best viewed from the Minaret Vista, off Highway 203 west of Mammoth Lakes.

🄯 Fodor's Choice ★ **Panorama Gondola.** Even if you don't ski, ride the gondola to see Mammoth Mountain, the aptly named dormant volcano that gives Mammoth Lakes its name. Gondolas serve skiers in winter and mountain bikers and sightseers in summer. The high-speed, eight-passenger gondolas whisk you from the chalet to the summit, where you can read about the area's volcanic history and take in top-of-the-world views. Standing high above the tree line, you can look west 150 miles across the state to the Coastal Range; to the east are the highest peaks of Nevada and the Great Basin beyond. You won't find a better view of the Sierra High Country without climbing. Remember, though, that the air is thin at the 11,053-foot summit; carry water, and don't overexert yourself. The boarding area is at the Main Lodge. ✉ *Off Hwy. 203* ☎ *760/934–2571 information, 3850 gondola station* 🎟 *$24* ⏲ *July 4–Oct., daily 9–4:30; Nov.–July 3, daily 8:30–4.*

Village at Mammoth. This huge complex of shops, restaurants, and luxury accommodations is the town's tourist center. Parking can be tricky, even seemingly impossible. There's a parking lot across the street on Minaret Road; cross your fingers and pay attention to time limits.

WHERE TO EAT

$$$ STEAKHOUSE 🍴 **The Mogul.** This longtime favorite the place to go when you want a straightforward steak and salad bar. The only catch is that the waiters cook your steak—and the result depends on the waiter's experience. But generally you can't go wrong. And kids love it. The knotty-pine walls lend a woodsy touch and suggest Mammoth Mountain before all the development. [$] *Average main: $24* ✉ *1528 Mammoth Tavern Rd., off Old Mammoth Rd.* ☎ *760/934–3039* 🌐 *www.themogul.com* ⏲ *No lunch.*

$$$ AMERICAN 🍴 **Petra's Bistro & Wine Bar.** The ambience at Petra's—quiet, dark, and warm—complements the carefully prepared meat main dishes and seasonal sides, and the more than two dozen California wines from behind the bar. The service is top-notch. Downstairs, the Clocktower Cellar bar provides a late-night, rowdy alternative—or chaser. [$] *Average main: $28* ✉ *6080 Minaret Rd.* ☎ *760/934–3500* 🌐 *www.petrasbistro.com* ✍ *Reservations essential* ⏲ *Closed Mon. No lunch.*

$$$ AMERICAN 🍴 **Restaurant at Convict Lake.** Tucked in a tiny valley ringed by mile-high peaks, Convict Lake is one of the most spectacular spots in the eastern Sierra. Thank heaven the food lives up to the view. The chef's specialties include beef Wellington, rack of lamb, and pan-seared local trout, all beautifully prepared. The woodsy room has a vaulted knotty-pine ceiling and a copper-chimney fireplace that roars on cold nights. Natural light abounds in the daytime, but if it's summer, opt for a table outdoors under the white-barked aspens. Service is exceptional, as is the wine list, with reasonably priced European and California varietals. [$] *Average main: $32* ✉ *Convict Lake Rd. off U.S. 395, 4 miles south of Mammoth Lakes* ☎ *760/934–3803* 🌐 *www.convictlake.com* ✍ *Reservations essential* ⏲ *No lunch early Sept.–July 4.*

$$ WINE BAR 🍴 **Side Door Café.** Half wine bar, half café, this is a laid-back spot for an easy lunch or a long, lingering afternoon. The café serves grilled panini sandwiches, sweet and savory crepes, and espresso. At the wine bar, order cheese plates and charcuterie platters, designed to pair with the 25 wines (fewer in summertime) available by the glass. If you're lucky, a winemaker will show up and hold court at the bar. [$] *Average main: $18* ✉ *Village at Mammoth, 1111 Forest Trail, Unit 229* ☎ *760/934–5200* 🌐 *www.sidedoormammoth.com.*

$$ AMERICAN 🍴 **The Stove.** A longtime family favorite for down-to-earth, folksy cooking, this is the kind of place you take the family to fill up before a long car ride. The omelets, pancakes, huevos rancheros, and meat loaf won't win any awards, but they're tasty. The room is cozy, with gingham curtains and dark-wood booths, and service is friendly. Breakfast and lunch are the best bets here. [$] *Average main: $16* ✉ *644 Old Mammoth Rd.* ☎ *760/934–2821* *Reservations not accepted* ⊙ *No dinner Mon. and Tues.*

WHERE TO STAY

$ B&B/INN **Alpenhof Lodge.** The owners of Alpenhof lucked out when developers built the fancy-schmancy Village at Mammoth across the street from their mom-and-pop motel, which remains a simple lodging offering basic comforts and a few niceties like attractive pine furniture. **Pros:** convenient for skiers; good price. **Cons:** could use an update; rooms above the pub can be noisy. **TripAdvisor:** "cozy hotel in stunning location," "nice 'Austrian' hotel," "a delightful retreat." [$] *Rooms from: $119* ✉ *6080 Minaret Rd., Box 1157* ☎ *760/934–6330, 800/828–0371* 🌐 *www.alpenhof-lodge.com* *54 rooms, 3 cabins.*

$$ B&B/INN **Cinnamon Bear Inn Bed and Breakfast.** In a business district off Main Street, this bed-and-breakfast feels more like a small motel, with nicely decorated rooms, many with four-poster beds. **Pros:** comparatively quiet; affordable; friendly. **Cons:** a bit tricky to find; limited parking. **TripAdvisor:** "delicious breakfast," "a lovely friendly place," "quirky." [$] *Rooms from: $149* ✉ *113 Center St.* ☎ *760/934–2873, 800/845–2873* 🌐 *www.cinnamonbearinn.com* *22 rooms* 🍴 *Breakfast.*

$$$ RESORT **Double Eagle Resort and Spa.** You won't find a better spa retreat in the eastern Sierra than the Double Eagle, which is in a spectacularly beautiful spot under towering peaks and along a creek, near June Lake, 20 minutes north of Mammoth Lakes. **Pros:** pretty setting; generous breakfast; good for families. **Cons:** expensive, remote. **TripAdvisor:** "beautiful spot," "great mountain getaway," "great location." [$] *Rooms from: $229* ✉ *5587 Hwy. 158, Box 736, June Lake* ☎ *760/648–7004, 877/648–7004* 🌐 *www.doubleeagleresort.com* *16 2-bedroom cabins, 16 cabin suites, 1 3-bedroom cabin.*

$$ RESORT **Juniper Springs Lodge.** Tops for slope-side comfort, these condominium-style units have full kitchens and ski-in ski-out access to the mountain. **Pros:** bargain during summer; direct access to the slopes; good views. **Cons:** no nightlife within walking distance; no air-conditioning. [$] *Rooms from: $159* ✉ *4000 Meridian Blvd.* ☎ *760/924–1102, 800/626–6684* 🌐 *www.mammothmountain.com* *10 studios, 99 1-bedrooms, 92 2-bedrooms, 3 3-bedrooms.*

$$ RESORT **Mammoth Mountain Inn.** If you want to be within walking distance of the Mammoth Mountain Main Lodge, this is the place. **Pros:** great location; big rooms; a traditional place to stay. **Cons:** can be crowded in ski season; won't be around for many more years. **TripAdvisor:** "service at its best," "ski-in ski-out," "very conveniently located." [$] *Rooms from: $129* ✉ *Minaret Rd., 4 miles west of Mammoth Lakes 760/934–2581, 800/626–6684* 🌐 *www.mammothmountain.com* *124 rooms, 91 condos.*

$$ RESORT Fodor's Choice ★ **Tamarack Lodge Resort & Lakefront Restaurant.** Tucked away on the edge of the John Muir Wilderness Area, where cross-country ski trails loop through the woods, this original 1924 lodge looks like something out of a snow globe, and the lake it borders is serenely beautiful. **Pros:** rustic

9

but not run-down; plenty of eco-sensitivity; tons of nearby outdoor activities. **Cons:** thin walls; some main lodge rooms have shared bathrooms. **TripAdvisor:** "rustic hotel in beautiful spot," "lots of character," "wonderful helpful staff." [$] *Rooms from: $169* ✉ *Lake Mary Rd., off Hwy. 203* ☎ *760/934–2442, 800/626–6684* 🌐 *www.tamaracklodge.com* ⇨ *11 rooms, 35 cabins.*

$$$ RESORT 🏨 **The Village Lodge.** At the epicenter of Mammoth's dining and nightlife scene, this cluster of four-story timber-and-stone condo buildings nods to Alpine style, with exposed timbers and peaked roofs. **Pros:** central location; clean; big rooms; lots of good restaurants nearby. **Cons:** pricey; can be noisy outside. **TripAdvisor:** "beautiful room," "great condos in a great location," "city living in the mountains." [$] *Rooms from: $189* ✉ *100 Canyon Blvd.* ☎ *760/934–1982, 800/626–6684* 🌐 *www.mammothmountain.com* ⇨ *277 units.*

SPORTS AND THE OUTDOORS

BICYCLING

Mammoth Mountain Bike Park. The park opens when the snow melts, usually by July, and has 70-plus miles of single-track trails—from mellow to super-challenging. Chairlifts and shuttles provide trail access, and rentals are available. Various shops around town also rent bikes and provide trail maps, if you don't want to ascend the mountain. ✉ *Mammoth Mountain Ski Area* ☎ *760/934–0706* 🌐 *www.mammothmountain.com.*

FISHING

The fishing season runs from the last Saturday in April until the end of October. Crowley Lake is the top trout-fishing spot in the area; Convict Lake, June Lake, and the lakes of the Mammoth Basin are other prime spots. One of the best trout rivers is the San Joaquin, near Devils Postpile. Hot Creek, a designated Wild Trout Stream, is renowned for fly-fishing (catch-and-release only).

Kittredge Sports. This outfit rents rods and reels and also conducts guided trips. ✉ *3218 Main St., at Forest Trail* ☎ *760/934–7566* 🌐 *www.kittredgesports.com.*

Sierra Drifters Guide Service. To maximize your time on the water, get tips from local anglers, or better yet, book a guided fishing trip with this service. ☎ *760/935–4250* 🌐 *www.sierradrifters.com.*

HIKING

Hiking in Mammoth is stellar, especially along the trails that wind through the pristine alpine scenery around the Lakes Basin. Carry lots of water; and remember, you're above 8,000-foot elevation, and the air is thin.

U.S. Forest Service Ranger Station and Welcome Center. Stop at the ranger station, just east of the town of Mammoth Lakes, for an area trail map and permits for backpacking in wilderness areas. ✉ *2510 Main St., Hwy. 203* ☎ *760/924–5500* 🌐 *www.fs.usda.gov/main/inyo.*

HORSEBACK RIDING

Stables around Mammoth are typically open from June through September.

Mammoth Lakes Pack Outfit. This company runs day and overnight horseback trips, or will shuttle you to the high country. ⊠ *Lake Mary Rd., between Twin Lakes and Lake Mary* ☎ *888/475–8747* ⊕ *www. mammothpack.com.*

McGee Creek Pack Station. These folks customize pack trips or will shuttle you to camp alone. ☎ *760/935–4324, 760/878–2207, 800/854–7407* ⊕ *www.mcgeecreekpackstation.com.*

SKIING

In winter, check the On the Snow website or call the Snow Report for information about Mammoth weather conditions.

June Mountain Ski Area. In their rush to Mammoth Mountain, most people overlook June Mountain, a compact, low-key resort 20 miles north of Mammoth. Snowboarders especially dig it. Two freestyle terrain areas are for both skiers and boarders, including a huge 16-foot-wall super pipe. Best of all, there's rarely a line for the lifts—if you want to avoid the crowds but must ski on a weekend, this is the place. And in a storm, June is better protected from wind and blowing snow than Mammoth Mountain. (If it starts to storm, you can use your Mammoth ticket at June.) Expect all the usual services, including a rental-and-repair shop, ski school, and sports shop, but the food quality is better at Mammoth. Lift tickets cost $72, with discounts for multiple days. ⊠ *3819 Hwy. 158, off June Lake Loop, June Lake* ☎ *760/648–7733, 888/586–3686* ⊕ *www.junemountain.com* ⊲ *35 trails on 500 acres, rated 35% beginner, 45% intermediate, 20% advanced. Longest run 2½ miles, base 7,510 feet, summit 10,174 feet. Lifts: 7.*

Fodor's Choice   **Mammoth Mountain Ski Area.** One of the West's largest and best ski areas,
★   Mammoth has more than 3,500 acres of skiable terrain and a 3,100-foot vertical drop. The views from the 11,053-foot summit are some of the most stunning in the Sierra. Below, you'll find a 6½-mile-wide swath of groomed boulevards and canyons, as well as pockets of tree-skiing and a dozen vast bowls. Snowboarders are everywhere on the slopes; there are three outstanding freestyle terrain parks of varying technical difficulty, with jumps, rails, tabletops, and giant super pipes (this is the location of several international snowboarding and, in summer months, mountain-bike competitions). Mammoth's season begins in November and often lingers into May. Lift tickets cost $89. Lessons and equipment are available, and there's a children's ski and snowboard school. Mammoth runs free shuttle-bus routes around town and to the ski area, and the Village Gondola runs from the Village complex to Canyon Lodge. However, only overnight guests are allowed to park at the Village for more than a few hours. Warning: The main lodge is dark and dated, unsuited in most every way for the crush of ski season. Within a decade, it's likely to be replaced. ⊠ *Minaret Rd., west of Mammoth Lakes* ☎ *760/934–2571, 800/626–6684, 760/934–0687 shuttle* ⊲ *150 trails on 3,500 acres, rated 30% beginner, 40% intermediate, 30% advanced. Longest run 3 miles, base 7,953 feet, summit 11,053 feet. Lifts: 27, including 9 high-speed and 2 gondolas.*

Tamarack Cross Country Ski Center. Trails at the center, adjacent to Tamarack Lodge, meander around several lakes. Rentals are available.

9

The all-day inclusive rate is $55. ✉ *Lake Mary Rd., off Hwy. 203* ☎ *760/934–5293, 760/934–2442* ⊕ *www.tamaracklodge.com.*

SKI RENTALS AND RESOURCES

★ **Footloose.** When the U.S. Ski Team visits Mammoth and needs boot adjustments, everyone heads to Footloose, the best place in town—and possibly all California—for ski-boot rentals and sales, as well as custom insoles (ask for Kevin or Corty). ✉ *3043 Main St., at Mammoth Rd.* ☎ *760/934–2400* ⊕ *www.footloosesports.com.*

Kittredge Sports. Advanced skiers should consider this outfit, which has been around since the 1960s. ✉ *3218 Main St.* ☎ *760/934–7566* ⊕ *www.kittredgesports.com.*

Mammoth Sporting Goods. This company rents good skis for intermediates and sells equipment, clothing, and accessories. ✉ *1 Sierra Center Mall, Old Mammoth Rd.* ☎ *760/934–3239.*

OntheSnow.com ⊕ *www.onthesnow.com/california/mammoth-mountain-ski-area/skireport.html.*

Snow Report. For information on winter conditions around Mammoth, call the Snow Report. ☎ *760/934–7669, 888/766–9778.*

EAST OF YOSEMITE NATIONAL PARK

Most people enter Yosemite National Park from the west, having driven out from the Bay Area or Los Angeles. The eastern entrance on Tioga Pass Road (Highway 120), however, provides stunning, sweeping views of the High Sierra. Gray rocks shine in the bright sun, with scattered, small vegetation sprinkled about the mountainside. To drive from Lee Vining to Tuolumne Meadows is an unforgettable experience, but keep in mind the road tends to be closed for at least seven months of the year.

LEE VINING

20 miles east of Tuolumne Meadows via Hwy. 120 to U.S. 395; 30 miles north of Mammoth Lakes on U.S. 395.

Tiny Lee Vining is known primarily as the eastern gateway to Yosemite National Park (summer only; ⇨ *Chapter 10*) and the location of vast and desolate Mono Lake. Pick up supplies at the general store year-round, or stop here for lunch or dinner before or after a drive through the high country. In winter the town is all but deserted, except for the ice climbers who come to scale frozen waterfalls. You can meet these hearty souls at Nicely's restaurant, where climbers congregate for breakfast around 8 on winter mornings. To try your hand at ice climbing, contact Doug Nidever (☎ *760/937–6922* ⊕ *www.themountainguide.com*), aka the Mountain Guide.

GETTING HERE AND AROUND

Lee Vining is on U.S. 395, just north of the road's intersection with Highway 120 and on the south side of Mono Lake. Yosemite Area Regional Transportation System (YARTS; ⊕ *www.yarts.com*) can get you here from Yosemite Valley, but you'll need a car to explore the area.

ESSENTIALS

Visitor Information **Lee Vining Chamber of Commerce** *760/647–6629* 🌐 *www.leevining.com.* **Mono Lake** ☎ *760/647–6595* 🌐 *www.monolake.org.*

EXPLORING

★ **Mono Lake.** Since the 1940s Los Angeles has diverted water from this lake, exposing striking towers of tufa, or calcium carbonate. Court victories by environmentalists have meant fewer diversions, and the lake is rising again. Although to see the lake from U.S. 395 is stunning, make time to walk about South Tufa, whose parking lot is 5 miles east of U.S. 395 off Highway 120. There during the summer you can join the naturalist-guided **South Tufa Walk,** which lasts about 1½ hours. The sensational **Scenic Area Visitor Center,** on U.S. 395, is open daily from June through September (Sunday–Thursday 8–5, Friday and Saturday 8–7), it's closed December through March and open weekends the rest of the year. The center's hilltop and sweeping views of Mono Lake, along with its interactive exhibits inside, make this one of California's best visitor centers. Rangers and naturalists lead walking tours of the tufa daily in summer and on weekends (sometimes on cross-country skis) in winter. In town at U.S. 395 and 3rd Street, the **Mono Lake Committee Information Center & Bookstore** has more information about this beautiful area. ✉ *Hwy. 120, east of Lee Vining* ☎ *760/647–3044.*

EN ROUTE

June Lake Loop. Heading south from Lee Vining, U.S. 395 intersects the June Lake Loop. This gorgeous 17-mile drive follows an old glacial canyon past Grant, June, Gull, and other lakes before reconnecting with U.S. 395 on its way to Mammoth Lakes. The loop is especially colorful in fall. ✉ *Hwy. 158 W.*

WHERE TO EAT AND STAY

For expanded reviews, facilities, and current deals, visit Fodors.com.

$ AMERICAN

🍴 **Nicely's.** Artworks for sale decorate the walls of this vintage diner. The country cooking isn't fancy—think blueberry pancakes for breakfast and chicken-fried steak for dinner—but this is a good spot for families with kids and unfussy eaters looking for a square meal. It's the kind of place where the waitress walks up with a pot of coffee and asks, "Ya want a warm-up, hon?" [$] *Average main: $15* ✉ *U.S. 395 and 4th St.* ☎ *760/647–6477* 🕒 *Closed Tues. and Wed. in winter.*

$ AMERICAN ★

🍴 **Tioga Gas Mart & Whoa Nelli Deli.** This might be the only gas station in the United States that serves cocktails, but its appeal goes way beyond novelty. The mahimahi tacos are succulent, the gourmet pizzas tasty, and the herb-crusted pork loin with berry glaze elegant. Order at the counter and grab a seat inside or out. [$] *Average main: $14* ✉ *Hwy. 120 and U.S. 395* ☎ *760/647–1088* 🌐 *www.whoanelliedeli.com* 🕒 *Closed mid-Nov.–mid-Apr.*

$ B&B/INN

🏨 **Lake View Lodge.** Enormous rooms and lovely landscaping, which includes several shaded sitting areas, set this motel apart from its competitors in town. **Pros:** attractive; clean; friendly staff. **Cons:** could use updating. **TripAdvisor:** "convenient to Tioga pass," "no frills no fuss," "clean and comfortable." [$] *Rooms from: $89* ✉ *51285 U.S. 395* ☎ *760/647–6543, 800/990–6614* 🌐 *www.lakeviewlodgeyosemite.com* 🛏 *76 rooms, 12 cottages.*

9

BODIE STATE HISTORIC PARK

23 miles northeast of Lee Vining via U.S. 395 to Hwy. 270.

The historic town of Bridgeport is the gateway to Bodie State Historic Park, and the only supply center for miles around. The scenery is spectacular, with craggy, snowcapped peaks looming over vast prairies. Tiny and for tourist purposes worth nothing more than a place to sleep and eat, Bridgeport's claim to fame is that most of the 1947 film-noir classic *Out of the Past* was filmed here. In winter, much of Bridgeport shuts down.

GETTING HERE AND AROUND

You need to get here by private car. About 15 miles north of Lee Vining (7 miles south of Bridgeport), look for signs pointing you east toward the ghost town, another 13 miles via Highway 270. The last 3 miles are unpaved, and possibly treacherous depending on erosion and the weather. You might need a snowmobile to get here in the winter.

EXPLORING

★ **Bodie Ghost Town.** The mining village of Rattlesnake Gulch, abandoned mine shafts, and the remains of a small Chinatown are among the sights at this fascinating ghost town. The town boomed from about 1878 to 1881, but by the late 1940s all its residents had departed. A state park was established here in 1962, with a mandate to preserve everything in a state of "arrested decay." Evidence of Bodie's wild past survives at an excellent museum, and you can tour an old stamp mill where ore was crushed into fine powder to extract gold and silver. The town is 23 miles from Lee Vining, north on U.S. 395, then east on Highway 270; the last 3 miles are unpaved. Snow may close Highway 270 from late fall through early spring. No food, drink, or lodging is available in Bodie. ⊠ *Main and Green Sts., Bodie* ☎ *760/647–6445* ⊕ *www.bodie. com* ☞ *Park $5, museum free* ⊙ *Park: late May–early Sept., daily 8–7; early Sept.–late May, daily 8–4. Museum: late May–early Sept., daily 9–6; early Sept.–late May, hrs vary.*

9

SOUTH OF SEQUOIA AND KINGS CANYON: THREE RIVERS

200 miles north of Los Angeles via I–5 to Hwy. 99 to Hwy. 198; 8 miles south of Ash Mountain/Foothills entrance to Sequoia National Park on Hwy. 198.

In the foothills of the Sierra along the Kaweah River, the serpentine hamlet of Three Rivers serves as the main gateway town to Sequoia and Kings Canyon national parks (⇨ *Chapter 21, Sequoia and Kings Canyon National Parks).* Its livelihood depends largely on tourism from the parks, courtesy of two markets, a few service stations, banks, a post office, and several lodgings, which are good spots to find a room when park accommodations are full (or if you dislike camping and would like to save money).

GETTING HERE AND AROUND

From Memorial Day through Labor Day, you can ride the city of Visalia's Sequoia Shuttle (☎ *877/404–6473* 🌐 *www.ci.visalia.ca.us*) to and from Three Rivers, up to and down from Sequoia National Park. You probably should count on driving here yourself, however, via Highway 198. The town is slender and long, and to walk from your hotel to a restaurant might wear you out before you set foot in the national park.

WHERE TO EAT AND STAY

For expanded reviews, facilities, and current deals, visit Fodors.com.

$ ECLECTIC 🍴 **We Three Bakery.** This friendly, popular-with-the-locals spot packs lunches for trips into the nearby national parks; it's also open for breakfast. Baked goods for the windy road ahead, anyone? [$] *Average main: $10* ✉ *43688 Sierra Dr.* ☎ *559/561–4761.*

$$ B&B/INN 🏨 **Buckeye Tree Lodge.** Every room at this two-story motel has a patio facing a sun-dappled grassy lawn, right on the banks of the Kaweah River. **Pros:** near the park entrance; fantastic river views; friendly staff. **Cons:** can fill up quickly in the summer; could use a little updating. **TripAdvisor:** "gorgeous location," "friendly people," "comfortable accommodations." [$] *Rooms from: $123* ✉ *46000 Sierra Dr., Hwy. 198* ☎ *559/561–5900* 🌐 *www.buckeyetree.com* 🛏 *11 rooms, 1 cottage* 🍽 *Breakfast.*

SPORTS AND THE OUTDOORS

RAFTING

Kaweah White Water Adventures. From April through July, this outfit conducts two-hour and full-day rafting trips, with some Class III rapids. Longer trips may include some Class IV. ☎ *559/561–1000, 800/229–8658* 🌐 *www.kaweah-whitewater.com* 🎟 *$50 to $140 per person.*

Yosemite
National Park

WORD OF MOUTH

"I tried cross-country skiing for the first time in Yosemite. An avid downhill skier, I quickly learned that cross-country is more physically demanding, slower going, but scenically spectacular. I chose to use the time to find the perfect shot of Half Dome."

—photo by Sarah Corley, Fodors.com member

WELCOME TO YOSEMITE

TOP REASONS TO GO

★ **Wet and wild:** An easy stroll brings you to the base of Lower Yosemite Falls, where roaring springtime waters make for misty lens caps and lasting memories.

★ **Tunnel vision:** Approaching Yosemite Valley, Wawona Road passes through a mountainside and emerges before one of the park's most heart-stopping vistas.

★ **Inhale the beauty:** Pause to smell the light, pristine air as you travel about the High Sierra's Tiago Pass and Tuolumne Meadows, where 10,000-foot granite peaks just might take your breath away.

★ **Walk away:** Leave the crowds behind—but do bring along a buddy—and take a hike somewhere along Yosemite's 800 miles of trails.

★ **Powder your nose:** Winter's hush floats into Yosemite on snowflakes. Lift your face to the sky and listen to the trees.

1 Yosemite Valley. At an elevation of 4,000 feet, in roughly the center of the park, beats Yosemite's heart. This is where you'll find the park's most famous sights and biggest crowds.

2 Wawona and Mariposa Grove. The park's southern tip holds Wawona, with its grand old hotel and pioneer history center, and the Mariposa Grove of Big Trees, filled with giant sequoias. These are closest to the South Entrance, 35 miles (a one-hour drive) south of Yosemite Village.

3 Tuolumne Meadows. The highlight of east-central Yosemite is this wildflower-strewn valley with hiking trails, nestled among sharp, rocky peaks. It's a two-hour drive northeast of Yosemite Valley along Tioga Road (closed mid-October–late May).

4 Hetch Hetchy. The most remote, least visited part of Yosemite accessible by automobile, this glacial valley is dominated by a reservoir and veined with wilderness trails. It's near the park's western boundary, about a half-hour drive north of the Big Oak Flat Entrance.

CALIFORNIA

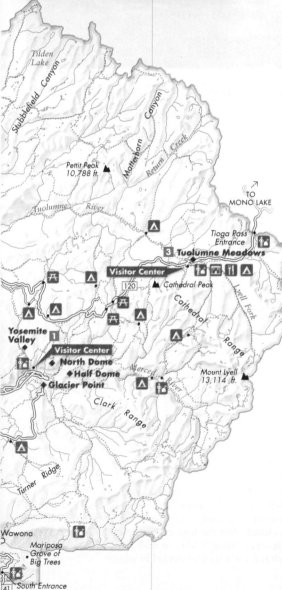

Tilden
Lake

Stubblefield Canyon

Matterhorn Canyon

Return Creek

Pettit Peak
10,788 ft.

Tuolumne River

TO
MONO LAKE

Tioga Pass
Entrance

3 **Tuolumne Meadows**

Visitor Center

120

Cathedral Peak

Cathedral Range

Lyell Fork

Yosemite Valley **1**

Visitor Center

◆ North Dome

◆ Half Dome

◆ Glacier Point

Merced River

Mount Lyell
13,114 ft.

Clark Range

Turner Ridge

Wawona

Mariposa
Grove of
Big Trees

South Entrance

41

GETTING ORIENTED

Yosemite is so large that you can think of it as five parks. Yosemite Valley, famous for waterfalls and cliffs, and Wawona, where the giant sequoias stand, are open all year. Hetch Hetchy, home of less-used backcountry trails, is most accessible from late spring through early fall. The subalpine high country, Tuolumne Meadows, is open for summer hiking and camping; in winter it's accessible via cross-country skis or snowshoes. Badger Pass Ski Area is open in winter only. Most visitors spend their time along the park's southwestern border, between Wawona and Big Oak Flat Entrance; a bit farther east in Yosemite Valley and Badger Pass Ski Area; and along the east–west corridor of Tioga Road, which spans the park north of Yosemite Valley and bisects Tuolumne Meadows.

10

Updated by
Reed Parsell

By merely standing in Yosemite Valley and turning in a circle, you can see more natural wonders in a minute than you could in a full day pretty much anywhere else. Half Dome, Yosemite Falls, El Capitan, Bridalveil Fall, Sentinel Dome, the Merced River, white-flowering dogwood trees, maybe even bears ripping into the bark of fallen trees or sticking their snouts into beehives—it's all in Yosemite Valley.

In the mid-1800s, when tourists were arriving to the area, the valley's special geologic qualities, and the giant sequoias of Mariposa Grove 30 miles to the south, so impressed a group of influential Californians that they persuaded President Abraham Lincoln to grant those two areas to the state for protection. On Oct. 1, 1890—thanks largely to lobbying efforts by naturalist John Muir and Robert Underwood Johnson, the editor of *Century Magazine*—Congress set aside 1,500 square miles for Yosemite National Park.

YOSEMITE PLANNER

WHEN TO GO

During extremely busy periods—such as the 4th of July—you will experience delays at the entrance gates. ■ TIP➜ For smaller crowds, visit mid-week. Or come mid-April through Memorial Day or mid-September through October, when the park is only a bit busy and the days usually are sunny and clear.

Summer rainfall is rare. In winter, heavy snows occasionally cause road closures, and tire chains or four-wheel drive may be required on the roads that remain open. The road to Glacier Point beyond the turnoff for Badger Pass is closed after the first major snowfall; Tioga Road is closed from late October through May or mid-June. Mariposa Grove Road is typically closed for a shorter period in winter.

GETTING HERE AND AROUND
BUS TRAVEL
Once you're in Yosemite you can take advantage of the free shuttle buses, which operate on low emissions, have 21 stops, and run every 10 minutes or so from 9 am to 6 pm year-round; a separate (but also free) summer-only shuttle runs out to El Capitan. Also during the summer, you can pay to take the morning "hikers' bus" from Yosemite Valley to Tuolumne or the bus up to Glacier Point. Bus service from Wawona is geared for people who are staying there and want to spend the day in Yosemite Valley. Free and frequent shuttles transport people between the Wawona Hotel and Mariposa Grove. During the snow season, buses run regularly between Yosemite Valley and Badger Pass Ski Area.

CAR TRAVEL
Roughly 200 miles from San Francisco, 300 miles from Los Angeles, and 500 miles from Las Vegas, Yosemite takes a while to reach—and its many sites and attractions merit much more time than what rangers say is the average visit: four hours. Most people arrive via automobile or tour bus, but public transportation (courtesy of Amtrak and the regional YARTS bus system) also can get you to the valley efficiently.

Of the park's four entrances, Arch Rock is the closest to Yosemite Valley. The road that goes through it, Route 140 from Merced and Mariposa, is a scenic western approach that snakes alongside the boulder-packed Merced River. Route 41, through Wawona, is the way to come from Los Angeles (or Fresno, if you've flown in and rented a car). Route 120, through Crane Flat, is the most direct route from San Francisco. The only way in from the east is Tioga Road, which may be the best route in terms of scenery—though due to snow accumulation it's open for a frustratingly short amount of time each year (typically early June through mid-October).

There are few gas stations within Yosemite (Crane Flat, Tuolumne Meadows, and Wawona; none in the valley), so fuel up before you reach the park. From late fall until early spring, the weather is especially unpredictable, and driving can be treacherous. You should carry chains.

10

PARK ESSENTIALS
PARK FEES AND PERMITS
The admission fee, valid for seven days, is $20 per vehicle or $10 per individual.

If you plan to camp in the backcountry or climb Half Dome, you must have a wilderness permit. Availability of permits, which are free, depends upon trailhead quotas. It's best to make a reservation, especially if you will be visiting May through September. You can reserve two days to 24 weeks in advance by phone (*209/372–0740 or 209/372–0739*); a $5-per-person processing fee is charged if and when your reservations are confirmed. Requests must include your name, address, daytime phone, the number of people in your party, trip date, alternative dates, starting and ending trailheads, and a brief itinerary. Without a reservation, you may still get a free permit on a first-come, first-served basis at wilderness permit offices at Big Oak Flat, Hetch Hetchy, Tuolumne,

Plants and Wildlife in Yosemite

Dense stands of incense cedar and Douglas fir—as well as ponderosa, Jeffrey, lodgepole, and sugar pines—cover much of the park, but the stellar standout, quite literally, is the *Sequoia sempervirens*, the giant sequoia. Sequoias grow only along the west slope of the Sierra Nevada between 4,500 and 7,000 feet in elevation. Starting from a seed the size of a rolled-oat flake, each of these ancient monuments assumes remarkable proportions in adulthood; you can see them in the Mariposa Grove of Big Trees. In late May the valley's dogwood trees bloom with white, starlike flowers. Wildflowers, such as black-eyed Susan, bull thistle, cow parsnip, lupine, and meadow goldenrod, peak in June in the valley and in July at higher elevations.

The most visible animals in the park—aside from the omnipresent western gray squirrel—are the mule deer. Though sightings of bighorn sheep are infrequent in the park itself, you can sometimes see them on the eastern side of the Sierra Crest, just off Route 120 in Lee Vining Canyon. You may also see the American black bear, which often has a brown, cinnamon, or blond coat. The Sierra Nevada is home to thousands of bears, and you should take all necessary precautions to keep yourself—and the bears—safe. For one, do not feed the bears. Bears that acquire a taste for human food can become very aggressive and destructive and often must be destroyed by rangers.

Watch for the blue Steller's jay along trails, near public buildings, and in campgrounds, and look for golden eagles soaring over Tioga Road.

Wawona, the Wilderness Center in Yosemite Village, and Yosemite Valley in summer. From fall to spring, visit the Valley Visitor Center.

PARK HOURS
The park is open 24/7 year-round. All entrances are open at all hours, except for Hetch Hetchy Entrance, which is open roughly dawn to dusk. Yosemite is in the Pacific time zone.

TOURS

★ **Ansel Adams Photo Walks.** Photography enthusiasts shouldn't miss these 90-minute guided camera walks offered a few mornings each week by professional photographers. All are free, but participation is limited to 15 people. Meeting points vary. and advance reservations are essential. ☎ *209/372–4413, 800/568–7398* ⊕ *www.anseladams.com* ✉ *Free.*

☾ **Wee Wild Ones.** Designed for kids under seven, this 45-minute program includes animal-theme games, songs, stories, and crafts. The event is held outdoors before the regular Yosemite Lodge or Curry Village evening programs in summer and fall; it moves to the Ahwahnee's big fireplace in winter and spring. All children must be accompanied by an adult. ☎ *209/372–1240* ✉ *Free.*

VISITOR INFORMATION
PARK CONTACT INFORMATION
Yosemite National Park ☎ *209/372–0200* ⊕ *www.nps.gov/yose.*

VISITOR CENTERS

Le Conte Memorial Lodge. This small but striking National Historic Landmark, with its granite walls and steeply pitched shingle roof, is Yosemite's first permanent public information center. Step inside to see the cathedral-like interior, which contains a library and environmental exhibits. To find out about evening programs, check the kiosk out front. ✉ *Southside Dr., about ½ mile west of Curry Village* ☉ *Memorial Day–Labor Day, Wed.–Sun. 10–4.*

Valley Visitor Center. Learn how Yosemite Valley's geology, vegetation, and human inhabitants at this visitor center. Don't leave without watching *Spirit of Yosemite*, a 23-minute introductory film that runs every half hour in the theater behind the visitor center. Strangely, the film shows no animals other than one deer. ✉ *Yosemite Village* ☎ *209/372–0299* ☉ *Late May–early Sept., daily 9–7:30; early Sept.–late May, daily 9–5.*

EXPLORING

HISTORIC SITES

Ahwahneechee Village. This solemn smattering of structures, accessed by a short loop trail behind the Yosemite Valley Visitor Center, is a look at what Native American life might have been like in the 1870s. One interpretive sign points out that the Miwok people referred to the 19th-century newcomers as "Yohemite" or "Yohometuk," which have been translated as meaning "some of them are killers." ✉ *Northside Dr., Yosemite Village* 🏷 *Free* ☉ *Daily sunrise–sunset.*

Pioneer Yosemite History Center. Some of Yosemite's first structures—those not occupied by Native Americans, that is—were relocated here in the 1950s and 1960s. You can spend a pleasurable and informative half-hour walking about them and reading the signs, perhaps springing for a self-guided-tour pamphlet (50¢) to further enhance the history lesson. Weekends and some weekdays in summer, costumed docents conduct free blacksmithing and "wet-plate" photography demonstrations, and for a small fee you can take a stagecoach ride. ✉ *Rte. 41, Wawona* ☎ *209/375–9531, 209/379–2646* 🏷 *Free* ☉ *Building interiors are open mid-June–Labor Day, Wed. 2–5, Thurs.–Sun. 10–1 and 2–5.*

10

SCENIC STOPS

★ **El Capitan.** Rising 3,593 feet—more than 350 stories—above the valley, El Capitan is the largest exposed-granite monolith in the world. Since 1958, people have been climbing its entire face, including the famous "nose." You can spot adventurers with your binoculars by scanning the smooth and nearly vertical cliff for specks of color. ✉ *Off Northside Dr., about 4 miles west of the Valley Visitor Center.*

Fodor'sChoice **Glacier Point.** If you lack the time, desire, or stamina to hike more than
★ 3,200 feet up to Glacier Point from the Yosemite Valley floor, you can drive here—or take a bus from the valley—for a bird's-eye view. You are likely to encounter a lot of day-trippers on the short, paved trail

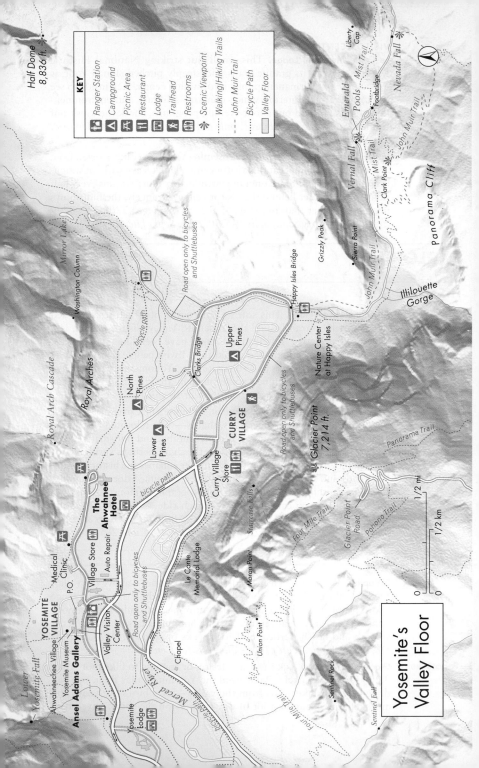

Yosemite's Valley Floor

KEY

- 🏛 Ranger Station
- ⛺ Campground
- 🍴 Picnic Area
- 🍴 Restaurant
- 🏨 Lodge
- 🥾 Trailhead
- 🚻 Restrooms
- ✳ Scenic Viewpoint
- · · · · Walking/Hiking Trails
- – – – John Muir Trail
- ········ Bicycle Path
- ▢ Valley Floor

Half Dome 8,836 ft.

Liberty Cap

Nevada Fall

Mist Trail

Emerald Pools

Footbridge

John Muir Trail

Vernal Fall

Mist Trail

Clark Point

Panorama Cliff

Grizzly Peak

Sierra Point

Illilouette Gorge

Happy Isles Bridge

Nature Center at Happy Isles

Mirror Lake

Washington Column

Road open only to bicycles and Shuttlebuses

bicycle path

Royal Arch Cascade

Royal Arches

Clarks Bridge

Upper Pines

North Pines

Lower Pines

CURRY VILLAGE

Curry Village Store

Road open only to bicycles and Shuttlebuses

Glacier Point 7,214 ft.

Panorama Trail

The Ahwahnee Hotel

Medical Clinic

P.O.

Village Store

Auto Repair

bicycle path

Le Conte Memorial Lodge

Staircase Falls

Moran Point

Four Mile Trail

Glacier Point Road

Pohono Trail

YOSEMITE VILLAGE

Ahwahneechee Village

Yosemite Museum

Ansel Adams Gallery

Valley Visitor Center

Road open only to bicycles and Shuttlebuses

Chapel

Union Point

Sentinel Rock

Lower Yosemite Fall

Yosemite Lodge

Merced River

bicycle path

Four Mile Trail

Sentinel Fall

1/2 mi

1/2 km

0

"This is us taking a break before conquering the top of Lembert Dome, while enjoying the beautiful view over Yosemite's high country." —photo by Rebalyn, Fodors.com member

that leads from the parking lot to the main overlook. Take a moment to veer off a few yards to the Geology Hut, which succinctly explains and illustrates how the valley looked like 10 million, 3 million, and 20,000 years ago. ⊠ *Glacier Point Rd., 16 miles northeast of Rte. 41* ☎ *209/372–1240.*

★ **Half Dome.** Visitors' eyes are continually drawn to this remarkable granite formation that tops out at more than 4,700 feet above the valley floor. Despite its name, the dome is actually about three-quarters intact. You can hike to the top of Half Dome on an 8.5-mile (one-way) trail whose last 400 feet must be ascended while holding onto a steel cable. For the past few years wilderness permits have been required (and checked on the trail). Back down in the valley, see Half Dome reflected in the Merced River by heading to Sentinel Bridge just before sundown. The brilliant orange light on Half Dome is a stunning sight.

Hetch Hetchy Reservoir. When Congress approved the O'Shaughnessy Dam in 1913, pragmatism triumphed over aestheticism. Some 2.4 million residents of the San Francisco Bay Area continue to get their water from this 117-billion-gallon reservoir, and spirited efforts are being made to restore the Hetch Hetchy Valley to its former, pristine glory. Eight miles long, the reservoir is Yosemite's largest body of water, and one that can be seen up close from several trails. ⊠ *Hetch Hetchy Rd., about 15 miles north of the Big Oak Flat entrance station.*

★ **Mariposa Grove of Big Trees.** Of Yosemite's three sequoia groves—the others being Merced and Tuolumne, both near Crane Flat well to the north—Mariposa is by far the largest and easiest to walk around.

GOOD READS

■ *The Photographer's Guide to Yosemite*, by Michael Frye, is an insider's guide to the park, with maps for shutterbugs looking to capture perfect images.

■ John Muir penned his observations of the park he long advocated for in *The Yosemite*.

■ *Yosemite and the High Sierra*, edited by Andrea G. Stillman and John Szarkowski, features beautiful reproductions of landmark photographs by Ansel Adams, accompanied by excerpts from the photographer's journals written when Adams traveled in Yosemite National Park in the early 20th century.

■ An insightful collection of essays accompanies the museum-quality artworks in *Yosemite: Art of an American Icon*, by Amy Scott.

■ Perfect for beginning wildlife watchers, *Sierra Nevada Wildflowers*, by Karen Wiese, identifies more than 230 kinds of flora growing in the Sierra Nevada region.

Grizzly Giant, whose base measures 96 feet around, has been estimated to be one of the largest in the world. Perhaps more astoundingly, it's about 2,700 years old. On up the hill, you'll find many more sequoias, a small museum, and fewer people. Summer weekends are especially crowded here. Consider taking the free shuttle from Wawona. ✉ *Rte. 41, 2 miles north of the South Entrance station.*

★ **Tuolumne Meadows.** The largest subalpine meadow in the Sierra (at 8,600 feet) is a popular way station for backpack trips along the Pacific Crest and John Muir trails. The setting is not as dramatic as Yosemite Valley, 56 miles away, but the almost perfectly flat basin, about 2½ miles long, is intriguing, and in July it's resplendent with wildflowers. The most popular day hike is up Lembert Dome, atop which you'll have breathtaking views of the basin below. Keep in mind that Tioga Road rarely opens before June and usually closes by mid-October. ✉ *Tioga Rd. (Rte. 120), about 8 miles west of the Tioga Pass entrance station.*

WATERFALLS

Yosemite's waterfalls are at their most spectacular in May and June. When the snow starts to melt (usually peaking in May), streaming snowmelt spills down to meet the Merced River. By summer's end, some falls, including the mighty Yosemite Falls, trickle or dry up. Their flow increases in late fall, and in winter they may be hung dramatically with ice. Even in drier months, the waterfalls can be breathtaking. If you choose to hike any of the trails to or up the falls, be sure to wear shoes with no-slip soles; the rocks can be extremely slick. Stay on trails at all times.

■**TIP→** Visit the park during a full moon and you can stroll without a flashlight and still make out the ribbons of falling water, as well as silhouettes of the giant granite monoliths.

Bridalveil Fall. This 620-foot waterfall is often diverted dozens of feet one way or the other by the breeze. It is the first marvelous site in Yosemite

Valley you will see if you enter via Route 41. ⊠ *Yosemite Valley, access from parking area off Wawona Rd.*

Nevada Fall. Climb Mist Trail from Happy Isles for an up-close view of this 594-foot cascading beauty. If you don't want to hike (the trail's final approach is quite taxing), you can see it—albeit distantly—from Glacier Point. Stay safely on the trail, as three people died in 2011 when they climbed over the railing and onto the slippery rocks. ⊠ *Yosemite Valley, access via Mist Trail from Nature Center at Happy Isles.*

Ribbon Fall. At 1,612 feet, this is the highest single fall in North America. It's also the first waterfall to dry up in summer; the rainwater and melted snow that create the slender fall evaporate quickly at this height. Look just west of El Capitan for the best view of the fall from the base of Bridalveil Fall. ⊠ *Yosemite Valley, west of El Capitan Meadow.*

Vernal Fall. Fern-covered black rocks frame this 317-foot fall, and rainbows play in the spray at its base. You can get a distance view from Glacier Point, or hike to see it close up. You'll get wet, but the view is worth it. ⊠ *Yosemite Valley, access via Mist Trail from Nature Center at Happy Isles.*

Fodor'sChoice
★
Yosemite Falls. Actually three falls, they together constitute the highest waterfall in North America and the fifth-highest in the world. The water from the top descends a total of 2,425 feet, and when the falls run hard, you can hear them thunder across the valley. If they dry up—that sometimes happens in late summer—the valley seems naked without the wavering tower of spray. ∎TIP➔ If you hike the mile-long loop trail (partially paved) to the base of the Lower Falls in May, prepare to get wet. You can get a view of the falls from the lawn of Yosemite Chapel, off Southside Drive. ⊠ *Yosemite Valley, access from Yosemite Lodge or trail parking area.*

EDUCATIONAL OFFERINGS

CLASSES AND SEMINARS

Art Classes. Professional artists conduct workshops in watercolor, etching, drawing, and other mediums. Bring your own materials or purchase the basics at the Art Activity Center, next to the Village Store. Children under 13 must be accompanied by an adult. ⊠ *Art Activity Center, Yosemite Village* ☎ *209/372–1442* ⊕ *www.yosemitepark.com* ⊠ *Free* ⊙ *Early Apr.–early Oct., Mon.–Sat., 10 am–2 pm.*

Yosemite Outdoor Adventures. Naturalists, scientists, and park rangers lead multi-hour to multiday educational outings on topics from woodpeckers to fire management to pastel painting. Most sessions take place spring through fall, but a few focus on winter phenomena. ⊠ *Various locations* ☎ *209/379–2321* ⊕ *www.yosemite.org* ⊠ *$82–$465.*

RANGER PROGRAMS

Junior Ranger Program. Children ages 3 to 13 can participate in the informal, self-guided Little Cub and Junior Ranger programs. A park activity handbook ($4) is available at the Valley Visitor Center or the Nature Center at Happy Isles. Once kids complete the book, rangers present them with a certificate and a badge. ⊠ *Valley Visitor Center or the Nature Center at Happy Isles* ☎ *209/372–0299.*

Ranger-Led Programs. Rangers lead entertaining walks and give informative talks several times a day from spring to fall. The schedule is more limited in winter, but most days you can find a program somewhere in the park. In the evenings at Yosemite Lodge and Curry Village, lectures, slide shows, and documentary films present unique perspectives on Yosemite. On summer weekends, Camp Curry and Tuolumne Meadows Campground host sing-along campfire programs. Schedules and locations are posted on bulletin boards throughout the park.

SPORTS AND THE OUTDOORS

BICYCLING

One enjoyable way to see Yosemite Valley is to ride a bike beneath its lofty granite monoliths. The eastern valley has 12 miles of paved, flat bicycle paths across meadows and through woods, with bike racks at convenient stopping points. For a greater challenge but at no small risk, you can ride on 196 miles of paved park roads—but bicycles are not allowed on hiking trails or in the backcountry. Kids under 18 must wear a helmet.

TOURS AND OUTFITTERS
Yosemite bike rentals. You can arrange for rentals from Yosemite Lodge and Curry Village bike stands. Bikes with child trailers, baby-jogger strollers, and wheelchairs are also available. The cost is about $10 per hour. ⊠ *Yosemite Lodge or Curry Village* ☎ *209/372–1208* ⊕ *www. yosemitepark.com* ☾ *Apr.–Oct.*

BIRD-WATCHING

Nearly 250 bird species have been spotted in the park, including the sage sparrow, pygmy owl, blue grouse, and mountain bluebird. Park rangers lead free bird-watching walks in Yosemite Valley one day each week in summer; check at a visitor center or information station for times and locations. Binoculars sometimes are available for loan.

10

HIKING

TOURS AND OUTFITTERS
Wilderness Center. This facility provides free wilderness permits, which are required for overnight camping (advance reservations are available for $5 and are highly recommended for popular trailheads in summer and on weekends). The staff here also provides maps and advice to hikers heading into the backcountry. ☎ *209/372–0308.*

Yosemite Mountaineering School and Guide Service. From April to November, Yosemite Mountaineering School and Guide Service leads two-hour to full-day treks, as well as backpacking and overnight excursions. Reservations are recommended. ⊠ *Yosemite Mountain Shop, Curry*

Village ☎ *209/372–8344* ⊕ *www.yosemitepark.com/Activities_Rock-Climbing.aspx.*

EASY

★ **Yosemite Falls Trail.** This is the highest waterfall in North America. The upper fall (1,430 feet), the middle cascades (675 feet), and the lower fall (320 feet) combine for a total of 2,425 feet and, when viewed from the valley, appear as a single waterfall. The ¼-mile trail leads from the parking lot to the base of the falls. Upper Yosemite Fall Trail, a strenuous 3½-mile climb rising 2,700 feet, takes you above the top of the falls. *Easy.* ⊠ *Trailhead off Camp 4, north of Northside Dr.*

MODERATE

★ **Mist Trail.** Except for Lower Yosemite Falls, more visitors take this trail (or portions of it) than any other in the park. The trek up to and back from Vernal Fall is 3 miles. Add another 4 miles total by continuing up to 594-foot Nevada Fall; the trail becomes quite steep and slippery in its final stages. The elevation gain to Vernal Fall is 1,000 feet, and to Nevada Fall an additional 1,000 feet. Merced River tumbles down both falls on its way to a tranquil flow through the valley. *Moderate.* ⊠ *Trailhead at Happy Isles.*

★ **Panorama Trail.** Few hikes come with the visual punch that this 8½-mile trail provides. The star attraction is Half Dome, visible from many intriguing angles, but you also see three waterfalls up close and walk through a manzanita grove. Before you begin, look down on Yosemite Valley from Glacier Point, a special experience in itself. *Moderate.* ⊠ *Trailhead at Glacier Point.*

DIFFICULT

Fodor'sChoice **John Muir Trail to Half Dome.** Ardent and courageous trekkers continue on
★ from Nevada Fall to the top of Half Dome. Some hikers attempt this entire 10- to 12-hour, 16¾-mile round-trip trek in one day; if you're planning to do this, remember that the 4,800-foot elevation gain and the 8,842-foot altitude will cause shortness of breath. Another option is to hike to a campground in Little Yosemite Valley near the top of Nevada Fall the first day, then climb to the top of Half Dome and hike out the next day. Get your wilderness permit (required for a one-day hike to Half Dome, too) at least a month in advance. Be sure to wear hiking boots and bring gloves. The last pitch up the back of Half Dome is very steep—the only way to climb this sheer rock face is to pull yourself up using the steel cable handrails, which are in place only from late spring to early fall. Those who brave the ascent will be rewarded with an unbeatable view of Yosemite Valley below and the high country beyond. *Difficult.* ⊠ *Trailhead at Happy Isles.*

HORSEBACK RIDING

Reservations for guided trail rides must be made in advance at the hotel tour desks or by phone. For overnight saddle trips, which use mules, call ☎ *559/253–5673* on or after September 15 to request a lottery application for the following year. Scenic trail rides range from two hours to a full day; six-day High Sierra saddle trips are also available.

TOURS AND OUTFITTERS

Tuolumne Meadows Stables. Tuolumne Meadows Stables runs two-, four-, and eight-hour trips that start at $64, as well as four- to six-day camping treks on mules that begin at $625. Reservations are essential. ✉ *Off Tioga Rd., 2 miles east of Tuolumne Meadows Visitor Center* ☎ *209/372–8427* ⊕ *www.yosemitepark.com.*

Wawona Stables. Wawona Stables has two- and five-hour rides starting at $64. Reservations are recommended. ✉ *Rte. 41, Wawona* ☎ *209/375–6502.*

Yosemite Valley Stables. You can tour the valley and the start of the high country on two-hour, four-hour, and daylong rides at Yosemite Valley Stables. Reservations are strongly recommended for the trips, which start at $64. ✉ *At entrance to North Pines Campground, 100 yards northeast of Curry Village* ☎ *209/372–8348* ⊕ *www.yosemitepark.com.*

RAFTING

Rafting is permitted only on designated areas of the Middle and South forks of the Merced River. Check with the Valley Visitor Center for closures and other restrictions.

OUTFITTERS

Curry Village raft stand. The per-person rental fee at Curry Village raft stand covers the four- to six-person raft, two paddles, and life jackets, plus a shuttle to the launch point on Sentinel Beach. ✉ *South side of Southside Dr., Curry Village* ☎ *209/372–8319* ⊕ *www.yosemitepark. com* 🎫 *$20.50* ☉ *Late May–July.*

ROCK CLIMBING

Fodor'sChoice
★

The granite canyon walls of Yosemite Valley are world renowned for rock climbing. El Capitan, with its 3,593-foot vertical face, is the most famous, but there are many other options here for all skill levels.

TOURS AND OUTFITTERS

Yosemite Mountaineering School and Guide Service. The one-day basic lesson at Yosemite Mountaineering School and Guide Service includes some bouldering and rappelling, and three or four 60-foot climbs. Climbers must be at least 10 and in reasonably good physical condition. Intermediate and advanced classes include instruction in first aid, anchor building, multi-pitch climbing, summer snow climbing, and big-wall climbing. There's a nordic program in the winter. ✉ *Yosemite Mountain Shop, Curry Village* ☎ *209/372–8344* ⊕ *www.yosemitepark. com* 🎫 *$80–$190* ☉ *Apr.–Nov.*

10

WINTER SPORTS

ICE-SKATING

Curry Village Ice Rink. Winter visitors have skated at this outdoor rink for decades, and there's no mystery why: it's a kick to glide across the ice while soaking up views of Half Dome and Glacier Point. ✉ *South*

DID YOU KNOW?

Yosemite's granite forma-
tions provide sturdy ground
for climbers of all skill levels.
The sheer granite monolith
El Capitan—simply "El Cap"
to climbers—is the most
famous, climbed by even
Captain Kirk (if you believe
the opening scene of *Star
Trek V: The Final Frontier*), but
climbers tackle rock faces up
in the mountains, too.

side of Southside Dr., Curry Village ☎ *209/372–8319* 🎟 *$9 per session, $3 skate rental* 🕒 *Mid-Nov.–mid-Mar. afternoons and evenings daily, morning sessions weekends (hrs vary).*

SKIING AND SNOWSHOEING

Badger Pass Ski Area. California's first ski resort has five lifts and 10 downhill runs, as well as 90 miles of groomed cross-country trails. Free shuttle buses from Yosemite Valley operate between December and early April, weather permitting. Lift tickets are $42, downhill equipment rents for $31, and snowboard rental with boots is $35. ✉ *Badger Pass Rd., off Glacier Point Rd., 18 miles from Yosemite Valley* ☎ *209/372–8430.*

Yosemite Ski School. The gentle slopes of Badger Pass make Yosemite Ski School an ideal spot for children and beginners to learn downhill skiing or snowboarding for as little as $28 for a group lesson. ☎ *209/372–8430* 🌐 *www.yosemitepark.com*

Yosemite Mountaineering School. Yosemite Mountaineering School conducts snowshoeing, cross-country skiing, telemarking, and skate-skiing classes starting at $35. ✉ *Badger Pass Ski Area* ☎ *209/372–8344* 🌐 *www.yosemitepark.com*

Yosemite Cross-Country Ski School. The highlight of Yosemite's cross-country skiing center is a 21-mile loop from Badger Pass to Glacier Point. You can rent cross-country skis for $23 per day at the Cross-Country Ski School, which also rents snowshoes ($22.50 per day), telemarking equipment ($29.50), and skate-skis ($27). ☎ *209/372–8444* 🌐 *www.yosemitepark.com*

WHERE TO EAT

10

In addition to the dining options listed here, you'll find fast-food grills and cafeterias, plus temporary snack bars, hamburger stands, and pizza joints lining park roads in summer. Many dining facilities in the park are open summer only. *Prices in the reviews are the average cost of a main course at dinner or, if dinner is not served, at lunch.*

$$$$ EUROPEAN Fodor's Choice ★

🍴 **Ahwahnee Hotel Dining Room.** Rave reviews about the dining room's appearance are fully justified—it features towering windows, a 34-foot-high ceiling with interlaced sugar-pine beams, and massive chandeliers. Although many continue to applaud the food, others have reported that they sense a dip in the quality both in the service and what is being served. Diners must spend a lot of money here, so perhaps that inflates the expectations and amplifies the disappointments. In any event, the $40 Sunday brunch is consistently praised. Reservations are always advised, and the attire is "resort casual." [$] *Average main: $38* ✉ *Ahwahnee Hotel, Ahwahnee Rd., about ¾ mile east of Yosemite Valley Visitor Center, Yosemite Village* ☎ *209/372–1489* ✍ *Reservations essential.*

$$$ AMERICAN ★

🍴 **Mountain Room.** Though good, the food becomes secondary when you see Yosemite Falls through this dining room's wall of windows—almost every table has a view. The chef makes a point of using locally

sourced, organic ingredients, so you can be assured of fresh vegetables. The Mountain Room Lounge, a few steps away in the Yosemite Lodge complex, has a broad bar with about 10 beers on tap. $ *Average main: $23 ✉ Yosemite Lodge, Northside Dr. about ¾ mile west of the visitor center, Yosemite Village ☎ 209/372–1281 ⏲ No lunch.*

$ FAST FOOD 🍴 **Tuolumne Meadows Grill.** Serving continuously throughout the day until 5 or 6 pm, this fast-food eatery cooks up breakfast, lunch, and snacks. Stop in for a quick meal before exploring the Meadows. $ *Average main: $8 ✉ Tioga Rd. (Rte. 120), 1½ miles east of Tuolumne Meadows Visitor Center ☎ 209/372–8426 ⏲ Closed Oct.–Memorial Day.*

$$ AMERICAN 🍴 **Tuolumne Meadows Lodge.** At the back of a small building that contains the lodge's front desk and small gift shop, this restaurant serves hearty American fare at breakfast and dinner. The decor is ultra-woodsy, with dark-wood walls and red-and-white-checkered tablecloths. Meals are mostly of the meat-and-potato variety, but vegetarians' requests are honored. If you have any dietary restrictions, let the front desk know in advance and the cooks will not let you down. $ *Average main: $18 ✉ Tioga Rd. (Rte. 120) ☎ 209/372–8413 ✍ Reservations essential ⏲ Closed late Sept.–Memorial Day. No lunch.*

$$$ AMERICAN ★ 🍴 **Wawona Hotel Dining Room.** Watch deer graze on the meadow while you dine in the romantic, candlelit dining room of the whitewashed Wawona Hotel, which dates from the late 1800s. The American-style cuisine favors fresh ingredients and flavors; trout is a menu staple. There's also a Sunday brunch Easter through Thanksgiving, and a barbecue on the lawn Saturday evenings in summer. A jacket is required at dinner. $ *Average main: $25 ✉ Wawona Hotel, Rte. 41, Wawona ☎ 209/375–1425 ✍ Reservations essential ⏲ Closed Jan. and Feb.*

PICNIC AREAS

Considering how large the park is and how many visitors come here—some 4 million people every year, most of them just for the day—it is somewhat surprising that Yosemite has so few formal picnic areas, though in many places you can find a smooth rock to sit on and enjoy breathtaking views along with your lunch. The convenience stores all sell picnic supplies, and prepackaged sandwiches and salads are widely available. Those options can come in especially handy during the middle of the day, when you might not want to spend precious daylight hours in such a spectacular setting sitting in a restaurant for a formal meal.

WHERE TO STAY

Prices in the reviews are the lowest cost of a standard double room in high season. For expanded hotel reviews, visit Fodors.com.

$$$$ HOTEL Fodor's Choice ★ 🏨 **Ahwahnee Hotel.** A National Historic Landmark, the hotel is constructed of sugar-pine logs and features Native American design motifs. **Pros:** best lodge in Yosemite; helpful concierge. **Cons:** expensive rates; some reports that service has slipped in recent years. **TripAdvisor:**

"splendid views," "rustic luxury in an incomparable location," "bucket list contender." $Rooms from: $485 ⊠ Ahwahnee Rd., about ¾ mile east of Yosemite Valley Visitor Center, Yosemite Village ☎ 559/252–4848 ⊕ www.yosemitepark.com ⤳ 99 lodge rooms, 4 suites, 24 cottage rooms.

$ | **Curry Village.** Opened in 1899 as
HOTEL | a place for budget-conscious travelers, Curry Village has plain accommodations: standard motel rooms, simple cabins, and tent cabins with rough wood frames and canvas walls. **Pros:** comparatively economical; family-friendly atmosphere. **Cons:** can be crowded; sometimes a bit noisy. **TripAdvisor:** "very comfortable," "amazing experience," "absolutely stunning." $Rooms from: $91 ⊠ South side of Southside Dr. ☎ 559/252–4848 ⊕ www.yosemitepark.com ⤳ 18 rooms, 390 cabins ⏺ No meals.

$$ | **Wawona Hotel.** This 1879 National Historic Landmark sits at Yosemite's
HOTEL | southern end, a 15-minute drive from the Mariposa Grove of Big Trees. **Pros:** lovely building; peaceful atmosphere. **Cons:** few modern amenities; an hour's drive from Yosemite Valley. **TripAdvisor:** "old-world charm," "a can't miss experience," "beautiful." $Rooms from: $135 ⊠ Hwy. 41, Wawona ☎ 559/252–4848 ⊕ www.yosemitepark.com ⤳ 104 rooms, 50 with bath ⊗ Closed Jan. and Feb.

$ | **White Wolf Lodge.** Set in a subalpine meadow, the rustic accommoda-
HOTEL | tions at White Wolf Lodge make it an excellent base camp for hiking the backcountry. **Pros:** quiet location; convenient for hikers; good restaurant. **Cons:** far from the valley; not much to do here. **TripAdvisor:** "rustic charm," "great high country lodging," "absolute heaven." $Rooms from: $100 ⊠ Off Tioga Rd. (Rte. 120), 25 miles west of Tuolumne Meadows and 15 miles east of Crane Flat ☎ 559/252–4848 ⤳ 24 tent cabins, 4 cabins ⊗ Closed mid-Sept.–early June.

$$ | **Yosemite Lodge at the Falls.** This 1915 lodge near Yosemite Falls more
HOTEL | closely resembles a 1960s resort with its numerous two-story structures tucked beneath the trees. **Pros:** centrally located; dependably clean rooms; lots of tours leave from out front. **Cons:** can feel impersonal; appearance is little dated. **TripAdvisor:** "love the renovated rooms," "best location in the park," "old school Yosemite." $Rooms from: $124 ⊠ Northside Dr. about ¾ mile west of the visitor center, Yosemite Village ☎ 559/252–4848 ⊕ www.yosemitepark.com ⤳ 245 rooms.

LODGING TIP

Reserve your room or cabin in Yosemite as far in advance as possible. You can make a reservation up to a year before your arrival (within minutes after the reservation office makes a date available, the Ahwahnee, Yosemite Lodge, and Wawona Hotel often sell out their weekends, holiday periods, and all days between May and September).

10

Best Campgrounds in Yosemite

If you are going to concentrate solely on valley sites and activities, you should endeavor to stay in one of the "Pines" campgrounds, which are clustered near Curry Village and within an easy stroll from that busy complex's many facilities. For a more primitive and quiet experience, and to be near many backcountry hikes, try one of the Tioga Road campgrounds.

National Park Service Reservations Office. Reservations are required at most of Yosemite's campgrounds, especially in summer. ☎ 800/436–7275 ⊕ www.recreation.gov ⊙ Daily 7–7.

Bridalveil Creek. This campground sits among lodgepole pines at 7,200 feet, above the valley on Glacier Point Road. From here, you can easily drive to Glacier Point's magnificent valley views. ⊠ From Hwy. 41 in Wawona, go north to Glacier Point Rd. and turn right; entrance to campground is 25 miles ahead on right side.

Camp 4. Formerly known as Sunnyside Walk-In, this is the only valley campground available on a first-come, first-served basis. ⊠ Base of Yosemite Falls Trail, just west of Yosemite Lodge on Northside Dr., Yosemite Village.

Crane Flat. This camp on Yosemite's western boundary, south of Hodgdon Meadow, is just 17 miles from the valley but far from its bustle. ⊠ From Big Oak Flat entrance on Hwy. 120, drive 10 miles east to campground entrance on right.

Housekeeping Camp. Composed of three walls (usually concrete) and covered with two layers of canvas, each unit has an open-ended fourth side that can be closed off with a heavy white canvas curtain. You rent "bedpacks," consisting of blankets, sheets, and other comforts. ⊠ Southside Dr., ½ mile west of Curry Village.

Lower Pines. This moderate-size campground sits directly along the Merced River; it's a short walk to the trailheads for the Mirror Lake and Mist trails. ⊠ At east end of valley.

Porcupine Flat. Sixteen miles west of Tuolumne Meadows, this campground sits at 8,100 feet. If you want to be in the high country, this is a good bet. ⊠ 16 miles west of Tuolumne Meadows on Hwy. 120.

Tuolumne Meadow. In a wooded area at 8,600 feet, just south of its namesake meadow, this is one of the most spectacular and sought-after campgrounds in Yosemite. ⊠ Hwy. 120, 46 miles east of Big Oak Flat entrance station.

Upper Pines. This is the valley's largest campground and the closest one to the trailheads. Expect large crowds in the summer—and little privacy. ⊠ At east end of valley, near Curry Village.

Wawona. Near the Mariposa Grove, just downstream from a popular fishing spot, this year-round campground has larger, less densely packed sites than campgrounds in the valley. ⊠ Hwy. 41, 1 mile north of Wawona.

White Wolf. Set in the beautiful high country at 8,000 feet, this is a prime spot for hikers. ⊠ From Big Oak Flat entrance, go 15 miles east on Tioga Rd.

Sequoia and Kings Canyon National Parks

WORD OF MOUTH

"On arrival, I oriented myself at the Visitor's Center in Grant Grove Village, and then took a short hike in Grant's Grove, taking in the General Grant tree, among the other giant sequoias. Their size is mind boggling. . . . Next up was a drive along the Kings Canyon Scenic Byway. I highly recommend this beautiful drive."

—Iregeo

WELCOME TO SEQUOIA AND KINGS CANYON NATIONAL PARKS

TOP REASONS TO GO

★ **Gentle giants:** You'll feel small—in a good way—walking among some of the world's largest living things in Sequoia's Giant Forest and Kings Canyon's Grant Grove.

★ **Because it's there:** You can't even glimpse it from the main part of Sequoia, but the sight of majestic Mt. Whitney is worth the trek to the eastern face of the High Sierra.

★ **Underground exploration:** Far older even than the giant sequoias, the gleaming limestone formations in Crystal Cave will draw you along dark, marble passages.

★ **A grander-than-Grand Canyon:** Drive the twisting Kings Canyon Scenic Byway down into the jagged, granite Kings River Canyon, deeper in parts than the Grand Canyon.

★ **Regal solitude:** To spend a day or two hiking in a subalpine world of your own, pick one of the 11 trailheads at Mineral King.

1 Giant Forest–Lodgepole Village. The most heavily visited area of Sequoia lies at the base of the "thumb" portion of Kings Canyon National Park and contains major sights such as Giant Forest, General Sherman Tree, Crystal Cave, and Moro Rock.

2 Grant Grove Village–Redwood Canyon. The "thumb" of Kings Canyon National Park is its busiest section, where Grant Grove, General Grant Tree, Panoramic Point, and Big Stump are the main attractions.

3 Cedar Grove. Most visitors to the huge, high-country portion of Kings Canyon National Park don't go farther than Roads End, a few miles east of Cedar Grove on the canyon floor. Here, the river runs through Zumwalt Meadow, surrounded by magnificent granite formations.

4 Mineral King. In the southeast section of Sequoia, the highest road-accessible part of the park is a good place to hike, camp, and soak up the unspoiled grandeur of the Sierra Nevada.

5 Mount Whitney. The highest peak in the Lower 48 stands on the eastern edge of Sequoia; to get there from Giant Forest you must either backpack eight days through the mountains or drive nearly 400 miles around the park to its other side.

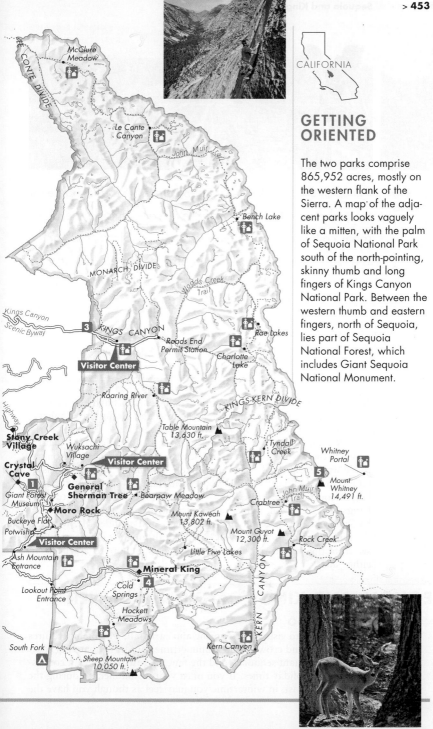

CALIFORNIA

GETTING ORIENTED

The two parks comprise 865,952 acres, mostly on the western flank of the Sierra. A map of the adjacent parks looks vaguely like a mitten, with the palm of Sequoia National Park south of the north-pointing, skinny thumb and long fingers of Kings Canyon National Park. Between the western thumb and eastern fingers, north of Sequoia, lies part of Sequoia National Forest, which includes Giant Sequoia National Monument.

(Map labels:)

McClure Meadow
LE CONTE DIVIDE
Le Conte Canyon
John Muir Trail
Bench Lake
MONARCH DIVIDE
Woods Creek Trail
Kings Canyon Scenic Byway
3 KINGS CANYON
Roads End Permit Station
Rae Lakes
Charlotte Lake
Visitor Center
Roaring River
Highway
KINGS-KERN DIVIDE
Table Mountain 13,630 ft.
Tyndall Creek
Whitney Portal
Stony Creek Village
Wuksachi Village
Visitor Center
Crystal Cave
1
Giant Forest Museum
General Sherman Tree
Bearpaw Meadow
5
Mount Whitney 14,491 ft.
John Muir Trail
Crabtree
Moro Rock
Buckeye Flat
Mount Kaweah 13,802 ft.
Potwisha
Mount Guyot 12,300 ft.
Rock Creek
Visitor Center
Little Five Lakes
Ash Mountain Entrance
KERN CANYON
Lookout Point Entrance
Mineral King
4
Cold Springs
Hockett Meadows
South Fork
Sheep Mountain 10,050 ft.
Kern Canyon

Updated by
Reed Parsell

Although *Sequoiadendron giganteum* is the formal name for the redwoods that grow here, everyone outside the classroom calls them sequoias, big trees, or Sierra redwoods. Their monstrously thick trunks and branches, remarkably shallow root systems, and neck-craning heights are almost impossible to believe, as is the fact they can live for more than 2,500 years. Many of these towering marvels are in the Giant Forest stretch of Generals Highway, which connects Sequoia and Kings Canyon national parks.

Next to or a few miles off the 43-mile road Generals Highway are most of Sequoia National Park's main attractions and Grant Grove Village, the orientation hub for Kings Canyon National Park. The two parks share a boundary that runs west–east, from the foothills of the Central Valley to the Sierra Nevada's dramatic eastern ridges. Kings Canyon has two portions: the smaller is shaped like a bent finger and encompasses Grant Grove Village and Redwood Mountain Grove (the two parks' largest concentration of sequoias), and the larger is home to stunning Kings River Canyon, whose vast, unspoiled peaks and valleys are a backpacker's dream. Sequoia is in one piece and includes Mt. Whitney, the highest point in the Lower 48 states (although it is impossible to see from the western part of the park and is a chore to ascend from either side).

SEQUOIA AND KINGS CANYON PLANNER

WHEN TO GO

The best times to visit are late spring and early fall, when temperatures are moderate and crowds thin. Summertime can draw hoards of tourists to see the giant sequoias, and the few, narrow roads mean congestion at peak holiday times. If you must visit in summer, go during the week. By contrast, in wintertime you may feel as though you have the parks all to yourself. But because of heavy snows, sections of the main park roads can be closed without warning, and low-hanging clouds can move in and obscure mountains and valleys for days. Check road and weather conditions before venturing out mid-November to late April.

GETTING HERE AND AROUND
CAR TRAVEL
Sequoia is 36 miles east of Visalia on Route 198; Kings Canyon is 53 miles east of Fresno on Route 180. There is no automobile entrance on the eastern side of the Sierra. Routes 180 and 198 are connected by Generals Highway, a paved two-lane road that sometimes sees delays at peak times due to ongoing improvements. The road is extremely narrow and steep from Route 198 to Giant Forest, so keep an eye on your engine temperature gauge, as the incline and congestion can cause vehicles to overheat; to avoid overheated brakes, use low gears on downgrades.

If you are traveling in an RV or with a trailer, study the restrictions on these vehicles. Do not travel beyond Potwisha Campground with an RV longer than 22 feet on Route 198; take straighter, easier Route 180 instead. Maximum vehicle length on Generals Highway is 40 feet, or 50 feet combined length for vehicles with trailers.

Generals Highway between Lodgepole and Grant Grove is sometimes closed by snow. The Mineral King Road from Route 198 into southern Sequoia National Park is closed 2 miles below Atwell Mill either on November 1 or after the first heavy snow. The Buckeye Flat–Middle Fork Trailhead Road is closed mid-October–mid-April when the Buckeye Flat Campground closes. The lower Crystal Cave Road is closed when the cave closes in November. Its upper 2 miles, as well as the Panoramic Point and Moro Rock–Crescent Meadow roads, are closed with the first heavy snow. Because of the danger of rockfall, the portion of Kings Canyon Scenic Byway east of Grant Grove closes in winter. For current conditions, call ☎ *559/565–3341 Ext. 4.*

■TIP➔ Snowstorms are common late October through April. Unless you have four-wheel drive with snow tires, you should carry chains and know how to apply them to the tires on the drive axle.

PARK ESSENTIALS
PARK FEES AND PERMITS
The admission fee is $20 per vehicle and $10 for those who enter by bus, on foot, bicycle, motorcycle, or horse; it is valid for seven days in both parks. U.S. residents over the age of 62 pay $10 for a lifetime pass, and permanently disabled U.S. residents are admitted free.

If you plan to camp in the backcountry, you need a permit, which costs $15 for hikers or $30 for stock users (e.g., horseback riders). One permit covers the group. Availability of permits depends upon trailhead quotas. Reservations are accepted by mail or fax for a $15 processing fee, beginning March 1, and must be made at least 14 days in advance (☎ *559/565–3766).* Without a reservation, you may still get a permit on a first-come, first-served basis starting at 1 pm the day before you plan to hike. For more information on backcountry camping or travel with pack animals (horses, mules, burros, or llamas), contact the Wilderness Permit Office (☎ 530/565–3761).

PARK HOURS
The parks are open 24/7 year-round. They are in the Pacific time zone.

VISITOR INFORMATION
PARK CONTACT INFORMATION
Sequoia and Kings Canyon National Parks ✉ 47050 Generals Hwy.(Rte. 198), Three Rivers ☎ 559/565–3341, 559/565–3134 ⊕ www.nps.gov/seki.

SEQUOIA VISITOR CENTERS
Foothills Visitor Center. Exhibits focusing on the foothills and resource issues facing the parks are on display here. You can also pick up books, maps, and a list of ranger-led walks, and get wilderness permits. ✉ *Generals Hwy. (Rte. 198), 1 mile north of the Ash Mountain entrance* ☎ 559/565–3135 ☉ Oct.–mid-May, daily 8–4:30; mid-May–Sept., daily 8–5.

Lodgepole Visitor Center. Along with exhibits on the area's geologic history, wildlife, and longtime American Indian inhabitants, the center screens an outstanding 22-minute film about bears. You can also buy books and maps here. ✉ *Generals Hwy. (Rte. 198), 21 miles north of Ash Mountain entrance* ☎ 559/565–4436 ☉ *June–Oct., daily 7–6; Nov.–May, weekends 7–6.*

KINGS CANYON VISITOR CENTERS
Cedar Grove Visitor Center. Off the main road and behind the Sentinel Campground, this small ranger station has books and maps, plus information about hikes and other things to do in the area. ✉ *Kings Canyon Scenic Byway, 30 miles east of park entrance* ☎ 559/565–3793 ☉ *Mid-May–late Sept., daily 9–5.*

Grant Grove Visitor Center. Acquaint yourself with the varied charms of this two-section national park by watching a 15-minute film and perusing the center's exhibits on the canyon, sequoias, and human history. Books, maps, and free wilderness permits are available, as are updates on the parks' weather and air-quality conditions. ✉ *Generals Hwy. (Rte. 198), 3 miles northeast of Rte. 180, Big Stump entrance* ☎ 559/565–4307 ☉ *Summer, daily 8–6; mid-May–late Sept., daily 9–4:30; winter, daily 9:30–4:30.*

SEQUOIA NATIONAL PARK

EXPLORING

SCENIC DRIVES
★ **Generals Highway.** One of the most scenic drives in a state replete with them is this 43-mile road, the main asphalt artery between Sequoia and Kings Canyon national parks. Named after the landmark Grant and Sherman trees that leave so many visitors awestruck, it runs from the Foothills Visitor Center north to Grant Grove Village. Along the way, it passes the turnoff to Crystal Cave, the Giant Forest Museum, Lodgepole Village, and Sequoia National Park's other most popular attractions.

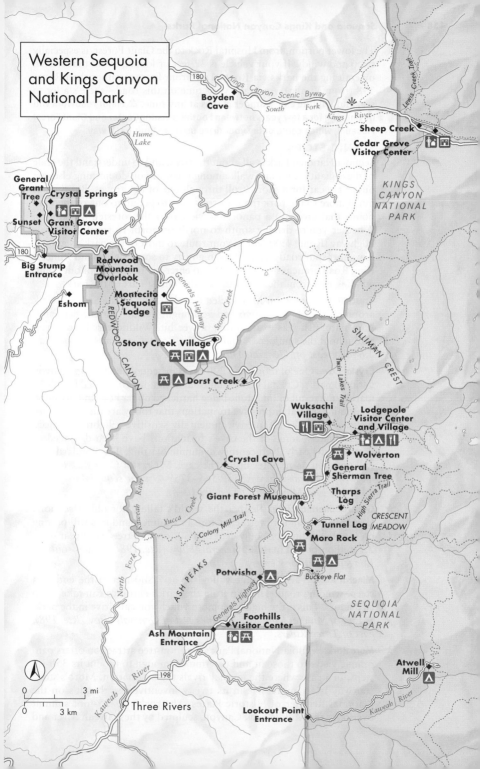

Western Sequoia and Kings Canyon National Park

Boyden Cave

Kings Canyon Scenic Byway

South Fork

Kings River

Lewis Creek Trail

180

Sheep Creek

Cedar Grove Visitor Center

KINGS CANYON NATIONAL PARK

Hume Lake

General Grant Tree

Crystal Springs

Grant Grove Visitor Center

Sunset

180

Big Stump Entrance

Redwood Mountain Overlook

Generals Highway

Eshom

Montecito Sequoia Lodge

REDWOOD CANYON

Stony Creek

Stony Creek Village

SILLIMAN CREST

Dorst Creek

Twin Lakes Trail

Wuksachi Village

Lodgepole Visitor Center and Village

Wolverton

Crystal Cave

General Sherman Tree

Kaweah River

Tharps Log

High Sierra Trail

CRESCENT MEADOW

Giant Forest Museum

Yucca Creek

Colony Mill Trail

Tunnel Log

Moro Rock

North Fork

ASH PEAKS

Buckeye Flat

Potwisha

SEQUOIA NATIONAL PARK

Generals Highway

Foothills Visitor Center

Ash Mountain Entrance

0   3 mi
0   3 km

Kaweah River

198

Three Rivers

Lookout Point Entrance

Atwell Mill

Kaweah River

The lower portion, from Hospital Rock to the Giant Forest, is especially steep and windy. If your vehicle is 22 feet or longer, avoid that stretch by entering the parks via Route 180 (from Fresno) rather than Route 198 (from Visalia). And take your time on this road—there's a lot to see, and wildlife can scamper across at any time. ⚠ Major roadwork will be ongoing for a few years between Foothills Visitor Center and Giant Forest Museum, which could delay your drive up to an hour each way.

SCENIC STOPS

Sequoia National Park is all about the trees, and to understand the scale of these giants you must walk among them. If you do nothing else, get out of the car for a short stroll through one of the groves. But there is much more to the park than the trees. Try to get up to one of the vista points that give you a panoramic view over the forested mountains. Whether you're driving south to north or north to south, Generals Highway (Route 198) will be your route to most of the park's sights. A few short spur roads lead off the highway to some sights, and Mineral King Road branches off Route 198 to enter the park at Lookout Point, winding east from there into the southernmost part of the park.

Crescent Meadow. John Muir called this the "gem of the Sierra." Walk around for an hour or two and you might decide that the Scotland-born naturalist was exaggerating a wee bit. Wildflowers bloom here throughout the summer. ✉ *End of Moro Rock–Crescent Meadow Rd., 2.6 miles east off Generals Hwy.*

★ **Crystal Cave.** One of more than 200 caves in Sequoia and Kings Canyon national parks, Crystal Cave is unusual in that it's composed largely of marble, the result of limestone being hardened under heat and pressure. It contains several impressive formations that today are much easier to make out, thanks to an environmentally sensitive relighting project. Unfortunately, some of the cave's formations have been damaged or destroyed by early 20th-century dynamite blasting. The standard tour will give you 45 minutes inside the cave. ✉ *Crystal Cave Rd., 6 miles west off Generals Hwy.* ☎ *559/565–3759* ⊕ *www.sequoiahistory.org* 🎫 *$13* 🕐 *Mid-May–mid-Oct., daily 10–4.*

★ **General Sherman Tree.** Neither the world's tallest nor oldest sequoia, General Sherman is nevertheless tops in volume—and it is still putting on weight, adding the equivalent of a 60-foot-tall tree every year to its 2.7 million-pound mass. ✉ *Generals Hwy. (Rte. 198), 2 miles south of Lodgepole Visitor Center.*

Mineral King. This subalpine valley sits at 7,800 feet at the end of a steep, winding road. The trip from the park's entrance can take up to two hours. This is the highest point to which you can drive in the park. ✉ *End of Mineral King Rd., 25 miles east of Generals Hwy. (Rte. 198), east of Three Rivers.*

★ **Moro Rock.** Sequoia National Park's best non-tree attraction offers panoramic views to those fit and determined enough to mount its 350-ish steps. In a case where the journey rivals the destination, Moro's stone stairway is so impressive in its twisty inventiveness that it's on the National Register of Historic Places. The rock's 6,725-foot summit overlooks the Middle Fork Canyon, sculpted by the Kaweah River and approaching the depth of Arizona's Grand Canyon, although hazy air often compromises the view. ⊠ *Moro Rock–Crescent Meadow Rd., 2 miles east off Generals Hwy. (Rte. 198) to parking area.*

Tunnel Log. It's been almost 45 years since you could drive through a standing sequoia—and that was in Yosemite National Park's Mariposa Grove, not here. This 275-foot tree fell in 1937, and soon a 17-foot-wide, 8-foot-high hole was cut through it for vehicular passage that continues today. Large vehicles take the nearby bypass. ⊠ *Moro Rock–Crescent Meadow Rd., 2 miles east of Generals Hwy. (Rte. 198).*

EDUCATIONAL OFFERINGS
CLASSES AND SEMINARS
Evening Programs. In summer, the park shows documentary films and slide shows, and has evening lectures. Locations and times vary; pick up a schedule at any visitor center or check bulletin boards near ranger stations. ☎ 559/565–3341.

★ **Seminars.** Expert naturalists lead seminars on a range of topics, including birds, wildflowers, geology, botany, photography, park history, backpacking, and pathfinding. Some courses offer transferable credits. Reserve in advance.

Sequoia Natural History Association. For information and prices, pick up a course catalogue at any visitor center or contact the Sequoia Natural History Association. ☎ 559/565–3759 ⊕ *www.sequoiahistory.org*

Sequoia Sightseeing Tours. The only licensed tour operator in either park offers daily interpretive sightseeing tours in a 10-passenger van with a friendly, knowledgeable guide. Reservations are essential. The company also offers private tours of Kings Canyon. ☎ 559/561–4489 ⊕ *www. sequoiatours.com* ⊠ *$65 half-day tour, $88 full-day tour.*

RANGER PROGRAMS
Free Nature Programs. Almost any summer day, half-hour to 1½-hour ranger talks and walks explore subjects such as the life of the sequoia, the geology of the park, and the habits of bears. Giant Forest, Lodgepole Visitor Center, Wuksachi Village, and Dorst Creek Campground are frequent starting points. Check bulletin boards throughout the park for the week's offerings.

SPORTS AND THE OUTDOORS

The best way to see Sequoia is to take a hike. Unless you do so, you'll miss out on the up-close grandeur of mist wafting between deeply scored, red-orange tree trunks bigger than you've ever seen. If it's winter, put on some snowshoes or cross-country skis and plunge into the snow-swaddled woodland. There are not too many other outdoor options: no off-road driving is allowed in the parks, and no special provisions have been made for bicycles. Boating, rafting, and snowmobiling are also prohibited.

BIRD-WATCHING
More than 200 species of birds inhabit Sequoia and Kings Canyon national parks. Not seen in most parts of the United States, the white-headed woodpecker and the pileated woodpecker are common in most

mid-elevation areas here. There are also many hawks and owls, including the renowned spotted owl. Species are diverse in both parks due to the changes in elevation, and range from warblers, kingbirds, thrushes, and sparrows in the foothills to goshawk, blue grouse, red-breasted nuthatch, and brown creeper at the highest elevations. Ranger-led birdwatching tours are held on a sporadic basis. Call the park's main information number to find out more about these tours.

Sequoia Natural History Association. The association's highly regarded Sequoia Field Institute conducts single-day and mulitiday "EdVenture" tours that include backpacking hikes, natural-history walks, and kayaking excursions. ☏ *559/565–3759* ⊕ *www.sequoiahistory.org.*

CROSS-COUNTRY SKIING

Wuksachi Lodge. Rent skis here. Depending on snowfall amounts, instruction may also be available. Reservations are recommended. Marked trails cut through Giant Forest, just 5 miles south of the lodge. ⊠ *Off Generals Hwy. (Rte. 198), 2 miles north of Lodgepole* ☏ *559/565–4070* ⌨ *$18–$25 ski rental* ⊗ *Nov.–May (unless no snow), daily 9–4.*

HIKING

The best way to see the park is to hike it. The grandeur and majesty of the Sierra is best seen up close. Carry a hiking map—available at any visitor center—and plenty of water. Check with rangers for current trail conditions, and be aware of rapidly changing weather. As a rule of thumb, plan on trekking about a mile per hour.

EASY

★ **Congress Trail.** This easy 2-mile trail, arguably the best hike in the parks in terms of natural beauty, is a paved loop that begins near General Sherman Tree and winds through the heart of the sequoia forest. You'll get close-up views of more big trees here than on any other Sequoia hike. Watch for the clusters known as the House and Senate. An easy offshoot leads to Crescent Meadow, where in summer you can catch free shuttles back to the Sherman parking lot. *Easy.* ⊠ *Trail begins off Generals Hwy. (Rte. 198), 2 miles north of Giant Forest.*

★ **Crescent Meadow Trails.** John Muir reportedly called Crescent Meadow the "gem of the Sierra." Brilliant wildflowers bloom here by midsummer, and a 1.8-mile trail loops around the meadow. A 1.6-mile trail begins at Crescent Meadow and leads to Tharp's Log, a cabin built from a fire-hollowed sequoia. *Easy.* ⊠ *Trail begins end of Moro Rock–Crescent Meadow Rd., 2.6 miles east off Generals Hwy. (Rte. 198).*

MODERATE

Tokopah Falls Trail. This moderate trail follows the Marble Fork of the Kaweah River for 1.75 miles one way and dead-ends below the impressive granite cliffs and cascading waterfall of Tokopah Canyon. It takes 2½ to 4 hours to make the 3.5-mile round-trip journey. The trail passes through a mixed-conifer forest. *Moderate.* ⊠ *Trail begins off Generals Hwy. (Rte. 198), ¼ mile north of Lodgepole Campground.*

DIFFICULT

Mineral King Trails. Many trails to the high country begin at Mineral King. The two most popular day hikes are Eagle Lake and Timber Gap, both of which are somewhat strenuous. At 7,800 feet, this is the highest point to which one can drive in either of the parks. Get a map and provisions, and check with rangers about conditions. *Difficult.* ⊠ *Trailhead at end of Mineral King Rd., 25 miles east of Generals Hwy. (Rte. 198).*

HORSEBACK RIDING

Trips take you through redwood forests, flowering meadows, across the Sierra, or even up to Mt. Whitney. Costs per person range from $35 for a one-hour guided ride to around $250 per day for fully guided trips for which the packers do all the cooking and camp chores.

TOURS AND OUTFITTERS

Horse Corral Pack Station. Hourly, half-day, full-day, or overnight trips through Sequoia are available for beginning and advanced riders. ⊠ *Off Big Meadows Rd., 12 miles east of Generals Hwy. (Rte. 198) between Sequoia and Kings Canyon national parks* ☎ *559/565–3404 in summer, 559/564–6429 in winter* 🖂 *$35–$145 day trips* ☼ *May–Sept.*

Mineral King Pack Station. Day and overnight tours in the high-mountain area around Mineral King are available here. ⊠ *End of Mineral King Rd., 25 miles east of East Fork entrance* ☎ *559/561–3039 in summer, 928/855–5885 in winter* ⊕ *mineralking.tripod.com* 🖂 *$30–$85 day trips* ☼ *July–late Sept. or –early Oct.*

SLEDDING AND SNOWSHOEING

The Wolverton area, on Route 198 near Giant Forest, is a popular sledding spot, where sleds, inner tubes, and platters are allowed. You can buy sleds and saucers, starting at $8, at the Wuksachi Lodge (☎ *559/565–4070*), 2 miles north of Lodgepole.

You can rent snowshoes for $18–$25 at the Wuksachi Lodge (☎ *559/565–4070*), 2 miles north of Lodgepole. Naturalists lead snowshoe walks around Giant Forest and Wuksachi Lodge, conditions permitting, on Saturdays and holidays. Snowshoes are provided for a $1 donation. Make reservations and check schedules at Giant Forest Museum (☎ *559/565–4480*) or Wuksachi Lodge.

KINGS CANYON NATIONAL PARK

EXPLORING

SCENIC DRIVES

★ **Kings Canyon Scenic Byway.** About 10 miles east of Grant Grove Village is Jackson View, where you'll first see Kings River Canyon. Near Yucca Point, it's thousands of feet deeper than the much more famous Grand Canyon. Continuing through Sequoia National Forest past Boyden Cavern, you'll enter the larger portion of Kings Canyon National Park and, eventually, Cedar Grove Village. Past there, the U-shape canyon becomes broader. Be sure to allow an hour to walk through Zumwalt Meadow. Also, be sure to park and take the less-than-five-minute walks

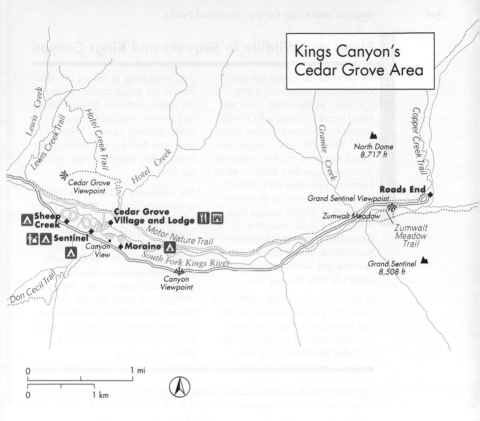

Kings Canyon's Cedar Grove Area

Lewis Creek
Lewis Creek Trail
Hotel Creek Trail
Hotel Creek
Cedar Grove Viewpoint
Granite Creek
Copper Creek Trail
North Dome 8,717 ft
Roads End
Grand Sentinel Viewpoint
Sheep Creek
Cedar Grove Village and Lodge
Zumwalt Meadow
Sentinel
Motor Nature Trail
Canyon View
Moraine
South Fork Kings River
Zumwalt Meadow Trail
Canyon Viewpoint
Grand Sentinel 8,508 ft
Don Cecil Trail

0 ——— 1 mi
0 ——— 1 km

to the base of Grizzly Falls and Roaring River Falls. The drive dead-ends at a big parking lot, the launch point for many backpackers. Driving the byway takes about one hour each way (without stops).

HISTORIC SITES

★ **Fallen Monarch.** This Sequoia's hollow base was used in the second half of the 19th century as a home for settlers, a saloon, and even to stable U.S. Cavalry horses. As you walk through it (assuming entry is permitted, which has not always been the case in recent years), check out how little the wood has decayed, and imagine yourself tucked safely inside, sheltered from a storm or protected from the searing heat. ⊠ *Trailhead 1 mile north of Grant Grove Visitor Center.*

SCENIC STOPS

Canyon View. There are many places along the scenic byway to pull over for sightseeing, but this special spot showcases evidence of the canyon's glacial history. Here, maybe more than anywhere else, you'll understand why John Muir compared Kings Canyon vistas with those in Yosemite. ⊠ *Kings Canyon Scenic Byway (Rte. 180), 1 mile east of the Cedar Grove turnoff.*

★ **Redwood Mountain Grove.** If you are serious about sequoias, you should consider visiting this, the world's largest big-tree grove. Within its 2,078 acres are 2,172 sequoias whose diameters exceed 10 feet. Your

Plants and Wildlife in Sequoia and Kings Canyon

The parks can be divided into three distinct zones. In the west (1,500–4,500 feet) are the rolling, lower elevation foothills, covered with shrubby chaparral vegetation or golden grasslands dotted with oaks. Chamise, red-barked manzanita, and the occasional yucca plant grow here. Fields of white popcorn flower cover the hillsides in spring, and the yellow fiddleneck flourishes. In summer, intense heat and absence of rain cause the hills to turn golden brown. Wildlife includes the California ground squirrel, noisy blue-and-gray scrub jay, black bears, coyotes, skunks, and gray fox.

At middle elevation (5,000–9,000 feet), where the giant sequoia belt resides, rock formations mix with meadows and huge stands of evergreens—red and white fir, incense cedar, and

ponderosa pines, to name a few. Wildflowers like yellow blazing star and red Indian paintbrush, bloom in spring and summer. Mule deer, golden-mantled ground squirrels, Steller's jays, mule deer, and black bears (most active in fall) inhabit the area, as does the chickaree.

The high alpine section of the parks is extremely rugged, with a string of rocky peaks reaching above 13,000 feet to Mt. Whitney's 14,494 feet. Fierce weather and scarcity of soil make vegetation and wildlife sparse. Foxtail and whitebark pines have gnarled and twisted trunks, the result of high wind, heavy snowfall, and freezing temperatures. In summer you can see yellow-bellied marmots, pikas, weasels, mountain chickadees, and Clark's nutcrackers.

options range from the distant (pulling off the Generals Highway onto an overlook) to the intimate (taking a 6- to 10-mile hike down into its richest regions, which include two of the world's 25 heaviest trees). ⊠ *Drive 5 miles south of Grant Grove on Generals Hwy. (Rte. 198), then turn right at Quail Flat; follow it 1½ miles to the Redwood Canyon trailhead.*

SPORTS AND THE OUTDOORS

CROSS-COUNTRY SKIING
Roads to Grant Grove are easily accessible during heavy snowfall, making the trails here a good choice over Sequoia's Giant Forest when harsh weather hits.

HIKING
You can enjoy many of Kings Canyon's sights from your car, but the giant gorge of the Kings River Canyon and the sweeping vistas of some of the highest mountains in the United States are best seen on foot. Carry a hiking map—available at any visitor center—and plenty of water. Check with rangers for current trail conditions, and be aware of rapidly changing weather.

Road's End Permit Station. If you're planning to hike the backcountry, you can pick up a permit and information on the backcountry at Road's End Permit Station. You can also rent or buy bear canisters, a must for campers. When the station is closed, you can still complete a self-service

Hiking in the Sierra Mountains is a thrilling experience, putting you amid some of the world's highest trees.

permit form. ⊠ *5 miles east of Cedar Grove Visitor Center, at the end of Kings Canyon Scenic Byway* ⊘ *Late May–late Sept., daily 7–3:30.*

EASY

Fodor's Choice
★
Zumwalt Meadow Trail. Rangers say this is the best (and most popular) day hike in the Cedar Grove area. Just 1.5 miles long, it offers three visual treats: the South Fork of the Kings River, the lush meadow, and the high granite walls above, including those of Grand Sentinel and North Dome. *Easy.* ⊠ *Trailhead 4½ miles east of Cedar Grove Village turnoff from Kings Canyon Scenic Byway.*

MODERATE

★ **Big Baldy.** This hike climbs 600 feet and 2 miles up to the 8,209-feet summit of Big Baldy. Your reward is the view of Redwood Canyon. The round-trip hike is 4 miles. *Moderate.* ⊠ *Trailhead 8 miles south of Grant Grove on Generals Hwy. (Rte. 198).*

★ **Redwood Canyon Trail.** Avoid the hubbub of Giant Forest and its General Sherman Tree by hiking down to Redwood Canyon, the world's largest grove of sequoias. Opt for the trail toward Hart Tree, and you'll soon lose track of how many humongous trees you pass along the 6-mile loop. Count on spending four to six peaceful hours here—although some backpackers linger overnight (wilderness permit required). *Moderate.* ⊠ *Trail begins off Quail Flat. Drive 5 miles south of Grant Grove on Generals Hwy. (Rte. 198), then turn right at Quail Flat; follow it 1½ miles to the Redwood Canyon trailhead.*

DIFFICULT

★ **Hotel Creek Trail.** For gorgeous canyon views, take this trail from the canyon floor at Cedar Grove up a series of switchbacks until it splits. Follow the route left through chaparral to the forested ridge and rocky outcrop known as Cedar Grove Overlook, where you can see the Kings River Canyon stretching below. This strenuous 5-mile round-trip hike gains 1,200 feet and takes three to four hours to complete. For a longer hike, return via Lewis Creek Trail for an 8-mile loop. *Difficult.* ⊠ *Trailhead at Cedar Grove pack station, 1 mile east of Cedar Grove Village.*

HORSEBACK RIDING

One-day destinations by horseback out of Cedar Grove include Mist Falls and Upper Bubb's Creek. In the backcountry, many equestrians head for Volcanic Lakes or Granite Basin, ascending trails that reach elevations of 10,000 feet. Costs per person range from $35 for a one-hour guided ride to around $250 per day for fully guided trips for which the packers do all the cooking and camp chores.

TOURS AND **Cedar Grove Pack Station.** Take a day or overnight trip along the Kings
OUTFITTERS River Canyon with Cedar Grove Pack Station. Popular routes include the Rae Lakes Loop and Monarch Divide. ⊠ *Kings Canyon Scenic Byway, 1 mile east of Cedar Grove Village* ☎ *559/565–3464 in summer, 559/337–2314 off-season* ✉ *Call for prices* ☉ *May–Oct.*

Grant Grove Stables. A one- or two-hour trip through Grant Grove leaving from Grant Grove Stables is a good way to get a taste of horseback riding in Kings Canyon. ⊠ *Rte. 180, ½ mile north of Grant Grove Visitor Center* ☎ *559/335–9292 mid-June–Sept., 559/594–9307 Oct.–mid-June* ✉ *$40–$60* ☉ *June–Labor Day, daily 8–6.*

SLEDDING AND SNOWSHOEING

In winter, Kings Canyon has a few great places to play in the snow. Sleds, inner tubes, and platters are allowed at both the Azalea Campground area on Grant Tree Road, ¼ mile north of Grant Grove Visitor Center, and at the Big Stump picnic area, 2 miles north of the lower Route 180 entrance to the park.

Snowshoeing is good around Grant Grove, where you can take naturalist-guided snowshoe walks on Saturdays and holidays mid-December through mid-March as conditions permit.

WHERE TO EAT

Prices in the reviews are the average cost of a main course at dinner or, if dinner is not served, at lunch.

SEQUOIA

$ ✕ **Lodgepole Market and Snack Bar.** The choices here run the gamut from
CAFÉ simple to very simple, with the three counters only a few strides apart in a central eating complex. For hot food, venture into the snack bar. The deli sells prepackaged sandwiches along with ice cream scooped from tubs. You'll find other prepackaged foods and souvenirs in the

market. $ *Average main: $5* ✉ *Next to Lodgepole Visitor Center* ☎ *559/565–3301* ☾ *Closed late Sept.–mid-Apr.*

$$$
BARBECUE

✗ **Wolverton Barbecue.** Weather permitting, diners congregate on a wooden porch that looks directly out onto a small but strikingly verdant meadow. In addition to the predictable meats such as ribs and chicken, the all-you-can-eat buffet has sides that include baked beans, corn on the cob, and potato salad. Following the meal, listen to a ranger talk and clear your throat for a campfire sing-along. Purchase tickets at Lodgepole Market, Wuksachi Lodge, or Wolverton Recreation Area's office. $ *Average main: $22* ✉ *Wolverton Rd., 1½ miles northeast off Generals Hwy. (Rte. 198)* ☎ *559/565–4070, 559/565–3301* ☾ *Closed Mon.–Thurs. and early Sept.–mid-June. No lunch.*

$$
AMERICAN
★

✗ **Wuksachi Village Dining Room.** Huge windows run the length of the high-ceilinged dining room, and a large fireplace on the far wall warms both the body and the soul. The diverse dinner menu—by far the best in the two parks—includes filet mignon, rainbow trout, and vegetarian pasta dishes, in addition to the ever-present burgers. The children's menu is economically priced. Breakfast and lunch also are served. $ *Average main: $20* ✉ *Wuksachi Village* ☎ *559/565–4070* ⌂ *Reservations essential.*

KINGS CANYON

$
AMERICAN

✗ **Cedar Grove Restaurant.** For a small operation, the menu here is surprisingly extensive, with dinner entrées such as pasta, pork chops, and steak. For breakfast, try the biscuits and gravy, French toast, pancakes, or cold cereal. Burgers (including vegetarian patties) and hot dogs dominate the lunch choices. Outside, a patio dining area overlooks the Kings River. $ *Average main: $13* ✉ *Cedar Grove Village* ☎ *559/565–0100* ☾ *Closed Oct.–May.*

$$
AMERICAN

✗ **Grant Grove Restaurant.** In a no-frills, open room, order basic American fare such as pancakes for breakfast or hot sandwiches and chicken for later meals. Vegetarians and vegans will have to content themselves with a simple salad. Take-out service is available. $ *Average main: $21* ✉ *Grant Grove Village* ☎ *559/335–5500.*

WHERE TO STAY

Prices in the reviews are the lowest cost of a standard double room in high season. For expanded reviews, facilities, and current deals, visit Fodors.com.

SEQUOIA

$$$
HOTEL
Fodor'sChoice
★

🛏 **Wuksachi Lodge.** The striking cedar-and-stone main building here is a fine example of how a structure can blend effectively with lovely mountain scenery. **Pros:** best place to stay in the parks, lots of wildlife. **Cons:** rooms can be small, main lodge is a few minutes' walk from guest rooms. **TripAdvisor:** "comfortable rooms," "great location," "beautiful setting." $ *Rooms from: $185* ✉ *Wuksachi Village* ☎ *559/565–4070, 888/252–5757 reservations* ⊕ *www.visitsequoia.com* ⇥ *102 rooms.*

CLOSE UP

Mt. Whitney

At 14,494 feet, Mt. Whitney is the highest point in the contiguous United States and the crown jewel of Sequoia National Park's wild eastern side. The peak looms high above the tiny, high-mountain desert community of Lone Pine, where numerous Hollywood Westerns have been filmed. The high mountain ranges, arid landscape, and scrubby brush of the Eastern Sierra are beautiful in their vastness and austerity.

Despite the mountain's scale, you can't see it from the more traveled west side of the park because it is hidden behind the Great Western Divide. The only way to access Mt. Whitney from the main part of the park is to circumnavigate the Sierra Nevada via a 10-hour, nearly 400-mile drive outside the park. No road ascends the peak; the best vantage point from which to catch a glimpse of the mountain is at the end of Whitney Portal Road. The 13 miles of winding road leads from U.S. 395 at Lone Pine to the trailhead for the hiking route to the top of the mountain. Whitney Portal Road is closed in winter.

KINGS CANYON

$$$
HOTEL

⚀ **John Muir Lodge.** This modern, timber-sided lodge is nestled in a wooded area in the hills above Grant Grove Village and offers year-round accommodations. **Pros:** common room stays warm; it's far enough from the main road to be quiet. **Cons:** check-in is down in the village. **TripAdvisor:** "surprisingly comfortable," "peace and quiet in the forest," "terrific location and service." $ *Rooms from: $195* ✉ *Kings Canyon Scenic Byway, ¼ mile north of Grant Grove Village* ☎ *559/335–5500, 866/522–6966* ⊕ *www.sequoia-kingscanyon.com* ⌲ *24 rooms, 6 suites.*

Sacramento and the Gold Country

WORD OF MOUTH

"The twin mining towns of Nevada City and Grass Valley are two of my favorite towns in California. They both have many well preserved historical buildings, B&Bs, restaurants, and interesting shops."

—Otis_B_Driftwood

WELCOME TO SACRAMENTO AND THE GOLD COUNTRY

TOP REASONS TO GO

★ **Rush to the past:** Marshall Gold Discovery State Park and Hangtown's Gold Bug & Mine conjure up California's mid-19th century boom.

★ **Capital connections:** Sedate Sacramento offers enough attractions to engage out-of-towners for a day or two, especially its Capitol, historic Old Sacramento, and dining scene.

★ **Bon appetit:** Sacramento is home to the California state fair in July and many ethnic food festivals. Nevada City and environs are known for summer mountain music festivals and Victorian and Cornish winter holiday celebrations.

★ **Vintage calm:** With bucolic scenery and friendly tasting rooms, the Shenandoah Valley is the Gold Country's laid-back answer to Napa.

★ **Ups and downs:** Calaveras Big Trees State Park is filled with giant sequoias, and Moaning Cavern's main chamber is big enough to hold the Statue of Liberty.

1 Sacramento and Vicinity. The gateway to the Gold Country, the seat of state government, and an agricultural hub, Sacramento plays many important contemporary roles. About 2.5 million people live in the metropolitan area, which offers up more sunshine and lower housing costs than coastal California.

2 The Gold Country—South. South of its junction with U.S. 50, Highway 49 traces in asphalt the famed Mother Lode. The peppy former gold-rush towns strung along the road have for the most part been restored and made presentable to visitors with an interest in one of the most frenzied episodes of American history.

3 The Gold Country—North. Highway 49 north of Placerville links the towns of Coloma, Auburn, Grass Valley, and Nevada City. Most are gentrified versions of once-rowdy mining camps, vestiges of which remain in roadside museums, old mining structures, and restored homes now serving as inns.

12

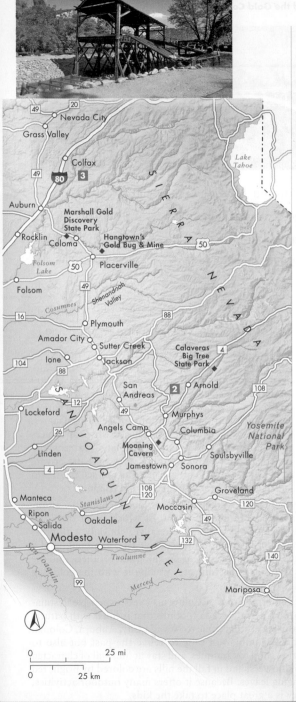

GETTING ORIENTED

The Gold Country is a largely laid-back and lower-tech destination for those seeking to escape Southern California and the Bay Area. Sacramento, Davis, and Woodland are in an enormous valley bordered to the east by the Sierra Nevada mountain range. Foothill communities Nevada City, Placerville, and Sutter Creek were products of the gold rush.

Updated by
Reed Parsell

A new era dawned for California when James Marshall turned up a gold nugget in the tailrace of a sawmill he was constructing along the American River. Before January 24, 1848, Mexico and the United States were still wrestling for ownership of what would become the Golden State. With Marshall's discovery, the United States tightened its grip on the region, and prospectors from all over the world came to seek their fortunes in the Mother Lode.

As gold fever seized the nation, California's population of 15,000 swelled to 265,000 within three years. The mostly young, mostly male adventurers who arrived in search of gold—the 49ers—became part of a culture that discarded many of the conventions of the eastern states. It was also a violent time. Yankee prospectors chased Mexican miners off their claims, and California's leaders initiated a plan to exterminate the local Native American population. Bounties were paid and private militias were hired to wipe out the Native Americans or sell them into slavery. California was now to be dominated by the Anglo.

The gold rush boom lasted scarcely 20 years, but it changed California forever. It produced 546 mining towns, of which fewer than 250 remain. The hills of the Gold Country were alive, not only with prospecting and mining but also with business, the arts, gambling, and a fair share of crime. Opera houses went up alongside brothels, and the California State Capitol, in Sacramento, was built with the gold dug out of the hills.

Today the Gold Country is one of California's less expensive destinations, a region of the Sierra Nevada foothills that is filled with natural and cultural pleasures. Visitors come to Nevada City, Auburn, Coloma, Sutter Creek, and Columbia not only to relive the past but also to explore art galleries, shop for antiques, and stay at inns full of character. Spring brings wildflowers, and in fall the hills are colored by bright red berries and changing leaves. Because it offers many outdoor activities, the Gold Country is a great place to take the kids.

Visiting Old Sacramento's museums is a good way to immerse yourself in history, but the Gold Country's heart lies along Highway 49, which winds the 325-mile north–south length of the historic mining area. The highway, often a twisting, hilly, two-lane road, begs for a convertible with the top down.

12

PLANNING

WHEN TO GO
The Gold Country is most pleasant in spring, when the wildflowers are in bloom, and in fall. Summers can be hot: temperatures of 100°F are fairly common. Sacramento winters tend to be cool with occasionally foggy and/or rainy days; many Sacramentans drive to the foothills (or to the coast) to get some winter sunshine. Throughout the year Gold Country towns stage community and ethnic celebrations. In December many towns are decked out for Christmas.

GETTING HERE AND AROUND
AIR TRAVEL
Sacramento International Airport (SMF), which unveiled a new terminal in late 2011, is served by Aeromexico, Alaska, American, Delta, Frontier, Hawaiian, JetBlue, Southwest, United, and US Airways. A private taxi from the airport to downtown Sacramento costs about $40; the Super Shuttle fare is $25. Public buses *(see Bus and Light-Rail Travel)* are also an option.

Contacts **Sacramento International Airport** ⊠ *6900 Airport Blvd., 12 miles northwest of downtown off I–5, Sacramento* ☎ *916/929–5411* ⊕ *www. sacramento.aero/smf.* **Super Shuttle** ☎ *800/258–3826* ⊕ *www.supershuttle.com.*

BUS AND LIGHT-RAIL TRAVEL
Yolobus public buses No. 42A and 42B connect SMF airport and downtown Sacramento, West Sacramento, Davis, and Woodland. Greyhound serves Sacramento, Davis, Auburn, and Placerville. It's a two-hour trip from San Francisco's Temporary Transbay Terminal, at Folsom and Beale streets, to the Sacramento Greyhound Station, at Richards and Sequoia Pacific boulevards. Sacramento Regional Transit serves the capital area with buses and light-rail vehicles.

Contacts **Greyhound** ☎ *800/231–2222* ⊕ *www.greyhound.com.* **Sacramento Regional Transit** ☎ *916/321–2877* ⊕ *www.sacrt.com.* **Yolobus** ☎ *530/666–2837, 916/371–2877* ⊕ *www.yolobus.com.*

CAR TRAVEL
Interstate 5 (north–south) and Interstate 80 (east–west) are the two main routes into and out of Sacramento. From Sacramento, three highways fan out toward the east, all intersecting with historic Highway 49: Interstate 80 heads northeast 34 miles to Auburn; U.S. 50 goes east 40 miles to Placerville; and Highway 16 angles southeast 45 miles to Plymouth. Highway 49 is an excellent two-lane road that winds and climbs through the foothills and valleys, linking the principal Gold Country towns. Traveling by car is the only practical way to explore the Gold Country.

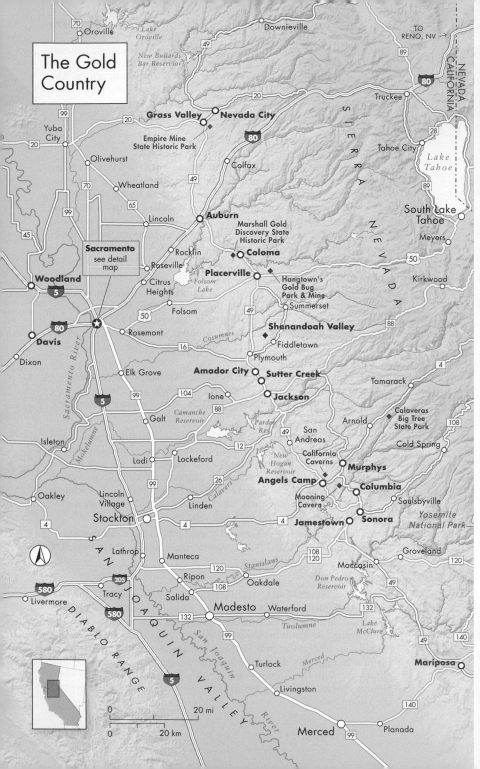

The Gold Country

Oroville
Lake Oroville
New Bullards Bar Reservoir
Downieville
TO RENO, NV
NEVADA CALIFORNIA
70
49
89
80
Yuba City
20
Grass Valley
Nevada City
Empire Mine State Historic Park
Truckee
99
20
20
80
Colfax
Tahoe City
28
Lake Tahoe
Olivehurst
70
65
Wheatland
49
SIERRA
89
Lincoln
Auburn
Marshall Gold Discovery State Historic Park
South Lake Tahoe
45
99
Rocklin
Coloma
NEVADA
Meyers
Sacramento see detail map
Roseville
Placerville
Woodland
Citrus Heights
Hangtown's Gold Bug Park & Mine
50
Kirkwood
5
Folsom Lake
Summerset
80
50
Folsom
49
88
Davis
Rosemont
Cosumnes
Shenandoah Valley
Dixon
16
Fiddletown
4
Elk Grove
Plymouth
Tamarack
104
Amador City
Sutter Creek
Galt
Ione
88
Jackson
Arnold
Calaveras Big Tree State Park
108
Isleton
Camanche Reservoir
Pardee Res.
San Andreas
Cold Spring
Mokelumne
Lodi
12
49
California Caverns
Lockeford
New Hogan Reservoir
Murphys
99
26
Calaveras
Columbia
Oakley
Linden
Angels Camp
Moaning Cavern
Soulsbyville
Lincoln Village
Jamestown
Sonora
Yosemite National Park
Stockton
4
4
4
Lathrop
Manteca
108 120
Moccasin
Groveland
120
Ripon
Stanislaus
Don Pedro Reservoir
49
580
120
Oakdale
108
132
Livermore
Tracy
Salida
132
205
Modesto
Waterford
Tuolumne
Lake McClure
49
140
580
DIABLO RANGE
132
San Joaquin River
99
Merced River
Mariposa
5
Turlock
SAN JOAQUIN VALLEY
Livingston
140
0   20 mi
0   20 km
Merced
99
Planada

Sacramento River

TRAIN TRAVEL

Amtrak trains serve Sacramento and Davis from San Jose, Oakland, and Emeryville (Amtrak buses transport passengers from San Francisco's Ferry Building to Emeryville). The trip takes 2½ hours. Amtrak also runs trains and connecting motor coaches from the Central Valley.

Contacts **Amtrak** ☎ 800/872-7245 ⊕ www.amtrakcalifornia.com.

HEALTH AND SAFETY

In an emergency, dial 911. Each of the following medical facilities has an emergency room open 24 hours a day.

Hospitals **Mercy Hospital of Sacramento** ✉ 4001 J St., Sacramento ☎ 916/453-4545 ⊕ www.mercygeneral.org. **Sutter General Hospital** ✉ 2801 L St., Sacramento ☎ 916/733-8900 ⊕ www.suttermedicalcenter.org. **Sutter Memorial Hospital** ✉ 52nd and F Sts., Sacramento ☎ 916/733-1000 ⊕ www.suttermedicalcenter.org.

VISITOR INFORMATION

Contacts **Amador County Chamber of Commerce & Visitors Bureau** ✉ 115 Main St., Jackson ☎ 209/223-0350 ⊕ www.amadorcountychamber.com. **El Dorado County Visitors Authority** ✉ 542 Main St., Placerville ☎ 530/621-5885, 800/457-6279 ⊕ visit-eldorado.com. **Grass Valley/Nevada County Chamber of Commerce** ✉ 422 Henderson St., Grass Valley ☎ 530/273-4667, 800/655-4667 ⊕ www.grassvalleychamber.com. **Mariposa County Visitors Bureau** ✉ 5158 Hwy. 140, Mariposa ☎ 209/966-7081, 866/425-3366 ⊕ www.yosemiteexperience.com. **Tuolumne County Visitors Bureau** ✉ 542 W. Stockton Rd., Sonora ☎ 209/533-4420, 800/446-1333 ⊕ www.tcvb.com.

RESTAURANTS

American, Italian, and Mexican are common Gold Country fare, but chefs also prepare ambitious European, French, and California cuisine. Grass Valley's meat- and vegetable-stuffed *pasties*, introduced by 19th-century gold miners from Cornwall, are one of the region's more unusual treats.

HOTELS

Full service hotels, budget motels, and small inns can be found in Sacramento. Larger towns along Highway 49—among them Jackson, Placerville, Auburn, and Nevada City—have chain motels and inns. Many Gold Country bed-and-breakfasts occupy former mansions, miners' cabins, and other historic buildings.

HOTEL AND RESTAURANT COSTS

Prices in the restaurant reviews are the average cost of a main course at dinner or, if dinner is not served, at lunch (excluding sales tax). Prices in the hotel reviews are the lowest cost of a standard double room in high season. Prices do not include taxes (as high as 14%, depending on the region).

Contacts **Gold Country Inns of Tuolumne County** ⊕ www.goldbnbs.com. **Historic Inns of Grass Valley and Nevada City** ☎ 530/477-6634 ⊕ goldcountryinns.net. **Tour Amador County** ☎ 209/267-9249, 877/868-7262 ⊕ www.touramador.com/accommodations.

SACRAMENTO AND VICINITY

California's capital is one of the country's most ethnically diverse cities, with sizable Hmong and Ukrainian populations, among many others.

SACRAMENTO

87 miles northeast of San Francisco on I–80; 384 miles north of Los Angeles on I–5.

All around the Golden State's seat of government you'll experience echoes of the gold-rush days, most notably in Old Sacramento, whose wooden sidewalks and horse-drawn carriages on cobblestone streets lend the waterfront district a 19th-century feel. The California State Railroad Museums and other venues hold artifacts of state and national significance, and historic buildings house shops and restaurants. River cruises and train rides are fun family diversions for an hour or two.

Due east of Old Sacramento is downtown, whose noteworthy landmarks are the Capitol building and the surrounding Capitol Park. The convention center is also here. A persistent homeless problem and a scattering of boarded-up storefronts diminish the area's appeal somewhat.

Farther east, starting at about 15th Street, lies the city's most interesting neighborhood, midtown, a vibrant mix of genteel Victorian edifices, ultramodern lofts, and innovative restaurants and cozy wine bars. The neighborhood, which is so cool it's got its own magazine (⊕ *www. midtownmonthly.net*), springs to life on the second Saturday evening of the month, when art galleries hold open houses and the sidewalks are packed. A few intersections are jumping most evenings when the weather's good; they include the corner of 20th and L streets in what's known as Lavender Heights, the center of the city's gay and lesbian community.

GETTING HERE AND AROUND

Most people drive to Sacramento and get around by car. Taxis are a minor presence. Bike lanes abound, but often they come to sudden ends and leave riders in dicey circumstances.

Bus Travel Sacramento Regional Transit (⊕ www.sacrt.com) buses and light-rail vehicles serve the Sacramento area. The No. 30 DASH (Downtown Area Shuttle) bus links Old Sacramento, midtown, and Sutter's Fort.

Car Travel Assuming that traffic is not a factor, though it can be, Sacramento is a 90-minute drive from San Francisco (and a seven-hour drive from Los Angeles). Parking garages serve Old Sacramento and other tourist spots, but except on weekends street parking downtown can be difficult to find.

ESSENTIALS

Visitor Information Old Sacramento Visitor Information Center ✉ *1002 2nd St., at K St.* ☎ *916/442-7644* ⊕ *www.oldsacramento.com* ◷ *Daily 10–5.* **Old Sacramento Events Hotline** ☎ *916/558-3912.* **Sacramento Convention and Visitors Bureau** ✉ *1608 I St., Suite 600* ☎ *916/808-7777, 800/292-2334* ⊕ *www.discovergold.org.*

12

EXPLORING

California Automobile Museum. More than 150 vintage automobiles—including Model Ts, Hudsons, Studebakers, Pontiacs, and other bygone makes and models—are on display at this diverting museum that pays tribute to automotive history and car culture. A 1920s roadside café and garage exhibit re-creates the early days of motoring, and the friendly docents are ready to explain everything you see. The museum is near downtown and Old Sacramento, with ample free parking. ✉ 2200 Front St., 1 block off Broadway, Downtown ☎ 916/442–6802 ⊕ www.calautomuseum.org ✍ $8 ⊙ Daily 10–6, 3rd Thurs. of the month, 10–9.

California Museum. Some of the exhibits at this celebration of all things California are high-tech and interactive, but there are also scores of archival drawers that you can pull out to see the real artifacts of history and culture—from the California State Constitution to surfing magazines. Board a 1949 cross-country bus to view a video on immigration, visit a Chinese herb shop maintained by a holographic proprietor, or find familiar names inducted into the annually expanded California Hall of Fame. There's also a café that's open weekdays until 2:30 pm. ✉ 1020 O St., at 11th St., Downtown ☎ 916/653–7524 ⊕ www.californiamuseum.org ✍ $9 ⊙ Mon.–Sat. 10–5, Sun. noon–5.

The California State Railroad Museum is North America's most popular railroad museum.

🄲 **California State Railroad Museum.** Near what was once the terminus of the

Fodor's Choice transcontinental and Sacramento Valley railroads, this 100,000-square-

★ foot museum—the best of its kind in the region, if not the country—
has 21 locomotives and railroad cars on display along with dozens of
other exhibits. You can walk through a post-office car and peer into
cubbyholes and canvas mailbags, enter a sleeping car that simulates
the swaying on the roadbed and the flashing lights of a passing town
at night, or glimpse the inside of the first-class dining car. One thousand vintage toy trains constitute a much-heralded permanent exhibit,
and the "Last Spike" room is compelling. Kids have lots of fun here,
especially in the big play area upstairs. ⊠ *125 I St., at 2nd St., Old
Sacramento* ☎ *916/445–6645* ⊕ *www.csrmf.org* ⊡ *$9* ⊙ *Daily 10–5.*

★ **Capitol.** The lacy plasterwork of the Capitol's 120-foot-high rotunda has
the complexity and colors of a Fabergé egg. Underneath the gilded dome
are marble floors, glittering chandeliers, monumental staircases, reproductions of century-old state offices, and legislative chambers decorated
in the style of the 1890s (the Capitol was built in 1869). Guides conduct tours of the building and the 40-acre Capitol Park, which contains
a rose garden, an impressive display of camellias (Sacramento's city
flower), and the California Vietnam Veterans Memorial. ■TIP→ The
photogenic front of the building is best captured in late-afternoon light.
⊠ *Capitol Mall and 10th St., Downtown* ☎ *916/324–0333* ⊕ *www.
statecapitolmuseum.com* ⊡ *Free* ⊙ *Daily 9–5; tours hourly 10–4.*

🄲 **Central Pacific Railroad Passenger Station.** At this reconstructed 1876 depot
there's rolling stock to admire, a typical waiting room, and a small
restaurant. On weekends April through September, and for special

occasions October through December, a train ($10) departs hourly from the freight depot, south of the passenger station, making a 40-minute out-and-back trip between the Sacramento River and, less interestingly, Interstate 5. ✉ *930 Front St., at J St., Old Sacramento* ☎ *916/445–6645* 🎫 *$4, free with same-day ticket from California State Railroad Museum* 🕓 *Daily 10–4.*

★ **Crocker Art Museum.** The oldest art museum in the American West has a collection of art from Europe, Asia, and California, including *Sunday Morning in the Mines* (1872), a large canvas by Charles Christian Nahl depicting aspects of the original mining industry, and the magnificent *Great Canyon of the Sierra, Yosemite* (1871), by Thomas Hill. An expansion completed in 2010 tripled the Crocker's size; it now rivals San Francisco's best art museums in scope if not quite in permanent collections. ✉ *216 O St., at 3rd St., Downtown* ☎ *916/808–7000* 🌐 *www.crockerartmuseum.org* 🎫 *$10* 🕓 *Tues., Wed. 10–5, and Fri.–Sun.; Thurs. 10–9.*

★ **Governor's Mansion.** This 15-room house was built in 1877 and used by the state's chief executives from the early 1900s until 1967, when Ronald Reagan vacated it in favor of an upscale private residence. Many of the Italianate mansion's interior decorations were ordered from the Huntington, Hopkins & Co. hardware store, one of whose partners, Albert Gallatin, was the original occupant. Each of the seven marble fireplaces has a petticoat mirror that ladies strolled past to see if their slips were showing. State funding difficulties could lead to this site's closure or to diminished hours, so check before you visit. ✉ *1526 H St., at 16th St., Midtown* ☎ *916/323–3047* 🎫 *$5* 🕓 *Daily 10–5; tours hourly, last tour at 4.*

QUICK BITES

Tapa the World. As the name implies, this cozy bar and restaurant serves tapa—small plates of meats, seafood, chicken, and veggies shared at the table—daily from 11:30 am until midnight in the heart of midtown. [$] *Average main: $12* ✉ *2115 J St., near 21st St., Midtown* ☎ *916/442–4353* 🌐 *www.tapatheworld.com.*

Old Sacramento Schoolhouse Museum. Sacramento's first school welcomed students in August 1849 and closed permanently four months later. Five years passed before another public school opened. Today it's a kid-friendly attraction that shows what one-room schoolhouses were like in the California Central Valley and foothills in the late 1800s.

👶 **State Indian Museum.** Among the interesting displays at this well-organized museum a few strides from Sutter's Fort is one devoted to Ishi, the last Yahi Indian to emerge from the mountains, in 1911. Ishi provided scientists with insight into the traditions and culture of this group of Native Americans. Arts-and-crafts exhibits, a demonstration village, and an evocative 10-minute video bring to life the multifaceted past and present of California's native peoples. ✉ *2618 K St., at 27th St.* ☎ *916/324–0971* 🌐 *www.parks.ca.gov* 🎫 *$3* 🕓 *Daily 10–5.*

👶 ★ **Sutter's Fort.** German-born Swiss immigrant John Augustus Sutter founded Sacramento's earliest Euro-American settlement in 1839. Audio speakers give information at each stop along a self-guided tour that includes a blacksmith's shop, bakery, prison, living quarters, and livestock areas. Costumed docents sometimes reenact fort life, demonstrating crafts, food preparation, and firearms maintenance. ✉ *2701 L St., at 27th St., Midtown* ☎ *916/445–4422* 🌐 *www.parks.ca.gov* 🎟 *$5 most days, $7 on interpretive program days* ⏲ *Tues.–Sun. 10–5.*

WHERE TO EAT

$$$ ITALIAN Fodor's Choice ★ 🍴 **Biba.** Owner Biba Caggiano is a nationally recognized authority on Italian cuisine. The Capitol crowd flocks here for homemade ravioli, osso buco, grilled pork loin, and veal and rabbit specials. A pianist adds to the upscale ambience nightly. [$] *Average main: $28* ✉ *2801 Capitol Ave., at 28th St., Midtown* ☎ *916/455–2422* 🌐 *www.biba-restaurant.com* ✍ *Reservations essential* ⏲ *Closed Sun. No lunch Mon. or Sat.*

$ MEXICAN 🍴 **Ernesto's Mexican Food.** Customers wait up to an hour for a table on Friday and Saturday evenings at this popular restaurant. Fresh ingredients are stressed in the wide selection of entrées, and the margaritas are especially refreshing. Sister restaurant **Zocalo** (✉ *1801 Capitol Ave.,* ☎ *916/441–0303*) has a striking indoor-outdoor atmosphere and is a popular launching spot for nights out on the town. [$] *Average main: $14* ✉ *1901 16th St., at S St., Midtown* ☎ *916/441–5850* 🌐 *www.ernestosmexicanfood.com.*

$$$$ AMERICAN Fodor's Choice ★ 🍴 **The Firehouse.** Consistently ranked by local publications as one of the city's top restaurants, this formal and historic restaurant has a full bar, courtyard seating (its signature attraction), and creative American cooking, such as char-grilled spring rack of lamb served with roasted French fingerling potatoes and baby artichoke and fava bean succotash. Visitors who can afford to treat themselves to a fine and leisurely meal can do no better in Old Sacramento—although they might also opt for the less-pricey **Ten 22.** Located a block away and under the same ownership as the Firehouse, it serves pizza and other fancified comfort food. [$] *Average main: $36* ✉ *1112 2nd St., at L St., Old Sacramento* ☎ *916/442–4772* 🌐 *www.firehouseoldsac.com* ⏲ *No lunch Sat.*

$ ECLECTIC 🍴 **The Park Downtown.** Atmosphere is what it's all about at this complex of sophisticated eateries across from Capitol Park. Ma Jong's Asian Diner has inexpensive fare, some suitable for vegetarians; the indoor-outdoor Park Lounge is a supermodern bar and dance club; and the Park To Go puts a classy spin on breakfasts and lunches for people to take away. [$] *Average main: $12* ✉ *1116 15th St., at L St., Downtown* ☎ *916/492–1960* 🌐 *www.theparkdowntown.com.*

WHERE TO STAY

For expanded reviews, facilities, and current deals, visit Fodors.com.

$$ B&B/INN ★ 🏨 **Amber House Bed & Breakfast Inn.** This B&B about a mile from the Capitol encompasses two homes: the original house is a Craftsman-style home with five bedrooms, and the second is an 1897 Dutch colonial–revival home. **Pros:** midtown location; attentive service. **Cons:** a few blocks' walk from midtown's main drags. **TripAdvisor:** "bliss," "wonderful getaway," "amazing anniversary trip." [$] *Rooms from: $169* ✉ *1315 22nd St., Midtown* ☎ *916/444–8085, 800/755–6526* 🌐 *www.amberhouse.com* 🛏 *10 rooms* 🍽 *Breakfast.*

$$$ HOTEL 🏨 **Citizen Hotel.** Billed as Sacramento's first luxury boutique hotel, the Citizen makes its home in the 1926 Cal Western Life building. **Pros:** all the modern amenities with older-world charms; within easy walking distance of the Capitol and other downtown attractions. **Cons:** pricey; smallish bathrooms. **TripAdvisor:** "lovely older hotel," "lots of character and service," "charming." [$] *Rooms from: $189* ✉ *926 J St., Downtown* ☎ *916/447–4460* 🌐 *www.jdvhotels.com* 🛏 *175 rooms, 23 suites* 🍴 *Breakfast.*

$$ HOTEL 🏨 **Delta King.** The best staterooms of this grand old riverboat, now permanently moored on Old Sacramento's waterfront, are on the river side toward the back. **Pros:** intimate; many historic sights nearby; creaky floors add to ambience. **Cons:** area can be dull at night; amenities aren't very modern; creaky floors. **TripAdvisor:** "quirky," "cute room," "an enjoyable stay." [$] *Rooms from: $172* ✉ *1000 Front St., Old Sacramento* ☎ *916/444–5464, 800/825–5464* 🌐 *www.deltaking.com* 🛏 *44 rooms* 🍴 *Breakfast.*

$$$ HOTEL ★ 🏨 **Hyatt Regency Sacramento.** With a marble-and-glass lobby and luxurious rooms, this hotel across from the Capitol and adjacent to the convention center is arguably Sacramento's finest. **Pros:** beautiful Capitol Park is across the street; some rooms have small balconies. **Cons:** nearby streets can be dodgy at night; somewhat impersonal. **TripAdvisor:** "business or pleasure," "beautiful view," "great staff." [$] *Rooms from: $195* ✉ *1209 L St., Downtown* ☎ *916/443–1234, 800/633–7313* 🌐 *www.hyatt.com* 🛏 *500 rooms, 24 suites.*

NIGHTLIFE AND THE ARTS

NIGHTLIFE

Blue Cue. A billiard lounge known for its large selection of single-malt scotches, the Blue Cue is upstairs from the popular Mexican restaurant Centro. ✉ *1004 28th St., at J St., Midtown* ☎ *916/441–6810* 🌐 *www.bluecue.com.*

Fox and Goose. This casual pub with live music is a big draw for weekend breakfasts. Traditional pub food (fish-and-chips, Cornish pasties) is served on weekday evenings until 9:30. ✉ *1001 R St., at 10th St., Downtown* ☎ *916/443–8825* 🌐 *www.foxandgoose.com.*

Harlow's. Harlow's draws a young crowd to its art-deco bar-nightclub for live music after 9 pm. ✉ *2708 J St., at 27th St., Midtown* ☎ *916/441–4693* 🌐 *www.harlows.com.*

Streets of London Pub. A favorite among Anglophiles, Streets is open after midnight every night. ✉ *1804 J St., at 18th St., Midtown* ☎ *916/498–1388* 🌐 *streetsoflondon.net.*

THE ARTS

California Musical Theatre. The California Musical Theatre presents Broadway shows at the Sacramento Community Center Theater. The group presents its summer Music Circus offerings (think *Fiddler, Grease*) at the spacious Wells Fargo Pavilion. ✉ *1419 H St., at 14th St., Downtown* ☎ *916/557–1999* 🌐 *www.calmt.com.*

Crest Theatre. The art-deco Crest is a beloved venue for classic and art-house films, along with concerts and other cultural events. ✉ *1013 K St., at 10th St., Downtown* ☎ *916/442–7378* 🌐 *www.thecrest.com.*

12

Sacramento Box Office. Tickets to major comedy, music, theater, and other cultural and sports events are sold through this online vendor. ⊠ *Downtown, Sacramento* ☏ *888/546–8561* ⊕ *sacramentoboxoffice.com.*

SHOPPING

Greater Sacramento is filled with shops you've heard of. To try something new, wander through Midtown, especially J, K, and L streets between 16th and 26th streets.

The Galleria at Roseville. The Sacramento region's largest shopping complex is a sprawling, heavily trafficked collection of chain stores and restaurants. It's always jumping. ⊠ *1151 Galleria Blvd., north of Sacramento off I–80 Exit 105A, Roseville* ⊕ *www.westfield.com/galleriaatroseville.*

Scout Living. The members of this collective are specialists in home accessories and antique, vintage, and modern furniture. Even if you're not looking to redecorate, the shop's a wonder to walk through. ⊠ *1215 18th St., at L St. Capitol Mall Alley, Sacramento* ☏ *916/594–7971,* ⊕ *www.scoutliving.com.*

WOODLAND

20 miles northwest of Sacramento on I–5.

In its heyday, Woodland was among California's wealthiest cities. Established by gold seekers and entrepreneurs, it later became an agricultural gold mine. The legacy of the old land barons can be seen in the restored Victorian and Craftsman architecture downtown; the best examples can be found south of Main Street on College, Elm, 1st, and 2nd streets. Budget cuts have led to extremely reduced hours for the Yolo Historical Museum (⊕ *www.gibsonhouse.org*) and the 1896 Woodland Opera House (⊕ *www.woodlandoperahouse.org*), so the town's undisputed top attraction is the delightful Heidrick Ag History Center.

GETTING HERE AND AROUND

Yolobus (⊕ *www.yolobus.com*) serves downtown Woodland from Sacramento, though most visitors arrive by car.

ESSENTIALS

Visitor Information Woodland Chamber of Commerce ⊠ *307 1st St., at Dead Cat Alley* ☏ *530/662–7327* ⊕ *www.woodlandchamber.org.*

EXPLORING

☾ **Heidrick Ag History Center Tractor & Truck Museum.** This gigantic space
★ provides a marvelous overview of the entire history of motorized agricultural vehicles. Souped-up and shiny, the antique threshers, harvesters, combines, tractors, and proto-tractors on display here look ready to service the farms of their eras all over again. And there's more. A separate wing surveys the evolution of the truck, with an emphasis on ones used for farm work. ⊠ *1962 Hays La., off County Rd. 102* ☏ *530/666–9700* ⊕ *www.aghistory.org* ⊡ *$8* ⊘ *Mid-Mar.–early Nov., Wed.–Sun. 10–5; early Nov.–mid-Mar., 10–4 daily.*

DAVIS

10 miles west of Sacramento on I–80.

Davis began as a rich agricultural area and remains one, but it doesn't feel like a cow town. It's home to the University of California at Davis, whose students hang at downtown cafés, galleries, and bookstores (most of the action takes place between 1st and 4th and C and G streets), lending the city a vaguely cosmopolitan feel.

GETTING HERE AND AROUND

Most people arrive here and tour by car. Yolobus (⊕ *www.yolobus.com*) serves Davis from Sacramento. Downtown is compact and walkable. Touring by bicycle is also an option—Davis is mostly flat.

ESSENTIALS

Visitor Information Davis Chamber of Commerce ⊠ *640 3rd St., at E St.* ☎ *530/756–5160* ⊕ *www.davischamber.com.*

EXPLORING

University of California Davis. A top research university, UC Davis educates many of Wine Country's vintners and grape growers. Campus tours depart from Buehler Alumni and Visitors Center. On a tour or not, worthy stops include the well-tended **Arboretum** (⊕ *arboretum. ucdavis.edu*)—this is a major agricultural school, and it shows—and the **Mondavi Center for the Performing Arts** (⊕ *www.mondaviarts.org*), a striking modern glass structure that books top-tier artists. ⊠ *Visitor Center, Alumni La.* ☎ *530/752–8111* ⊕ *visit.ucdavis.edu* ☉ *Visitor-center weekdays 8–5, Sat. 10–2; campus tours Sat. at 11:30.*

THE GOLD COUNTRY—SOUTH

This hilly region has an old-timey vibe. It's rich with antiques shops, quaint coffee shops, and delightfully appointed Victorian B&Bs.

PLACERVILLE

10 miles south of Coloma on Hwy. 49; 44 miles east of Sacramento on U.S. 50.

It's hard to imagine now, but in 1849 about 4,000 miners staked out every gully and hillside in Placerville, turning the town into a rip-roaring camp of log cabins, tents, and clapboard houses. The area was then known as Hangtown, a graphic allusion to the nature of frontier justice. It took on the name Placerville in 1854 and became an important supply center for the miners. ("Placer" is defined roughly as valuable minerals found in riverbeds or lakes.) Mark Hopkins, Philip Armour, and John Studebaker were among the industrialists who got their starts here.

GETTING HERE AND AROUND

Placerville is a 45-minute drive east of downtown Sacramento via U.S. 50. There is no public bus link worth mentioning. You'll need a car to get here and around.

EXPLORING

Apple Hill. During the fall harvest season (from September through December), the members of the Apple Hill Growers Association open their orchards and vineyards for apple and berry picking, picnicking, and wine and cider tasting. Many sell baked items and picnic food. At other times of the year, various roadside stands sell produce and other items. The association's website has a map you can download. ⚠ **Traffic on October weekends is often backed up.** ✉ *About 5 miles east of Hwy. 49; take Camino exit from U.S. 50* ☎ *530/644–7692* 🌐 *www.applehill.com.*

★ **Hangtown's Gold Bug Park & Mine.** Hangtown's Gold Bug Park & Mine, owned by the City of Placerville, centers on a fully lighted mine shaft open for self-guided touring. ■ **TIP→ An audio tour is included with admission and greatly enriches the experience. A shaded stream runs through the park, and there are picnic facilities.** ✉ *2635 Goldbug La., off Bedford Ave., 1 mile off U.S. 50* ☎ *530/642–5207* 🌐 *www.goldbugpark.org* 🎟 *$5* 🕒 *Apr.–Oct., daily 10–4; Nov.–Mar., weekends noon–4. Gift shop Apr.–Oct., daily 10–4.*

WHERE TO EAT AND STAY

$ VEGETARIAN 🍴 **The Cozmic Cafe.** Crowds convene here at any time of day for healthful wraps, burritos, sandwiches, salads, and the like, plus breakfasts (served anytime), smoothies, and coffee drinks. The portions are big, prices are low, and the ambience is distinctive. The eatery is in the 1859 Pearson's Soda Works Building and extends back into the side of a mountain, into what used to be a mineshaft. The live music here is among the best in the foothills, and an upstairs pub beckons with local wines and microbrews; unwind with yoga classes in the ballroom there before the evening's libations. [$] *Average main: $9* ✉ *594 Main St., at Bedford Ave.* ☎ *530/642–8481* 🌐 *www.ourcoz.com.*

$$ B&B/INN 🏨 **Seasons Bed & Breakfast.** A 10-minute walk from downtown, one of Placerville's oldest homes has been transformed into a lovely and relaxing oasis. **Pros:** quiet setting; attentive hosts; great breakfasts. **Cons:** B&B environment not for everyone. **TripAdvisor:** "beautiful escape," "top-notch service," "pampered beyond our wildest dreams." [$] *Rooms from: $135* ✉ *2934 Bedford Ave.* ☎ *530/626–4420* 🌐 *www.theseasons.net* 🛏 *1 room, 2 suites* 🍽 *Breakfast.*

SHENANDOAH VALLEY

20 miles south of Placerville on Shenandoah Rd., east of Hwy. 49.

The most concentrated Gold Country wine-touring area lies in the hills of the Shenandoah Valley, east of Plymouth. Robust Zinfandel is the primary grape grown here, but vineyards also produce other varietals. Most wineries are open on weekend afternoons; several have shaded picnic areas, gift shops, and galleries or museums; all have tasting rooms. ■ **TIP→ This region is gaining steam as a less-congested alternative to the Napa Valley.**

Continued on page 490

EUREKA! CALIFORNIA'S GOLD RUSH

When James W. Marshall burst into John Sutter's Mill on January 24, 1848, carrying flecks of gold in his hat, the millwright unleashed the glittering California gold rush with these immortal words:

 "Boys, I believe I've found a gold mine!"

Before it was over, drowsy San Francisco had become the boomtown of the Golden West, Columbia's mines alone yielded $87,000,000, and California's Mother Lode—a vein of gold-bearing quartz that stretched 150 miles across the Sierra Nevada foothills—had been nearly tapped dry. Even though the gold rush soon became the gold bust, today you can still strike it rich by visiting the historic sites where it all happened.

Journey down the Gold Country Highway—a serpentine, nearly 300-mi-long two-lane route appropriately numbered 49—to find pure vacation treasure: fascinating mother lode towns, rip-roaring mining camps, and historic strike sites. In fact, in Placerville—as the former Hangtown, this spot saw so much new money and crime that outlaws were hanged in pairs—you can still pan the streams. And after you've seen the sights, the prospects remain just as golden: the entire region is a trove of gorgeous wineries, fun eateries, and Victorian-era hotels.

by: Reed Parsell and Robert I.C. Fisher

ALL THAT GLITTERED: '49ER FEVER

From imagination springs adventure, and perhaps no event in the 19th century provoked more wild adventures than the California gold rush of 1848 to 1855.

James Marshall

1856 U.S. quarter

John Sutter

GOLD IN THEM THAR HILLS California's golden lava was discovered purely by accident. Upon finding his cattle ranch had gone to ruin while he was away fighting in the Mexican-American War, New Jersey native James W. Marshall decided to build a sawmill, with John Sutter, outside the town of Coloma, 40 miles upstream of Sutter's Fort on the American River. To better power the mill, he had a wider siphon created to divert the river water and, one morning, spotted golden flakes in the trench. Rich fur magnate Sutter tried to keep the mother strike quiet, but his own staff soon decamped to pan the streams and the secret was out. The gold rush's impact was so profound that, practically overnight, it catapulted San Francisco into one of the nation's—and the world's—wealthiest cities.

BROTHER, CAN YOU SPARE AN INGOT? After Marshall, 37 at the time, saw his fledgling mill abandoned by workers who went to pan the streams, he left Coloma for almost a decade. During the 1860s he made some money as a vintner there—a dicey profession for a reported alcoholic. Eventually Marshall's wine business dried up, and he returned to prospecting in the 1870s. But without success. For six years starting in 1872, the state Legislature gave him a small pension as an acknowledgment of his gold rush importance, but for the last years of his life he was practically penniless. He died on Aug. 10, 1885, at age 74.w

THE GOLD CRUSH Before the gold rush ended, in 1855, it is estimated that it drew 300,000 people—Americans, Europeans, and Chinese—to the Sierra Nevada foothills to seek their fortune. Sadly, accidents, disease, and skirmishes with Native Americans took their toll on both the prospectors and the environment. In addition, the gold lust of '49er fever left more than a thousand murders in its wake (not counting the infamous "suspended" sentences meted out at Hangtown).

BOOM TO BUST

Jan. 24, 1848: James W. Marshall spies specks of bright rock in the streambed at his sawmill's site; Sutter certifies they are gold.
May, 1848: California's coastal communities empty out as prospectors flock to the hills to join the "forty-eighters."
Aug. 19, 1848: The *New York Herald* is the first East Coast newspaper to report a gold rush in California.
Oct. 13, 1849: California's state constitution is approved in Monterey. The state's new motto becomes "Eureka!"
1855: The California gold rush effectively ends, as digging for the precious mineral becomes increasingly difficult, and large corporations monopolize mining operations.

DID YOU KNOW?

You can still pan the streams, but any shiny stuff will usually be worthless iron pyrite. Here a young prospector tries his hand at Marshall Gold Discovery State Park.

GOING FOR THE GOLD

Marshall Gold Discovery State Park

If you want to go prospecting for the best sightseeing treasures in Gold Country, just follow this map.

Coloma

Empire Mine State Historic Park, Grass Valley: During the century that it was operating, Empire Mine produced some 5.6 million ounces of gold. More than 350 miles of tunnels were dug, most under water. Operations ceased in 1956, but today visitors to the 800-acre park can go on 50-minute guided tours of the mines and enjoy great hiking trails and picnic spots.

Marshall Gold Discovery State Historic Park, Coloma: Here's where it all began—a can't-miss gold rush site. See the stone cairn that marks the spot of James Marshall's discovery, the huge statue of him that rests on his grave site, and visit—together with crowds of schoolchildren—the updated museum, and more.

Hangtown's Gold Bug Park & Mine, Placerville: Put on a hardhat and step into the 19th century at Gold Bug, located a few miles south of Marshall's jackpot site. Take a self-guided audio tour of a mine that opened in 1888, or a special tour of a mine opened in the 1850s, and do some "placering" (panning for gold) yourself, outside the gift shop. "Fool's gold" (used for billiard tables and chalkboards) was mostly found here before digging stopped in 1942.

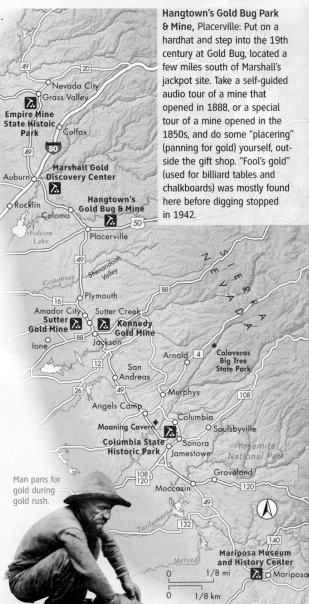
Man pans for gold during gold rush.

Empire Mine State Historic Park　　　　Gold sifting pan　　　　Columbia State Historic Park

Sutter Gold Mine: Between Amador City and Sutter Creek off Highway 49, this is the place to see how the so-called "Forty-Niner" individual prospectors were succeeded by large, deep-pocket mining companies. One-hour tours, offered daily April through most of October, take visitors deep into a hard-rock mine, where they can see ore veins that contain gold and learn the basics of hydraulic extraction.

Kennedy Gold Mine, Jackson: At 5,912 feet below ground, this is one of the world's deepest mines. Its head frame is one of the most dominant man-made sights along Highway 49's 295 miles. In operation from 1880 until World War II, the mine produced tens of millions of dollars of gold. One-hour tours, offered weekends and holidays from March through October, include a look inside the stately Mine Office.

Columbia State Historic Park. Just north of Sonora, this is the best extant example of a gold rush-era town as it appeared in the mid-19th century. During its "golden" years, Columbia yielded more than $85 million in gold. Since World War II, the town has been restored. Fandango halls, Wells Fargo stage coaches, and a costumed staff bring a working 1850's mining town to life again.

Gold dollars

Mariposa Museum and History Center, Mariposa: Find all sorts of mining equipment, including a five-stamp ore mill, at this modest museum in the gold rush region's southernmost area. Also here is the fascinating California State Mining and Mineral Museum, home to a famous 13-pound golden nugget.

A PROSPECTING PRIMER

Grab any non-Teflon-coated pan with sloping sides and head up to "them thar hills." Find a stream—preferably one containing black sand—you can stoop beside, and then:

■ Scoop out sediment to fill your pan.

■ Add water, then gently shake the pan sideways, back and forth. This allows any gold to settle at the bottom.

■ Pick out and toss away any larger rocks.

■ Keep adding water, keep shaking the pan, and slowly pour the loosened waste gravel over the rim of the pan, making sure not to upend the pan while doing so.

■ If you're left with gold, yell "Eureka!" then put it in a glass container. Your findings may not make you rich, but will entitle you to bragging rights for as long as you keep the gold handy to show friends.

■TIP→ If you'd rather not pan on your own, plenty of attractions and museums in the Gold Country will let you try your hand at prospecting. See listings in this chapter for more details on these historic sites.

Columbia State Historic Park

GETTING HERE AND AROUND

Reach the Shenandoah Valley by turning east on Fiddletown Road in Plymouth, between Placerville and Sutter Creek. You will need a car to explore the valley and its vineyards.

EXPLORING

Charles Spinetta Winery. Here, you can see a wildlife art gallery in addition to tasting the wine. The Zinfandel and Syrah are popular. ✉ *12557 Steiner Rd., off Shenandoah Rd.* ☎ *209/245–3384* 🌐 *www.charlesspinettawinery.com* 🕓 *Mon., Thurs., and Fri. 8–4; weekends 9–5.*

Shenandoah Vineyards. The gallery at this Sobon-affiliated winery (one of the valley's original four) displays contemporary art, and sells pottery, framed photographs, and souvenirs. ✉ *12300 Steiner Rd.* ☎ *209/245–4455* 🌐 *www.sobonwine.com* 🕓 *Daily 10–5.*

Sobon Estate. Exhibits in the winery's Shenandoah Valley Museum illustrate pioneer life and wine making in the valley. The family-owned business is listed as a California State Historic Landmark. ✉ *14430 Shenandoah Rd., east of Ostrom Rd.* ☎ *209/245–4455* 🌐 *www.sobonwine.com* 🕓 *Daily 9:30–5.*

AMADOR CITY

6 miles south of Plymouth on Hwy. 49.

The history of tiny Amador City mirrors the boom-bust-boom cycle of many Gold Country towns. With an output of $42 million in gold, its Keystone Mine was one of the most productive in the Mother Lode. After all the gold was extracted, the miners cleared out, and the area suffered. Amador City now derives its wealth from tourists, who come to browse through its antiques and specialty shops, most of them on or just off Highway 49.

GETTING HERE AND AROUND

Park where you can along Old Highway 49 (a bypass diverts Highway 49 traffic around Sutter Creek and Amador City), and walk around this blink-and-you'll-miss-it town.

WHERE TO STAY

For expanded reviews, facilities, and current deals, visit Fodors.com.

$ B&B/INN ★ 🏨 **Imperial Hotel.** The whimsically decorated mock-Victorian rooms at this 1879 hotel give a modern twist to the excesses of the era; the antique furnishings include iron-and-brass beds, gingerbread flourishes, and, in one room, art-deco appointments. **Pros:** comfortable; good restaurant and bar; tiny-town charm. **Cons:** the town's got no nightlife. **TripAdvisor:** "dinner is first class," "take a step back in time," "charming." [$] *Rooms from: $120* ✉ *14202 Old Hwy. 49* ☎ *209/267–9172* 🌐 *www.imperialamador.com* 🛏 *6 rooms, 3 suites* 🍴 *Breakfast.*

12

SUTTER CREEK

★ *2 miles south of Amador City on Hwy. 49.*

Sutter Creek is a charming conglomeration of balconied buildings, Victorian homes, and neo–New England structures. The stores on Main Street (formerly part of busy Highway 49, which was rerouted around town) are worth visiting for works by the many local artists and craftspeople.

GETTING HERE AND AROUND

There are no public transportation options here, but Sutter Creek is very walkable once you've found a parking spot.

EXPLORING

Monteverde Store Museum. This store, opened 1896, is a relic from the past. Forty years ago, its final owner walked out without telling a soul and never returned, but you can still visit everything he left behind on the shelves including typical wares from the turn of the 20th century, an elaborate antique scale, and a chair-encircled potbellied stove in the corner. The store is open Thursday through Monday provided there are volunteers available. ✉ *3 Randolph St.* ☎ *209/267–0493.*

Sutter Creek Visitor Center. The visitor center organizes walking tours and has a helpful website. ✉ *71A Main St.* ☎ *209/267–1344, 800/400–0305* 🌐 *www.suttercreek.org.*

WHERE TO EAT AND STAY

$$ AMERICAN 🍴 **Susan's Place.** Fresh produce, prompt and attentive service, and a lovely patio (especially so on warm summer evenings) distinguish this local favorite a half block off the main drag. The serving of wine is a big deal here; there's even a "mystery wine" option that leaves the bottle (or glass) choice up to the owner. Try the eggplant and Portobello mushrooms on grilled panini bread. [$] *Average main: $16* ✉ *15 Eureka St.* ☎ *209/267–0945* 🕒 *Closed Mon.–Wed.*

$$ B&B/INN ★ 🏨 **Eureka Street Inn.** The lead- and stained-glass windows and the original redwood paneling, wainscoting, and beams—and, oh yes, those gas-log fireplaces in most rooms—lend the Eureka Street Inn a cozy feel. **Pros:** quiet location; lovely porch; engaging owners; WiFi; large private bathrooms. **Cons:** only four rooms. **TripAdvisor:** "friendly and relaxing," "pleasant experience," "incredibly fantastic." [$] *Rooms from: $125* ✉ *55 Eureka St.* ☎ *209/267–5500, 800/399–2389* 🌐 *www.eurekastreetinn.com* 🛏 *4 rooms* 🍽 *Breakfast.*

$$ B&B/INN ★ 🏨 **The Foxes Inn of Sutter Creek.** The rooms in this 1857 white-clapboard house are handsome, with high ceilings, antique beds, and armoires; five have gas fireplaces. **Pros:** lovely inside and out; friendly owners. **Cons:** pricey. **TripAdvisor:** "best bed and breakfast," "so close and so good," "absolutely fabulous." [$] *Rooms from: $160* ✉ *77 Main St.* ☎ *209/267–5882, 800/987–3344* 🌐 *www.foxesinn.com* 🛏 *5 rooms, 2 suites* 🍽 *Breakfast.*

$ HOTEL 🏨 **Sutter Creek Days Inn.** If you're on a budget, this hotel is a good choice; the rooms have coffeemakers, and most have queen-size beds. **Pros:** affordable; convenient; clean. **Cons:** can feel a bit impersonal. **TripAdvisor:** "simple but friendly," "clean and presentable," "well situated."

§ *Rooms from: $89* ✉ *271 Hanford St.* ☎ *209/267–9177* ⊕ *www.daysinn.com/suttercreek* ↝ *52 rooms* ⦿| *Breakfast.*

JACKSON

8 miles south of Sutter Creek on Hwy. 49.

Jackson wasn't the Gold Country's rowdiest town, but the party lasted longer here than most anywhere else: "girls' dormitories" (aka brothels) and nickel slot machines flourished until the mid-1950s. Jackson also had the world's deepest and richest gold mines, the Kennedy and the Argonaut, which together produced $70 million in gold. These were deep-rock mines with tunnels extending as much as a mile underground. Most of the miners who worked the lode were of Serbian or Italian origin, and they gave the town a European character that persists to this day. Jackson has pioneer cemeteries whose headstones tell the stories of local Serbian and Italian families.

GETTING HERE AND AROUND
Arrive here via automobile on Highway 49. You'll need a car to see Jackson and the nearby sites.

EXPLORING
St. Sava Serbian Orthodox Church. The terraced cemetery on the grounds of the handsome church is the town's most impressive burial grounds. ✉ *724 N. Main St.*

WHERE TO EAT
$ ✕ **Mel and Faye's Diner.** For more than a half-century this roadside (loom-
AMERICAN ing over Highway 49 on a small hill) diner has been a local hangout, with its signature "Moo Burger" (so big it still makes cow sounds, presumably). Mel and Faye's son now runs the business and has supplemented the menu with slightly more sophisticated fare for breakfast, lunch, and dinner. § *Average main: $10* ✉ *31 Main St.* ☎ *209/223–0853* ⊕ *melandfayesdiner.com* ⊘ *Closed Tues. No dinner.*

ANGELS CAMP

20 miles south of Jackson on Hwy. 49.

Angels Camp is famous chiefly for its May jumping-frog contest, based on Mark Twain's short story "The Celebrated Jumping Frog of Calaveras County." The writer reputedly heard the story of the jumping frog from Ross Coon, proprietor of Angels Hotel, which has been in operation since 1856.

GETTING HERE AND AROUND
Angels Camp is at the intersection of Highway 49 and Highway 4, which from here heads northeast past Murphys up into the Sierra Nevada. You'll need a car to get here and around.

EXPLORING
Angels Camp Museum. Here you'll find gold-rush relics, including photos, rocks, petrified wood, old blacksmith and mining equipment, and a horse-drawn hearse. The carriage house out back holds 31 carriages and an impressive display of mineral specimens. ✉ *753 S. Main St.*

12

209/736–2963 ⊕ *www.angelscampmuseumfoundation.org* $5
⊙ *Jan. and Feb., weekends 10–4; Mar.–Dec., daily 10–4.*

Ⓒ **California Cavern.** A ½-mile subterranean trail winds through large chambers and past underground streams and lakes. There aren't many steps to climb, but it's a strenuous walk with some narrow passageways and steep spots. The caverns, at a constant 55°F, contain crystalline formations not found elsewhere, and the 80-minute guided tour explains local history and geology. Call ahead to check on hours of operation, which are subject to change. ⊠ *9 miles east of San Andreas on Mountain Ranch Rd., then about 3 miles on Cave City Rd.* 209/736–2708 ⊕ *www.caverntours.com* $14.75 ⊙ *Mar. and Apr., daily 10–4; May–Oct., daily 10–5; Nov.–Feb. weekends 10–4.*

Ⓒ **Moaning Cavern.** A 235-step spiral staircase leads into this vast cavern. More adventurous sorts can rappel into the chamber—ropes and instruction are provided. Otherwise, the only way inside is via the 45-minute tour, during which you'll see giant (and still growing) stalactites and stalagmites and an archaeological site that holds some of the oldest human remains yet found in America (an unlucky person has fallen into the cavern about once every 130 years for the last 13,000 years). ■TIP➔ Caves are a great place to visit on rainy or especially hot days. Outside there are three zip lines, starting at $39 per person. ⊠ *5350 Moaning Cave Rd., off Parrots Ferry Rd., about 2 miles south of Vallecito* 209/736–2708 ⊕ *www.caverntours.com* $14.75 ⊙ *May–Oct., daily 9–6; Nov.–Apr., weekdays 10–5, weekends 9–5.*

Fodor'sChoice ★

MURPHYS

10 miles northeast of Angels Camp on Hwy. 4.

Murphys is a well-preserved town of white-picket fences, Victorian houses, and interesting shops that exhibits an upscale vibe, with its nearby wineries and free-spending Bay Area visitors. Horatio Alger and Ulysses S. Grant came through here, staying at Murphys Historic Hotel & Lodge when they, along with many other 19th-century tourists, came to see the giant sequoia groves in nearby Calaveras Big Trees State Park.

GETTING HERE AND AROUND

Although Murphys is 10 miles off Highway 49, the diversion on Highway 4 is worth it, as Murphys presents the Gold Country's most compact, orderly town, with enough shops and restaurants to keep most families busy for at least a half-day. You'll need to drive here, and parking can be a challenge on busy summer weekends.

EXPLORING

Calaveras Big Tree State Park. The Calavaras Big Tree State Park protects hundreds of the largest and rarest living things on the planet—magnificent giant sequoia redwood trees. Some are 3,000 years old, 90 feet around at the base, and 250 feet tall. There are campgrounds and picnic areas; swimming, wading, fishing, and sunbathing on the Stanislaus River are popular in summer. ⊠ *Off Hwy. 4, 15 miles northeast of Murphys, 4 miles northeast of Arnold, Angels Camp* 209/795–2334 ⊕ *www.parks.ca.gov/?page_id=551* $6 per vehicle day use; campsites

DID YOU KNOW?

A stately giant sequoia rises above it all at Calaveras Big Trees State Park, which pro-tects the northernmost grove of giant sequoias known to exist.

$20 ⏲ Park daily sunrise–sunset day use. Visitor center May–Oct., daily 11–3; Nov.–Apr., weekends 11–3.

Ironstone Vineyards. Tours take you through the spectacular gardens and into underground tunnels cooled by a waterfall from a natural spring, and include a performance on a massive automated pipe organ. ■ **TIP→ It's worth a visit even if you don't drink wine.** The winery schedules concerts during summer in its huge outdoor amphitheater, plus art shows and other events on weekends. On display is a 44-pound specimen of crystalline gold. Visit the deli for lunch. ✉ *From Jones St. in town, head south on Scott St., 1894 6 Mile Rd.* ☎ *209/728–1251* 🌐 *www.ironstonevineyards.com* ⏲ *Daily 10–5; open until 6 in summer.*

WHERE TO EAT AND STAY

$$ AMERICAN 🍴 **Grounds.** Light entrées, grilled vegetables, chicken, seafood, and steak are the specialties at this bustling bistro and coffee shop. Sandwiches, salads, and homemade soups are served for lunch. The crowd is friendly and the service attentive. [$] *Average main: $18* ✉ *402 Main St.* ☎ *209/728–8663* 🌐 *www.groundsrestaurant.com* ⏲ *No dinner Mon.–Tues.*

$ HOTEL 🏨 **Murphys Historic Hotel & Lodge.** This 1855 stone hotel, whose register has seen the signatures of Mark Twain and the bandit Black Bart, figured in Bret Harte's short story "A Night at Wingdam." **Pros:** historical ambience; great bar; in the middle of downtown. **Cons:** dated; creaky. **TripAdvisor:** "historic and fun," "quaint and convenient," "homey." [$] *Rooms from: $109* ✉ *457 Main St.* ☎ *209/728–3444, 800/532–7684* 🌐 *www.murphyshotel.com* 🛏 *29 rooms, 20 with bath.*

COLUMBIA

14 miles south of Angels Camp via Hwy. 49 to Parrots Ferry Rd.

Columbia is the gateway for Columbia State Historic Park, which is one of the Gold Country's most visited sites.

GETTING HERE AND AROUND

The only way to get here is by private automobile. Consider bringing picnic supplies, as there are several inviting spots within and around the town.

EXPLORING

👶 Fodor's Choice ★ **Columbia State Historic Park.** Though definitely showing wear from state budget cuts, Columbia comes as close to a gold-rush town in its heyday as any site in the Gold Country. Usually, you can ride a stagecoach, pan for gold, and watch a blacksmith working at an anvil. Street musicians perform in summer. Restored or reconstructed buildings include a Wells Fargo Express office, a Masonic temple, stores, saloons, two hotels, a firehouse, churches, a school, and a newspaper office. At times, all are staffed to simulate a working 1850s town. The park also includes the **Historic Fallon House Theater,** where entertainment is presented much of the year. The town's two 19th-century historic lodgings, the Fallon Hotel ($) and City Hotel ($–$$) recently reopened; find out more at 🌐 *www.cityhotel.com.* ✉ *11175 Washington St.* ☎ *209/532–0150* 🌐 *www.parks.ca.gov/?page_id=552* 🎟 *Free* ⏲ *Daily 9–5.*

SONORA

4 miles south of Columbia via Parrots Ferry Rd. to Hwy. 49.

Miners from Mexico founded Sonora and made it the biggest town in the Mother Lode. Following a period of racial and ethnic strife, the Mexican settlers moved on, and Yankees built the commercial city that is visible today. Sonora's historic downtown section sits atop the Big Bonanza Mine, one of the richest in the state. Another mine, on the site of nearby Sonora High School, yielded 990 pounds of gold in a single week in 1879. Reminders of the gold rush are everywhere in Sonora, in prim Victorian houses, typical Sierra-stone storefronts, and awning-shaded sidewalks. Reality intrudes beyond the town's historic heart, with strip malls, shopping centers, and modern motels.

GETTING HERE AND AROUND

Sonora represents a bit of a parking challenge, what with its busy main drag (Washington Street, which is Highway 49) and its narrow, often very steep side roads.

EXPLORING

Tuolumne County Museum and History Center. The small museum occupies a historic gold rush–era building that served as a jail until 1960. Vintage firearms and paraphernalia, gold specimens, and MiWuk baskets are among the many artifacts on display. ⊠ *158 W. Bradford St., at Lower Sunset Dr.* ☎ *209/532–1317* ⊕ *www.tchistory.org* ⊠ *Free* ☉ *Weekdays 10–4, Sat. 10–3:30.*

WHERE TO EAT AND STAY

$ ✕ **Diamondback Grill and Wine Bar.** The bright decor and refined atmo-
AMERICAN   sphere suggest more ambitious fare, but burgers are what this place is about. Locals crowd the tables, especially after 6 pm, for the ground-meat patties, beer-battered onion rings, veggie burger, and fine wines. $ *Average main: $11* ⊠ *93 S. Washington St., at Linoberg St.* ☎ *209/532–6661* ⊕ *www.thediamondbackgrill.com* ☉ *Closed Sun.*

$$ ⊡ **Barretta Gardens Bed and Breakfast Inn.** This inn is perfect for a roman-
B&B/INN   tic getaway, with elegant Victorian rooms varying in size, all furnished with period pieces. **Pros:** lovely grounds; yummy breakfasts; romantic. **Cons:** only seven rooms. **TripAdvisor:** "ultimate B&B," "cozy and charming," "great ambience." $ *Rooms from: $155* ⊠ *700 S. Barretta St.* ☎ *209/532–6039, 800/206–3333* ⊕ *www.barrettagardens.com* ➷ *7 rooms* ⊙l *Breakfast.*

JAMESTOWN

4 miles south of Sonora on Hwy. 49.

Compact Jamestown supplies a touristy view of gold rush–era life. Shops in brightly colored buildings along Main Street sell antiques and gift items. You can try your hand at panning for gold here or, if state budget cuts haven't forced its complete closure, visit Railtown 1897 (⊕ *www.railtown1897.org*), the local (mostly) outdoor railroad museum.

12

GETTING HERE AND AROUND

Jamestown is a car town. Highway 108 bisects the town east–west.

EXPLORING

🪙 **Gold Prospecting Adventures.** You'll get a real feel (sort of) for the life of a prospector on the three-hour gold-panning excursions led by this outfit's congenial, steeped-in-history tour guides. You might even strike gold (people do) at the Jimtown Mine, and though it probably won't even cover your costs, you're likely to enjoy the experience, especially if traveling with kids. ✉ *18170 Main St.* ☎ *209/984–4653, 800/596–0009* ⊕ *www.goldprospecting.com.*

WHERE TO STAY

For expanded reviews, facilities, and current deals, visit Fodors.com.

$$
HOTEL
⛳ **National Hotel.** The National has been in business since 1859, and the furnishings—brass beds, regal comforters, and lace curtains—are authentic but not overly embellished. **Pros:** wonderful historic feel; great brunches—especially the crepes. **Cons:** only nine rooms. **TripAdvisor:** "beautiful stay," "food is fantastic," "this place is a gem." 🟊 *Rooms from: $140* ✉ *18183 Main St.* ☎ *209/984–3446, 800/894–3446 in CA* ⊕ *www.national-hotel.com* 🛏 *9 rooms* ⧄ *Breakfast.*

MARIPOSA

50 miles south of Jamestown on Hwy. 49.

Mariposa marks the southern end of the Mother Lode. Much of the land in this area was part of a 44,000-acre land grant Colonel John C. Fremont acquired from Mexico before gold was discovered and California became a state.

GETTING HERE AND AROUND

Many people stop here on the way to Yosemite National Park, about an hour's drive east on Highway 140. YARTS (⊕ *www.yarts.com*), the regional transit system, is a cheap and dependable way to travel among Merced (off the Central Valley's busy Highway 99), Mariposa, and Yosemite Valley. YARTS partners with Amtrak so that riders on the Central Valley's San Joaquin line can detrain in Merced and catch a bus right at the train station. Otherwise, you'll need a car to get here.

WHERE TO EAT AND STAY

$$$
AMERICAN
✕ **Charles Street Dinner House.** Ever since Ed Uebner moved here from Chicago to become the owner-chef in 1980, Charles Street has been firmly established as the classiest dinner joint in town—plus, it's centrally located. The extensive menu includes beef, chicken, pork, lamb, duck, and lobster; recently a few vegetarian options were added. 🟊 *Average main: $25* ✉ *Hwy. 140 and 7th St.* ☎ *209/966–2366* ⊕ *www.charlesstreetdinnerhouse.com* ⊘ *No lunch.*

$
B&B/INN
⛳ **Little Valley Inn.** Historical photos and old mining tools add a little charm to this modern lodging, located about 7 miles south of Mariposa. **Pros:** quiet; comfortable; small. **Cons:** about an hour from Yosemite National Park. **TripAdvisor:** "nice comfortable stay," "charming rooms," "a mountain of hospitality." 🟊 *Rooms from: $115* ✉ *3483*

Brooks Rd., off Hwy. 49 ☎ *209/742–6204, 800/889–5444* 🌐 *www.littlevalley.com* 🛏 *6 cabins, 1 suite* 🍴 *Breakfast.*

THE GOLD COUNTRY—NORTH

Gold has had a significant presence along this northern stretch of Highway 49, whose highlights include the bucolic Empire State Historic Park and Coloma, where the discovery of a few nuggets triggered the gold rush.

COLOMA

8 miles northwest of Placerville on Hwy. 49.

The California gold rush started in Coloma. "My eye was caught with the glimpse of something shining in the bottom of the ditch," James Marshall recalled. Marshall himself never found any more "color," as gold came to be called.

GETTING HERE AND AROUND

The only practical way to get here is by car. Once you've parked, it's easy enough to walk about town and see all the worthwhile sites.

EXPLORING

★ **Marshall Gold Discovery State Historic Park.** Most of Coloma lies within the historic park. Though crowded with tourists in summer, Coloma hardly resembles the mob scene it was in 1849, when 2,000 prospectors staked out claims along the streambed. The town's population grew to 4,000, supporting seven hotels, three banks, and many stores and businesses. But when reserves of the precious metal dwindled, prospectors left as quickly as they had come. A working reproduction of an 1840s mill lies near the spot where James Marshall first saw gold. A trail leads to a sign marking his discovery. **■ TIP→ The museum is not as interesting as the outdoor exhibits.** ✉ *310 Back St., off Hwy. 49* ☎ *530/622–3470* 🌐 *www.parks.ca.gov/?page_id=484* 🎟 *$5 per vehicle, day use* 🕑 *Park daily 8–sunset. Museum daily 10–3.*

WHERE TO STAY

For expanded reviews, facilities, and current deals, visit Fodors.com.

$$ B&B/INN 🏨 **Coloma Country Inn.** Four of the rooms at this B&B on 2½ acres in the state historic park are inside an 1850s farmhouse, and two suites with kitchenettes occupy the carriage house. **Pros:** convenient to the park; quiet; leisurely ambience. **Cons:** no nightlife. **TripAdvisor:** "charming accommodations," "beautiful grounds," "pleasant and relaxing getaway." [$] *Rooms from: $125* ✉ *345 High St.* ☎ *530/622–6919* 🌐 *www.colomacountryinn.com* 🛏 *4 rooms, 2 suites* 🍴 *Breakfast.*

AUBURN

18 miles northwest of Coloma on Hwy. 49; 34 miles northeast of Sacramento on I–80.

Auburn is the Gold Country town most accessible to travelers on Interstate 80. An important transportation center during the gold rush,

Auburn has a small Old Town district with narrow climbing streets, cobblestone lanes, wooden sidewalks, and many original buildings. ■ **TIP→ Fresh produce, flowers, baked goods, and gifts are for sale at the farmers' market, held Saturday morning year-round.**

GETTING HERE AND AROUND

You can get here via Amtrak or Greyhound. Otherwise, count on driving and needing a car to see all other Gold Country attractions.

EXPLORING

Bernhard Museum Complex. Party like it's 1889 at this diverting complex, whose main structure opened in 1851 as the Traveler's Rest Hotel and for 100 years was the residence of the Bernhard family. The congenial docents, dressed in Victorian garb, describe the family's history and 19th-century life in Auburn. ✉ *291 Auburn–Folsom Rd., at Fairgate Rd.* ☎ *530/889–6500* 🎫 *Free* 🕒 *Tues.–Sun. 11–4.*

👶 **Gold Country Museum.** You'll get a feel for life in the mines at this museum whose highlights include a re-created mine tunnel, a gold-panning stream, and a reproduction saloon. ✉ *1273 High St., off Auburn–Folsom Rd.* ☎ *530/889–6500* 🎫 *Free to museum, $3 to pan for gold* 🕒 *Tues.–Sun. 11–4.*

Placer County Courthouse. Auburn's standout structure is the Placer County Courthouse. The classic gold-dome building houses the Placer County Museum, which documents the area's history—Native American, railroad, agricultural, and mining—from the early 1700s to 1900. ✉ *101 Maple St., at Lincoln Way* ☎ *530/889–6500* 🎫 *Free* 🕒 *Daily 10–4.*

WHERE TO EAT AND STAY

$ AMERICAN 🍴 **Awful Annie's.** Big patio umbrellas (and outdoor heaters when necessary) allow patrons to take in the Old Town view from this popular spot for lunch or breakfast—one specialty is a chili omelet. Find an Awful Annie's outlet in nearby Lincoln. [$] *Average main: $10* ✉ *160 Sacramento St., at Washington St.* ☎ *530/888–9857* 🌐 *www.awfulannies.com* 🕒 *No dinner.*

$$ ECLECTIC 🍴 **Latitudes.** Delicious multicultural cuisine is served in an 1870 Victorian. The menu (with monthly specials from diverse geographical regions) includes meat entrées prepared with the appropriate Mexican spices, curries, cheeses, or teriyaki sauce. Vegetarians and vegans have several inventive choices, including tofu and tempeh dishes. Sunday brunch is deservedly popular. [$] *Average main: $16* ✉ *130 Maple St., at Auburn-Folsom Rd.* ☎ *530/885–9535* 🌐 *www.latitudesrestaurant.com* 🕒 *Closed Mon. and Tues.*

$$ HOTEL 🏨 **Holiday Inn.** On a hill above the freeway across from Old Town, this hotel has a welcoming lobby and chain-standard but attractively furnished rooms. **Pros:** convenient; clean; large rooms. **Cons:** rooms near parking lot can be noisy. **TripAdvisor:** "on the way to Tahoe," "met expectations," "a nice friendly place." [$] *Rooms from: $124* ✉ *120 Grass Valley Hwy.* ☎ *530/887–8787, 800/814–8787* 🌐 *www.auburnhi.com* 🛏 *96 rooms, 6 suites.*

Almost 6 million ounces of gold were extracted from the Empire Mine.

GRASS VALLEY

24 miles north of Auburn on Hwy. 49.

More than half of California's total gold production was extracted from mines around Grass Valley, including the Empire Mine, which, along with the North Star Mining Museum, is among the Gold Country's most fascinating attractions.

GETTING HERE AND AROUND

Highway 20 arrives here from Interstate 5 to the west and Interstate 80 to the east; otherwise, you'll likely get here via Highway 49 from Placerville. Gold Country Stage vehicles (☎ 530/447–0103 ☺ *Weekdays 7–6*) serve some attractions here. Expect to wait, though.

EXPLORING

☺ **Empire Mine State Historic Park.** The hard-rock gold mine at Empire Mine
★ State Historic Park was one of California's richest. An estimated 5.8 million ounces were extracted from its 367 miles of underground passages between 1850 and 1956. On the 50-minute tours you can walk into a mine shaft, peer into the mine's deeper recesses, and view the owner's "cottage," which has exquisite woodwork. With its shaded picnic areas and gentle hiking trails, this is a pleasant place for families. ✉ *10791 E. Empire St., south of Empire St. exit of Hwy. 49* ☎ *530/273–8522* ⊕ *www.parks.ca.gov/?page_id=875* ☞ *$5* ☺ *May–Aug., daily 9–6; Sept.–Apr., daily 10–5. Tours May–Aug., daily on hr 11–4; Sept.–Apr., weekends at 1 (cottage only) and 2 (mine yard only), weather permitting.*

12

Holbrooke Hotel. The landmark hotel, built in 1851, hosted entertainer Lola Montez and writer Mark Twain as well as a stream of U.S. presidents including Ulysses S. Grant. Its restaurant-saloon is one of the oldest operating west of the Mississippi. ⊠ *212 W. Main St., at N. Church St.* ☎ *530/273–1353, 800/933–7077* ⊕ *www.holbrooke.com.*

Lola Montez House. In the center of town, on the site of the original, stands a reproduction of the home of Lola Montez, the notorious dancer, singer, and courtesan whose popularity with gold-rush-era miners derived from her suggestive "spider dance." Lola repaired to Grass Valley after wearing out her welcome in Europe, where her lovers included the composer Franz Liszt and the ill-fated King Ludwig of Bavaria. (Her calls for democracy contributed to Ludwig's overthrow and her banishment as a witch—or so the story goes.) Religion has recently found Lola: A local church bought her repro house in late 2011. ⊠ *248 Mill St., at Walsh St.*

☺ **North Star Mining Museum.** Housed in the former North Star powerhouse, the museum displays the 32-foot-high enclosed Pelton Water Wheel, said to be the largest ever built. It was used to power mining operations and was a forerunner of the modern turbines that generate hydroelectricity. Hands-on displays are geared to children. There's a picnic area nearby. ⊠ *10933 Allison Ranch Rd., north of Empire St. exit of Hwy. 49* ☎ *530/273–4255* ⊕ *nevadacountyhistory.org* ✉ *Donation requested* ☉ *May–mid-Oct., daily 10–5.*

WHERE TO EAT AND STAY

$

BRITISH

✗ **Cousin Jack Pasties.** Meat- and vegetable-stuffed pasties are a taste of the region's history, having come across the Atlantic with Cornish miners and their families in the mid-19th century. The flaky crusts practically melt in your mouth. A simple food stand, Jack's is nonetheless a local landmark. $ *Average main: $8* ⊠ *100 S. Auburn St., at Main St.* ☎ *530/272–9230* ▭ *No credit cards.*

$$

ITALIAN

✗ **Villa Venezia Restaurant.** Pasta and seafood are the specialties served up in a cozy, warm Victorian building with an intimate patio area. Seafood stew is one of the most-ordered entrées. $ *Average main: $21* ⊠ *124 Bank St., at Stewart St.* ☎ *530/273–3555* ⊕ *www.villavenezia.info* ☉ *No lunch Sat.–Thurs.*

$

HOTEL

⌂ **Holiday Lodge.** This modest hotel is close to many of the town's main attractions, and its staff can help arrange historical tours of Nevada City, Grass Valley, and the small town of Washington. **Pros:** good price; friendly staff. **Cons:** feels a bit dated. **TripAdvisor:** "great family environment," "good value," "comfortable and very clean." $ *Rooms from: $77* ⊠ *1221 E. Main St.* ☎ *530/273–4406, 800/742–7125* ⊕ *www. holidaylodge.biz* ↻ *35 rooms* ⦿| *Breakfast.*

NEVADA CITY

4 miles north of Grass Valley on Hwy. 49.

Nevada City, once known as the Queen City of the Northern Mines, is the most appealing of the northern Mother Lode towns. The iron-shutter brick buildings that line the narrow downtown streets contain antiques shops, galleries, boutiques, B&Bs, restaurants, and a winery. Horse-drawn carriage tours add to the romance, as do gas street lamps. At one point in the 1850s, Nevada City had a population of nearly 10,000—enough to support much cultural activity. Today, about 3,000 people live here.

GETTING HERE AND AROUND

Highway 20 arrives here from Interstate 5 to the west and Interstate 80 to the east; otherwise, you'll likely get here via Highway 49. Gold Country Stage vehicles (☎ *530/447–0103* 🕒 *Weekdays 7–6)* serve some attractions here.

ESSENTIALS

Visitor Information Nevada City Chamber of Commerce ✉ *132 Main St.* ☎ *530/265–2692* 🌐 *www.nevadacitychamber.com.*

EXPLORING

Firehouse No. 1. With its gingerbread-trim bell tower, Firehouse No. 1 is one of the Gold Country's most distinctive buildings. A museum, it houses gold-rush artifacts and the altar from a Chinese joss house (temple). ✉ *214 Main St., at Coyote St.* ☎ *530/265–5468* 🎟 *Donation requested* 🕒 *May–Nov., Tues.–Sun. 1–4.*

Miners Foundry. The Miners Foundry, erected in 1856, produced machines for gold mining and logging. The Pelton Water Wheel, a power source for the mines (the wheel also jump-started the hydroelectric power industry), was invented here. The cavernous building hosts plays, concerts, receptions, and other events. ✉ *325 Spring St., at Bridge St.* ☎ *530/265–5040* 🌐 *www.minersfoundry.org.*

Nevada City Winery. You can watch wine being created while you sip at the Nevada City Winery, where the tasting room overlooks the production area. ✉ *Miners Foundry Garage, 321 Spring St., at Bridge St.* ☎ *530/265–9463, 800/203–9463* 🌐 *www.ncwinery.com* 🎟 *Free* 🕒 *Tastings Sun.–Thurs. noon–5, Fri. and Sat. noon–6.*

Nevada Theatre. This redbrick edifice, constructed in 1865, is California's oldest theater building. Mark Twain, Emma Nevada, and many other notable people appeared on its stage. These days, plays and old films are presented here. ✉ *401 Broad St., at Commercial St.* ☎ *530/265–6161, 530/274–3456 for film showtimes* 🌐 *www.nevadatheatre.com.*

WHERE TO EAT AND STAY

$$$ ECLECTIC 🍴 **Friar Tuck's.** Popular Friar T's specializes in aromatic, interactive fondues and has an extensive seafood menu. The sparkling interior has a late-19th century ambience—it's one of Nevada City's best indoor spaces. [$] *Average main: $23* ✉ *111 N. Pine St., at Broad St.* ☎ *530/265–9093* 🌐 *friartucks.com* 🕒 *No lunch.*

$$$ AMERICAN 🍴 **New Moon Cafe.** An attractively lighted room gives diners a cozy feeling, though loyal patrons have been known to complain about the high noise level. Organic flours and free-range meats are used when available. [$] *Average main: $25* ✉ *203 York St., at Commercial St.*

12

☎ *530/265–6399* 🌐 *www.thenewmooncafe.com* 🕓 *Closed Mon. No lunch weekends.*

$ AMERICAN 🍴 **South Pine Cafe.** Locals flock here, especially for brunch. Although lobster and beef are on the menu, the real attention-grabbers are vegetarian entrées and side dishes, such as breakfast potatoes and apple-ginger muffins. A regional hit, South Pine also has branches in Grass Valley and Auburn. [$] *Average main: $11* ✉ *110 S. Pine St., at Spring St.* ☎ *530/265–0260* 🌐 *www.southpinecafe.com* 🕓 *Daily 8–3.*

$$ B&B/INN Fodor's Choice ★ 🏨 **Red Castle Historic Lodgings.** Handsome antique furnishings and Oriental rugs decorate the rooms of this 1857 Gothic-revival mansion, a fine option for those who appreciate the finer points of Victorian interior design. **Pros:** friendly owners; spectacular food; fascinating architecture; hillside setting overlooking town. **Cons:** you'll get a workout walking up the hill from downtown. **TripAdvisor:** "romantic," "authentic historical experience," "very accommodating." [$] *Rooms from: $155* ✉ *109 Prospect St.* ☎ *530/265–5135, 800/761–4766* 🌐 *www.redcastleinn.com* 🛏 *4 rooms, 3 suites* 🍽 *Breakfast.*

Lake Tahoe

WITH RENO, NEVADA

WORD OF MOUTH

"Lake Tahoe is quiet after Labor Day. The weather is beautiful and all of the activities . . . the hiking, touring the lake by paddlewheel boat, dining, and shopping, are still open and running."

—artjoanne

WELCOME TO LAKE TAHOE

TOP REASONS TO GO

★ **The lake:** Blue, deep, and alpine pure, Lake Tahoe is far and away the main reason to visit this high Sierra paradise.

★ **Snow, snow, snow:** Daring black-diamond runs or baby-bunny bumps—whether you're an expert, a beginner, or somewhere in between, there are many slopes to suit your skills at the numerous Tahoe-area ski parks.

★ **The great outdoors:** A ring of national forests and recreation areas, linked by miles of trails make Tahoe a nature-lover's paradise.

★ **Dinner with a view:** You can picnic lakeside at state parks or dine in restaurants perched along the shore.

★ **A date with lady luck:** Whether you want to roll dice, play the slots, or hope the blackjack dealer goes bust before you do, you'll find round-the-clock gambling at the casinos in Reno and on the Nevada side of the lake.

1 California Side. With the exception of Stateline, Nevada—which, aside from its casino-hotel towers, seems almost indistinguishable from South Lake Tahoe, California—the California side is more developed than the Nevada side. Here you can find both commercial enterprises—restaurants, motels, lodges, resorts, residential subdivisions— and public-access facilities, such as historic sites, parks, campgrounds, marinas, and beaches.

2 Nevada Side. You don't need a highway sign to know when you've crossed from California into Nevada: the flashing lights and elaborate marquees of casinos announce legal gambling in garish hues. But you'll find more here than tables and slot machines. Reno, the Biggest Little City in the World, has a vibrant art scene and a serene downtown RiverWalk. And when you really need to get away from the chip-toting crowds, you can hike through pristine wilderness at Lake Tahoe–Nevada State Park, or hit the slopes near Incline Village.

GETTING ORIENTED

In the northern section of the Sierra Nevada mountain range, the Lake Tahoe area covers portions of five national forests, several state parks, and rugged wilderness areas with names like Desolation and Granite Chief. Lake Tahoe, the star attraction, straddles California and Nevada and is one of the world's largest, clearest, and deepest alpine lakes. The region's proximity to the Bay Area and Sacramento to the west and Reno to the east draws thrill-seekers during ski season and summer, when water sports, camping, and hiking are the dominant activities.

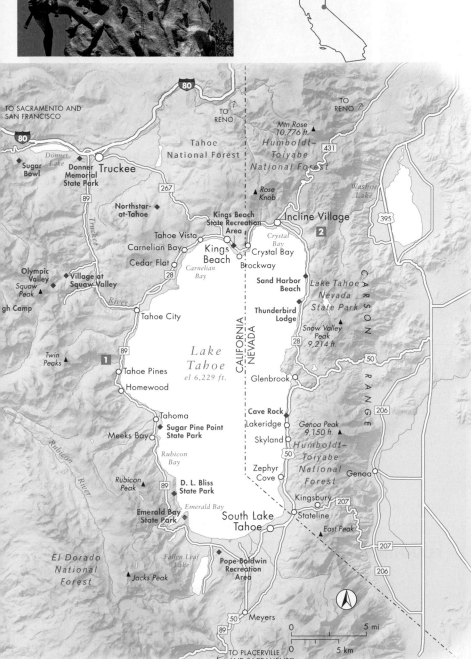

TO SACRAMENTO AND
SAN FRANCISCO

80

80

Donner
Lake

Sugar
Bowl

Donner
Memorial
State Park

Truckee

Tahoe
National Forest

TO
RENO

TO RENO

Mtn Rose
10,776 ft.

Humboldt–
Toiyabe
National Forest

431

267

Rose
Knob

395

Washoe
Lake

Northstar-
at-Tahoe

Kings Beach
State Recreation
Area

Incline Village

2

Tahoe Vista

Crystal
Bay

89

Carnelian Bay

**Kings
Beach**

Crystal Bay

Cedar Flat

28

Carnelian
Bay

Brockway

Sand Harbor
Beach

Lake Tahoe
Nevada
State Park

Olympic
Valley
*Squaw
Peak*

Village at
Squaw Valley

Thunderbird
Lodge

gh Camp

River

Tahoe City

89

Twin
Peaks

1

Tahoe Pines

Homewood

*Lake
Tahoe*
el 6,229 ft.

CALIFORNIA

NEVADA

Snow Valley
Peak
9,214 ft.

28

Glenbrook

CARSON RANGE

50

206

Tahoma

Sugar Pine Point
State Park

Cave Rock

Lakeridge

Genoa Peak
9,150 ft.

Meeks Bay

*Rubicon
Bay*

Skyland

50

Humboldt–
Toiyabe
National
Forest

Zephyr
Cove

Genoa

Rubicon River

Rubicon
Peak

89

D. L. Bliss
State Park

Kingsbury

207

Emerald Bay
State Park

Emerald Bay

**South Lake
Tahoe**

Stateline

East Peak

207

El Dorado
National
Forest

*Fallen Leaf
Lake*

Pope-Baldwin
Recreation
Area

206

Jacks Peak

50

Meyers

89

0   5 mi

0   5 km

TO PLACERVILLE
AND SACRAMENTO

Updated by Christine Vovakes

Stunning Lake Tahoe is the largest alpine lake in North America, famous for its clarity, cobalt-blue water, and surrounding snowcapped peaks. Straddling the state line between California and Nevada, it lies 6,225 feet above sea level in the Sierra Nevada.

The border gives this popular resort region a split personality. About half its visitors are intent on low-key sightseeing, hiking, fishing, camping, and boating. The rest head directly for the Nevada side, where bargain dining, big-name entertainment, and the lure of a jackpot draw them into the glittering casinos.

The typical way to explore the Lake Tahoe area is to drive the 72-mile road that follows the shore through wooded flatlands and past beaches, climbing to vistas on the rugged southwest side of the lake and passing through busy commercial developments and casinos on its northeastern and southeastern edges. Another option is to actually go out *on* the 22-mile-long, 12-mile-wide lake on a sightseeing cruise or kayaking trip.

The lake, the communities around it, the state parks, national forests, and protected tracts of wilderness are the region's main draws, but other nearby destinations are gaining in popularity. Truckee, with an Old West feel and hot new restaurants, entices visitors looking for a relaxed pace and easy access to Tahoe's north shore and Olympic Valley ski parks. And today Reno, once known only for its casinos, attracts tourists with its buzzing arts scene, revitalized downtown riverfront, and campus events at the University of Nevada.

PLANNING

WHEN TO GO

A sapphire-blue lake shimmering deep in the center of an ice-white wonderland—that's Tahoe in winter. But those blankets of snow mean lots of storms that often close roads and force chain requirements on the interstate. In summer the roads are open, but the lake and lodgings are clogged with visitors seeking respite from valley heat. If you don't ski, the best times to visit are early fall—September and October—and late spring. The crowds thin, prices dip, and you can count on Tahoe being beautiful.

Most Lake Tahoe accommodations, restaurants, and even a handful of parks are open year-round, but many visitor centers, mansions, state parks, and beaches are closed from October through May. During those months, winter-sports enthusiasts swamp Tahoe's downhill resorts and cross-country centers, North America's largest concentration of skiing facilities. In summer it's cooler here than in the scorched Sierra Nevada foothills, the clean mountain air is bracingly crisp, and the surface temperature of Lake Tahoe is an invigorating 65°F to 70°F (compared with 40°F to 50°F in winter). This is also the time, however, when it may seem as if every tourist at the lake—100,000 on peak weekends—is in a car on the main road circling the shoreline (especially on Highway 89, just south of Tahoe City; on Highway 28, east of Tahoe City; and on U.S. 50 in South Lake Tahoe). Christmas week and July 4th are the busiest times, and prices go through the roof; plan accordingly.

GETTING HERE AND AROUND

AIR TRAVEL

The nearest airport to Lake Tahoe is Reno–Tahoe International Airport (RNO), in Reno, 50 miles northeast of the closest point on the lake. Airlines serving RNO include Alaska, American, Delta, Southwest, United, and US Airways. These airlines plus Frontier, Hawaiian, and JetBlue serve Sacramento International Airport (SMF), 112 miles from South Lake Tahoe. North Lake Tahoe Express runs buses ($40 one way, $75 round-trip) between RNO and towns on the lake's western and northern shores, plus Incline Village, Truckee, and Squaw Valley. South Tahoe Express runs buses ($27.50 one-way, $49 round-trip) between Reno–Tahoe Airport and resort hotels in the South Lake Tahoe area.

Airports Reno–Tahoe International Airport ⊠ *2001 E. Plumb La., off U.S. 395, Exit 65B, Reno, Nevada* ☎ *775/328–6400* ⊕ *www.renoairport.com.* **Sacramento International Airport** ⊠ *6900 Airport Blvd., 12 miles northwest of downtown off I–5, Sacramento, California* ☎ *916/929–5411* ⊕ *www.sacramento.aero/smf.*

Transfers North Lake Tahoe Express ☎ *866/216–5222* ⊕ *www. northlaketahoeexpress.com.* **South Tahoe Express** ☎ *775/325–8944, 866/898– 2463* ⊕ *www.southtahoeexpress.com.*

BUS TRAVEL

Greyhound stops in Sacramento, Truckee, and Reno. BlueGO ($2 per ride) provides year-round local service in South Lake Tahoe, Nifty 50 Trolley service to parks and other attractions during summer. On the north shore, Tahoe Area Regional Transit (TART; $1.75) operates buses between Tahoma and Incline Village and runs shuttles to Truckee. RTC RIDE buses ($2) serve the Reno area. All local rides require exact change.

In winter, BlueGO provides free ski shuttle service from South Lake Tahoe hotels and resorts to various Heavenly Mountain ski lodge locations. Most of the major ski resorts offer shuttle service to lodgings near them.

13

Bus Contacts Greyhound ☎ *800/231–2222* ⊕ *www.greyhound.com.***BlueGO**
☎ *530/541–7149* ⊕ *www.bluego.org.* **RTC RIDE** ☎ *775/348–7433* ⊕ *www.*
rtcwashoe.com. **Tahoe Area Regional Transit (TART)** ☎ *530/550–1212,*
800/736–6365 ⊕ *www.laketahoetransit.com.*

CAR TRAVEL

Lake Tahoe is 198 miles northeast of San Francisco, a drive of less than
four hours in good weather and light traffic—if possible avoid heavy
weekend traffic, particularly leaving the San Francisco area for Tahoe
on Friday afternoon and returning on Sunday afternoon. The major
route is Interstate 80, which cuts through the Sierra Nevada about 14
miles north of the lake. From there Highway 89 and Highway 267
reach the west and north shores, respectively. U.S. 50 is the more direct
route to the south shore, a two-hour drive from Sacramento. From
Reno you can get to the north shore by heading south on U.S. 395 for
10 miles, then west on Highway 431 for 25 miles. For the south shore,
head south on U.S. 395 through Carson City, and then turn west on
U.S. 50 (50 miles total).

The scenic 72-mile highway around the lake is marked Highway 89 on
the southwest and west shores, Highway 28 on the north and northeast
shores, and U.S. 50 on the east and southeast. Sections of Highway 89
sometimes close during snowy periods, usually at Emerald Bay because
of avalanche danger, which makes it impossible to complete the circular drive around the lake. Interstate 80, U.S. 50, and U.S. 395 are all-
weather highways, but there may be delays while snow is cleared during
major storms. Interstate 80 is a four-lane freeway; much of U.S. 50 is
only two lanes with no center divider. Carry tire chains from October
through May, or rent a four-wheel-drive vehicle. Most rental agencies
do not allow tire chains to be used on their vehicles; ask when you book.

Contacts California Highway Patrol ☎ *530/577–1001 South Lake Tahoe*
⊕ *www.chp.ca.gov.***Caltrans Current Highway Conditions** ☎ *800/427–7623*
⊕ *www.dot.ca.gov.***Nevada Department of Transportation Road Informa-**
tion ☎ *877/687–6237* ⊕ *www.safetravelusa.com/nv.***Nevada Highway Patrol**
☎ *775/687–5300* ⊕ *www.nvdpspub.gov/nhp/roadhazard.aspx.*

TRAIN TRAVEL

Amtrak's cross-country rail service makes stops in Truckee and Reno.
Amtrak also operates several buses daily between Reno and Sacramento
to connect with coastal train routes.

Train Contact Amtrak ☎ *800/872–7245* ⊕ *www.amtrak.com.*

HEALTH AND SAFETY

In an emergency dial 911.

Hospital Contacts Barton Memorial Hospital ✉ *2170 South Ave., at 4th*
St., South Lake Tahoe ☎ *530/541–3420* ⊕ *www.bartonhealth.org.* **St. Mary's**
Regional Medical Center ✉ *235 W. 6th St., at N. Arlington Ave., Reno, Nevada*
☎ *775/770–3000 general information* ⊕ *www.saintmarysreno.org.* **Tahoe For-**
est Hospital ✉ *10121 Pine Ave., at Levon Ave., off Donner Pass Rd., Truckee*
☎ *530/587–6011* ⊕ *www.tfhd.com.*

OUTDOORS AND BACKCOUNTRY TIPS

If you're planning to spend any time outdoors around Lake Tahoe, whether hiking, climbing, skiing, or camping, be aware that weather conditions can change quickly in the Sierra. To avoid a life-threatening case of hypothermia, always bring a pocket-size, fold-up rain poncho (available in all sporting-goods stores) to keep you dry. Wear long pants and a hat. Carry plenty of water. Because you'll likely be walking on granite, wear sturdy, closed-toe hiking boots, with soles that grip rock. If you're going into the backcountry, bring a signaling device (such as a mirror), emergency whistle, compass, map, energy bars, and water purifier. When heading out alone, tell someone where you're going and when you plan to return.

13

If you plan to ski, be aware of resort elevations. In the event of a winter storm, determine the snow level before you choose the resort you'll ski. Often the level can be as high as 7,000 feet, which means rain at some resorts' base areas but snow at others.

BackCountry, in Truckee, operates an excellent website with current information about how and where to (and where not to) ski, mountain bike, and hike in the backcountry around Tahoe. The store also stocks everything from crampons to transceivers. For storm information, check the National Weather Service's website; for ski conditions, visit ⊕ *ontheSnow.com.* For reservations at campgrounds in California state parks, contact Reserve America. If you plan to camp in the backcountry of the national forests, you'll need to purchase a wilderness permit, which you can pick up at the forest service office or at a ranger station at any forest entrance. If you plan to ski the backcountry, check the U.S. Forest Service's recorded information for conditions.

Contacts and Information BackCountry ✉ *11400 Donner Pass Rd., at Meadow Way, Truckee* ☎ *530/582–0909 Truckee* ⊕ *www.thebackcountry.net.* **National Weather Service** ⊕ *www.wrh.noaa.gov/rev.* **Reserve America** ☎ *800/444–7275* ⊕ *www.reserveamerica.com.* **U.S. Forest Service** ✉ *Office, 35 College Dr., South Lake Tahoe* ☎ *530/543–2600 general information, 530/587–3558 backcountry recording* ⊕ *www.fs.fed.us/r5/ltbmu.*

TOUR OPTIONS

The 312-passenger *Tahoe Queen,* a glass-bottom paddle wheeler, departs from South Lake Tahoe daily for 2½-hour sightseeing cruises year-round by reservation and 3-hour dinner-dance cruises daily from late spring to early fall (weekly the rest of the year). Fares range from $46 to $75. In winter the boat becomes a waterborne ski shuttle: $125 covers boat transportation from South Lake Tahoe to the Hyatt Regency dock at Incline Village and back again, a bus transfer to Northstar Ski Resort, a half-day lift ticket, and breakfast. From May through September, the *Sierra Cloud,* a 41-passenger catamaran, departs from the Hyatt Regency beach at Incline Village and cruises the north shore area. The fare is $60. The 520-passenger MS *Dixie II,* a stern-wheeler, sails year-round from Zephyr Cove to Emerald Bay on sightseeing, lunch, and dinner cruises. Fares range from $39 to $69.

Also in Zephyr Cove, Tahoe Boat Cruises operates the *Woodwind II,* a 50-passenger catamaran that sails on regular and champagne cruises from April through October. Fares range from $34 to $49. The company's *Safari Rose,* an 80-foot-long wooden motor yacht, departs from Tahoe Keys Marina for half-day cruises around the lake; $105, including lunch.

Lake Tahoe Balloons flies over the lake from May through October; the hour-long trips cost $250. The entire experience takes four hours total.

Tour Contacts Lake Tahoe Balloons ☎ *530/544-1221, 800/872-9294* ⊕ *www.laketahoeballoons.com.* **MS Dixie II** ✉ *Zephyr Cove Marina, 760 U.S. Hwy. 50, near Church St., Zephyr Cove, Nevada* ☎ *775/589-4906, 888/896-3830* ⊕ *www.zephyrcove.com/cruises.* **Sierra Cloud** ✉ *Hyatt Regency Lake Tahoe, 111 Country Club Dr., Incline Village* ☎ *775/831-4386* ⊕ *www.awsincline.com.* **Tahoe Queen** ✉ *Ski Run Marina, 900 Ski Run Blvd., off U.S. 50, South Lake Tahoe* ☎ *530/543-6191, 888/896-3830* ⊕ *www.zephyrcove.com/cruises.* **Tahoe Boat Cruises** ✉ *Zephyr Cove Resort, 760 U.S. Hwy. 50, near Church St., Zephyr Cove* ☎ *775/588-1881, 888/867-6394* ⊕ *www.tahoecruises.com.*

RESTAURANTS

On weekends and in high season, expect a long wait in the more popular restaurants. And expect to pay resort prices almost everywhere. Some restaurants are only open 6 out of 12 months a year; during the "shoulder seasons" (from April to May and September to November), some places may close temporarily or limit their hours, so call ahead. Also, check local papers for deals and discounts during this time, especially two-for-one coupons. Many casinos use their restaurants to attract gamblers. Marquees often tout "$8.99 prime rib dinners" or "$1.99 breakfast specials." Some of these meals are downright lousy and they are usually available only in the coffee shops and buffets, but at those prices, it's hard to complain. The finer restaurants in casinos deliver pricier food, as well as reasonable service and a bit of atmosphere. Unless otherwise noted, even the most expensive area restaurants welcome customers in casual clothes. *Prices in the reviews are the average cost of a main course at dinner or, if dinner is not served, at lunch.*

HOTELS

Quiet inns on the water, suburban-style strip motels, casino hotels, slope-side ski lodges, and house and condo rentals throughout the area constitute the lodging choices at Tahoe. The crowds come in summer and during ski season; reserve as far in advance as possible, especially for holiday periods when prices skyrocket. Spring and fall give you a little more leeway and lower—sometimes significantly lower—rates. Check hotel websites for the best deals.

Head to South Lake Tahoe for the most activities and the widest range of lodging options. Heavenly Village in the heart of town has an ice rink, cinema, shops, fine dining restaurants, and simple cafés, plus a gondola that will whisk you up to the ski park. Walk two blocks south from downtown, and you can hit the casinos.

Tahoe City, on the west shore, has a small-town atmosphere and is accessible to several nearby ski resorts. A few miles northwest of the lake, Squaw Valley USA has its own self-contained upscale village, a gondola to the slopes, and numerous outdoor activities once the snow melts.

Looking for a taste of old Tahoe? The north shore with its woodsy backdrop is your best bet, with Carnelian Bay and Tahoe Vista on the California side. And across the Nevada border are casino resorts where Hollywood's glamour-stars once romped. *Prices in the reviews are the lowest cost of a standard double room in high season. For expanded reviews, facilities, and current deals, visit Fodors.com.*

13

SKIING AND SNOWBOARDING

The mountains around Lake Tahoe are bombarded by blizzards throughout most winters and sometimes in fall and spring; 10- to 12-foot bases are common. Indeed, the Sierra often have the deepest snowpack on the continent, but because of the relatively mild temperatures over the Pacific, falling snow can be very heavy and wet—it's nicknamed Sierra Cement for a reason. The upside is that you can sometimes ski and board as late as July (snowboarding is permitted at all Tahoe ski areas). The major resorts get extremely crowded on weekends. If you're going to ski on a Saturday, arrive early and quit early. Avoid moving with the masses: eat at 11 am or 1:30 pm, not noon. Also consider visiting the ski areas with few high-speed lifts or limited lodging and real estate at their bases: Alpine Meadows, Sugar Bowl, Homewood, Mt. Rose, Sierra-at-Tahoe, Diamond Peak, and Kirkwood. And to find out the true ski conditions, talk to waiters and bartenders—most of whom are ski bums.

The Lake Tahoe area is also a great destination for Nordic skiers. "Skinny" (i.e., cross-country) skiing at the resorts can be costly, but you get the benefits of machine grooming and trail preparation. If it's bargain Nordic you're after, take advantage of thousands of acres of public forest and parkland trails.

VISITOR INFORMATION

Contacts Lake Tahoe Visitors Authority ✉ *169 U.S. Hwy. 50, Stateline* ☎ *775/588–5900, 800/288–2463* ∰ *tahoesouth.com.* **OntheSnow.com** ∰ *www. onthesnow.com/california/skireport.html.* **U.S. Forest Service** ☎ *530/587–2158 backcountry recording* ∰ *www.fs.usda.gov/tahoe.*

THE CALIFORNIA SIDE

The most hotels, restaurants, ski resorts, and state parks are on the California side of the lake, but you'll also encounter the most congestion and developed areas.

SOUTH LAKE TAHOE

50 miles south of Reno on U.S. 395 and U.S. 50; 198 miles northeast of San Francisco on I–80 and U.S. 50.

The city of South Lake Tahoe's raison d'être is tourism: the casinos of adjacent Stateline, Nevada; the ski slopes at Heavenly Mountain; the beaches, docks, bike trails, and campgrounds all around the south shore; and the backcountry of Eldorado National Forest and Desolation Wilderness. The main road into town, however, shows less attractive features: a mix of older motels, strip malls, and low-rise prefab-looking buildings that line both sides of U.S. 50. Though there are plenty of places to stay, we haven't recommended many because they're not top choices. The small city's saving grace is its convenient location and bevy of services, as well as its gorgeous lake views.

GETTING HERE AND AROUND

U.S. 50, the main route into South Lake Tahoe, changes its name to Lake Tahoe Boulevard and is the major road through the city. Arrive by car or, if coming from Reno Airport, take the South Tahoe Express bus. BlueGO operates daily bus service in the south shore area year-round, plus a ski shuttle from the large hotels to Heavenly Ski Resort in the winter.

ESSENTIALS

Visitor Information Lake Tahoe Visitors Authority ✉ *Visitor Center, 169 U.S. Hwy. 50, at Kingsbury Grade, Stateline, Nevada* ☎ *775/588–5900, 800/288–2463* 🌐 *ltva.org* ✉ *Visitor Center, 3066 Lake Tahoe Blvd., at San Francisco Ave.* ☎ *530/554–5050.*

EXPLORING

Fodor's Choice ★ **Heavenly Gondola.** Whether you ski or not, you'll appreciate the impressive view of Lake Tahoe from the Heavenly Gondola. Its eight-passenger cars travel from the middle of town 2.4 miles up the mountain in 15 minutes. When the weather's fine, you can take one of three hikes around the mountaintop and then have lunch at Tamarack Lodge. Heavenly also offers day care for children. ✉ *4080 Lake Tahoe Blvd.* ☎ *775/586–7000, 800/432–8365* 🌐 *www.skiheavenly.com* 🎫 *$32* ⏲ *Hrs vary; summer, daily 10–5; winter, daily 9–4.*

Heavenly Village. At the base of the gondola the Heavenly Village is the centerpiece of South Lake Tahoe's efforts to reinvent itself and provide a focal point for tourism. Essentially a pedestrian mall, it includes some good shopping, a cinema, an arcade for kids, and the Heavenly Village Outdoor Ice Rink. ✉ *U.S. 50 and Heavenly Village Way.*

WHERE TO EAT

$ ECLECTIC 🍴 **Blue Angel Café.** A favorite of locals, who fill the dozen or so wooden tables, this cozy spot serves basic sandwiches and salads along with internationally inspired dishes like chipotle shrimp tacos and Thai curry. The café has Wi-Fi. [$] *Average main: $12* ✉ *1132 Ski Run Blvd., at Larch Ave.* ☎ *530/544–6544.*

$ MEXICAN 🍴 **The Cantina.** A casual Tahoe favorite, the Cantina serves traditional Mexican dishes—huge burritos, enchiladas, and rellenos—as well as stylized Southwestern fare such as smoked-chicken polenta with grilled vegetables, and crab cakes in jalapeño cream sauce. The bartenders make great margaritas and serve 30 different kinds of beer. [$] *Average main: $13* ✉ *765 Emerald Bay Rd., Hwy. 89, at 10th St.* ☎ *530/544–1233* 🌐 *www.cantinatahoe.com* ✍ *Reservations not accepted.*

$$$ ECLECTIC 🍴 **Evan's American Gourmet Cafe.** Its excellent service, world-class food, and superb wine list make this the top choice for high-end dining in South Lake. Inside a converted cabin, the restaurant serves creative American cuisine that includes catch-of-the-day seafood offerings and meat dishes such as roasted rack of lamb with citrus couscous. Some

Continued on page 522

TAHOE A LAKE FOR ALL SEASONS

by Christine Vovakes

Best known for its excellent skiing, Lake Tahoe is a year-round resort and outdoor sports destination. All kinds of activities are available, from snowboarding some of the best runs in North America and gliding silently along the lakeshore on cross-country skis in winter, to mountain biking through lush forests and puttering around the alpine lake in a classic yacht in summer. Whatever you do—and whenever you visit—the sapphire lake is at the center of it all, pulling you out of your posh resort or rustic cabin rental like a giant blue magnet. There are many ways to enjoy and experience Lake Tahoe, but here are some of our favorites.

(top) Heavenly Mountain Resort,
(bottom) Sand Harbor Beach.

WINTER WONDERLAND

Home to a host of world-famous Sierra resorts, Tahoe is a premier ski destination. Add sledding, ice skating, cross-country skiing, and jingly sleigh rides under the stars to the mix, and you begin to get a glimpse of Tahoe's cold-weather potential.

DOWNHILL SKIING AND SNOWBOARDING

Even if you've never made it off the bunny hill before, you should definitely hit the slopes here at least once. The Lake Tahoe region has the deepest snowpack in North America, and you can ski from Thanksgiving until it melts—which is sometimes July.

One of the top-rated resorts in the country, Olympic Valley's **Squaw Valley USA** hosted the 1960 Winter Olympics that put Tahoe on the map. A great classic resort is **Sugar Bowl,** where you can revel in a bit of Disney nostalgia while you swoop down the slopes. Walt helped start the resort, which opened in 1939 and had Tahoe's first chair lift.

Even if you're not hitting the slopes at South Lake Tahoe's **Heavenly Mountain,** be sure to take a ride on their **Heavenly Gondola** so you can take in awe-inspiring views of the frozen circle of white ice that rings the brilliant lake.

(top) Skiing in Lake Tahoe,. (above left) Cross-country skiing, (above right) Snow boarding at Heavenly Mountain.

SKI RESORT	LOCATION	TRAILS	ACRES	BEGIN.	INTER.	ADV./ EXP.
CALIFORNIA						
Alpine Meadows	Tahoe City	100	2,400	25%	40%	35%
Heavenly Mountain	South Lake Tahoe	94	4,800	20%	45%	35%
Homewood Mountain	Homewood	60	1,260	15%	50%	35%
Kirkwood	Kirkwood	72	2,300	15%	50%	35%
Northstar-at-Tahoe	Truckee	97	3,000	13%	60%	27%
Sierra-at-Tahoe	South Lake Tahoe	46	2,000	25%	50%	25%
Squaw Valley USA	Olympic Valley	170	4,000	25%	45%	30%
Sugar Bowl	Truckee	95	1,500	17%	45%	38%
NEVADA						
Diamond Peak	Incline Village	30	655	18%	46%	36%
Mt. Rose Ski Tahoe	Incline Village	61	1,200	20%	30%	50%

CROSS-COUNTRY SKIING

Downhill skiing may get all the glory here, but Lake Tahoe is also a premier cross-country (or Nordic) skiing destination. "Skinny" skiers basically have two options: pony up the cash to ski the groomed trails at a resort, or hit the more rugged (but cheaper—or free) public forest and parkland trails.

Beautiful **Royal Gorge** is the country's largest cross-country ski resort. Other resorts with good skinny skiing include **Kirkwood, Squaw Valley USA, Tahoe Donner,** and **Northstar-at-Tahoe.** Private operators **Spooner Lake Cross Country** and **Hope Valley Cross Country** will also have you shushing through pristine powder in no time.

For bargain Nordic on public trails, head to **Sugar Pine Point State Park.** Other good low-cost cross-country skiing locations include **Donner Memorial State Park, Lake Tahoe—Nevada State Park,** and **Tahoe Meadows** near Incline Village.

CAUTION⚠ Cross-country skiing is relaxing and provides a great cardiovascular workout—but it's also quite strenuous. If it's your first time out or you're not in great shape, start out slow.

SLEDDING AND TUBING

Kirkwood, Squaw Valley USA, Boreal, Soda Springs, and many other Tahoe resorts have areas where you can barrel down hills on inflatable tubes. Some good non-resort sledding spots are **Tahoe National Forest** and **Tahoe Meadows,** near Incline Village.

ICE SKATING

Want to work on your triple lutz? You can skate seasonally at **Heavenly Village Outdoor Ice Rink,** or year-round at the **South Tahoe Ice Arena.** Other great gliding spots include **Squaw Valley USA's Olympic Ice Pavilion.**

WARMING UP

To defrost your ski-stiff limbs, take a dip in a resort's heated pool, de-stress in a hotel spa... or enjoy a brandy by the fire at a cozy restaurant. Our favorite places to warm up and imbibe include Graham's of Squaw Valley and Soule Domain, near Crystal Bay.

Lake Tahoe
Outdoor Activities

FROSTY CATCH

Too cold to fish? Nonsense. South Lake's Tahoe Sport Fishing runs charters year-round with crews that will clean and package your catch.

IN THE WARM CALIFORNIA SUN

Summer in Tahoe means diving into pure alpine waters, hiking a mountain trail with stunning lake views, or kayaking on glorious Emerald Bay. From tennis to golf to fishing, you can fill every waking moment with outdoor activity—or just stretch out on a sunny lakeside beach with a good book and a cool drink.

HIKING

The lake is surrounded by protected parkland, offering countless opportunities to take jaunts through the woods or rambles along lakeside trails.

One of the most unique hiking experiences in Tahoe is at Heavenly Mountain Resorts, where the **Heavenly Gondola** runs up to three nice trails. When you're done enjoying sky-high views of the lake, grab lunch at the nearby Tamarack Lodge.

Another out-of-the-ordinary option is a romantic moonlit trek. **Camp Richardson** has lots of trails and a long curve of lake to catch the moonlight.

In **Eldorado National Forest and Desolation Wilderness,** you can hike a small portion of the famous Pacific Crest Trail and branch off to discover beautiful back-country lakes. Nearby **Eagle Falls** has stunning views of Emerald Bay.

One of Tahoe's best hikes is a 4½-mi trail at **D.L. Bliss State Park;** it has lovely views of the lake and leads to bizarre **Vikingsholm** (*see box on next page*).

Other great places to hike in Lake Tahoe include **Sugar Pines Point State Park, Olympic Valley's Granite Chief Wilderness, Squaw Valley USA's High Camp, Donner Memorial State Park,** and **Lake Tahoe—Nevada State Park.**

You can pick up hiking maps at the **U.S. Forest Service** office at the **Lake Tahoe Visitor Center.**

HIT THE BEACH

Lake Tahoe has some gorgeous lakeside sunbathing terrain; get to perennial favorite **Kings Beach State Recreation Area** early to snag a choice spot. Or, if you never want to be far from the water, reserve one of the prime beachside spots at **D.L. Bliss State Park Campground.**

(left) Fannette Island in Emerald Bay. (right) A young man leaps off a cliff into Lake Tahoe.

MOUNTAIN BIKING AND CYCLING

You don't need to be preparing for the Tour de France to join the biking fun. While there are myriad rugged mountain biking trails to choose from, the region is also blessed with many flat trails.

Truly intrepid cyclists take the lift up **Northstar-at-Tahoe** and hit the resort's 100 mi of trails. Another good option is **Sugar Pine Point State Park,** where you can hop on a 10-mi trail to Tahoe City.

Tahoe Sports in South Lake Tahoe is a good place for bike rentals and tips for planning your trip. **Cyclepath Mountain Bikes Adventures** in Truckee leads guided mountain biking tours, and **Flume Trail Bikes** on the Nevada side of the lake, near Glenbrook, rents bikes and operates a bike shuttle to popular trails.

LAKE TOURS AND KAYAKING

One of the best ways to experience the lake is by getting out on the water.

The *Tahoe Queen* is a huge glass-bottomed paddle-wheel boat that offers sightseeing cruises and dinner-dance cruises; in winter, it's the only water-

borne ski shuttle in the world. The *Sierra Cloud, MS Dixie II,* and *Woodwind II* also ply the lake, offering a variety of enjoyable cruises. *(See Tour Options in the Planner section of this chapter for contact info.)*

Another enjoyable option is taking a throwback wooden cruiser from Tahoe Keys Marina in South Lake Tahoe to tour **Thunderbird Lodge,** the meticulously crafted stone mansion built in 1936 by socialite George Whittell.

For a more personal experience, rent a kayak and glide across **Emerald Bay. Kayak Tahoe** in South Lake Tahoe will have you paddling in no time.

VIKINGS?

As you kayak around Tahoe, you'll see many natural wonders...and a few manmade ones as well. One of the most impressive and strangest is **Vikingsholm,** a grand 1929 estate that looks like an ancient Viking castle. You can see it from **Emerald Bay** (which, appropriately, resembles a fjord), or hike to it via a steep one-mile trail.

(left top) Biking along the shore. (left bottom) Kayaking. (right) Steamboat cruise.

diners find the table spacing a tad close. Evan's is intimate, to be sure, but the food always pleases. [$] *Average main: $30* ✉ *536 Emerald Bay Rd., Hwy. 89, at 15th St.* ☎ *530/542–1990* 🌐 *www.evanstahoe.com* 🕓 *No lunch.*

$$$$ ASIAN 🍴 **Kalani's.** Fresh-off-the-plane seafood gets flown directly from the Honolulu fish market to Heavenly Village's sexiest (and priciest) restaurant. The sleek, white-tablecloth dining room is decked out with carved bamboo, a burnt-orange color palette, and a modern-glass sculpture, all of which complement contemporary Pacific Rim specialties such as melt-from-the-bone baby back pork ribs with sesame-garlic soy sauce. Sushi selections with inventive rolls and sashimi combos, plus less expensive vegetarian dishes, add depth to the menu. [$] *Average main: $33* ✉ *1001 Heavenly Village Way, at U.S. 50* ☎ *530/544–6100* 🌐 *www.kalanis.com* 🕓 *No lunch weekdays in winter.*

$ AMERICAN 🍴 **Red Hut Café.** A vintage-1959 Tahoe diner, all chrome and red plastic, the Red Hut is a tiny place with a wildly popular breakfast menu: huge omelets; banana, pecan, and coconut waffles; and other tasty vittles. A second branch, the only one that serves dinner (there's also a soda fountain), is also in South Lake, and there's a third location in Stateline. [$] *Average main: $8* ✉ *2723 Lake Tahoe Blvd., near Blue Lake Ave.* ☎ *530/541–9024* 🌐 *www.redhutcafe.com* ✍ *Reservations not accepted* 💳 *No credit cards* 🕓 *No dinner at either location.*

$$ ITALIAN 🍴 **Scusa! Italian Ristorante.** This longtime favorite moved recently, but the kitchen still turns out big plates of veal scallopine, chicken piccata, and linguine with clams—straightforward Italian-American food (and lots of it), served in an intimate dining room warmed by a crackling fire. The new location has an outdoor patio that's open in warm weather. [$] *Average main: $18* ✉ *2543 Lake Tahoe Blvd., near Silver Dollar Ave.* ☎ *530/542–0100* 🌐 *www.scusalaketahoe.com* 🕓 *No lunch.*

WHERE TO STAY

For expanded reviews, facilities, and current deals, visit Fodors.com.

$$$ B&B/INN Fodor's Choice ★ 🏨 **Black Bear Inn Bed and Breakfast.** South Lake Tahoe's most luxurious inn feels like one of the grand old lodges of the Adirondacks. **Pros:** intimate; serene, woodsy grounds; within walking distance of good restaurants. **Cons:** not appropriate for children under 16; pricey. **TripAdvisor:** "extremely accommodating," "amazing gardens," "great place to be pampered."[$] *Rooms from: $225* ✉ *1202 Ski Run Blvd.* ☎ *530/544–4451, 877/232–7466* 🌐 *www.tahoeblackbear.com* 🛏 *5 rooms, 4 cabins* 🍽 *Breakfast.*

$$ HOTEL 👶 🏨 **Camp Richardson.** An old-fashioned family resort that is built around a 1920s lodge, this property features a few dozen cabins and a small inn, all tucked beneath giant pine trees on 80 acres fronting Lake Tahoe. **Pros:** lakeside location; wide choice of lodgings. **Cons:** dated style; no phones or TVs in some rooms. **TripAdvisor:** "retro stay right on the lake," "beautiful place to stay," "no wonder Lucky Baldwin lived here."[$] *Rooms from: $105* ✉ *1900 Jameson Beach Rd.* ☎ *530/541–1801, 800/544–1801* 🌐 *www.camprichardson.com* 🛏 *27 lodge rooms, 40 cabins, 7 inn rooms, 212 campsites; 100 RV sites.*

$$ HOTEL ★ 🏨 **Inn by the Lake.** Across the road from a beach, the "inn" is essentially a high-end motel, with spacious, spotless rooms and suites.

Pros: great value; stellar service; short drive from Heavenly Mountain. **Cons:** on busy Lake Tahoe Boulevard. **TripAdvisor:** "a heavenly holiday," "nice location," "very relaxing." [$] *Rooms from: $140* ✉ *3300 Lake Tahoe Blvd.* ☎ *530/542–0330, 800/877–1466* 🌐 *www.innbythelake.com* 🛏 *90 rooms, 10 suites.*

WORD OF MOUTH

"Bike trails are wonderful from Camp Richardson (near South Shore). It's like hiking in the middle of the woods, but on a bicycle. You can bike from beach to beach. Take a picnic lunch." —elnap29

$$$ RESORT ★ 🏨 **Marriott's Grand Residence and Timber Lodge.** You can't beat the location of these two gigantic, modern condominium complexes right at the base of Heavenly Gondola, smack in the center of town. **Pros:** central location; great for families; within walking distance of excellent restaurants. **Cons:** can be jam-packed on weekends. **TripAdvisor:** "great facilities," "great service," "perfect location and large rooms." [$] *Rooms from: $159* ✉ *1001 Heavenly Village Way* ☎ *530/542–8400, 800/627–7468* 🌐 *www.marriott.com* 🛏 *431 condos.*

$$ RESORT 🏨 **Sorensen's Resort.** Escape civilization by staying in a log cabin at this woodsy 165-acre resort within the Eldorado National Forest, 20 minutes south of town. **Pros:** gorgeous, rustic setting. **Cons:** nearest nightlife is 20 miles away in South Lake Tahoe. **TripAdvisor:** "cozy cabins," "amazing rustic hospitality," "gorgeous setting." [$] *Rooms from: $135* ✉ *14255 Hwy. 88, Hope Valley* ☎ *530/694–2203, 800/423–9949* 🌐 *www.sorensensresort.com* 🛏 *2 rooms with shared bath, 35 cabins, 5 houses.*

$$ HOTEL 🏨 **Tahoe Seasons Resort.** It's a 150-yard walk to California Lodge of Heavenly Mountain Resort from this all-suites time-share hotel, where every room has a two-person sunken hot tub. [$] *Rooms from: $175* ✉ *3901 Saddle Rd.* ☎ *530/541–6700 front desk, 800/540–4874 reservations* 🌐 *www.tahoeseasons.com* 🛏 *160 suites.*

NIGHTLIFE

Most of the area's nightlife is concentrated in the casinos over the border in Stateline. To avoid slot machines and blinking lights, try the California-side nightspots in and near Heavenly Village. The Marriott Timber Lodge bars are always dependable.

The Fresh Ketch. The lively bar at this popular seafood restaurant hosts bands on Tuesday, Thursday, and Friday year-round, Saturdays in summer. ✉ *2435 Venice Dr., off Tahoe Keys Blvd.* ☎ *530/541–5683* 🌐 *www.thefreshketch.com.*

Mc P's Irish Pub & Grill. You can hear live bands—rock, jazz, blues, alternative—on most nights at Mc P's, across the street from the Heavenly Gondola. ✉ *4093 Lake Tahoe Blvd., near Friday Ave.* ☎ *530/542–4435* 🌐 *www.mcpspubtahoe.com.*

SPORTS AND THE OUTDOORS

FISHING **Tahoe Sport Fishing.** One of the area's largest and oldest fishing-charter services offers morning and afternoon trips. Outings include all necessary gear and bait, and the crew cleans and packages your catch. ✉ *900*

Ski Run Blvd., off U.S. 50 ☎ *530/541–5448, 800/696–7797 in CA* ⊕ *www.tahoesportfishing.com.*

GOLF **Lake Tahoe Golf Course.** The 18-hole, par-71 course also has a driving range. Greens fees cost from $64 to $84; a cart (mandatory Friday to Sunday) costs $25. Twilight rates drop as low as $39. ⊠ *2500 Emerald Bay Rd, Hwy. 89/U.S. 50* ☎ *530/577–0788* ⊕ *www.laketahoegc.com.*

HIKING The south shore is a great jumping-off point for day treks into nearby Eldorado National Forest and Desolation Wilderness.

Desolation Wilderness. Trails at the 100-square-mile wilderness lead to gorgeous backcountry lakes and mountain peaks. It's called Desolation Wilderness for a reason, so bring a topographic map and compass, and carry water and food. In summer, you can access this area by boarding a boat taxi ($10 one way) at **Echo Chalet** (⊠ *9900 Echo Lakes Rd., off U.S. 50* ☎ *530/659–7207* ⊕ *www.echochalet.com*) and crossing Echo Lake. The Pacific Crest Trail also traverses Desolation Wilderness. ⊠ *El Dorado National Forest Information Center* ☎ *530/644–6048* ⊕ *www. fs.usda.gov/eldorado.*

Pacific Crest Trail. Hike a couple of miles on this famous mountain trail that stretches from Mexico to Canada. ⊠ *Echo Summit, about 12 miles southwest of South Lake Tahoe off U.S. 50* ☎ *916/285–1846, 888/728–7245* ⊕ *www.pcta.org.*

ICE-SKATING **Heavenly Village Outdoor Ice Rink.** If you're here in winter, practice your jumps and turns at this rink between the gondola and the cinema. ⊠ *1001 Heavenly Village Way* ☎ *530/542–4230* ⊠ *$20, includes skate rentals* ⊙ *Nov.–Mar., daily 10–8, weather permitting.*

South Tahoe Ice Arena. For year-round fun, head to this city-operated NHL regulation size indoor rink where you can rent equipment and sign up for lessons. In the evening the lights are turned low and a disco ball lights up the ice. Call ahead to check on the irregular hours. ⊠ *1176 Rufus Allen Blvd.* ☎ *530/542–6262* ⊠ *$9, plus $3 skate rental* ⊙ *Daily.*

KAYAKING **Kayak Tahoe.** Sign up for lessons and excursions (to the south shore, Emerald Bay, and Sand Harbor), offered from May through September. You can also rent a kayak and paddle solo on the lake. ⊠ *Timber Cove Marina, 3411 Lake Tahoe Blvd., at Balbijou Rd.* ☎ *530/544–2011* ⊕ *www.kayaktahoe.com.*

MOUNTAIN BIKING **Tahoe Sports Ltd.** You can rent road and mountain bikes and get tips on where to ride from the friendly staff at this full-service sports store. ⊠ *Tahoe Crescent V Shopping Center, 4000 Lake Tahoe Blvd., near Heavenly Valley Way* ☎ *530/542–4000* ⊕ *www.tahoesportsltd.com.*

SKIING If you don't want to pay the high cost of rental equipment at the resorts, you'll find reasonable prices and expert advice at Tahoe Sports *(see Mountain Biking, above).*

Fodor'sChoice **Heavenly Mountain Resort.** Straddling two states, vast Heavenly Moun-
★ tain Resort—composed of nine peaks, two valleys, and four base-lodge areas, along with the largest snowmaking system in the western United States—has terrain for every skier. Beginners can choose wide, well-groomed trails, accessed from the California Lodge or the gondola from

downtown South Lake Tahoe; kids have short and gentle runs in the Enchanted Forest area all to themselves. The Sky Express high-speed quad chair whisks intermediate and advanced skiers to the summit for wide cruisers or steep tree-skiing. Mott and Killebrew canyons draw experts to the Nevada side for steep chutes and thick-timber slopes. For snowboarders and tricksters, there are four different terrain parks.

The ski school is big and offers everything from learn-to-ski packages to canyon-adventure tours. Call about ski and boarding camps. Skiing lessons are available for children ages four and up; there's day care for infants older than six weeks. ⊠ *Ski Run Blvd., off U.S. 50* ☎ *775/586–7000, 800/432–8365 ⊕ www.skiheavenly.com ⟳ 94 trails on 4,800 acres, rated 20% beginner, 45% intermediate, 35% expert. Longest run 5½ miles, base 6,540 feet, summit 10,067 feet. Lifts: 30, including 1 aerial tram, 1 gondola, 2 high-speed 6-passenger lifts, and 8 high-speed quads.*

Hope Valley Cross Country. Operating from a yurt at Pickett's Junction, Hope Valley provides lessons and equipment rentals to prepare you for cross-country skiing and snowshoeing. The outfit has 60 miles of trails through Humboldt–Toiyabe National Forest, 10 of which are groomed. ⊠ *Hwy. 88 at Hwy. 89, Hope Valley* ☎ *530/694–2266 ⊕ www.hopevalleyoutdoors.com.*

★ **Kirkwood Ski Resort.** Thirty-six miles south of Lake Tahoe, Kirkwood Ski Resort is the hard-core skiers' and boarders' favorite south-shore mountain, known for its craggy gulp-and-go chutes, sweeping cornices, steep-aspect glade skiing, and high base elevation. But there's also fantastic terrain for newbies and intermediates down wide-open bowls, through wooded gullies, and along rolling tree-lined trails. Tricksters can show off in the Stomping Grounds terrain park on jumps, wall rides, rails, and a half-pipe, all visible from the base area. The mountain gets hammered with more than 500 inches of snow annually, and often has the most in all of North America. If you're into out-of-bounds skiing, check out Expedition Kirkwood, a backcountry-skills program that teaches basic safety awareness. Kirkwood is also the only Tahoe resort to offer Cat-skiing. If you're into cross-country, the resort has 80 km (50 miles) of superb groomed-track skiing, with skating lanes, instruction, and rentals. Nonskiers can snowshoe, snow-skate, and go dogsledding or snow-tubing. The children's ski school has programs for ages 4 to 12. ⊠ *1501 Kirkwood Meadows Dr., off Hwy. 88, 14 miles west of Hwy. 89, Kirkwood* ☎ *209/258–6000 downhill, 209/258–7248 cross-country, 209/258–7293 lodging information, 877/547–5966 snow phone ⊕ www.kirkwood.com ⟳ 65 trails on 2,300 acres, rated 15% beginner, 50% intermediate, 20% advanced, 15% expert. Longest run 2½ miles, base 7,800 feet, summit 9,800 feet. Lifts: 14, including 2 high-speed quads.*

Sierra-at-Tahoe. Often overlooked by skiers and boarders rushing to Heavenly or Kirkwood, Sierra-at-Tahoe has meticulously groomed intermediate slopes, some of the best tree-skiing in California, and gated backcountry access. Extremely popular with local snowboarders, Sierra also has six terrain parks, including a super-pipe with 17-foot

13

walls. For nonskiers there's a snow-tubing hill. Sierra has a low-key atmosphere that's great for families. Kids and beginners take the slow routes in the Mellow Yellow Zone. ⊠ *1111 Sierra-at-Tahoe Rd., 12 miles from South Lake Tahoe off U.S. 50, near Echo Summit, Twin Bridges* ☎ *530/659–7453* ⊕ *www.sierraattahoe.com* ☞ *46 trails on 2,000 acres, rated 25% beginner, 50% intermediate, 25% advanced. Longest run 2½ miles, base 6,640 feet, summit 8,852 feet. Lifts: 14, including 3 high-speed quads.*

POPE-BALDWIN RECREATION AREA

5 miles west of South Lake Tahoe on Hwy. 89.

To the west of downtown South Lake Tahoe, U.S. 50 and Highway 89 come together, forming an intersection nicknamed "the Y." If you head northwest on Highway 89, also called Emerald Bay Road, and follow the lakefront, commercial development gives way to national forests and state parks. One of these is Pope-Baldwin Recreation Area.

GETTING HERE AND AROUND

The entrance to the Pope-Baldwin Recreation Area is on the east side of Emerald Bay Road. In summer, BlueGO's Nifty 50 Trolley serves the area from South Lake Tahoe. From the northern and western communities, take a TART bus to Tahoma and transfer to the trolley. The area is closed to vehicles in winter, but you can cross-country ski here.

EXPLORING

Tallac Historic Site. Stroll or picnic lakeside, then explore **Pope House,** the magnificently restored 1894 mansion of George S. Pope, who made his money in shipping and lumber and played host to the business and cultural elite of 1920s America. There are two other estates here. One belonged to entrepreneur "Lucky" Baldwin; today it houses the **Baldwin Museum,** a collection of family memorabilia and Washoe Indian artifacts. The **Valhalla** (⊕ *www.valhallatahoe.com*), with a spectacular floor-to-ceiling stone fireplace, belonged to Walter Heller. Its Grand Hall and a lakeside boathouse, refurbished as a theater, host summertime concerts, plays, and cultural activities. Docents conduct tours of the Pope House in summer; call for tour times. In winter you can cross-country ski around the site. ⊠ *Hwy. 89* ☎ *530/541–5227* ⊕ *www. tahoeheritage.org* ☛ *Free; Pope House tour $5* ☉ *Grounds daily sunrise–sunset. Pope House and Baldwin Museum late May–mid-June, weekends 11–3; mid-June–early Sept., daily 11–4.*

☾ **Taylor Creek Visitor Center.** At this center operated by the U.S. Forest Service you can visit the site of a Washoe Indian settlement; walk self-guided trails through meadow, marsh, and forest; and inspect the Stream Profile Chamber, an underground display with windows right into Taylor Creek (in fall you may see spawning kokanee salmon digging their nests). In summer U.S. Forest Service naturalists organize discovery walks and evening programs (call ahead). ⊠ *Hwy. 89, 3 miles north of junction with U.S. 50* ☎ *530/543–2674 June–Oct., 530/543– 2600 year-round* ⊕ *www.fs.usda.gov/recmain/ltbmu/recreation* ☛ *Free* ☉ *Memorial Day–late Sept., daily 8–5; Oct., daily 8–4.*

Fjordlike Emerald Bay is quite possibly the prettiest part of Lake Tahoe.

EMERALD BAY STATE PARK

4 miles west of Pope-Baldwin Recreation Area on Hwy. 89.

GETTING HERE AND AROUND

The entrance to Emerald Bay State Park is on the east side of a narrow, twisty section of Highway 89. Caution is the keyword for both drivers and pedestrians. In summer, BlueGO's Nifty 50 Trolley serves the area from South Lake Tahoe. From the northern and western communities, take a TART bus to Tahoma and transfer to the trolley. The park is closed to vehicles in the winter.

EXPLORING

Fodor's Choice
★

Emerald Bay. A massive glacier millions of years ago carved this 3-mile-long and 1-mile-wide fjordlike inlet. Famed for its jewel-like shape and colors, the bay surrounds Fannette, Tahoe's only island. Highway 89 curves high above the lake through Emerald Bay State Park; from the Emerald Bay lookout, the centerpiece of the park, you can survey the whole scene. This is one of the don't-miss views of Lake Tahoe. The light is best in mid- to late morning, when the bay's colors really pop. ⊠ *Hwy. 89* ☎ *530/525–7232* ⊕ *www.parks.ca.gov.*

Vikingsholm. A steep 1-mile-long trail from the Emerald Bay lookout leads down to Vikingsholm, a 38-room estate completed in 1929. The original owner, Lora Knight, had this precise copy of a 1,200-year-old Viking castle built out of materials native to the area. She furnished it with Scandinavian antiques and hired artisans to build period reproductions. The sod roof sprouts wildflowers each spring. There are picnic tables nearby and a gray-sand beach for strolling. The hike back up is hard (especially if you're not yet acclimated to the elevation), but there are benches and stone culverts to rest on. At the 150-foot peak of Fannette Island are the ruins of a stone structure known as the Tea House, built in 1928 so that Knight's guests could have a place to enjoy afternoon refreshments after a motorboat ride. The island is off-limits from February through June to protect nesting Canada geese. The rest of the year it's open for day use. ⊠ *Hwy. 89* ☎ *530/541–6498 summer, 530/525–3345 year-round* ⊕ *www.vikingsholm.com* ✉ *Day-use parking fee $8, mansion tour $8* ⊙ *Late May–Sept., daily 10–4.*

SPORTS AND THE OUTDOORS

HIKING   **Eagle Falls.** Leave your car in the parking lot for Eagle Falls picnic area (near Vikingsholm; arrive early for a good spot), and head to these falls, a short but fairly steep walk-up canyon. You'll have a brilliant panorama of Emerald Bay from this spot, near the boundary of Desolation Wilderness. For a strenuous full-day hike, continue 5 miles, past Eagle Lake, to Upper and Middle Velma Lakes. Pick up trail maps at Taylor Creek Visitor Center in summer, or year-round at the main U.S. Forest Service Office in South Lake Tahoe, at 35 College Drive. ⊠ *Hwy. 89, South Lake Tahoe.*

D.L. BLISS STATE PARK

3 miles north of Emerald Bay State Park on Hwy. 89; 17 miles south of Tahoe City.

GETTING HERE AND AROUND

The entrance to D.L. Bliss State Park is on the east side of Highway 89 just north of Emerald Bay. In summer, BlueGO's Nifty 50 Trolley serves the area from South Lake Tahoe. From the northern and western communities, take a TART bus to Tahoma and transfer to the trolley.

EXPLORING

D.L. Bliss State Park. This park takes its name from Duane LeRoy Bliss, a 19th-century lumber magnate. At one time Bliss owned nearly 75% of Tahoe's lakefront, along with local steamboats, railroads, and banks. The park shares 6 miles of shoreline with Emerald Bay State Park; combined the two parks cover 1,830 acres, 744 of which the Bliss family donated to the state. At the north end of Bliss is Rubicon Point, which overlooks one of the lake's deepest spots. Short trails lead to an old lighthouse and Balancing Rock, which weighs 250,000 pounds and balances on a fist of granite. A 4.5-mile trail—one of Tahoe's premier hikes—leads to Vikingsholm and provides stunning lake views. Two white-sand beaches front some of Tahoe's warmest water. ⊠ *Hwy. 89* ☎ *530/525–3345, 800/777–0369* ⊕ *www.parks.ca.gov* ✉ *$8 per vehicle, day use* ⊙ *Late May–Sept., daily sunrise–sunset.*

SUGAR PINE POINT STATE PARK

8 miles north of D.L. Bliss State Park on Hwy. 89; 10 miles south of Tahoe City.

GETTING HERE AND AROUND

The entrance to Sugar Pine Point is on the east side of Highway 89, about a mile south of Tahoma. In summer, BlueGO's Nifty 50 Trolley serves the area from South Lake Tahoe. From the northern and western communities, take a TART bus to Tahoma and transfer to the trolley for the short ride to the entrance. There's also a bike trail that links Tahoe City to the park.

EXPLORING

★ **Ehrman Mansion.** The main attraction at Sugar Pine Point State Park is Ehrman Mansion, a 1903 stone-and-shingle summer home furnished in period style. In its day it was the height of modernity, with a refrigerator, an elevator, and an electric stove. Also in the park are a trapper's log cabin from the mid-19th century, a nature preserve with wildlife exhibits, a lighthouse, the start of the 10-mile biking trail to Tahoe City, and an extensive system of hiking and cross-country skiing trails. If you're feeling less ambitious, you can relax on the sun-dappled lawn behind the mansion and gaze out at the lake. ⊠ *Hwy. 89* ☎ *530/525–7982 mansion in season, 530/525–7232 year-round* ⊕ *www.parks.ca.gov* ⊠ *$8 per vehicle, day use; mansion tour $8* ⊙ *Mansion Memorial Day–Labor Day, daily 11–4.*

Sugar Pine Point State Park. Lake Tahoe's largest state park has 2,000 acres of dense forests and nearly 2 miles of shore frontage. A popular spot during snow season, Sugar Pine provides cross-country trails and winter camping on a first-come, first-served basis. Rangers lead three full-moon snowshoe tours from January to March. ⊠ *Hwy. 89, 1 mile south of Tahoma* ⊕ *www.parks.ca.gov.*

TAHOMA

1 mile north of Sugar Pine Point State Park on Hwy. 89; 23 miles south of Truckee on Hwy. 89.

With its rustic waterfront vacation cottages, Tahoma exemplifies life on the lake in its quiet early days before bright-lights casinos and huge crowds proliferated. In 1960 Tahoma was host of the Olympic Nordic-skiing competitions. Today there's little to do here except stroll by the lake and listen to the wind in the trees, making it a favorite home base for mellow families and nature buffs.

GETTING HERE AND AROUND

Approach Tahoma by car on Highway 89, called West Lake Boulevard in this section. In summer, BlueGO's Nifty 50 Trolley serves the area from South Lake Tahoe. From the northern and western communities, take a TART bus to Tahoma. A bike trail links Tahoe City to Tahoma.

WHERE TO STAY

For expanded reviews, facilities, and current deals, visit Fodors.com.

13

$$ B&B/INN ★ **Tahoma Meadows B&B Cottages.** It's hard to beat this serene property for atmosphere and woodsy charm; it's a great retreat for families and couples. **Pros:** lovely setting; good choice for families; close to Homewood ski resort. **Cons:** far from the casinos. **TripAdvisor:** "exceptional service," "nice accommodations," "best breakfast ever." [$] *Rooms from: $149* ✉ *6821 W. Lake Blvd.* ☎ *530/525–1553, 866/525–1553* 🌐 *www.tahomameadows.com* *16 cabins* 🍴 *Breakfast.*

SPORTS AND THE OUTDOORS

SKIING **Homewood Mountain Resort.** Schuss down these slopes for fantastic views—the mountain rises across the road from the Tahoe shoreline. This smaller, usually uncrowded resort is the favorite area of locals on a fresh-snow day, because you can find lots of untracked powder. It's also the most protected and least windy Tahoe ski area during a storm; when every other resort's lifts are on wind hold, you can almost always count on Homewood's to be open. There's only one high-speed chairlift, but there are rarely any lines, and the ticket prices are some of the cheapest around—kids 5 to 12 ski for $10, and those 4 and under are free. The resort may look small as you drive by, but most of it isn't visible from the road. ✉ *5145 W. Lake Blvd., Hwy. 89, 6 miles south of Tahoe City, Homewood* ☎ *530/525–2992* 🌐 *www.skihomewood.com* ☞ *60 trails on 1,260 acres, rated 15% beginner, 50% intermediate, and 35% advanced. Longest run 2 miles, base 6,230 feet, summit 7,880 feet. Lifts: 4 chairlifts, 4 surface lifts.*

TAHOE CITY

★ *10 miles north of Sugar Pine Point State Park on Hwy. 89; 14 miles south of Truckee on Hwy. 89.*

Tahoe City is the only lakeside town with a charming downtown area good for strolling and window-shopping. Stores and restaurants are all within walking distance of the Outlet Gates, where water is spilled into the Truckee River to control the surface level of the lake. You can spot giant trout in the river from Fanny Bridge, so-called for the views of the backsides of sightseers leaning over the railing.

GETTING HERE AND AROUND

Tahoe City is at the junction of Highway 28, also called North Lake Boulevard, and Highway 89 where it turns northwest toward Squaw Valley and Truckee. TART buses serve the communities along the north and west shores, and connects them to Truckee. Or you could arrive in Truckee via Greyhound bus or Amtrak, rent a car there, and drive to Tahoe City.

ESSENTIALS

Visitor Information North Lake Tahoe Resort Association ☎ *530/583–3494, 888/434–1262* 🌐 *www.gotahoenorth.com.*

EXPLORING

★ **Gatekeeper's Cabin Museum.** This museum preserves a little-known part of the region's history. Between 1910 and 1968 the gatekeeper who lived on this site was responsible for monitoring the level of the lake, using a hand-turned winch system (still used today) to keep the water at the correct level. Also on this site, the fantastic Marian Steinbach Indian Basket Museum displays 800 baskets from 85 tribes. ✉ *130 W. Lake Blvd.* ☎ *530/583–1762* 🌐 *www.northtahoemuseums.org* 🎟 *$5* ⏲ *May–Sept., Wed.–Mon. 10–5; Oct.–Apr., Fri. and Sat. 11–5.*

Watson Cabin Living Museum. In the middle of town sits a 1909 log cabin built by Robert M. Watson and his son. Now a museum, it's filled with century-old furnishings and many reproductions. Docents are available to answer questions and will lead tours if you call ahead. ✉ *560 N. Lake Blvd.* ☎ *530/583–8717, 530/583–1762* 🌐 *www.northtahoemuseums.org* 🎟 *$2 donation suggested* ⏲ *Late May–early Sept., Thurs.–Mon. 10–5.*

13

WHERE TO EAT

$$$ AMERICAN

🍴 **Christy Hill.** Huge windows give diners here some of the best lake views in Tahoe. The menu features solid Euro–Cal preparations of fresh seafood, filet mignon, or vegetarian selections. The extensive wine list and exceptionally good desserts earn accolades, as do the gracious service and casual vibe. If the weather is balmy, have dinner on the deck. In any season, this is the romantic choice for lake gazing and wine sipping. [$] *Average main: $24* ✉ *Lakehouse Mall, 115 Grove St., at N. Lake Blvd.* ☎ *530/583–8551* 🌐 *www.christyhill.com* ⏲ *No lunch.*

$ AMERICAN

🍴 **Fire Sign Café.** Watch the road carefully or you'll miss this great little diner 2 miles south of Tahoe City on Highway 89. There's often a wait for breakfast and lunch, but it's worth it. The pastries are made from scratch, the salmon is smoked in-house, the salsa is hand cut, and there's real maple syrup for the many types of pancakes and waffles. Leave room for dessert; a fruit cobbler is almost always on the menu. [$] *Average main: $9* ✉ *1785 W. Lake Blvd., at Fountain Ave.* ☎ *530/583–0871* ✍ *Reservations not accepted* ⏲ *No dinner.*

$$$ ECLECTIC

🍴 **Wolfdale's.** Consistent, inspired cuisine makes Wolfdale's one of the top restaurants on the lake. Seafood is the specialty on the changing menu; the imaginative entrées merge Asian and European cooking (drawing on the chef-owner's training in Japan) and lean toward the light and healthful, rather than the heavy and overdone. Everything from teriyaki glaze to smoked fish is made in-house. Request a window table, and book early enough to see the lake view from the elegantly simple dining room. [$] *Average main: $27* ✉ *640 N. Lake Blvd., near Grove St.* ☎ *530/583–5700* 🌐 *www.wolfdales.com* ✍ *Reservations essential* ⏲ *Closed Tues. No lunch.*

WHERE TO STAY

For expanded reviews, facilities, and current deals, visit Fodors.com.

$$ B&B/INN

🏨 **Cottage Inn.** Avoid the crowds by staying in one of these charming circa-1938 log cottages under the towering pines on the lake's west shore. **Pros:** romantic, woodsy setting; each room has a fireplace; full breakfast. **Cons:** no kids under 12. **TripAdvisor:** "lovely cottages," "nice location and facilities," "charming and comfortable." [$] *Rooms from: $145* ✉ *1690 W. Lake Blvd., Box 66* ☎ *530/581–4073, 800/581–4073* 🌐 *www.thecottageinn.com* 🛏 *22 rooms.*

$$ HOTEL

🏨 **River Ranch Lodge.** Tucked into a bend of the Truckee River, this intimate lodge is a short distance from major ski resorts and the town center. **Pros:** beautiful river site; lounge with a gorgeous curved wall of windows. **Cons:** rooms fill quickly. **TripAdvisor:** "not bad at all," "retro charm," "cozy inn." [$] *Rooms from: $120* ✉ *Hwy. 89 at Alpine Meadows Rd.* ☎ *530/583–4264, 866/991–9912* 🌐 *www.riverranchlodge.com* 🛏 *19 rooms* 🍴 *Breakfast.*

$$$ HOTEL ★ 🏨 **Sunnyside Steakhouse and Lodge.** The views are superb at this pretty little lodge right on the lake, 3 miles south of Tahoe City. **Pros:** complimentary Continental breakfast and afternoon tea; most rooms have balconies overlooking the lake. **Cons:** can be pricey for families. **TripAdvisor:** "a great getaway spot," "friendly and lovely," "excellent in every way." [$] *Rooms from: $200* ✉ *1850 W. Lake Blvd., Box 5969* ☎ *530/583–7200, 800/822–2754* 🌐 *www.sunnysideresort.com* 🛏 *18 rooms, 5 suites* 🍴 *Breakfast.*

SPORTS AND THE OUTDOORS

GOLF **Tahoe City Golf Course.** Golfers use pull carts or caddies at this 9-hole course, which opened in 1917. ■ **TIP→ All greens break toward the lake.** Though rates vary by season, the maximum greens fees are $40 for 9 holes, $75 for 18; a power cart costs $15 to $25. ✉ *251 N. Lake Blvd.* ☎ *530/583–1516* 🌐 *www.tahoecitygolf.com.*

MOUNTAIN BIKING **Cyclepaths Mountain Bike Adventures.** This combination full-service bike shop and bike-adventure outfitter offers instruction in mountain biking, guided tours, tips for self-guided bike touring, bike repairs, and books and maps on the area. ✉ *10200 Donner Pass Rd., off I–80/Hwy. 89, Truckee* ☎ *530/582–1890* 🌐 *www.cyclepaths.com.*

RIVER RAFTING 👶 **Truckee River Rafting.** In summer you can take a self-guided raft trip down a gentle 5-mile stretch of the Truckee River. The outfitters will shuttle you back to Tahoe City at the end of your two- to three-hour trip. On a warm day, this makes a great family outing. ✉ *175 River Rd., near W. Lake Blvd.* ☎ *530/583–1111* 🌐 *www.truckeeriverrafting.com.*

SKIING ★ **Alpine Meadows Ski Area.** The locals' favorite place to ski on the north shore is also the unofficial telemarking hub of the Sierra. With 495 inches of snow annually, Alpine has some of Tahoe's most reliable conditions. It's usually one of the first areas to open in November and one of the last to close in May or June. Alpine isn't the place for arrogant show-offs; instead, you'll find down-to-earth alpine fetishists. The two peaks here are well suited to intermediate skiers, with a number of runs for experts only. Snowboarders and hot-dog skiers will find a terrain park with a super-pipe, rails, and tabletops, as well as a boarder-cross course. Alpine is a great place to learn to ski and has a ski school that teaches and coaches those with physical and mental disabilities. On Saturday, because of the limited parking, there's more acreage per person than at other resorts. ✉ *2600 Alpine Meadows Rd., off Hwy. 89, 6 miles northwest of Tahoe City and 13 miles south of Truckee* ☎ *530/583–4232, 800/441–4423, 530/581–8374 snow phone* 🌐 *www.skialpine.com* ☞ *100 trails on 2,400 acres, rated 25% beginner, 40% intermediate, 35% advanced. Longest run 2½ miles, base 6,835 feet, summit 8,637 feet. Lifts: 14, including 1 high-speed 6-passenger lift and 2 high-speed quads.*

Squaw Valley USA has runs for skiers of all ability levels—from beginner trails to cliff drops for experts.

Tahoe Dave's Skis and Boards. You can rent skis, boards, and snowshoes at this shop, which touts the area's best selection of downhill rental equipment. ⊠ *590 N. Lake Blvd.* ☎ *530/583–0400.*

OLYMPIC VALLEY

7 miles north of Tahoe City via Hwy. 89 to Squaw Valley Rd.; 8½ miles south of Truckee via Hwy. 89 to Squaw Valley Rd.

Olympic Valley got its name in 1960, when Squaw Valley USA, the ski resort here, hosted the Winter Olympics. Snow sports remain the primary activity, but once summer comes, you can hike into the adjacent Granite Chief Wilderness, explore wildflower-studded alpine meadows, or lie by a swimming pool in one of the Sierra's prettiest valleys.

GETTING HERE AND AROUND

Squaw Valley Rd., the only way into Olympic Valley, branches west off Highway 89 about 8 miles south of Truckee. TART connects the Squaw Valley ski area with the communities along the north and west shores, and Truckee, with year-round public transportation. Squaw Valley Ski Resort provides a free shuttle to many stops in those same areas.

EXPLORING

High Camp. You can ride the Squaw Valley Aerial Tram to this activity hub, which at 8,200 feet commands superb views of Lake Tahoe and the surrounding mountains. In summer, go for a hike, sit by the pool, or have a cocktail and watch the sunset. In winter, you can ski, ice-skate, or snow-tube. There's also a restaurant, a lounge, and a small Olympic museum. ⊠ *Aerial Tram Bldg., Squaw Valley* ☎ *530/581–7278 High*

Camp ⊕ *www.squaw.com/the-village* ⊠ *Aerial Tram, $29* ⊙ *Daily; call for hrs.*

⊛ **Village at Squaw Valley.** The centerpiece of Olympic Valley is a pedestrian mall at the base of several four-story ersatz Bavarian stone-and-timber buildings, where you'll find restaurants, high-end condo rentals, boutiques, and cafés. ⊠ *1750 Village East Rd.* ☎ *530/584–1000, 530/584–6205, 888/805–5022 condo reservations* ⊕ *www.squaw.com/the-village.*

WHERE TO EAT

$$$

ECLECTIC

✕ **Graham's of Squaw Valley.** Sit by a floor-to-ceiling river-rock hearth under a knotty-pine peaked ceiling in the intimate dining room in the Christy Inn Lodge. The southern European–inspired menu changes often, but expect hearty entrées such as fillet of beef with wild mushroom sauce, along with lighter-fare small plates like quail with red wine demi-glace. You can also stop in at the fireside bar for appetizers and wine from Graham's highly regarded wine list. $ *Average main: $26* ⊠ *1650 Squaw Valley Rd.* ☎ *530/581–0454* ⊙ *Closed Mon. No lunch.*

$$

JAPANESE

✕ **Mamasake.** The hip and happening spot for sushi at Squaw serves stylized presentations. In the evening, sit at the bar and watch extreme ski movies, many of which were filmed right outside the window. Or drop in from 3 to 5 to enjoy the inexpensive afternoon special: a spicy-tuna or salmon hand roll and a can of Bud for five bucks. $ *Average main: $16* ⊠ *1800 Village South Rd., off Squaw Valley Rd.* ☎ *530/584–0110* ⊕ *www.mamasake.com.*

$$$

AMERICAN

Fodor'sChoice

★

✕ **PlumpJack Café.** The best restaurant at Olympic Valley is also the finest in the entire Tahoe Basin, the epitome of discreet chic and a must-visit for all serious foodies. The menu changes seasonally, but look for roasted quail in an orange sauce, crispy sweetbreads, and butter poached lobster tail. Rather than complicated, heavy sauces, the chef uses simple reductions to complement a dish. The result: clean, dynamic, bright flavors. The wine list is exceptional for its variety and surprisingly low prices. A less expensive but equally adventurous menu, including lunch, is served at the bar. $ *Average main: $28* ⊠ *1920 Squaw Valley Rd.* ☎ *530/583–1578, 800/323–7666* ⊕ *www.plumpjackcafe.com* ⚓ *Reservations essential.*

WHERE TO STAY

For expanded reviews, facilities, and current deals, visit Fodors.com.

$$$

HOTEL

Fodor'sChoice

★

⌂ **PlumpJack Squaw Valley Inn.** If style and luxury are a must, make PlumpJack your first choice. **Pros:** small; intimate; lots of attention to details. **Cons:** not the best choice for families with small children. **TripAdvisor:** "perfect location," "best food and lodging in Tahoe," "great staff." $ *Rooms from: $210* ⊠ *1920 Squaw Valley Rd.* ☎ *530/583–1576, 800/323–7666* ⊕ *www.plumpjacksquawvalleyinn.com* ⇒ *56 rooms, 8 suites* ⦿ *Breakfast.*

$$$

HOTEL

⌂ **The Village at Squaw Valley USA.** Right at the base of the slopes, at the center point of Olympic Valley, the Village's condominiums were built in 2000 and still look fresh. **Pros:** family-friendly; near Village restaurants and shops. **Cons:** claustrophobia-inducing crowds on weekends. **TripAdvisor:** "great location," "good service," "comfortable condo."

[$] *Rooms from: $179* ✉ *1750 Village East Rd.* ☎ *530/584–1000, 866/818–6963* 🌐 *www.squaw.com/the-village/lodging* 🛏 *198 suites.*

SPORTS AND THE OUTDOORS

GOLF **Resort at Squaw Creek Golf Course.** This narrow, challenging 18-hole par-71 championship course was designed by Robert Trent Jones Jr. Greens fees range from $60 for afternoon play to $95 for prime time, and include the use of a cart. ✉ *400 Squaw Creek Rd.* ☎ *530/583–6300* 🌐 *www.squawcreek.com.*

HIKING **High Camp.** The Granite Chief Wilderness and the high peaks surrounding Olympic Valley are accessible by foot, but save yourself a 2,000-foot elevation gain by riding the Squaw Valley Aerial Tram to High Camp, the starting point for several hikes. Pick up trail maps at the tram building. High Camp offers sunset hikes in summer, and full moon hikes in winter. ☎ *530/583–6985* 🌐 *www.squaw.com.*

ICE-SKATING 👶 **Olympic Ice Pavilion.** Ice-skate here from late November to mid-March. A ride up the mountain in the Aerial Tram costs $29, plus $12 for skate rental and one hour of skate time. End your outing in the hot tub ($10). In summer, the pavilion converts into a roller-skating rink. Year-round, you get fabulous views of the lake and the Sierra Nevada. ✉ *1960 Squaw Valley Rd., High Camp, Squaw Valley* ☎ *800/403–0206, 530/581–7246* 🌐 *www.squaw.com.*

MINIATURE GOLF 👶 ★ **Squaw Valley Adventure Center.** Next to the Olympic Village Lodge, on the far side of the creek, this activities center has an 18-hole miniature golf course, a ropes course, and sometimes a bungee trampoline, a blast for kids. ✉ *1960 Squaw Valley Rd.* ☎ *530/583–7673* 🌐 *www.squawadventure.com.*

ROCK CLIMBING **Headwall Climbing Wall.** Before you rappel down a granite monolith, hone your skills at this challenging wall at the base of the Aerial Tram. ✉ *Squaw Valley Adventure Center, 1960 Squaw Valley Rd.* ☎ *530/583–7673* 🌐 *www.squawadventure.com.*

SKIING **Resort at Squaw Creek.** Cross-country skiers enjoy looping through the valley's giant alpine meadow. The resort rents equipment and provides trail maps. ✉ *400 Squaw Creek Rd.* ☎ *530/583–6300* 🌐 *www.squawcreek.com.*

Fodor's Choice ★ **Squaw Valley USA.** Known for some of the toughest skiing in the Tahoe area, this park was the centerpiece of the 1960 Winter Olympics. Today it's the definitive North Tahoe ski resort and among the top-three megaresorts in California (the other two are Heavenly and Mammoth). Although Squaw has changed significantly since the Olympics, the skiing is still world-class and extends across vast bowls stretched between six peaks. Experts often head directly to the untamed terrain of the infamous KT-22 face, which has bumps, cliffs, and gulp-and-go chutes, or to the nearly vertical Palisades, where many famous Warren Miller extreme-skiing films have been shot. Fret not, beginners and intermediates: you have plenty of wide-open, groomed trails at High Camp (which sits at the *top* of the mountain) and around the more challenging Snow King Peak. Snowboarders and show-off skiers can tear up the three fantastic terrain parks, which include a giant super-pipe. Lift prices include night skiing until 8 pm. ⊠ *1960 Squaw Valley Rd., off Hwy. 89, 7 miles northwest of Tahoe City* ☎ *530/583–6985, 800/545–4350 lodging reservations, 530/583–6955 snow phone* ⊕ *www.squaw. com* ↻ *170 trails on 4,000 acres, rated 25% beginner, 45% intermediate, 30% advanced. Longest run 3.2 miles, base 6,200 feet, summit 9,050 feet. Lifts: 33, including a gondola-style funitel, a tram, 7 high-speed chairs, and 18 fixed-grip chairs.*

Tahoe Dave's Skis and Boards. If you don't want to pay resort prices, you can rent and tune downhill skis and snowboards at this shop. ⊠ *3039 Hwy. 89, at Squaw Valley Rd.* ☎ *530/583–5665* ⊕ *www.tahoedaves. com.*

TRUCKEE

13 miles northwest of Kings Beach on Hwy. 267; 14 miles north of Tahoe City on Hwy. 89.

Formerly a decrepit railroad town in the mountains, Truckee is now the trendy first stop for many Tahoe visitors. The town was officially established around 1863, and by 1868 it had gone from a stagecoach station to a major stopover for trains bound for the Pacific via the new transcontinental railroad. Freight trains and Amtrak's California Zephyr still stop every day at the depot right in the middle of town. Stop inside the depot for a walking-tour map of historic Truckee. Across from the station, where Old West facades line the main drag, you'll find galleries, gift shops, boutiques, old-fashioned diners, and several remarkably good restaurants. Look for outlet stores, strip malls, and discount skiwear shops along Donner Pass Road, north of the freeway. Because of its location on Interstate 80, Truckee is a favorite stopover for people traveling from the San Francisco Bay Area to the north shore of Lake Tahoe, Reno, and points east.

GETTING HERE AND AROUND

Truckee is just off Interstate 80 between Highways 89 and 267. Greyhound and Amtrak stop here, Enterprise and Hertz provide car rentals, and TART buses serve Truckee and north shore communities.

ESSENTIALS

Visitor Information Truckee Donner Chamber of Commerce and the California Welcome Center ⊠ *Amtrak depot, 10065 Donner Pass Rd., near Spring St.* ☎ *530/587–8808* ⊕ *www.truckee.com.*

EXPLORING

Donner Memorial State Park and Emigrant Trail Museum. The park and museum commemorate the Donner Party, westward-bound pioneers—about 90; historians debate the exact number—who became trapped in the Sierra in the winter of 1846–47 in snow 22 feet deep. Barely more than half the pioneers survived, some by resorting to cannibalism. The Emigrant Trail Museum details the Donner Party's plight, and other displays explain railroad development through the Sierra. In the park, you can picnic, hike, camp, and go boating, fishing, and water-skiing in summer; winter brings cross-country skiing and snowshoeing on groomed trails. Slated for a late-summer 2013 debut, a new High Sierra Crossing Museum will contain exhibits about the Donner Party, regional Native Americans, and railroad and transportation development through Donner Pass. ✉ *12593 Donner Pass Rd., off I–80, 2 miles west of Truckee* ☎ *530/582–7892 museum, 800/444–7275 camping reservations* 🌐 *www.parks.ca.gov* 🎫 *$8 parking, day use* 🕒 *Museum late May–early Sept., daily 9–4; closed Tues. and Wed. early Sept.–late May.*

OFF THE BEATEN PATH

Tahoe National Forest. Draped along the Sierra Nevada Crest above Lake Tahoe, the national forest offers abundant outdoor recreation: picnicking and camping in summer, and in winter, snowshoeing, skiing, and sledding over some of the deepest snowpack in the West. The **Big Bend Visitor Center** occupies a state historic landmark within the forest, 10 miles west of Donner Summit. This area has been on major cross-country routes for centuries, ever since Native Americans passed through trading acorns and salt for pelts, obsidian, and other materials. Between 1844 and 1860, more than 200,000 emigrants traveled to California along the Emigrant Trail, which passed nearby; you can see rut marks left by wagon wheels scraping the famously hard granite. Later the nation's first transcontinental railroad ran through here (and still does), as do U.S. 40 (the old National Road) and its successor, Interstate 80. Exhibits in the visitor center explore the area's transportation history. ✉ *49685 Hampshire Rocks Rd., Rainbow–Big Bend exit off I–80, Soda Springs* ☎ *530/426–3609, 530/265–4531* 🌐 *www.fs.usda.gov/tahoe* 🎫 *Free* 🕒 *Summer months only, hrs vary; call ahead.*

WHERE TO EAT

$$$ ECLECTIC

🍴 **Cottonwood.** Perched above town on the site of North America's first chairlift, the Cottonwood restaurant is a veritable institution. The bar is decked out with old wooden skis, sleds, skates, and photos of Truckee's early days. The dining area serves an ambitious menu—everything from grilled New York strip steak to baby back short ribs with Cajun spices to butternut squash enchiladas, plus fresh-baked breads and desserts—but people come here mainly for the atmosphere and hilltop views. [$] *Average main: $23* ✉ *10142 Rue Hilltop, off Brockway Rd., ¼ mile south of downtown* ☎ *530/587–5711* 🌐 *www.cottonwoodrestaurant.com* 🕒 *No lunch.*

$$ ASIAN

🍴 **Dragonfly.** Flavors are bold and zingy at this Cal-Asian spot, where every dish is well executed and stylishly presented. Southeast Asian cooking inspires most dishes, which you can savor in the bright, contemporary dining rooms—one for sushi—or an outdoor terrace overlooking Main Street and the train depot. Lunch is a bargain, and there are many choices for vegetarians. Look for the staircase: the restaurant is on the second floor, not at street level. [$] *Average main: $22* ✉ *10118 Donner Pass Rd., at Spring St.* ☎ *530/587–0557* 🌐 *www.dragonflycuisine.com.*

$$ AMERICAN

🍴 **FiftyFifty Brewing Company.** In this Truckee brewpub, warm red tones and comfy booths, plus a pint of the Donner Party Porter, will take the nip out of a cold day on the slopes. The lunch menu includes salads, burgers, and the house specialty, a pulled-pork sandwich. After 5 pm, you can tuck into barbecued ribs and pan-seared salmon. Order one of their inventive pizzas anytime. There's a full bar along with the brews, and lots of après-ski action. $ *Average main: $19* ✉ *11197 Brockway Rd.* ☎ *530/587–2337* ⊕ *www.fiftyfiftybrewing.com.*

$$$ ✗ **Moody's Bistro Bar & Beats.** Head here for contemporary-Cal cuisine
ECLECTIC in a sexy dining room with pumpkin-color walls, burgundy velvet banquettes, and art-deco fixtures. The earthy, sure-handed cooking features organically grown ingredients: look for ahi poke, snazzy pizzas bubbling-hot from a brick oven, pan-roasted wild game, fresh seafood, and organic grass-fed steak. Lunch fare is lighter. In summer dine alfresco surrounded by flowers. From Thursday through Saturday there's music in the borderline-raucous bar that gets packed with Truckee's bon vivants. $ *Average main: $23* ✉ *10007 Bridge St., at Church St.* ☎ *530/587–8688* ⊕ *www.moodysbistro.com.*

WHERE TO STAY
For expanded reviews, facilities, and current deals, visit Fodors.com.

$$$ ⊡ **Cedar House Sport Hotel.** Cedar House ups the ante for lodging at
HOTEL Tahoe: the clean, spare lines of the wooden exterior evoke a modern European feel, while energy-saving heating, cooling, and lighting systems, countertops made from recycled paper, and other green features emphasize the owners' commitment to sustainability. **Pros:** an environmentally friendly; comfortable; hip. **Cons:** some bathrooms on the small side. **TripAdvisor:** "excellent European feel," "ultra comfortable," "impeccable service." $ *Rooms from: $175* ✉ *10918 Brockway Rd.* ☎ *530/582–5655, 866/582–5655* ⊕ *www.cedarhousesporthotel. com* ↝ *41 rooms* ‖○‖ *Breakfast.*

$$$$ ⊡ **Northstar-at-Tahoe Resort.** The area's most complete destination resort
RESORT is perfect for families, thanks to its many sports activities—from golf and tennis to skiing and snowshoeing—and its concentration of restaurants, shops, recreation facilities, and accommodations. **Pros:** array of lodging types; on-site shuttle, several dining options in Northstar Village. **Cons:** family accommodations are very pricey. **TripAdvisor:** "beautiful condos," "excellent skiing," "great location." $ *Rooms from: $229* ✉ *Hwy. 267, 6 miles southeast of Truckee, Box 129* ☎ *530/562–1010, 800/466–6784* ⊕ *www.northstarattahoe.com* ↝ *250 units.*

$$$$ ⊡ **Ritz-Carlton Highlands Court, Lake Tahoe.** The first luxury hotel built in
RESORT the Tahoe area in decades, the Ritz-Carlton opened in December 2009. **Pros:** superb service; gorgeous setting. **Cons:** prices as breathtaking as the views; must go off-site for golf and tennis. **TripAdvisor:** "serene," "majestic beauty," "world class." $ *Rooms from: $819* ✉ *13031 Ritz-Carlton Highlands Court* ☎ *530/562–3000, 800/241–3333* ⊕ *www. ritzcarlton.com/laketahoe* ↝ *153 rooms, 17 suites.*

$$ ⊡ **River Street Inn.** On the banks of the Truckee River, this 1885 wood-
B&B/INN and-stone inn was at times a boardinghouse and a brothel. **Pros:** nice rooms; good value. **Cons:** parking is a half block from inn. **TripAdvisor:** "thoughtful and supportive proprietors," "the ambience was exceptional," "great accommodations and service." $ *Rooms from: $130* ✉ *10009 E. River St.* ☎ *530/550–9290* ⊕ *www.riverstreetinntruckee. com* ↝ *11 rooms* ‖○‖ *Breakfast.*

SPORTS AND THE OUTDOORS

GOLF **Coyote Moon Golf Course.** This course is challenging and beautiful, with no houses to spoil the view. Fees range from $95 to $149, including cart. ⊠ *10685 Northwoods Blvd., off Donner Pass Rd.* ☎ *530/587–0886* ⊕ *www.coyotemoongolf.com.*

Northstar. The course here has open links–style play and tight, tree-lined fairways, including water hazards. Fees range from $45 to $80, including cart. ⊠ *Hwy. 267, at Northstar Dr.* ☎ *530/562–3290* ⊕ *www. northstarattahoe.com.*

Old Greenwood. At north Lake Tahoe's only Jack Nicklaus signature course, the water hazards are trout streams where you can actually fish. The $100–$185 fee includes a cart. ⊠ *12915 Fairway Dr., off Overland Trail Rd., off I–80, Exit 190* ☎ *530/550–7010* ⊕ *www.oldgreenwood. com.*

MOUNTAIN **Northstar-at-Tahoe.** In summer you can rent a bike and ride the lifts to
BIKING the mountain-biking park for 100 miles of challenging terrain. The lift ride is $42 for ages 13 and above; $27 for ages 9–12. The season extends from mid-June through September with varying hours. ⊠ *Hwy. 267, at Northstar Dr.* ☎ *530/562–2268* ⊕ *www.northstarattahoe.com.*

SKIING Several smaller resorts around Truckee give you access to the Sierra's slopes for less than half the price of the big resorts. Though you'll sacrifice vertical rise, acreage, and high-speed lifts, you can ski or ride and still have money left over for room and board. These are great places for first-timers and families with kids learning to ski.

Boreal. These slopes have 480 skiable acres and 500 vertical feet of terrain visible from the freeway; lift-served snow-tubing and night skiing go until 9. ⊠ *19749 Boreal Ridge Rd., at I–80, Boreal/Castle Peak exit, Soda Springs* ☎ *530/426–3666* ⊕ *www.rideboreal.com.*

Donner Ski Ranch. This ski park has 505 acres and 750 vertical feet and sits across from the more challenging Sugar Bowl (⇨ *below*). ⊠ *19320 Donner Pass Rd., Norden* ☎ *530/426–3635* ⊕ *www.donnerskiranch. com.*

Northstar-at-Tahoe. With two tree-lined, northeast-facing, wind-protected bowls, this park is the ideal place in a storm, and just may be the best all-around family ski resort at Tahoe. Hotshot experts unfairly call the mountain "Flatstar," but the meticulous grooming and long cruisers make it an intermediate skier's paradise. Boarders are especially welcome, with awesome terrain parks, including a 420-foot-long super-pipe, a half-pipe, rails and boxes, and lots of kickers. Experts can ski the steeps and bumps off Lookout Mountain, where there's rarely a line for the high-speed quad. Northstar-at-Tahoe's cross-country center has 25 miles of groomed trails, including double-set tracks and skating lanes. The school has programs for skiers ages four and up, and day care is available for tots two and older. The mountain gets packed on busy weekends but when there's room on the slopes, Northstar is loads of fun. ⊠ *100 Northstar Dr., off Hwy. 267, 6 miles southeast of Truckee* ☎ *530/562–1010, 800/466–6784, 530/562–1330 snow phone* ⊕ *www.northstarattahoe.com* ☞ *93 trails on 3,000 acres, rated 13% beginner, 60% intermediate, 27% advanced. Longest run 1.4 miles,* base 6,330 feet, summit 8,610 feet. Lifts: 19, including a gondola and 6 high-speed quads.

★ **Royal Gorge.** If you love to cross-country, don't miss Royal Gorge, which serves up 93 miles of 18-foot-wide track for all abilities, 65 trails on a whopping 9,172 acres, a ski school, and eight warming huts. Two trailside cafés and two lodges round out the facilities. Since it's right on the Sierra Crest, the views are drop-dead gorgeous, and the resort feels like it goes on forever. ✉ 9411 Hillside Dr., off I–80, Soda Springs/ Norden exit, Soda Springs ☎ 530/426–3871 ⊕ www.royalgorge.com.

Soda Springs. Along with 200 acres and 652 vertical feet, this ski park also has lift-served snow-tubing. ✉ 10244 Soda Springs Rd., I–80 Soda Springs exit, Soda Springs ☎ 530/426–3901 ⊕ www.skisodasprings. com.

Sugar Bowl. Opened in 1939 by Walt Disney, this is the oldest—and one of the best—resorts at Tahoe. Atop Donner Summit, it receives an incredible 500 inches of snowfall annually. Four peaks are connected by 1,500 acres of skiable terrain, with everything from gentle groomed corduroy to wide-open bowls to vertical rocky chutes and outstanding tree skiing. Snowboarders can hit two terrain parks with numerous boxes, rails, and jumps. Because it's more compact than some of the area's megaresorts, there's a certain gentility here that distinguishes Sugar Bowl from its competitors, making this a great place for families and a low-pressure, low-key place to learn to ski. It's not huge, but there's some very challenging terrain (experts: head to the Palisades). There's limited lodging at the base area. ✉ 629 Sugar Bowl Rd., off Donner Pass Rd., 3 miles east of I–80 Soda Springs/Norden exit, 10 miles west of Truckee, Norden ☎ 530/426–9000 information and lodging reservations, 530/426–1111 snow phone, 866/843–2695 lodging referral ⊕ www.sugarbowl.com ⌖ 95 trails on 1,500 acres, rated 17% beginner, 45% intermediate, 38% advanced. Longest run 3 miles, base 6,883 feet, summit 8,383 feet. Lifts: 13, including 5 high-speed quads.

Tahoe Dave's. You can save money by renting skis and boards at this shop, which has the area's best selection and also repairs and tunes equipment. ✉ 10200 Donner Pass Rd., near Spring St. ☎ 530/582–0900 ⊕ www.tahoedaves.com.

Tahoe Donner. Just north of Truckee, this park covers 120 acres and 560 vertical feet; the cross-country center includes 51 trails on 114 km (71 miles) of groomed tracks on 4,800 acres, with night skiing on Wednesday in January and February. ✉ 11509 Northwoods Blvd., at Muhlebach Way ☎ 530/587–9444 ⊕ www.tahoedonner.com.

CARNELIAN BAY TO KINGS BEACH

5–10 miles northeast of Tahoe City on Hwy. 28.

The small lakeside commercial districts of Carnelian Bay and Tahoe Vista service the thousand or so locals who live in the area year-round and the thousands more who have summer residences or launch their boats here. Kings Beach, the last town heading east on Highway 28 before the Nevada border, is to Crystal Bay what South Lake Tahoe is to Stateline: a bustling California town full of basic motels and rental condos, restaurants, and shops, used by the hordes of hopefuls who pass through on their way to the casinos.

GETTING HERE AND AROUND

To reach Kings Beach and Carnelian Bay from the California side, take Highway 89 north to Highway 28 north and then east. From the Nevada side, follow Highway 28 north and then west. TART provides public transportation in this area.

BEACHES

☺ **Kings Beach State Recreation Area.** The 28-acre Kings Beach State Recreation Area, one of the largest such areas on the lake, is open year-round. The 700-foot-long sandy beach gets very crowded in summer with people swimming, sunbathing, jet-skiing, riding in paddleboats, spiking volleyballs, and tossing Frisbees. If you're going to spend the day, come early enough to snag a table in the picnic area; there's also a good playground. **Amenities:** food and drink; parking (fee); toilets; water sports. **Best For:** sunrise; swimming; windsurfing. ✉ *8318 N. Lake Blvd., Hwy. 28, Kings Beach* ☎ *530/546–7248* 🎫 *$8 parking fee* 🕐 *Daily.*

WHERE TO EAT AND STAY

For expanded reviews, facilities, and current deals, visit Fodors.com.

$$$ ECLECTIC 🍴 **Gar Woods Grill and Pier.** The view's the thing at this lakeside stalwart, where you can watch the sun shimmer on the water through the dining room's plate-glass windows or from the heated outdoor deck. Grilled steak and fish are menu mainstays, but be sure to try specialties like crab chiles rellenos and chipotle chicken salad. At all hours in season, the bar gets packed with boaters who pull up to the restaurant's private pier. [$] *Average main: $28* ✉ *5000 N. Lake Blvd., Hwy. 28, Carnelian Bay* ☎ *530/546–3366* 🌐 *www.garwoods.com.*

$$ AMERICAN 🍴 **Spindleshanks.** This handsome roadhouse, decorated with floor-to-ceiling knotty pine, serves mostly classic American cooking—ribs, steaks, and seafood updated with adventurous sauces—as well as house-made ravioli. On cold nights request seating near the crackling fireplace and enjoy a drink from the full bar or the extensive wine list. Reservations are recommended. [$] *Average main: $20* ✉ *6873 N. Lake Blvd, Tahoe Vista* ☎ *530/546–2191* 🌐 *www.spindleshankstahoe.com* 🕐 *No lunch.*

$ HOTEL ☺ 🏨 **Ferrari's Crown Resort.** The family-owned and -operated Ferrari's has straightforward motel rooms in a resort setting, great for families with kids. **Pros:** family-friendly; lakeside location. **Cons:** older facility. **TripAdvisor:** "everything we needed," "room was amazing," "beautiful view." [$] *Rooms from: $99* ✉ *8200 N. Lake Blvd., Kings Beach* ☎ *530/546–3388, 800/645–2260* 🌐 *www.tahoecrown.com* 🛏 *71 rooms* 🍽 *Breakfast.*

$$$$ B&B/INN ★ 🏨 **Shore House.** Every room has a gas fireplace, down comforter, and featherbed at this lakefront B&B in Tahoe Vista. **Pros:** waterfront honeymoon cottage; massage appointments available. **Cons:** pricey (even off-season). **TripAdvisor:** "perfect for a romantic getaway," "relaxing," "Tahoe perfected." [$] *Rooms from: $265* ✉ *7170 N. Lake Blvd., Tahoe*

Vista ☎ *530/546–7270, 800/207–5160* 🌐 *www.shorehouselaketahoe.com* 🛏 *8 rooms, 1 cottage* 🍴 *Breakfast.*

THE NEVADA SIDE

The difference on the Nevada side of the lake is, of course, gambling, with all its repercussions.

CRYSTAL BAY

1 mile east of Kings Beach on Hwy. 28; 30 miles north of South Lake Tahoe, U.S. 50 to Hwy. 28.

Right at the Nevada border, Crystal Bay has a cluster of casinos that look essentially the same, but have a few minor differences. These casinos tend toward the tacky, and most of the lodging is pretty lackluster.

GETTING HERE AND AROUND

From the California side, reach Crystal Bay via Highway 89 or 267 to Highway 28. TART serves the communities along the north and west shores.

EXPLORING

Cal-Neva Lodge. Bisected by the state line, the Cal-Neva Lodge opened in 1927 and has weathered many scandals. The largest involved former owner Frank Sinatra (he lost his gaming license in the 1960s for alleged mob connections). The secret tunnel that Frank built so that he could steal away unnoticed to Marilyn Monroe's cabin is definitely worth a look; call for tour times. ✉ *2 Stateline Rd.* ☎ *800/225–6382* 🌐 *www.calnevaresort.com.*

Crystal Bay Club. Known for its classic steak and lobster dinner, the restaurant here has a distinctive open-truss ceiling. ✉ *14 Hwy. 28, near Stateline Rd.* ☎ *775/833–6333* 🌐 *www.crystalbaycasino.com.*

Jim Kelley's Tahoe Nugget. Nearly 90 kinds of beer highlight the bar scene at Jim Kelley's Tahoe Nugget. In fact, they're the highlight of the entire casino, which has no table games, only slots and video poker. ✉ *20 Hwy. 28, near Stateline Rd.* ☎ *775/831–0455.*

Tahoe Biltmore. A daily happy hour keeps this old favorite hopping. The circular Tahoe Biltmore sign is a 1962 "Googie-style" architectural riff off the Seattle Space Neeedle, which debuted the same year. ✉ *5 Hwy. 28, at Stateline Rd.* ☎ *800/245–8667* 🌐 *www.tahoebiltmore.com.*

WHERE TO EAT

$$$ ECLECTIC 🍴 **Soule Domain.** Rough-hewn wood beams and a vaulted wood ceiling lend high romance to this cozy 1927 pine-log cabin next to the Tahoe Biltmore. Chef-owner Charlie Soule's specialties include curried almond chicken, fresh sea scallops poached in champagne with kiwi and mango cream sauce, and a vegan sauté with ginger, jalapeños, and tofu, but you'll find the chef's current passion in the roster of nightly specials. Some find Soule Domain pricey, but if you're looking for a place with a sterling menu where you can hold hands by candlelight, this is it. [$] *Average main: $26* ✉ *9983 Cove Ave., ½ block up Stateline Rd.*

off Hwy. 28, Kings Beach ☎ *530/546–7529* ⊕ *www.souledomain.com* ⚑ *Reservations essential* ☾ *No lunch.*

INCLINE VILLAGE

3 miles east of Crystal Bay on Hwy. 28.

Incline Village dates to the early 1960s when an Oklahoma developer bought 10,000 acres north of Lake Tahoe. His idea was to sketch out a plan for a town without a central commercial district, hoping to prevent congestion and to preserve the area's natural beauty. One-acre lakeshore lots originally fetched $12,000 to $15,000; today you couldn't buy the same land for less than several million.

13

GETTING HERE AND AROUND

From the California side, reach Incline Village via Highway 89 or 267 to Highway 28. From South Lake Tahoe, take U.S. 50 north to Highway 28 north. TART serves the communities along Lake Tahoe's north and west shores from Incline Village to Tahoma.

ESSENTIALS

Visitor Information Lake Tahoe Incline Village/Crystal Bay Visitors Bureau ⊠ *969 Tahoe Blvd.* ☎ *775/832–1606, 800/468–2463* ⊕ *www.gotahoenorth.com.*

EXPLORING

Lakeshore Drive. Take this beautiful drive to see some of the most expensive real estate in Nevada. The route is discreetly marked: to find it, start at the Hyatt hotel and drive westward along the lake.

Fodor's Choice
★

Thunderbird Lodge. George Whittell, a San Francisco socialite who once owned 40,000 acres of property along the lake, built the lodge in 1936. You can tour the mansion and the grounds by reservation only, and though it's pricey to do so, you'll get a rare glimpse back to a time when only the very wealthy had homes at Tahoe. The lodge is accessible via a bus from the Incline Village Visitors Bureau, a catamaran from the Hyatt in Incline Village ($110), or a 1950 wooden cruiser from Tahoe Keys Marina in South Lake Tahoe, which includes Continental breakfast and lunch ($135). ☎ *775/832–8750 lodge info, 800/468–2463 reservations, 775/588–1881, 888/867–6394 Tahoe Keys boat, 775/831–4386 Hyatt Incline catamaran* ⊕ *www.thunderbirdlodge.org/tours* ⊠ *$39 bus tour, $110 & 135 for boat tours* ☾ *May–Oct., Tues.–Sat., call for tour times.*

BEACHES

Lake Tahoe–Nevada State Park and Sand Harbor Beach. Protecting much of the lake's eastern shore from development, the park comprises several sections that stretch from Incline Village to Zephyr Cove. Beaches and trails provide access to a wilder side of the lake, whether you're into cross-country skiing, hiking, or just relaxing at a picnic. With a gently sloping beach for lounging, crystal clear water for swimming and snorkeling, and a picnic area shaded by cedars and pines, **Sand Harbor Beach** is so popular that it sometimes fills to capacity by 11 am on summer weekends. Boaters have two launch ramps. A handicap-accessible nature trail has interpretive signs and beautiful lake views. Pets are not allowed. **Amenities:** food and drink; parking ($12 mid-Apr.–mid-Oct.,

$7 rest of the year; toilets; water sports. **Best For:** snorkeling; sunset; swimming; walking. ✉ *Sand Harbor Beach, Hwy. 28, 3 miles south of Incline Village* ☎ *775/831–0494* 🌐 *parks.nv.gov/parks/sand-harbor.*

WHERE TO EAT AND STAY

For expanded reviews, facilities, and current deals, visit Fodors.com.

$$$ ECLECTIC 🍴 **Frederick's.** Copper-top tables lend a chic look to the dining room at this intimate bistro. The menu consists of a mélange of European and Asian dishes, most of them prepared with organic produce and free-range meats. Try the braised short ribs, roasted duck with caramel-pecan glaze, or the deliciously fresh sushi rolls. Ask for a table by the fire. [$] *Average main: $28* ✉ *907 Tahoe Blvd., at Village Blvd.* ☎ *775/832–3007* 🌐 *fredricksbistro.com* ✍ *Reservations essential* 🕒 *Closed Sun. and Mon. No lunch.*

$$$ FRENCH 🍴 **Le Bistro.** Incline Village's hidden gem serves expertly prepared French-country cuisine in a relaxed, romantic dining room. The chef-owner makes everything himself, using organically grown ingredients. Expect such dishes as pâté de campagne, porcini mushroom bisque en croute, escargot, and herb-crusted roast lamb loin. Try the five-course prix-fixe menu ($50), which can be paired with award-winning wine selections. Service is gracious and attentive. Be sure to ask directions when you book, because the restaurant is hard to find. [$] *Average main: $30* ✉ *120 Country Club Dr., off Lakeshore Blvd.* ☎ *775/831–0800* 🌐 *www.lebistrorestaurant.net* 🕒 *Closed Sun. and Mon. No lunch.*

$ SOUTHERN 🍴 **T's Rotisserie.** There's nothing fancy about T's (it looks like a small snack bar), but the mesquite-grilled chicken and tri-tip steaks are delicious and inexpensive—a rare combination in pricey Incline Village. It's mainly a take-out spot; seating is limited. [$] *Average main: $8* ✉ *901 Tahoe Blvd., at Village Blvd.* ☎ *775/831–2832* 💳 *No credit cards.*

$$$$ RESORT 🏨 **Hyatt Regency Lake Tahoe.** A full-service destination resort on 26 acres of prime lakefront property, the Hyatt has a range of luxurious accommodations, from tower-hotel rooms to lakeside cottages. **Pros:** incredible views; first-class spa. **Cons:** pricey (especially for families). **TripAdvisor:** "beautiful resort," "the best staff I have ever experienced," "nice room."[$] *Rooms from: $298* ✉ *111 Country Club Dr.* ☎ *775/832–1234, 888/899–5019* 🌐 *www.laketahoe.hyatt.com* 🛏 *386 rooms, 36 suites.*

SPORTS AND THE OUTDOORS

GOLF **Incline Championship.** Robert Trent Jones Sr. designed this 18-hole, par-72 course with a driving range. The $179 greens fee includes an optional cart. ✉ *955 Fairway Blvd., at Northwood Blvd., north off Hwy. 28* ☎ *866/925–4653* 🌐 *www.inclinegolf.com.*

Incline Mountain. This executive (shorter) 18-hole par 58 course has greens fees that start at $65, including optional cart. ✉ *690 Wilson Way, at Golfer's Pass, south off Hwy. 431* ☎ *866/925–4653* 🌐 *www.inclinegolf.com.*

MOUNTAIN BIKING **Flume Trail Bikes.** You can rent bikes and get helpful tips from company, which also operates a bike shuttle to popular trailheads. Ask about the secluded backcountry rental cabins for overnight rides. ✉ *Spooner*

Get to Sand Harbor Beach in Lake Tahoe–Nevada State Park early; the park sometimes fills to capacity before lunchtime in summer.

Summit, Hwy. 28, ¾ mile north of U.S. 50, Glenbrook ☎ *775/749–5349* ⊕ *www.theflumetrail.com.*

SKIING **Diamond Peak.** A fun family mood prevails at Diamond Peak, which has affordable rates and many special programs. Snowmaking covers 75% of the mountain, and runs are groomed nightly. The ride up the 1-mile Crystal Express rewards you with fantastic views. Diamond Peak is less crowded than the larger areas and provides free shuttles to nearby lodging. A great place for beginners and intermediates, it's appropriately priced for families. Though there are some steep-aspect black-diamond runs, advanced skiers may find the acreage too limited. For snowboarders there's a small terrain park. ⊠ *1210 Ski Way, off Country Club Dr.* ☎ *775/832–1177* ⊕ *www.diamondpeak.com* ☞ *30 trails on 655 acres, rated 18% beginner, 46% intermediate, 36% advanced. Longest run 2½ miles, base 6,700 feet, summit 8,540 feet. Lifts: 6, including 2 high-speed quads.*

Mt. Rose Ski Tahoe. At this park, ski some of Tahoe's highest slopes and take in bird's-eye views of Reno, the lake, and Carson Valley. Though more compact than the bigger Tahoe resorts, Mt. Rose has the area's highest base elevation and consequently the driest snow. The mountain has a wide variety of terrain. The most challenging is the Chutes, 200 acres of gulp-and-go advanced-to-expert vertical. Intermediates can choose steep groomers or mellow, wide-open boulevards. Beginners have their own corner of the mountain, with gentle, wide slopes. Boarders and tricksters have three terrain parks to choose from, on opposite sides of the mountain, allowing them to follow the sun as it tracks across the resort. The mountain gets hit hard in storms; check conditions before heading up during inclement weather or on a windy day. ✉ *22222 Mt. Rose Hwy., Hwy. 431, 11 miles north of Incline Village, Reno* ☎ *775/849–0704, 800/754–7673* ⊕ *www.skirose.com* ✆ *61 trails on 1,200 acres, rated 20% beginner, 30% intermediate, 40% advanced, 10% expert. Longest run 2½ miles, base 8,260 feet, summit 9,700 feet. Lifts: 8, including 2 high-speed 6-passenger lifts.*

> ### TAHOE TESSIE
>
> Local lore claims this huge sea monster slithers around Lake Tahoe. Skeptics laugh, but true believers keep their eyes peeled for surprise sightings.

Spooner Lake Cross-Country. You'll find superbly groomed tracks and fabulous views of Lake Tahoe while you skim along about 50 miles of trails on more than 9,000 acres. Two secluded cabins are available for rent for overnight treks. ✉ *Spooner Summit, Hwy. 28, ½ mile north of U.S. 50, Glenbrook* ☎ *775/749–5349* ⊕ *www.spoonerlake.com.*

Tahoe Meadows Snowplay Area. This is the most popular area near the north shore for noncommercial cross-country skiing, sledding, tubing, snowshoeing, and snowmobiling. ✉ *Hwy. 431, between Incline Village and Mt. Rose.*

ZEPHYR COVE

22 miles south of Incline Village via Hwy. 28 to U.S. 50.

The largest settlement between Incline Village and the Stateline area is Zephyr Cove, a tiny resort. It has a beach, marina, campground, picnic area, coffee shop in a log lodge, rustic cabins, and nearby riding stables.

GETTING HERE AND AROUND

From the north shore communities, reach Zephyr Cove by following Highway 28 along the eastern side of the lake. From South Lake Tahoe, take U.S. 50 north and then west. Public transportation isn't available in Zephyr Cove.

EXPLORING

★ **Cave Rock.** Near Zephyr Cove, this 75 feet of solid stone at the southern end of Lake Tahoe–Nevada State Park is the throat of an extinct volcano. Tahoe Tessie, the lake's version of the Loch Ness monster, is reputed to live in a cavern below the impressive outcropping. Cave Rock towers over a parking lot, a lakefront picnic ground, and a boat launch. The views are some of the best on the lake; this is a good spot to stop and take a picture. However, this area is a sacred burial site for the Washoe Indians, and climbing up to the cave, or through it, is prohibited. ✉ *U.S. 50, 4 miles north of Zephyr Cove* ☎ *775/831–0494.*

WHERE TO STAY

For expanded reviews, facilities, and current deals, visit Fodors.com.

$$$ 🏨 **Zephyr Cove Resort.** Beneath towering pines at the lake's edge stand 29
RENTAL cozy, modern vacation cabins with peaked knotty-pine ceilings. **Pros:**
♻ family-friendly. **Cons:** lodge rooms are very basic; can be noisy. **Trip-Advisor:** "a cabin with a beautiful view," "fresh peaceful scenery," "tranquility."Ⓢ *Rooms from: $199* ✉ *760 U.S. 50, 4 miles north of*

Stateline ☎ *775/589–4907, 888/896–3830* 🌐 *www.zephyrcove.com* 🛏 *29 cabins.*

STATELINE

5 miles south of Zephyr Cove on U.S. 50.

Stateline is the archetypal Nevada border town. Its four high-rise casinos are as vertical and contained as the commercial district of South Lake Tahoe, on the California side, is horizontal and sprawling. And Stateline is as relentlessly indoors oriented as the rest of the lake is focused on the outdoors. This strip is where you'll find the most concentrated action at Lake Tahoe: restaurants (including typical casino buffets), showrooms with famous headliners and razzle-dazzle revues, tower-hotel rooms and suites, and 24-hour casinos.

13

GETTING HERE AND AROUND

From South Lake Tahoe take U.S. 50, also called Lake Tahoe Boulevard, north across the Nevada border to reach Stateline and its casinos. If coming from Reno's airport, take U.S. 395 south to Carson City, and then head west on U.S. 50 to the lake and head south. Or take the South Tahoe Express bus. BlueGO operates daily bus service in the south shore area year-round, plus a ski shuttle from the large hotels to Heavenly in the winter.

BEACHES

Nevada Beach. Although less than a mile long, this is the widest beach on the lake and especially good for swimming (many Tahoe beaches are rocky). You can boat and fish here, and there are picnic tables, barbecue grills, and a campground beneath the pines. This is the best place to watch the July 4th or Labor Day fireworks, but most of the summer the subdued atmosphere attracts families and those seeking a less-touristy spot. **Amenities:** parking ($7 fee); water sports; toilets. **Best For:** sunrise; swimming; walking. ✉ *Elk Point Rd., off U.S. 50, 3 miles north of Stateline* ☎ *530/543–2600* 🌐 *www.fs.usda.gov/ltbmu* ⏲ *Daily late May–Oct.* ☞ *No pets.*

WHERE TO EAT AND STAY

For expanded reviews, facilities, and current deals, visit Fodors.com.

$$$ FRENCH 🍴 **Mirabelle.** Don't be put off by this restaurant's nondescript exterior. Inside there's an airy dining room with creamy yellow walls and white tablecloths. Enticing scents drift from the kitchen, where the Alsatian-born chef-owner, Camille Schwartz, prepares everything from puff pastry to meringues to homemade bread. Specialties include sautéed veal sweetbreads, garlicky escargot, and rack of lamb with fresh thyme. There's always a fresh fish entrée, plus a $29.50 prix-fixe "casual menu." [$] *Average main: $25* ✉ *290 Kingsbury Grade, off U.S. 50* ☎ *775/586–1007* 🌐 *www.mirabelletahoe.com* ⏲ *Closed Mon. No lunch.*

$$ HOTEL 🏨 **Harrah's Tahoe Hotel/Casino.** The hotel's major selling point is that every room has two full bathrooms, each with a television and telephone, a boon if you're traveling with family. **Pros:** central location; great midweek values. **Cons:** can get noisy. **TripAdvisor:** "nice surprise,"

"amazing," "great location."$ Rooms from: $110 ✉ 15 U.S. 50, at Stateline Ave. ☎ 775/588–6611, 800/427–7247 ⊕ www.harrahstahoe. com ↘ 470 rooms, 62 suites.

$$
HOTEL
☷ **Harveys Resort Hotel/Casino.** The resort began as a cabin in 1944, and now it's Tahoe's largest casino-hotel. **Pros:** hip entertainment; just a few blocks south of the Heavenly Gondola. **Cons:** can get loud at night. **TripAdvisor:** "great rooms," "very nice," "not your typical casino hotel."$ Rooms from: $80 ✉ 18 U.S. 50, at Stateline Ave. ☎ 775/588–2411, 800/648–3361 ⊕ www.harrahs.com ↘ 705 rooms, 38 suites.

$
HOTEL
☷ **MontBleu.** The contemporary, slightly kitschy MontBleu has guest rooms with oversize tubs, king-size beds, and views of Lake Tahoe and the surrounding mountains. **Pros:** indoor pool; first-class spa; great specials online. **Cons:** looking careworn in places; can get noisy; some rooms overlook parking lot's glaring lights. **TripAdvisor:** "nice location," "many amenities," "great weekend stay."$ Rooms from: $99 ✉ 55 U.S. 50 ☎ 775/588–3515, 800/648–3353 ⊕ www.montbleuresort. com ↘ 328 rooms, 109 suites.

NIGHTLIFE

Each of the major casinos has its own showroom, featuring everything from comedy to magic acts to sexy floor shows to Broadway musicals.

Harveys Outdoor Summer Concert Series. The casino presents outdoor concerts on weekends in summer with headliners such as Sugarland, Brad Paisley, the Rascal Flats, and Toby Keith. ☎ 800/427–7247 ⊕ www. harveystahoe.com.

South Shore Room. Old-school (Rick Springfield) and really old-school (Eric Burdon) rockers play Harrah's big showroom, along with relatively less nostalgia-oriented headliners such as Los Lobos and—combining most of the above attributes—Chickenfoot. ✉ Harrah's, 15 U.S. 50 ☎ 775/588–6611.

Vex. You can dance the night away at this club with a semi-Vegas feel. ✉ Harrah's, 15 U.S. 50 ☎ 775/588–6611.

SPORTS AND THE OUTDOORS

GOLF
Edgewood Tahoe. This highly scenic lakeside course, 18 holes, par 72, has a driving range. The greens fee, $160–$240, includes an optional cart. ✉ 100 Lake Pkwy., at U.S. 50 ☎ 775/588–3566, 888/881–8659 ⊕ www.edgewood-tahoe.com.

RENO

32 miles east of Truckee on I–80; 38 miles northeast of Incline Village via Hwy. 431 and U.S. 395.

Established in 1859 as a trading station at a bridge over the Truckee River, Reno grew along with the silver mines of nearby Virginia City and the transcontinental railroad that chugged through town. Train officials named it in 1868, but gambling—legalized in 1931—put Reno on the map.

Today a sign over the upper end of Virginia Street proclaims Reno "The Biggest Little City in the World." This is still a gambling town, with most of the casinos crowded into five square blocks downtown, but a thriving university scene and outdoor activities also bring tourists to the area.

Though parts of downtown are sketchy, things are changing. Several defunct casinos are being converted into condominiums, and downtown is undergoing an urban renewal, sparked by the development of the riverfront, with new shops, boutiques, and nongaming, family-friendly activities like kayaking on the Truckee River. Excellent restaurants have sprung up outside the hotels. Temperatures year-round in this high-mountain-desert climate are warmer than at Tahoe, though it rarely gets as hot here as in Sacramento and the Central Valley, making strolling around town a pleasure.

RENO'S RIVERWALK

Stroll along the Truckee River and check out the art galleries, cinema, specialty shops, theater, and restaurants that line this lively refurbished section of town near Reno's casino district.

13

GETTING HERE AND AROUND

Interstate 80 bisects Reno east–west, U.S. 395 north–south. Greyhound and Amtrak stop here, and several airlines fly into Reno-Tahoe International Airport. RTC Ride provides bus service in the greater Reno area.

ESSENTIALS

Bus Contact RTC Ride ⌧ *Transit Center, E. 4th and Lake Sts.* ☎ *775/348–0400* ⊕ *rtcwashoe.com.*

Visitor Information Reno-Sparks Convention and Visitors Authority ⌧ *4001 S. Virginia St.* ☎ *775/827–7650, 800/367–7366* ⊕ *www.visitrenotahoe. com.*

EXPLORING
TOP ATTRACTIONS

Downtown RiverWalk. Once dilapidated, Reno's waterfront district got a gentrified makeover when the Downtown RiverWalk brought in street performers, art exhibits, shops, and a lovely park. The 2,600-foot-long Truckee River white-water kayaking course runs right through downtown and has become a major attraction for water-sports enthusiasts. On the third Saturday of each month, from 2 to 5, local merchants host a **Wine Walk.** The cost is $20; stop inside the RiverWalk's participating shops, galleries, and boutiques to refill your wine glass. In July look for stellar outdoor art, opera, dance, and kids' performances as part of the monthlong **Artown festival** (⊕ *www.renoisartown.com*), presented mostly in Wingfield Park, along the river. ⌧ *S. Virginia St. and the Truckee River* ⊕ *www.renoriver.org.*

Eldorado. Action packed, with lots of slots and popular bar-top video poker, this casino also has good coffee-shop and food-court fare. Don't miss the Fountain of Fortune with its massive Florentine-inspired sculptures. ⌧ *345 N. Virginia St., at W. 4th St.* ☎ *775/786–5700, 800/648–5966* ⊕ *www.eldoradoreno.com.*

Fleischmann Planetarium. Digital star shows provide the glittering lights inside this facility that aims to make learning about astronomy entertaining for kids and adults. ⌧ *University of Nevada, 1650 N. Virginia*

St., near E. 15th St. ☎ *775/784–4811* 🌐 *www.planetarium.unr.nevada.edu* 🎫 *Exhibits free, films and star shows $7* 🕐 *Mon.–Thurs. noon–5, Fri. noon–9, Sat. 10–9, Sun. 10–5.*

👶 ★ **National Automobile Museum.** Antique and classic automobiles, including an Elvis Presley Cadillac, a Mercury coupe driven by James Dean in the movie *Rebel Without a Cause,* and the experimental and still futuristic-looking 1938 Phantom Corsair are all on display here. ✉ *10 S. Lake St., at Mill St.* ☎ *775/333–9300* 🌐 *www.automuseum.org* 🎫 *$10* 🕐 *Mon.–Sat. 9:30–5:30, Sun. 10–4.*

★ **Nevada Museum of Art.** A dramatic structure designed by Will Bruder houses this splendid museum's collection, which focuses on themes such as the Sierra Nevada/Great Basin and altered-landscape photography. Important traveling exhibitions often come here. ✉ *160 W. Liberty St., and Hill St.* ☎ *775/329–3333* 🌐 *www.nevadaart.org* 🎫 *$10* 🕐 *Wed. and Fri.–Sun. 10–5, Thurs. 10–8.*

★ **Peppermill.** A few miles from downtown, this casino is known for its excellent restaurants and neon-bright gambling areas. The Fireside cocktail lounge is a blast. ✉ *2707 S. Virginia St., at Peppermill La.* ☎ *775/826–2121, 800/648–6992* 🌐 *www.peppermillreno.com.*

WORTH NOTING

👶 **Circus Circus.** Families with kids in tow head to this casino, where a midway above the floor has clowns, games, fun-house mirrors, and circus acts. ✉ *500 N. Sierra St., at W. 5th St.* ☎ *775/329–0711, 800/648–5010* 🌐 *www.circusreno.com.*

Harrah's. Occupying two city blocks, this landmark property has a sprawling casino and an outdoor promenade. ✉ *219 N. Center St., at E. 2nd St.* ☎ *775/786–3232, 800/648–3773* 🌐 *www.harrahsreno.com.*

Silver Legacy. A 120-foot-tall mining rig and video poker games draw gamblers to this razzle-dazzle casino. ✉ *407 N. Virginia St., at W. 4th St.* ☎ *775/329–4777, 800/687–8733* 🌐 *www.silverlegacy.com.*

WHERE TO EAT

$$$ AMERICAN ★ 🍴 **4th St. Bistro.** For deliciously simple, smart cooking, head to this charming little bistro on the edge of town. The chef-owner uses organic produce and meats in her soulful preparations of dishes like grilled Moroccan spiced chicken breast with garbanzo beans and couscous. Ocher-color sponge-painted walls and a roaring fireplace warm the white-tablecloth dining room. [$] *Average main: $30* ✉ *3065 W. 4th St.* ☎ *775/323–3200* 🌐 *www.4thstbistro.com* 🕐 *Closed Sun. and Mon. No lunch.*

$ THAI 🍴 **Bangkok Cuisine.** To eat well but not break the bank, come to this busy Thai restaurant and sample the delicious soups, salads, stir-fries, and curries. [$] *Average main: $10* ✉ *55 Mt. Rose St., at S. Virginia St.* ☎ *775/322–0299* 🌐 *www.bangkokcuisinereno.com* 🕐 *No lunch Sun.*

$$$ FRENCH 🍴 **Beaujolais Bistro.** Consistently spot-on, this restaurant serves earthy, country-style French food with zero pretension—classics like beef bourguignonne, roast duck, escargots, and steak frites béarnaise, all lovingly prepared and seasoned just right. Less expensive small plates are also on the menu, plus a nightly $39 prix-fixe offering. The airy dining

room has an inviting, casual vibe. [$] *Average main: $28* ✉ *130 West St.* ☎ *775/323–2227* 🌐 *www.beaujolaisbistro.com* ⏲ *Closed Mon. No lunch weekends.*

$ CAFÉ 🍴 **Chocolate Bar.** Part café, part cocktail bar, this hip little spot close to the river makes killer truffles, chocolate fondue, fabulous fruity cocktails, gourmet appetizers, and stellar hot chocolate, served at a long curved bar or at several tables and leather banquettes. Chocolate Bar is open late each night for those craving dessert, a fabulous chocolate cocktail, or a simple, unadorned cognac. [$] *Average main: $13* ✉ *95 N. Sierra St., at W. 1st St.* ☎ *775/337–1122* 🌐 *www.thechocbar.com.*

WHERE TO STAY

For expanded reviews, facilities, and current deals, visit Fodors.com.

$ HOTEL 🏨 **Eldorado.** In the middle of glittering downtown, the resort's huge tower has rooms overlooking either the mountains or the lights of the city. **Pros:** fun; good food; amusingly kitschy decor. **Cons:** noisy. [$] *Rooms from: $65* ✉ *345 N. Virginia St.* ☎ *775/786–5700, 800/648–5966* 🌐 *www.eldoradoreno.com* 🛏 *679 rooms, 137 suites.*

$ HOTEL 🏨 **Harrah's.** Of the big-name casino hotels in downtown Reno, double-towered Harrah's does a good job, with no surprises. **Pros:** sets the standard for downtown Reno; great midweek rates. **Cons:** huge property. **TripAdvisor:** "another wonderful stay," "it's almost all about the bed," "one of the few good ones downtown."[$] *Rooms from: $67* ✉ *219 N. Center St.* ☎ *775/786–3232, 800/648–3773* 🌐 *www.harrahs.com* 🛏 *876 rooms, 52 suites.*

$ HOTEL ★ 🏨 **Peppermill.** A few miles removed from downtown Reno's flashy main drag, this property generates its own glitz with a dazzling neon-filled casino. **Pros:** luxurious rooms; casino decor; good (and inexpensive) coffee shop. **Cons:** deluge of neon may be offputting to some. **TripAdvisor:** "the only place to stay," "always a great experience," "beautiful room."[$] *Rooms from: $99* ✉ *2707 S. Virginia St.* ☎ *775/826–2121, 800/648–6992* 🌐 *www.peppermillreno.com* 🛏 *915 rooms, 720 suites.*

The Far North

WITH LAKE SHASTA, MT. SHASTA, AND LASSEN VOLCANIC NATIONAL PARK

WORD OF MOUTH

"Lassen is one of those best-kept-secret spots. It has a little bit of everything: peaks, waterfalls, snow, trees, awesome flowers, a mini Yellowstone, and not tons of folks everywhere."

—spirobulldog

WELCOME TO THE FAR NORTH

TOP REASONS TO GO

★ **Mother Nature's wonders:** California's Far North has more rivers, streams, lakes, forests, and mountains than you'll ever have time to explore.

★ **Rock and roll:** With two volcanoes to entice you—Lassen and Shasta—you can learn firsthand what happens when a mountain blows its top.

★ **Fantastic fishing:** Whether you like casting from a riverbank or letting your line bob beside a boat, you'll find fabulous fishing in all the northern counties.

★ **Cool hops:** On a hot day there's nothing quite as inviting as a visit to Chico's world-famous Sierra Nevada Brewery. Take the tour and then savor a chilled glass on tap at the adjacent brewpub.

★ **Shasta:** Wonderful in all its forms: lake, dam, river, mountain, forest, and town.

1 **From Chico to Mt. Shasta.** The Far North is bisected, south to north, by Interstate 5, which passes through several historic towns and state parks, as well as miles of mountainous terrain. Halfway to the Oregon border is Lake Shasta, a favorite recreation destination, and farther north stands the spectacular snowy peak of Mt. Shasta.

2 **The Backcountry.** East of Interstate 5, the Far North's main corridor, dozens of scenic two-lane roads crisscross the wilderness, leading to dramatic mountain peaks and fascinating natural wonders. Small towns settled in the second half of the 19th century seem frozen in time, except that they are well equipped with tourist amenities.

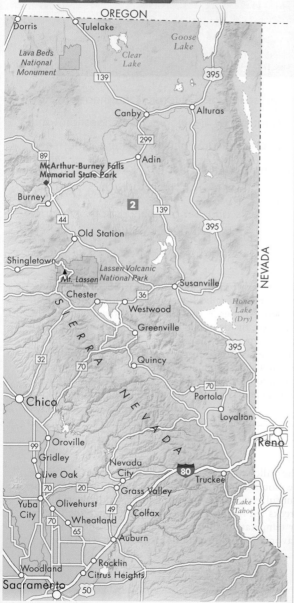

GETTING ORIENTED

The Far North is a vast area that stretches from the upper reaches of the Sacramento Valley north to the Oregon border and east to Nevada. The region includes all or part of eight counties with sparsely populated rural farming and mountain communities, as well as thriving small cities in the valley. Much of the landscape was shaped by two volcanoes—Mt. Shasta and Mt. Lassen—that draw amateur geologists, weekend hikers, and avid mountain climbers to their rugged terrain. An intricate network of high mountain watersheds feeds lakes large and small, plus streams and rivers that course through several forests.

14

Updated
by Christine
Vovakes

The wondrous landscape of California's northeastern corner, relatively unmarred by development, congestion, and traffic, is the product of volcanic activity. At the southern end of the Cascade Range, Lassen Volcanic National Park is the best place to witness the Far North's fascinating geology. Beyond the sulfur vents and bubbling mud pots, the park owes much of its beauty to 10,457-foot Mt. Lassen and 50 wilderness lakes.

The most enduring image of the region, though, is Mt. Shasta, whose 14,162-foot snowcapped peak beckons outdoor adventurers of all kinds. There are many versions of Shasta to enjoy—the mountain, the lake, the river, the town, the dam, and the forest—all named after the Native Americans known as the Shatasla, or Sastise, who once inhabited the region. The Far North's soaring mountain peaks, wild rivers teeming with trout, and almost unlimited recreational possibilities make it the perfect destination for sports lovers. You won't find many hot nightspots or cultural enclaves, but you will find superlative hiking and fishing.

FAR NORTH PLANNER

WHEN TO GO
Heat scorches the valley in summer. Temperatures above 110°F are common, but the mountains provide cool respite. Fall throughout the Far North is beautiful, rivaled only by spring, when wildflowers bloom and mountain creeks fed by the snowmelt splash through the forests. Winter is usually temperate in the valley, but cold and snowy in high country. A few favorite tourist attractions are closed in winter.

GETTING HERE AND AROUND
AIR TRAVEL

For the cheapest fares, fly into Sacramento (⇨ *Chapter 12, Sacramento and the Gold Country*) and then rent a car—you'll need one anyway—and drive north. Chico and Redding, both served by United Express, have small airports. Neither has shuttle service, but you can take a taxi for about $30 to downtown Redding and $21 to downtown Chico.

Air Contacts **Chico Municipal Airport** ✉ *150 Airpark Blvd., off Cohasset Rd., Chico* ☎ *530/896–7200* ⊕ *www.chico.ca.us/airport/home_page.asp.* **Redding Municipal Airport** ✉ *6751 Woodrum Circle, off Airport Rd., Redding* ☎ *530/224–4320* ⊕ *www.ci.redding.ca.us/transeng/airports/rma.htm.*

Ground Transportation **Taxi Service, Chico** ☎ *530/893–4444, 530/342–2929.* **Taxi Service, Redding** ☎ *530/246–0577, 530/222–1234.*

BUS TRAVEL

Greyhound buses stop in Burney, Chico, Red Bluff, Redding, Susanville, and Weed. Various transit authorities provide local bus transportation *(see individual town listings for details)*, though few tourists avail themselves of it.

Bus Contact **Greyhound** ☎ *800/231–2222* ⊕ *www.greyhound.com.*

CAR TRAVEL

Interstate 5 runs up the center of California through Red Bluff and Redding. Chico is east of Interstate 5 on Highway 32. Lassen Volcanic National Park can be reached by Highway 36 from Red Bluff or (except in winter) Highway 44 from Redding. Highway 299 connects Weaverville, Redding and Alturas. U.S. 395 leads from Susanville to Alturas. Highway 89 will take you from Mt. Shasta to Quincy. Highway 36 links Chester and Susanville. Check weather reports and carry detailed maps, warm clothing, and tire chains whenever you head into mountainous terrain in winter.

Road Conditions **Caltrans Current Highway Conditions** ☎ *800/427–7623* ⊕ *www.dot.ca.gov.*

TRAIN TRAVEL

Amtrak serves Chico, Redding, and Dunsmuir.

Train Contacts **Amtrak** ☎ *800/872–7245* ⊕ *www.amtrakcalifornia.com.*

RESTAURANTS

Redding, the urban center of the Far North, and college-town Chico have the greatest selection of restaurants. Cafés and simple eateries are the rule in the smaller towns, though trendy, innovative restaurants have been popping up. Dress is always informal. *Prices in the reviews are the average cost of a main course at dinner or, if dinner is not served, at lunch.*

HOTELS

Aside from the large chain hotels and motels in Redding and Chico, most accommodations in the Far North blend rusticity, simplicity, and coziness. Rooms in Redding, Chico, and Red Bluff usually are booked solid only during popular local events. Wilderness resorts close in fall

14

and reopen after the snow season ends in May. For summer holiday weekends in towns such as Mt. Shasta, Dunsmuir, and Chester, and at camping sites within state or national parks, make lodging reservations well in advance. *Prices in the reviews are the lowest cost of a standard double room in high season. For expanded reviews, facilities, and current deals, visit Fodors.com.*

B&B Info California Association of Bed & Breakfast Inns ⊕ *www.cabbi.com/ region/Mount-Shasta.*

VISITOR INFORMATION

Contacts Lassen County Chamber of Commerce ✉ *75 N. Weatherlow St., Susanville* ☏ *530/257-4323* ⊕ *www.lassencountychamber.com.* **Shasta Cascade Wonderland Association** ✉ *1699 Hwy. 273, Anderson* ☏ *530/365-7500, 800/474-2782* ⊕ *www.shastacascade.com.* **Visit Siskiyou** ☏ *800/926-4865* ⊕ *www.visitsiskiyou.org.*

FROM CHICO TO MT. SHASTA

From the blooming almond orchards of the fertile Sacramento River valley, through the forested mountains and to the dominating peak of a dormant volcano, this section of the Far North entices tourists in all seasons.

CHICO

180 miles from San Francisco, east on I–80, north on I–505 to I–5, and east on Hwy. 32; 86 miles north of Sacramento on Hwy. 99.

Chico (which is Spanish for "small") lies in the Sacramento Valley and offers a welcome break from the monotony of Interstate 5. The Chico campus of California State University, the scores of local artisans, and the area's agriculture (primarily almond orchards) all influence the culture here. Chico's true claim to fame, however, is the popular Sierra Nevada Brewery, which keeps beer drinkers across the country happy with its distinctive microbrews.

GETTING HERE AND AROUND

Both Highway 99, coming north from Sacramento or south off Interstate 5 at Red Bluff, and Highway 32, going east off Interstate 5 at Orland, intersect Chico. Amtrak and Greyhound stop here, and United Express flies into the Chico airport. Butte Regional Transit's B-Line buses serve Chico and nearby towns. Anchored by a robust university scene, the downtown neighborhoods are great for walking.

ESSENTIALS

Bus Contact B-Line ☏ *530/342-0221, 800/822-8145* ⊕ *www.blinetransit.com.*

Visitor Information Chico Chamber of Commerce ✉ *300 Salem St., at W. 3rd St.* ☏ *530/891-5556, 800/852-8570* ⊕ *www.chicochamber.com.*

EXPLORING

★ **Bidwell Mansion State Historic Park.** Built between 1865 and 1868 by General John Bidwell, the founder of Chico, this mansion was designed by Henry W. Cleaveland, a San Francisco architect. Bidwell and his wife welcomed many distinguished guests to their distinctive pink Italianate home, including President Rutherford B. Hayes, naturalist John Muir, suffragist Susan B. Anthony, and General William T. Sherman. A one-hour tour takes you through most of the mansion's 26 rooms. ✉ *525 The Esplanade, at Memorial Way* ☎ *530/895–6144* 🎟 *$6* 🕓 *Mon. noon–5, weekends 11–5; last tour at 4* 🕓 *Closed Tues.–Thurs.*

★ **Bidwell Park.** The sprawling 3,670-acre Bidwell Park is a community green space straddling Big Chico Creek, where scenes from *Gone With the Wind* and the 1938 version of *Robin Hood* (starring Errol Flynn) were filmed. The region's recreational hub, it includes a golf course, swimming areas, and paved biking, hiking, and in-line skating trails. One of the largest city-run parks in the country, Bidwell starts as a slender strip downtown and expands eastward 11 miles toward the Sierra foothills. ✉ *300 S. Park Dr., off Hwy. 99* ☎ *530/896–7800* 🌐 *www.bidwellpark.org.*

★ **Sierra Nevada Brewing Company.** This pioneer of the microbrewery movement still has a hands-on approach to beer making. Tour the brew house and see how the beer is produced—from the sorting of hops through fermentation and bottling. You can also visit the gift shop and enjoy a hearty lunch or dinner in the brewpub where tastings are available (for a fee). ✉ *1075 E. 20th St., at Sierra Nevada St.* ☎ *530/345–2739* 🌐 *www.sierranevada.com* 🎟 *Free* 🕓 *Tours daily, call for times.*

WHERE TO EAT

$$$ STEAKHOUSE 🍴 **5th Street Steakhouse.** Hand-cut steak is the star in this refurbished early 1900s building, the place to come when you're craving red meat and a huge baked potato. Exposed redbrick walls warm the small dining area. A long mahogany bar catches the overflow crowds that jam the place on weekends. Lunch is served on Friday only. No reservations are accepted on Friday and Saturday, but it's worth the wait. [$] *Average main: $27* ✉ *345 W. 5th St., at Normal Ave.* ☎ *530/891–6328* 🌐 *www.5thstreetsteakhouse.com* 🕓 *No lunch Sat.–Thurs.*

$ AMERICAN 🍴 **Madison Bear Garden.** This downtown favorite two blocks south of the Chico State campus is a great spot for checking out the vibrant college scene while enjoying a burger and a brew. [$] *Average main: $8* ✉ *316 W. 2nd St., at Salem St.* ☎ *530/891–1639* 🌐 *www.madisonbeargarden.com.*

$$$ MEDITERRANEAN 🍴 **Red Tavern.** With its burgundy carpet, white linen tablecloths, and mellow lighting, this is one of Chico's coziest restaurants. The Mediterranean-influenced menu, inspired by fresh local produce, changes seasonally. There's a great California wine list, and also a full bar. [$] *Average main: $24* ✉ *1250 The Esplanade, at E. 3rd Ave.* ☎ *530/894–3463* 🌐 *www.redtavern.com* 🕓 *Closed Sun. No lunch.*

WHERE TO STAY

For expanded reviews, facilities, and current deals, visit Fodors.com.

$$$ HOTEL ★ **Hotel Diamond.** Crystal chandeliers and gleaming wood floors and banisters elegantly welcome guests into the foyer of this restored gem in downtown Chico near the university. **Pros:** refined; great location; excellent breakfast buffet included in room rate. **Cons:** pricey; not a good choice for families. **TripAdvisor:** "beautiful antique hotel," "quality service," "you will not be disappointed." [$] *Rooms from: $175* ✉ *220 W. 4th St.* ☎ *530/893-3100, 866/993-3100* 🌐 *www.hoteldiamondchico.com* 🛏 *39 rooms, 4 suites* 🍴 *Breakfast.*

$ B&B/INN **Johnson's Country Inn.** Nestled in an almond orchard a five-minute drive from downtown, this Victorian-style farmhouse with a wraparound veranda is a welcome change from motel row. **Pros:** rural setting; antique furnishings; expected modern conveniences; beautifully maintained; serene walks. **Cons:** a car is essential. **TripAdvisor:** "quiet country setting," "beautiful home and grounds," "lovely people." [$] *Rooms from: $95* ✉ *3935 Morehead Ave.* ☎ 📠 *530/345-7829* 🌐 *www.chico.com/johnsonsinn* 🛏 *4 rooms* 🍴 *Breakfast.*

SHOPPING

Made in Chico. Made in Chico sells locally made goods, including pottery, olives, almonds, and Woof and Poof creations—whimsical home decor items, such as stuffed Santas, elves, animals, and pillows. ✉ *127 W. 3rd St., between Main St. and Broadway* ☎ *530/894-7009.*

Needham Studios. Beautiful custom-made etched, stained, and beveled glass is created at Needham Studios. ✉ *237 Broadway, at 3rd St.* ☎ *530/345-4718* 🌐 *www.needhamstudios.com.*

RED BLUFF

41 miles north of Chico on Hwy 99.

Historic Red Bluff is a gateway to Lassen Volcanic National Park. Established in the mid-19th century as a shipping center and named for the color of its soil, the town is filled with dozens of restored Victorians. It's a great home base for outdoor adventures in the area.

GETTING HERE AND AROUND

Access Red Bluff via exits off Interstate 5, or by driving north on Highway 99. Highway 36 is a long, twisting road that begins near the Pacific Coast and goes to Red Bluff, then east to the towns near Lassen Volcanic National Park. Greyhound buses stop here and also provide connecting service to Amtrak. TRAX (Tehama Rural Area Express) serves Red Bluff and neighboring towns.

ESSENTIALS

Bus Information TRAX ✉ *Red Bluff* ☎ *530/385-2877* 🌐 *www.taketrax.com.*

Visitor Information Red Bluff–Tehama County Chamber of Commerce ✉ *100 Main St., at Rio St.* ☎ *530/527-6220* 🌐 *www.redbluffchamber.com.*

EXPLORING

★ **William B. Ide Adobe State Historic Park.** Named for the first and only president of the short-lived California Republic of 1846, William B. Ide Adobe State Historic Park is on an oak-lined bank of the Sacramento River. The Bear Flag Party proclaimed California a sovereign nation, separate from Mexican rule, and the republic existed for 22 days before it was taken over by the United States. The republic's flag has survived, with minor refinements, as California's state flag. The park's main attraction is an adobe home built in the 1850s and outfitted with period furnishings. ✉ *21659 Adobe Rd., at Park Pl.* ☎ *530/529–8599* 🌐 *www.parks.ca.gov/?page_id=458* 🎫 *$6 per vehicle* 🕓 *Park and picnic facilities; adobe home and historic sites open Fri.–Sun., varying hrs.*

RED BLUFF ROUND-UP

Check out old-time rodeo at its best during the Red Bluff Round-Up. Held the third weekend of April, this annual event attracts some of the best cowboys in the country. For more information, visit 🌐 *www.redbluffroundup.com.*

WHERE TO EAT AND STAY

For expanded reviews, facilities, and current deals, visit Fodors.com.

$$ STEAKHOUSE 🍴 **Green Barn Steakhouse.** You're likely to find cowboys sporting Stetsons and spurs feasting on sizzling porterhouse, baby back ribs, and prime rib at Red Bluff's premier steak house. For lighter fare, there's rainbow trout or clam fettuccine. Don't miss the bread pudding with rum sauce. The lounge is usually hopping, especially when there's an event at the nearby rodeo grounds. [$] *Average main: $19* ✉ *5 Chestnut Ave., at Antelope Blvd.* ☎ *530/527–3161* ✍ *Reservations not accepted* 🕓 *Closed Sun.*

$ B&B/INN 🏨 **The Jeter Victorian Inn.** The four guest rooms of this 1881 Victorian home are elegantly decorated with antiques and period furnishings; two have private baths, and the Imperial Room has a Jacuzzi. **Pros:** quiet residential area; within walking distance of restaurants. **Cons:** no Internet access. [$] *Rooms from: $85* ✉ *1107 Jefferson St.* ☎ *530/527–7574* 🌐 *www.jetervictorianinn.com* 🛏 *4 rooms, 3 with bath; 1 cottage* 🍽 *Breakfast.*

REDDING

32 miles north of Red Bluff on I–5.

As the largest city in the Far North, Redding is an ideal headquarters for exploring the surrounding countryside.

GETTING HERE AND AROUND

Reach Redding from exits off Interstate 5 or via Highway 299, which originates near coastal Eureka and crosses Weaverville and Redding before heading northeast to Burney and Alturas. Highway 44 stretches from Susanville past Lassen Park's north entrance before ending in Redding. United Express serves the Redding airport. Amtrak and Greyhound make stops here.

Fisherman under Santiago Calatrava's striking Sundial Bridge next to Turtle Bay Exploration Park.

ESSENTIALS

Bus Information **Redding Area Bus Authority** ☎ *530/241–2877* 🌐 *www.rabaride.com.*

Visitor Information **Redding Convention and Visitors Bureau** ✉ *2334 Washington Ave., Suite B* ☎ *530/225–4100, 800/874–7562* 🌐 *www.visitredding.com.*

EXPLORING

Fodor's Choice ★ **Turtle Bay Exploration Park.** Here you find walking trails, an arboretum and botanical gardens, and lots of interactive exhibits for kids, including a gold-panning area and the seasonal butterfly exhibit. The main draw is the stunning **Sundial Bridge,** which links the Sacramento River Trail and the park's arboretum and gardens. Access to the bridge and arboretum is free, but there's a fee for the museum. ✉ *840 Sundial Bridge Dr., off Hwy. 44* ☎ *530/243–8850* 🌐 *www.turtlebay.org* 🎟 *$14 for museum* 🕒 *Apr.–mid-Sept., Mon.–Sat. 9–5, Sun. 10–5; mid-Sept.–Mar., Wed.–Sat. 9–4, Sun. 10–4.*

WHERE TO EAT AND STAY

For expanded reviews, facilities, and current deals, visit Fodors.com.

$ SEAFOOD 🍴 **Buz's Crab.** This casual restaurant in central Redding shares space with a bustling seafood market where locals snap up fresh-from-the-ocean Dungeness crab in season. The fish-and-chips and seafood combos are popular, but crab is what keeps the customers coming back. [$] *Average main: $13* ✉ *2159 East St., at Pine St.* ☎ *530/243–2120* 🌐 *www.buzscrab.com.*

$$$ STEAKHOUSE 🍴 **Jack's Grill.** Famous for its 16-ounce steaks, this popular bar and steak house also serves shrimp and chicken. A town favorite, the place is

usually jam-packed and noisy. $ *Average main: $23* ⊠ *1743 California St., at Sacramento St.* ☎ *530/241–9705* ⊕ *www.jacksgrillredding.com* ⊘ *Closed Sun. No lunch.*

$
AMERICAN
✗ **Klassique Kafe.** Two sisters run this small, bustling restaurant that caters to locals looking for simple but hearty breakfast and lunch fare. The hot luncheon specials served daily might include butter beans and ham with corn bread, or chicken and dumplings. $ *Average main: $9* ⊠ *2427 Athens Ave., at Locust St.* ☎ *530/244–4939* ⊘ *Closed Sat. No dinner.*

$$
HOTEL
🏨 **The Red Lion.** Close to Redding's convention center and regional recreation sites, this hotel is a top choice for both business and vacation travelers. **Pros:** family-friendly; close to a major shopping area. **Cons:** busy area. **TripAdvisor:** "nice people," "awesome hospitality and comfortable beds," "convenient." $ *Rooms from: $119* ⊠ *1830 Hilltop Dr., Hwy. 44/299 exit off I-5* ☎ *530/221–8700, 800/733–5466* ⊕ *www. redlion.com* ⤴ *192 rooms, 2 suites.*

SPORTS AND THE OUTDOORS

Fly Shop. The Fly Shop sells fishing licenses and has information about guides, conditions, and fishing packages. ⊠ *4140 Churn Creek Rd., at Denton Way* ☎ *530/222–3555* ⊕ *www.flyshop.com.*

WEAVERVILLE

46 miles west of Redding on Hwy. 299.

A man known only as Weaver struck gold here in 1849, and the fledgling community that developed at the base of the Trinity Alps was named after him. With its impressive downtown historic district, today Weaverville is a popular headquarters for family vacations and biking, hiking, fishing, and gold-panning excursions.

GETTING HERE AND AROUND

Highway 299 becomes Main Street down the center of Weaverville. Take the highway either east from the Pacific Coast or west from Redding. Highway 36 from Red Bluff to Highway 3 heading north leads to Weaverville. Trinity Transit provides minimal local bus service plus a line that links Weaverville to Interstate 5 at Redding.

EXPLORING

Trinity County Courthouse. Trinity County Courthouse, built in 1856 as a store, office building, and hotel, was converted to county use in 1865. The Apollo Saloon, in the basement, became the county jail. It's the oldest courthouse still in use in California. ⊠ *Court and Main Sts.*

★ **Trinity County Historical Park.** For a vivid sense of Weaverville's past, visit the Trinity County Historical Park, especially its **Jake Jackson Memorial Museum,** which has a blacksmith shop and a stamp mill (where ore is crushed) from the 1890s that is still in use. Also here are the original jail cells of the Trinity County Courthouse. ⊠ *780 Main St., at Bartlett La.* ☎ *530/623–5211* ⊘ *Jan.–Mar., Wed. and Sat. noon–4; Apr., daily noon–4; May–Oct., daily 10–5; Nov. and Dec., Wed.–Sat. 11–4.*

Fodor's Choice
★
Weaverville Joss House. Weaverville's main attraction is the Joss House, a Taoist temple built in 1874 and called Won Lim Miao ("the temple

of the forest beneath the clouds") by Chinese miners. The oldest continuously used Chinese temple in California, it attracts worshippers from around the world. With its golden altar, antique weaponry, and carved wooden canopies, the Joss House is a piece of California history that can best be appreciated on a guided 30-minute tour. The original temple building and many of its furnishings—some of which came from China—were lost to fire in 1873, but members of the local Chinese community soon rebuilt it. ⊠ *630 Main St., at Oregon St.* ☎ *530/623–5284* 🖾 *Museum free; guided tour $4* ☉ *Thurs. and Sun. 10–5; last tour at 4.*

WHERE TO EAT

$$

AMERICAN

✕ **La Grange Café.** In two brick buildings dating from the 1850s (they're among the oldest edifices in town), this eatery serves buffalo and other game meats, pasta, fresh fish, and farmers' market vegetables when they're available. There's a full premium bar, and the wine list is extensive. $ *Average main: $19* ⊠ *520 Main St.* ☎ *530/623–5325* ☉ *Hrs sometimes sporadic in winter.*

SPORTS AND THE OUTDOORS

Fly Stretch. Below the Lewiston Dam, east of Weaverville on Highway 299, is the Fly Stretch of the Trinity River, an excellent fly-fishing area.

Pine Cove Boat Ramp. This ramp on Lewiston Lake provides fishing access for those with disabilities—decks here are built over prime trout-fishing waters.

Weaverville Ranger Station. Check here for maps and information about hiking trails in the Trinity Alps Wilderness. ⊠ *360 Main St.* ☎ *530/623–2121.*

LAKE SHASTA AREA

★   *12 miles north of Redding on I-5.*

When you think of the Lake Shasta Area picture water, wilderness, dazzling stalagmites—and a fabulous man-made project in the midst of it all.

GETTING HERE AND AROUND

Interstate 5 north of Redding is the main link to the entire Lake Shasta area. Get to the dam by passing through tiny City of Shasta Lake. There is no local bus service.

ESSENTIALS

Shasta Cascade Wonderland Association ⊠ *1699 Hwy. 273, Anderson* ☎ *530/365–7500, 800/474–2782* ⊕ *www.shastacascade.com.*

EXPLORING

Lake Shasta. Twenty-one types of fish inhabit the lake, including rainbow trout and salmon. The lake region also has the largest nesting population of bald eagles in California. You can rent fishing boats, ski boats, sailboats, canoes, paddleboats, Jet Skis, and windsurfing boards at one of the many marinas and resorts along the 370-mile shoreline.

Fodor's Choice
★

Lake Shasta Caverns. Stalagmites, stalactites, flowstone deposits, and crystals entice visitors to the Lake Shasta Caverns. To see this impressive spectacle, you must take the two-hour tour, which includes a catamaran ride across the McCloud arm of Lake Shasta and a bus ride up Grey Rock Mountain to the cavern entrance. The caverns are 58°F year-round, making them a cool retreat on a hot summer day. The most awe-inspiring of the limestone rock formations is the glistening Cathedral Room, which appears to be gilded. During peak summer months (June through August), tours depart every half hour; in April, May, and September it's every hour. A gift shop is open from 8 to 4:30. ✉ *20359 Shasta Caverns Rd., off I–5, 17 miles north of Redding, Lakehead* ☎ *530/238–2341, 800/795–2283* ⊕ *www.lakeshastacaverns.com* 🎫 *$24* ⊙ *June–Aug., tours on the ½ hr, daily 9–4; Apr., May, and Sept., tours on the hr, daily 9–3; Oct.–Mar., tours at 10, noon, and 2 daily.*

★ **Shasta Dam.** This is the second-largest concrete dam in the United States (only Grand Coulee in Washington is bigger). The visitor center has computerized photographic tours of the dam construction, video presentations, fact sheets, and historical displays. Hour-long guided tours inside the dam and its powerhouse leave from the center. ✉ *16349 Shasta Dam Blvd., off Lake Blvd., Shasta Lake* ☎ *530/275–1554* ⊕ *www.usbr.gov/mp/ncao* 🎫 *Free* ⊙ *Visitor center daily 8–5; call for tour times.*

14

SPORTS AND THE OUTDOORS

FISHING

The Fishen Hole. A couple of miles from the lake, this bait-and-tackle shop sells fishing licenses and provides information about conditions. ✉ *3844 Shasta Dam Blvd., Shasta Lake City* ☎ *530/275–4123.*

HOUSEBOATING

Houseboats here come in all sizes except small. As a rule, rentals are outfitted with cooking utensils, dishes, and most of the equipment you'll need—you supply the food and the linens. When you rent a houseboat, you receive a short course in how to maneuver your launch before you set out. You can fish, swim, sunbathe on the flat roof, or sit on the deck and watch the world go by. The shoreline of Lake Shasta is beautifully ragged, with countless inlets; it's not hard to find privacy. Expect to spend a minimum of $350 a day for a craft that sleeps six. A three-day, two-night minimum is customary. Prices are often lower during the off-season (September through May). Bridge Bay Resort rents houseboats, fishing boats, ski boats, and patio boats. Shasta Cascade offers general information.

Bridge Bay Resort ✉ *10300 Bridge Bay Rd., Redding* ☎ *800/752–9669.*

Shasta Cascade Wonderland Association ✉ *Anderson* ☎ *530/365–7500, 800/474–2782* ⊕ *www.shastacascade.com.*

DUNSMUIR

10 miles south of Mt. Shasta on I–5.

Castle Crags State Park surrounds the tiny town of Dunsmuir, which was named for a 19th-century Scottish coal baron who offered to build a fountain if the town were renamed in his honor. The town's other major attraction is the Railroad Park Resort, where you can spend the night in restored railcars.

GETTING HERE AND AROUND

Reach Dunsmuir via exits off Interstate 5 at the north and south ends of town. When snow hasn't closed the route, you can take Highway 89 from the Lassen Park area toward Burney then northeast to Interstate 5 at Mt. Shasta. From there it's a 10-mile drive south to Dunsmuir. Amtrak stops here; Greyhound stops in Weed, 20 miles north. On weekdays, STAGE buses serve Dunsmuir.

> **FINE FISHING**
>
> The upper Sacramento River near Dunsmuir is consistently rated one of the best fishing spots in the country. Check with the chamber of commerce for local fishing guides.

ESSENTIALS

Bus Information STAGE ☎ *530/842-8295* 🌐 *www.co.siskiyou.ca.us.*

Visitor Information Dunsmuir Chamber of Commerce ✉ *5915 Dunsmuir Ave., Suite 100* ☎ *530/235-2177* 🌐 *dunsmuir.com.*

EXPLORING

★ **Castle Crags State Park.** Named for its 6,000-foot glacier-polished crags, which tower over the Sacramento River, this park offers fishing in Castle Creek, hiking in the backcountry, and a view of Mt. Shasta. The crags draw climbers and hikers from around the world. The 4,350-acre park has 28 miles of hiking trails, including a 2.75-mile access trail to **Castle Crags Wilderness,** part of the **Shasta-Trinity National Forest.** There are excellent trails at lower altitudes. Because of budget cuts, the state parks department proposed closing Castle Crags, but nonprofit groups hope to keep this stunning space open. Call ahead to check status. ✉ *6 miles south of Dunsmuir, Castella/Castle Crags exit off I–5* ☎ *530/235-2684* 🎟 *$8 per vehicle, day use.*

WHERE TO EAT AND STAY

For expanded reviews, facilities, and current deals, visit Fodors.com.

$$ MEDITERRANEAN 🍴 **Café Maddalena.** The chef here gained experience working in top San Francisco restaurants before moving up north to prepare adventurous Mediterranean fare with a French influence. Selections change seasonally but always feature a vegetarian dish, along with entrées such as Pacific salmon with Meyer lemon sauce, and lamb shoulder with cassoulet. Wines from Spain, Italy, and France complement the meals. [$] *Average main: $18* ✉ *5801 Sacramento Ave.* ☎ *530/235-2725* 🌐 *www.cafemaddalena.com* 🕒 *Closed Mon.–Wed. and Jan.–mid-Feb. No lunch.*

$ HOTEL 👶 🏨 **Railroad Park Resort.** The antique cabooses here were collected over more than three decades and have been converted into cozy motel rooms in honor of Dunsmuir's railroad legacy. **Pros:** gorgeous setting; kitschy fun. **Cons:** cabooses can feel cramped; restaurant open mid-May through September. **TripAdvisor:** "what a fun place," "railroad buff's delight," "quite different." [$] *Rooms from: $115* ✉ *100 Railroad Park Rd.* ☎ *530/235-4440* 🌐 *www.rrpark.com* 🛏 *23 cabooses, 4 cabins.*

MT. SHASTA

34 miles north of Lake Shasta on I–5.

GETTING HERE AND AROUND

Three exits off Interstate 5 lead to the town of Mt. Shasta. When snow hasn't closed the route, you can take Highway 89 from the Lassen Park area toward Burney then northeast to Mt. Shasta. The ski park is off Highway 89. Greyhound stops at Weed, 10 miles north; Amtrak stops at Dunsmuir, 10 miles south. There's no local bus system.

ESSENTIALS

Visitor Information Mt. Shasta Chamber of Commerce and Visitors Bureau ✉ *300 Pine St., at W. Lake St.* ☎ *530/926–3696, 800/926–4865* ⊕ *www. visitsiskiyou.org.*

EXPLORING

Mt. Shasta. The crown jewel of the 2.5-million-acre Shasta-Trinity National Forest, Mt. Shasta, a 14,162-foot-high dormant volcano, is a mecca for day hikers. It's especially enticing in spring, when fragrant Shasta lilies and other flowers adorn the rocky slopes. The paved road reaches only as far as the timberline; the final 6,000 feet are a tough climb of rubble, ice, and snow (the summit is perpetually ice packed). Only a hardy few are qualified to make the trek to the top.

The town of Mt. Shasta has real character and some fine restaurants. Lovers of the outdoors and backcountry skiers abound, and they are more than willing to offer advice on the most beautiful spots in the region, which include out-of-the-way swimming holes, dozens of high mountain lakes, and a challenging 18-hole golf course with 360 degrees of spectacular views.

WHERE TO EAT AND STAY

For expanded reviews, facilities, and current deals, visit Fodors.com.

$$
ECLECTIC
✕ **Lilys.** This restaurant in a white-clapboard home, framed by a picket fence and arched trellis, serves everything from steaks and pastas to Mexican and vegetarian dishes. Daily specials include prime rib and a fresh fish entrée. For innovative vegetarian fare try a *dal* burger, which is made with walnuts, fresh veggies, garbanzo beans, and rice. $ *Average main: $19* ✉ *1013 S. Mt. Shasta Blvd., at Holly St.* ☎ *530/926–3372* ⊕ *www.lilysrestaurant.com.*

$
CAFÉ
✕ **Seven Suns Coffee and Cafe.** A favorite gathering spot for locals, this small coffee shop serves specialty wraps for breakfast and lunch, plus soup and salad selections. Pastries, made daily, include muffins and scones, and blackberry fruit bars in season. If the weather's nice, grab a seat on the patio. $ *Average main: $8* ✉ *1011 S. Mt. Shasta Blvd., at Holly St.* ☎ *530/926–9701* ⊕ *www.mtshastacoffee.com.*

$$$
RENTAL
★
🏨 **Mount Shasta Resort.** Private chalets are nestled among tall pine trees along the shore of Lake Siskiyou, all with gas-log fireplaces and full kitchens. **Pros:** incredible views; romantic woodsy setting. **Cons:** kids may get bored. **TripAdvisor:** "fabulous views and surroundings," "it's all service and ambience," "beautiful." $ *Rooms from: $169* ✉ *1000 Siskiyou Lake Blvd.* ☎ *530/926–3030, 800/958–3363* ⊕ *www. mountshastaresort.com* ⤴ *65 units.*

14

SPORTS AND THE OUTDOORS

HIKING **Mt. Shasta Forest Service Ranger Station.** Check in here for current trail conditions and avalanche reports. ✉ *204 W. Alma St., at Pine St.* ☎ *530/926–4511, 530/926–9613.*

MOUNTAIN **Fifth Season Mountaineering Shop.** The shop rents skiing and climbing
CLIMBING equipment and operates a recorded 24-hour climber-skier report. ✉ *300 N. Mt. Shasta Blvd.* ☎ *530/926–3606, 530/926–5555* ⊕ *www. thefifthseason.com.*

Shasta Mountain Guides. These guides lead hiking, climbing, and ski-touring groups to the summit of Mt. Shasta. ☎ *530/926–3117* ⊕ *www. shastaguides.com.*

SKIING **Mt. Shasta Board & Ski Park.** On the southeast flank of Mt. Shasta, this
Ⓒ ski park has three triple-chair lifts and one surface lift on 425 skiable acres. Three-quarters of the trails are for beginning or intermediate skiers. The area's vertical drop is 1,435 feet, with a top elevation of 6,600 feet. The longest of the 32 trails is 1.75 miles. A package for beginners, available through the ski school, includes a lift ticket, ski rental, and a lesson. The school also runs ski and snowboard programs for children. There's night skiing for those who want to see the moon rise as they schuss. The base lodge has a simple café, a ski shop, and a ski-snowboard rental shop. ✉ *Hwy. 89 exit east from I–5, south of Mt. Shasta* ☎ *530/926–8610, 800/754–7427* ⊕ *www.skipark.com* ⊙ *Winter ski season schedule: Sun.–Wed. 9–4, Thurs.–Sat. 9–9.*

Mt. Shasta Nordic Center. The center, run by a nonprofit, maintains 15 miles of groomed cross-country ski trails. ✉ *Ski Park Hwy., off Hwy. 89 (take I–5's McCloud exit)* ☎ *530/926–2142* ⊕ *www.mtshastanordic. org.*

THE BACKCOUNTRY

The Far North's primitive, rugged backcountry is arguably full of more natural wonders than any other region in California.

MCARTHUR–BURNEY FALLS MEMORIAL STATE PARK

Hwy. 89, 52 miles southeast of Mt. Shasta and 41 miles north of Lassen Volcanic National Park.

GETTING HERE AND AROUND

To see some stunning falls, head east off Interstate 5 on Highway 89 at Mt. Shasta. The drive is 52 miles. From Interstate 5 in Redding, head east 55 miles on Highway 299 to connect with Highway 89; follow signs 6 miles to the park. From Alturas, head west on Highway 299 for about 86 miles hook up with Highway 89.

EXPLORING

Ⓒ **McArthur–Burney Falls Memorial State Park.** Just inside the park's southern
Fodor'sChoice boundary, Burney Creek wells up from the ground and divides into
★ two falls that cascade over a 129-foot cliff into a pool below. Count-less ribbonlike streams pour from hidden moss-covered crevices; resi-dent bald eagles are frequently seen soaring overhead. You can walk

a self-guided nature trail that descends to the foot of the falls, which Theodore Roosevelt—according to legend—called "the eighth wonder of the world." On warm days, swim at Lake Britton; lounge on the beach; rent motorboats, paddleboats, and canoes; or relax at one of the campsites or picnic areas. The camp store is open from early May to the end of October. ⊠ *24898 Hwy. 89, Burney* ☎ *530/335–2777* ⊞ *$8 per vehicle, day use.*

ALTURAS

86 miles northeast of McArthur–Burney Falls Memorial State Park on Hwy. 299.

Alturas is the county seat and largest town in Modoc County. The Dorris family arrived in the area in 1874, built Dorris Bridge over the Pit River, and later opened a small wayside stop for travelers. As in the past, travelers today come to see eagles and other wildlife, the Modoc National Forest, and active geothermal areas.

14

GETTING HERE AND AROUND

To get to Alturas from Susanville take Main Street/Highway 36 south for about 4 miles; turn left at U.S. 395 and stay on that highway for 99 miles. From Redding, take the Lake Blvd./299E exit off Interstate 5, head east and stay on Highway 299 for 140 miles. Sage Stage buses serve Alturas from Redding and Susanville.

ESSENTIALS

Bus Information Modoc County Sage Stage ☎ *530/233–3883, 530/233–6410* ⊕ *www.sagestage.com.*

Visitor Information Alturas Chamber of Commerce ⊠ *600 S. Main St.* ☎ *530/233–4434* ⊕ *www.alturaschamber.org.*

EXPLORING

Modoc National Forest. Encompassing 1.6 million acres, Modoc National Forest protects 300 species of wildlife, including Rocky Mountain elk, wild horses, mule deer, and pronghorn antelope. In spring and fall, watch for migratory waterfowl as they make their way along the Pacific Flyway above the forest. Hiking trails lead to Petroglyph Point, one of the largest panels of rock art in the United States. ⊠ *Park Headquarters, 800 W. 12th St.* ☎ *530/233–5811* ⊕ *www.fs.usda.gov/modoc.*

Modoc National Wildlife Refuge. The 7,021-acre Modoc National Wildlife Refuge was established in 1961 to protect migratory waterfowl. You might see Canada geese, sandhill cranes, mallards, teal, wigeon, pintail, white pelicans, cormorants, and snowy egrets. The refuge is open for hiking, bird-watching, and photography, but one area is set aside for hunters. Regulations vary according to season. ⊠ *U.S. 395, 1½ miles south of Alturas* ☎ *530/233–3572* ⊕ *www.fws.gov/modoc/* ⊞ *Free* ☉ *Daily dawn–dusk.*

WHERE TO EAT

$$

SPANISH

✕ **Brass Rail.** Prix-fixe dinners at this authentic Basque restaurant include wine, homemade bread, soup, salad, side dishes, coffee, and ice cream. Steak, lamb chops, fried chicken, shrimp, and scallops are among the

best entrée selections. A lounge with a full bar adjoins the dining area. [$] *Average main: $20* ✉ *395 Lake View Dr., at Lake Rd.* ☎ *530/233–2906* ⏲ *Closed Mon.*

SUSANVILLE

104 miles south of Alturas via U.S. 395; 65 miles east of Lassen Volcanic National Park via Highway 36.

Susanville, established as a trading post in 1854, tells the tale of its rich history through murals painted on buildings in the historic uptown area. You can take a self-guided tour around the original buildings and stop for a bite at one of the restaurants now housed within them. If you'd rather work up a sweat, you can hit the Bizz Johnson Trail and Eagle Lake recreation areas just outside of town.

GETTING HERE AND AROUND

U.S. 395 connects Susanville and Alturas, about a 100-mile trip. From Red Bluff, take Interstate 5's Highway 36E/Fairgrounds exit and drive east for about 3 miles; turn left at Highway 36E and continue through the mountains for 103 miles. Lassen Rural Bus serves Susanville and surrounding areas on weekdays only.

ESSENTIALS

Bus Information Lassen Rural Bus ☎ *530/252–7433* 🌐 *www.lassentransportation.org.*

Visitor Information Lassen County Chamber of Commerce ✉ *75 N. Weatherlow St., off Main St.* ☎ *530/257–4323* 🌐 *www.lassencountychamber.com.*

EXPLORING

Bizz Johnson Trail. Bizz Johnson Trail follows a defunct line of the Southern Pacific Railroad for 25 miles. Known to locals as the Bizz, the trail is open for hikers, walkers, mountain bikers, horseback riders, and cross-country skiers. It skirts the Susan River through a scenic landscape of canyons, bridges, and forests abundant with wildlife. ✉ *Trailhead, 601 Richmond Rd., near N. Railroad Ave.* ☎ *530/257–0456* 🌐 *www.blm.gov/ca/eaglelake/bizztrail.html* 🎟 *Free.*

Eagle Lake. Anglers travel great distances to fish the waters of large Eagle Lake, whose rainbow trout is prized for its size and fighting ability. Surrounded by high desert to the north and alpine forests to the south, the lake is also popular for picnicking, hiking, boating, waterskiing and windsurfing, and bird-watching—ospreys, pelicans, and many other waterfowl visit the lake. On land you might see mule deer, small mammals, and even pronghorn antelope—and be sure to watch for bald-eagle nesting sites. ✉ *16 miles north of Susanville, Eagle Lake Rd. off Hwy. 139* ☎ *530/257–0456 for Eagle Lake Recreation Area, 530/825–3454 for Eagle Lake Marina* 🌐 *www.blm.gov/ca/eaglelake.*

WHERE TO EAT AND STAY

$ MEXICAN 🍴 **Mazatlan Grill.** The sauces and tortillas are prepared on-site in this friendly, family-run restaurant and lounge, which serves lunch and dinner daily. The dining room is simple and tidy, with comfortable upholstered booths. The extensive menu offers authentic, inexpensive

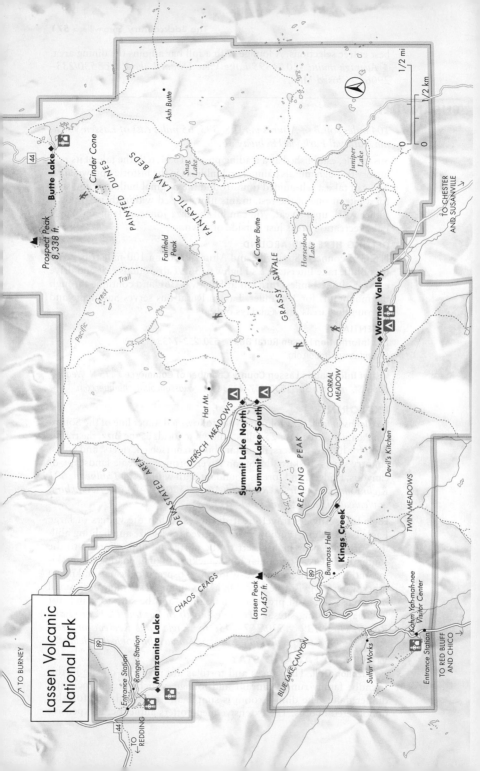

Lassen Volcanic National Park

TO BURNEY

TO REDDING

TO
REDDING

Entrance Station

Ranger Station

Manzanita Lake

CHAOS CRAGS

Lassen Peak
10,457 ft.

BLUE LAKE CANYON

DEVASTATED AREA

DERSCH MEADOWS

Hat Mt.

Summit Lake North
Summit Lake South

READING PEAK

Bumpass Hell

Kings Creek

Sulfur Works

Kohm Yah-mah-nee
Visitor Center

Entrance Station

TO RED BLUFF
AND CHICO

TWIN MEADOWS

Devil's Kitchen

CORRAL MEADOW

GRASSY SWALE

Warner Valley

TO CHESTER
AND SUSANVILLE

Horseshoe Lake

Juniper Lake

Crater Butte

Fairfield Peak

Snag Lake

PAINTED DUNES

FANTASTIC LAVA BEDS

Cinder Cone

Ash Butte

Butte Lake

Prospect Peak
8,338 ft.

Pacific Crest Trail

1/2 mi
1/2 km
0
0

Mexican fare ranging from fajitas and enchiladas to a vegetarian burrito. $ *Average main: $10* ⊠ *1535 Main St., at Park St.* ☎ *530/257–1800.*

$

HOTEL

⚎ **High Country Inn.** Rooms are spacious in this colonial-style motel on the eastern edge of town. **Pros:** great mountain views; heated pool. **Cons:** lots of traffic in the area. **TripAdvisor:** "everything was great," "quiet," "a very nice property." $ *Rooms from: $84* ⊠ *3015 Riverside Dr.* ☎ *530/257–3450, 866/454–4566* ⊕ *www.high-country-inn.com* ⥾ *66 rooms* ⦿ *Breakfast.*

LASSEN VOLCANIC NATIONAL PARK

45 miles east of Redding on Hwy. 44; 48 miles east of Red Bluff on Hwy. 36.

14

GETTING HERE AND AROUND

Whether coming from the west or the east, reach the park's southern entrance via Highway 36E, and turn onto Highway 89 for a short drive to the park. The northwest entrance is reached via Highway 44 from Redding and Susanville. No buses serve the area.

EXPLORING

Chaos Jumbles. More than 350 years ago, an avalanche from the Chaos Crags lava domes scattered hundreds of thousands of rocks—many of them 2–3 feet in diameter—over a couple of square miles. ⊠ *Lassen Park Rd., 2 miles northeast of the northwest entrance ranger station.*

Fodor's Choice
★

Lassen Scenic Byway. This 185-mile scenic drive begins in Chester and loops through the forests, volcanic peaks, geothermal springs, and lava fields of Lassen National Forest and Lassen National Park, providing for an all-day excursion into dramatic wilderness. Parts of the road are inaccessible in winter. From Chester, take Route 36 west to Route 89 north through the park, then Route 44 east to Route 36 west. ☎ *800/427–7623.*

Fodor's Choice
★

Lassen Volcanic National Park. A dormant plug dome, Lassen Peak is the focus of Lassen Volcanic National Park's 165.6 square miles of distinctive landscape. The peak began erupting in May 1914, sending pumice, rock, and snow thundering down the mountain and gas and hot ash billowing into the atmosphere. Lassen's most spectacular outburst occurred in 1915 when it blew a cloud of ash some 7 miles into the stratosphere. The resulting mudflow destroyed vegetation for miles in some directions; the evidence is still visible today, especially in Devastated Area. The volcano finally came to rest in 1921. Now fumaroles, mud pots, lakes, and bubbling hot springs create a fascinating but dangerous landscape that can be viewed throughout the park, especially via a hiked descent into Bumpass Hell. Because of its significance as a volcanic landscape, Lassen became a national park in 1916. Several volcanoes—the largest of which is now Lassen Peak—have been active in the area for roughly 600,000 years. The four types of volcanoes found in the world are represented in the park, including shield (Prospect Peak), plug dome (Lassen Peak), cinder cone (Cinder Cone), and composite (Brokeoff Volcano). Lassen Park Road (the continuation of Highway 89 within the park) and 150 miles of hiking trails provide access to many of these volcanic wonders. Caution is key here: signs warn visitors to stay on the trails and railed boardwalks to avoid falling into boiling water or through dangerous thin-crusted areas of the park. Although the park is closed to cars in winter, it's usually open to intrepid cross-country skiers and snowshoers. The Kohm Yah-mah-nee Visitor Center, at the southwest entrance to the park, is open year-round. ⊕ *www.nps. gov/lavo* ≋ *$10 per car, $5 per person if not in a car.*

🝐 **Sulphur Works Thermal Area.** Proof of Lassen Peak's volatility becomes evident shortly after you enter the park at the southwest entrance. Sidewalks skirt boiling springs and sulphur-emitting steam vents. This area is usually the last site to close because of snow. ⊠ *Lassen Park Rd., 1 mile from the southwest entrance ranger station.*

SPORTS AND THE OUTDOORS

HIKING **Bumpass Hell Trail.** Boiling springs, steam vents, and mudpots highlight
Fodor'sChoice this 3.2-mile round-trip hike. Expect the loop to take about three hours.
★ During the first mile of the hike there's a gradual climb of 500 feet before a steep 250-foot descent to the basin. You'll encounter rocky patches, so wear hiking boots. Stay on trails and boardwalks near the thermal areas, as what appears to be firm ground may be only a thin crust over scalding mud. *Moderate.* ⊠ *Trailhead at end of paved parking area off Lassen Park Rd., 6 miles from the southwest entrance ranger station.*

Fodor'sChoice **Lassen Peak Hike.** This trail winds 2½ miles to the mountaintop. It's a
★ tough climb—2,000 feet uphill on a steady, steep grade—but the reward is a spectacular view. At the peak you can see into the rim and view the entire park (and much of California's far north). Bring sunscreen, water, and a jacket since it's often windy and much cooler at the summit. ■**TIP**→ A multiyear restoration project means all or part of the trail will be closed at certain times, so call ahead. At this writing trail work was expected to be complete in 2014. *Difficult.* ⊠ *Trailhead past a paved parking area off Lassen Park Rd., 7 miles north of the southwest entrance ranger station* ☎ *530/595–4480.*

CHESTER

36 miles west of Susanville on Hwy 36.

The population of this small town on Lake Almanor swells from 2,500 to nearly 5,000 in summer as tourists come to visit. Chester serves as a gateway to Lassen Volcanic National Park.

GETTING HERE AND AROUND

Chester is on Highway 36E. When snow doesn't close Highway 89, the main road through Lassen Park, visitors can take Highway 44 from Redding to Highway 89 through the park and to Highway 36E and onto Chester and Lake Almanor. Plumas County Transit connects Chester to the Quincy area.

ESSENTIALS

Bus Information Plumas County Transit ⊠ *Chester* ☎ *530/283–2538* ⊕ *www. plumastransit.com.*

Lassen Volcanic National Park's King Creek Falls Hike, which takes you through forests and meadows dotted with wildflowers, is a good hike for nature photographers.

Visitor Information **Chester–Lake Almanor Chamber of Commerce** ✉ *529 Main St., at Farrar Dr.* ☎ *530/258–2426, 800/350–4838* 🌐 *www.lakealmanorarea.com.*

EXPLORING

Lake Almanor. Lake Almanor's 52 miles of shoreline lie in the shadow of Mt. Lassen, and are popular with campers, swimmers, water-skiers, and anglers. At an elevation of 4,500 feet, the lake warms to above 70°F for about eight weeks in summer. ✉ *Off Hwys. 89 and 36* ☎ *530/258–2426.*

WHERE TO EAT AND STAY

For expanded reviews, facilities, and current deals, visit Fodors.com.

$ AMERICAN 🍴 **Kopper Kettle Cafe.** Locals return again and again to this tidy restaurant that serves home-cooked lunches and dinners. Head here for breakfast whenever you've got a hankering for scrambled eggs or biscuits and gravy. [$] *Average main: $13* ✉ *243 Main St., at Myrtle St.* ☎ *530/258–2698.*

$ MEXICAN 🍴 **Maria's Mexican Restaurant.** A festive atmosphere prevails in this family-friendly restaurant and lounge, where traditional south-of-the-border fare is served. It's one of the few restaurants in the area with a full bar, a great place to enjoy a margarita at the end of a long day spent hiking. [$] *Average main: $10* ✉ *159 Main St., at Willow Way* ☎ *530/258–2262* 🕒 *Closed Sun.*

$$ HOTEL 🏨 **Best Western Rose Quartz Inn.** Down the road from Lake Almanor and close to Lassen Volcanic National Park, this small-town inn balances traditional decor and up-to-the-minute amenities like Wi-Fi. **Pros:** near national park; modern conveniences. **Cons:** standard rooms on the

pricey side. **TripAdvisor:** "comfortable," "great night's sleep," "friendly place to stay."$ *Rooms from: $120* ✉ *306 Main St.* ☎ *530/258–2002, 888/571–4885* ⊕ *www.bestwesterncalifornia.com/chester-hotels* ⌁ *50 rooms* ⍓*Breakfast.*

$ 🛏 **Bidwell House.** Some guest rooms at this 1901 ranch house have wood-
B&B/INN burning stoves, claw-foot tubs, and antique furnishings; a separate
Fodor's Choice cottage with a kitchen sleeps six. **Pros:** unique decor in each room; beau-
★ tiful wooded setting; near Lake Almanor. **Cons:** not ideal for kids. **Trip-Advisor:** "these folks know how to do hospitality," "peaceful place," "great breakfasts."$ *Rooms from: $115* ✉ *1 Main St.* ☎ *530/258–3338* ⊕ *www.bidwellhouse.com* ⌁ *14 rooms, 12 with bath* ⍓*Breakfast.*

QUINCY

67 miles southwest of Susanville via Hwys. 36 and 89.

A center for mining and logging in the 1850s, Quincy is nestled against the western slope of the Sierra Nevada. The county seat and largest community in Plumas County, the town is rich in historic buildings that have been the focus of preservation and restoration efforts. The four-story courthouse on Main Street, one of several stops on a self-guided tour, was built in 1921 with marble posts and staircases. The arts are thriving in Quincy, too: catch a play or a bluegrass performance at the Town Hall Theatre.

GETTING HERE AND AROUND

Quincy is on Highway 70 and is accessible from all directions via mountain roads. Highway 70 goes through the Feather River Canyon to Highway 149, then Highway 99 to Chico and Red Bluff, a 198-mile trip. From Quincy, Highway 70 connects to Highway 89 and then to Highway 36E toward Susanville in the east, or westward toward Chester and Lassen Park. Plumas County Transit serves Chester and Quincy. Lassen Rural Bus connects Quincy and Susanville.

ESSENTIALS

Bus Information Lassen Rural Bus ☎ *530/252–7433* ⊕ *www. lassentransportation.org.***Plumas County Transit** ☎ *530/283–2538* ⊕ *www. plumastransit.com.*

Visitor Information Quincy Chamber of Commerce ✉ *464 Main St., at Bradley St.* ☎ *530/283–0188* ⊕ *www.quincychamber.com.*

EXPLORING

Plumas County Museum. The cultural, home arts, and industrial history displays at the Plumas County Museum contain artifacts dating to the 1850s. Highlights include collections of Maidu Indian basketry, pioneer weapons, and rooms depicting life in the early logging and mining days of Plumas County. Out in the Exhibit Yard are a working blacksmith shop, a restored goldminer's cabin, and a railroad exhibit. ✉ *500 Jackson St., at Coburn St.* ☎ *530/283–6320* ⊕ *www.plumasmuseum.org* ✉ *$2* ⊗ *Tues.–Sat. 10–4.*

Plumas National Forest. Plumas County is known for its wide-open spaces, and the 1.2-million-acre Plumas National Forest, with its high alpine lakes and crystal-clear woodland streams, is a beautiful example.

Hundreds of campsites are maintained in the forest, and picnic areas and hiking trails abound. You can enter the forest along Highways 70 and 89. ✉ *U.S. Forest Service, 159 Lawrence St., near W. Main St.* ☎ *530/283–2050* 🕒 *Office weekdays 8–4:30.*

WHERE TO EAT AND STAY

For expanded reviews, facilities, and current deals, visit Fodors.com.

$ AMERICAN 🍴 **Sweet Lorraine's.** Hearty fare served in this casual, bustling restaurant in Quincy's historic downtown area includes meaty dishes like St. Louis ribs as well as vegetarian selections and lighter items; there's also a good selection of wines. If the weather is mild, dine alfresco on the patio. [$] *Average main: $15* ✉ *384 Main St., at Harbison Ave.* ☎ *530/283–5300* 🕒 *Closed Sun. and Mon.*

14

$ RENTAL Fodor's Choice ★ 🏨 **Ada's Place.** This place is actually four uniquely beautiful cottages, secluded on a quiet street one block from the county courthouse and downtown Quincy. **Pros:** on-site owners' meticulous upkeep. **Cons:** not a good choice for children. **TripAdvisor:** "fabulous tranquil retreat," "a most wonderful oasis," "absolutely wonderful."[$] *Rooms from: $100* ✉ *562 Jackson St., near Court St.* ☎ *530/283–1954, 877/234–2327* 🌐 *www.adasplace.com* 🛏 *4 cottages.*

$ B&B/INN 🏨 **Feather Bed.** The quaint romanticism of an 1893 Queen Anne Victorian plus proximity to Quincy's town center are the draws here. **Pros:** great location for exploring the town on foot. **Cons:** some rooms are small. **TripAdvisor:** "caring and nurturing place to stay," "friendly owners," "nice location."[$] *Rooms from: $120* ✉ *542 Jackson St.* ☎ *530/283–0102, 800/696–8624* 🌐 *www.featherbed-inn.com* 🛏 *5 rooms, 2 cottages* 🍽 *Breakfast.*

Travel Smart
Northern
California

WORD OF MOUTH

"Highway 1 is an awesome drive, but it took us a lot longer to do than we had initially planned, so give yourself enough time including stops for photos at beautiful empty beaches along the way."

—Elyse_Dorm

www.fodors.com/community

GETTING HERE AND AROUND

Wherever you plan to go in Northern California, getting there will likely involve driving, even if you fly. Major airports are usually far from main attractions. (In San Francisco, it's a 30-minute-plus trip between any Bay Area airport and downtown.) Northern California's major airport hub is SFO in San Francisco, but satellite airports can be found around most major cities. When booking flights, it pays to check these locations, as you may find more convenient times and a better location in relation to your hotel. Most small cities have their own commercial airports, with connecting flights to larger cities—but service may be extremely limited, and it may be cheaper to rent a car and drive from San Francisco.

▌ AIR TRAVEL

Flying time to California is about 6 hours from New York and 4½ hours from Chicago. Travel from London to San Francisco is 11 hours and from Sydney approximately 14. Flying between San Francisco and Los Angeles takes about 90 minutes.

AIRPORTS

California's gateways are Los Angeles International Airport (LAX), San Francisco International Airport (SFO), San Diego International Airport (SAN), Sacramento International Airport (SMF), and San Jose International Airport (SJC). Oakland International Airport (OAK) is another option in the Bay Area, and other Los Angeles airports include Long Beach (LGB), Bob Hope Airport (BUR), LA/Ontario (ONT), and John Wayne Airport (SNA).

Airport Information Bob Hope Airport ☎ 818/840-8840 ⊕ www.burbankairport. com. **John Wayne Airport** ☎ 949/252-5200 ⊕ www.ocair.com. **LA/Ontario International Airport** ☎ 909/937-2700 ⊕ www.flyontario. com. **Long Beach Airport** ☎ 562/570-2600

⊕ www.lgb.org. **Los Angeles International Airport** ☎ 310/646-5252 ⊕ www.lawa. org/lax. **Oakland International Airport** ☎ 510/563-3300 ⊕ www.flyoakland.com. **Sacramento International Airport** ☎ 916/929-5411 ⊕ www.sacramento.aero/smf. **San Diego International Airport** ☎ 619/400-2404 ⊕ www.san.org. **San Francisco International Airport** ☎ 650/821-8211, 800/435-9736 ⊕ www.flysfo.com. **San Jose International Airport** ☎ 408/392-3600 ⊕ www.flysanjose. com.

FLIGHTS

United, with hubs in San Francisco and Los Angeles, has the greatest number of flights into and within California. But most national and many international airlines fly to the state. Southwest Airlines connects smaller cities within California, often from satellite airports near major cities.

Airline Contacts Air Canada ☎ 888/247-2262 ⊕ www.aircanada.com. **Alaska Airlines/Horizon Air** ☎ 800/252-7522 ⊕ www. alaskaair.com. **American Airlines** ☎ 800/433-7300 ⊕ www.aa.com. **British Airways** ☎ 800/247-9297 ⊕ www.britishairways.com. **Cathay Pacific** ☎ 800/233-2742 ⊕ www. cathaypacific.com. **Delta Airlines** ☎ 800/221-1212 for U.S. reservations, 800/241-4141 for international reservations ⊕ www.delta. com. **Frontier Airlines** ☎ 800/432-1359 ⊕ www.frontierairlines.com. **Japan Air Lines** ☎ 800/525-3663 ⊕ www.jal.com. **JetBlue** ☎ 800/538-2583 ⊕ www.jetblue.com. **Qantas** ☎ 800/227-4500 ⊕ www.qantas.com. au. **Southwest Airlines** ☎ 800/435-9792 ⊕ www.southwest.com. **Spirit Airlines** ☎ 800/772-7117 ⊕ www.spirit.com. **United Airlines** ☎ 800/864-8331 for U.S. reservations, 800/538-2929 for international reservations ⊕ www.united.com. **US Airways** ☎ 800/428-4322 for U.S. and Canada reservations, 800/622-1015 for international reservations ⊕ www.usairways.com.

■ BOAT TRAVEL

CRUISES

A number of major cruise lines offer trips that begin or end in California. Most voyages sail north along the Pacific Coast to Alaska or south to Mexico. California cruise ports include Los Angeles, San Diego, and San Francisco.

Cruise Lines Carnival Cruise Line ☎ 305/599–2600, 800/227–6482 ⊕ www. carnival.com. **Celebrity Cruises** ☎ 800/647–2251, 800/437–3111 ⊕ www.celebritycruises. com. **Crystal Cruises** ☎ 310/785–9300, 800/446–6620 ⊕ www.crystalcruises.com. **Holland America Line** ☎ 206/281–3535, 877/932–4259 ⊕ www.hollandamerica.com. **Norwegian Cruise Line** ☎ 305/436–4000, 800/327–7030 ⊕ www.ncl.com. **Princess Cruises** ☎ 661/753–0000, 800/774–6237 ⊕ www.princess.com. **Regent Seven Seas Cruises** ☎ 954/776–6123, 800/477–7500 ⊕ www.rssc.com. **Royal Caribbean International** ☎ 305/539–6000, 800/327–6700 ⊕ www.royalcaribbean.com. **Silversea Cruises** ☎ 954/522–4477, 800/722–9955 ⊕ www. silversea.com.

■ BUS TRAVEL

Greyhound is the major bus carrier in California. Regional bus service is available in metropolitan areas.

Bus Information Greyhound ☎ 800/231–2222 ⊕ www.greyhound.com.

■ CAR TRAVEL

There are two basic north–south routes in California: Interstate 5 runs inland most of the way from the Oregon border to the Mexican border; and U.S. 101 hugs the coast for part of the route from Oregon to Mexico. A slower but much more scenic option is to take California State Route 1, also referred to as Highway 1 and the Pacific Coast Highway, which winds along much of the California coast and provides an occasionally hair-raising, but breathtaking, ride.

From north to south, the state's east–west interstates are Interstate 80, Interstate 15, Interstate 10, and Interstate 8. Much of California is mountainous, and you may encounter winding roads, frequently cliffside, and steep mountain grades. In winter, roads crossing the Sierra from east to west may close at any time due to weather. Also in winter, Interstate 5 north of Los Angeles closes during snowstorms.

The flying and driving times in the accompanying charts represent best-case scenario estimates, but know that the infamous California traffic jam can occur at any time.

GASOLINE

Gasoline prices in California vary widely, depending on location, oil company, and whether you buy it at a full-service or self-serve pump. It's less expensive to buy fuel in the southern part of the state than in the north. If you're planning to travel near Nevada, you can save a bit by purchasing gas over the border. Gas stations are plentiful throughout the state. Most stay open late (24 hours along major highways and in big cities), except in rural areas, where Sunday hours are limited and where you may drive long stretches without a chance to refuel.

ROAD CONDITIONS

Rainy weather can make driving along the coast or in the mountains treacherous. Some of the smaller routes over mountain ranges and in the deserts are prone to flash flooding. When the rains are severe, coastal Highway 1 can quickly become a slippery nightmare, buffeted by strong winds and obstructed by falling debris from the cliffs above. When the weather is particularly bad, Highway 1 may be closed due to mud and rock slides.

Many smaller roads over the Sierra Nevada are closed in winter, and if it's snowing, tire chains may be required on routes that are open, most notably those to Yosemite and Lake Tahoe. From October through April, if it's raining along the coast, it's usually snowing at higher elevations. Consider renting a four-wheel-drive vehicle, or purchase chains before you get to the mountains. (Chains or cables generally cost $30 to $70, depending on tire size; cables are easier to attach than chains, but chains are more durable.) If you delay and purchase them in the vicinity of the chain-control area, the cost may double. Be aware that most rental-car companies prohibit chain installation on their vehicles. If you choose to risk it and do not tighten them properly, they may snap—your insurance likely will not cover any resulting damage. Uniformed chain installers on Interstate 80 and U.S. 50 will apply them at the checkpoint for $35 or take them off for less than that. Chain installers are independent business people, not highway employees, and set their own fees. They are not allowed to sell or rent chains. On smaller roads, you're on your own. Always carry extra clothing, blankets, water, and food when driving to the mountains in the winter, and keep your gas tank full to prevent the fuel line from freezing.

Road Conditions Caltrans Current Highway Conditions ☎ 800/427-7623 ⊕ www.dot. ca.gov.

Weather Conditions National Weather Service ☎ 707/443-6484 northernmost California, 831/656-1725 San Francisco Bay area and central California, 775/673-8100 Reno, Lake Tahoe, and northern Sierra, 805/988-6610 Los Angeles area, 858/675-8700 San Diego area ⊕ www.weather.gov.

ROADSIDE EMERGENCIES

Dial 911 to report accidents on the road and to reach the police, the California Highway Patrol (CHP), or the fire department. On some rural highways and on most interstates, look for emergency phones on the side of the road.

RULES OF THE ROAD

All passengers must wear seat belts at all times. A child must be secured in a federally approved child passenger restraint system and ride in the back seat until at least eight years of age or until the child is at least 4 feet 9 inches tall. Children who are eight but don't meet the height requirement must ride in a booster seat or a car seat. Unless otherwise indicated, right turns are allowed at red lights after you've come to a full stop. Left turns between two one-way streets are allowed at red lights after you've come to a full stop.

Drivers with a blood-alcohol level higher than 0.08 who are stopped by police are subject to arrest, and police officers can detain those under 21 with a level of 0.05 if they appear impaired. California's drunk-driving laws are extremely tough—violators may have their licenses immediately suspended, pay hefty fines, and spend the night in jail.

The speed limit on many interstate highways is 70 mph; unlimited-access roads are usually 55 mph. In cities, freeway speed limits are between 55 mph and 65 mph. Many city routes have commuter lanes during rush hour.

Those 18 and older must use a hands-free device for their mobile phones while driving; those under 18 may not use mobile phones or wireless devices while driving. Texting on a wireless device is illegal for all drivers. Smoking in a vehicle where a minor is present is an infraction. For more information refer to the Department of Motor Vehicles driver's handbook at ⊕ www.dmv.ca.gov.

CAR RENTAL

When you reserve a car, ask about cancellation penalties, taxes, drop-off charges (if you're planning to pick up the car in one city and leave it in another), and surcharges (for being under or over a certain age, for additional drivers, or for driving across state or country borders or beyond a specific distance from your point of rental). All of these things can add substantially to your costs. Request car seats and extras such as GPS when you book.

Rates are sometimes—but not always—better if you book in advance or reserve through a rental agency's website. There are other reasons to book ahead, though: for popular destinations, during busy times of the year, or to ensure that you get certain types of cars (vans, SUVs, exotic sports cars).

■**TIP**➔ Make sure that a confirmed reservation guarantees you a car. Agencies sometimes overbook, particularly for busy weekends and holiday periods.

A car is essential in most parts of California, though in compact San Francisco it's better to use public transportation to avoid parking headaches.

Rates statewide for the least expensive vehicle begin as low as $30 a day, usually on weekends, and less than $200 a week (though they increase rapidly from here). This does not include additional fees or the tax on car rentals, which is 8.5% in San Francisco. Be sure to shop around— you can get a decent deal by carefully shopping the major car rental companies' websites. Compare prices by city before you book, and ask about "drop charges" if you plan to return the car in a city other than the one where you rented the vehicle. If you pick up at an airport, there may also be a facility charge of as much as $12 per rental; ask when you book.

In California, you must have a valid driver's license and be 21 to rent a car; rates may be higher if you're under 25. Some agencies will not rent to those under 25; check when you book. Non-U.S. residents must have a license with text that is in the Roman alphabet that is valid for the entire rental period. Though it need not be entirely written in English, it must have English letters that clearly identify it as a driver's license. In addition, most companies also require an international license; check in advance.

If you dream of driving down the coast with the top down, or you want to explore the desert landscape not visible from the road, consider renting a specialty vehicle. Agencies that specialize in convertibles and sport-utility vehicles will often arrange airport delivery in larger cities. Unlike most of the major agencies, the following companies guarantee the car class that you book.

Specialty Car Agencies Specialty Rentals ☎ *800/400–8412 locations in San Francisco and Los Angeles* ⊕ *www.specialtyrentals.com.*

Major Rental Agencies Alamo ☎ *800/462–5266* ⊕ *www.alamo.com.* **Avis** ☎ *800/331–1212* ⊕ *www.avis.com.* **Budget** ☎ *800/527–0700* ⊕ *www.budget.com.* **Hertz** ☎ *800/654–3131* ⊕ *www.hertz.com.* **National Car Rental** ☎ *877/222–9058* ⊕ *www. nationalcar.com.*

■ TRAIN TRAVEL

One of the most beautiful train trips in the country, Amtrak's *Coast Starlight,* begins in Los Angeles and hugs the Pacific Coast to San Luis Obispo before it turns inland for the rest of its journey to Seattle. The *California Zephyr* travels from Chicago to Oakland via Denver; the *Pacific Surfliner* connects San Diego and San Luis Obispo via Los Angeles and Santa Barbara with multiple departures daily; and the *Sunset Limited* runs from Los Angeles to New Orleans via Arizona, New Mexico, and Texas.

Information Amtrak ☎ *800/872–7245* ⊕ *www.amtrakcalifornia.com.*

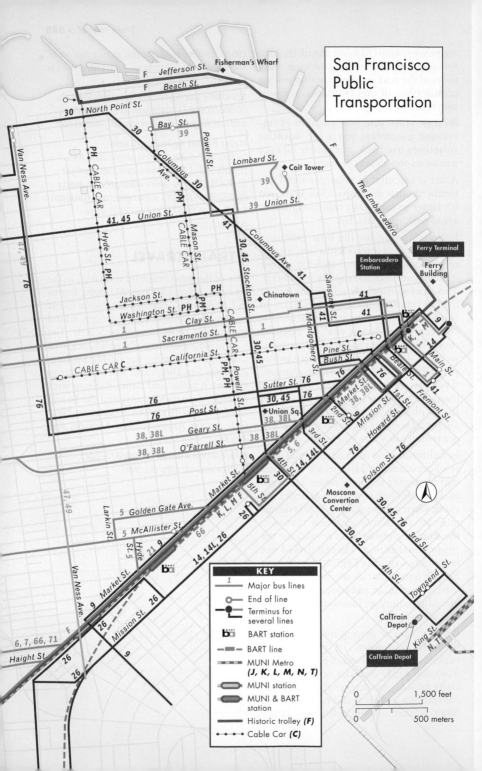

San Francisco Public Transportation

ESSENTIALS

■ ACCOMMODATIONS

The lodgings we review are the cream of the crop in each price category. For a full list of the facilities that are available at each property, please see the expanded review on ⊕ *www.fodors.com*. We don't specify whether the facilities cost extra; when pricing accommodations, ask what's included and what costs extra. ⇨ *For price information, see the planner in each chapter.*

Most hotels require you to give your credit-card details before they will confirm your reservation. If you don't feel comfortable emailing this information, ask if you can fax it (some places even prefer faxes). However you book, get confirmation in writing and have a copy of it handy when you check in.

Be sure you understand the hotel's cancellation policy. Some places allow you to cancel without any kind of penalty— even if you prepaid to secure a discounted rate—if you cancel at least 24 hours in advance. Others require you to cancel a week in advance or penalize you the cost of one night. Small inns and B&Bs are most likely to require you to cancel far in advance. Most hotels allow children under a certain age to stay in their parents' room at no extra charge, but others charge for them as extra adults; find out the cutoff age for discounts.

Many B&Bs are entirely nonsmoking, and hotels and motels are decreasing their inventory of smoking rooms; if you require one, ask when you book if any are available.

BED-AND-BREAKFASTS

California has more than 1,000 bed-and-breakfasts. You'll find everything from simple homestays to lavish luxury lodgings, many in historic hotels and homes. The California Association of Bed and Breakfast Inns has about 300 member properties that you can locate and book through its website.

Reservation Services Bed & Breakfast.com ☎ 512/322–2710, 800/462–2632 ⊕ *www.bedandbreakfast.com.* **Bed & Breakfast Inns Online** ☎ 310/280–4363, 800/215–7365 ⊕ *www.bbonline.com.* **BnB Finder.com** ☎ 212/480–0414, 888/547–8226 ⊕ *www.bnbfinder.com.* **California Association of Bed and Breakfast Inns** ☎ 800/373–9251 ⊕ *www.cabbi.com.*

■ COMMUNICATIONS

INTERNET

Internet access is widely available in urban areas, but it's usually more difficult to get online in the state's rural areas. Most hotels offer some kind of connection—usually broadband or Wi-Fi. Many hotels charge a daily fee (about $10) for Internet access. Cybercafés are located throughout California.

Contacts Cybercafés ⊕ *www.cybercafes.com.*

■ EATING OUT

California has led the pack in bringing natural and organic foods to the forefront of American cooking. Though rooted in European cuisine, California cooking sometimes has strong Asian and Latin influences. Wherever you go, you're likely to find that dishes are made with fresh produce and other local ingredients.

The restaurants we list are the cream of the crop in each price category. ⇨ *For price information, see the planner in each chapter.*

CUTTING COSTS

■ TIP→ If you're on a budget, take advantage of the "small plates" craze sweeping California by ordering several appetizer-size portions and having a glass of wine at the bar, rather than having a full meal. Also, the better grocery and specialty-food stores have grab-and-go sections, with prepared foods on par with restaurant cooking, perfect for picnicking. At resort areas in the off-season (such as Lake Tahoe in October and May), you can often find two-for-one dinner specials at upper-end restaurants; check coupon apps or local papers or with visitor bureaus.

RESERVATIONS AND DRESS

Regardless of where you are, it's a good idea to make a reservation if you can. We only mention reservations specifically when they are essential (there's no other way you'll ever get a table) or when they are not accepted. For popular restaurants, book as far ahead as you can (often 30 days), and reconfirm as soon as you arrive. (Large parties should always call ahead to check the reservations policy.) We mention dress only when men are required to wear a jacket or a jacket and tie.

Online reservation services make it easy to book a table before you even leave home. OpenTable covers many California cities.

Contacts OpenTable ⊕ *www.opentable.com.*

WINES, BEER, AND SPIRITS

Throughout the state, most famously in the Napa and Sonoma valleys, you can visit wineries, many of which have tasting rooms and offer tours. Microbreweries are an emerging trend in the state's cities and in some rural areas in northern California. The legal drinking age is 21.

▌ HEALTH

Do not fly within 24 hours of scuba diving. Smoking is illegal in all California bars and restaurants, including on outdoor dining patios in some cities.

▌ HOURS OF OPERATION

Banks in California are typically open weekdays from 9 to 6 and Saturday morning; most are closed on Sunday and most holidays. Smaller shops usually operate from 10 to 6, with larger stores remaining open until 8 or later. Hours vary for

museums and historical sites, and many are closed one or more days a week, or for extended periods during off-season months. It's a good idea to check before you visit a tourist site.

▌ MONEY

San Francisco tends to be an expensive city to visit, and rates at coastal resorts are almost as high. Hotel rates average $150 to $250 a night (though you can find cheaper places), and dinners at even moderately priced restaurants often cost $20 to $40 per person. Costs in the Gold Country and the Far North region are considerably less—many fine Gold Country bed-and-breakfasts charge around $100 a night, and some motels in the Far North charge $70 to $90.

CREDIT CARDS

It's a good idea to inform your credit-card company before you travel. Otherwise, the credit-card company might put a hold on your card owing to unusual activity—not a good thing halfway through your trip. Record all your credit-card numbers—as well as the phone numbers to call if your cards are lost or stolen—in a safe place, so you're prepared should something go wrong. Both MasterCard and Visa have general numbers you can call (collect if you're abroad) if your card is lost, but you're better off calling the number of your issuing bank, since MasterCard and Visa normally just transfer you to your bank; your bank's number is usually printed on your card.

Reporting Lost Cards American Express ☏ 800/992–3404 in U.S., 336/393–1111 collect from abroad ⊕ www.americanexpress.com. **Discover** ☏ 800/347–2683 in U.S., 801/902–3100 collect from abroad ⊕ www.discovercard. com.**Diners Club** ☏ 800/234–6377 in U.S., 514/877–1577 collect from abroad ⊕ www. dinersclub.com. **MasterCard** ☏ 800/622–7747 in U.S., 636/722–7111 collect from abroad ⊕ www.mastercard.com. **Visa** ☏ 800/847–2911 in U.S., 303/967–1096 collect from abroad ⊕ www.visa.com.

SAFETY

California is a safe place to visit, as long as you take the usual precautions. In large cities ask the concierge or desk clerk to point out areas on your map that you should avoid. Lock valuables in a hotel safe when you're not using them. (Some hotels have in-room safes large enough to hold a laptop computer.) Keep an eye on your handbag when you're out in public. Security is high (but mostly invisible) at theme parks and resorts.

TAXES

Sales tax in California varies from about 7.25% to 9.75% and applies to all purchases except for food purchased in a grocery store; food consumed in a restaurant is taxed but take-out food purchases are not. Hotel taxes vary widely by region, from about 8% to 15%.

TIME

California is in the Pacific time zone. Pacific daylight time (PDT) is in effect from mid-March through early November; the rest of the year the clock is set to Pacific standard time (PST).

TIPPING

Most service workers in California are fairly well paid compared to those in the rest of the country, and extravagant tipping is not the rule here. Exceptions include wealthy enclaves such as Beverly Hills, La Jolla, and San Francisco as well as the most expensive resort areas.

TIPPING GUIDELINES FOR CALIFORNIA	
Bartender	$1 per drink, or 10%–15% of tab per round of drinks
Bellhop	$1–$5 per bag, depending on the level of the hotel
Hotel Concierge	$5 or more, if he/she performs a service for you
Hotel Doorman	$1–$2 if he/she helps you get a cab
Valet Parking Attendant	$2 when you get your car
Hotel Maid	$2–$3 per person, per day; more in high-end hotels
Waiter	15%–20% (20% is standard in upscale restaurants); nothing additional if a service charge is added to the bill
Skycap at Airport	$1–$3 per bag
Hotel Room-Service Waiter	15%–20% per delivery, even if a service charge was added since that fee goes to the hotel, not the waiter
Taxi Driver	15%–20%, but round up the fare to the next dollar amount
Tour Guide	10% of the cost of the tour, more depending on quality

TOURS

Guided tours are a good option when you don't want to do it all yourself. You travel along with a group (sometimes large, sometimes small), stay in prebooked hotels, eat with your fellow travelers (the cost of meals is sometimes included in the price of your tour, sometimes not), and follow a schedule.

But not all guided tours are an if-it's-Tuesday-this-must-be-Yosemite experience. A knowledgeable guide can take you places that you might never discover on your own, and you may be pushed to see more than you would have otherwise. Tours aren't for everyone, but they can be just the thing for trips to places where making travel arrangements is difficult or time-consuming.

Whenever you book a guided tour, find out what's included and what isn't. A "land-only" tour includes all your travel (by bus, in most cases) in the destination, but not necessarily your flights to and from or even within it. Also, in most cases prices in tour brochures don't include fees and taxes. And remember that you'll be expected to tip your guide (in cash) at the end of the tour.

SPECIAL-INTEREST TOURS

BIKING

Bicycling is a popular way to see the California countryside, and commercial tours are available throughout the state. Most three- to five-day trips are all-inclusive—you'll stay in delightful country inns, dine at good regional restaurants, and follow experienced guides. The Northern California wine country, with its flat valley roads, is one of the most popular destinations. When booking, ask about level of difficulty, as nearly every trip will involve some hill work. Tours fill up early, so book well in advance.

■TIP→ Most airlines accommodate bikes as luggage, provided they're dismantled and boxed.

Contacts Napa and Sonoma Valley Bike Tours ✉ 6795 Washington St., Bldg. B, Yountville ☎ 800/707–2453 ⊕ www. napavalleybiketours.com. **Bicycle Adventures** ✉ 29700 S.E. High Point Way, Issaquah, Washington ☎ 800/443–6060 ⊕ www. bicycleadventures.com.

▌VISITOR INFORMATION

The California Travel and Tourism Commission's website takes you to each region of California, with digital visitor guides in multiple languages, driving tours, maps, welcome center locations, information on local tours, links to bed-and-breakfasts, and a complete booking center. It also links you—via the Explore California menu—to the websites of city and regional tourism offices and attractions. *For the numbers and websites of regional and city visitor bureaus and chambers of commerce see the "Planning" sections in each chapter.*

Contacts California Travel and Tourism Commission ✉ Box 1499, Sacramento ☎ 916/444–4429 information, 800/862–2543 brochures ⊕ www.visitcalifornia.com.

INDEX

A

PHOTO CREDITS

1, Yuen Kwan, Fodors.com member. 3, Heavenly Mountain Resort. Chapter 1: Experience California: 6-7, Jay Anderson, Fodors.com member. 9, Helio San Miguel. 10 (top), Clinton Steeds/Flickr. 10 (bottom), Jose Vigano, Fodors.com member. 11, comfortablynirm, Fodors.com member. 13, vathomp, Fodors.com member. 14, Robert Holmes. 15 (left), sd_foodies, Fodors.com member. 15 (right), Lisa M. Hamilton. 16 (left), Christophe Testi/iStockphoto. 16 (top right), Corbis. 16 (bottom right), Warren H. White. 17 (top left), Alan A. Tobey/iStockphoto. 17 (bottom left), Janet Fullwood. 17 (right), Aaron Kohr/iStockphoto. 18, Warren H. White. 19, Thomas Kranzel/Venture Media. 20, Andrew Zarivny/ iStockphoto. 22, yummyporky/Flickr. 23 (top and bottom), Lisa M. Hamilton. 24 (top), Janine Bolliger/ iStockphoto. 24 (bottom), Lise Gagne/iStockphoto. 25, iStockphoto. 26 (top), Evan Meyer/ iStockphoto. 26 (center), Kyle Maass iStockphoto. 26 (bottom left), iStockphoto. 26 (bottom right), iStockphoto. 27, Tom Baker/Shutterstock. 28 (left), SuperStock/age fotostock. 28 (top right), CURAphotography/Shutterstock. 28 (bottom right), Michael Almond/iStockphoto. 29 (top), iStockphoto. 29(bottom), Lise Gagne/iStockphoto. 30 (top), Ross Stapleton-Gray/iStockphoto. 30 (center), Jay Spooner/iStockphoto. 30 (bottom), TebNad/Shutterstock. 31 (top), Jay Spooner/iStockphoto. 31 (bottom), Lise Gagne/iStockphoto. 32, John Elk III/Alamy. Chapter 2: The Central Coast: 33, TweetieV, Fodors.com member. 34, Stephen Walls/iStockphoto. 35 (top), Bart Everett/iStockphoto. 35 (bottom), Robert Holmes. 36, David M. Schrader/Shutterstock. 46, S. Greg Panosian/iStockphoto. 47, Ruben G. Mendoza. 48 (top), Richard Wong/www.rwongphoto.com/Alamy. 48 (bottom), Ruben G. Mendoza. 49 (top left), Witold Skrypczak/ Alamy. 49 (top right), S. Greg Panosian/iStockphoto. 49 (bottom), Janet Fullwood. 50 (top left), GIPhotoStock Z/Alamy. 50 (top right), Craig Lovell/Eagle Visions Photography/Alamy. 50 (bottom) and 51 (top), S. Greg Panosian/iStockphoto. 51 (bottom), Eugene Zelenko/wikipedia.org. 56, David M. Schrader/Shutterstock. 65, Doreen Miller, Fodors.com member. 76, Robert Holmes. 92-93, Valhalla I Design & Conquer, Fodors.com member. Chapter 3: The Monterey Bay Area: 99, mellifluous, Fodors. com member. 100, Janet Fullwood. 101 (top), vittorio sciosia/age fotostock. 101 (bottom). Jeff Greenberg/age fotostock. 102, Brent Reeves/Shutterstock. 109, Robert Holmes.116, Holger Mette/iStockphoto. 123, laurel stewart/iStockphoto. Chapter 4: San Francisco: 143-146, Brett Shoaf/Artistic Visuals Photography. 155, Brett Shoaf/Artistic Visuals Photography. 156 (top), Arnold Genthe. 156 (bottom), Library of Congress Prints and Photographs Division. 157 (left), Sandor Balatoni/SFCVB. 157 (right), Detroit Publishing Company Collection, Photography Collection, Miriam and Ira D. Wallach Division of Art, Prints and Photographs, The New York Public Library, Astor, Lenox and Tilden Foundation. 158, Brett Shoaf/Artistic Visuals Photography. 159 (top), Gary Soup/Flickr. 159 (bottom), Albert Cheng/Shutterstock. 160 (top), Sheryl Schindler/SFCVB. 160 (center), Ronen/Shutterstock. 160 (bottom), Robert Holmes. 165, Walter Bibikow/age fotostock. 171, travelstock44/Alamy. 173, Brett Shoaf/Artistic Visuals Photography. 174, San Francisco Municipal Railway Historical Archives. 181, Lewis Sommer/SFCVB. 190, Robert Holmes. 199, aprillilacs, Fodors.com member. 203, Rafael Ramirez Lee/iStockphoto. 210, rick/Flickr. 211 (top), Ei-Lun Tsai/Flickr. 211 (bottom), Cathleen Clapper/Shutterstock. *228 (top), Fairmont Hotels, Resorts. 228 (center left), The Huntington Hotel. 228 (center right), David Phelps/Argonaut Hotel. 228 (bottom), Cesar Rubio/Joie de Vivve Hospitality. 229 (top), The Ritz-Carlton, San Francisco. 229 (center left & center right), Joie de Vivre Hospitality. 229 (bottom), Cris Ford/Union Street Inn. 230, Queen Anne Hotel. 238, Rough Guides/Alamy. 241, Robert Holmes. Chapter 5: The Bay Area: 245 and 246, Robert Holmes. 247, Jyeshern Cheng/iStockphoto. 248, Brett Shoaf/Artistic Visuals Photography. 253, Robert Holmes. 267, Mark Rasmussen/iStockphoto. 269, Robert Holmes. 276, S. Greg Panosian/iStockphoto. 280 and 292, Robert Holmes. Chapter 6: The Wine Country: 299 Robert Holmes. 300, iStockphoto. 301, Robert Holmes. 302, Warren H. White. 308, Robert Holmes. 309 (top), kevin miller/iStockphoto. 309 (bottom), Far Niente+Dolce+Nickel & Nickel. 310 (top and bottom) Robert Holmes. 311 (top) Domaine Carneros. 311 (bottom), star5112/Flickr. 312 (top left), Rubicon Estate. 312 (top right and bottom) and 313 (top and bottom), Robert Holmes. 314 (top), Philippe Roy/Alamy. 314 (center), Agence Images/Alamy. 314 (bottom), Cephas Picture Library/Alamy. 315 (top), Napa Valley Conference Bureau. 315 (second and third from top), Wild Horse Winery (Forrest L. Doud). 315 (fourth from top), Napa Valley Conference Bureau. 315 (fifth from top), Panther Creek Cellars (Ron Kaplan). 315 (sixth from top), Clos du Val (Marvin Collins). 315 (seventh from top), Panther Creek Cellars (Ron Kaplan). 315 (bottom), Warren H. White. 316 and 319, Robert Holmes. 329, Far Niente+Dolce+Nickel & Nickel. 332, Terry Joanis/Frog's Leap. 340, Chuck Honek/Schramsberg Vineyard. 342, Castello di Amorosa. 355, 356, 362-363, and 364, Robert Holmes. Chapter 7: The North Coast:373, Thomas Barrat/Shutterstock. 374 (all), Robert Holmes. 375 (top), Russ Bishop/age fotostock. 375 (bottom), Robert Holmes. 376, Janet Fullwood. 383, 389, and 393 Robert Holmes. Chapter 8: Redwood National Park: 403, iStockphoto. 404 (top), Michael Schweppe/wikipedia.org. 404 (center), Agnieszka Szymczak/ iStockphoto. 404 (bottom), Natalia Bratslavsky/Shutterstock. 406, WellyWelly/Shutterstock. Chapter 9:

The Southern Sierra: 411, Randall Pugh, Fodors.com member. 412, Craig Cozart/iStockphoto. 413 (top), David T Gomez/iStockphoto. 413 (bottom left and bottom right), Robert Holmes. 414, christinea78, Fodors.com member. 419, moonjazz/Flickr. 426, Douglas Atmore/iStockphoto. Chapter 10: Yosemite National Park: 429, Sarah P. Corley, Fodors.com member. 430, Yosemite Concession Services. 431 (top), Andy Z./Shutterstock. 431 (bottom), Greg Epperson/age fotostock. 432, Doug Lemke/Shutterstock. 437, Rebalyn, Fodors.com member. 439, Nathan Jaskowiak/Shutterstock. 444, Greg Epperson/age fotostock. 446-47, Katrina Leigh/Shutterstock. Chapter 11: Sequoia and Kings Canyon National Parks: 451 and 452, Robert Holmes. 453 (top), Greg Epperson/age fotostock. 453 (bottom) and 454, Robert Holmes. 461, urosr/Shutterstock. 465, Robert Holmes. Chapter 12: Sacramento and the Gold Country: 469 and 471 (top and bottom), Robert Holmes. 472, Andy Z./Shutterstock. 478, Marcin Wichary/Flickr. 485, Image Asset Management/age fotostock. 486 (left) and 486 (right), wikipedia.org. 486 (center), Charles Danek. 487, Ambient Images Inc./Alamy. 488 (top), Trailmix.Net/Flickr. 488 (center), oger jones/Flickr. 488 (bottom), L. C. McClure/wikipedia.org. 489 (top left), Russ Bishop/age fotostock. 489 (top center), vera bogaerts/iStockphoto. 489 (top right and bottom left), Walter Bibikow/age fotostock. 489 (bottom right), Charles Danek. 494, Janet Fullwood. 500, RickC/Flickr. Chapter 13: Lake Tahoe: 505, Tom Zikas/North Lake Tahoe. 506 (top), Rafael Ramirez Lee/iStockphoto. 506 (bottom) and 507, Janet Fullwood. 508, Jay Spooner/iStockphoto. 515 (top), Heavenly Mountain Resort. 515 (bottom), Jake Foster/iStockphoto. 516 (top), Lake Tahoe Visitors Authority. 516 (bottom left), iStockphoto. 516 (bottom right), Heavenly Mountain Resort. 519 and 520 (left), Andrew Zarivny/iStockphoto. 520 (right), Harry Thomas/iStockphoto. 521 (top left), Joy Strotz/Shutterstock. 521 (bottom left), iStockphoto. 521 (right), Jennifer Stone/Shutterstock. 527, Jay Spooner/iStockphoto. 533, Tom O'Neill. 545, Christopher Russell/iStockphoto. Chapter 14: The Far North: 553, NPS. 554 (top and bottom), Robert Holmes. 555 (top), Andy Z./Shutterstock. 555 (bottom), NPS. 556, ThreadedThoughts/Flickr. 562, Robert Holmes. 570, kathycsus/Flickr. 575, NPS.